The VM/ESA User's and

Applications Handbook

The VM/ESA User's and Applications Handbook

Philip H. Smith III

Gabriel Goldberg

McGraw-Hill, Inc.

New York San Francisco Washington, D.C. Auckland Bogotá
Caracas Lisbon London Madrid Mexico City Milan
Montreal New Delhi San Juan Singapore
Sydney Tokyo Toronto

Library of Congress Cataloging-in-Publication Data

Smith, Philip H., III.
    The VM/ESA user's and applications handbook / Philip H. Smith III,
Gabriel Goldberg.
       p.   cm.
    Includes index.
    ISBN 0-07-0-07-023703-4 (alk. paper)
    1. Operating systems (Computers) 2 VM/ESA. I. Goldberg,
Gabriel. II. Title.
QA76.76.063S588 1994
005.4'429—dc20   93-33994
                                                    CIP

1 2 3 4 5 6 7 8 9 0 DOC/DOC 9 9 8 7 6 5 4 3

ISBN 0-07-023703-4

*The sponsoring editor for this book was Jerry Papke, the editing super-
visor was David E. Fogarty, and the production supervisor was
Suzanne W. Babeuf.*

Printed and bound by R. R. Donnelley & Sons Company.

This book is printed on acid-free paper.

Contents

PART 2: Exploiting VM/ESA

PART 3:   VM/ESA Application Development

PART 4:   VM/ESA Resources

Introduction

By Bob Thomas
Enterprise Systems Journal

"Is the mainframe dead?" As publisher of *Enterprise Systems Journal*, a monthly magazine reporting on IBM mainframe issues since 1986, I am often asked that question or variations of it.

The answer to the question is as close as your telephone. Make a call. Call American Airlines to check on your frequent flier account. Call Master-Card to determine your credit limit. Dial your local Social Security Administration office to see when the last check was direct deposited into your bank account. Hundreds of millions of records stored in huge databases could not be accessed without the speed provided by the mainframe.

Thus, while mainframes are certainly evolving, they are by no means dead. So how do we explain the fact that with dreary regularity, pundits foretell the mainframe's imminent demise? Well, pundits who make pronouncements about the future of this or that technology are not well-served by the record.

Since the dawn of the information age, the mainframe computer has been—and remains—an inexorable part of the fabric that defines economic and social life in the last decade of the Twentieth Century. The unique role that mainframes have accepted in the functioning of modern society has been misinterpreted since the inception of information processing.

When mainframes were first introduced commercially in the 1950s—remember names such as Sperry, Univac, and Burroughs?—many pundits were decidedly skeptical. They thought that the computational problems mainframes were designed to address applied to perhaps five or six organizations in the country. Sure, they said, the Strategic Air Command—charged with defending all of North America from missiles—probably had an application that mainframes could conceivably handle. The Social Security Administration might use mainframe computer number-crunching power. The Census Bureau, which had requested the automation that led to development of mainframe technology, probably had enough data to justify such a big-ticket item.

However, for the vast majority of businesses, mainframes were a solution looking for a problem. Or so conventional wisdom went. In the early 1950s, in fact, a respected market research firm predicted the total United States mainframe market to be about 25 units.

They could not have been more wrong, of course. Over the next 40 years, virtually every enterprise worthy of the name installed a mainframe computer. It is difficult, in retrospect, to imagine the business environment without centralized, mainframe computers anchoring our largest organizations, maintaining repositories of the information that increasingly drives our lives.

Why did thousands of organizations spend individual sums literally in the millions of dollars on these machines? It was not out of a sense of adventure or desire to explore the limits of computing science. Without exception, mainframe computer systems were purchased by flint-hearted executives who were convinced the machines represented the best alternative for their most pressing business issue—staying competitive. If they had concluded that gerbils with green eyeshades could do the job better, the best-selling item in company cafeterias across the country would be Purina Gerbil Chow.

They put their money in mainframe technology because mainframes demonstrated the ability to tirelessly process huge amounts of data day after day. Virtually single-handedly, the mainframe computing environment created the information-based, online world on which we rely. Without mainframes, none of the applications we use every day—automated teller machines, airline reservation systems, overnight delivery services—would be possible.

So when people ask if mainframes' days are numbered, I ask them if the numbers business organizations have to deal with are shrinking. In fact, the problems for which mainframes were designed are getting **more**, not **less**, complicated. Data to be manipulated grows exponentially. People's demand for up-to-the-second information is insatiable. Everyone wants service to be faster, cheaper, more reliable, and more secure than ever before. When it comes to processing large amounts of information quickly, reliably, and securely, mainframes are still the best and sometimes only technology for the job.

Of course, it is not the mainframe that is important. It is the mainframe's power—the speed and functionality to solve business problems—that is at issue. In this sense, a mainframe is more a process than a piece of hardware. As the process changes, the hardware does too. The mainframe was designed to serve many people by not working very closely with any of them. This orientation must change because business conditions have changed.

As business needs change, the mainframe's architecture evolves. In such global trends as downsizing and client/server systems, we see a paradigm shift in the way businesses consider information. Today, businesses are determined to bring business processes—including information processing—as close to end-users as possible. The personal computer (PC) revolution is partly a cause and partly a result of this trend. Mainframes have never been a static technology. PC development has simply forced mainframes to change faster.

Many tasks required of mainframes in the past can be done better and cheaper by PCs. That is good, because downsizing or shifting workloads to the most efficient processing platform is good for business. Modern business practice calls for decentralized systems: bringing information processing as close to the end-user or customer as possible. This is good, because quality improves when the distance between customers and those who serve them decreases. As a result, a lot of work formerly done by mainframes has been offloaded to networked PCs and minicomputers.

Is anything left for mainframes to do? It turns out that the mainframe retains the role for which it was designed: to be the system's traffic cop. As organizations deploy geographically dispersed PC-based systems connected to computers made by different vendors, system administration tasks quickly become problematic. While PCs and workstations can no doubt take over many of the information processing tasks formerly handled by mainframes, they are not ready to accept the huge information management chores—preserving information integrity and security, to name just two—created by those configurations.

There is no reversing the IS revolution. Everything that used to have a spring or a motor, everything that moves or measures, is being computerized in some fashion. What will we use to manage all these computers? The mainframe, in whatever guise it may appear, will be available to ensure that information processing is orderly, secure, and error-free.

This book and its companion, *The VM/ESA Systems Handbook*, were written by several dozen experts in areas such as database, client/server, image applications, communications, mainframe architecture and hardware, performance analysis and system tuning, application design and development, and end-user facilities such as REXX and XEDIT. They all strive to maximize the benefits of using VM systems to solve today's and tomorrow's real-world business problems, and they present information from practical and applied, rather than theoretical, viewpoints. The combination of IBM, vendor, and customer authors illustrates the breadth of the VM community, and shows that the entire VM—and mainframe—story has not yet been written.

Editors' Notes

In editing a work of this scope, with chapters by numerous authors, a dilemma arises: whether to enforce similarity in voice and tone among authors. We have attempted to preserve each chapter's flavor, while editing for consistency.

Another challenge is resolving potential or real overlap between chapter topics, resulting in duplicated information. Again, the solution was to leave most things alone. This allows authors to present material in different levels of detail and from different viewpoints on topics such as exploiting CMS, XEDIT, REXX, and the Shared File System.

Romney White's "Interludes" on data spaces and CMS session services are personal and focused descriptions of two key VM functions.

To address the next stages of VM evolution, Mark Cathcart's chapter Chapter 2, *Wide-Open VM,* on page 35 on VM as an "open" system describes how VM application portability and interoperability will be improved by support of standard application and system programming interfaces.

A companion volume, *The VM/ESA Systems Handbook*, describes VM evaluation, installation, maintenance, performance and tuning, operation, security, and exploiting functions and features (e.g., data spaces, CMS Pipelines, DCSS and NSS architecture, and VM/ESA Release 2 enhancements).

Contributors' biographies appear at the end of the book.

Readers are invited to provide feedback on and updates to the book by contacting the editors.

VM Evolution and Terminology

In the beginning

It has been noted that VM innovated functions of **personal computing**, **local area networks**, **workgroup computing**, and **client/server computing** decades before the terms were coined. What could be more personal than a CMS virtual machine? What could be more local and better connected than colleagues sharing a VM system? What more epitomizes client/server function than a VM service machine responding to dozens—or hundreds, or thousands—of user requests? Today's VM builds on fundamental architecture to provide enterprise-level client/server function, LAN services and administration, and many other mission-critical application enablers. Perhaps most significantly, these functions are scalable, allowing VM to operate efficiently on processors from the smallest to the largest. This book describes the newest VM, which is truly descended from the first VM.

VM versions

VM has evolved steadily over the past twenty years, through numerous versions and releases, with different names. Many chapters refer to current VM releases without naming them; others mention features added at various points.

The same is true of IBM documentation: some chapters cite manuals by name. The same information may appear in different manuals in different VM releases.

We have sought a consistent nomenclature for different VM releases, allowing precise determination of what features are available in what release. Unfortunately, prior to VM/ESA, VM facilities in a given version or release were not necessarily a superset of those in previous VM editions. VM/XA (Migration Aid, System Facility, and System Product) and VM/SP HPO Release 6, in particular, were evolutionary mutations which were not suitable for installations which fully exploited (for example) VM/SP Release 6 or VM/SP HPO Release 5. VM/ESA ESA feature offers a convergence of prior VM function and a starting point for future development.

Release	Full name and description

VM/370   Virtual Machine Facility/370; the no-charge precursor to VM/SP. Did not include REXX, EXEC 2, or XEDIT.

VM/SP 1–5   Virtual Machine/System Product Release 1 through Release 5; introduced in 1981. Included **CMS 1** through **CMS 5.**

VM/XA SP   Virtual Machine/Extended Architecture System Product; VM for System/370-Extended Architecture (370/XA) hardware. Introduced in 1988, VM/XA SP had two releases and a subrelease (VM/XA SP Releases 1 and 2, plus VM/XA SP Release 2.1); these included **CMS 5.5** for Releases 1 and 2, and **CMS 5.6** for VM/XA SP Release 2.1.

VM/SP 6   Virtual Machine/System Product Release 6; introduced in late 1988, but not installed by many installations. Included **CMS 6**.

VM/ESA   Virtual Machine/Enterprise Systems Architecture; announced in 1990, with Releases 1.0 (available December 1990) and 1.1 (available December 1991). Release 1 included two options, the **370 feature** (essentially VM/SP Release 7) and the **ESA feature** (essentially VM/XA SP Release 3). It converged functional differences between VM/SP and VM/XA SP, providing a single CMS Level 7 or simply **CMS 7**. Release 1.1, available as ESA feature only, provides data space support for system and application exploitation. Release 1.1 includes CMS Level 8. IBM has strongly and officially indicated that there will be no 370 feature enhancements after Release 1.0, though rumors and unofficial statements indicate that the issue is not settled. Unless stated or implied by the context, references to VM/ESA denote the ESA feature.

Release 2.0 was announced in June 1992 and available in December 1992. Confusion was introduced about the true term to describe the successor to Release 1.1: it has been called both Release **1.2** and Release **2.0**. The confusion stems from IBM's occasional use of a **version** number to describe software products. The 1992 VM/ESA is Version 1, so the successor to Release 1.1 is in fact Version 1 Release 2, sometimes abbreviated 1.2. The clearest and most commonly used term is **VM/ESA Release 2**. Release 2 includes CMS Level 9.

Release 2.1 was announced in May 1993 and available in July 1993. This "fractional" release added a few significant functions, but was not different enough to be considered an entirely new release. Rather than release the new function as part of the normal service process, IBM chose a subrelease to fulfill requirements from user groups to avoid large changes through service.

Software execution modes

VM/XA introduced new architectures for I/O and machine instructions, necessitating new terms to describe modes of software execution. Terms such as **370 mode**, **370 only**, **XA mode**, **XA tolerant**, **XA exploitative**, and **XA only** usually apply to CMS software and applications, but can also apply to CP enhancements. VM/ESA Release 1.1 introduced data space exploitation and an additional virtual machine architecture, **XC mode**.

370 mode   A virtual machine in 370 mode emulates the System/370 hardware architecture, as defined in *System / 370 Principles of Operation*. If such a machine attempts to execute an instruction not defined by the *Principles*, an operation exception occurs. In VM versions prior to VM/XA, all virtual machines were "370 virtual machines", as they are often called.

XA mode   A virtual machine in XA (Extended Architecture) mode emulates the System/370-XA architecture, as defined in *System / 370-XA Principles of Operation*. Major differences between 370 and XA mode include different I/O instructions and PSW formats, and the ability to address more than 16MB of storage in XA mode. XA-mode virtual machines can select 24-bit (up to 16MB) addressing mode or 31-bit (up to 2GB) addressing mode via a bit in the PSW; this enables execution of many older applications in XA-mode virtual machines (see **370 only**, **XA tolerant**, and **XA exploitative** below). If an XA-mode virtual machine attempts to execute an instruction defined in 370 mode but **not** defined in XA mode, an operation exception occurs.

VM/XA introduced XA-mode virtual machines; as its descendant, VM/ESA ESA feature continues to support them. However, on System/370-ESA or System/390 hardware, an XA-mode virtual machine is really an ESA-mode virtual machine: all ESA features are available to the VM. The only difference is in the results of CP commands such as CP `QUERY SET` which return the mode as **XA**.

ESA mode

A virtual machine in ESA (Enterprise Systems Architecture) mode emulates the System/370-ESA or System/390 architecture, depending on the hardware, as defined in *System/370-ESA Principles of Operation* or the *System/390 Principles of Operation*. ESA mode includes all features of XA mode, plus the ability to access multiple address spaces, or **data spaces**.

VM/XA introduced ESA-mode virtual machines, for ESA-capable hardware only; as the VM/ESA ESA feature runs only on ESA-capable hardware, it supports ESA-mode virtual machines on all platforms on which it operatess.

XC mode

A virtual machine in XC (Extended Configuration) mode emulates the System/390-XC architecture, as defined in *System/390-XC Principles of Operation*. XC-mode virtual machines are supported only under VM/ESA ESA feature on System/390 hardware (although VM/ESA ESA feature will run on System/370-ESA hardware). Unlike System/370, System/370-XA, System/370-ESA, or System/390, and despite the existence of the *System/390-XC Principles of Operation*, XC mode does **not** map to a defined hardware: instead, it is a VM-specific virtual machine mode, introduced in VM/ESA Release 1.1 to aid virtual machine exploitation of VM/ESA data spaces.

XC mode includes all features of ESA mode, with minor changes to enable use of VM data spaces.

370 only   Software which is 370 only can execute only in a 370-mode machine, because it uses instructions which do not exist in XA mode. By definition, 370-only software runs in 24-bit mode, addressing up to 16MB of storage.

XA tolerant   Software which is XA-tolerant can execute in a 370-mode machine *or* in an XA-mode machine, but runs in 24-bit mode, and must reside "below the line"—at a address below 16MB. Such software usually does not perform any architecture-specific operations such as I/O instructions; if it does, it examines the machine mode and issues appropriate instructions.

XA exploitative   Software which is XA exploitative can execute in a 370-mode machine *or* in an XA-mode machine, and, in XA mode, will execute in 31-bit mode, addressing up to 2GB of storage and need not reside "below the line". XA-exploitative software examines the machine mode and issues I/O and other instructions appropriate to the mode.

XA only   Software which is XA only can execute only in an XA-mode machine, because it requires more than 16MB of storage or uses instructions which do not exist in XA mode.

ESA only   Software which is ESA only can execute only in an ESA-mode machine, because it requires access to ESA hardware features such as data spaces. The VM/ESA ESA feature Control Program (CP) is an example of ESA-only software.

XC only   Software which is XC only can execute only in an XC-mode virtual machine, because it requires access to VM data spaces.

User groups and conferences

Some chapters refer to **SHARE**, **GUIDE**, or **VMSHARE**. SHARE and GUIDE are IBM user groups, meeting four and three times a year, respec-

tively, in major North American cities. Meetings consist of presentations by
IBM, customers, and vendors on a wide variety of topics, including IBM and
vendor hardware and software. User groups also produce **requirements**,
which provide formal input to the IBM planning and development process.

SHARE and GUIDE memberships are free, but require certain IBM hardware and software. Affiliate membership is available to user groups, companies, and individuals not qualified for full membership. SHARE's telephone number is (312) 822-0932; GUIDE's is (312) 644-6610.

VMSHARE is a VM-specific electronic bulletin board, conference, and EMail service, available to SHARE and GUIDE members for a fee of US$1200 a year. Residing at McGill University in Montreal, Canada, VMSHARE is considered a "must" by many VM system programmers for its timely and correct information on VM problems, and the access to VM experts it provides. Some local user groups offer electronic conferences and bulletin boards, some of which "shadow" (maintain read-only copies of) VMSHARE.

Document References

Many chapters refer to publications issued by IBM and other vendors. Products such as VM and SQL/DS (among many others) evolve rapidly, and are described by similarly evolving documentation. Chapter authors cite specific titles and order numbers of publications used at their installations or for reference when writing their chapters. Consider these references to be somewhat generic; determine the document editions which are applicable to your environment or requirements. Chapter 27, *VM/ESA References,* on page 653 lists full citations for referenced publications.

The Future

From the perspective of 20 years of VM history, it is obvious that a reason for VM's success is its implementation of (then unnamed) personal computing, client/server, and local area network computing paradigms. VM is evolving more rapidly in 1993 than it has since the early days of VM/SP in the 1980s. Fundamental user interfaces and operational characteristics are being enhanced to meet long-standing desires of the VM community. Future editions of this book will likely show VM's client/server and enterprise hub roles in more detail and breadth, representing a return to the verities of VM's origins.

Trademarks

The following are registered trademarks of International Business Machines: IBM, MicroChannel and PS/2.

The following are trademarks or service marks of International Business Machines: ACF/VTAM, AD/Cycle, AIX, AIX/ESA, AIX/600, Big Blue, BookManager, BookMaster, Bright Sized, Bright Sizing, CALLUP, CICS/VSE, Common User Access, CSP, CUA, CustomPac/VM, Distributed Relational Database Architecture, DrawMaster, DRDA, Enterprise System Architecture/370, Enterprise System Architecture/390, ES/4381, ES/9000, ESA, ESA/390, FunctionPac/VM, GDDM, IBM, IBMLink, MVS/ESA, NetView, OfficeVision, OpenEdition, OS/2, OS/400, PR/SM, PS/2, RISC, RISC System/6000, S/390, SAA, Service Director, Software Analysis Test Tool, SoftwareXcel, SoftwareXcel SystemPac/VM, SQL, SQL/DS, System/360, System/370, System/390, System/6000, Systems Application Architecture, SystemView, The Integrated Reasoning Shell, TIRS, Virtual Machine/Enterprise Systems Architecture, Virtual Machine/Extended Architecture, VM/ESA, VM/SP, VM/XA, VSE, VTAM, Workstation Interactive Test Tool, Workstation Platform/2, "Yes We're Open", and 3090.

AES is a trademark of the Open Software Foundation, Inc.
ANSI is a trademark of the American National Standards Institute.
Apple is a trademark of Apple Computer, Inc.
BACHMAN is a trademark of Bachman Information Systems.
CADAM is a registered trademark of Cadam, Inc.
DEC is a trademark of Digital Equipment Corporation.
DECdts is a trademark of Digital Equipment Corporation.
Easel is a trademark of Easel Corporation.
Encina is a trademark of Transarc Corporation.
Episode is a trademark of Transarc Corporation.
Ethernet is a trademark of Xerox Corporation.
FOCUS is a trademark of Information Builders, Inc.
IEEE is a trademark of the Institute of Electrical and Electronic Engineers.
Kerberos is a trademark of the Massachusetts Institute of Technology.
Lotus 1-2-3/M is a trademark of Lotus Development Corporation.
Macintosh is a trademark of Apple Computer, Inc.
Microsoft is a registered trademark of Microsoft Corporation.
MOSAIC is a trademark of Science Applications International Corporation.
Motif is a trademark of the Open Software Foundation, Inc.
MUMPS is a registered trademark of Massachusetts General Hospital.
MUSIC is a trademark of McGill University.
MUSIC/SP is a trademark of McGill University.

Acknowledgments

Gerry Hackett of the IBM Endicott Programming Laboratory helped with management, legal, and logistical issues. She provided calm continuity through the entire project, and greatly facilitated author recruiting.

Pam Christina of IBM Endicott was a cheerleader and multitalented factotum, even on Mondays. In addition to writing the *Softcopy Publications* Chapter and the bibliography, she recruited numerous IBM contributors, encouraged IBM writers throughout production, and edited several chapters.

Chip Coy of IBM Endicott joined the project early, delivered two assigned chapters, then cheerfully volunteered to fill a large gap in the book's material. He also recruited other IBM authors to tell the complete and current story in several key areas.

Pat McGrew of GenText in Dallas provided the foundation for producing the final book format, and assisted during design and production.

Pam Christina, Linda Green, Pat Hayes, and Steve Jones, of IBM Endicott, and Janet Gobeille of the IBM Washington Systems Center, supported EMail connectivity and communication.

Jerry Papke of McGraw-Hill served as negotiator and lightning rod for the million-and-one details required to move a book from inspiration to bookstore.

Jay Ranade of Merrill Lynch and McGraw-Hill provided motivation and consistent encouragement for this project.

Paul Loftus, formerly director of the IBM Endicott Programming Laboratory, helped launch this book with early and vigorous resources and staffing support. He is now president of the Services Sector Division in IBM's Application Solutions line of business.

Leslie Wilkes, director of the IBM Endicott Programming Laboratory, embraced the project by continuing staff support and providing the introduction.

Relay Technology, Inc. (formerly VM Systems Group, Inc.) provided "time and furniture" for the many tasks required to produce this book. Access to facilities and people helped in numerous ways.

IBM supported and contributed to the book with people and logistical facilities.

Dave Bishop of IBM Atlanta provided key electronic communication via IBMLink which greatly accelerated and facilitated various tasks.

The global VM community was immensely supportive of this book. Many people provided suggestions and guidance which helped shape the book. Several others helped by advising individual authors or reviewing chapters.

The VMSHARE electronic conference at McGill University provided communication with authors around the world, facilitated by several human gateways.

Chapter authors merged major writing and editing tasks into otherwise busy lives, making personal and professional sacrifices. We are especially grateful to authors who joined the project near the end, and completed their tasks on a greatly compressed schedule: Bill Bitner, Mark Cathcart, Dave Hemsath, Dan Hunsinger, Peter Kohlmann, Tom Kumpf, Ray Parker, Ross Patterson, and Terrence Sole.

Reviewers provided a final quality and consistency check: Karen Jones of BMC Software, Inc.; Aimee Kratts of Relay Technology, Inc.; William Mosteller of Sterling Software, Inc.; Ross A Patterson of Sterling Software, Inc.; Jeffrey Savit of Merrill Lynch; and Romney White of Velocity Software. Errors and omissions are, of course, our responsibility.

Philip H. Smith III
Gabriel Goldberg
1993

The VM/ESA User's and

Applications Handbook

Introduction to VM/ESA

This section introduces VM/ESA fundamentals, components, and architecture. It describes the characteristics, use, and power of three essential VM tools: CMS, XEDIT, and REXX.

1

VM/ESA Fundamentals, Features, and Components

By Ray Parker and Tom Kumpf

Introduction

This chapter provides an overview of VM/ESA. Some experience with VM is assumed, but a few significant concepts are explained for less experienced readers. With noted exceptions, only components that are part of the base VM/ESA product are discussed; add-on software is discussed in more detail in other chapters.

What Is VM/ESA?

Virtual Machine/Enterprise Systems Architecture (VM/ESA) is the latest in a series of IBM operating systems that implement the **virtual machine** metaphor: the idea that the resources of a physical machine can be managed such that multiple users each believe and act as if the entire system was dedicated to serving them, without ever needing to be aware that the environment is being shared. This simple concept provides the framework of today's premier platform for interactive mainframe computing.

Do not let that description be misleading. VM's true power lies not in its considerable ability, but in its adaptability and extensibility. Inside the VM/ESA box are tools and building blocks which, though powerful in their own right, can be combined in countless ways to produce solutions for today's business needs. No other mainframe environment provides the breadth and variety of possible solutions found in every VM/ESA installation.

What Is a Virtual Machine?

A **virtual machine** is simply the programmatic equivalent of a real machine. Using hardware architecture, VM creates a software environment that supports attributes and capabilities of a real computer: memory, DASD storage, console for operator communication, and various peripheral devices. Within virtual machines, users can load and run programs that obey conventions established by the System/370, 370/XA, or ESA/390 architectures—from simple "Hello, world" programs to complex operating systems. In the realm of VM system programmers, it is quite common to find that the program loaded and running in this virtual machine environment is in fact VM/ESA itself!

The Two Principal VM Components: CP and CMS

That many users see VM as a single entity exemplifies the seamless integration a properly administered VM system should present to non-technical users. The reality, however, is that VM is a collection of individual parts, each of which plays an important role in providing users a place to work. The two most important of these are **CP** and **CMS**.

What Is CP?

The Control Program (CP) is the heart of VM, and is the framework upon which all other VM function is laid. It is also true that CP, due to its very nature, is something most VM users see very little of, since it is least visible when doing its job well.

CP's first major objective is to provide a runtime environment for software that is indistinguishable from a real, dedicated computer, and it succeeds in spectacular fashion. Unless a loaded program chooses to, it will not detect the difference between virtual and real machines, and typically does not care. This is an instance where the overused phrase "transparent to the user" has real meaning, and clearly exhibits one of the critical successes of VM: the ability to run any program that follows the hardware architecture without modification, awareness, or allowances for the fact that execution is not on a real computer.

CP's second major objective is to accomplish the above while sharing physical machine resources with other programs. CP manages access to real VM/ESA system resources and distributes those resources to operating systems under its control. These resources include:

- Main storage
- Auxiliary storage
- Expanded storage
- SPOOLing
- Input/Output operations
- CPU allocation

CP's greatest achievement is thus exploiting the hardware's potential by taking the concept of virtual storage one step farther and managing a workload of heterogeneous users, each of whom runs a private operating system.

The last major objective for CP is to provide support services for virtual machines which desire them, so that programs within virtual machines can do things such as communicate with other virtual machines, query and/or change the characteristics of the real or virtual environment, and exploit CP's ability to simulate hardware functions.

While addressing the first two of these objectives, the question of deciding exactly what the correct response is to a given program request occurs repeatedly. In answer to this, it is said that CP is the benefactor of the most exhaustively complete program specifications ever written: the *Principles of Operation*.

Starting with the System/360 and continuing to the current ESA/390, the *Principles of Operation* has been used as the mandate and final arbiter for CP's management of the virtual machine environment.

CP features and capabilities

The VM/ESA Control Program simultaneously supports System/370, 370/XA, and ESA/390 (when running on an ESA/390 processor) virtual machine architectures, and supports three types of virtual machine storage configurations:

V=R **Virtual=Real**, which has a fixed, contiguous area of storage starting at page 0 of real storage.

V=F **Virtual=Fixed**, which also has a fixed, contiguous area of storage, but the area does not start at page 0.

V=V **Virtual=Virtual**, which has no permanently resident storage in the real system.

V=R and V=F virtual machines have special capabilities provided for them by CP, and are referred to as **preferred** virtual machines. CP provides additional support including hardware-assisted storage protection, dedicated processor I/O support when running on a real multiprocessor, fast-path I/O processing, and use of Start Interpretive Execution (SIE) assist. Preferential treatment for these virtual machines can provide performance and throughput levels approaching those achieved when running natively on real machines. (Indeed, some operating systems such as VSE/SP which do not exploit features such as dynamic channel pathing for I/O can *exceed* native performance under CP as a V=R or V=F virtual machine!)

Processor Resource/Systems Manager (PR/SM), necessary for support of V=F machines, is a hardware feature available on certain processors. PR/SM can operate in either of two modes: **basic** mode and **logically partitioned** (LPAR) mode. The PR/SM mode affects preferred virtual machine support as follows:

- Without PR/SM, CP supports only V=R and V=V machines
- With PR/SM in basic mode, CP supports V=R, V=F, and V=V machines
- With PR/SM in LPAR mode, CP supports only V=V machines

A uniquely powerful feature of CP is V=R guest machine recovery. A guest machine is defined as a virtual machine running an operating system, and although strictly speaking this definition is true of all virtual machines, it generally denotes operating systems such as VM/ESA itself, VSE/ESA, MVS/ESA, AIX/ESA, and PICK/370. The V=R recovery feature allows a V=R guest to survive recoverable CP

ABENDs, where real system storage is left intact; the effect is that the V=R guest simply halts processing for the time that CP needs to recover, then resumes. There are some restrictions to this feature, but it is worth the time to set up.

Configuration and runtime options define and control guest processors, both real and virtual. If a real machine has multiple processors, CP lets one or more of them be dedicated to virtual machines. Virtual machine definitions can also include statements that create a virtual multiprocessor (MP) environment for 370-XA, ESA/370, and ESA/390 mode virtual machines, and a virtual attached processor (AP) environment for System/370 virtual machines.

CP initialization

When a CP nucleus is built, a copy must be written to the system residence device so that it can be the object of an **Initial Program Load** or **IPL**. The CP nucleus consists of two parts—**resident** and **pageable**. The resident CP nucleus contains frequently used routines and those providing functions that must remain independent of paging operations, such as ABEND recovery routines.

The pageable CP nucleus contains less frequently used routines and is part of CP's virtual storage. These routines are brought into main storage (paged in) as required, thus conserving main storage. The performance impact of referencing the pageable nucleus is minimal, since frequently used pageable modules tend to remain resident except under severe storage constraints.

Loading the CP nucleus

Module HCPLOD loads the CP nucleus into storage. The following events cause HCPLOD to gain control:

1. Hardware or virtual IPL of CP
2. Software restart after a CP ABEND
3. SHUTDOWN REIPL request

When HCPLOD receives control, it begins by loading into main storage the checkpoint module (HCPCKP) and modules referenced by HCPCKP. HCPCKP performs a checkpoint if one was not done during the previous CP termination and returns control to

HCPLOD, which then loads the remaining resident portion of the CP nucleus, along with initialization-dependent pageable modules.

Storage initialization

Module HCPIST initializes CP's real and virtual storage. A query of the real processor obtains information about the hardware configuration and determines the amount, if any, of expanded storage. If a V=R guest is defined, the CP nucleus is moved above the preferred virtual machine's recovery area (storage reserved as a workarea for V=R guest recovery). Next, a list of reserved page frames for CP use—the free storage reserved frame list—is acquired. Finally, the RIO370 area is initialized, if defined. This area is reserved for DIAGNOSE X'98' LOCK requests on behalf of 24-bit addressing mode virtual machines. The size of the above areas are determined by installation-specified parameters and by the amount of real memory installed. Whatever storage remains is allocated as the **dynamic paging area**.

The dynamic paging area contains:

- Pageable CP modules (CP virtual storage)
- Free storage for CP requests
- CP Trace tables
- Virtual storage for VM guests
- CP SPOOL buffers
- Prefix pages for multiple CPUs, containing important information about each processor: status, PSWs, etc.

Information on real storage layout is contained in module HCPRSM. It contains all anchors, counts, and locks which map real storage.

I/O device initialization

Modules HCPIIO and HCPIID initialize I/O devices defined to the system. Each device defined in HCPRIO is tested with an I/O operation to determine whether it is physically attached (in VM/ESA Release 2 and later, devices may be detected dynamically rather than being defined in HCPRIO). Condition code 3 from an I/O request tells CP that the device is not operational. These devices are marked offline and are unavailable to the system. The following modules are called for specific functions:

HCPIDT	Tests each direct access storage device (DASD)
HCPITT	Tests each tape drive
HCPIMT	Tests unit record devices, terminals, and other device classes

Miscellaneous initialization tasks

After I/O device initialization, CP does the following:

- Initializes timers and clocks
- Brings the directory online
- Allocates system DUMP space
- Initializes expanded storage
- Restarts V=R guest if necessary
- Activates any alternate CPUs
- Activates missing interrupt detector
- Builds system operator's VMDBK and segment tables
- Logs on system operator
- Starts SPOOLing devices
- AUTOLOGs error recording, symptom recording, and accounting virtual machines
- Enables online terminals

CP termination

CP can terminate either through the privileged SHUTDOWN command, by an unrecoverable error such as a program check in CP or a machine check which causes an ABEND, or by invoking a hardware restart. Module HCPWRP controls the events that quiesce CP.

SHUTDOWN processing

The SHUTDOWN command causes an orderly shutdown of the control program. Major events include:

- Parsing the SHUTDOWN command for possible REIPL option
- Notifying system operator of SHUTDOWN processing
- Varying alternate CPUs offline
- Disabling all terminals
- Quiescing the I/O subsystem
- Loading disabled wait PSW (unless REIPL was specified)

V=R guest recovery

In most cases, CP attempts to recover and restart a preferred virtual machine running as a V=R guest upon CP reinitialization. This can only be accomplished if the system restarts itself through a SHUTDOWN REIPL request or from successful ABEND processing. If the system enters a disabled wait state, subsequent IPL processing resets the I/O unit and channel status required for successful guest recovery. The preferred virtual machine is reinitialized between loading the CP nucleus and logging on the system operator. Once this is accomplished, the preferred guest must invoke its own recovery procedure to continue operating.

Soft ABENDs

Some software errors are isolated to a specific virtual machine and do not prevent CP from continuing normal operation. In these cases a **soft ABEND** occurs and system operation continues.

During a soft ABEND, the virtual machine associated with the problem is notified, if possible, and placed in stopped state. A dump of CP pages and selected page frames relevant to the virtual machine is written to the dump device. These pages contain information such as virtual machine registers and prefix pages, the VMDBK, and CP's trace table entries.

Hard ABENDs

A hard ABEND occurs when an unrecoverable error occurs, or if system integrity is in question. Module HCPWRP performs the following tasks in this case:

- Obtains system termination lock
- Preserves prefix-page information
- Stops all CPUs except the one it is running on
- Saves vector facility status
- Disables all devices
- Takes a system dump, if required
- Performs a system checkpoint
- Records and saves V=R user environment
- Attempts to restart the system

Real CPU management

During CP initialization and termination, execution is in uniprocessor mode, that is, as if the system had a single CPU. CP detects, as part of initialization, CPUs in a multiprocessing system and initializes them. After CP initialization, all processors present on a multiprocessor system are available for work and CP controls their use.

In this environment, virtual machines can run on multiple processors. In order to maintain system integrity, CP uses serialization techniques to prevent the same module or virtual machine from running on more than one processor at a time or more than one processor attempting to change the same area of storage simultaneously. The most common serialization techniques used are **locks**.

Locks are either **formal** or **informal**, that is, either controlled by lock managers, or by routines attempting to use them. Informal locks are released and obtained outside the control of a lock manager. VM/ESA has four lock managers:

- HCPIOL manages I/O locks
- HCPLCK manages general locks
- HCPLOC manages symbolic locks
- HCPSYN manages spin locks

Semaphore locks

Both I/O and general locks are **semaphore** locks, which are static locks, allocated with an associated control block (VMDBK, SYSCM, etc.), and are always present whether the lock is in use or not. Semaphore locks are mapped by HCPLKWRD, which contains information such as:

- Number of shared requests
- Pointer to queued defer requests
- Control flags

If a module attempts to obtain a semaphore lock, CP checks whether it is in use. If not, the lock is set and control returns to the requester immediately. If the lock is in use, CP creates a CPEBK (CP execution block) and queues it behind the current lock holder and any prior pending requests for that lock. As modules release the lock, queued requests are dequeued in FIFO (first in, first out) order and processing resumes.

Examples of semaphore locks are:

- TOD synchronization
- Minidisk shared access
- VMDBK IUCV transactions
- Logical device operations
- Master processor switching
- Tape I/O processing
- Directory locks

Symbolic locks

Symbolic locks are similar to semaphores, except that they are created dynamically, as needed. A symbolic lock consists of an eight-character name called a **lock symbol**. Like the semaphore lock, requests for symbolic locks are queued via CPEBKs if unavailable, or given immediately if available.

Both semaphore and symbolic locks are referred to as **defer locks** and can be requested as **exclusive** or **shared**. If a module requests a shared defer lock, and no other module currently has an exclusive request on it, the lock request is granted. If the lock is held exclusively, requests for shared access are queued until the exclusive lock is released.

Spin locks

Spin locks are held only by CPUs. The term **spin** means that modules loop, testing lock availability without relinquishing processor control. There are **conditional** and **unconditional** spin lock requests. A conditional spin lock request indicates that the module only wants the lock if it is available immediately, that is, it does **not** want to spin on the lock. This allows the module to perform other tasks if the lock is unavailable.

An example of a spin lock request is HCPSYM, the symbolic lock manager, that must obtain a lock on the symbolic lock list in order to update it without allowing another processor to do the same thing simultaneously.

Real storage management

There are several types of real storage pages, or **frames**. Each page frame is represented by a frame table entry control block (FRMTE). The collection of FRMTEs make up the frame table located in a contiguous area of the resident CP nucleus, addressed by field RSAAVLFP in HCPRSM. The frame table appears in order of frame address, that is, the first FRMTE represents address X'0', the second represents address X'1000', and so on. Frames allocated during system IPL include:

- CP resident nucleus
- V=R guest storage
- RIO370 area
- Trace tables

These areas require little management since they are allocated for the duration of a system IPL, unless explicitly released by the operator. Most CP storage management is devoted to **available** and **user-owned** frames.

Available frames are maintained from an anchor (RSAAVLAN) in HCPRSM. From this list, CP satisfies free storage requests and CP storage as needed. If there is no storage on the available list, CP attempts to obtain a frame from the dynamic paging area. If unsuccessful, CP obtains a page from the free storage reserved frames list. If still unsuccessful, CP cannot continue, and ABENDs with a FRF002.

It is possible to obtain contiguous frames of free storage under VM/ESA. These requests are made through:

- The DEFINE STORAGE command
- HCPGETST macro
- Saved segments

These requests are conditional—if unsuccessful, the requester must employ appropriate procedures to handle the condition.

User-owned frames are those allocated to a specific virtual machine. If a frame is allocated to a virtual machine, a field in the FRMTE points to the user's page table entry in the page management control block (PGMBK).

Another type of storage, called **expanded storage**, is optional and, if installed, can be partitioned into guest and CP areas. CP uses its partition for high-speed paging and minidisk caching.

VM data spaces

VM data spaces are address spaces that can be used as repositories for large amounts of data. A virtual machine running in ESA/XC (eXtended Configuration) mode is assigned a **primary address space**. Additional spaces can be requested by the virtual machine, and can range in size from 64KB to 2GB (2 billion bytes) each. These address spaces can be accessed by other virtual machines—even non-XC virtual machines—if the owning virtual machine makes them sharable. Address spaces are created by the ADRSPACE macro, using the CREATE operand. The ADRSPACE macro can also return a sharable space to a private state (ADRSPACE ISOLATE) and delete an address space (ADRSPACE DESTROY).

Programs can run only in the primary address space; thus the term **data spaces** describes additional address spaces. Each address space is associated with an address space name and Address Space Identification Token (ASIT).

Identifying address spaces

The address space name (ASN) of the primary address space is BASE, which is assigned by CP. All other address spaces within a virtual machine must have unique 1- to 24-character names assigned by the virtual machine. This name is preceded by the creating userid and a colon to form the **space ID**. The ASIT is an eight-character system-wide token assigned by CP, unique among address spaces. This token is never used more than once throughout a system IPL, even if the address space is destroyed.

Accessing address spaces

Address spaces can be accessed directly by XC-mode virtual machines running in access-register mode. There are 16 access registers and an instruction set for using them; for example, LAM is the Load Access Multiple instruction.

For 370-, XA-, and ESA-mode virtual machines, address spaces are accessed indirectly through DIAGNOSE X'248' (copy-to-primary service).

SPOOL management

SPOOLing (**S**imultaneous **P**eripheral **O**perations **OnL**ine) is a method by which images of reader, printer, and punch input/output are kept on high-speed DASD. SPOOLing allows each user to perform private unit-record operations without having dedicated real devices. It also allows passing information among virtual machines by transferring it in SPOOL files. CP itself uses SPOOL to hold system data files that contain:

- Named saved systems (NSSs)
- Discontiguous saved segments (DCSSs)
- Trace files (TRF)
- National language support (NLS) repositories
- User-class override (UCR) files
- 3800 image libraries (IMG)

These files differ from normal SPOOL files and are called **System Data Files** (SDFs). For example, if the system is cold-started at IPL time, all normal SPOOL files are purged, while SDFs are preserved.

SPOOL files are represented by **SPOOL file control blocks** (SPFBKs). SPFBKs are anchored by one of three pointers in the system common area (SYSCM)—SYSINQ (reader files, CP dumps, VM dumps), SYSOUTQ (printer/punch files), or SYSDATQ (system data files). SPOOL data and CCWs are placed on a page of DASD called the SPOOL file data page block (SPDBK). All SPDBKs for a file are recorded on a SPOOL file map block (SPMBK). For virtual SPOOLing, another block—the SPOOL file allocation block (SPABK)—collects information about SPDBKs between SPMBK updates. The relationship between these blocks is discussed in the next section.

CP maintains a file ID table (FILID) in CP virtual storage which contains pointers to SPOOL queue anchors and the first SPFBK for each user that has a SPOOL file. A user entry is made the first time a user creates a SPOOL file, and remains in the table throughout the system IPL. Even after a user's last SPOOL file is deleted, the FILID entry remains until it is reconstructed at the next system IPL.

CP also maintains a SPOOL file index block (SFNDX) in the warm start area on DASD, which contains pointers to the first SPMBK of each file in the system. The number of pages in the

SFNDX is determined by the size of the warm start area. This is calculated by HCPGEN by multiplying the number of warm start cylinders by the number of pages per cylinder. Each 4K page contains 1,022 file pointers. The number of pages for the SFNDX is stored in field SYSSFNDX and the maximum number of files is contained in field SYSMSPID, both found in the system common area (HCPSYSCM). A copy of the SFNDX is maintained in CP virtual memory starting just after the pageable CP nucleus. External symbol @LOADEND in the CP nucleus marks this area.

During WARM or FORCE starts, CP uses the SFNDX to read the first SPMBK of each SPOOL file. The SPMBK contains a copy of the SPFBK which is used to reconstruct the SPOOLing queues.

SPOOL files are chained system-wide using forward and backward pointers (SPFFPNT/SPFBPNT); SPOOL files for particular users are chained using forward pointers only (SPFPNT).

SPOOL files contain data and CCWs required by the target device to process that data. When printed output, for example, is sent to a real device, CP writes SPOOL data and CCWs to the printer which processes the SPOOL file as if the originating program had written it directly to the printer itself.

Each real unit-record device is represented by a **real SPOOLing control block** (RSPBK) which gives CP information about the device and the file being processed. This information includes:

- SPFBK address for active file
- Real device address
- Pointer to real device block (RDEVBK)
- List of SPOOLing classes device will accept
- Character set and forms information

Virtual SPOOLing

Virtual machines can define virtual unit-record devices (readers, printers, punches), each of which is represented by a virtual device block (VDEVBK). To applications, these devices act exactly as their real counterparts, and no special programming is needed. CP manages data flow to and from these virtual devices through the control block relationships mentioned earlier. As an illustration, consider a virtual machine writing output to a virtual printer:

- When the virtual printer is defined, either in the user's directory entry or by the CP DEFINE command, a VDEVBK is created. A virtual SPOOLing device block (VSPBK) is also created, and its address is placed in the VDEVBK.

- The first line of output causes creation of an SPFBK, an SPABK, an SPMBK, and an SPDBK.
- The address of the SPABK is placed in the VSPBK.
- The first SPDBK is written to SPOOL and retained in memory.
- As each memory page is filled with output data, it is written to an assigned DASD SPOOL slot (SPDBK).
- The DASD address of each page is placed into the SPABK. The SPABK can hold up to 16 DASD slot addresses.
- After 16 DASD pages are consumed, their DASD addresses are written to the SPMBK and the SPABK is cleared for the next set.
- Each SPMBK can hold 960 slot addresses. When this is exhausted, a new SPMBK is created, and is chained to the old SPMBK by a pointer in the old SPMBK.
- When the file is closed, any remaining DASD slot addresses in the SPABK are written to the SPMBK and the current output frame is written to DASD. The SPABK pointer in the VDEVBK is cleared.

Virtual machine creation

When a user logs onto VM/ESA, CP creates a virtual machine. The control block that describes this virtual machine is the **virtual machine definition block** (VMDBK). The VMDBK contains important information about the user such as:

- Userid
- Accounting number
- Virtual machine registers
- Virtual machine state
- Pointers to other control blocks
- Virtual storage size

VMDBKs are chained in a cyclical list off the system VMDBK, which is not itself on the chain. This chain is referred to as the **global cyclical list**. A chain called the **local cyclical list** chains VMDBKs for virtual machines with more than one virtual CPU, such as a multiprocessor MVS guest. The VMDBK assigned at logon, called the **origin VMDBK**, contains a pointer to any other local VMDBKs, and also appears on the chain itself.

In this case, virtual CPUs are represented by separate VMDBKs, and are chained together by field VMDLCYCL. The VMDBK that owns user storage is called the **base VMDBK**, and may or may not be the origin VMDBK. Another pointer, VMDBASE, points to the base VMDBK.

Scheduling and dispatching the virtual machine

CP allocates processor resources based on virtual machine **timeslice** and **priority**. This task is performed by the scheduler.

HCPISR calculates the user (VMDBK) timeslice—the amount of time the running VMDBK may execute before the next VMDBK is **dispatched** (given control of the processor). It is calculated based on the processor's speed, by executing a predetermined set of instructions and noting the time consumed. This value then becomes the **minor timeslice**.

The optimum value is one that allows maximum execution for a task while ensuring adequate service to all users on the dispatch list. This value can also be set using the CP SET SRM DSPSLICE command. Overly small values cause unnecessary overhead and poor performance because of frequent scheduler intervention, while excessively high values cause inadequate interactive response time.

The scheduler maintains a list called the **dispatch vector** that contains VMDBK addresses of virtual machines ready for processing resources. If the scheduler determines that there is not enough memory to service a virtual machine, it is placed on the **eligible list** instead of the dispatch list.

A user's priority determines when a user moves from the Eligible to the Dispatch list. The methods used to calculate this priority are very complex, taking many factors about virtual machine settings and performance into account. This process is well-documented in HCPSCH.

In general, E0 users are placed on the dispatch list as soon as resources become available with no further consideration. E1 users (interactive) get the next-highest priority, followed by E2 users and finally E3 users. Keep in mind that higher-priority users get a smaller timeslice while lower priority users get a larger timeslice. These settings are continually monitored and adjusted during CP's scheduling of VMDBKs. The eligible list contains four parts, E0 through E3:

E0 Special list for users such as QUICKDSP virtual machines; added to the dispatch list without waiting.
E1 Short-running tasks
E2 Medium-running tasks
E2 Long-running tasks

Virtual machines begin by entering the dispatch list as E1 tasks. If a machine exhausts its timeslice and is dropped involuntarily, it becomes an E2 task. If it uses up its timeslice again, it becomes an E3 task. To ensure a fair and responsive interactive environment, short-running tasks get their small timeslice more frequently than longer-running tasks. Conversely, long running tasks get a larger timeslice but less frequently. In short, a one-minute task would enter the dispatch list ten times more frequently than a ten-minute task. This method prevents CPU-intensive tasks from dominating the CPU and causing "lumpy" (uneven) response time. Virtual machines not ready for processing are placed on the dormant list.

The dispatcher is responsible for passing control of the real processor to the virtual machine. Each processor in the real complex has a **processor-local dispatch vector**, commonly referred to as the **runlist**. In addition to a local runlist, the master processor also has another list, the **master-only processor-local dispatch vector**, which contains tasks which cannot run on an alternate processor. Most CP commands are executed on the master processor.

The dispatcher checks the system VMDBK for work to perform before dispatching virtual machines. On the master processor, the master-only dispatch vector is checked before the processor-local dispatch vector. On non-master processors, the dispatcher checks its local dispatch vector and, if empty, searches the local dispatch vector of other processors for work. Dedicated processor work is only dispatched from the local dispatch vector.

PSW states

While CP is dispatching virtual machines, it operates in one of two states: **disabled wait** or **active wait**.

When the dispatcher has searched all dispatch vectors without finding any work to do, it enters an active wait state. For uniprocessors, this is done by loading an enabled wait PSW under which new work is recognized by an interrupt. In a multiprocessing environment, or when running as a guest under VM, CP loads an enabled PSW in PSW key 3. This allows CP to respond to interrupts from any processor. Module HCPWAI performs the active wait method appropriate for the type of processor. When in PSW key 3 active wait, HCPWAI loops through the dispatch vectors looking for work. If a task is found, HCPWAI exits the active wait state for that processor.

Virtual storage management

Each megabyte of virtual storage is represented by a **page management control block** (PGMBK), a 4K storage block with five sections:

- Page table
- Page status table
- ASA table
- Flags and status area
- Time stamps

When a virtual machine references a page not in storage, a page fault occurs. This signals CP to acquire a real storage frame for the user. Once a frame is acquired, its address is placed in the page table entry for that user's virtual address.

The real page address for a user virtual address can be identified by the following process:

1. Locate user's VMDBK (CP LOCATE *userid*).
2. Find address of segment table origin (STO) at VMDPSTO (for virtual machines up to 32MB, the segment table is kept in the first 32 words of the VMDBK at VMDLSEG; for machines larger than 32MB, separate pages are allocated).
3. Each word in the STO represents one segment, that is, one megabyte of virtual storage. For example, if looking for virtual zero, use the first word; this is the address of the PGMBK for that segment. The last 6 bits are used by CP as control information for that segment, and not used as part of the address; substitute 0s. If the high-order bit (X'80') is on, the segment represents non-addressable storage for this user.

4. The first 256 words of the PGMBK represent each page in the segment. Locate the page in question. Again, zero is the first entry. The low-order 12 bits are used for control information; substitute 000 to form the address. If bit X'04' is on in the third byte, the page is invalid, i.e., is not resident in real storage.

5. To find the ASA (DASD entry) for a page with no real associated page, start at PGMBK+X'800'. Each word there represents the DASD slot associated with a page that has been referenced, but paged out (stolen).

6. If there is no page table entry or ASA for a virtual page, it has not been referenced by the virtual machine.

I/O management

I/O instructions are privileged operations under VM/ESA. CP intercepts these instructions and performs necessary functions that either translate CCWs, pass I/O to real devices, or simulate I/O to logical and virtual devices. The results of I/O operations are reflected to a virtual machine exactly as if the virtual machine performed I/O to a real device. Each I/O device in the system configuration is represented by a **real device control block** (RDEVBK).

The types of I/O CP intercepts are:

- DIAGNOSE I/O
- Start I/O (SIO) (370 mode)
- Halt I/O (HIO) (370 mode)
- Start I/O, fast release (SIOF) (370 mode)
- Start subchannel (SSCH) (370/XA mode)
- Halt subchannel (HSCH) (370/XA mode)
- Clear subchannel (CSCH) (370/XA mode)

Each I/O request is assigned an **I/O request and response information block** (IORBK). This block contains important information CP uses to perform the I/O under VM/ESA and to return proper responses to the requester. Functions CP performs on the I/O request include:

Virtual-to-real translation: I/O data addresses are converted to real addresses before issuing the I/O request. The virtual device address is converted as necessary.

Cylinder relocation: I/O to specific minidisk cylinders almost always references a different real cylinder.

CCW translation: Non-ESA CCWs must be converted to their ESA counterparts.

Logical device simulation: Logical devices are graphic terminals that do not physically exist, such as those defined by IBM's VM/Pass-Through program product.

Virtual device simulation: I/O to virtual printers, readers, and punches are converted to SPOOLing operations.

Reserve/release processing: This permits shared DASD access.

Device error recovery: CP attempts to recover from I/O errors; if unsuccessful, it notifies the virtual machine.

Interrupt management

Interrupts are generated by hardware, a virtual machine, or CP itself. They are either solicited, that is, in response to a request; or unsolicited, as in the interrupt generated by an attention key on a 3270 device. In any event, CP handles these interrupts and reflects their status to the requester as the hardware itself would respond.

Interrupts are handled by **first level interrupt handlers** (FLIHs) and **second level interrupt handlers** (SLIHs). The FLIHs intercept the following interrupts:

- Restart
- External
- SVC
- Program check
- Machine check
- I/O

The entry-point address for each FLIH routine is stored in the corresponding new hardware PSW. When an interrupt occurs, hardware loads the appropriate new PSW, saving the interrupting address (the current PSW) in the old PSW location. First-level interrupt handlers execute disabled, that is, they prevent other interrupts from occurring while they handle the current one. If the interrupt is for a virtual machine, CP places this information in the virtual machine's page zero. The virtual machine then receives the interrupt when it is next dispatched.

If a second-level interrupt handler is required, CP prepares a control block and stacks a request. Typical events requiring second-level interrupt handlers are:

- Clock comparator external interrupts
- I/O interrupts
- Correctable machine checks

Virtual machine instruction processing

When a virtual machine is dispatched, it receives control of the real processor, and can issue 370 and ESA instructions. Some instructions are simulated by CP, while others are intercepted, such as I/O and the DIAGNOSE instruction. Under VM/ESA, virtual machines use the **SIE** instruction, in **interpretive execution mode**.

SIE (Start Interpretive Execution) is a facility by which most privileged and non-privileged instructions are handled by the hardware without requiring CP intervention. This allows the virtual machine to exploit the hardware's speed while preventing the virtual machine from modifying CP and other virtual machines in the system. On some processors, the interpretive execution facility also supports Virtual Machine Assist (VMA), which intercepts and executes privileged instructions and supervisor calls to improve VM/SP and VM/HPO performance.

What Is CMS?

The second major ingredient in the VM toolbox is the **Conversational Monitor System** (CMS). This is the VM facet with which users are most familiar, since it produces most of the data that occupies a terminal screen. By traditional definition, CMS is a single-tasking operating system dedicated to serving the needs of one terminal user. At one point in its history, CMS could run as a stand-alone system on a real machine, but it has long since been so heavily optimized to allow for efficient running in a CP virtual machine that this is no longer possible.

CMS is a tool that provides the ability to perform tasks associated with computing in an interactive, friendly way, including loading and executing user programs, and creating and saving data files. It includes hundreds of individual functions, covering such a broad range of computing needs that most users never use them all. Several features mentioned in this chapter have entire chapters dedicated to them later in this book, so only a limited description of them is given here.

CMS features and capabilities

CMS has two modes of operation: **command line** and **full-screen** (formally called **CMS Session Services**, and sometimes referred to as **CMS Windows**). Command line mode is the traditional mode, and the choice of most experienced CMS users, since it provides both a more familiar environment and more direct access to the CMS command set they already know well. The full-screen CMS facility allows users to define and manipulate multiple, potentially overlapping windows that contain results of requests to edit files, issue CMS commands, receive messages from other users, and more.

Regardless of CMS interface chosen, all users also benefit from the tremendous range of support that CMS provides, including two of the most productive and popular applications ever to grace a computer: the **System Product Editor** (**XEDIT**), an extremely powerful editor; and **Procedures Language VM/REXX** (**REXX**), an interpreted high-level programming language. These are discussed in more detail in Chapter 4, *Exploiting XEDIT,* on page 107 and Chapter 5, *Exploiting REXX,* on page 141.

Other significant CMS features and facilities are:

CMS Pipelines: A powerful tool for processing data that involves passing it from one step to the next using a "pipeline" metaphor, that is, manipulating it with predefined programs at each stage until it exists in the form desired by the user.

Shared File System (SFS): The SFS allows data and DASD storage space to be shared among a pool of users, with security options available to control access to files in the pool.

Advanced Program-To-Program Communication (APPC): Two facilities for APPC programming interfaces exist: **APPC/VM** for assembler language programs, and **Common Programming Interface for Communications** (CPIC) for high-level languages.

A program can use either to communicate with a partner program on the same or a different system.

Coordinated Resource Recovery (CRR): This facility implements Systems Network Architecture (SNA) LU6.2 sync-point architecture, and is designed to allow users to create applications that have interdependencies when updating data files, so that an application may be assured that all updates it requests are completed successfully (**committed**), or none are completed (**rolled back**).

Callable Services Library (CSL): The CMS CSL contains many useful routines, callable from seven supported CSL languages, that provide facilities such as program-to-program communication (using SAA CPIC), access to SFS functions, access to CRR functions, and access to information derived from the current virtual machine execution environment.

Online HELP: HELP information is available online for all IBM-supplied CMS commands; installations and users can further extend HELP for local commands or enhancements to IBM commands.

Programming Simulation Services: Aside from its own native program support, CMS simulates a limited environment for generating and executing OS and VSE programs.

High-level Language Support: CMS supports many high-level programming languages, including OS/VS COBOL, VS COBOL II, VS FORTRAN, VS Pascal, PL/I, REXX, and C.

Other VM Components

Multiple virtual machines working together: GCS

The Group Control System (GCS) provides multitasking dispatching services within individual virtual machines and common storage capability across virtual machine boundaries, making it unique in the VM world. This facility allows several virtual machines to work in concert to provide a service, each running independently of others except when necessary to communicate.

GCS exists and is used today primarily to provide support for Virtual Telecommunication Access Method (VTAM) under VM without requiring a guest virtual machine such as VSE or MVS. To fully support the requirement, GCS is implemented as a true multitasking supervisor. The nucleus provides mechanisms for controlling and allocating nucleus memory (as common storage), and allocating memory in individual virtual machines (as private storage).

Virtual machines running the same GCS Saved System are members of the same GCS group, and can access the common storage in the GCS nucleus. Using this, members of the group can exchange data simply by placing it in the common storage area and notifying another group member with some variety of message. Alternatively, a program can be initialized in the same virtual machine as the program with which it needs to exchange data, and the notification process can be handled by the simpler task-to-task processes supported in all multitasking environments.

An additional GCS capability is the GCS Recovery Machine, defined to the GCS nucleus, which is the first virtual machine to initialize GCS in its storage. No common programming tasks associated with normal processing are done here; rather, this userid runs a task which is notified by the GCS supervisor when either a subtask or an entire virtual machine ABENDs within the group. Using information provided, the recovery task can clean up the environment left behind by the ABENDed task, doing things such as freeing acquired storage, closing files, and notifying other tasks of the problem. The recovery task can also restart the failed task, thus effecting a complete ABEND recovery.

Multiple CPUs working together: Cross System Extensions

Cross System Extensions (CSE), a built-in VM/ESA facility, connects up to four real processors running VM/ESA in a **complex** that appears to users as single machine. All systems must be connected by channel-to-channel adapters, or a 3088 Multisystem Channel Communications Unit. With this feature, systems in a complex can share SPOOL files and minidisks, command queries include information from all processors, and messages can be issued to users logged on any system in the complex. For some large installations, CSE is the best way to combine the power of several real machines in a way that does not significantly add to system complexity for users. CSE is the function successor to products from IBM (Inter-

System Facilities for VM/SP HPO) and VM/CMS Unlimited (Single System Image for VM/SP and VM/SP HPO).

Program-to-program communication

The VM/ESA protocol for inter-program communication, **Advanced Program-to-Program Communication/VM** (APPC/VM), implements the APPC architecture as defined by Systems Network Architecture (SNA).

Transparent Services Access Facility (TSAF) transports APPC/VM protocols throughout a group of interconnected systems, called a **collection**. This use of TSAF supports APPC/VM communication calls from a program on any machine in the collection, to another program on any other machine, without the programs themselves being concerned about where they reside. The TSAF collection can be connected by VTAM-driven communication links, or by several communication links directly supported by TSAF. Use of CSL functions from high-level languages facilitates creating programs capable of this type of communication. TSAF supports the "protected" conversation mode required for support of Coordinated Resource Recovery.

APPC/VM VTAM Support (AVS) is an extension to TSAF, and is aimed at communicating with other programs that reside anywhere in an SNA network; thus it is not limited to the scope of a single TSAF collection. AVS, a task that runs in the same GCS virtual machine as VTAM, handles translations between APPC/VM and APPC/VTAM during sessions. Again, CSL functions make this capability easily available from high-level programming languages. Like TSAF, AVS supports "protected" conversations.

Integrating the workstation

Workstations of all varieties are increasingly part of VM/ESA configurations. Rather than just supporting workstations as fancy 3270 terminals, VM/ESA allows workstations to access an array of host services. With the Enhanced Connectivity Facility (ECF) operating in a virtual machine, a workstation with a connected session to the host can:

- Use host DASD storage as if it were on the workstation
- Access host resident files directly

- Use host system printing facilities
- Copy files between workstation and host, with automatic data format conversions
- Access host resident databases as if on the workstation

Open Systems Interconnection/Communications Subsystem (OSI/CS), a facility that allows VM/ESA users to participate in multivendor Open Systems Interconnection (OSI) networks, supports common OSI requirements such as file and message transfer. Using OSI/CS, an application program running on a VM/ESA system can communicate with an application on another system that is using a compatible set of OSI protocols.

IBM's Workstation Data Save Facility/VM (WDSF/VM) program product allows backing up, archiving, and restoring workstation files to and from host VM systems from workstations executing PC-DOS, OS/2, AIX/RT PC, or AIX Version 3 for RISC/6000. WDSF/VM can create and use full or incremental backups, and can be scheduled to run automatically to allow for convenience. This process essentially uses the VM host as a data repository, and depends also on the host backup methodology to provide some of its function. See Chapter 14, *VM/ESA–Workstation Synergy,* on page 375 for more information on WDSF and other VM/ESA–workstation connectivity facilities.

Problem diagnosis: dump examination tools

No matter how stable an environment, situations will arise that require in-depth examination, and VM/ESA provides tools for this. Dump Viewing Facility (DVF) and its predecessor Interactive Problem Control System (IPCS, shipped with VM/ESA 1.0 370 Feature) assist users in problem determination after ABENDs occur. When a virtual machine, or the VM/ESA system itself, encounters a problem where operation cannot continue, it has the option of taking a snapshot of its memory to facilitate further problem analysis. Since these memory dumps exist as files on the VM/ESA system, DVF and IPCS use the power of the computer to make information in these files more presentable to the human eye, allowing users to focus on understanding the sequence of events that led to the problem, rather than the data extraction techniques. DVF also allows creating REXX macro commands to provide further assistance by automating information-gathering.

KPROBE, a program product from Relay Technology, Inc. (formerly VM Systems Group, Inc.), provides an alternative to IPCS and DVF, offering enhanced functionality and usability.

Data storage simplified: System-Managed Storage

In order to assist VM/ESA installations with management of the typical ever-growing pool of external storage devices, Data Facility/System-Managed Storage for VM/ESA (DFSMS/VM) automates many administrative processes required to manage the resources effectively. Based on site definitions, DFSMS/VM attempts to match needs of the data to the appropriate physical storage medium. It also allows new storage devices to be added to an existing configuration with minimal impact, since use of and migration to new devices can be controlled automatically and staged as desired through DFSMS/VM.

DFSMS/VM function is available through the Interactive Storage Management Facility (ISMF), a full-screen, menu-driven application that simplifies the command interface to the storage management subsystem, thus minimizing effort and time required to manage the environment effectively.

Automated operations: PROP

Another resource in the VM/ESA toolbox is the Programmable Operator (PROP), which automates operation of anything from a single virtual machine to a complete CSE complex. Many everyday actions on VM systems can be automated, and PROP is a simple but highly effective mechanism for accomplishing this.

PROP operates by examining the text of messages received, and using a site- or user-specified table to determine what (if any) action is to be taken. If it finds a match, PROP calls the action routine specified in the table to respond to the situation indicated by the message. Action routines are simply locally written programs that do such things as query task status, issue commands, notify another user, or log a message about the problem. These routines can be written in REXX, making them almost trivial to create. With proper action routines, many messages issued by virtual machines or by VM/ESA can be handled without human intervention.

Tools for smaller jobs: CMS Utilities Feature

While standard CMS command facilities are extremely robust, there are occasional requirements for specific functions for which there are no native commands. IBM's CMS Utilities Feature (CUF) demonstrates how easy it is to extend capabilities of the basic environment, simply by creating a program to do the function desired. This package consists of a suite of programs that have proven useful, in some cases over many years, and includes many familiar names:

ACCOUNT   Processes VM/ESA accounting records
BROWSE   Provides full-screen, read-only access to CMS files
DCSSBKUP Saves CMS saved segments as CMS files
DCSSRSAV Restores segments saved by DCSSBKUP
DEPRINT   Writes print-format reader files to disk, saving carriage control commands
FLIST   Provides full-screen file list
WAKEUP   Puts virtual machine into dormant state until predetermined event occurs

How VM Is Used

Most VM/ESA users can be categorized as one of the following: guest operating system, interactive user, or service virtual machine. It is testimony to VM's power and flexibility that these three categories have such diverse needs and benefits.

Guest operating systems

As mentioned, any program that respects the hardware architecture can execute in a virtual machine. In order to maximize shared use of hardware resources, virtual machines frequently contain operating systems such as VM/ESA itself, MVS/ESA, VSE/ESA, and others. These operating systems do not execute in degraded mode, but are as fully functional as if running on a real system.

Operating these systems as guests under VM can provide more benefits than just sharing physical resources: due to CP's ability to virtualize hardware function, it is possible to create a virtual communications path between two virtual machines that functions exactly as its hardware counterpart, sometimes even more efficiently than real devices! This is frequently done with creation of virtual channel-to-channel adapters that connect a VSE/ESA VTAM system with VM/VTAM, or an MVS/ESA Job Entry Subsystem (JES) connected directly to a Remote Spooling Communications System (RSCS) service machine.

An interesting situation occurs when VM/ESA itself runs in a virtual machine, because another critical VM attribute is recognized: the ability to use VM as a tool for testing itself, with other users isolated from adverse affects. As a matter of trivia, the real recursion limit is not known, but VM execution nested in five levels of virtual machines has been observed with no apparent negative effects other than confusing the terminal operator (and relatively poor performance, due to multiple levels of translation and paging).

Personal computing for interactive users

VM's most obvious use is providing a terminal user the capability to perform work. The range of tasks that can be accomplished by a single user is limitless, including such common activities as managing an appointment calendar, exchanging communications with other users, creating REXX procedures to automate normal daily work, and even identifying resources consumed while performing all the other tasks. There are as many ways to exploit VM/ESA as there are individual VM/ESA users; no matter how complex the tasks at hand, the interactive environment makes accomplishing a task as easy as possible.

Client serving: service virtual machines

The last of the three primary modes of operation is that of service virtual machines (SVMs). This highlights another critical attribute of VM: adaptability and extensibility of the environment to the needs of the moment. If any task remains to be accomplished, a service machine can accommodate it.

When the need arose to manage the driver program to support advanced printing capabilities of IBM's 3812 printer, a service machine was created. When a user must compile a test program without disabling the interactive session, the compile can be performed in a CMS Batch service machine, with output routed back to the user for later examination. When a security facility must access its database to perform logon password verification, a communication request is issued from CP to a service machine, and the proper response is given to the user. When a user needs data from a database, most likely an SQL/DS server machine will provide the required answer. When a VM/ESA installation connects to a world-wide SNA network, a service machine runs VTAM, VSCS, and AVS to provide terminal and program communication throughout the network. When a VTAM network change is tested, another VTAM service machine replicates the production configuration to isolate the test environment.

The last example, simple as it may seem, further proves the power of the virtual machine concept: VM is the only VTAM host capable of running multiple VTAM copies; due to operating system design limitations, MVS/ESA and VSE/ESA cannot do this.

Today's industry excitement regarding client/server computing echoes 20 years of VM use. Client/server computing recognizes the power and simplicity of VM's service machine architecture, and applies it to heterogeneous and distributed applications. VM's past and future role in client/server computing is demonstrated by IBM's naming it as the first component in the Client/Server Computing Unit organization.

VM and local area networks

Through use of IBM's Transmission Control Protocol/Internet Protocol (TCP/IP) program product, VM/ESA lets users work on a multivendor Internet network that uses the TCP/IP protocol set, through a connection to a Local Area Network (LAN). Users can transfer files and log on to remote systems anywhere in the network. This capability uses a channel-attached controller such as an IBM 3174 to connect to the desired network. Network protocols supported include IBM Token Ring LAN, Ethernet LAN, and X.25.

The VM community

VM has for many years had strong and vocal support from its many users; the common theme from the beginning has been "Users united in sharing information". This remains true, and the entire VM community realizes the benefit of this attitude. Many VM/ESA features were added through efforts of users and organizations who worked with IBM to enhance the product, and gave it more tools to perform functions needed in the business of everyday life.

Well-organized user groups such as SHARE and GUIDE have a long history of improving VM, as well as serving as meeting points for world-wide users to exchange information, ideas, and, often, program code as well. These meetings, open to users from all environments, typically last about five days, and are attended by as many as 5000 people, many of whom have a primary interest in VM.

The VMSHARE electronic conference was created expressly as a communication vehicle for people involved in VM-related SHARE activities, but has outgrown that limited role and become the center of all discussion, technical and otherwise, related to VM. Currently supported by McGill University, it is used by hundreds of people every day to exchange information.

The University of Waterloo in Ontario, Canada, has for many years served as a clearinghouse for VM-based programs and ideas that have been placed in the public domain through the generosity of their authors. For a small processing fee, the current VM public domain library is available to anyone.

The annual VM Workshop is a very informal, very friendly, very intense gathering of VM technicians and users where information is the price of attendance: attendees are asked (although not required) to offer a presentation or contribution of some kind. The reward for attendance at the workshop is the **VM Tools Tape**, a set of tapes containing a snapshot of the current VMSHARE and PCSHARE conference databases, a copy of the current University of Waterloo VM library, individual contributions from workshop attendees, and occasionally public domain libraries from VM user groups around the world. This meeting, usually sponsored by a university to reduce costs, draws an average attendance of about 300 people.

Beyond this, many smaller local user groups serve the needs of users closer to home, by offering support, encouragement, and information. These groups typically meet on a regular basis, for half- or full-day sessions. Most local user groups do not have formal membership requirements, so anyone is welcome to attend; depending on geographical concentration of VM installations, attendance varies from 20 to 200 people.

VM/ESA Benefits

Benefits of running VM have been demonstrated repeatedly to and by the many VM users and installations that depend on VM to provide function and support to succeed in daily business. VM/ESA is the most powerful, full-featured VM ever, and represents a far-reaching and integrated platform for consolidation of users of earlier VM versions.

Today's businesses must respond quickly to competitive pressures, and the rapid prototyping and development capabilities that VM affords continue to provide timely answers to problems they face. The wide range of hardware platforms on which VM is available—from single-user workstations to the largest processor complex—provides tremendous flexibility in matching problem solutions to economic need. The ability to create a service virtual machine to handle the most obscure or complex requirement produces confidence that today's tools will build tomorrow's solutions.

The richness of function provided by VM/ESA is astounding and gratifying. The world of data processing is changing by leaps and bounds, and a clear picture of the service provider that will address these changes is beginning to take shape. What makes VM/ESA fit into that picture is not what it can do today, but what it will do tomorrow.

2

Wide-Open VM

By Mark Cathcart

Outline

This chapter addresses several topics relating to VM in the open systems world:

- VM's current position
- Requirements for open systems
- Definitions and explanations
- Techniques for interoperability in heterogeneous computing environments
- A preview of things VM will do to support such an environment

Because this chapter describes VM/ESA's promise to deliver major open systems standards, it is a "work in progress", as availability of these standards on VM is emerging.

If you have concerns about currency of information in this chapter, contact the author directly or via your IBM account team.

Introduction

VM past

Since its birth, VM has been amongst the most popular of IBM System/370, System/370-XA, and System/390 operating systems. It has always spanned the range of IBM "mainframe" processors, from the smallest to the very largest.

Today, it can run on systems from an IBM PS/2-based processor through the latest 8-way water cooled ES/9000 technology; it has also been demonstrated running on processors with 32 CPU engines.[1]

Of all the computer industry's operating systems, it is one of the least architecturally constrained, supporting gigabytes of real and virtual storage, up to 64 processors per system image, and thousands of I/O devices and concurrent users.[2]

The power and flexibility this offers, combined with the fact that much of the operating system is provided in source code program format to its licensed customers, has led to there being over 20,000[3] VM systems world-wide with an estimated 9,000,000 daily users.

Through to the mid-1980s, VM was seen as one of the more open operating systems, as its users can quickly and easily modify and tailor VM to meet their own needs.

It pioneered techniques such as program-to-program communication, and concepts such as personal computing, groupware, client/server computing, and local area networking have been commonplace in VM since its inception in the late 1960s.

However, since the rise of the personal computer and, later, RISC-based workstations running Unix derivatives, VM has increasingly been viewed as a proprietary operating system offering little to the new worlds of open computing and both formal and informal standards. Nothing could be further from the truth.

---

[1]   An IBM prototype (PPCS) processor at CERN in Geneva, Switzerland.

[2]   Today in the UK, an IBM customer runs with greater than 5,000 concurrent users.

[3]   April 1993

VM future

In February 1993, IBM announced a "statement of direction" to support the Open Software Foundation (OSF) Distributed Computing Environment (DCE) on VM, as well as selected POSIX (Portable Operating System Interfaces for computer environments) standards as defined by the IEEE (Institute of Electrical and Electronic Engineers).

Today's Environment

Information infrastructure objectives

As IS organizations seek to build information infrastructures for their businesses, their real objective must be to enhance the effectiveness of system users—from the executive office to the loading bay—with increased **range** and **reach**.

Range   Today's computing systems can provide a broad range of information system services, starting with simple computer messages, increasing to access to corporate databases, incorporating more users and functions in various applications, and, finally, integrating all users in all applications, as needed by the business.

In the past, it was important to focus use of technology to improve individual work locations or disciplines. Now, particularly with increased consolidation of time as a competitive factor, the focus must be extended to involve all operational facets. An example of this is the feedback provided in retail distribution from automated point-of-sale devices. These systems update store inventory databases, which are amalgamated into company-wide EDI (electronic data interchange) ordering systems that replenish seasonal merchandise only at stores that are below a certain "safe" stock level.

Reach   In a similar respect, today's computing can reach out to users, growing from departmental solutions, through division line-of-business applications, extending to enterprise-wide data-intensive programs, and encompassing suppliers, business partners, and customers.

As the world moves to a global economy, it is important to focus not only on intra-enterprise capabilities, but also on inter-enterprise communications, data access, and applications.

Why Open?

X/OPEN, a group dedicated to creating a set of standard interfaces, surveyed its members and in January 1992 published a report entitled *The Open Systems Directive*. It identified their top five strategic requirements:

1. Interoperability across heterogeneous systems and networks
2. Overall architecture for enterprise open systems computing
3. Heterogeneous, networked database access and management
4. Integrated open and proprietary network management
5. Open systems access to data on proprietary mainframe applications

These requirements will be no surprise to many IBM customers, especially members of one of the main user groups [GUIDE, SHARE, SHARE Europe and Australian SHARE/GUIDE (ASG)], all of which have written papers or submitted requirements to match these.

In order to progress beyond these user requirements it is first necessary to refine them into a set of open infrastructure requirements:

Multivendor interoperability: The basis for this is connectivity—the capability to support varied networking options across and beyond enterprises.

Transparent access to data: Information, wherever it resides, must be accessible in a transparent and non-disruptive way. Applications and user tools must be able to transcend vendor and protocol barriers, while protecting sensitive information from theft, manipulation, and destruction.

Remote application access: Authorized users, both people and programs, must be able to access applications, wherever they may reside, to complete tasks.

Multivendor systems management: Tools and mechanisms are needed to manage all system resources.

Transaction processing across systems: For the evolving distributed processing environment, users require an open transaction processing environment which supports standard communication protocols, allows effective applications to interoperate between platforms, and permits user and application portability.

Multivendor security: As enterprises open resources through interoperability to both their own users and those of partners and customers, facilities must be available to protect these assets from accidental and intentional misuse or destruction.

Consistent user interface: For users to operate productively in mixed environments, they need consistent interfaces to the varied systems and applications.

View and print anywhere: Users need the ability to display and create printed output through use of a consistent set of view and print capabilities across enterprises. They want to do this with the assurance that what was edited on the workstation will be the same as that which is produced elsewhere on a high speed (or other) printer.

Application flexibility: For application developers, provide a consistent development capability across platforms, and support the flexibility of running applications on varied systems, both IBM and others.

Integrated application solutions: Users need a consistent application solution. This is particularly important, they say, for applications that form a core part of their business operations.

As the above shows, open systems is a style—a view—a *concept* of computing based on and responsive to the growing requirements of computing in the 1990s. It is the part of the information infrastructure that allows information technology to be implemented across a multivendor environment.

By facilitating portability and interoperability, open systems enhance the ability to protect investments, particularly those made with open systems criteria.

Portability

For many users, portability just means being able to run applications on other platforms without any changes. This is important,

but portability is also about data, and about people and their skills.
It is valuable to the business:

- To give freedom to change hardware and software vendors,
  and yet protect investment in applications
- To provide flexibility in changing systems platforms
  ("rightsizing") to match changing business needs
- To allow the same application to be used across several busi-
  ness units, each of which may have chosen different systems
- To be able to use "shrink-wrapped" application packages
- To allow copies of data to be readily transferred and reused
- To make it easier for staff to move between departments and
  between systems
- To shorten the learning curve for new applications

To achieve portability, interfaces must be standard across systems:

- To port **applications** requires not only standard languages,
  but also standard interfaces to services provided by the
  system: file and database access, communications, user interface, etc.
- To port **data** requires standard formats; a basic but pervasive example is the ASCII flat file. A richer but more
  context-specific example is the IGES (Initial Graphics
  Exchange Specification) for engineering design data; there
  are many others.
- To enable **people** to move readily, requires a standard user
  interface, as defined (for example) by IBM's Common User
  Access (CUA).

Standardization is rarely absolute and complete, and therefore
portability is rarely perfect. It is the level at which the interface is
standard which determines the amount and ease of portability: the
higher the level, the greater the portability and the greater the
resulting value.

In general, alas, the higher the level, the less a standard exists;
the process of developing and approving standards has mainly
worked "bottom-up". This is clearly seen, for example, in communication protocols, using the ISO (International Standards Organization) seven-layer reference model: far more of the lower levels have
been standardized than of the upper.

Interoperability

Most enterprises today possess a mix of computer equipment from several vendors. They also have an urgent business need: to enable people to share data and applications across these systems. This may be *ad hoc*—for example, retrieval of data for use in a PC-based spreadsheet; or it may involve new integrated applications, such as a banking system providing a complete view of all accounts for bank customers. Further, the return on investment in systems will be improved by wider access to them. So heterogeneous systems must work well together. This is what interoperability means.

Most customers now consider interoperability to be their highest priority for open systems, as seen in the X/OPEN survey. Often, interoperability is confused with connection or communication. **Connection** just means that there is a physical path between systems. **Communication** means that they can send data to each other. **Interoperability** defines the ability to recognize and use information within the data. This can take several forms:

- At the most basic level, simple messaging, where a system sends a message to another system which acts upon the message

- File transfer, in which a complete file can be copied from one system for temporary use on another

- More sophisticated file- and database-sharing, where data is kept on one system—or several distributed systems—and can be accessed and updated from other systems

- Remote application access, in which a user or process on one system can initiate a process on another system, and may or may not wait for process completion and return of results

- "Transparent" sharing of processor power, in which a process runs somewhere in the computer network, depending on what processors are available at that moment.

Like portability, interoperability depends upon standards for functions and for interfaces; over time, the standards are moving up the levels. Interoperability exists at multiple levels—the higher the level, the more it contributes to productivity of users and application developers. Much of the interoperation needed and expected by business today is above the level which the standards have currently defined. So interoperation is built on standards, but also involves proprietary products with interfaces which are yet to be standardized.

Distributed Computing Environment (DCE), produced by OSF, seems to have such a strong industry acceptance that it is becoming a *de facto* standard. Many *de facto* standards evolve into *de jure* standards over time. This enables solutions which address today's requirements and which lead to the standards of tomorrow.

IBM Strategy

Aspects of an open system

There are many definitions of what makes up an open system. To some people, open systems means increased choice; to others it means Unix; to others—and most importantly—it means interoperability.

IBM believes that the Unix environment provides an effective alternative to implementing open computing solutions and therefore delivers AIX. It also believes in other effective alternatives to open computing, and delivers many standards in all of its operating systems.

To this end, IBM has adopted a standard definition of open systems:

> An **open** systems environment supports a comprehensive and consistent set of international information technology standards and functional standards profiles that specify interfaces, services, and supporting formats to accomplish interoperability and portability of applications, data, and people.

This definition is contained in IEEE 1003.0 (Draft 15, June 1992).

However, as the IEEE definition and our customers confirm, standards are not an end in themselves. They must solve real business problems relating to interoperability. It means the flexibility to enhance existing applications or install new ones, without being constrained to a single system environment, and without unnecessary replication of data and software. Applications should be able to draw upon databases, files, or other applications wherever they reside.

Investments in hardware, operating systems, applications, and skills must be protected. New and emerging technologies, however, must also be used to enhance productivity and efficiency.

Open enterprise

It is therefore IBM's strategy to provide the ability to implement an infrastructure to support the open enterprise; this will be done using these strategic initiatives:

- Commitment to standards
- Technology and innovation
- Integrated infrastructure
- Extensive services and support

Both IBM's Systems SAA and AIX family definitions provide the foundation for implementing IBM's open systems solution. VM has contributed much to the SAA definition and has long been a leading implementor of it.

Today both the SAA and AIX family support a significant number of open standards and interfaces and support a multivendor environment. In the future they will be extended to embrace additional multivendor environment capabilities and provide enhanced flexibility for current and new IBM customers.

Systems Application Architecture (SAA)

SAA remains a cornerstone of IBM's strategy and has itself become a *de facto* standard for cross-platform IBM software which runs on the VM, MVS, OS/400, and OS/2 operating systems.

SAA is a layered software structure with common interfaces for users, for application developers, and for communications with other systems. This enables development of end-user applications with a degree of commonality across platforms.

SAA has also made its mark well outside its original scope of IBM systems. For example X/Open has adopted the SAA CI (Communications Interface) as the model for conversational inter-process communication, which is the basis for much transaction processing.

SAA and AIX interoperability offers:

- The best of Unix, SAA, and other systems across the organization
- The ability to mix and match resources at desktop, workgroup, and corporate levels to meet business requirements with fewer technical constraints
- A broad and solid basis for application software development and use

In addition to products and standards referenced in the "VM Open Enterprise Product Selection Guide" on page 66, VM's current strategy towards open encompasses two major standards areas:

- OSF's DCE
- POSIX compliance

Key Current and Emerging Standards

Before concentrating in detail on OSF DCE and POSIX, it is worth reviewing current and emerging standards. The presence of an item on this chart does not necessarily indicate that IBM will announce support for it, or that if adopted into the SAA or AIX family definition, that VM will choose to implement it.

Function	Current Requirement	Emerging Technology
End-user interface	SAA/CUA OSF-MOTIF	ISO end-user interface standards
CASE and programming languages	ISO COBOL 85 ISO FORTRAN 77 ISO C 89	ECMA PCTE; ANSI REXX; ISO FORTRAN 90
Application data exchange	ANSI SGML ISO MHS (X.400) ANSI X12 (EDI) EDIFACT CCITT G3/G4; ISO CGM ISO IGES	ISO ODA/ODIF; ISO PDES/STEP

Function	Current Requirement	Emerging Technology
Data management services SAA DRDA ISO FTAM NFS	ISO SQL 89	ISO data dictionary; OSF-distributed file system (DFS); ISO RDA
Presentation services	ISO GKS ISO PHIGS X Window System	Multimedia
Distributed computing services	SAA CPI-C NCS	OSF DCE Time Services; OSF DCE Remote Procedure Call (RPC); OSF DCE Directory Services; ISO Directory Services (X.500); ISO OSI TP
Network transport	TCP/IP SNA OSI	X/OPEN transport interface (XTI); OSI intermediate system to intermediate system; OSI NMF-managed objects
Systems management	SNMP	OS CMIP/CMIS
Security	ISO security framework data encryption	OSF DCE security
System services	IEEE 1003.1 XPG	Internationalization

OSF

The Open Software Foundation is a not-for-profit research and development organization developing and delivering an open software environment based on standards for the benefit of the information processing industry. OSF uses an innovative open process, soliciting technologies from the industry at large, and delivering the technologies in source code form.

OSF has more than 300 members and approximately 275 employees in locations around the world. IBM is a charter member of OSF. OSF uses a Request For Technology (RFT) process to address key open computing requirements. Completed and/or in-process technology definitions by OSF include:

- Application Environment Specification (AES)
- Architecture-Neutral Distribution Format (ANDF)
- Motif Graphical User Interface (GUI)
- Distributed Computing Environment (DCE)

Application Environment Specification (AES)

OSF's Application Environment Specification (AES) defines programming interfaces needed to develop portable applications for an open systems environment. Major standards and specifications from other sources, as well as some definitions from OSF, are included in this. AES consists of the following components:

- XPG3 (X/OPEN)
- ANSI C
- POSIX

Architecture-Neutral Distribution Format (ANDF)

ANDF is a compiler intermediate language technology that enables developers to develop and distribute applications in a format that can be installed and run on diverse open systems architectures. This technology, a hardware-independent software distribution format, provides a consistent development and distribution environment for multiple platforms.

ANDF thus facilitates creation of highly portable, high-performance applications for the open systems marketplace. OSF has selected TDF technology from the Electronics Division of the Defence

Research Agency of the U.K. (formerly the Royal Signals and Radar Establishment), for the core technology of ANDF.

Motif Graphical User Interface (GUI)

Motif provides a three-dimensional environment based on the X Window System. It is supported by a style guide for GUI design, and libraries and toolkits for building applications that can be independent of the implementing platforms. Although not a formal standard, Motif has been widely adopted by numerous hardware and software vendors.

OSF Distributed Computing Environment (DCE)

OSF's Distributed Computing Environment (DCE) is a comprehensive, integrated set of services that supports development, use, and maintenance of distributed applications. Availability of a uniform set of services anywhere in the network enables applications to effectively harness the power that tends to lie unused in many networks.

The OSF DCE services are organized into two categories:

1. Fundamental distributed services
   - Remote Procedure Call
   - Naming Service
   - Time Service
   - Security Service
   - Threads Service
2. Data sharing services
   - Distributed File System
   - Diskless Support
   - Personal computer integration (DOS file and printer support services)

The DCE architecture draws on submitted architectures from a multitude of organizations, including Digital Equipment Corporation, SUN Microsystems, Hewlett-Packard, and MIT Project Athena. Though the DCE architecture has its roots in the Unix environment, and many vendors implementing DCE are doing so on Unix-based operating systems such as Digital's Ultrix, it is by no means limited to Unix. Proprietary non-Unix-based systems, such as IBM's MVS and VM operating systems, will be adapted for the DCE technology.

OSF's DCE is a layer between the operating system and network software and the distributed application software:

```
┌─────────────────────────────────────┐
│      Distributed Applications        │
├─────────────────────────────────────┤
│          DCE Technology              │
├─────────────────────────────────────┤
│      Operating System and            │
│      Network Services                │
└─────────────────────────────────────┘
```

OSF has also produced its first system **kernel**, OSF/1. The kernel is the part of the operating system closest to the hardware.[4] The OSF/1 kernel was developed by the Transarc Corporation. Of the IBM operating systems, AIX/ESA has first complete implementation of OSF/1. IBM supplied commands and utilities to accompany the Transarc kernel, and together they form OSF/1.

For the benefit of many VM users for whom OSF DCE will be new, the following overview of OSF DCE is included.

The next diagram shows a DCE **cell**. A cell is a collection of inter-connected DCE client and server applications. A DCE cell may exist entirely on one computer, on tightly coupled processors or, more commonly, on several loosely coupled or connected processors. VM/ESA will be able to participate in a DCE cell.

A cell is often called a **domain**: the portion of a network that an administrator has control over. Each cell must provide four core services: **Remote Procedure Call**, **Directory**, **Security**, and **Time**.

---

[4] In a VM environment the kernel can be viewed as either the Control Program (CP) which manages real hardware, or something that runs in a virtual machine, such as CMS.

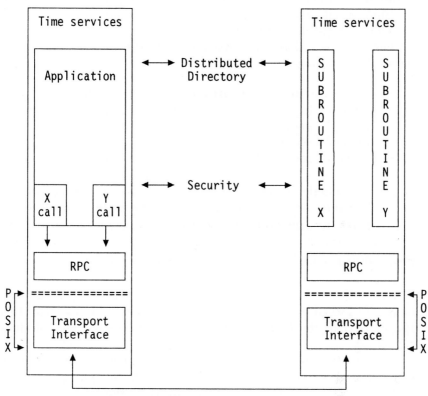

Communications

OSF DCE Remote Procedure Call (RPC)

The OSF Remote Procedure Call (RPC) technology is based on the programming construct called the procedure call, with which control of the program execution is passed from one segment of code to another, and then returned to the original segment.

For the distributed computing environment, this concept was generalized from the single system environment to a network of systems; the RPC mechanism provides a facility for calling a procedure on a remote system as if it were a local procedure.

DCE RPC technology automatically transforms the client's procedure call into network messages so that the client's procedure is executed on the server with which it is communicating. The RPC mechanism provides a high-level programming model which hides communication details, and which enhances application portability by removing system and hardware dependencies.

There are essentially two components to the DCE Remote Procedure Call technology:

- An **Interface Definition Language** and associated compiler to simplify development of distributed applications through generation of portable source code that allows Remote Procedure Calls to act as local procedure calls
- A **Run-time Facility** which allows distributed applications to run across multiple, heterogeneous systems, thus allowing individual system architectures and underlying connection technologies and protocols connecting systems to be transparent to application procedures

RPC Interface Definition Language (IDL)

The Interface Definition Language (IDL) is a tool for programmers to specify procedures designed to run on remote systems. The DCE IDL is similar to ANSI C in terms of data types and bindings supported.

When writing distributed applications, application programmers define the RPC interfaces (groups of operations that servers can perform) and associated data types in IDL files, using the DCE Interface Definition Language. The Interface Definition Language allows transfer of procedural information in known data types and constructs appropriate for a network environment.

Programmers compile IDL files using the Interface Definition Language compiler. The compiler translates the IDL interface definitions into output in one of two forms: a high-level programming language such as C, or object code. Three pieces of output are created: a **client** stub, a **server** stub, and a **header**. The stubs will be bound or linked to applications running on the client and on the server. The stubs copy arguments to and from the Remote Procedure Call packets flowing over the underlying connection technology, and call the RPC Run-time Facility.

This relieves programmers of some tasks which would otherwise have to be written by hand. If necessary, the stubs also convert data representations to those understood by the client and the server.

Binding is the process though which a client finds a server. In some cases, a client may receive the location of the server directly—that is, the location may be contained within a file or hard-coded as a value within a program. Alternatively, the client may use DCE Directory Services to locate the server which handles the interface in which the client is interested. The server must be "advertised" within the Directory Service for the client to locate it. In this case, the client does not directly call the Cell Directory Service; rather, the binding is supported by the Name Service Independent application programming interface.

RPC Run-time Facility

After the distributed application is written, the client and server stubs are compiled and linked. The RPC Run-time Facility provides the mechanism for transferring requests from clients to servers, and for transmitting and receiving responses over the network.

The Run-time Facility may be viewed as a set of routines which implement communications between clients and servers.

Two specific transport implementations are supported by RPC:

TCP/IP   Transmission Control Protocol/Internet Protocol, a connection-oriented transport

UDP/IP   User Datagram Protocol/Internet Protocol, a connectionless transport.

The distributed application programmer can specify the underlying RPC protocol, but the semantics of the RPC calls are the same whether the transport is connection-oriented (TCP/IP) or connectionless (UDP/IP).

The RPC process is asymmetric and synchronous by nature; it can be made asynchronous, however. This is done by first creating another thread and using that to issue the synchronous RPC. Data used in RPC is handled under the covers, through a process called **marshalling**.

OSF DCE Naming (Directory)

Directory services allow applications and users to locate and share information, including people, places, applications and services, within the distributed computing environment. In this environment, anything that can be accessed individually is called an **object**. An **entry** is a listing in the Directory Service that describes its corresponding object. The description may contain several attributes, including name and location. A **directory** is a list of name entries.

Directories may be organized in various ways. They may be structured into hierarchies in which objects are defined by their names; some directories contain a list of other directories. Directories may also be partitioned into several distinct and co-operating Directory servers to allow different directories to reside on different computer systems. Directories may be replicated on multiple systems to improve availability and reliability in case of computer failure.

The global X.500 Directory Services definition is being adopted as an international standard for accessing names worldwide. DCE support for Directory Services is compatible with the X.500 support. DCE uses an application programming interface (API) based on the X/Open Directory Service (XDS) for access to both local DCE and X.500 Directory Services. XDS is the API that application programmers use to make all Directory Service calls to both the Cell Directory Service and Global Directory Service. DCE directory support allows distributed computing environment clients to tie into X.500 Directory Services, and provides support to allow X.500 users to access local names. Applications that use the XDS programming interface can exploit the DCE and the X.500 Directory Services without software application changes.

A group of DCE systems—including users, administrators, and servers—connected via a network, that work together, and that are administered as a single unit is called a **cell**. It is the domain covered by a directory. A department or a collection of systems on a local area network are examples of cells.

The distributed computing environment must support communication between different cells, since users and applications often need to communicate with others who may not be in the same cell. Each cell has at least one Cell Directory Service (CDS) that contains the name and attributes of each resource located within that cell.

A Global Directory Service (GDS) is used to look up a name not located within the same local cell; it acts as a connector between independent cells, and allows them to find out about and interact with each other. Because the Global Directory Service is based on the CCITT X.500 international standard, it can work with other X.500 implementations and participate in world-wide X.500 Directory Services. The GDS can own and administer a portion of X.500 namespace.

A Domain Name Service (DNS) is another standard Directory Service widely used in the Internet community. Like GDS, it can act as a high-level connector of DCE cells.

A Cell Directory Service which needs to communicate with other cells' Directory Services uses a Global Directory Agent (GDA). A Global Directory Agent acts as a naming gateway that allows multiple Cell Directory Services to be connected, and is used as an intermediary between Cell Directory Services and Global Directory Services. The GDA handles CDS calls that are directed to foreign cells. The foreign cells must be registered in either the X.500 or the Domain Name Service global Directory Service. The following diagram illustrates the three DCE Directory Services components.

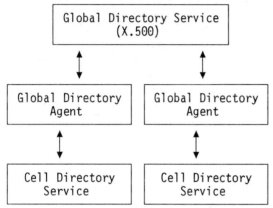

The Directory Services component of OSF's DCE is integrated with other DCE technologies: distributed file service, Remote Procedure Call, and security. The DCE distributed file service technology uses the Directory Services to locate files. The authentication and authorization features of the DCE security component are used by the Directory Services to verify that clients and servers are who they claim to be and to control access to resources. RPC is the standard communications interface used by clients for communicating with DCE Directory Services.

OSF DCE Security

The Security Services of DCE include three key functions, described on the next page.

Authentication: Verify that users are who they say they are
Authorization: Control access to resources
Communication Integrity: Protect integrity and privacy of messages sent over network

Authentication

In discussions of DCE Security Services, clients and servers are referred to as **principals**. Principals prove their identities to each other by exchanging secret messages called **tickets** or **credentials**. The tickets or credentials contain user information, such as name and location, and a secret key. The secret key is used to encode and decode secret messages used to verify the credentials.

DCE technology contains multiple types of Security servers:

- **Authentication** servers and **Ticket Granting** servers support the Kerberos authentication protocol for verifying identity of computers in the network.

- **Privilege** servers determine if a user should be granted access requested to resources controlled by the server. This server is an extension of Kerberos which supports group memberships and inter-realm operation. A **realm** is an authentication domain.

- **Registry** servers are database systems of users, passwords, servers, security policies, encryption keys, and other related information for maintaining a list of valid principals. They are usually replicated on multiple systems. Their domain is usually a single cell.

In addition, the **Login Facility** initializes a user's DCE security environment through interactions with both the Authentication and Privilege servers. Using the user's password, the Login Facility authenticates the user to the Security server. The Security server returns credentials which then authenticate the user to distributed services, such as Distributed File Services, accessed during the user's session.

The Kerberos authentication services require third-party verification. The client and the server each share a secret key with a third party, but not with each other, to verify their identity. Users typically get credentials from Security servers for later use—to be presented, for example, to application servers when they wish to perform some operation. The scenario for authenticating a client to an application server is as follows:

1. Client asks Security server for credentials to present to the application server.
2. Security server returns encrypted packet of information to client. The information is known only to the client and Security server.
3. The client uses a private key to decrypt the packet of information. The packet contains a Kerberos ticket and a session key.
4. The client uses this new session key to encrypt the request to be made of the application server, and then forwards the encrypted request and Kerberos ticket to the application server.
5. The application server decrypts the incoming ticket. The ticket was encrypted using a key shared only between the security server and the application server. The ticket has the client's name and the same session key previously provided to the client.
6. The application server uses that session key to decrypt the incoming request. Using the client's name provided in the ticket, the application server decides whether to honor the client's request.

Using a similar procedure, the application server would identify itself and prove its identity to the client.

Authorization

Authorization is verification that users are permitted to perform operations they have requested on information they have tried to access. **Access control lists** (ACLs) are used by DCE technology for authorization purposes. An access control list is associated with each resource and identifies the principals (user names) and types of operations (such as read, write, execute) each is permitted to perform on the resource. The names in the list may refer to individual users or groups of users.

The registry editor is a security administration application used for maintaining the access control lists. The access control lists may be remotely administered from any server on which the administrator has authority.

The access control lists supported by OSF distributed computing environment are a superset of those specified by the POSIX 1003.6 Access Control List working group. POSIX access control lists are designed to control access only to files. The DCE access control lists extensions make the POSIX access control lists useful in the distributed computing environment.

Communication Integrity

The DCE security component is integrated with the DCE Remote Procedure Call (RPC) mechanism in a number of ways which help ensure the privacy and integrity of communications over the network. RPC is used by the registry editor; for communications between users and Security servers; and for communications between users and application servers in the OSF distributed computing environment. Each DCE server provides a remote RPC-based interface for maintaining the access control lists.

Rather than having application code handle retrieval of Kerberos tickets, the RPC run-time code performs this operation. The RPC run-time code decodes the incoming tickets, performs required security checks, and provides server application code with the client's identity. This eliminates the need for the application server to understand Kerberos protocols and the format of incoming security information packets.

RPC uses trusted third-party secret key encryption as the method for distributing secret encryption keys to both principals in secure communications.

RPC uses mathematical operations called **cryptographic data checksums** to determine if the data was modified or corrupted during its passage through the network.

RPC automatically encrypts data according to the level of security specified by the application developer. The level of security may be selected by specifying a specific value for a byte in the RPC header. The RPC application programming interface extension verbs allow either the client or server to choose the security level. The security level may range from private (all data is encrypted) to non-private (no data is encrypted). The seven levels of security from which the application developer may choose are listed on the next page.

0 No Authentication (anyone may access)
1 Assert Id (user identifies self)
2 Authentication per connection
3 Authentication per call
4 Authentication per packet
5 Strong Integrity Check (DES CBC)
6 Privacy (DES encryption)

OSF DCE Threads

A single, sequential flow of control within a program is called a **thread**. Threading technology allows an application to be structured to allow it to exploit multitasking.

Threads use reentrant programming techniques. That is, the DCE threads component is written to handle multiple threads executing simultaneously. This allows program designs that are more simple than other parallelism alternatives such as exploitation of asynchronous operations and multiprocess implementations using shared memory.

DCE threads can be used as-is or can be mapped to an existing threads facility provided by the host operating system.

The Concert Multithread Architecture (CMA), by Digital Equipment Corporation, selected by OSF for the Distributed Computing Environment technology implementation, has the following characteristics:

- User-space (non-kernel)
- Single process
- Co-routine-based
- Support for easy-to-use synchronous primitives
- Varied scheduling policies
- Thread pre-emption
- Thread cancellation
- Support for POSIX 1003.4a interface specifications
- Can be ported to use native kernel-supported threads package (integrated with in-kernel threads implementation)
- Designed to be easily ported to diverse machines and operating systems

OSF DCE Time Service

Individual computer systems have a single clock to determine the time of day. In a distributed system with multiple computer systems working together to provide services to users, clocks of computers in the network must be synchronized so that each has the same idea of the current time. A single, co-ordinated time value is important both for services (for example, authentication) and applications (for example, distributed file systems). Computers working together to provide services such as these compare dates and times to determine relative order of events, compute the time between events, and schedule events.

Clocks have a tendency to drift from the synchronized time at different rates, so there is usually a slight discrepancy between each clock's notion of the current time as they drift between synchronizations. For this reason, and because it takes a certain amount of time to exchange messages about what time it is, distributed time is usually expressed as a range, rather than as a single point.

In a distributed system, clients (Time **clerks**) take time from servers (Time **servers**) and servers take time from each other. Time servers are designated to answer time queries. As a safeguard against the possibility that any given server may fail or be inaccurate, servers request time from several other servers and then select the correct time.

In addition, Time Services includes an interface to primary, high-quality time providers, such as atomic clocks or radio stations. The purpose of distributed Time Service is two-fold:

- Provide a way to periodically synchronize the local computer's clock with that of other computer systems in the network so they all have the same notion of what time it is.
- Provide a way to keep that synchronized time close to the Co-ordinated Universal Time (UTC), an international time standard, so that the time is meaningful in the rest of the world.

The distributed Time Service technology selected by OSF for the distributed computing environment is Digital Equipment Corporation's Distributed Time Synchronization Services (DECdts), which:

- Runs over the environment's Remote Procedure Call, and therefore uses thread services

- Uses authentication services
- Uses naming services
- Has a simple algorithm for synchronizing time
- Has management and maintenance tools

OSF DCE Distributed File System (DFS)

The distributed file system technology allows a user on a computer in a network the ability to access, modify, and store data in files on another computer. It extends the local file system model to remote systems. The file server is the computer on which data is stored; the client is the computer requesting use of that data.

Several components make up DCE distributed file system support.

On the client:

- The Cache Manager runs in any system acting as a DFS client. The cache manager requests data on behalf of the client either from the local system cache copy, if one exists, or from the File Server machine.

On the file server:

- The File Exporter handles requests from remote clients for the files that it manages. In conjunction with the Token Manager, the file exporter co-ordinates synchronization of different clients which may concurrently access the same file, and then returns requested information to the client.
- The Token Manager synchronizes access to files by multiple clients by issuing tokens. Tokens represent the ability to perform operations (such as lock, for locking a portion of a file, or open, for opening a file). The Token Manager works with the Token Management Layer in the client's Cache Manager to manage the tokens. If a client requests an operation on a file that conflicts with a token held by another client for that file, the conflicting token is revoked by the Token Manager before the requested operation is allowed to proceed.
- The DCE Local File System (DCE LFS) is the physical file system provided with DCE. It manages the storage of files on disk.

The key components of the DCE distributed file system support are shown below. Note that the client and server communicate via Remote Procedure Call operations.

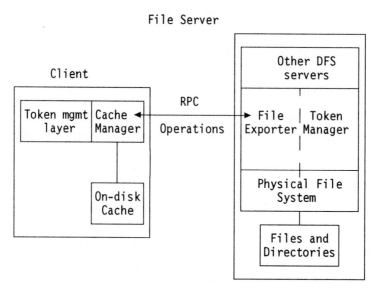

Although the Network File System (NFS) protocol version 2 from Sun Microsystems is the current *de facto* standard file system in the distributed computing environment, it has some weaknesses and limitations. OSF sought an improved distributed file system for the distributed computing environment that:

- Supported NFS protocols for compatibility
- Supported an improved protocol for POSIX 1003.1 semantics (NFS protocol limits it to partial implementation of POSIX 1003.1 semantics)
- Supported consistent naming for directories and files across all systems in the network
- Enables coherent management of the system from any location
- Protects and controls access to resources
- Has high availability of data
- Is scalable to very large configurations without significant performance degradation
- Is usable in systems designed to support NFS without requiring restructuring of the operating system kernel

OSF selected the technology based on AFS Version 4.0 from the Transarc Corporation as the technology of choice for a distributed file system because it exceeded the criteria. In addition, OSF supports the NFS protocol in the OSF/1 operating system.

The OSF/DCE distributed file system has seven key characteristics:

1. Data consistency is obtained through token management. Caching is the mechanism employed to allow a user to manipulate data stored on a file server. A copy of the data being accessed is stored on the client computer. When a copy of the data is on the client, the user can read and modify it. When the user is finished, the data is written back to the file server. Tokens are used by the server to keep track of information cached by each client. The server allocates a particular type of token to the client when the client caches data: the token may be a read token if the client wants only to read data, or a write token if the client wishes to modify data. If a client modifies the data, the server revokes tokens of other clients who have cached that data to signal that their copy is no longer current. In this way, the DFS server ensures that clients do not perform conflicting operations on shared files and that they do not see inconsistent copies of the same file.

2. Uniform access to data is obtained through **uniform name space**, a mechanism that allows the filename to look the same to all computers in the network on which the file resides. DCE distributed file systems specifies a naming convention to which adherence is enforced.

3. Security is maintained through authentication and authorization. Kerberos authentication services prove that users are who they claim to be. Client and file server exchange encrypted information during this process. Access control lists are used by the file server during the authorization process. Using the access control lists, the file server grants permission to clients to perform specific operations they have requested on resources they have requested.

4. Reliability is obtained with file or database replication. Multiple copies of files or databases are distributed to multiple servers to protect against the loss of data needed by users to complete their tasks. Duplicate files on distributed servers are simultaneously kept up to date. Since files and

databases are replicated on several servers, the failure of a particular server does not prevent clients from continuing operation. They simply switch to a server with replicated information.

5. Availability of data to clients is obtained through:
   - The capability to perform routine maintenance tasks of the server's hardware, software, and data while the file server is in operation and available to users.
   - Replication of files and databases on multiple servers, allowing an administrator to perform file system backups while the system is up and running.
   - Caching techniques in which copies of files are cached on DFS clients making it possible for users to access files which have been cached in the event of a network failure.
   - Allowing administrators to move files from one disk to another while the system is available, possible because the file name is independent of its physical location.
   - DFS LFS is a **log-based** file system in which the file system logs every disk operation that occurs between updates of the housekeeping information used to reconstruct the system in the event of a system failure.

6. Good performance: since there are fewer data requests to the file server because client caching of files and directory data is used, system and network loads may decrease.

7. Manageability is provided through use of distributed databases to track configuration information such as file location, authentication, and access control lists used by file servers and clients, and through the use of tools by which the file server is self-configuring and easy to operate.

In addition, the distributed file system support offered by OSF for the distributed environment is compliant with IEEE POSIX 1003.1 file system semantics and uses protocol gateways so that it can interoperate with the NFS client.

The DCE distributed file system support is integrated with other DCE technology as well, including authentication, authorization, naming, and Time Services. It is an in-kernel implementation built on top of a virtual file system switch with extensions (called **vfs+**).

The physical file system used by AFS Version 4, the basis of the DCE DFS support, is called **Episode**. [Currently, some are also referring to it as the "Logging File System" (LFS)]. Episode, Transarc's version of a Unix file system, is based on logical partitions called **filesets**. Filesets are a convenient grouping of files and directories for administrative purposes. Filesets can be configured independently from underlying physical partitions. In addition, Episode supports an interface to access control lists for authorization.

OSF DCE Personal Computer Integration (PCI)

OSF defines personal computer integration as interoperability between systems not based on DOS and systems based on DOS. With OSF distributed computing environment, the DOS environment is extended by offering DOS systems a way to use resources that exist on other non-DOS systems such as Unix systems.

In this environment, OS/2-based systems are considered an alternative to, not a replacement or extension of, DOS-based systems, since OS/2 systems normally do not have the architectural limitations (such as single-tasking environment and minimal memory capacity) imposed on DOS-based systems.

OSF's definition of interoperability and personal computer integration include two basic services. **File services** provide the capability for DOS users to store files on non-DOS systems. **Print services** provide the capability for DOS users to queue files to be printed on non-DOS systems.

There may be some additional, or auxiliary services for personal computer integration, above OSF's definition. These additional services may include application programming interfaces between DOS and non-DOS systems, electronic mail, the capability for remote execution on a non-DOS system, and terminal emulation. OSF's technology implementation of personal computer integration provides the server only, and no client services. The server executes on non-DOS systems and interoperates with DOS clients on Intel architectures.

OSF DCE Management

OSF recognizes that managing systems in a distributed environment is important and calls for integration of management facilities throughout implementation of DCE technologies.

In addition, OSF has integrated a set of management facilities into an offering called the Distributed Management Environment (DME). DME works in conjunction with DCE, but is not a part of the DCE offering from OSF.   DME provides a framework which links system administration and network management over a wide variety of systems, from standalone computers to distributed systems.

It is operating system-independent and supports both *de facto* and *de jure* network and system and system management standards.

IEEE—POSIX

The Institute of Electrical and Electronics Engineers (IEEE) Technical Committee on Open Systems (TCOS) has defined a base set of operating environments.   These standards are known as **POSIX**—Portable Operating System Interface for Computer Environments—and were developed in an open forum by technical professionals from many companies, including IBM.

POSIX is really a set of things. It is a term used to refer to a set of work groups which are defining interfaces for open systems. At this time only the standard form group 1003.1 has been completed and accepted. This standard has in turn become part of the U.S. Federal Information Processing Standard 151-1.   1003.1 addresses the base system services of an operating environment.   VM will support POSIX 1003.1

The following POSIX workgroups are also being developed:

1003.0	Overall Workplan (guide to POSIX Open System Environment)
1003.1	System Interfaces
1003.1a	System Interfaces (API) extensions
1003.2	Shell/Utilities
1003.2a	Shell/Utilities User Portability Extensions
1003.3	Testing Methods
1003.4	Real Time Extensions
1003.4a	Threads
1003.5	ADA Language Bindings
1003.6	Security
1003.7	Systems Management
1003.8	Transparent File System
1003.9	Fortran Language Bindings
1003.10	Supercomputer Profile
1003.11	Transaction Processing Profile
1003.12	Protocol Independent Network

1003.13	Real Time Profile
1003.14	Multiprocessing Profile
1003.15	Batch Services
1003.16	C Language Bindings
1003.17	Directory Services
1003.18	POSIX Base Platform Profile
1201	Windowing Toolkit and EUI
1224	X.400 API and ASN.1 Object API
1238	Common Connection management

At this time, POSIX thus offers specifications for selected aspects of computing. OSF recommends some instances of POSIX-compliance in its DCE technology. However, not all POSIX standards are reflected in the DCE technology, and OSF does not recommend POSIX compliance for all its DCE technology.

VM will support POSIX where the POSIX function provides a functional need in VM; VM will *not* support POSIX services without a perceived use for such services. Where VM provides a corresponding native service it might be reasonable to expect a POSIX interface to that service.[5]

Currently, VM plans to support both 1003.1 and 1003.4a. Providing support for 1003.1 will also mean that many of the shell/utilities in POSIX 1003.2 will also be provided. At this time VM support for 1003.2 has not been announced.

Significance of POSIX

POSIX in 1990s will provide the essential services that were provided by OS simulation in the 1970's and 1980's. Without OS simulation, most language compilers and many products would not run on VM today; in addition, the ability to do cross-platform development would be missing.

---

[5] This is in fact, exactly how MVS currently provides POSIX compliance in its MVS OpenEdition. It should be noted that the MVS OpenEdition is still some nine months from general availability (GA) and the implementation being used at trade shows may change before it is delivered to customers.

VM Open Enterprise Product Selection Guide

The tables on the following pages give the current availability of IBM and IBM co-operative software products that implement key international, national, and *de facto* standards in the VM environment.

This list is not exhaustive and there may be both IBM and non-IBM products which adhere to or support major international standards but are unknown to the author at this time.

Programming languages

Standard	Product	Available	Notes and References
Ada ANSI Ada	ADA/370	Now	ADA/370 also supports FIPS PUB 119 and ISO 8652:1987
C ANSI C	SAA AD/Cycle C/370	Now	C/370 also supports ISO/IEC 9899:1990
COBOL ANSI COBOL 85	SAA AD/Cycle COBOL/370 VS COBOL II	Now	see Additional Notes
FORTRAN ANSI FORTRAN 77	VS FORTRAN V2R5	Now	VS FORTRAN V2 supports ISO/IEC 1539:1980
PASCAL ANSI Pascal 83	VS Pascal V1R2	Now	VS Pascal V1 R2 supports ISO/IEC 7185:1983 level 0 and FIPS PUB 109

Standard	Product	Available	Notes and References
REXX	VM/ESA SAA REXX/370	Now	Interpreter and Compiler
Additional Notes:			
COBOL	SAA AD/Cycle COBOL/370 supports the subset of ISO/IEC 1989:1985 and FIPS PUB 21-3 (intrinsic Function Module Flagging)		
COBOL	VS COBOL 11 R3.1 and higher support the high subset of ISO/IEC 1989:1985 and FIPS PUB 21.3 (ANSI and ISO COBOL is composed of all the language elements and the highest level of all required modules at the time of announcement; this is the "high subset", frequently called the **high level** in IBM announcements)		

Service protocols

Standard	Product	Available	Notes and References
POSIX 1003.1-1990 Draft 1003.4A	(none)	SoD	VM/ESA has a statement of direction to implement selected elements of POSIX
Berkley Sockets BSD 4.3	TCP/IP for VM V2.2	Now	
CICS	(none)		CICS/CMS and CICS/VM have been withdrawn from marketing

Standard	Product	Available	Notes and References
CPI-C	VM/ESA	Now	
Database SQL-89 Level 2	DB2/VM (formerly SQL/DS V3 R3/R4)	Now	DRDA Remote Unit of Work support
DCE Security Services Directory Services Time Service RPC Service Threads Service PC Integration Distributed File System	(none)	SoD	VM/ESA has SOD to implement parts of DCE, will interoperate fully in DCE cells
EDI	(none)		
Graphics PHIGS GKS CGM	GDDM/ graPHIGS V2.2 GDDM-GKS V1 GDDM/XA V2.3 GDDM/VM V3.1	Now	
FIPS 151	(none)	SOD	

Standard	Product	Available	Notes and References
XPG4 Base Band (CAE)	(none)		

Additional Notes:

Database SQL/DS V3R2 and higher support FIPS PUB 127-1 and ISO/IEC 9075:1989 (without the optional Enhancement Integrity feature).

Graphics GDDM/graPHIGS programming interface V2 is based on the ANSI and ISO standards. V2.2.3 supports the 1991 interim draft PHIGS C bindings (ISO/IEC 9593-4). The C and FORTRAN bindings of GDDM/graPHIGS programming interface V2.2.4 have some limitations. GDDM-GKS is an implementation of level 2b of GKS, ISO GKSM metafile. GDDM-GKS supports ANS GKS and ISO GKS with some limitations. GDDM/VM V3.1, GDDM/XA V2R3 and higher can both receive and generate ISO/IEC 8632 CGM binary.

Communication protocols: OSI

Application Layer Standard	Product	Available	Notes and References
ACSE Classes 1&2 (ISO/IEC 8650)	OSI/CS	Now	
FTAM (ISO/IEC 8571)	OSI/FS	Now	

Application Layer Standard	Product	Available	Notes and References
X.400	Open Network Distribution Services/VM	Now	
CMIS/CMIP (ISO/IEC 9595, 9596) Draft proposal level — Manager — Agent	OSI/CS	Now	
CMIS/CMIP (ISO/IEC 9595, 9596) Standard Level — Agent	OSI/CS	SOD	
Directory Services Subset of X.500	OSI/CS	Now	X.500 provides directory accessed by subset of draft ISO/IEC 9594 based on CCITT X.500-X.521 subset
Directory Services X.500 — User Agent — System Agent			

Presentation Layer Standard	Product	Available	Notes and References
Kernel (ISO/IEC 8823)	OSI/CS	Now	
ASN.1 (ISO/IEC 8824, 8825)	OSI/CS	Now	

Session Layer Standard	Product	Available	Notes and References
Versions 1&2 (ISO/IEC 8327)	OSI/CS	Now	

Transport Layer Standard	Product	Available	Notes and References
Classes 0,2,4 (ISO/IEC 8073)	OSI/CS	Now	

Network Layer Standard	Product	Available	Notes and References
CLNS (ISO/IEC 8473)	OSI/CS	Now	
CONS (ISO/IEC 8208)	OSI/CS	Now	
X.25 (ISO/IEC 8208)	ACF/VTAM ACF/NCP X.25 NPSI	Now Now Now	

Network Layer Standard	Product	Available	Notes and References
ISDN (ISC/IEC 9574, Q.931)			

Link Layer Standard	Product	Available	Notes and References
Logical Link Control (ISO/IEC 8802-2)		Now	
Token Ring (ISO/IEC 8802-5)		SOD	
CSMA/CD (ISO/IEC 8802-3)		Now	Using 3172 Interconnect controller
X.25 LAPB (ISO/IEC 7776)		Now	
ISDN (ISO/IEC 9574, Q.921)			

Communication protocols: TCP

Application Layer Standard	Product	Available	Notes and References
FTP — Client — Server	TCP/IP for VM	Now	
SMTP — Client — Server	TCP/IP for VM	Now	
Remote Logon (Telnet) — Client — Server	TCP/IP for VM	Now	
REXEC — Client — Server	TCP/IP for VM	Now	
NFS — Client — Server — ONC RPC	TCP/IP for VM		
NCS	TCP/IP for VM	Now	
OSF/Motif V1.1.2	TCP/IP for VM V2	Now	
X Window V11 — Client — Server	TCP/IP for VM	Now	Announcement does not state X Window System release implemented

Application Layer Standard	Product	Available	Notes and References
SNMP — Agent — Monitor	TCP/IP for VM	Now	
LPR/LPD — Client (LPD) — Server (LPR)	TCP/IP for VM	Now	
Kerberos — Client — Server	TCP/IP for VM	Now	

Additional Notes:

Kerberos Due to U.S. Government regulations, the Kerberos Data Encryption Standard (DES) algorithm cannot be shipped outside North America without a special export license; thus Kerberos is offered as two features for TCP/IP Version 2 for VM: one for the U.S. and Canada, the other for the remaining countries

Common Transport Semantics	Product	Available	Notes and References
MPTN TCP/IP sockets over SNA SNA APPC over TCP/IP SNA LU 0,1,2,3 over TCP/IP			

Transport Layer Protocols	Product	Available	Notes and References
TCP		Now	
UDP		Now	

Internet Layer Protocols	Product	Available	Notes and References
IP		Now	
ICMP		Now	
ARP		Now	

Network	Product	Available	Notes and References
X.25		Now	
Ethernet		Now	
Token Ring (ISO/IEC 8802-5)		Now	
CSMA/CD (IEEE 802.3)		Now	
SLIP			
FDDI		Now	

Additional Notes:

Network PC Network, SNALINK, and HYPERChannel protocols are supported.

SAA/SNA protocols

In addition to any references given, the supporting reference document for SNA is the *SAA Common Communications Support Summary*, GC31-6810.

Application Services Standard	Product	Available	Notes and References
SNA/MS	NetView ACF/VTAM	Now Now	
SNA/DS			
DIA			
DDM Level 2 Files			
DDM Level 3 Database	SQL/DS V3R3	Now	DDM L3 is part of DRDA
DRDA	SQL/DS V3R3	Now	

Session Services	Product	Available	Notes and References
LU 6.2	VM/ESA APPC/VM ACF/VTAM	Now	VM/CMS, ACF/VTAM together support LU 6.2 for VM

Objects	Product	Available	Notes and References
PTOCA	DW/370 PSF/VM	Now	
IOCA FS10	GDDM PSF/VM DW/370	Now	
IOCA FS11			
GOCA	GDDM PSF/VM DW/370	Now	
FOCA	GDDM PSF/VM DW/370	Now	Generator
FD:OCA	SQL/DS V3R3	Now	FD:OCA is part of DRDA
BDOCA	PSF/VM	Now	

Data Streams	Product	Available	Notes and References
3270DS	GDDM	Now	
IPDS	GDDM PSF/VM	Now	
RFT:DCA	DW/370	Now	
MO:DCA-P IS/1	PSF/VM	Now	
MO:DCA-P IS/2			

Data Streams	Product	Available	Notes and References
MO:DCA-L			
CDRA	SQL/DS V3R3	Now	CDRA is part of DRDA

Common Transport Semantics	Product	Available	Notes and References

MPTN
  TCP/IP
    sockets over
    SNA
  SNA APPC
    over TCP/IP
  SNA LU
    0,1,2,3 over
    TCP/IP			

Network	Product	Available	Notes and References
Type 2.1 Node APPN-EN		SoD	
Type 2.1 Node APPN-NN	Hardware	Now	IBM 3174
Type 2.1 Node LEN	ACF/VTAM ACF/NCP	Now	
ISDN (Q.931)			

Data Link Control	Product	Available	Notes and References
SDLC		Now	
Token Ring (8802-5)		Now	
X.25		Now	
ISDN (Q.921, Q.922)		Now	
ISO/IEC 8802.3		Now	For LU 6.2
Ethernet V2		Now	

VM interoperability

From	To	Available	Notes and References
TCP/IP SMTP	OV/2 OV/MVS	Now	Available from Soft-Switch
TCP/IP SMTP	OV/400 OV/VM cc:Mail	Now	
OSI X.400	OV/2 OV/400 OV/MVS	Now	
OfficeVision/VM	TCP/IP SMTP OSI X.400	Now	
SNA to/from	DECnet	Now	

From	To	Available	Notes and References
SQL/DS via DRDA	AIX/6000 OS/2 DOS OS/400 DBM MVS DB2 VSE		AIX DDCS/6000 in limited availability status
AIX V3 Sun Microsystems DEC	SQL/DS	Now	
VM	AIX: INGRES MVS: DB2, IMS/DB, Model 204, FOCUS, System 2000, IDMS, VSAM VMS: Rdb, RMS, Oracle, INGRES	Now	CrossAccess
AIX MVS DEC VMS	SQL/DS Oracle	Now	CrossAccess

From	To	Available	Notes and References
VM Applications	Novell Netware 3.11 server-held data and printer queues	Now	LANRES/VM
Novell Netware 3.11	S/390 host server-based disk and printer resources	Now	LANRES/VM
OS/2 LAN TCP/IP NFS Client	S/390 host server-based disk services	Now	OS/2, NFS clients can share data with dynamic locking, file transformation
VM	Numerous Databases	Now	Using EDA/SQL
AIX V3 OS/2 Apple Macintosh SunOS DOS Microsoft Windows Netware 386	Backup to VM	Now	Many clients supported now by WDSF/VM, additional clients supported by DFDSM
VM applications	LAN Attached printers	Now	PSF/VM PSF/2

Client/Server Computing

People think of Client/Server in many ways:

- Shift of control to the user
- "Down-sizing", replacing mainframes with networked PCs to save cost (such hopes are not always realized—cheaper hardware may be outweighed by greater system complexity and "hidden" people costs)
- Modular software design with a simple program interface
- Enabling easier access to applications and data, wherever they may be located
- Using graphical user interface with its proven and measured effect on users' productivity and happiness
- Integrating and exploiting PCs in the enterprise

The common themes in the list above are user effectiveness and distributing functions to most appropriate system.   Local area networks and their servers are becoming pervasive, but client/server is equally about use of wide area networks and large central servers.

While it is true that client/server products normally fall in the category of open systems, they might typically use industry standard programming interfaces.   It is also true that client/server products can help manage the enterprise and exploit the shifting workstation technology paradigm.

IBM and its business partners offer products, skills, and resources to help build Open Client/Server Enterprises, including:

- OS/2 LAN-based resource sharing, OS/2 LAN server and Netware from IBM[6]
- Front-ending existing mainframe applications with EASEL
- For access to data files, the industry standard NFS; and for access to relational databases, the SQL API supported by

---

6   Netware, based on Novell products, can be extended to IBM mainframes for large file storage and central systems management of many LANs, using IBM's LANRES software under VM or MVS. The OS/2 LAN server can share resources with its users, users of the IBM mainframe, and TCP/IP NFS clients using the LAN File Services/ESA product. LFS/ESA is available for both VM and MVS systems and supersedes the WLFS/VM product. LFS/ESA provides transparent transformation of files across a disparate set of computer architectures; it also allows locking individual bytes of data held on IBM mainframe systems.

products implementing the Distributed Relational Database Architecture (DRDA)

- Transaction management and support via CICS

IBM is evolving its products to exploit open standards and technology including OSF DCE, while at the same time continuing to develop and provide the higher-level functions and interfaces required for effective use of client/server.

Summary

As VM returns to the open systems arena, it is clear that in many respects it never left. There have been and still are many standards conforming products and services available to VM users.

Activities planned in the arena of open systems and VM are:

- Announced statements of direction for OSF DCE on VM
- Announced statements of direction for POSIX 1003.1 and 1003.4a (threads)
- Looking to provide X Window System support where base VM functions (such as file manager, mail manager, and others) are X-clients
- Providing hardware and software platforms on the IBM PS/2 to run VM as a single-user workstation for development of client/server applications
- Providing hardware and software platforms on the PS/2 to run VM as a multi-user LAN (at competitive cost) so existing VM applications can be "Bright-sized" into a LAN environment, thus enabling applications that can already communicate between VM systems to communicate between LANs and VM hosts

By adding support for DCE and POSIX, VM/ESA is positioned not only as a leader in traditional computing services on which businesses depend, but also to have the unique capability of integrating new and emerging applications technologies. Many enterprises will have VM as well as other IBM and non-IBM operating environments. These enterprises will be able to keep existing VM applications that are important to their businesses and also integrate newer DCE- and POSIX-compliant applications onto VM/ESA. This allows VM/ESA to interoperate with other environments, letting businesses choose where and how VM can provide specific value.

VM has been a strong player in the past regarding open and emerging technologies. Traditionally, it has been an excellent platform allowing businesses to run applications on VM as well as develop applications that could be ported to other platforms. With these strengths, VM can now incorporate facilities and interfaces, such as DCE and POSIX, that will continue to make it a strong player in the world of open systems. Considering its past, present and future, VM is *OPEN* to nearly anything!

References and Bibliography

- "References and Bibliography", *VM/ESA Distributed Computing Environment Overview and Technical Strategy*; Susan Franznick, IBM Endicott

- *The Open Enterprise* Presentation and Reference Guide; R. J. McCann, IBM Open Systems Marketing, Dallas, TX

- *A Guide to Open Enterprise Computing*; G811-1844; produced by the Open Enterprise Group, IBM Europe, Basingstoke UK

- *Open Enterprise Product Guide*, Seventh Edition; A.J. Cubbon, IBM Open Systems Marketing, Dallas, TX

- *Introduction to DCE*, Revision 1.0; Open Software Foundation, Cambridge, MA

- *OSF Distributed Computing Environment Overview*, Open Software Foundation, Cambridge, MA

- *Directory Services for a Distributed Computing Environment*, Open Software Foundation, Cambridge, MA

- "VM/ESA in the Open World", Cathcart and Nettleship, in *VM/ESA—Today's Proven Client/Server Solution!* supplement to July 1993 *Enterprise Systems Journal*

Acknowledgments

The author thanks Susan Franznick from IBM Endicott Technical Strategy for her co-operation and contributions to this chapter; the Open Enterprise Group of IBM Europe in Basingstoke, UK for their

Guide to Open Enterprise Computing; R. J. McCann and A. J. Cubbon of IBM US Open Systems Marketing. (See *References* and *Bibliography* for details.)

3

Exploiting CMS

By Ross A. Patterson

Introduction

Most VM users run the Conversational Monitor System (CMS) as
their virtual operating system. CMS and CP together provide an
environment similar to that of a personal computer on a Local Area
Network (LAN), but with the power and facilities of a large mainframe computer. CMS provides a powerful set of end-user and
programming facilities, all of which can be combined with programs
supplied with CMS, by IBM and independent software vendors, or
written locally, to build applications to meet a company's needs.

This chapter covers major facilities of CMS briefly, including the
editor (XEDIT), the System Product Interpreter (REXX), and the
Shared File System (SFS). These parts of the CMS environment are
covered in greater detail in later chapters. The most recent addition
to the CMS family, CMS Pipelines, is also covered briefly here. The
bulk of this chapter is concerned with the structure of CMS and
interfaces available when writing applications to run under it.

CMS Facilities

CMS is comprised of several separate, yet interrelated, subsystems and facilities. Some, such as the REXX programming language and the XEDIT editor, are visible to the casual user. Others, such as the command interpreter and the file system, form the background against which all else is observed.

The main facilities in CMS are:

XEDIT   The standard editor, often used for terminal interaction.

REXX   The most advanced of the three **EXEC** languages.

File system   Provides data, program, and command storage. In CMS, most commands are simply files.

Command interpreter
                  Reads commands from the terminal, finds the appropriate routines, and executes them.

S-disk   A large collection of commands, supplied by IBM and available on all CMS systems.

Nucleus   A collection of performance-critical commands, device-support routines, and other operating-system routines, pre-loaded for speed or because they cannot reside on the S-disk.

These areas are covered, to varying degrees, in the following sections.

REXX

Originally designed as a replacement for the first CMS command-procedure language (called simply EXEC), REXX has grown into a programming language in its own right, with implementations on many differing systems. Although REXX is usually interpreted, several compilers exist, with varying degrees of performance gain over the interpreters.

REXX posesses all the usual attributes of third-generation programming languages (block structure, variable scoping, and sophisticated control forms), with several differences that make it ideally suited to its role as a command language. REXX has only one data type, the character string, upon which all operations are performed. Variables can be set, examined, created, or destroyed by non-REXX programs run from REXX expressions. Block structure and variable scoping are dynamic, following execution flow rather than program structure.

The typical REXX program, with between 10 and 100 lines of code, centers around coordinated execution of a small number of commands. Atypical programs, in excess of 5000 lines, are not hard to find, and have proven the value of REXX in complex applications. Two attributes make REXX so valuable: it has one of the most flexible text parsers ever designed into a language and smooth integration of host commands. Any expression written on its own (i.e., not as part of an assignment statement) passes its result to the host environment (CMS, XEDIT, etc.) for execution as a command.

XEDIT

XEDIT is the standard data and program editor in CMS. Although primarily a screen-oriented editor, it has a reasonable line-oriented mode, and most subcommands function in both modes. XEDIT offers a rich set of subcommands, and has the ability to write new subcommands as REXX programs. The entire subcommand set is available to REXX programmers, as well as subcommands designed specifically to aid in building other subcommands (e.g., EXTRACT, PRESERVE, etc.). Many examples of the XEDIT extensibility have been widely circulated in the VM community, including several implementations of "cut and paste" block editing. One of the more complex extensions is XCOL, an excellent XEDIT add-on available from IBM that provides column-oriented editing in a fashion similar to line-oriented editing.

XEDIT is often used as the underlying screen manager for applications written in REXX. The SET RESERVED subcommand can override the normal screen output, and the READ subcommand lets applications (often called **macros**) control terminal input. Because XEDIT supports a large number of files, data can be stored in and moved between file buffers easily. There is also an interface to file buffers that mimics the CMS file system interface, making it easy to access XEDIT buffers instead of disk files.

Pipelines

The most recent addition to CMS is **CMS Pipelines**, which supports a programming method very different from what most programmers are familiar with, called the **data flow** model. While most CMS commands manipulate specific types of input and output devices, CMS Pipelines encourages device-independent programming.

CMS Pipelines subprograms, called **stages**, are usually divided into two classes. **Device drivers** read input from or write output to specific device types. Drivers exist for disk files, magnetic tapes, card readers, printers, SQL/DS databases, and many more. Data read is passed to the next pipeline stage. Data written is passed in from the preceding stage. **Filters** accept data from the preceding stage, perform some transformation upon it, and pass the result to the next stage. CMS Pipelines provides a clean, seamless interface between stages and handles the implicit multitasking that is required. This ensures that data is processed through the pipeline quickly, with a minimum of overhead, and without using intermediate files.

CMS Pipelines originated as an internal IBM tool, created by John Hartmann of IBM Denmark. It has been available in Europe for many years, and was recently released in the United States as a PRPQ (Programming Request for Price Quotation, an obscure method of product delivery). While this made CMS Pipelines available to some users, the most gratifying change has been its inclusion in the CMS base product, beginning in VM/ESA Release 1.1. Widespread availability allows programmers to share CMS Pipelines programs freely and software vendors to build products that use pipelines.

The **data flow** programming model can take some getting used to. It differs in subtle ways from traditional procedure-oriented methods. Pipeline stages tend to be much smaller than other programs, performing a small number (often one) of operations upon the incoming data, and then passing it on to the next stage.

CMS Pipelines' numerous built-in filters include such functions as:

- Mass alteration of data (spec)
- Sorting (sort)
- Merging (merge)
- Counting (count)
- Record selection (find, between, locate, etc.)
- Data blocking (block, deblock)
- Data compression (pack, unpack)

More than forty built-in device driver stages are also supplied, allowing simple I/O to and from various devices, including:

- Disk files (`<`, `>`, etc.)
- Tapes (`tape`)
- SPOOL (`printmc`, `punch`, etc.),
- SQL/DS databases (`sql`)
- IUCV connections (`starmsg`)
- Program stack (`stack`)
- Virtual console (`console`, `fullscr`)
- CMS and CP commands (`CMS`, `command`, `CP`)
- REXX variables (`stem`, `var`, `varload`)

Most importantly, users can write pipeline stages, either filter or device driver, and use them in a pipeline exactly as if they were built-in. Stages may be written in assembler, REXX, PL/I, or C with the IBM C/370 compiler. Thomas Denier of the University of Pennsylvania has succeeded in adapting the IBM C interface to the SAS/C compiler, and has shared that code by uploading it to NOTE PIPELINE on VMSHARE.

Similarly, Chuck Boeheim of the Stanford Linear Accelerator Laboratory has provided the VM community with an excellent debugger for pipelines, available on VMSHARE in NOTE PIPEDEMO. PIPEDEMO provides an on-screen, stage-by-stage animation of a pipeline and data flowing through it. It allows programmers to observe transformations applied by each stage, and to determine easily where things go awry. It is common to begin coding a pipeline with PIPEDEMO, switching to CMS Pipelines only when satisfied with the behavior of the pipeline. Not surprisingly, PIPEDEMO is itself a CMS Pipelines program.

CMS Structure

CMS is divided into several relatively separate functional units. This modularity has allowed some parts to mature over time without wreaking havoc on unrelated areas. In the 15 releases so far, native CMS has had three different file systems, three different command languages, and two different editors. In fact, VM/SP Release 6 had all eight at the same time.

The major functional components of CMS are explained in detail below.

Commands

CMS commands fall into several classes. Some are **nucleus resident**, built into CMS and always available. Others are **disk resident**, stored as MODULE files, and must be loaded into memory before execution (CMS does this automatically). MODULEs may be preloaded into memory as **nucleus extensions**, bypassing both the load process and some of the command search process.

File systems

CDF

The original CMS file system, using minidisks blocked at 800 bytes, is now known as the Conventional Disk Format (CDF). Since release of the VM/System Extensions Program Product (VM/SEPP) in 1979, CDF has become obsolete. CDF is not supported by VM/ESA, and nothing further will be said of it.

EDF

The immediate successor to CDF, the Extended Disk Format (EDF) file system allows larger files and larger minidisks. EDF minidisks can be blocked at 512, 1024, 2048, or 4096 bytes. The default block size used by the CMS FORMAT command is 4096 bytes on most devices, encouraging efficient I/O at the expense of wasting some space on small files. The EDF file system attempts to improve application performance by reading several data blocks at a time, helping to assure that data is in memory when needed.

SFS

The Shared File System (SFS), introduced with VM/SP Release 6, allows CMS users on the same or different systems to have shared-write access to files and directories of files. The external view of SFS resembles that of MS-DOS or Unix closely enough that casual CMS users with PC backgrounds should feel—almost—at home. Although the EDF file system has been faster to use than SFS in past releases, IBM reports that use of shared data spaces by SFS in VM/ESA 1.1 brings it to the same or better level of performance as EDF for read-only directories. SFS cannot be used for either the

S-disk or the Y-disk, but seems well-suited to most other shared-disk environments, particularly when the data is not changed frequently.

Nucleus

The CMS nucleus is a collection of assorted routines, subsystems, and data which is always in memory in every CMS virtual machine. It is loaded at IPL, and remains until LOGOFF. In most systems, there is only one copy of the nucleus, shared between all CMS users. This results in less use of real memory, and improved performance for both the individual CMS user and for the system as a whole. Programs are part of the nucleus for several reasons. They may be general-purpose subroutines, which ought to be shared between programs in the same virtual machine.   They may be used frequently (like XEDIT or REXX), in which case performance is improved if they are in memory at all times. They may be used at times when files cannot be read in from disk, such as during interrupt handling. Lastly, they may perform disk I/O.

NUCON

The primary data area in CMS, called **NUCON,** resides at address 0 in every virtual machine. This single 4K data page is different for each virtual machine, and contains pointers both into the nucleus and to major data structures.   Many CMS routines are found through address constants in NUCON, although most are undocumented.   Every control block chain is also anchored here. NUCON is mapped by the CMS macro NUCON, contained in DMSGPI MACLIB.

Nucleus extensions

CMS allows user programs to receive many benefits of nucleus residency through the Nucleus Extension facility. The NUCEXT assembler macro defines, deletes, and obtains information about these extensions (or **NUCEXTS**). Programs running in a virtual machine may add their own commands to CMS, replace or "front-end" existing CMS commands and functions, add end-of-command processing, or perform other useful functions. Nucleus extensions may be defined in several ways:

- Loaded as part of a running program and defined by the NUCEXT macro. These extensions should be deleted at or before program termination.
- Loaded from a MODULE file by the NUCXLOAD command.
- Loaded from a LOADLIB member by the NUCXLOAD command.
- Loaded into storage obtained by the CMSSTOR macro and defined by the NUCEXT macro.

Nucleus extensions loaded via NUCXLOAD with the SYSTEM option will be entered in key 0 and supervisor state, with all interrupts disabled. Nucleus extensions defined via the NUCEXT macro can request key 0 by the KEY=NUCLEUS option, and can choose which interrupts to accept through the INTTYPE= option.

When deleted by NUCEXT macro or NUCXDROP command, normal nucleus extensions are simply removed. Those defined with the SERVICE option on NUCXLOAD or the SERVICE=YES option on NUCEXT are called with a parameter list indicating that a PURGE operation is taking place. The extension cannot refuse deletion, but it can perform any necessary clean-up functions. Nucleus extensions with the SERVICE option will also be called during ABEND processing.

A nucleus extension can be given a **user word** when it is defined via the NUCEXT macro. This 32-bit value can be obtained from field SCBWKWRD in the SCBLOCK during execution. The SCBLOCK address is passed in register 2 whenever the extension is called. The userword is commonly used as a pointer to the main storage area for the extension. This allows multiple instances of the extension to be co-resident in memory and yet have distinct workareas.

Nucleus extension calling conventions are:

```
R0   - Address of the Extended Parameter List
R1   - Address of the Tokenized Parameter List
R2   - Address of the SCBLOCK
R3-R11 - Unspecified
R12  - Entry point address
R13  - Address of a USERSAVE save area
R14  - Return address
R15  - Entry point address (same as R12)
```

The executor

The executor is the interface between CMS and the command language processors. It is invoked either explicitly by the EXEC command, or implicitly (and most commonly) by invoking an EXEC

from the terminal. CMS supports three standard command
language processors, and allows dynamically adding others. The
executor examines the program being requested, decides (based on
the first line) which processor is needed, and calls it to run the
program. Programmers can freely intermix all of these, deciding
which meets their needs best on a case-by-case basis. The executor
is one of the best examples of modular function in CMS. Little
inside of it is exposed, and what is exposed works for all three
languages as appropriate.

The first standard processor is called **EXEC**, or occasionally
EXEC 1 or **EXEC Classic**. EXEC came first and is a very simple
language. There are few functions, and strings are arbitrarily
uppercased and truncated to eight characters, in a process called
tokenization. It is rarely used today, except for driving mass alterations of large numbers of files. The CMS EXEC program produced by
the EXEC option of the LISTFILE command is written in EXEC.

EXEC 2, released next, bears a strong resemblence to EXEC.
Many of the restrictions of EXEC were relaxed (though rarely
removed) in EXEC 2, and crude versions of several modern
programming structures were added. EXEC 2 is well-known both
for low overhead and code which can be difficult to read.

REXX is the most recent command language and certainly the
most powerful yet seen in CMS. It has a rich set of functions and
programming structures, and performance that approaches EXEC 2
in most cases. REXX is the language of choice for larger applications.

The most recent addition to the executor, called the **alternate
EXEC processor**, allows users to supply private command language
processors. Programs written for these alternate processors are
marked with a special sequence in the first record, indicating that
they require an alternate processor, and specifying its name. This
support was initially added to support IBM's REXX compiler, but is
supported as a general interface. At least one other vendor has
written a command language processor based on this capability.

Subcommands

Programs that allow users to invoke REXX programs as subcommands often provide a **subcommand environment** to which the
REXX programs may send commands (via the ADDRESS instruction,
which controls the target of non-REXX statements in REXX

programs). These subcommands function just as any other command issued from REXX, setting the RC (return code) variable, and in some cases setting REXX variables. XEDIT uses this capability extensively, and IBM ships many XEDIT **macros** as part of CMS. Any program may define a subcommand environment by using the assembler SUBCOM macro. All subcommand environments are destroyed when CMS issues the Ready; message.

CMS Programming

CMS has three distinct Application Programming Interfaces (APIs), each with its own purpose and target environment. Many functions are available in more than one API, although there are some extreme differences between the APIs.

Callable Services API

The newest interface is the **Callable Services Library** (CSL) API. CMS provides many routines in VMLIB CSLLIB, which can be loaded by name into memory via the RTNLOAD command or on demand. Programs in most languages (COBOL, FORTRAN, PL/I, C, assembler, REXX) can invoke these **CSL calls** through their native subroutine calling mechanism. The list of CSL functions is long, and includes:

SFS I/O:

DMSCRDIR	Create a directory
DMSEXIDI	Check if a directory exists
DMSOPDIR	Open a directory for input
DMSGETDI	Read from a directory
DMSCLDIR	Close an open directory
DMSEXIFI	Check if a file exists
DMSOPEN	Open a file for input or output
DMSREAD	Read from a file
DMSWRITE	Write to a file
DMSCLOSE	Close an open file
DMSCRALI	Create an alias for a file
DMSERASE	Erase a file, alias, or directory
DMSRELOC	Move a file or directory

Resource serialization:

DMSREG	Register a Resource Adapter
DMSCOMM	Commit
DMSGETER	Get errors
DMSGETRS	Get recovery server information
DMSGETSP	Get syncpoint errors
DMSROLLB	Rollback
DMSUNREG	Unregister a Resource Adapter

Program-to-program communcations:

CMINIT	Initialize a conversation
CMALLC	Connect with the other program
CMACCP	Accept a connection
CMSEND	Send data
CMRCV	Receive data
CMDEAL	Disconnect from the other program

REXX program execution and interaction:

DMSCCE	Call an EXEC
DMSCDR	Drop a variable
DMSCGR	Get the value of a variable
DMSCGS	Get arguments, fileid, etc.
DMSCGX	Get next variable
DMSCSR	Set a variable

CMS information:

DMSERP	Extract or replace information

CSL programming example

The following example illustrates the calling conventions for CSL routines. The RUNEXEC program runs as a CMS command and takes two arguments. The first argument is the filename of an EXEC to run, and the second is passed to the EXEC as its argument. The CMS service that runs an EXEC is DMSCCE, which expects the parameters shown on the next page.

CL8'DMSCCE'	Routine name for CSL interface
F	The return code from DMSCCE
CL8'execname'	Filename of the EXEC
F'nargs'	Number of arguments for the EXEC
A(arg1)	Address of the first argument
F'arg1l'	Length of the first argument
...	Other arguments (up to 10)
A(retval)	Address of a buffer for the EXEC's return value
F'retvall'	The length of the return value buffer

```
RUNEXEC  CSECT  ,                             CSL usage sample program
         LR     R12,R15                       Set the base register
         USING  RUNEXEC,R12                   and tell the assembler.
         STM    R0,R15,SAVEAREA               Save the registers.
         MVC    EXECNAME,8(R1)                Set name of EXEC file.
         MVC    ARG1,16(R1)                   Pass one 8-byte arg.
         CALL   DMSCSL,(RTNNAME,RC,EXECNAME,NUMARGS,ARG1,       X
                ARG1L,RETVAL,RETL),VL    Run the EXEC.
         L      R15,RC                        Pass out DMSCCE's RC.
         LM     R0,R14,SAVEAREA               Restore other registers.
         BR     R14                           Return to CMS.
SAVEAREA DS     16F                           Save area for registers.
RTNNAME  DC     CL8'DMSCCE'                   Name of CSL to run an EXEC.
EXECNAME DC     CL8'none'                     Name of EXEC to run.
ARG1     DC     CL8'none'                     One 8-byte argument.
RETVAL   DC     CL8' '                        A buffer for the RESULT value.
RC       DS     F                             Return code from DMSCCE.
NUMARGS  DC     F'1'                          Only one argument.
ARG1L    DC     F'8'                          Length of the argument.
RETL     DC     F'8'                          Length of the RESULT buffer.
         REGEQU ,
         END    ,
```

Assembler Language API

Assembler language programmers have access to many CMS services through macros. Each macro eventually results in execution of an SVC instruction, either SVC 202, 203 or 204. These macros are clearly documented in the *CMS Application Development Reference for Assembler* SC24-5453.

CMS assembler macros are stored in several MACLIBs, depending on their intended use. They are identified as either **Preferred** or **Compatibility**, with the former consisting of more recent additions.

Preferred Group

Macros in the **Preferred Group** can access data in storage above the 16MB line, and can generate reentrant code. Some are "old friends" with changes to support these goals, but most are new attempts at services provided in part by macros in the Compatibility Group. The Preferred Group includes macros to:

Read and write files on minidisks and in SFS:

FSSTATE	Determine if a file exists
FSOPEN	Open a file for input or output
FSPOINT	Locate a specific record
FSREAD	Read records from a file
FSWRITE	Write records to a file
FSCLOSE	Close an open file
FSERASE	Erase a file

Obtain and release storage:

SUBPOOL	Define, delete, and query storage subpools
CMSSTOR	Obtain and release storage

Manage nucleus additions:

SUBCOM	Define, delete, and query subcommand environments
NUCEXT	Define, delete, and query nucleus extensions
IMMCMD	Define, delete, and query immediate commands

Interact with the virtual console:

CONSOLE	Perform full-screen input and output
APPLMSG	Write an error message to the console
LINERD	Read a line from the console
LINEWRT	Write a line to the console
CMSSTACK	Put a line in the console stack

Communicate with other virtual machines and CP:

CMSIUCV	Perform IUCV communications
HNDEXT	Process external interrupts
HNDIUCV	Process IUCV events

Perform other input and output:

HNDIO	Process I/O interrupts
PRINTL	Write a line to the virtual printer
PUNCHC	Write a line to the virtual punch
RDCARD	Read a line from the virtual reader

TAPECTL   Perform tape control operations
TAPESL   Process standard labeled tapes
RDTAPE   Read a block from a tape drive
WRTAPE   Write a block to a tape drive

Compatibility Group

Compatibility Group macros are remnants of older CMS releases that were not XA-capable. These macros cannot process data or parameter lists that reside above the 16MB line, and most cannot generate reentrant code. The following table shows some Compatibility Group macros, their replacements, and their function.

Compatibility Group macro	Replacement macro	Function
DMSFREE	CMSSTOR	Obtain storage
DMSFRET	CMSSTOR	Release storage
LINEDIT	APPLMSG	Edit/write error message
RDTERM	LINERD	Read line from console
WRTERM	LINEWRT	Write line to console

Command/Function API

Although few CMS users realize it, the entire CMS command language is itself an API. Any command in the nucleus, or loaded as a nucleus extension, can be invoked through either SVC 202 or the CMSCALL macro. Commands that load in the user or transient areas can also be used in the same way, provided that those areas are not already in use. Each word of the command text is left-aligned in an 8-byte field, and SVC 202 or CMSCALL is invoked with the address of the first word in register 1. Command return codes are returned in register 15.

A small number of CMS **functions** also use the SVC 202 interface, but are not usable as commands from the console or from EXECs. Like the assembler macros, these functions are also identified as either **Preferred Group** or **Compatibility Group**. Most Compatibility Group functions are replaced by Preferred Group assembler macros. The Preferred Group functions are:

Function   Purpose
DISKID   Get information about RESERVEd minidisks
LANGADD   Define an NLS language for an application
LANGFIND   Search for an NLS language definition

Most Compatibility Group functions are replaced by assembler macros in the Preferred Group. The functions and their macro replacements are:

Function   Macro and purpose
ATTN   CMSSTACK—Place a line in the program stack
NUCEXT   NUCEXT—Define, delete, and query nucleus extensions
SUBCOM   SUBCOM—Define, delete, and query subcommand environments
TODACCNT   None—Obtain program execution time
WAITRD   LINERD—Read a line from the console or stack

Services

Storage management

CMS storage is divided into groups called **subpools**, and managed through the SUBPOOL and CMSSTOR assembler macros. The SUBPOOL macro creates, queries, and destroys storage subpools. Subpools may be known within a program (LOCAL) or by all programs in the virtual machine (GLOBAL).

Within a subpool, blocks of storage are managed by the CMSSTOR macro. CMSSTOR ensures that programs are given storage that is not in use by other programs, and that storage released was obtained from the same subpool.

The following example demonstrates the use of the SUBPOOL and CMSSTOR macros. It builds, uses, and deletes a storage pool called Mine.

1.   The SUBPOOL CREATE macro builds a new storage subpool named Mine, which is not shared with any other programs running in the virtual machine.

2. The CMSSTOR OBTAIN macro gets a block of 256 bytes from the storage pool.

3. The CMSSTOR RELEASE macro gives back 64 of those 256 bytes, at the start of the block.

4. The STORMAP (SUBPOOL Mine command displays the current allocations in this storage pool.

5. The SUBPOOL DELETE macro deletes the storage pool, and gives back the 192 bytes that were not already given back.

6. The STORMAP (SUBPOOL Mine command shows that the storage pool is gone.

```
SUBPSAMP CSECT ,
         LR     R12,R15             Set the base register
         USING  SUBPSAMP,R12        and tell the assembler
         STM    R0,R15,SAVEAREA     Save the registers
* Define a subpool named Mine, not shared with anyone else
         SUBPOOL CREATE,NAME='Mine',TYPE=PRIVATE
* Obtain some storage from our new subpool
         CMSSTOR OBTAIN,BYTES=256,SUBPOOL='Mine'
         LR     R2,R1               Remember the address
* Release one quarter of what we got
         CMSSTOR RELEASE,BYTES=64,ADDR=(2)
* Display what we've got left
         APPLMSG TEXT='After CMSSTOR RELEASE...',APPLID=SUB
         CMSCALL PLIST=STMAPCMD,EPLIST=STMAPEPL
* Delete the subpool.  This will also release any remaining storage
         SUBPOOL DELETE,NAME='Mine',TYPE=PRIVATE
* Prove the subpool is gone
         APPLMSG TEXT='After SUBPOOL DELETE...',APPLID=SUB
         CMSCALL PLIST=STMAPCMD,EPLIST=STMAPEPL
         SR     R15,R15             Set RC=0
         LM     R0,R14,SAVEAREA     Restore other registers
         BR     R14                 Return to CMS
* Data areas
SAVEAREA DS     16F                 Save area for registers
*
         DS     0D                  STORMAP command
STMAPCMD DC     CL8'STORMAP'        - Command name
STMAPARS DC     CL8'('              - Options separator
         DC     CL8'SUBPOOL'        - SUBPOOL option
         DC     CL8'Mine'             and value
STMAPARE DC     8X'FF'              - Fence
*
STMAPEPL DC     A(STMAPCMD,STMAPARS,STMAPARE)  EPlist for STORMAP
*
         REGEQU ,
         END    ,
```

National Language Support

CMS supports separation of command syntax, message content, and program execution through the **National Language Support** facility. Command syntax and message content are supplied in replaceable files, allowing installations to customize them, or to wholly replace them. CMS messages are available from IBM in various languages. It is also possible to define commands and messages for other programs, and to load these definitions into a running CMS virtual machine.

CMS supplies two commands that compile the definitions. The GENCMD command reads a Definition Language for Command Syntax (DLCS) file and generates two object files named *xxx*UPA*xx* and *xxx*USY*xx* that contain the syntax and synonyms.

The following example of a **Definition Language for Command Syntax** (DLCS) file is used by a program in a later example. The file specifies the American English translation of the syntax for the SAMPLE CHEQUE and SAMPLE VERSION commands. The file translates CHECK to CHEQUE and the TOD and NOTOD options to TIME and NOTIME.

```
:* This file is "SAMPLE DLCS".
:* Comments begin with colon-star and cannot be continued.
:* All other statements end with colon-semicolon.

:* Applid is "SMP", this is an American English syntax :;
:DLCS SMP USER AMENG :;

   :* The first command is "SAMPLE".  Its translation in American
   :* English is "SAMPLE".  Its unique-id is "SMP_CMD1".
   :CMD SMP_CMD1 SAMPLE SAMPLE 6 :;

      :* The first command format is the "CHEQUE" format. Syntax is:
      :* "SAMPLE CHEQUE fn ft <fm> ( <<NO>TIME>".
      :* "fn" and "ft" are a required filename and filetype;
      :* "fm" is an optional filemode or "*".
      :* "TIME" and "NOTIME" are the only acceptable options.
      :* In American English, the command is entered as
      :* "SAMPLE CHECK fn ft {fm} ({{NO}TOD}".
      :KW.1 CHEQUE 4 CHECK 4 :;
         :OPR FCN(FN) :;
         :OPR FCN(FT) :;
         :OPR FCN(FM, STRING('*')) OPTIONAL :;
         :OPT KWL(<TIME 2 TOD 2> <NOTIME 4 NOTOD 4>) :;

      :* The second command format is the "VERSION" format. Syntax
      :* is "SAMPLE VERSION", with no other operands or options.
      :KW.1 VERSION 7 :;
```

The GENMSG command reads a message repository source (REPOS) file and generates an object file with the same name containing the messages. The filename should be aaaUMEcc, where aaa is the application identifier (**applid**) and cc is the two-character language identifier (or null); otherwise CMS will not be able to locate the object file. These three object files must be made available to CMS before any of the NLS commands or macros can be used. The

SET LANGUAGE command is used to load the object files and make
them available.

The following example of a message repository is used by a
program in a later example. The file contains three messages, each
with one or more substitution fields.

```
*
* This file is "SMPUME REPOS".
*
* Line one specifies the substitution-character ("&") and the number
* of message digits to display for messages below 1000 ("3").
*
& 3
* Message SMPVER001I is the response from the "SAMPLE VERSION" command.
0001    I SAMPLE version &1.
* Messages SMPSHO002I and SMPSHO003E are the responses from the
* "SAMPLE CHEQUE" command.
0002    I &1 File &2 &3 &4 exists.
0003    E &1 File &2 &3 &4 does not exist.
```

CMS has several commands and assembler macros to ease access
to these definitions. These interfaces depend on a unique three-
character value, called an **application identifier** (or **applid**), to
connect the definitions and executing program.

The assembler macros are:

APPLMSG   Issue an error message
PARSECMD   Parse a parameter list

Commands, intended for EXEC 2 and REXX programs, are:

XMITMSG   Issue an error message
PARSECMD   Parse a parameter list

The APPLMSG macro and XMITMSG command perform similar functions for different environments. Both allow substitution of variable
data into constant message texts. Both will obtain the constant text
from the current macro repository, although APPLMSG also allows the
programmer to specify the text directly. Both offer a variety of
output editing and display options.

The PARSECMD command is used to separate and validate the operands and options on a command. The PARSECMD command obtains
the command string either from the arguments passed to the
invoking REXX or EXEC 2 program or from the STRING option on
the command. It applies the parsing rules specifed in the DLCS file
(as compiled by GENCMD), and returns the results in two variable
arrays: Token. and Code..

The PARSECMD macro performs the same function for assembler programs. The command string must be supplied by the caller, and the results are returned in a chain of control blocks mapped by the PARSERCB and PVCENTRY macros.

The following example illustrates the use of DLCS and message repositories to rewrite commands and messages. The REXX program processes two commands:

```
SAMPLE CHEQUE fn ft <fm=A> (TIME|NOTIME:
```

and issues either message SMPSH0002I or SMPSH0003E, depending on whether or not the file exists. If the TIME option is specified, the message begins with the time of day.

```
SAMPLE VERSION:
```

Displays the version of the SAMPLE command (i.e., 1.0).

```
/* Sample showing usage of PARSECMD and XMITMSG */
/* Load the DLCS and REPOS information */
   'SET LANGUAGE (USER ADD SMP'
/* Parse the command using the DLCS information */
   'PARSECMD SMP_CMD1 (APPLID SMP'
   if rc <> 0 then exit rc
/* Is this a VERSION or a CHEQUE command? */
   select
       when token.2 = 'CHEQUE' then call cheque
       when token.2 = 'VERSION' then call version
/* PARSECMD guarantees it's one of the above */
       otherwise nop
   end
/* All done */
   exit

CHEQUE:
   procedure expose token. code.
/* The FN and FT are required, so they're definitely here */
   fn = token.3
   ft = token.4
/* The next token to look at is */
   next = 5
/* The FM is optional, so let's see if it's really there */
   if code.0 >= next & code.next <> 'OPTSTART' then do
       fm = token.next /* It's there */
       next = next+1
   end
   else fm = 'A' /* It's missing, default to "A" */
/* Process the options */
   timeopt = 0 /* Default is "NOTIME" */
   if code.0 >= next & code.next = 'OPTSTART'
   then do next = next+1 to code.0
       if token.next = 'TIME' then timeopt = 1
       if token.next = 'NOTIME' then timeopt = 0
   end
   if timeopt then time = time()
```

```
      else time = ''
/* See if the file exists */
   address command 'ESTATE' fn ft fm
   if rc = 0
   then 'XMITMSG 002 TIME FN FT FM (APPLID SMP CALLER SHO ERRMSG'
   else 'XMITMSG 003 TIME FN FT FM (APPLID SMP CALLER SHO ERRMSG'
   return

VERSION:
   procedure expose token. code.
/* Tell the user that we're version 1.0 */
   'XMITMSG 001 "1.0" (APPLID SMP CALLER VER ERRMSG'
   return
```

Conclusion

This chapter has touched on several parts of CMS. Other chapters provide more detail on topics such as REXX, XEDIT, and SFS. Many areas have been ignored, since a full treatment of CMS would require at least one full book of its own. For reference material, IBM's *CMS Application Development Reference for Assembler* and *CMS Application Development Reference* are very useful. IBM's *CMS Application Development Guide for Assembler* and *CMS Application Development Guide* provide a useful, if stilted, introduction to some of the topics covered here, and many more.

4

Exploiting XEDIT

By Philip H. Smith III

The XEDIT editor is one of VM's strongest assets. Its ease-of-use, native power, and extensibility endear it to VM users, and have even led to its implementation on non-VM and non-IBM platforms.

While almost all VM users use XEDIT, most do not exploit it fully; this chapter discusses features and techniques which can increase personal productivity through improved XEDIT exploitation on VM/ESA.

History

XEDIT's introduction with VM/SP Release 1 in 1980 was welcome news for VM sites. For almost 10 years, they had struggled with CMS EDIT, which was usable but nobody's idea of wonderful.

In fact, EDIT was disliked enough that IBM offered a priced alternative called **EDGAR**, which exploited the 3270 architecture much like XEDIT, and many of whose ideas were adopted in XEDIT.

Many user installations had also invested significant effort enhancing CMS EDIT, adding many subcommands and even interfaces to the CMS EXEC processor, thus enabling rudimentary macros. The University of Waterloo and the Perkin-Elmer Corporation were among these; their EDIT enhancements numbered in tens of thousands of lines of code.

XEDIT's obvious power and extensibility rapidly eclipsed EDIT even at these installations, and few would consider using EDIT for anything today. In early releases of VM/SP, XEDIT was actively developed and enhanced. More recently, including VM/XA SP and VM/ESA releases, it has largely been relegated to "maintenance mode", meaning that bug fixes are the only changes. A notable exception to this was conversion to XA-exploitation mode for VM/ESA, enabling use of storage above the 16MB line.

Like REXX, XEDIT was largely the work of a single individual. Xavier de Lamberterie of IBM Geneva originally developed it as a labor of love, and distributed it via the IBM internal network. Since its inclusion in the VM product, XEDIT has been enhanced and maintained by the CMS development organization; however, Xavier is still consulted occasionally to resolve theological questions of "proper" behavior.

XEDIT has often been cited as an example of an excellent product, despite a high initial reported bug rate. In XEDIT's case, this bug rate reflects a rich environment which users tend to push to and beyond its limits, rather than weak code containing many errors.

Why XEDIT?

It has been said that "editors are theology": that is, the one most often used becomes the religion of choice for that user. XEDIT is certainly not immune to this phenomenon, and some users prefer other editors, even under VM. However, even they often acknowledge XEDIT's great power. XEDIT is unique in that while its many strengths are for the most part available elsewhere, it offers a combination of features unparalleled by any other mainframe editor.

XEDIT can be used for tasks far beyond simple editing:

- Automated text processing—for example, creating a configuration file for a program after prompting the user for input.
- Display management—presenting system performance data, database search results, or any output suitable for full-screen viewing.
- Editing extensions—through macros, XEDIT can be extended without limit, providing application-specific "subcommands" to perform specialized editing tasks.

As mentioned earlier, most VM users use XEDIT, but few are truly proficient at it. As in any rich environment, it is possible to perform useful work while exploiting only a fraction of facilities available. In fact, most XEDIT users are familiar with perhaps a dozen or so subcommands and settings—out of almost 200!

Though the average XEDIT user is quite productive, adding knowledge of other XEDIT facilities can speed and simplify editing tasks, as well as open doors to further XEDIT exploitation through macros and non-editing uses as discussed above.

Besides learning how to do things not possible without these "power tools", better understanding of XEDIT often illustrates better ways to achieve commonly performed functions. An obvious example is the novice who, lacking knowledge of the CHANGE subcommand, makes manual global alterations to a file: learning CHANGE can be a revelation which improves that user's productivity dramatically.

The remainder of this chapter examines some of these often-underused facilities. It assumes familiarity with basic XEDIT subcommands and concepts.

Line Targets

One of XEDIT's most powerful yet least-understood features is the **line target**. Line targets are arguments to subcommands such as LOCATE. There are four varieties of line target:

Absolute   A file line number, with a leading colon. Examples:

:18   Line 18, or end-of-file if fewer lines exist

:197 line 197, or end-of-file if fewer lines exist

An absolute line number that is past end-of-file (EOF) or end-of-range (EOR) is legal, and indicates EOF or EOR; thus it seems that any absolute line target should always be valid. However, if a line is excluded from the display using ALL or other selective line editing (see "Selective Line Editing" on page 134), attempts to address that line as an absolute line target will fail with a message indicating that the target was not found.

Relative   A number of lines relative to the current line, in either direction. Examples:

5   Five lines down from the current line, or EOF/EOR if fewer lines remain

+11   11 lines down from the current line, or EOF/EOR if less than 11 lines remain

-8   Eight lines up from the current line, or EOF/EOR if less than 8 lines remain

*   Always indicates EOF/EOR

String   A delimited string; multiple strings may be combined with logical AND and OR operators; logical NOT sign specifies "not this string". Examples:

/abc/   the next line, looking downward in the file, containing abc

-/def/   the next line, looking upward, containing def

¬/the /   the next line, looking downward, which does not contain the

/x/|/y/   the next line containing x or y, or both

¬,VM/ESA,|,VM/SP, the next line containing neither VM/ESA nor VM/SP

-¬/the/&/x/|¬/the /&/y/
           the next line, looking upward, which does not contain the but which does contain x or y

Traditionally, a slash ("/") is used to delimit string targets; however, any non-blank character can be used. In fact, another character *must* be used if the string itself contains a slash, as in the fifth example above.

The last example above illustrates a weakness of logical capabilities of string targets: no support for parentheses. At first, the second ¬/the / appears unnecessary; however, if omitted, *any* line containing "y" would match the target, because OR takes precedence over AND.

Named   A name for a line, set by SET POINT or the .*xxxx* prefix subcommand. Examples:

.a   the line named a if one exists

.here   the line named here if one exists

A given name can only exist for one line at a time. The SET POINT subcommand fails if an attempt is made to name a line when that name is already in use; SET POINT .*xxxx* OFF must be issued first. The .*xxxx* prefix subcommand does not suffer from this restriction, and, when issued using LPREFIX, may be as easy to use: lp .x names the current line x whether that name was previously in use or not. Names for lines case-sensitive and are subject to translation by the current CASE setting. Thus when CASE is U, all names set are uppercase, and mixed-case line names cannot be located without setting CASE M first.

A novel concept for many users is that operations need not proceed downward in a file. It is important to understand this when exploiting line targets: when line target :3 is issued from line 400, the operation proceeds upward in the file, rather than starting at line 3 and proceeding downward to the current line. In most cases this distinction is irrelevant; however, if an operation is terminated—for example, a CHANGE ends because data is truncated from the end of a line—it becomes extremely important.

Any of the four types of line targets may be specified *anywhere* a line target is required. This includes most subcommands; for example, CHANGE uses a line target for the third operand:

```
change/dog/cat/target
```

The best example of line target use is the LOCATE subcommand, whose function is really just "go to this line target".

An excellent XEDIT usability feature is that unrecognized commands are parsed as possible line targets, and, if valid, are passed to LOCATE for resolution. This is called an **implicit LOCATE**. Thus /banana/ is identical to LOCATE /banana/.

Since any of the four line target types is valid for LOCATE, this feature can save some typing. For example, instead of issuing down 5 to move downward five lines in the file, simply typing 5 performs the same function. Similarly, -11 moves upward 11 lines in the file.

In concert with the chained locate facility discussed below, implicit LOCATE is an amazingly powerful feature.

Chained LOCATEs

Any subcommand may follow a LOCATE subcommand on the same command line. If the LOCATE succeeds, the subcommand is executed; if the LOCATE fails, the subcommand is ignored.

For example, to move down five lines in the file and delete the new current line, a single command can be typed:

```
5del
```

This allows chaining multiple LOCATEs together, allowing extremely complex and powerful sequences; each LOCATE is executed in turn until one fails:

```
.start /:h1/ /:ul/&¬/compact/
```

The above:

- Goes to named line .start, if it exists
- Locates the next first-level heading tag
- Locates the first unordered list tag after that heading which does not already have the compact attribute

This technique avoids terminal interactions and I/O (especially useful on overloaded systems, or when using slow dial-up lines), and allows primitive programming without writing macros:

```
/:h1./&/Topics/ 1 c/:h3./:h2./
```

This command:

- Locates the next line containing both :h1. and Topics
- Moves to the next line
- Changes :h3. to :h2.

The "dangerous" part of the command—the CHANGE—is executed only if the LOCATEs are successful (of course, the 1 to go to the next line cannot really fail). Thus this sequence is safer than simply chaining the commands together with linend characters:

```
/:h1./&/Topics/#1#c/:h3./:h2./
```

While the latter will produce the same result if a line containing both :h1. and Topics exists, it will have undesirable results if such a line does not exist: the LOCATE will fail, but the other two lines are still stacked, and so the change will be issued against the line following the current line.

Chained locates can also be combined with the REPEAT subcommand to execute a sequence like this repeatedly; see "REPEat—re-execute subcommand to target" on page 115 for details on using REPEAT.

Obscure Subcommands

This section discusses some XEDIT subcommands often unknown to general users.

The minimum truncation allowed for each subcommand is shown the first time the subcommand is listed: for example, **LPrefix** shows that the minimum truncation of the **LPREFIX** subcommand is **LP**.

LPrefix—Logical Prefix

The LPREFIX subcommand issues a logical prefix subcommand: that is, it is the equivalent of moving the cursor to the prefix area of the current line, typing a subcommand, and pressing ENTER.

Most XEDIT users are familiar with prefix subcommands such as M (move), MM (block move), D/DD (delete), and c/cc (copy), but few know or use LPREFIX.

This is unfortunate, since typing LP MM is certainly faster and easier than moving the cursor to the current line and then back into the prefix area and typing MM, especially on loaded systems with less-than-instantaneous response to pressing a CURSOR PF key.

Command-line subcommands are available to perform the same functions as most prefix subcommands. However, using prefix subcommands is often easier, since they offer "point and shoot" function—operations performed on lines marked, rather than on lines described via command-line syntax. Thus LPREFIX is often preferable.

For example, it is often necessary to delete an indeterminate number of lines from a file. The DELETE subcommand requires a target to determine the number of lines to be deleted; it is usually easier to mark the start of the block of lines to be deleted using DD, locate the end of the block, and complete the operation by marking it with another DD. The cursor will likely be on the command line, initially and/or after the end of the block has been located (by scrolling, or perhaps by using a LOCATE or FIND subcommand), so LP DD may be the fastest and easiest method to mark one or both ends of the block.

LPREFIX can also be combined with chained locates to great advantage; see "Chained LOCATEs" on page 112 for details.

COMPress/EXPand—reformat columns

Occasionally columnar data—information aligned in columns—must be manipulated, or data not aligned in columns must be rearranged.

COMPRESS and EXPAND work with tab stops to automate this process. COMPRESS condenses multiple blanks preceding a tab stop into a single character, and EXPAND reverses the process.

For example, given three fields delimited in a describable fashion—for example, each field surrounded by double quotes—which must be arranged in columns, a combination of SET, CHANGE, and EXPAND can easily align the fields in columns 10, 20, and 30:

```
SET TABS 1 10 20 30
ALTER " 05 * 3
EXPAND *
```

The SET command defines the tab columns; the ALTER changes the double quote delimiters to tab characters (a tab character is a hexadecimal '05'); and EXPAND aligns the data. (This example and those following assume that STAY is ON—see "SET and QUERY" on page 122 for discussion of SET STAY.)

This technique can be employed in any case where data must be placed in columns. Even if data is delimited only by blanks, tab characters can be inserted. Multiple blanks in the "before" state can be deleted by one or more CHANGE/ / /* * subcommands prior to issuing an ALTER 40 05 * to change the delimiting blank to a tab character.

Data already in columns occasionally must be realigned—the fields made wider or narrower. For example, suppose data has been defined in columns 10, 20, and 30 as above, and it is discovered that the second field (20–29) is not wide enough.

Most XEDIT users would manually (and painfully) add the extra blanks; a few would know that CINSERT with REPEAT, or SET ZONE followed by a CHANGE would work.

However, the simplest and most foolproof method is EXPAND, this time in concert with COMPRESS. The trick is changing tab stops after COMPRESSing and before EXPANDing:

- SET TABS 1 10 20 30
- COMPRESS *
- SET TABS 1 10 30 40
- EXPAND *

The initial SET may not be needed if tabs are already set; the COMPRESS converts all leading blanks before tab columns to a single tab character. Resetting tabs and re-EXPANDing the data realigns it as needed!

SHIFT—shift data columns

When data must be shifted left or right, several methods can be employed: CHANGE, CDELETE/CINSERT, and even the COMPRESS/EXPAND technique described above.

However, the easiest method is using the SHIFT subcommand provided for this very purpose. SHIFT moves data left or right between the ZONE columns. It is important to recognize that SHIFT changes *data*, not just the file view (as LEFT or RIGHT would): SHIFT will delete data if it "falls off" the left or right end of a line.

Although needed infrequently, SHIFT is well worth knowing about.

REPEat—re-execute subcommand to target

Some XEDIT subcommands such as column commands (CDELETE, CINSERT, CREPLACE) operate only on the current line. The REPEAT subcomand can execute these against multiple lines.

When issued without operands, REPEAT is the equivalent of typing NEXT followed by retyping the previous subcommand. For example, if REPEAT is issued after a CDELETE 3 has been executed, three characters at the current column pointer are deleted from the line *below* the current line (and that line becomes the new current line).

REPEAT accepts a line target: thus REPEAT *target* performs an action from the current line to the target, or until a non-zero return code results from the subcommand, whichever occurs first.

When combined with chained locates, this becomes increasingly powerful. For example, to change every *other* line in the file:

```
1c/x/y/
repeat *
```

Starting with the line after the current line, string **x** is changed to **y**. REPEAT * then moves forward a line and reissues the command; the leading implicit LOCATE moves forward a second line, and the CHANGE is repeated. Thus every other line in the file is altered (until EOF/EOR is reached or the CHANGE fails).

REPEAT, an underused subcommand, can save hours of repetitive typing, PF key pressing, and macro writing.

MErge—merge lines

The MERGE subcommand overlays groups of lines at a specified column position. Its operands include two line targets specifying the groups to merge, and a column position specifying where.

The documentation includes complex rules governing merging of mixed blank and non-blank data, and must be read and understood thoroughly or unexpected results may occur.

MERGE is complicated to use, but, when appropriate, is far more efficient than other techniques. It is usually best used in macros, where it can be controlled and documented.

RESET—cancel pending prefix subcommands

When a prefix subcommand has been entered but not yet executed, it is **pending**, and XEDIT displays a notice in the bottom right-hand corner of the screen to this effect.

Occasionally, one enters a potentially destructive prefix subcommand such as DD (half a block delete), and then a reconsideration of the problem results in a desire to remove the pending subcommand without executing it. If the DD is 500 lines from the current line, locating and clearing it can be tedious, requiring QUERY PENDING DD followed by moving to the line indicated, clearing the DD by typing over it or using LPREFIX with a blank operand, and then returning to the original current line.

Far easier is simply typing RESET, which clears all pending prefix subcommands.

UPPercase/LOWercase—convert text case

UPPERCASE and LOWERCASE convert file text between upper- and lowercase within the ZONE columns.

LOWERCASE is especially useful after one or more lines have been inadvertently uppercased by modifying them while in CASE U: it is usually faster and less error-prone to LOWERCASE the entire line(s) and then re-uppercase any specific characters than it is retype all the data in the appropriate case.

CANCEL—QUIT unmodified files

XEDIT can edit many files simultaneously. Sometimes after a long session, one must exit quickly from all files.

A poor—but all too common—solution is typing QQ and pressing ENTER repeatedly. This works, but can result in lost changes to one or more files.

Far preferable is typing CANCEL, which quits all unmodified files; an intelligent decision can then be made about any remaining files.

COUnt—count occurrences of a string

To count occurrences of a string, many use a "null" CHANGE:

```
c/dog/dog/*
```

This works, but actually changes the file, which may be undesirable (particularly in UPDATE mode).

XEDIT provides a COUNT subcommand for just this purpose. Like CHANGE, COUNT is case-sensitive and does not honor CASE IGNORE; this makes sense given the implementation, for COUNT merely follows a shortened path through the CHANGE code. Despite this limitation,

COUNT can be useful, especially for checking quote or parenthesis nesting:

```
count/'/*          (count all quotes in the file)
count/(/#count/)/  (count both types of parenthesis
                    on the current line)
```

LOAD—load file into memory

Perhaps the most obscure subcommand is LOAD, which is valid once per file and only in the profile. When the profile starts execution, the file to be edited has not yet been read from disk; LOAD does this.

While the value of this may not be obvious, it enables powerful processing to occur in the profile. For example, the profile can:

- Set a default filetype or even entire fileid to be edited—for example, select the last file edited when no fileid is specified
- Resolve partial fileids—for example, resolve THESIS S to THESIS SCRIPT
- Force options based on fileid—for example, WIDTH 255 for REXX programs

Executing any other XEDIT subcommand before a LOAD forces an implicit LOAD, and a subsequent explicit LOAD fails. Thus any CMS commands issued before a LOAD—for example, a GLOBALV to select the last fileid edited when defaulting—must be prefixed with ADDRESS COMMAND (in REXX) to avoid an implicit LOAD.

Many users exploit this facility to simplify specification of fileids to be edited; some have even created CMS utilities that access XEDIT control blocks to enable capabilities not otherwise possible, such as changing the MSGLINE setting *before* the LOAD. While not for the faint-of-heart, this facility can add flexibility to the XEDIT command itself; see "Another XEDIT API: DMSXMS" on page 134 for details.

An unfortunate limitation is that while the fileid need not be specified correctly or fully, XEDIT does parse options before invoking the PROFILE (it must do so to know which PROFILE, if any, to invoke), so "custom" options are not possible. However, parameters may be passed after a closing parenthesis on the XEDIT command itself:

```
xedit some file a (profile banana) peel
```

BANANA XEDIT can parse its argument string and access the PEEL operand after the closing parenthesis. Note that these arguments are uppercased and tokenized (truncated to eight characters).

Column Commands

XEDIT's current line concept is common to many editors and is thus usually well-understood. Less intuitive is the **column pointer**, which points to a column position (the "current column"). The column pointer is displayed at the top of the screen, on the SCALE line (if present), and is accessible via QUERY, TRANSFER, and EXTRACT.

Various column commands (CLOCATE, CDELETE, CINSERT) set and/or use the column pointer. Some of these also use a **column target** operand. Column targets are a subset of the line targets, and include absolute, relative, and string varieties; logical AND and OR are not available, nor are column names.

For example, CLOCATE sets the column pointer to a column target, and CDELETE deletes characters to a column target. SET STREAM ON allows column targets to span lines, a subtle but very useful capability, especially when working with languages such as REXX which allow statements to span lines.

CFIRST and CLAST set the column pointer to the first and second ZONE column, respectively; CINSERT, CREPLACE, and COVERLAY insert, replace, and overlay strings at the column pointer. These last three are often combined with REPEAT for multiline operation (see "REPEat—re-execute subcommand to target" on page 115). This often avoids the need for a "one-shot" macro.

The CAPPEND macro simulates "column append", although it is less than ideal: it actually appends text after any existing text, and leaves the column pointer at that point, which makes little sense. Many installations replace CAPPEND with a locally written APPEND to perform the same function but without altering the column pointer.

SOS Commands

Another seemingly obscure subcommand is SOS—not a synonym for HELP, but rather standing for Screen Operation Simulation. SOS functions simulate physical terminal actions—actual keystrokes, i.e., pressing 3270 keys; results are based on screen cursor position when SOS is issued. Intended for use from macros or as PF key settings, SOS is a legacy of EDGAR, the original add-on VM full-screen editor.

SOS functions transcend those available via single keystrokes, and include:

- Field tab: move cursor to next/previous 3270 field
- Command line tab: move cursor to next/previous command line (most meaningful when viewing multiple files or multiple views of a single file, and especially useful from macros which must affect all files being viewed)
- Save and restore (PUSH/POP) cursor position
- "Press" a PF key
- Add or remove trailing nulls from current line (default setting of PA2 key)
- Add or delete file line at cursor position (default PF2 key setting is SOS ADDLINE)

Unfortunately, SOS has not changed since XEDIT's original release, and has thus not kept pace with other XEDIT facilities added since its introduction: for example, VM/SP Release 3 added the ability to set PA keys and the ENTER key, yet there are no SOS functions to "press" these keys.

Despite its limited function, SOS is extremely useful.

Invocation Options

XEDIT, like many CMS commands, supports command line options. These are most often useful in XEDIT-based applications, although they are well worth knowing for occasional utility in mundane editing.

The most useful include:

PROFILE   Specifies name of an XEDIT macro to invoke instead of the default, PROFILE. This option—or NOPROFILE, which specifies that no macro is to be invoked on entry—should *always* be specified in XEDIT-based applications, to avoid unexpected results from options set and subcommands executed in user profiles. XEDIT lends itself to tailoring to such an extent that many users' XEDIT environments bear little resemblance to defaults, and most applications cannot tolerate such user profiles.

NOMSG   Suppresses XEDIT messages—that is, enters XEDIT with MSGMODE OFF. This avoids requiring SET MSGMODE

OFF, and simplifies debugging. Many XEDIT-based applications consist of short front-end EXECS which invoke XEDIT using application-specific profiles. It is thus often easy to invoke XEDIT manually *without* the NOMSG option to view messages generated by the profile, avoiding the need to edit application code.

NOCLEAR Avoids clearing the screen on entry to XEDIT. Normally this is undesirable, as it causes a MORE... condition if the terminal is not already in full-screen mode. However, it avoids a screen flash when entering a XEDIT from a full-screen application; this is especially useful on slow dial-up terminals. In addition, XEDIT applications which generate mixed full-screen and linemode output can use NOCLEAR to allow the user time to read the linemode output before displaying the next screen. In this case, the MORE... is desirable, and the user simply presses PA2 or CLEAR to continue after reading the output.

NOSCREEN Forces XEDIT into linemode (non-full-screen mode). This is useful only to test linemode operation. Many XEDIT subcommands and settings produce error messages if issued in linemode, and applications which must operate in both modes should be tested to avoid this.

Some programmers use NOSCREEN in XEDIT-based applications which will never display the screen, but doing so means that if the application terminates abnormally, the user is left in a VM READ with no indication of what action should be taken. If NOSCREEN is not used, a user on a 3270 terminal will instead see an XEDIT session—unexpected but familiar, and easy to exit from.

UPDATE Specifies that changes made during editing are to be placed in a file of filetype UPDATE. Such updates are in a special format which the CMS UPDATE command uses to generate changed data without directly modifying an original file, and is the preferred method of making VM source code changes. The CMS UPDATE scheme is discussed in more detail in Chapter 17, *Native Application Development and Execution,* on page 455.

CTL Specifies the name of a **control file** (filetype CNTRL) which lists **auxiliary control files** or **AUX** files, which, if they exist, list update filetypes to be applied to the base. This enables a multilevel update scheme providing granularity of changes and vastly simplifying removal of changes which are found to be in error. See Chapter 17, *Native Application Development and Execution,* on page 455 for details.

UNTIL   Specifies an update filetype after which XEDIT is to stop applying updates. This option implies XEDIT's update mode; however, without the CTL option, only a single update is ever applied, so UNTIL is useful only in conjunction with CTL.

SET and QUERY

Along with its almost 100 subcommands, XEDIT offers over 80 SET options. These provide extensive tailorability of the XEDIT environment—to the point that many users' XEDIT sessions bear little resemblance to others, both in screen layout and operation!

For example, with no user profile, the XEDIT screen looks like:

```
    J        J        A1   F 80   Trunc=80 Size=1 Line=0 Col=1 Alt=2




===== * * * Top of File * * *
       |...+....1....+....2....+....3....+....4....+....5....+....6....+....7..
===== This is some text.
===== * * * End of File * * *



====>
                                                      X E D I T  1 File
```

The author's profile makes the screen look like:

```
    J         J       A1  F 80   Trunc=72 Size=1 Line=0 Col=1 Alt=3              14:25



       0 * * * Top of File * * *
       1 This is some text.
       2 * * * End of File * * *




    ====>
```

Another sophisticated user's XEDIT looks like:

```
    J         J       A1  F 80   Trunc=80 Size=1 Line=0 Col=1 Alt=2
    ====>


    * * * Top of File * * *
    |...+....1....+....2....+....3....+....4....+....5....+....6....+....7....+....
    This is some text.
    * * * End of File * * *



     5 pre on  10 spltjoin 11 schange6 12 linedup  14 linedel  16 tab back
    17 pre off 18 cms       21 chcase U 22 chcase L 23 chcase M 24 xblock
```

XEDIT users often discover the extent of this tailorability when seeking to correct XEDIT's poorer defaults. For example, the default XEDIT screen includes a scale line in the middle, showing column positions. While the scale is useful at times, the average XEDIT novice has no use for it and wishes that it were not present. Once directed to the HELP menu for the XEDIT SET subcommand, they start customizing the environment to suit their taste.

Many users prefer the command line to be displayed at the top of the screen instead of the bottom, or the prefix areas at the right instead of the left, as well as moving or deleting the scale line mentioned above—which are all easy in XEDIT.

Another unfortunate default is STAY OFF. This means that most XEDIT subcommands—especially failed ones—move the current line, often to EOF/EOR. Pity the poor novice who, upon mistyping a subcommand, is suddenly thrown to EOF/EOR with no method of returning! SET STAY ON in the profile is one of the most common XEDIT options.

Other powerful SET options to consider include:

SET NUMBER ON	displays line numbers in the prefix area.
SET PREFIX NULLS	uses null characters instead of equals signs in the prefix area, and suppresses leading zeros on line numbers if NUMBER is ON. PREFIX NULLS enables typing prefix subcommands while in Insert mode, avoiding irritating keyboard lockups.
SET SHADOW OFF	suppresses "shadow" lines displayed after use of the ALL macro. While shadow lines can be useful, NUMBER ON allows an alternative method of determining where lines are omitted (by noting non-sequential line numbers in prefix areas), and maximizes the number of file lines visible on the screen.
SET MSGLINE ON 2 n OVERLAY	(where n is one less than the number of physical screen lines) allows display of more than two XEDIT messages on the screen without clearing and displaying the messages in linemode. The OVERLAY option indicates that a screen line need not be reserved (left blank) for the first XEDIT message, increasing the number of file lines displayed.
	As an alternative, consider a MSGLINE setting of -1 n OVERLAY in conjunction with CMDLINE TOP. Without this, CMDLINE TOP

users find their command line overlaid by message text whenever a message is displayed. Many XEDIT users move the command line, but are unaware of this option and suffer quietly.

SET CASE MIXED IGNORE (or UPPER IGNORE)

makes case irrelevant in LOCATE subcommands: uppercase and lowercase characters are treated identically. While this is usually the most useful setting, note that hexadecimal strings (entered using X'nn' after SET HEX ON) are also subject to CASE IGNORE: thus X'81' (lowercase a) matches X'C1' (uppercase A), much to the user's consternation.

SET SYNONYM   sets synonyms for XEDIT subcommands and macros. Far more powerful than the CMS SYNONYM facility, XEDIT not only allows simple command verb substitutions, but also symbolic operand rearrangement and even implicit logical linend characters—enabling execution of multiple subcommands via a single word, without requiring a macro.

NULLS and FULLREAD help avoid an artifact of the 3270 terminal architecture. With NULLS OFF and FULLREAD OFF (the defaults), screen lines are padded with blanks and thus cannot be extended while in Insert mode without first pressing PA2 to force null padding instead.

With NULLS ON, lines are padded with nulls, enabling use of Insert mode. However, attempts to place text past the existing end of a line after cursor movement using the cursor keys results in the text "leaping" to the left after the existing text when ENTER is pressed.

FULLREAD ON appears to offer the best of both worlds, but requires additional system resources every time the screen is read by VM, and is thus not ideal (and is in some cases explicitly not supported) when using non-locally attached terminals.

However, these options are well worth experimenting with, and many users use NULLS ON extensively.

An oddity of XEDIT syntax is that the word SET is optional on all SET subcommands except those which conflict with other subcommands (such as SET =, which, without SET, becomes the "=" subcommand). This feature, originally implemented to ease conversion from CMS EDIT, whose settings were changed in this manner, aids usability but leads to confusion and sloppy programming in macros.

For example, the user who has been typing CASE M for years to enter mixed-case mode may be unaware that this command is actually a short form for SET CASE MIXED. If CASE M is used in a macro, it may cause a problem on another userid, where CASE might be a synonym for another subcommand or macro.

While unlikely in this instance, such conflicts do occur, causing bewildering failures of otherwise robust macros. In addition, another programmer updating or attempting to understand a macro which omits the SET will find it much harder to locate HELP information on the CASE subcommand, since none exists. It is thus worth understanding which subcommands are SET functions, and specifying the full command in macros.

The QUERY subcommand displays current option settings. It is worth noting that there are a number of QUERY operands which have no corresponding SET, such as LENGTH (display the length of the current line, excluding trailing blanks), RING (show information about files being edited, such as names and line counts), TARGET (display the line numbers of the last target located), and others.

Finally, after changing the screen beyond recognition, the STATUS macro displays all current settings, or optionally writes them to a file for extraction or reuse.

327x Keys

In the early days of VM, most users worked on linemode terminals, commonly called **TTY** (teletype) terminals, or just **TTYs**. In fact, the first few releases of VM/370 in the early 1970s did not support 3270 terminals in full-screen mode—which explains CMS EDIT's relative lack of 3270 exploitation, as it dates to these first releases.

In those days, applications which supported only full-screen terminals were relatively rare, as only a few VM users could exploit them. Now, with workstation communications programs and full-screen emulators (both software and hardware) common, 3270-only operation is increasingly the standard. XEDIT was designed while linemode was still common, and so supports TTYs, though much XEDIT function is available only on 3270s. Most users, however, do not fully exploit the 3270 architecture.

Hardware (field) tab keys

For example, many users rarely or never use hardware (field) tab keys, choosing instead to move the cursor using the cursor movement (arrow) keys. Tab keys can move the cursor quickly back to the beginning of a line, or into the prefix area, much more efficiently than cursor movement keys.

RETURN

The RETURN key (the large key above the ENTER key on 3270 keyboards) is also useful: it moves the cursor to the first unprotected field below the line the cursor is on. If the cursor is on the command line (with the command line in the default position), RETURN twice moves the cursor to the first file line on the screen—by far the easiest way to perform this function.

FIELD MARK

The FIELD MARK key is interpreted as a tab key by XEDIT. When entering columnar data, or even program code such as assembler or FORTRAN which require entry in specific columns, FIELD MARK can speed input on a slow system by avoiding mainframe interaction to process a TABKEY PF key. Simply press FIELD MARK instead of the TABKEY PF key; when ENTER or another PF key is pressed later, the tabs will be expanded, much the same as using the EXPAND subcommand, discussed earlier.

For example, if tab stops were set at columns 1 10 16 30, a line of assembler could be entered as follows (the FIELD MARK characters are represented in the example by semicolons):

```
LABEL;DS;0H;This is a label
```

When ENTER is pressed after the end of the comment, the screen is redisplayed with tabs expanded:

```
LABEL    DS    OH                        This is a label
```

Use of this feature is subject to an obscure XEDIT setting, IMAGE. If IMAGE is OFF or CANON, tabs are not expanded automatically, although EXPAND still operates. By default, IMAGE is ON for most files, with the exception of filetypes SCRIPT, MACLIB, TEXT, and MODULE.

ERASE EOF

The ERASE EOF key also has a special XEDIT purpose. If a file line has been altered, but no attention-generating keys have been pressed (ENTER, PF keys, PA keys), moving the cursor back to the beginning of the line and pressing ERASE EOF *restores* the line when ENTER is pressed!

Inexperienced XEDIT users often find this undocumented feature bewildering, but it is extremely useful for restoring inadvertently modified lines. Blanking out lines requires entering a blank as well as pressing ERASE EOF.

CLEAR

Screen changes made before an interrupt is generated (ENTER or a PA or PF key is pressed) can be undone by the CLEAR key.

Entry Assist

Another terminal feature which few users exploit is **Entry Assist**. This 3270 architecture extension is available on terminals connected to most control units, and offers features such as word tabs, word delete, and automatic line wrap.

Entry Assist is enabled by pressing ALT and one of the blank keys along the left-hand edge of the keyboard, on most 3270s, or by some other key sequence on emulated 3270s. The word DOC and an arrow pointing downward appear at the bottom right edge of the terminal screen to indicate Entry Assist mode. When first enabled, Entry Assist tends to be more irritating than useful: the cursor cannot move past column 80 without the keyboard locking, and pressing a field tab key will not "wrap" the cursor from the bottom to the top of the screen. While the latter of these is inherent to Entry Assist and cannot be disabled, it can be avoided by learning to use the RETURN key.

The cursor-locking-at-column-80 problem can be rectified by reconfiguring Entry Assist, through another esoteric key sequence. On most 3270s:

1. Press ALT and the IDENT key (bottom left): the downward-pointing arrow next to the DOC will disappear.
2. Press the blank key used to enable Entry Assist: a scale line will replace the bottom (status) line on the screen.
3. Move the cursor to column 80 (by pressing the "cursor back" key, the left arrow).
4. Press the CURSOR SELECT key: the character displayed in column 80 will change from a greater than sign (">") to an OR bar ("|").
5. Press the blank key again.

After this procedure, the effects of Entry Assist are:

1. ALT+cursor left/right performs word tabbing instead of moving the cursor two characters.
2. ALT+DELETE deletes a word.
3. ALT+the key to the left of the RETURN key on the middle row performs a "typamatic" (repeating) character delete.
4. Pressing ALT+cursor up displays the cursor position on the status line (row/column).
5. The field tab keys cannot be used to "wrap" the cursor from bottom to top of screen (and vice-versa).

The benefits of Entry Assist (commonly called "DOC mode", from the indicator displayed) can be tremendous, but require the ability to "reprogram" one's fingers. Many users find this difficult, and dislike Entry Assist intensely. Fortunately, it can be disabled the same way it is enabled, and the configuration settings remain, so multiple users can share a terminal without arguing about whether to use Entry Assist.

Entry Assist is documented in detail in *IBM 3270 Information Display System: Entry Assist User's Guide*.

Programmable Keys (PF, PA, ENTER)

XEDIT has always allowed control over the PF keys; VM/SP Release 3 introduced the ability to set PA keys and even the ENTER key. Most users, however, do not set *any* keys.

This represents a missed opportunity for many. For example, PF1–12 are set the same as PF13–24, since some terminals have PF1–12 on the keypad and some have PF13–24. Users who commonly use a single terminal with 24 PF keys can set the "other" 12 in their profiles, doubling the number of functions available by PF key.

Other users may find that some default keys—PF1/13, set to HELP XEDIT MENU, or PF5/17, set to MACRO SCHANGE—are rarely used, and are thus available for more useful functions.

Users with SET NULLS ON in the profile garner no benefit from the default PA2, which sets nulls on for the line the cursor is on, and can thus change it, perhaps to CMS so that PA1 enters CP and PA2 enters CMS.

When setting keys, the BEFORE, AFTER, ONLY, and IGNORE operands control processing of commands typed on the command line before the key is pressed.

Some users set all keys, confusing others who must use their virtual machines—but maximizing their own productivity. When existing PF keys are insufficient, consider using a key as a "shift" key, toggling between two (or more) sets of PF key settings. This is perhaps best used with one or more RESERVED lines to indicate which set is in use, to minimize one's own confusion!

The ENTER key is an excellent candidate for customization. By default, it moves the cursor to the command line. If the cursor is already on the command line, the ENTER setting performs no useful purpose; in any case, PF12/24 (CURSOR HOME) achieves the same effect.

ENTER might be more useful set to invoke a macro, which might determine the cursor location and act accordingly. For example, if the cursor is on the command line, ENTER might perform a NEXT, enabling line-by-line scrolling; if in the file area, it might do a word tab. An example of such a macro is shown on the next page.

Other examples of ENTER function range from CURSOR HOME (freeing PF12/24 for other use) to invocation of complex macros that perform extensive processing, such as checking for unread electronic mail.

When setting the ENTER key, it is particularly important to understand the BEFORE, AFTER, ONLY, and IGNORE operands to avoid confusing results.

```
/* AUTONEXT XEDIT -- Do NEXT or word tab when ENTER pressed;
                  SET ENTER IGNORE MACRO AUTONEXT to use.  */
'EXTRACT /CURSOR/LINE/SIZE/MSGMODE'  /* Find out where we are */
select
    when cursor.3 = 0 | cursor.3 > size.1 then       /* TOF/EOF */
    'COMMAND CURSOR CMDLINE'
    when cursor.3 = -1 then                     /* Non-file area */
    'COMMAND NEXT'
    when cursor.4 = -1 then                       /* Prefix area */
    'COMMAND CURSOR FILE' cursor.3 1 'PRIORITY 21'
    otherwise                                       /* File line */
    'COMMAND LOCATE :'cursor.3 'COMMAND EXTRACT /LENGTH/CURLINE/'
    'COMMAND LOCATE :'line.1                         /* Go back */
    curline.3 = substr(curline.3, cursor.4)/* Get rest of line */
    if substr(curline.3, 1, 1) = ' ' then     /* If on a blank */
    c = wordindex(curline.3, 1) /* Find position of first word */
    else c = wordindex(curline.3, 2)    /* Else try second word */
    'COMMAND SET MSGMODE OFF'   /* Suppress any error messages */
    if c = 0 & length.1 = 0 then
    length.1 = cursor.4 - 2                          /* Fake it */
    if c = 0 then        /* Rest/all of line blank, go past end */
    'COMMAND CURSOR FILE' cursor.3 length.1 + 2 'PRIORITY 21'
    else           /* Non-blank, try putting it on next word */
    'COMMAND CURSOR FILE' cursor.3 c + cursor.4 - 1 'PRIORITY 21'
    if rc ¬= 0 then    /* That failed, try cursor on end-of-line */
    'COMMAND CURSOR FILE' cursor.3 length.1 'PRIORITY 22'
    if rc ¬= 0 then    /* That failed, try cursor where it was */
    'COMMAND CURSOR FILE' cursor.3 cursor.4 'PRIORITY 23'
    'COMMAND SET MSGMODE' msgmode.1                 /* Restore */
end
exit
```

Macros

XEDIT introduced the concept of application-specific macros written in the system procedures languages (originally EXEC 2, later adding REXX). This avoided the need to learn a new application-specific language for each application or environment, and was quickly embraced by VM users and developers. Today few would imagine creating an application-specific macro language for VM, and users and developers alike have benefited from this commonality.

XEDIT macros are invoked the same way as native subcommands—that is, by simply typing the macro name. They allow unlimited extensions to XEDIT, ranging from *ad hoc*, single-use macros for special tasks to huge programs with their own profiles and unique subcommand sets.

Almost *any* XEDIT behavior can be changed with a macro, although altering operation of native subcommands is discouraged to avoid confusion, as well as unexpected results from macros written by others expecting particular behavior (see "Macro tips" on page 133 for details on how to avoid such surprises).

A feature of XEDIT command parsing is that non-alphabetic tokens are parsed separately from alphabetics, even if they are not separated by blanks. Since native subcommands have alphabetic names, this means that a numeric first operand need not be separated from the command verb: down3 is parsed as down 3.

This simplifies command entry for users, but can lead to difficulty when invoking macros with non-alphabetic filenames. For example, typing THING2 invokes macro THING with operand 2.

Most XEDIT users discover this behavior at some point, often when working on successive generations of a macro: the "old" version (THING, in this case) keeps being invoked, with a spurious operand!

The solution is to use the MACRO subcommand to force normal tokenization of the command verb and invocation of the macro:

```
MACRO THING2
```

While many wish this behavior did not exist, it can be useful. If an XEDIT macro is created with particularly destructive behavior—for example, one which deletes every third line in a file—it might be named with a numeric in the filename, preventing accidental invocation.

Another use is in naming application-specific profiles for programs which might plausibly be invoked from within XEDIT. For example, if the BANANA application is XEDIT-based, it is tempting to create an EXEC called BANANA and a corresponding XEDIT profile called BANANA. However, if a user tries to invoke the application from within XEDIT by simply typing BANANA, the macro (the profile) will be executed directly, perhaps causing errors or lost work.

Of course, in some cases the profile can be designed such that direct invocation is detected and processed correctly. However, when this is impossible, naming the macro BANANA1 is preferable even to detecting direct invocation and error exiting, since it maintains intuitive operation.

Macro tips

Some XEDIT subcommands are particularly (or only) useful in macros:

EXTract   Places XEDIT environmental information in macro variables. Many EXTRACT options return information unavailable by other means.

PREServe   Saves most settings, for later restoration using RESTORE.

RESTore   Restores settings (inverse of PRESERVE).

CURsor   Positions the cursor on the screen. Operands enable positioning on the screen, command line, and specific file lines and columns.

COMMAND   Forces subcommand execution rather than macro or synonym substitution; see also MACRO.

MACRO   Forces macro execution rather than command or synonym substitution; see also COMMAND.

EMSG   Displays an error message and sounds the terminal alarm, if equipped.

MSG   Displays an informational (non-error) message.

CMSG   Places text on the XEDIT command line. CMSG is most useful for prompting, and for redisplaying invalid commands.

An XEDIT API: DMSXFLxx

Besides macros, XEDIT provides an assembler-level application programming interface (API). Four entry points to module DMSXFL manipulate files being edited, using an interface similar to the CMS file system interface.

Four functions are provided:

* Check existence of a file
* Read from a file
* Write to a file
* Locate a specific line

IBM utilities such as LISTFILE and NAMEFIND use DMSXFL for high-performance XEDIT data input/extraction; FILELIST and others depend on these to provide reasonable response time.

DMSXFL is a supported interface, and is documented in the *CMS Application Development Guide*; the comments in module DMSXFL provide the best documentation, however.

Another XEDIT API: DMSXMS

Another—and undocumented—API is used by module DMSXMS, which provides XEDIT's SORT function.

The SORT subcommand is actually a macro which front-ends DMSXMS, performing basic parsing and setup. DMSXMS uses the CMS SUBCOM (subcommand) interface to acquire pointers to XEDIT control blocks, and then sorts the lines in place. (For more information on SUBCOM, see "Subcommands" on page 95.)

This technique can create other high-performance, drop-in XEDIT enhancements. Existing examples include modules to delete blank lines; delete duplicates in a sorted file; perform Unix-style regular expression (GREP) searches; and to "unchange" a modified line when in UPDATE mode—to clear the bit which indicates that it has been modified, thus removing it from the resulting update file.

This last function would clearly be difficult or impossible to implement as a macro; the others are possible (and were prototyped as such), but with unacceptably poor performance.

This technique can also enable changing XEDIT settings *before* a LOAD subcommand is executed (see "LOAD—load file into memory" on page 118 for details). For example, when using UPDATE mode, application of more than two updates displays the messages about updates applied in linemode, since by default the MSGLINE only includes two lines (see "SET and QUERY" on page 122 for details on the MSGLINE setting). MSGLINE cannot normally be reset before LOAD, since doing so causes an implicit LOAD. An assembler program invoked using ADDRESS COMMAND from a REXX profile can maximize MSGLINE to include the entire screen.

CMS 5.5 and later provide documented assembler macros to exploit the SUBCOM interface, although it is available in earlier releases.

Selective Line Editing

Most XEDIT users are familiar with the ALL subcommand. ALL is actually a macro, which exploits a facility called **selective line**

editing. Added in VM/SP Release 3, selective line editing consists of three SET operands:

SELECT   Associate a numeric **selection level**—any positive numeric value—with one or more lines

DISPLAY   Select a range of selection levels to include in the display

SCOPE   Choose whether subcommands affect all lines, or only those included in the current DISPLAY range

After parsing arguments, ALL operation breaks down as follows:

1. SET SCOPE ALL to include all lines in the scope affected by subcommands.
2. LOCATE the string target provided.
3. SET SELECT 1 for the line located, to set its selection level.
4. Repeat the LOCATE and SET SELECT for the entire file or range.
5. SET DISPLAY 1 1 to include only the lines selected in the display.
6. SET SCOPE DISPLAY to include only displayed lines in the scope of subcommands.

Additional steps are required, of course, to handle cases such as an ALL issued after a previous ALL (since only the newly selected lines should be displayed), but the above is the mainline code path.

These three elegant and simple primitives can provide far more function than ALL (and the associated x/xx (eXclude) and s (Show) prefix subcommands) offer. For example, a TALL ("temporary ALL" or perhaps "toggle ALL") macro, to toggle between the partial display of selected lines and the entire display without having to re-enter the ALL subcommand, consists of about eight lines of code. Its value is so great that users accustomed to it almost invariably find themselves recreating it when forced to work where it is not available.

The code for TALL is quite short:

```
/* TALL XEDIT -- Toggle partial/complete display after ALL. */
   'COMMAND EXTRACT/LINE/DISPLAY/SELECT'     /* Find out stuff */
   if select.2 = 0 then exit       /* If no ALL done, just quit */
   if display.1 > 0 | display.2 < select.2 then
   'COMMAND SET DISPLAY 0' select.2
   else 'COMMAND SET DISPLAY 1' select.2
   'COMMAND SET SCOPE ALL'
   'COMMAND LOCATE :'line.1
   'COMMAND SET SCOPE DISPLAY'
```

Other examples of useful selective line editing macros include:

TN   Go to next selected line while viewing entire file, after
          ALL and TALL used
TU   Go to previous selected line while viewing entire file,
          after ALL and TALL used
ALSO   After ALL, include additional lines in selected display
          (for example, after changing ZONE)
EXCLUDE   After ALL, remove lines from selected display (inverse
          of ALSO)
ALLSIZE   Displays number of lines in current selective display

ALSO and EXCLUDE can both be created by modifying ALL; ALSO
consists of ALL without the code to reset existing selection levels
before setting new ones, and EXCLUDE is the same as ALSO except
that located lines' selection levels are set to 0 instead of 1. Many
installations have created ALSO and EXCLUDE, often with name variations, such as INCLUDE or SHOW for ALSO, or HIDE or ALLBUT for
EXCLUDE.

Prefix Macros

XEDIT prefix subcommands allow users to point to lines to be
affected rather than describing them using line targets.

As with subcommand extensions via macros, prefix subcommands
can be created using macros. In fact, several IBM-provided prefix
subcommands are actually macros: X/XX, S, >/>>, </<<, and SI.
Prefix macros have filetype XEDIT, as do regular macros; in fact, like
regular subcommands, *any* unrecognized prefix subcommand causes
a macro search.

Prefix subcommands usually have short names, consisting of one
or two characters. To avoid accidental command-line invocation,
and to help distinguish prefix macros from "normal" macros, the SET
PREFIX SYNONYM subcommand enables mapping prefix subcommands
to macros. This means that prefix macros can have names such as
PREFIXX (which provides the X and XX prefix subcommands), or
perhaps follow some other pattern.

Some simple examples of prefix macros one could create include:

G   (Get)—embed lines from another file, or from the   PUT
     temporary file (created by using PUT with no fileid specified)
R   (Recover)—Recover deleted lines

U   (Uppercase)—Convert lines to uppercase

L   (Lowercase)—Convert lines to lowercase

In fact, all of these can be implemented as a single macro:

```
/* PREFIXXX XEDIT -- General-purpose prefix macro, adds:
   G -- GET prefix subcommand
   R -- RECOVER prefix subcommand
   U -- UPPER prefix subcommand
   L -- LOWER prefix subcommand

   Designed to be used with:
   COMMAND SET PREFIX SYNONYM   G PREFIXXX
   COMMAND SET PREFIX SYNONYM   R PREFIXXX
   COMMAND SET PREFIX SYNONYM   U PREFIXXX
   COMMAND SET PREFIX SYNONYM   L PREFIXXX
*/
   arg p f 1 rest
   if f='CLEAR' | p<>'PREFIX' then exit
   parse source . . . . . pcmd .
   select
      when pcmd = 'G' then cmd = 'GET'
      when pcmd = 'R' then cmd = 'RECOVER'
      when pcmd = 'U' then cmd = 'UPPER'
      when pcmd = 'L' then cmd = 'LOWER'
      otherwise
      rc = 5
      signal ERROR
   end
   'EXTRACT /LINE/'
   'COMMAND LOCATE :'1
   'COMMAND' cmd rest
   r=rc
ERROR:
   if rc = 0 | rc = 1 then exit
   'COMMAND SET PENDING ERROR' pcmd rest
   exit
```

Prefix macros receive a special-format parameter list, which allows them to detect whether invocation was from the command line or as a prefix macro. This means that, when appropriate, macros can be written to support both command line and prefix-area invocation. Examples of this might include:

ETW   (Edit-To-Width)—Reformat paragraphs

RAC   (Right-Align Comments)—Right-justify REXX or C comments

As with macros, once users are aware of prefix macros, they can extend XEDIT without limit. An oddity of prefix macros is that XEDIT saves the current line and restores it after execution; thus prefix macros find it difficult to move the current line. This is possible, however, by deleting the current line and recovering it from within the macro: since the saved line no longer exists, XEDIT does not restore it after execution. This will, however, lose any selection level and names for the line, as well as adding it to the resulting update file, if in UPDATE mode. Another technique involves stacking a subcommand for execution after exiting—not particularly robust, and not recommended.

XEDIT Display Management

XEDIT is often used as a display manager. While it is serviceable in this mode, its primary design goal was to be an editor, not a display manager, and so several important display management functions are missing. Thus it is best used for small, simple applications, such as displaying one or several panels as part of a front end for an application. The advantage XEDIT offers over "true" screen managers is its portability—all VM systems support it.

Several XEDIT facilities exist to help with display management. SET RESERVED defines static lines on the screen, such as permanent prompts or headers.

Although complex to use, SET CTLCHAR extends RESERVED lines, allowing features such as user-defined input fields and highlighting.

The READ subcommand traps user input, placing it in the program stack for macro access. READ operands control how much data is stacked, and whether it is tagged to indicate its origin. For example, READ ALL TAG traps all screen input, including fields in RESERVED lines, and "tags" it with a three-letter indicator of its origin, with line and column numbers as appropriate. The NOCHANGE operand reflects changes made to the file on the screen without actually changing file contents. Finally, READ ALL NOCHANGE interprets CTLCHARs in file lines, not just RESERVED lines. This enables creation of "template" files for use by macros, which set appropriate CTLCHARs and then issue the READ ALL NOCHANGE to display the screen. This feature is undocumented, but is used heavily by the CMS HELP command, and is thus unlikely to be removed.

XEDIT Text Processing

A common application use of XEDIT is to alter a file under program control. For example, a skeleton configuration file might be provided for an application; command line options or responses filled in on a full-screen panel (perhaps driven by XEDIT) could be applied to this skeleton by an XEDIT profile.

While REXX and EXECIO can be used for the same purpose, XEDIT offers advantages such as the CHANGE subcommand, enabling global changes as a single operation, and simplifies deletion and insertion of lines. XEDIT's SORT subcommand is also faster than CMS SORT, and also offers in-memory sorting, avoiding the need for disk space to hold sort work files.

As noted in "Macros" on page 131, application-specific arguments can be passed to a profile after a closing parenthesis:

```
'XEDIT SOME TEXT A (NOMSG PROFILE SETITUP)' arg1 arg2 ...
```

These arguments, however, are uppercased and truncated to eight characters; longer or case-sensitive arguments can be passed in the program stack.

XEDIT applications of this type can return a failure indicator by using SAVE followed by QUIT with a return code rather than simply using FILE. Such applications might also set PF3/15 to COMMAND QUIT *n*, where *n* is a return code which the calling program will recognize as an error. This means that if an application error leaves the user in an unexpected XEDIT session, pressing PF3/15 will not only exit the session, but will signal the caller that the error occurred.

Hygiene

Some basic rules can avoid errors and other surprises when using XEDIT:

1. Prefix all subcommands in macros with COMMAND to force subcommand execution, avoiding user synonyms and macros.
2. Similarly, prefix all macro invocations with MACRO.
3. Avoid implicit SET subcommands in macros: include the SET keyword.
4. Avoid short names or synonyms for macros which may be destructive if invoked inadvertently.
5. Consider SET LINEND OFF in macros which execute or insert user input or file data to avoid execution errors or entering full-screen input mode inadvertently.
6. Spell out all subcommands and operands in macros to avoid confusion for others examining the program.

7. Consider using SET AUTOSAVE if the system is unstable.
8. *Always* save files when leaving the terminal or even just stopping to think—even stable systems fail! The SSAVE subcommand can be abbreviated SS, which is quick and easy to type.

XEDIT on Other Platforms

XEDIT's popularity on VM has led to its implementation on other platforms. Since these other platforms are not 3270-based, they operate somewhat differently in some areas; however, the basic "look and feel" is that of XEDIT. These other implementations greatly improve user productivity when forced to work on other platforms, since they reduce the learning curve associated with any new editor.

KEDIT from Mansfield Software Group is the original non-VM XEDIT implementation. Available for MS-DOS/PC-DOS and OS/2, it offers extremely similar function, with extensions to exploit workstation capabilities. It is a mature, popular product. KEDIT macros use Personal REXX (from Quercus Systems), IBM OS/2 REXX, or a built-in REXX subset called KEXX. Mansfield can be reached at (203) 429-8402.

uniXEDIT from The Workstation Group (TWG) implements XEDIT for Unix systems. A young product, it is a fairly complete XEDIT implementation, although not to the extent of KEDIT. uniXEDIT macros use uniREXX, from the same vendor. TWG can be reached at (708) 696-4450.

Summary

XEDIT is a powerful and rich environment, which offers more function than most people use. The good news is that even inexperienced users can add skills easily, increasing personal productivity.

XEDIT users who feel proficient should consider reading an XEDIT reference manual, noting unfamiliar facilities and experimenting with them to discover their power. Learning more not only eases one's own daily efforts, but increases the quality of work and thus one's value.

5

Exploiting REXX

By Philip H. Smith III

Since its introduction in VM/SP Release 3, the VM System Procedures Language, commonly called **REXX**, has grown far beyond its humble VM origins. This chapter briefly discusses REXX origins, history, and futures, and offers suggestions for maximizing REXX exploitation on VM/ESA. More information on REXX can be found in *The REXX Handbook* (McGraw-Hill, 1992; ISBN 0-07-023682-8). With 45 chapters by over three dozen authors, many from IBM, this book is the definitive work on REXX, describing both VM and non-VM platforms.

What Is a Procedures Language?

Any operating system needs a language for **procedures**: programs consisting of commands grouped together, enabling invocation of a set of operations via a single command.

Procedures languages provide "glue" between the operating system and applications and are, to many, the best-known programming languages. This is especially true because these languages are typically interpreted rather than compiled, simplifying exploitation by unsophisticated end-users.

Procedures language examples from other operating systems include **CLIST** for MVS/TSO; **DCL** for DEC VAX; **TACL** for Tandem Guardian; **BAT** for PC-DOS and MS-DOS; and **awk, sed, perl**, and many others for Unix.

A typical VM user owns several hundred REXX procedures, ranging from trivial to wildly complex, with hundreds or thousands more available in common system storage. These procedures may be written by end-users, support staff, system programmers, or vendors. They run the gamut from short, simple "command lists" which issue a single command with default parameter values; to large, moderately complex programs which prompt for input and build commands or data files for other applications; to entire application suites, often consisting of tens or hundreds of thousands of lines of REXX code in dozens or hundreds of programs, which invoke custom functions and utility routines in REXX, assembler, or high-level languages, and perhaps interact with databases, remote systems, or programmable workstations.

History and Origins

Since the earliest days of VM, many "built-in" operating system commands have been partially or completely implemented as procedures. These VM procedures are generally called **EXECs**, since the original VM procedures language was **EXEC**, and files written in this original language always have filetype EXEC. As VM has evolved, so have its procedures languages. VM/System Product Release 1, in 1980, introduced the **EXEC 2** language. EXEC 2 offered dramatic improvements over the original EXEC (often referred to as **EXEC 1** or **EXEC Classic** to differentiate it from EXEC 2), but severe limitations remained.

These limitations were recognized by an IBM programmer named Michael F. Cowlishaw, who undertook designing a replacement. After several years of internal IBM feedback and refinements, his language, called **REXX**, was added to VM in VM/SP Release 3. REXX was immediately embraced by the VM user community, rapidly eclipsing EXEC and EXEC 2 usage in most VM installations.

REXX Exploitation

Since all VM systems offer REXX to all users, most sophisticated
VM end-users and essentially all VM programmers claim to know
REXX. However, examination of their REXX code reveals that,
while their programs work, they often fail to exploit language functions and features which could make their code faster, more
powerful, and easier to create and maintain.

In addition, lack of understanding of REXX's full potential can
lead to inappropriate language choices, due to a mistaken belief that
something is impossible or difficult in REXX.

The remainder of this chapter offers tips and suggestions for
REXX exploitation. Some discussion is VM-specific; other portions
may be applicable to any REXX programming environment.

"Power" Uses for REXX

The average end-user uses REXX to write a PROFILE EXEC, or a
PROFILE XEDIT, and perhaps to string together a few frequently
issued commands.

However, REXX is ideally suited for many less-intuitive applications, including system debugging and diagnosis (when executed
from userids with appropriate privilege classes); front-ending end-
user commands (performing disk setup, prompting for missing
parameters, etc.); application prototyping (indeed, many such prototypes are robust and efficient enough that they become production);
and even as a rudimentary system monitor, summarizing performance data in a concise fashion.

Logical variables

REXX logical variables have values 1 or 0, and are tested implicitly:

```
if logical_variable then ...
```

This technique is more efficient and more readable than:

```
if non_logical_variable = 'YES' then ...
```

Logical variables can make complex IF statements much more
compact and readable:

```
if first & weekday & ¬holiday then ...
```

where FIRST, WEEKDAY, and HOLIDAY are all logical variables.

In REXX, unlike C, logical variables can *only* have values 0 or 1; any other value causes a REXX syntax error.

In fact, *any* REXX logical comparison (Boolean) resolves to a logical value of 0 or 1; TRACE output with the R option displays a 1 or 0 when tracing IF statements and other logical comparisons.

Comparisons can be used other than in IF and WHEN statements to improve efficiency. For example, when a logical variable is to be set as a result of a comparison, a single statement can replace an IF/THEN pair:

```
var = (a = 3)
```

rather than:

```
if a = 3 then var = 1
else var = 0
```

(the parentheses around the comparison are not required, but aid readability.)

Logical values are also useful as return values from function calls. In the example cited, if the day of the week is in variable DAY, the entire comparison might be:

```
if BUSINESSDAY(day) then ...
```

where function BUSINESSDAY looks something like:

```
BUSINESSDAY:
procedure expose first weekdays holidays
arg day
if find(weekdays, day) = 0 then return 0        /* Weekend */
if find(holidays, day) > 0 then return 0   /* But a holiday */
return first              /* Return 1 or 0 depending on FIRST */
```

This example is somewhat trivial, but when a complex function can be easily implied by a function call, programs can often be made more readable in this manner.

In addition, if several tests musts be performed, a function call can often improve performance and readability by avoiding unnecessary tests and/or extra DO nesting. Remember that REXX always evaluates all portions of a complex Boolean; that is, in the statement:

```
if a <> 0 & b/a > 1 then ...
```

a divide-by-zero error will occur despite the check for variable A being zero. This must be coded instead as:

```
if a <> 0 then
if b/a > 1 then ...
```

Similarly, in the statement:

```
if FUNCTIONA(x) & FUNCTIONB(y) & FUNCTIONC(z) then ...
```

all three functions will be called even if the first returns 0. When the functions are "expensive", that is, require significant resources to execute, this can lead to code such as:

```
if FUNCTIONA(x) then do
   if FUNCTIONB(y) then do
      if FUNCTIONC(z) then do
      ⋮
      end
   end
end
```

In this case, a function call would be more appropriate:

```
if FUNCTIONS(x, y, z) then ...
⋮
FUNCTIONS:
procedure
arg a, b, c
if ¬FUNCTIONA(a) then return 0
if ¬FUNCTIONB(b) then return 0
if ¬FUNCTIONC(c) then return 0
return 1
```

The mainline is much easier to read and maintain, and should a fourth function call be required, FUNCTIONS is easily extended.

Comparisons can also be used to build logical values to be returned. For example, to return a 1 if the return code is 28:

```
return (rc = 28)
```

A more complex and somewhat difficult to read, but sometimes useful, construct builds a logical value based on a return code of a specific value or 0, a fairly common case:

```
return (rc <> 28) * rc
```

This returns 0 if the return code is either 0 or 28, since if the return code is 0, the Boolean resolves to 1, but is then multiplied by 0; when the return code is 28, the Boolean resolves to 0, and 28 x 0 = 0. Clearly such coding warrants careful documentation!

Finally, logical values can occasionally be used in arithmetic. The quintessential example is calculation of the number of days in the current year, taking into account leap years:

```
days = 365 + (substr(date('O'), 1, 2)//4 = 0)
```

The Boolean in this statement divides the last two digits of the year by 4, and if the remainder is 0, resolves to a 1 (a leap year). This example does not account for century years, which are not leap years, but could be enhanced to do so.

PARSE

The REXX PARSE instruction is a powerful language feature, yet one which few use to advantage. This is likely due at least in part to the number of PARSE operands and the resulting bulk of documentation—an entire chapter in most REXX manuals! This is unfortunate, for much value can be gained from using PARSE without necessarily exploiting every feature.

The fact that other languages lack any equivalent to PARSE, but most include function calls similar to REXX function calls, magnifies this situation. As a result, beginning REXX programmers often use numerous function calls to achieve what a single PARSE statement can do.

REXX programmers should learn to exploit PARSE; examples below offer only a few of the many powerful techniques which this instruction offers.

PARSE input can be acquired from various sources, including arguments passed, the stack, function responses, and internal REXX information. The data may be PARSEd based on blank-delimited tokens, specific strings, absolute column positions, and relative column positions. The most common PARSE use is to divide a string—either an argument string or the contents of a variable—into separate tokens:

```
parse arg fname ftype fmode rest
```

This example parses the first blank-delimited token of the argument string into variable FNAME, the second and third into FTYPE and FMODE, and anything remaining into REST.

Most REXX users eventually learn to use simple PARSE statements such as this, and often include parsing based on specific strings:

```
parse upper arg fname ftype fmode rest '(' options ')'
```

This example is especially appreciated by former EXEC 2 programmers, for whom an argument string such as:

```
some file(width 255)
```

was especially troublesome, since EXEC 2 provided no easy way to tokenize the parentheses as required by CMS command parsing. The REXX fragment shown above would set FNAME and FTYPE to the strings SOME and FILE, respectively, FMODE and REST to null strings, and OPTIONS to WIDTH 255.

If options require further processing by the REXX program, a common technique is decomposing the option string:

```
do while options <> ''
   parse var options option options
   select
      when option = ...
```

This enables easy processing of each option in turn. For options with values following, such as the WIDTH 255 option in the example, lines following the WHEN instruction can further decompose the OPTIONS string.

When data of a known format such as a date is to be parsed into variables, PARSE is again the best method:

```
parse var date mm '/' dd '/' yy
```

not:

```
mm = substr(date, 1, 2)
dd = substr(date, 4, 2)
yy = substr(date, 7, 2)
```

Besides being faster and more compact than multiple SUBSTR calls, the PARSE has the advantage of correctly handling dates without leading zeros, which the SUBSTR would not.

PARSE VALUE is often useful to avoid otherwise useless intermediate variables:

```
parse value diag(8, 'QUERY FILES') with . rdrfiles . ','
```

not:

```
files = diag(8, 'QUERY FILES')
parse var files . rdrfiles ','
```

Of course, in the case where the FILES variable has other uses, the
latter might be preferable, but in many cases this technique avoids
assignment of a variable which will never be reused.

Stemmed variables and arrays

REXX supports not only simple scalar variables, but also vectors
and arrays. These are represented by variables with a period in
them, such as LINE.1, LINE.2, LINE.136, etc. REXX programmers
often refer to such variables as **stemmed variables**, since the
portion up to and including the period (LINE. in this case) is called
the **stem**. The portion after the period—the subscript, in most
languages—is called the **tail**.

Since REXX variables are not declared, the scope of such vectors
and arrays is indeterminate. That is, REXX programmers do not
declare an array as 10 elements by 10 elements, or any other size:
its dimensions are determined at execution time.

Further, REXX variable tails need not be numeric: LINE.BANANA
is just as valid as LINE.1. This enables *associative memory*, a
technique in which the tail indicates something about the variable
contents.

For example, an array of people's ages might be held in an array
with stem AGE. with the people's names as the tails: AGE.PHIL,
AGE.KATIE, etc. The REXX program could then look up each age,
assuming it has the person's name in variable NAME:

```
say age.name
```

This is simple, efficient, and easy to read.

When using associative memory, a program must keep track of
the defined tails: there is no REXX facility to traverse a set of
stemmed variables. This is commonly done by building a vector

containing the list of tails, and then either decomposing it or simply traversing it with the WORD function when the values of all tails are required.

The power of this technique is that when managing a set of related variables, the program can use stemmed variables for each, with the tail unique for each entity. This avoids having to associate each entity with a specific numeric subscript (tail) value, as would be required in other languages.

For example, a program which manipulates userid data might use the userid as the tail, and set stemmed variables with each value for the user. If variable RECORD contains the userid information in a known format, the program segment which parses records might resemble:

```
parse var record userid department '<' name '>' '<' title '>' age
userids = userids userid
department.userid = department
name.userid = name
title.userid = title
age.userid = age
```

In this example, variable USERIDS contains the list of known tails. The program could then access each userid's information easily:

```
do i = 1 to words(userids)
   userid = word(userids, i)
   say name.userid 'is a' title.userid 'in the' department.userid,
      'department, and is' age.userid 'years old. '
```

This example is not terribly interesting, since if only one record refers to each userid, it usually makes more sense to process each userid's information as it is encountered.

However, consider input containing multiple entries for each userid, each specifying some value to be accumulated such as CPU time consumed. In such cases, associative memory allows REXX to manage the list of variables, and the resulting program is much shorter and simpler than in other languages, as shown in the next example. Another feature of stemmed variables allows assigning a value to the stem itself. Rather than creating a variable with a null tail, this instead sets a default value for all variables using that stem (and in fact resets any defined previously). In a program which generates totals, this is invaluable, since it avoids having to initialize the total the first time a tail is encountered:

```
userids = ''                            /* No userids known yet */
cputime. = 0                            /* No total CPUTIMEs yet */
do forever
    parse value GETNEXT() with userid cputime .
    if userid = '' then leave           /* No more, we're done */
    cputime.userid = cputime.userid + cputime
    if find(userids, userid) = 0 then userids = userids userid
end
```

The default value set for the tail need not be 0; for example, the
default value might be set to unknown or ? before the input is processed. Subsequent references to a tail not already known will then
produce a recognizable and deterministic result.

It is important to recognize that while REXX allows multiply
subscripted variables (e.g., A.B.C.D.E), only the portion through the
first period is truly a stem. That is, the statement:

```
a.b. = 3
```

merely assigns a variable called A.B., and does *not* initialize a stem
for all variables starting A.B..

Nested function calls

Complex programs often use several functions on the same piece of
data. By nesting these function calls—using the output of one as
the input to another—programs can be made shorter and more
compact. For example, to get the last non-blank character in variable LINE before the occurrence of a colon:

```
last = right(strip(substr(line, 1, max(index(line, ':'), 1))), 1)
```

rather than:

```
n = index(line, ':')
n = max(n, 1)
line = substr(line, 1, n)
line = strip(line)
last = right(line, 1)
```

This technique has its limitations: nesting dozens of function calls
ensures that comprehension and problem diagnosis will be more
complex than necessary. It is usually best to nest only to the limits
of easy readability, perhaps splitting longer nestings between easily
described subfunctions.

For example, if the previous example were to be split, the following might be most intuitive because the two pieces can be easily described as "get the piece of the line before a colon, if any", and "get the last non-blank byte in that piece":

```
last = substr(line, 1, max(index(line, ':'), 1))
last = right(strip(line), 1)
```

Interactive tracing

One of REXX's most attractive features is its interactive debugging mode. Some compiled languages also support such debugging, but in most cases, programs must be recompiled with special options to enable it, which sometimes affects operation.

REXX interactive debugging is always available, has no effect on program operation, and can be invoked within a program, before starting execution via the CMS SET EXECTRAC ON command, or during execution via the CMS TS Immediate command.

In interactive debugging mode, the user can:

- Stop after each statement or resume normal execution
- Examine variables and change their values
- Re-execute the line traced, perhaps with changed variable values, by entering an = command
- Suppress host command execution (! option)
- Suppress tracing for a specified number of statements
- Trace without stopping for a specified number of statements

Subroutine calls are also traced, and tracing may be changed or disabled once a subroutine is entered without affecting mainline tracing.

Since tracing is inherent to the REXX language, it may be enabled conditionally by the program itself. For example, if a variable which should contain a numeric value causes a syntax error occasionally because it receives a non-numeric value, an IF can be inserted to enable tracing before the offending line, enabling examination of related variables and (presumably) diagnosis of the problem:

```
if ¬datatype(count, 'W') then trace ?r; nop
total = total + count
```

The NOP is added to force an instruction trace before the assignment; otherwise the error will occur before the user can examine the variables.

SIGNAL ON

SIGNAL ON and CALL ON provide condition trapping, similar to PL/I ON conditions. Five conditions can be trapped:

ERROR	Non-zero RC
FAILURE	Negative RC
SYNTAX	REXX syntax errors (SIGNAL only)
HALT	HI CMS Immediate command
NOVALUE	Uninitialized variable reference (SIGNAL only)

When a trapped condition is raised, control transfers to a program label which is the same as the condition name, or to a user-specified label. If the trap was via CALL ON, a RETURN instruction can be used to continue after the instruction which raised the condition; however, conditions such as syntax errors cannot be trapped via CALL ON. This is because the condition is raised in mid-statement, and it would make little sense to return either in mid-statement or after a syntactically incorrect statement.

When control transfers, special variable SIGL contains the line number which raised the condition; the SOURCELINE function can display this source line. After syntax errors, variable RC contains an error code; the ERRORTEXT function can display the error text.

The CONDITION function adds further diagnostics about the error; for example, for NOVALUE errors, it can return the name of the uninitialized variable.

These facilities enable elegant error-trapping, displaying diagnostic information and entering interactive debug to allow further problem diagnosis:

```
signal on SYNTAX
   :
SYNTAX:
say 'Syntax error' rc 'raised in line' sigl':'
say errortext(rc)
say 'Source line was:'
do i = sigl by 1 until right(strip(sourceline(i))) <> ','
   say sourceline(i) /* Show source line(s) in error */
end
trace ?r; nop     /* Need NOP to avoid immediate exit */
exit
```

The DO loop handles continued source lines, since the line number reported in variable SIGL reflects the start of the source statement, not the line where the error actually occurred.

Extensibility

Part of REXX's general applicability comes from its extensibility. There are several ways to extend the language: using subroutines internal to the mainline, using external REXX programs, and using assembler or even high-level language routines.

The next two sections discuss these techniques.

Internal and external functions

Internal REXX functions—not to be confused with **built-in** functions, which are those built into the interpreter—are subroutines in the program.

External REXX functions are separate REXX programs.

Both are invoked exactly like built-in functions or subroutines, with arguments passed and values returned in a manner indistinguishable to the caller from a built-in routine.

Internal functions can isolate variables through use of the PROCEDURE instruction, with selected variables made global as appropriate by the EXPOSE operand.

Variable stems can be EXPOSEd, shortening EXPOSE lists and simplifying identification of global variables; for example, using stem GLOBAL. for all global variables makes it obvious which have global scope. See "Literals" on page 165 for discussion of a caveat relating to this technique.

External routines have more difficulty sharing variables, and must resort to the CMS GLOBALV command, the stack, or application-specific files. However, external routines are often preferable in complex applications, as they simplify mainline maintenance through shorter code, and also enable code reuse when the application contains many REXX programs.

The PARSE SOURCE instruction returns, among other things, the way that a routine was invoked (COMMAND, FUNCTION, or SUBROUTINE). This enables "smart" routines which behave according to how they are invoked, perhaps typing output if called as a command, stacking it if called as a subroutine, and RETURNing it if called as a function.

When an application macro (with a filetype other than EXEC) invokes an external REXX function, REXX searches both for a routine with the same filetype as the invoking program and for one of filetype EXEC. This further simplifies code reuse, since common functions may be easily invoked even from application macros.

Assembler and high-level language functions

REXX functions can be written in assembler or even high-level languages, when necessary for functional or performance reasons. For example, a function which includes an interrupt handler cannot be written in REXX, which provides no native interrupt handling.

Such extensions, for example, a function called BANANA, may be named various ways:

- As RXBANANA MODULE;
- As part of RXUSERFN MODULE, RXSYSFN MODULE, or RXLOCFN MODULE, invoked by REXX with BANANA as an operand, and (perhaps) containing numerous functions;
- As BANANA MODULE

These programs may all be loaded as nucleus extensions.

REXX truncates long function names when searching for MODULEs. Thus if the program issues:

```
fruit = POMEGRANATE(27)
```

REXX would search for RXPOMEGR MODULE, or would invoke the RXxxxxFN MODULEs with operand POMEGRAN, or would search for POMEGRAN MODULE.

The most interesting of these approaches, the RXxxxFN function packages, are actually the least useful, since they cannot be cascaded, that is, only one of each may be used at a time. As a result, the RXxxxxxx MODULE approach is most common, as it enables easy identification of MODULEs which are in fact REXX functions, and is more efficient than simply naming the MODULE the same as the function.

These functions will be located and invoked *before* external routines written in REXX; this simplifies replacing a REXX prototype of an external routine with a higher-performance version written in assembler or a high-level language without having to delete the REXX version.

In complex environments, it is worth considering portability problems introduced by local functions: users may be unaware that a function is not built-in, include it in applications, and cause problems when those applications are subsequently run on other systems.

While there is no foolproof solution to this problem, one way to simplify detection and avoidance is to create a single local function with subfunctions. For example, the BANANA function listed above might be a subfunction of the LOCALFRUITS function, contained in module RXLOCALF:

```
peel = LOCALFRUITS('BANANA', 27)
```

While users must still know that LOCALFRUITS is not a built-in function, use of the word LOCAL in the name provides a hint; and a more appropriate name, perhaps including the company name (for example, LCLIBM for functions internal to IBM) would provide further guidance.

In addition, when use of the functions must be located in programs, the string LCLIBM can be located more deterministically than BANANA, since it is less likely to appear other than as a function name.

Special function uses: TRANSLATE

The TRANSLATE function performs character translations, on input strings, using input and output translate tables.

However, TRANSLATE also offers other uses. When input and output translate tables are omitted, it uppercases the input string:

```
bark = 'woof'
bark = translate(bark)                      /* Uppercase */
/* Now BARK contains WOOF */
```

This duplicates the function of the UPPER instruction; however, UPPER is not a part of any formal REXX language specification and is not implemented on most platforms. In programs which may be ported to other environments, TRANSLATE is thus preferable to UPPER.

An elegant but less intuitive use of TRANSLATE is rearranging column positions within a string.

In this method, the current ("old") column order is specified as the input string, and the desired ("new") column order is specified as the input translate table; the data itself is specified as the output translate table:

```
date = '01/31/90'
date = translate('78612345', date, '12345678')
/* Now DATE = '90/01/31' */
```

While totally obscure at first glance, this is much shorter and faster than using multiple SUBSTR calls, and is a useful technique when appropriate—with careful documentation of what is intended!

Note that the column positions need not be numeric; they simply must map to each other, or results will be unpredictable.

Special function uses: SPACE

The SPACE function places a specified number of blanks between tokens in a string.

Many programmers fail to realize that the number of blanks can be zero:

```
line = 'This is a line'
line = space(line, 0)                    /* Drop any blanks */
/* Now LINE = 'Thisisaline' */
```

In combination with TRANSLATE, SPACE can remove any occurrences of a specified character or characters:

```
date = date('U')             /* Assume today is 01/31/90 */
date = space(translate(date, ' ', '/'), 0)  /* Drop slashes */
/* Now DATE = '013190' */
```

or:

```
n = '199,467,221'
n = space(translate(n, ' ', ','), 0)            /* Drop commas */
>> Now NUMBER = '199467221'
```

This is somewhat unintuitive, but with careful documentation, it is far faster and easier than looping to decompose the string and "glueing" the tokens back together.

Functions

REXX offers more functions than most people ever use. Many functions overlap slightly; there are thus often several ways to perform a given task. It is worth reviewing the list of built-in functions periodically and considering some of the more obscure, as knowledge of their existence can avoid "reinventing the wheel" later.

Examples include:

INSERT	Insert a string into another
COMPARE	Determine where two strings differ
COPIES	Copy string specified number of times
DELSTR	Delete part of a string
LASTPOS	Determine last occurrence of string
REVERSE	Reverse string
RANDOM	Generate pseudo-random number
XRANGE	Generate hexadecimal value range

CMS commands mainly consist of blank-delimited words. REXX caters to this, offering many word-based functions. While much can be done with PARSE, knowing these functions also often simplifies coding:

SUBWORD	Take first n words of a string
DELWORD	Delete one or more words from a string
WORDINDEX	Return column position of nth word in a string
WORDPOS	Return token number of a word in a string
WORDLENGTH	Return length of nth word in a string
WORDS	Count words in a string
WORD	Get nth word from a string

The INTERPRET instruction

REXX is usually interpreted, although compilers exist. The INTERPRET instruction adds an extra level of interpretation to a REXX statement, enabling truly dynamic (and difficult to debug!) coding.

For example, with INTERPRET, the left-hand side of an assignment may be a variable; that is, if the *name* of a variable to be assigned is known, that variable may be set using INTERPRET. No other method exists in current native CMS REXX to do this. For example, if variable VNAME contains ABC and variable VVALUE contains SOME STRING:

```
interpret 'vname = vvalue'
```

sets variable ABC to SOME STRING.

INTERPRET is a subject of dispute for many REXX programmers, since it is expensive to process, and is not available with the IBM REXX compiler. Extended discussions of methods to avoid using INTERPRET arise periodically at user groups and on electronic forums. For example, in most cases, the example above could be avoided through use of a stemmed variable:

```
v.vname = vvalue
```

In this case, variable V.ABC will be set; unless the variable name is restricted due to conventions of a called application (ISPF is a particular problem in this area), this example avoids the INTERPRET.

There are occasions when no other method exists to solve a problem, and INTERPRET is a powerful tool in the programmer's arsenal.

INTERPRET also allows creation of a short program to execute REXX typed at the terminal:

```
/* REXX EXEC to execute from the terminal */
   signal DO_FOREVER                    /* Skip error handler */
SYNTAX:                                 /* Here if syntax error */
   say 'SYNTAX ERROR' rc': ' errortext(rc)
DO_FOREVER:                                  /* Main loop */
   signal on SYNTAX                  /* Catch syntax errors */
   do forever                           /* Loop until EXIT */
      parse external cmd                   /* Read a line */
      interpret cmd                     /* Execute the line */
   end
```

To use this program, which might simply be called REXX, one types the command REXX, and enters lines of REXX in response to the terminal read. The syntax error handler traps syntax errors and allows retries. Typing EXIT exits the program.

This is valuable for experimenting with programming techniques and learning REXX features. Loops can even be entered by separating statements with semicolons:

```
do i = 1 to 10;'CP MSG SERVER'i 'STOP';end
```

This is often useful to avoid creating a single-use REXX program.

The ADDRESS instruction

The ADDRESS instruction is poorly understood by many REXX programmers. It controls the execution environment for commands not recognized by REXX.

The current ADDRESS environment can be changed:

```
address banana
```

and restored to the previous environment by omitting an operand:

```
address
```

This is a toggle, not a stack: that is, if the environment has changed several times, ADDRESS with no operands simply switches back and forth between the last two, rather than allowing regression through the entire sequence.

The default ADDRESS environment for REXX programs with file-type EXEC is ADDRESS CMS. This choice reflects the REXX design philosophy of "minimal astonishment" (of making the language perform as intuitively as possible), since it lets commands issued from a REXX program perform normal CMS command search resolution. However, it is in some ways a poor default for programs to be used by others, because it incurs extra overhead resolving commands, and also allows user EXECs with the same names as called programs to "get in the way" and be invoked accidentally.

A better choice is ADDRESS COMMAND. This avoids surprises from user EXECs, and improves performance. It also allows manipulation of mixed-case fileids, something not possible with ADDRESS CMS.

A few CMS commands (ESTATE and LISTFILE, among others) also behave slightly differently when invoked under ADDRESS COMMAND, suppressing informational messages like FILE NOT FOUND. This can be more useful than it sounds; inexperienced REXX programmers often code sequences like:

```
'QUERY CMSTYPE (FIFO'
pull cmstype
'SET CMSTYPE HT'
'ESTATE' fn ft fm
saverc = rc
'SET CMSTYPE RT'
if saverc <> 0 then ...
```

With ADDRESS COMMAND, most of this is avoided:

```
'ESTATE' fn ft fm
if rc <> 0 then ...
```

Using ADDRESS COMMAND does require extra rigor. To invoke another EXEC, the word EXEC must precede the command name, and CP commands must similarly be prefixed with CP. However, improved performance and determinism make this worthwhile.

Even experienced REXX programmers often overlook benefits of ADDRESS, aside from automatically placing an ADDRESS COMMAND at the start of every program.

For example, programs such as the ubiquitous XUP EXEC (to XEDIT a source file in update mode) can be made more intuitive by adding awareness of invocation from XEDIT, and routing commands or output to the XEDIT screen instead of CMS.

This can be achieved by detecting the presence of XEDIT and using ADDRESS XEDIT to route the commands or output:

```
'SUBCOM XEDIT'                          /* Is XEDIT active? */
xedit = (rc = 0) & ¬(cmsflag('SUBSET'))       /* Remember */
  :
if xedit then address xedit 'MSG' ourmsg
else say ourmsg
  :
if xedit then address xedit
'XEDIT' fn ft fm '(UPDATE'
```

In this example, SUBCOM yields return code 0 if XEDIT is active in the virtual machine, and return code 1 if it is not. The CMSFLAG test avoids a false detection of XEDIT if CMS SUBSET mode has been entered from within XEDIT (although there are cases where this should be ignored). Assignment of variable XEDIT sets a logical value of 0 or 1 depending on whether commands and output should be routed to XEDIT.

Subsequent statements test this variable to determine whether output should be displayed via SAY or routed using the XEDIT MSG subcommand, as well as whether the ultimate result of the EXEC is a CMS XEDIT command or an XEDIT XEDIT subcommand.

A common misconception is that the operand of an ADDRESS statement should be enclosed in quotes. In fact, while it *may* be enclosed in quotes, it is not interpreted as a variable, and in fact enclosing it in quotes incurs measurable overhead. To set the ADDRESS environment based on the contents of a variable, use the VALUE operand:

```
something = 'XEDIT'
  :
address value something
```

This interprets the value of the variable SOMETHING, in this case setting the environment to XEDIT.

The CMS stack

The stack is an important part of CMS, which REXX exploits well. There are actually two logically connected CMS stacks: **console** and **program**. The console stack contains data entered at the keyboard, while the program stack contains data stacked by programs.

REXX programs which manipulate the stack should tolerate data stacked before their invocation, that is, they should not accidentally read or delete those lines.

Two CMS commands, MAKEBUF and DROPBUF, facilitate this by creating program **stack levels**. A program stack level is a numbered, logical division within the program stack.

A common misconception is that MAKEBUF and DROPBUF are parts of REXX. This is exacerbated by the fact that in some non-CMS REXX implementations, MAKEBUF and DROPBUF commands are provided with REXX, since they do not exist on that system; however, these are CMS commands, and should be specified in quotes (see "Literals" on page 165 for details on quoting commands).

Lines stacked in **FIFO** (First-In, First-Out) order are added at one end of the current program stack level, contiguous with any previously stacked lines in the program or console stacks; lines stacked in **LIFO** (Last-In, First-Out) order are stacked at the opposite end of the current program stack level, and are the first lines read by PARSE PULL or PULL instructions.

MAKEBUF's return code is a stack level. This can saved and be specified later on a DROPBUF to indicate to delete any lines stacked in that level or later, although this is usually not necessary, since correct stack maintenance will ensure that the current level is the one "owned" by the current program; using DROPBUF with an explicit stack level is usually necessary only when the program calls another application which is a terminal-based environment (such as XEDIT) or is known to be ill-behaved and to alter previously stacked lines inadvertently.

MAKEBUF and DROPBUF simplify delimiting stack usage by a program: issue a MAKEBUF before stacking any data, and a corresponding DROPBUF afterward, while being careful not to PULL more lines than were stacked.

The QUEUED and EXTERNALS functions return the number of lines in the program and console stacks, respectively; usually QUEUED is sufficient for correct stack management. For example:

```
lines = queued()              /* Remember count before starting */
'MAKEBUF'
'QUERY DISK (FIFO'
pull .                                     /* Drop header line */
do queued() - lines
   parse pull ...
end
'DROPBUF'
```

In this example, the MAKEBUF return code is not important, since there is no opportunity for the stack level to change before the DROPBUF.

Using MAKEBUF and DROPBUF in this manner also means that a program need not process all the lines it has stacked before leaving the loop: the DROPBUF deletes any remaining. This is sometimes useful, especially when searching stacked information for a specific value or condition. Even if all lines are read from the current stack level, the level is not decremented until the first line is read from the *next* level, so the DROPBUF is harmless in these cases.

A pictorial representation of stack levels might look like the diagram on the next page.

A program reading a line from the stack in this case would receive line 1. Stacking a line using REXX PUSH (LIFO) would add it as line 14, in the current stack level (PROGRAM stack level 3). Stacking a line using REXX QUEUE (FIFO) would add it between line 7 and line 8 in PROGRAM stack level 3.

A DROPBUF would delete line 8 through line 13, and the current stack level would then be 2. A MAKEBUF would produce return code 3, indicating that another (null) stack level has been created. Reading a line instead of the MAKEBUF would automatically delete the null stack level (PROGRAM stack level 2), and read line 7 from PROGRAM stack level 1.

DROPBUF 2 would delete line 8 through line 13 and also delete the null stack level.

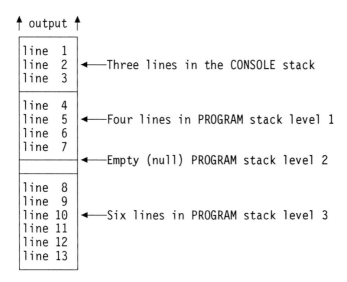

An older CMS command, DESBUF, deletes all stack levels, and also deletes any pending CMS output lines waiting to be typed.   DESBUF is usually a poor choice. A better method is to use DROPBUF 0, which deletes all lines from the program stack, perhaps in concert with a loop to read and discard any lines in the console stack:

```
'DROPBUF 0'
do while externals() > 0
   pull .
end
```

The SENTRIES command is identical to the QUEUED function except that it is a CMS command. Its return code is the number of stacked lines. It is designed for use from languages other than REXX, and there is no reason to use it in REXX, since QUEUED is more efficient.

DMSSEQ is yet another CMS command, introduced in VM/SP Release 6, which is the equivalent of SENTRIES but counts lines in the console stack rather than the program stack.

DROPping variables

The REXX DROP instruction destroys one or more variables, deleting their contents and returning them to the "undefined" state (such that the SYMBOL function returns LIT).

Variable stems can be dropped, deleting all variables starting with that stem.   As with assignments to stems, only the portion of a stemmed variable through the first period is truly a stem:

```
drop a x. y.z.
```

would delete variable A, all variables starting X., and variable Y.Z.; if variable Y.Z.23 were defined before the DROP, it would survive.

DROP's usefulness is often questionable. A common misconception is that since it reinitializes variables, it must conserve storage. This is not entirely true.   Storage is released only when stems are DROPped, for all such stemmed variables destroyed; other variables are merely marked in the internal variable tree as being undefined, so no storage is freed.

DROP is thus most useful for reinitializing in iterative routines, and, when stemmed variables are used, for conserving storage in complex, long-running applications.

Performance Tips

REXX offers excellent performance, especially for an interpreted language.   However, it is in most cases slower than compiled languages, and thus understanding and avoidance of performance pitfalls is often worthwhile.

In general, quoting literals (see "Literals" on page 165) and using ADDRESS COMMAND as appropriate (see "The ADDRESS instruction" on page 159) are the two easiest, most significant performance-related tactics.

Two other common programming choices which should be avoided are listed below.

Quoting function calls

Quotes can be placed around names of built-in REXX functions:

```
line = 'SUBSTR'(line, 1, 8)
```

This avoids the search for a local function (a subroutine in the program) with the same name, and thus *appears* to offer a performance boost; indeed, some REXX programmers quote all built-in function calls for this reason.

This is a mistake, for when an unquoted built-in function is invoked for the first time, REXX does indeed scan the entire program. However, when this scan is performed, "lookaside" entries for all labels are created, and when the function is subsequently found to be built-in, a lookaside entry is also created for it.

Lookasides are not created for quoted calls; thus although the first call will be faster, subsequent calls will be *slower* than if no quoting had been used, since the entire built-in function table will be searched each time.

It could be argued that if a function will only be used once, quoting it is worthwhile, since the lookaside will not be used; however, the extra effort of entering the quotes and maintaining them, along with the risk that later enhancements *will* use the function repeatedly, make this argument suspect.

Quoting function calls is best used *only* when an internal function has for some reason been created with the same name as a built-in function (usually a poor idea), and the built-in must be invoked directly.

Semicolons on statements

PL/I, C, and Pascal programmers find the REXX ";" statement delimiter familiar, and often end *all* REXX statements with it.

While this appears harmless, it in fact generates a null REXX clause internally, which requires some resources to manage.

In addition, if comments are placed to the right of code, as is commonly done:

```
size = 24;              /* Initialize default screen size */
```

interactive tracing shows each line's comments with the *next* line, since the semicolon delimits the statement.

Semicolons should be used *only* if multiple statements are entered on a single line (itself a questionable practice, for readability and maintainability reasons).

Literals

REXX literals—strings which are not to be interpreted as variables—should *always* be enclosed in quotes. This offers a significant performance boost (up to 20% less CPU in some cases), as well as avoiding unintuitive program errors. For example, consider the following CMS command in a REXX program:

```
copyfile myprof exec b profile exec a
```

This command operates as expected if all six variables named—for indeed, all six unique tokens are valid variable names and will thus be interpreted as such—are undefined, since in that case REXX returns the variable name as the value.

However, if, for example, variable A is used as an index in a loop later on:

```
do a = 1 to queued()
   pull line.a
end
```

and the COPYFILE is reissued, the command fails, because A has a numeric value and is not a valid filemode.

This common error has frustrated many beginning REXX programmers, and cost many hours of debugging for those who must fix programs written by those who did not understand this behavior.

It is thus important to understand when a non-REXX command is issued, and to enclose literals in quotes. For example, MAKEBUF and DROPBUF are CMS commands, not REXX instructions, but many programmers do not realize this, and fail to specify them in quotes.

In addition, many REXX function arguments are literals, and should also be quoted:

```
say date('U')
```

This is perhaps less intuitive, but is equally important: if variable U were defined and the DATE call did not specify the operand in quotes, results would not be as desired.

An exception to the rule is the ADDRESS environment, which can be specified in quotes but is not subject to variable substitution if it is not (see "The ADDRESS instruction" on page 159 for details on ADDRESS).

Fortunately, REXX offers the NOVALUE condition, which traps references to undefined variables. See "SIGNAL ON" on page 152 for information on REXX condition trapping. Use of this feature not only avoids errors, but helps beginning REXX programmers learn which operands are literals.

The one exception to the quoting rule is numeric values, which cannot be variables and thus need not be quoted. Quoting these is harmless, however, and some programmers choose to do so; others quote numbers only when the value "just happens" to be numeric, i.e., the value is sometimes a string and sometimes numeric:

```
what = 'unknown'
:
what = '27'   /* Quoted because "just happens" to be numeric */
```

A final area where literals require care relates to stemmed variable tails. In large applications, it is often desirable to use PROCEDURE to isolate variables, and to identify globally accessible variables with a common stem such as GLOBAL.. It is important in such cases to choose the tails carefully, for they are usually thought of as literals but will be interpreted as variables if defined.

For example, if variable GLOBAL.USER contains a userid, it is far too easy to write code which assigns local variable USER. Subsequent references to GLOBAL.USER in the same routine will then return a value different than expected, since the tail will be substituted with the value of USER.

A good technique in such cases is to use a unique character in all literal variable tails, such as an underscore ("_"):

```
global._user = 'OPERATOR'          /* Assign default userid */
:
global._user = user               /* Set new userid */
:
SOMEROUTINE:
procedure expose global.
:
parse var line user settings
:
'CP MSG' global._user 'The settings for' user 'were' settings
```

While the underscore is a valid character in variables—and variable _USER could in fact be assigned—it is not difficult to avoid such variables, and the small extra rigor required greatly improves program robustness.

REXX on Other Platforms

In 1987, when IBM announced its Systems Application Architecture (SAA)—its grand design for the future of IBM computing, guaranteeing similar "look and feel" among applications on differing IBM platforms—REXX was designated the SAA Procedures Language. This was important, for it promised REXX availability beyond VM, on all SAA platforms (MVS, OS/2, and OS/400), and—as SAA moves toward reality—guarantees that REXX usage will grow as new audiences discover it.

In fact, a large, non-VM audience had already discovered REXX. In 1985, a small company called Mansfield Software Group, Inc., introduced a REXX implementation for PC-DOS and MS-DOS called **Personal REXX**.

Originally popular with PC users who knew REXX from VM, Personal REXX has grown steadily in popularity, and has been credited with introducing REXX to many users who have never seen a VM system. Now marketed by Quercus Systems (its original developer), Personal REXX continues to be developed, with Windows and OS/2 versions now available.

Since IBM's SAA announcement, IBM has implemented REXX on all SAA platforms, and many non-IBM REXX implementations have become available as well, including:

- Commodore AmigaDOS (standard in AmigaDOS release 2)
- Unix (several implementations)
- Microsoft Windows (several implementations)
- Tandem Guardian
- VMS (DEC VAX)
- ... with promise of more to come

Future

The REXX language evolved under the watchful eye of its creator, Mike Cowlishaw, based on user feedback and his own ideas. One of his stated objectives was to "keep the language small", i.e., to avoid adding features whose benefit was less than the added complexity in learning, using, implementing, and maintaining the language. He succeeded admirably at this, and by making the language easily extensible (see "Extensibility" on page 153), most special needs can be met through environment-specific add-ons. However, once REXX became part of SAA and was thus destined to be used on other IBM platforms, it was clear that a more elaborate mechanism was required to ensure that the SAA Procedures Language would evolve to meet user and industry needs, while maintaining its original strengths and benefits.

Since the SAA announcement, the IBM REXX Architecture Review Board (ARB) has been created to perform this function. Consisting of IBM REXX developers, users, and planners, the ARB creates language definitions, called **levels**, which define how REXX operates in the IBM SAA environments. Not surprisingly, the SAA language levels differ only slightly from the original REXX language specification defined in Cowlishaw's book, *The REXX Language* (Prentice-Hall, 1985, 0-13-780651-5, second edition). SAA extensions thus far have been confined to support for extended character sets for foreign countries, and these extensions are defined in a "REXX-like" manner, thus ensuring that SAA REXX "looks and feels" like non-SAA REXX.

In 1991, an American National Standards Institute (ANSI) committee was formed to develop a REXX language standard. This committee, consisting of REXX vendors, users, and interested parties such as mainframe user groups, is open to any organization which can meet financial and attendance requirements.

The first draft of an ANSI REXX standard, targeted for 1994, will consist of a detailed specification for the language described in Cowlishaw's book. The next revision will include topics such as standard language extension mechanisms.

The ANSI committee is well aware of risks involved in defining a standard for an interpreted language which is used by end-users. With a compiled language such as C, older programs which are not compatible with a new standard continue to work, using older interfaces and program libraries. An interpreted language, on the other hand, is entirely dependent on the interpreter state every time the program is executed. If, for example, ANSI-standard REXX were likely to break many or most existing user programs, few or no vendors would likely adopt the standard. Fortunately, thanks to the clarity of Cowlishaw's original vision, all existing REXX implementations conform extremely closely to each other, suggesting that a true standard is possible.

Additionally, IBM has stated that the SAA Procedures Language specification will likely merge with the ANSI standard as soon as is practical.

Object-oriented REXX

Another area of REXX evolution deals with object-orientation. This new approach to programming has emerged in the last few years as a possible revolution, offering vastly improved productivity through reusable code libraries without "jumping through hoops" or perform-ance impacts. Object-oriented (OO) versions of other languages are available: C++ is an object-oriented C, and Modula-2 is an OO Pascal.

An IBM research project has explored OO REXX for several years, and is close to releasing an implementation. While OO REXX prom-ises even greater REXX power and flexibility, it is important to note that even the OO version is expected to remain compatible with current implementations: OO features will be added as new instructions and operators, enabling existing programs to continue execution unchanged.

Conclusions

The REXX procedures language is powerful, intuitive, easy to use, and spreading far beyond its VM origins. As such, becoming profi-cient in REXX is not only an investment in one's VM expertise, but in one's future value as a programmer for other environments.

This chapter offered hints on REXX exploitation under VM. There is always more to learn, and REXX's intuitive design and excellent interactive tracing facilities aid in understanding unfamiliar facili-ties. Skimming the REXX reference manual periodically usually results in adding a technique or two to one's REXX toolbox; at a minimum, a feature or two whose usefulness is not obvious usually surfaces at a later date—often surprisingly soon!

Chapter

6

Interlude: Exploiting CMS Session Services

By Romney White

Several years ago, I wanted to write a real-time monitor for VM/XA
and VM/ESA. One major component of such a program would be an
interactive user interface to let a performance analyst select and
view desired data. Writing such an interface in a conventional
programming language appeared to require substantial effort and
would have been difficult to change. So I looked for a way to reduce
programming effort, speed development, and simplify major changes.
I selected CMS Session Services, a little-known facility in CMS, as
my tool.

What Is CMS Session Services?

CMS Session Services is a high-level application programming interface. It is distinct from Fullscreen CMS and should not be confused
with the mode of operation produced by issuing SET FULLSCREEN ON.
While CMS Session Services can create windows in much the same

fashion as Fullscreen CMS does, it can also be used for other purposes.

It took me a while to understand that Fullscreen CMS and CMS Session Services were separate and distinct. Initial user community reaction to what was billed as CMS Windows was so negative that I avoided the whole area for a long time. I have since learned that many people discovered Session Services, much as I did, and that they too were pleasantly surprised.

Why CMS Session Services?

I selected CMS Session Services for several reasons. It was available on all current VM versions. This meant that one approach could be used to implement the user interface. Its non-proprietary nature would keep costs lower for customers, since no third-party software would be required. The interface to CMS Session Services consisted of CMS commands, so REXX programs could be used to develop a prototype. As a result, the approach was easy to try.

Session Services Basics

CMS Session Services introduces a few new concepts to CMS. Understanding them is fundamental to developing an appreciation for how Session Services works and how it can be used.

Virtual Screens

A **virtual screen** or **VSCREEN** is, as its name implies, the virtual equivalent of a 3270 screen. Since it is virtual, a VSCREEN may contain any number of lines and columns. It has a name that is used to refer to it and may have various characteristics (e.g., color, extended attributes) associated with real 3270 devices.

Windows

A **window** is a rectangular area on the physical 3270 screen. It is referred to by a user-specified name. A window is used to view part or all of a virtual screen.

Borders

A window may be surrounded by horizontal and vertical lines called a **border**. In addition to showing window boundaries, the border can receive commands that affect the window. For example, the window can be scrolled, hidden, or minimized by border commands.

Commands

Virtual screens and windows are defined and manipulated by CMS commands. The VSCREEN command manipulates virtual screens, while the WINDOW command creates and controls windows. Each command provides functions (e.g., DEFINE, DELETE, MAXIMIZE) that allow the two kinds of entities to be managed. To facilitate using windows interactively, these commands may be assigned to Program Function keys (PF keys). A related command, PSCREEN, allows the physical screen to be manipulated.

Environment

XAMON, a Velocity Software product, is a real-time monitor for VM/ESA and its predecessor, VM/XA. It consists of three CMS-based components:

XAMWRITE	Collects and analyzes VM performance data
XAMSERVE	Controls XAMWRITE and provides real-time and historical performance data to users
XAMON	Obtains data from XAMSERVE and prepares it for presentation

The XAMON component is the one of interest with regard to CMS Session Services. Since it presents data to users in tabular, menu, and graphical form, it needs a way to manage the display medium.

Using Session Services in XAMON

XAMON is implemented as a macro processor. When invoked, it establishes a subcommand environment and executes a specified macro. The macro is typically a REXX program with filetype XAMON. Usually, the macro uses XAMON subcommands to extract and present performance data.

I developed a standard viewing environment for XAMON by writing an XAMON macro named STDMON. STDMON XAMON interprets a description of a screen that tells what data to extract and how to display it. The display is produced using CMS Session Services.

STDMON defines a virtual screen that covers the physical screen and defines a full-screen window in which to display it. It then constructs and displays individual lines on the virtual screen. The output may be a table, menu, or character graph.

When the virtual screen has been constructed, it is presented in the window. Function keys and input areas on the screen may cause other actions, all of which are handled by the STDMON macro.

Results

Using CMS Session Services was a good way to approach the XAMON user interface design. It was easy to implement and has proven simple to extend. For example, I added a command line to the screen with about 30 lines of code in the STDMON macro. Its performance has been good enough that there is no need to rewrite the interface in a more traditional programming language. CMS Session Services provides valuable facilities for developing CMS applications.

Exploiting VM/ESA

This section describes tools and applications which enhance VM/ESA use and provide payback from its operation.

7

Exploiting Service Machines

By Gabriel Goldberg and Ross A. Patterson

Introduction

This chapter describes **service virtual machines,** sometimes called **servers, service machines, SVMs,** or **DVMs.** They are called SVMs throughout the chapter. This chapter's information facilitates evaluating and maintaining vendor products and public domain offerings which use SVMs; it also provides background, perspective, and details useful in designing and implementing SVM-based applications.

SVMs implement operating system function (security, automatic operation, terminal protocol conversion, etc.) outside the operating system (CP and CMS). The virtual machine architecture allows SVM-based functions to use rigid and well-defined interfaces to communicate with human users, other SVMs, or system services. These interfaces isolate SVM function and operation from other SVMs and system operation, providing compartmentation that improves overall system reliability. SVMs can be virtual machines with no special system privileges which accept requests from users and return information or perform actions on their behalf; SVMs can also be highly privileged virtual machines which act as "trusted assistants" to the operating system.

This chapter begins with detailed descriptions of RTM VM/ESA and CMSBATCH, two common SVMs. It then discusses SVM:

> Advantages
> Architectural decisions
> Building blocks
> Input (e.g., transactions, data, system status)
> Output (e.g., messages, files, actions)
> Control, initialization, and termination
> Performance and accounting
> Maintenance and debugging
> Security

The chapter concludes with brief descriptions of additional common SVMs (which are used as examples throughout the chapter), and rules and recommendations for SVM construction and operation.

Advantages of SVMs

SVM functions and typical implementations include resource serialization (SQL/DS), work scheduling (VMUTIL), batch job processing (CMSBATCH), resource allocation and control (DIRMAINT), system monitoring (RTM VM/ESA), CP extensions (Resource Access Control Facility, or RACF), and communication (Remote Spooling Communications Subsystem, or RSCS; VM/Pass-Through, or PVM). Implementing operating system function outside traditional operating system (CP and CMS) boundaries offers a number of benefits:

Isolation from operating system: SVMs usually rely on supplied system interfaces, and do not require source-level enhancements to CP or CMS. While such enhancements are sometimes required for specific functions, SVMs often avoid them. By using standard interfaces, SVMs can be made portable from one VM installation to another, and are likely to be isolated from changes in VM version or release.

Localized function protected from users: An SVM makes software available without compromising its integrity. An application executing in a user's virtual machine can be compromised by CP commands such as TRACE, STORE, and DISPLAY. Security or accounting based on user virtual machine software is not reliable. SVM execution is impervious to user penetration, except through the SVM's interfaces. If well designed, these disallow inappropriate user actions. SVM interfaces usually confine problems within a single SVM, preventing corrupted data from being shared with other SVMs and keeping programming errors in specialized functions from causing total system failures.

Enforcement of standard interfaces: An application that executes in a user's virtual machine to control access to LINKed minidisks can be subverted, providing direct and unrestricted access to the minidisks. SVM-owned resources are invisible to users, and can only be acquired through SVM interfaces.

Centralized control of resources: The system manager at an installation with multiple links to other sites would hardly want an operator to attach a telecommunication line to users wanting to transmit a file, confirm that transmission was complete, retrieve the line, and allocate it to the next waiting user. Similarly, it would not be practical to control access to multi-user database resources with passwords, because authorized users would likely embed passwords in application software. There would be periodic needs to change passwords, breaking many applications and imposing inconvenience on users. Centralized control allows a single SVM file or data repository to specify system-wide rules governing access, or granting specific user privileges. This allows SVM owners to easily monitor and change access to SVM resources.

History

When first introduced (announced August 1972, available November 1972), VM/370 lacked many features and options now taken for granted, such as PVM, RSCS, remote 3270 support, and more. Even worse, tools for building virtual machine applications were limited, lacking today's VMCF and IUCV for inter-virtual machine communication, the TAG command for routing SPOOL files, the DIAGNOSE to determine virtual memory size, and, not least, the capability of

DIAGNOSE 8 to capture responses from CP commands for interpretation.

Many installations implemented new function in CP which today would be placed in an SVM. An example of that was RASP, a large system for sophisticated cross-processor SPOOL file communication, which embedded file routing control in CP. While IBM initially supported remote 3270 terminals in CP, under VM/ESA these terminals are controlled by the VM/Pass-Through SVM. Similarly, while some (3203 or equivalent, 3800-1, etc.) printers are directly supported by CP, the trend in printer management is towards more function provided by SVMs. IBM, other vendors, and users recognize benefits of SVM implementation of operating system-like functions.

Sample Service Machines

Before introducing SVM building blocks, architectures, input/output, control, and the like, it is instructive to examine two common SVMs: RTM VM/ESA and CMSBATCH. These are described in detail to illustrate SVM operation and interfaces. For readers not familiar with SVM concepts, the external characteristics of these SVMs illustrate the elegance, power, and flexibility of providing operating system functions in SVMs.

Typical user interactions with SVMs

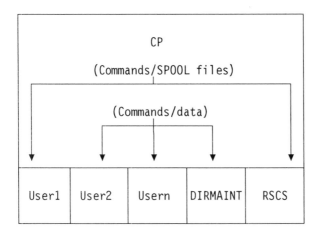

User1 communicates through CP SPOOL with RSCS to send and receive files, while User2 uses CP's VMCF to submit requests to DIRMAINT. Human users control the Usern virtual machines while DIRMAINT and RSCS operate disconnected.

RTM VM/ESA

IBM's Real Time Monitor VM/ESA (Program Number 5798-DWD) is a tool that provides an observation window into the performance of a running VM/ESA ESA CP system.

RTM periodically samples data within CP with the privileged DIAGNOSE 4 interface, processes the data in its virtual memory, and (on demand or at predefined intervals) displays or prints it. Requests for data and commands to control operation are sent to RTM from users via VMCF (Virtual Machine Communication Facility). The program performs no minidisk I/O after initialization is complete, and minimizes use of other CP and CMS services, to avoid affecting the system performance being measured.

While some RTM commands are non-privileged and available to all users, other commands affect RTM operation and are restricted. RTM usually executes disconnected, although it will display data on a console to which it is connected. Data is more commonly displayed on user terminals in response to specific requests.

RTM/ESA can function as an "early warning" system for VM problems. Many key system conditions are monitored; default values and conditions are defined which can be overridden by privileged commands. RTM can detect real I/O devices requiring manual intervention, limits exceeded for values such as CPU utilization or CP overhead, disconnected and disabled users (which will automatically be forced off by CP after 15 minutes), and many other potentially dangerous conditions. Out-of-bounds values are (at a minimum) logged; RTM can also be told to notify a specific user for each condition, either by message or VMCF.

CMSBATCH

The CMS Batch Facility is a facility that allows users to run noninteractive CMS jobs in another virtual machine dedicated to that purpose, freeing their own virtual machines for other work. This facility, more commonly called CMSBATCH (after the userid in which it usually executes) is described in the *VM/ESA CMS User's*

Guide. CMSBATCH in this chapter refers to the facility provided with VM; several vendors (including IBM) offer enhanced batch job processors, and several public domain implementations also exist.

Because CMS's interactive user interface is one of its greatest strengths, the term "CMS batch" seems oxymoronic. Some CMS applications and functions, however, do not capitalize on CMS's interactivity. If executed connected to a terminal, these can be disruptive if they inhibit normal terminal tasks such as accessing personal files or responding to electronic mail.

CMSBATCH allows CMS users to **multitask**—that is, to execute more than one computer task at a time. This is accomplished by submitting to the batch SVM a "job" (a SPOOLed card-image punch file) containing control cards, normal CMS commands, a subset of CP commands, and (optionally) data files. CMSBATCH reads the punch file, notifies the job's submitter or designee of the job's initiation, interprets control cards, executes commands, directs output where specified by supplied commands, and provides notification of job completion. No user or operator control functions exist.

Input (source programs, object decks, data files, etc.) can be supplied in the SPOOLed punch job file, or provided on minidisks LINKed and ACCESSed by commands in the job. Output (compiler listings, object decks, data files, etc.) can be routed by commands in the job or placed directly on a minidisk LINKed and ACCESSed writable by commands in the job. Returning output in SPOOL files requires slightly greater overhead than placing it directly on a minidisk, but can be used whether the minidisk owner is logged on or not, and (more importantly) prevents minidisk damage caused by two userids with simultaneous write access.

The Shared File System can provide data to or receive data from CMSBATCH jobs, although its use may create a security exposure, allowing other users' jobs inadvertent access to data.

CMSBATCH illustrates the SVM concepts of localized function (all users typically submit jobs to the same batch SVM) and defined interfaces (the batch SVM reads job files sequentially, executes commands, produces output).

Architecture

SVM architecture can be open, robust, general, and use standard interfaces. It can also be closed, fragile, overly specific, and use undocumented interfaces. These attributes are often not chosen explicitly, but rather are imposed by design and implementation decisions. This chapter describes CMS-based SVMs. SVM applications can also be stand-alone (run without any virtual machine operating system) or based on another operating system like MVS or VSE.

Open/closed

An **open** SVM provides documented external and internal interfaces, and is easily extended to provide unanticipated functions. It uses structured code with minimal dependencies between seemingly unrelated functions. An open SVM may have a main function driver, triggered by arriving transactions or timer events, which invokes specific functional action routines. Localized function and formalized interfaces simplify understanding operation, and facilitate adding or removing function or changing event processing without side effects. The openness may extend to packaging, so that functions are isolated in separate files, whether EXECs or other source files.

A **closed** SVM is a black box, presenting a set of actions and functions which cannot be easily changed. Closed SVMs are usually provided without source code, and may depend on undocumented system or application interfaces.

Robust/fragile

A robust SVM is insensitive to trivial (or larger) changes in operating environment. An SVM should not fail because it is executing on a new userid or processor or under a new version of VM. Misadventures like a full minidisk, a virtual machine program check, or an invalid command received should be noted without interruption of SVM operation.

General/specific

A general SVM provides an engine for implementation of specific functions without itself being application specific. RSCS is general in that it supports a variety of communication functions with a single nucleus which supports protocol-specific line drivers. Most earlier communication SVMs (and some today) required separate virtual machines and software for each communication line or protocol. Modern SVMs, such as IBM's Advanced Function Printing service machine, support multiple devices per SVM.

Standard/non-standard interfaces

Standard interfaces are documented as such in IBM manuals. While they sometimes change without notice, they are an attempt to create a formal definition of services and protocols which applications can use, and are increasingly stable. Examples are command syntax, CSL calls, and DIAGNOSE code parameters. SVMs should, as much as possible, use only standard interfaces.

Non-standard interfaces include direct use of data from operating system control blocks and undocumented side effects of standard system services. SVMs sometimes must acquire information not available from a defined interface, perform an action not supported by standard facilities, or rely on continuation of undocumented system behavior. Use of these non-standard interfaces makes an SVM (or any other application) vulnerable to IBM changes. Therefore, their use should be explicitly documented and grouped in one or a few modules to simplify future maintenance. RTM VM/ESA's use of DIAGNOSE X'04' to read CP storage is a standard interface, but its interpretation of CP control blocks and vulnerability to changes in CP is a non-standard interface.

CMS/non-CMS

While most SVMs operate under CMS, and are therefore relatively familiar in structure and operation to system programmers and users, some do not. Common non-CMS SVMs are RSCS, the GCS recovery machine, and the VTAM Service Machine. Non-CMS SVMs introduce special considerations, and are often not as flexible in operation as CMS SVMs; for example, the GCS environment lacks much function available in CMS.

Types

Different SVM characteristics satisfy different operational requirements.

Connected/disconnected

Connected refers to virtual machine execution with a real terminal (virtual machine console). **Disconnected** describes execution with no virtual machine console. Most SVMs execute disconnected, since their purpose is hands-off automation. Disconnected SVMs are usually logged on with the AUTOLOG command, though they can be logged on and then disconnected. Disconnected SVMs should execute with console SPOOLing started and directed to the SVM owner or (better) an SVM central repository for console files.

In special cases (e.g., a critical service provider, or when debugging or monitoring security violations) an SVM may execute connected. An MVS guest, for example, may execute connected to simplify operational tasks. Special care is needed to prevent a terminal MORE or HOLDING condition from blocking execution or delaying desired output. In VM/ESA Release 2, these conditions can be avoided using CP SET command options.

Always/sometimes logged on

An SVM can be logged on whenever VM service is offered, at certain time intervals, or only on demand. Most SVM services (e.g., terminal access, file transfer, and database functions) are expected to be constantly available. SVMs like these are usually AUTOLOGged by AUTOLOG1 or another system-initializing SVM when CP is IPLed. See "AUTOLOG1" on page 211 for a description of CP and SVM startup.

Some SVMs (e.g., a private SQL database server) may be best logged on only when needed, to avoid their holding unused resources. This can be accomplished manually, by requests to or instructions for the system operator; it can also be accomplished by time-of-day processing by another SVM or even by allowing any user who knows the password to AUTOLOG a requested SVM. A userid which is logged or AUTOLOGged periodically to execute a predefined application with no external interactions is actually a disconnected batch job rather than an SVM.

Synchronous/asynchronous

Synchronous communication makes the requester wait for the SVM response. Synchronous communication is simple, requires minimal handshaking, and is relatively impervious to the user's virtual machine environment. On the other hand, it tends to be application-specific and (should be) limited to servers that respond quickly. Synchronous execution couples the requesting user to the SVM until the requested function is complete. During this time, the requesting user's virtual machine is dedicated to waiting for completion and cannot perform any other tasks. RTM VM/ESA's synchronous execution provides mostly instantaneous execution of commands, but it is the reason that when the RTM SVM is "hung" (logged on and partly functional, but not able to process requests), issuing an RTM request can appear to delay execution in a user's virtual machine. SVC and DIAGNOSE requests are synchronous, in that the issuer waits until the requested function completes.

Asynchronous communication uncouples the requester's execution from the SVM response. Asynchronous communication is more general in nature and can be extended to support new applications. It is, however, more complex than synchronous communication, requiring overhead and handshaking transactions. It can be affected by changes in the user's virtual machine environment. Asynchronous execution allows a request to be submitted and normal interactive tasks to continue, with the SVM providing notification when the request is complete. CMSBATCH's asynchronous execution allows users to submit jobs without regard for the number of jobs awaiting execution. CMSBATCH notifies the submittor of a job when it starts and ends execution. The CP MSG command is asynchronous, in that it completes instantly for the sender, but the message is not displayed until the target user's terminal is available (i.e., not in MORE/HOLDING state or in full-screen mode).

Single-thread/multi-thread

An SVM's level of **threading** is the number of transactions it can handle simultaneously. Threading is a synonym for **tasking**, the number of tasks in simultaneous execution. Most simple SVMs like CMSBATCH and RTM VM/ESA are single-threaded. This requires arriving transactions to be queued until preceding transactions have completed. RTM transactions take hardly any time, so RTM appears to handle all requests instantly. An installation with a single CMSBATCH SVM and many users submitting jobs may find that queue length and service waits become unacceptable. Since CMSBATCH is, architecturally, single-threaded, a solution can be to create multiple batch servers (with different userids, of course). Users can then be allocated to a particular server or servers, or another SVM can be created to receive batch jobs and route them to available servers.

Most SVMs that provide end-user functions like protocol conversion, file transfer, or database access (VM/Pass-Through, RSCS, and SQL/DS) are multi-threaded.   Up to a point, this provides better overall service.   However, if an SVM is too overloaded, maintaining task queues and internal dispatching can be costly.   A tradeoff is to provide a maximum level of multi-threading, after which transactions are queued and wait for previous transactions to complete.

Single copy/multiple copy

This is the opposite of the single-thread/multi-thread decision. Usually, single copies of multi-threaded SVMs such as RSCS and PVM are used, while multiple copies of single-threaded SVMs such as CMSBATCH and the OfficeVision mailbox (MBX) SVM may be required for adequate turnaround or multiple device support.

Global/local/private resources

Servers that accept requests through the Advanced Program-to-Program Communication (APPC) facility are called **resources**.   They may be defined to be known on all systems in the SNA network (GLOBAL), on all systems in the same TSAF cluster (LOCAL), or not visible at all outside the SVM (PRIVATE).   Programs that define APPC resources can use Common Programming Interface for Communications (CPI-C) CSL routines to easily handle communications with requesters.   The best known APPC resources in VM systems are the Shared File System servers, and are known by the names of the file-pools they manage.

Building Blocks

SVM building blocks are all of VM's native interfaces, utilities, commands, macros, SVCs, together with those of any additional installed software.   A sampling of native and supplemental building blocks is discussed here, representing various types and sources.

Programmable Operator (PROP)

PROP, part of VM, can automate VM operation by intercepting messages and requests directed to its virtual machine and handling them according to preprogrammed actions. PROP commonly runs in the system operator's virtual machine to log selected messages, filter (ignore) common informational messages, and act on designated commands from authorized users. PROP activity is controlled by a routing table, a CMS file containing user authorizations, command definitions, and option specifications. Action routines are programs or EXECs invoked by the match of a message and a routing table entry. PROP can also be the foundation of non-system operator transaction-based applications.

REXX

REXX (Restructured EXtended eXecutor), also called the System Product Interpreter, is the language of choice for many CMS applications. Replacing the older EXEC and EXEC 2, it is particularly suited for command procedures (EXECs), user-defined XEDIT subcommands, prototyping, and general personal computing. Similar to PL/I, it has extensive debugging facilities.

Although REXX was originally an interpreted language, compilers have become available in recent years. Depending on the nature and complexity of the application, compilers can effect dramatic improvement on execution of a REXX program. In general, the larger and more complex the code, the more likely it will be to gain efficiency by compilation.

CP SET xxxx IUCV

Several classes of virtual machine console output (CPCONIO, EMSG, IMSG, MSG, SMSG, VMCONIO, and WNG) can be retrieved via IUCV. This allows programs to intercept and act on messages or interruptions generated by their own or other virtual machines.

Interrupt handling

Interrupts are asynchronous events presented by CP. Some interrupts emulate real hardware facilities, while others (e.g., VMCF and

IUCV) are CP-supplied extensions to System/390 architecture. Since SVMs typically run disconnected, assorted facilities for manually interrupting a virtual machine from the terminal (PA1, PA2, HX, HT, CP ATTN, etc.) are not available. Other virtual machine interrupts (program check, IUCV, VMCF, external, I/O, etc.) may occur as part of normal operation or errors. SVMs must handle anticipated interrupts without interfering with normal virtual machine operation and must avoid or not be damaged by error interrupts. Interrupts can be processed at a low architectural level (by replacing a new PSW with an SVM-specific PSW), an intermediate level (with interrupt-specific macros such as HNDIO or HNDSVC), or a higher level (capturing results of an interrupt without dealing with the interrupt protocol, such as happens with the CONSOLE macro).

PSW manipulation

The PSW (Program Status Word) is 64 bits of information which represents and controls virtual machine execution and status. An interrupt causes the current PSW to be saved and a new, interrupt-specific PSW to be loaded. It has been traditional to manipulate appropriate PSWs to direct specific interrupts (I/O, external, etc.) to application-specific interrupt handlers. For several reasons, this is no longer advisable:

- Many more flexible facilities have been added (assembler language macros, commands, language facilities, CMS subroutines) that are easier and more reliable to use.
- Complex SVMs use interrupts for multiple communication tasks or paths and use diverse interrupt types. PSW manipulation can disrupt this coexistence.
- 370-mode, ESA-mode, and XC-mode machines require different PSWs and low-level interrupt handling.

CMS macros

HNDEXT: traps external interrupts and passes control to a designated routine.

HNDINT: traps interrupts for one or more specified I/O devices and passes control to designated routines.

HNDSVC: traps interrupts for one or more specified SVC instructions and passes control to designated routines.

HNDIUCV: traps external interrupts for specific IUCV requests, passing control to a designated routine. HNDIUCV allows several programs in a virtual machine to share IUCV access concurrently without interference.

CMSIUCV: provides IUCV services through CMS, with much of the complexity of IUCV masked from the application.

CONSOLE: performs I/O to the virtual machine console or to an attached terminal, and provides all interrupt handling.

CMS Commands

WAKEUP: This command simplifies SVM interrupt handling. It suspends virtual machine operation until a designated event occurs. WAKEUP is part of IBM's **CMS Utilities Feature**, described later. It can detect and report time-of-day and time interval events, or console, external, I/O, VMCF, IUCV, and unit record interrupts. Options control interrupt processing and reporting. Since multiple events and interrupts can be awaited simultaneously, WAKEUP resumes execution when the first specified event/interrupt occurs, indicating what event occurred. WAKEUP is used by the CMS Utilities Feature VMUTIL SVM machine for event processing.

EXECIO: EXECIO is a general data transfer utility frequently used in SVMs. It reads from disk or reader files to the program stack or EXEC variables, writes from the program stack or variables to disk or SPOOL files, and executes CP commands with optional retrieval of resulting output.

Pipelines: CMS Pipelines is an extremely powerful and flexible non-procedural means of processing data. It is more powerful and offers better performance than EXECIO, and is thus usually preferred when available. It was integrated into CMS in VM/ESA Release 1.1, and is available for earlier VM releases as an add-on product. See Chapter 3, *Exploiting CMS*, on page 87 for more information.

CP SPOOL commands

Many SVMs process, are driven by, or create SPOOL files. CP has non-privileged commands to manipulate *virtual* SPOOL resources (files or devices), as well as privileged CP commands to manipulate *real* SPOOL devices and files belonging to other users.

CMS Utilities Feature

Before VM/ESA, IBM sold a product called **VM/Interactive Productivity Facility,** (IPF). The portion of IPF that provided a number of useful utility programs is now available on its own, as a separately orderable feature of VM/ESA, called the CMS Utilities Feature.

Its commands supplement those of CP and CMS, providing such functions as DCSS backup and restore, and SPOOL file manipulation without loss of printer carriage control. It also includes WAKEUP, described above.

Virtual Machine Communication Facility (VMCF)

VMCF, part of CP, lets a virtual machine exchange data with other virtual machines without performing I/O. It is occasionally used by SVMs to receive requests from and return answers and data to users, although it has been made largely obsolete by IUCV. VMCF includes data transfer and control functions, a special external interrupt code, and a special external interrupt message header.

The most glaring difference between VMCF and IUCV is the lack of support in CMS for sharing VMCF between programs in the same virtual machine. Programs using VMCF should take care not to invoke other VMCF-using programs, such as the RTM VM/ESA interface module, VMC.

Inter-User Communications Vehicle (IUCV)

IUCV, part of CP, lets a virtual machine communicate with other virtual machines, CP system services, and itself. IUCV communication paths can be restricted to certain users or quantities of users. It is the tool of choice for programmed exchanges of data between SVMs and clients. IUCV functions create and dismantle communication paths, send and reply to messages, receive or reject messages, and control the sequence of IUCV events.

CMS provides a layer of support above the CP IUCV instruction that allows programs in the same virtual machine to share use of IUCV without interfering with each other. This facility, implemented by the CMSIUCV and HNDIUCV assembler macros, is critical to the use of IUCV from CMS programs. Without this capability, it would be impossible to use IUCV in a virtual machine that was also accessing Shared File System files, or that was running Fullscreen CMS, as these facilities use IUCV for their communications.

CP DIAGNOSE functions

In general, CP creates virtual machines by emulating real hardware facilities (i.e., equipment that exists in the real world, even if not on a particular VM system). An exception is the DIAGNOSE facility which is used by virtual machines to request CP services. DIAGNOSE instructions are sometimes called **hypervisor calls**, since they request service from CP, the system hypervisor. The CP module that handles DIAGNOSE services is therefore named DMKHVC in VM/ESA 370 feature or HCPHVC in VM/ESA ESA feature. SVMs often use DIAGNOSE instructions to communicate with CP, request CP services, or to extract CP information. The DIAGNOSE instruction has no assembler language mnemonic, and must thus be created with:

```
DC  X'83xycccc'
    or
DIAG Rx,Ry,X'cccc'
```

instructions or macros such as DIAG, supplied in DMSGPI MACLIB. The DIAGNOSE operation code is 83 and cccc is the 4-hexadecimal-digit DIAGNOSE code (DIAGNOSE codes are always identified in hex). DIAGNOSE codes are multiples of 4. IBM reserves DIAGNOSE codes 0000–00FC and 0200–02FC (hex); installation-defined DIAGNOSE functions run from 0100 through 01FC. A subcode parameter selects a function for DIAGNOSE codes such as X'14' which perform multiple functions. Not all DIAGNOSE codes are used; sometimes a function (or particular subcode) is implemented only on some VM versions, so the associated DIAGNOSE code is missing from other VM versions. As the DIAGNOSE facility evolves with VM, often providing function for new IBM products, it supports new varieties of user or vendor SVMs. The *x/y* digits identify virtual machine registers which contain parameters for the DIAGNOSE code. Some codes use more than two register parameters by defining the contents of the *x*+1 and *y*+1 registers. DIAGNOSE codes can return data in registers or in virtual storage addressed by registers; status information is available in the PSW condition code after execution.

Some DIAGNOSE codes can be executed directly from REXX programs through the DIAG and DIAGRC functions, with appropriate notation for supplying parameters and receiving answers. While many DIAGNOSE functions are available to all users, others are restricted to users with particular command privileges. Execution of a privileged DIAGNOSE without proper privileges results in a virtual operation exception (program check); invalid DIAGNOSE parameters may cause virtual specification, protection, or addressing exceptions.

VM/ESA DIAGNOSE code information is provided in *VM/ESA CP Programming Services for 370* and *VM/ESA CP Programming Services*. If system programmers use the **User Class Restructure** facility to redefine privileges required for DIAGNOSE codes, the command class requirements listed in the manual may be misleading. The CP COMMANDS command displays the commands and DIAGNOSE codes available to a user.

CP system services

System services use a special form of IUCV that provides communication between virtual machines and CP. They allow SVMs and CP to present asynchronous messages to each other, and support a reasonably high transaction rate. For example, CP uses *RPI to request authorization from an access control SVM such as RACF for LOGON, LINK, and other resource-related transactions. CP functions required by installation-written SVMs can be added as new system services. CP modules DMKIUC (for VM/ESA 370) and HCPIUG (for VM/ESA ESA) contain a table of system services. System service names begin with "*" to indicate communication with CP instead of another virtual machine.

> ***ACCOUNT**   Provides an interface for receiving accounting records from CP. This service is not available

on VM/ESA 370 feature, where accounting records are written to SPOOL files instead.

*BLOCKIO Provides device-independent access to minidisks with support for multiple concurrently pending I/O requests.

*CCS (SNA Virtual Console Support) provides VM console capabilities to SNA terminals through a VTAM service machine (VSM) that acts as an interface between an SNA network and CP.

*CRM Allows an authorized virtual machine to connect to the Collection Resource Management System Service and become the TSAF virtual machine.

*IDENT Allows authorized TSAF virtual machines to identify themselves to CP as resource owners and to revoke resource ownership.

*LOGREC Lets an authorized virtual machine receive a copy of records written to the CP Error Recording Area.

*MONITOR Provides system performance and resource utilization data to an SVM. It replaces SPOOL files or tape volumes for data collection.

*MSG Allows incoming messages and responses from CP to be read by programs instead of being displayed on user terminals.

*MSGALL Receives all incoming messages in classes not currently directed to the *MSG system service. The primary use of *MSGALL is by Fullscreen CMS.

*RPI Provides a communication path over which an access control SVM (RACF, ACF2, etc.) can receive requests and return authorizations and rejections.

*SIGNAL Allows members of a virtual machine group to send signals to each other.

*SPL Lets an authorized virtual machine handle logical printer functions.

*SYMPTOM Allows an authorized virtual machine to receive data about CP problems, called **Symptom Records**.

Some system services are of most use to IBM-provided software (*CCS and *CRM), some may be used by IBM and non-IBM software

(*IDENT, *RPI, *SIGNAL), and some are of great use in IBM and non-IBM SVMs (*BLOCKIO, *LOGREC, *MSG, *MSGALL, *SPL).

Input Transaction Sources

Input transactions can be categorized by **source** (where they originate) and **type** (how they arrive at the SVM). Some SVMs handle multiple transaction sources and/or types.

Timer

Powerful SVMs exist which are purely driven by passage of time. RTM/ESA gathers system statistics and verifies system status at predetermined intervals. The WAKEUP command (described in "Building Blocks" on page 187) allows applications to suspend execution until a specified time is reached. To guard against invalid calculations causing too-soon or too-late execution, or execution resumed by extraneous interrupts, timer-driven SVMs must verify the time when execution resumes. Timing anomalies such as leap years, the year 2000, and repeated execution at the same time of day should be handled. Timer-driven SVMs should allow "escaping" from application code without requiring a LOGOFF or re-IPL.

System status or events

An SVM connected to CP via a system service must react asynchronously to events or changes in system status. For example, a member of a virtual machine group must respond to *SIGNAL input, and an SVM supporting logical printers must respond to *SPL input. Most SVMs which appear to be driven by system status or events (e.g., system SPOOL occupancy too high, a critical userid disconnected and disabled, CP free storage extended, etc.) are really timer-driven to interrogate and report their areas of interest.

User requests

User requests are functions invoked by a user at a terminal or a user-initiated process. A user accessing Shared File System (SFS) resources will generate implicit requests to the SFS SVM. User input (as opposed to input generated by an application front end or automatic process such as SFS) requires thorough validation.

Input Transaction Types

Virtual machine interrupts (I/O, timer)

SVMs written in high-level languages (EXEC 2, REXX, PL/I, C, etc.) generally cannot handle interrupts directly, but use tools such as WAKEUP or the Callable Services Library. Assembler language SVMs can either use these tools or handle interrupts directly with appropriate CMS macros. The technique of replacing the virtual machine new PSWs with application code PSWs (**PSW stealing**) has been made largely unnecessary with the availability of standard interrupt handling facilities provided by the HND*xxxx* macros described earlier. For SVMs that can run in XA- or ESA-mode, PSW stealing also presents an unneccesary complication, since the PSW formats and interrupt handling requirements differ greatly between these modes and 370 mode.

Secondary console

The Single Console Image Facility (SCIF) allows a user (or SVM) to control one or more disconnected SVMs. The controlling (secondary) user uses the CP SEND command to provide console input to (primary) SVM(s). Console output from primary SVMs is prefixed with the originating userid. While SCIF is a limited interface (only one userid can be the secondary console for a given SVM), it allows one userid to control multiple SVMs. The controlling userid can in fact be automated, submitting transactions with SEND and receiving responses and asynchronous primary user console output with a combination of CP SET CPCONIO (see "CP SET xxxx IUCV" on page 188) and SUPERMSG or equivalent. A disadvantage of SCIF is that, prior to VM/ESA Release 2, secondary users must be defined in the system directory (Release 2 adds privileged CP SET SECUSER commands).

User requests (MSG, SMSG, VMCF, IUCV)

User requests can be detected immediately by one of the interrupt-handling programs described in "Building Blocks" on page 187.

SPOOL files

The CP SPOOLing system was the first communication path between virtual machines. SPOOL files are easily understood, created, transmitted, detected by an SVM, read, and purged. Transactions in SPOOL files are automatically queued by CP in an SVM's virtual reader, independent of SVM status or activity level. This allows asynchronous transaction creation, processing, and purging. CMSBATCH receives transactions—batch jobs—in SPOOL files. SPOOLing, however, can cause system overhead out of proportion to the amount of data transmitted: creating and purging even small SPOOL files causes the system SPOOL checkpoint to be updated. SPOOL files are an adequate input mechanism for low-volume SVMs which need not provide crisp response.

SPOOL file arrival can be detected immediately by one of the interrupt-handling programs described in "Building Blocks" on page 187. The originator and characteristics of SPOOL files should be validated; files can be processed immediately or queued for later handling. Alternatively, if an SVM need not react instantly to arriving files, a timer-driven SVM which periodically checks for new SPOOL files will probably serve.

Problems can be caused by expected SPOOL files not arriving (if an SVM looks for files while SPOOL is being backed up by SPTAPE, which makes groups of SPOOL files invisible while they are processed) or arriving in the wrong order (if SPOOL files are restored by SPTAPE or the system is started CKPT).

Dialed-in terminal

Function is sometimes provided by multi-user SVMs which handle user terminals as dedicated or DIALed devices. Interactive end-user computing is provided by systems such as MUSIC and AIX/370 to users whose terminals are connected to the appropriate SVM instead of being logged on to VM. In these cases, other than providing SVMs with virtual machine functions and supporting connected terminals, CP is not involved in handling SVM input or output transactions.

This technique provides perhaps the most secure implementation of SVM function, because a user connected to the SVM is completely under the SVM's control and cannot directly invoke any CP or CMS functions to escape or subvert the SVM application. The CONSOLE macro can be used by a CMS application to handle attached terminals with the same ease as the virtual console.

Validation

Input provided to SVMs must be validated to prevent accidental or deliberate abuse of SVM applications.

Source

The source of transactions must be reliably known; an application front end executing in a user virtual machine can be used to impersonate another (perhaps more highly privileged) user. Use CP identification of the sender of VMCF, IUCV, and SPOOL file transactions, rather than information provided by the user's virtual machine.

Function

Unknown function types must be detected, rejected, and logged. Even a minimal SVM must filter commands based on SVM-specific specification of privileges.

Data

Similarly, all other aspects of input transactions must be validated. An SVM must detect invalid command syntax, conflicting options, and invalid data types without any problem (e.g., program check or EXEC branch error). Transactions containing invalid information should be rejected and logged, rather than partially processed or repaired.

Output

Most SVMs provide some form of output, rather than simply accepting user input with no resulting action or feedback.

Actions

SVM actions might include running a batch job (CMSBATCH or MVS), creating a logical terminal session (VM/Pass-Through), or executing a time-of-day set of commands. An SVM should provide the requesting user confirmation of action taken and results accomplished. Certain actions should be reported to the system operator or other authority, in the form of messages, electronic mail, or audit files.

Responses

Responses include reports of actions taken, database output, and answers to queries on system behavior. The form in which responses are provided (VMCF/IUCV transactions, message, message-noheader, SPOOL file) should be tailorable on a system-wide or individual user level.

Files

Data provided by SVMs should be available as SPOOL, minidisk, or SFS files, as alternatives to programmed interfaces such as VMCF/IUCV. Data in files can be processed at user convenience, enabling asynchronous request and output processing.

Validation

Most SVMs validate input transactions only, assuming that acceptable input transactions will produce proper output. An extremely sensitive application could post-process output to ensure that actions taken, responses issued, and files transmitted were appropriate to the environment (userid involved, day of week, time of day, system load, etc.). Significant events and improper requests shold be logged for reference.

Initialization

SVM initialization should ensure that the environment is correct and understood (minidisk configuration and space available, virtual machine size, virtual and real devices, other required SVMs) before beginning to accept transactions. Some adaptations may be required; for example, buffer allocation may depend on virtual machine size. If conditions are incorrect and cannot be corrected, an SVM should report initialization failure and log off or at least reject arriving transactions (with, of course, messages explaining the problem to transaction submitters). An SVM should guard against repeated failures to initialize in a short time interval. SVM console activity should be collected by the command:

```
CP SPOOL CONSOLE START
```

A specialized use of an **internal file** (described later) during initialization is a **profile** capability. An SVM profile is similar to a user's PROFILE EXEC or PROFILE XEDIT, which are executed after CMS IPL or when entering a file in XEDIT. Instead of being processed directly by CMS, the SVM profile is read by SVM application code during SVM startup. An SVM profile can execute CP and CMS commands, and execute an initial set of SVM commands to start communication links, define virtual I/O devices, synchronize action with other SVMs, and perform other SVM-specific actions. The SVM profile is distinct from the SVM's PROFILE EXEC, which can also issue CP/CMS commands but cannot perform SVM-specific functions.

It can be inefficient to allocate multiple SVM minidisks, each of which contains nothing but an SVM-specific PROFILE and perhaps a few additional files. A single minidisk can serve as a 191 disk for several SVMs, by controlling execution of the one PROFILE EXEC according to the userid under which it is executed. This is especially useful for managing multiple SVMs that run the same software, or groups of otherwise related SVMs. An IPL command option (PARM FPOOL) can direct CMS to execute a PROFILE from an SFS file pool, which can eliminate the need for SVM 191 minidisks.

Parameters used (by default or specified at startup) should be logged. Userids identified as owning or monitoring the SVM should be notified of startup, any problems, and availability for service. Some SVMs may need to recognize whether they are being restarted under a running VM system or being started as part of normal system startup. This can be done by passing a special parameter during system startup, or by the SVM comparing its logon time with the CP IPL time.

EXECs and XEDIT macros which are frequently executed or which reside on disks that may be RELEASEd later should be loaded into memory using the EXECLOAD command. This ensures that they will always be available, whether the disk is still ACCESSed or not, and that they will not need to be read from disk.

Operational Control (Parameters and Commands)

All but the simplest SVMs require some amount of operational control, for example, identification of privileged users, definition of communication nodes, choices of problem handling techniques, or specification of SPOOL file classes to handle. Initial and changed parameters and date/timestamps of parameter files should be logged in an SVM audit trail. Any means of providing parameters and commands to an SVM should allow inclusion of comment lines beginning with "*" which will be ignored by the SVM. SVM parameters can be provided in a variety of ways, with differing amounts of flexibility.

At startup

Simple parameters (e.g., SPOOL file class) can be provided on the CP AUTOLOG command which starts an SVM. The command:

```
AUTOLOG SPOOLER FEB31#EXEC SPOOLPRG CLASS P
```

would start an SVM called SPOOLER, with password FEB31, and execute SPOOLPRG with parameters CLASS P. The EXEC would presumably parse and act on the parameters. This technique is most suitable for a "private" SVM which is occasionally logged on by an individual user. It is too error-prone to be appropriate for "system" SVMs which must be reliably started with specific options. In addition, if SVMs are started by a set of AUTOLOG commands (perhaps executed by AUTOLOG1), changing parameters can be burdensome and impossible to audit.

Commands from outside sources

Parameters can be specified on commands accepted from authorized users. These commands (often sent by SMSG) can be handled by normal transaction processing in the SVM, and can take effect immediately. The command:

```
SMSG RSCS START LINKWEST CLASS Z
```

tells an RSCS SVM to process class Z files on communication link LINKWEST. All commands (and, for most SVMs, all transactions) should be logged. Since SQL/DS and PROFS servers do not accept external commands, it can be difficult to automate their operation. The combination of Single Console Image Facility (SCIF) and Programmable Operator (PROP) can allow authorized users to submit commands to these and other SVMs. PROP, running in the OPERATOR virtual machine, can detect messages from users submitting SVM commands and use routing tables and action routines to validate authorizations. Valid commands can be submitted to SVMs through SCIF.

```
/* Sample external RTM VM/ESA initialization commands */
address command
'CP SLEEP 10 MIN'
'VMC SMART SET LOGM 1  ON   USER OPERATOR LIMIT 1'
'VMC SMART SET LOGM 6  OFF USER OPERATOR LIMIT 1'
'VMC SMART INTERVAL DISPLAY 3'
```

These commands, executed from a privileged user, set RTM VM/ESA SVM options because RTM has no "profile" capability.

Commands from the SVM

Internal commands are executed from SVM-owned files. These files specify actions to take at SVM startup, specified intervals, or particular times of day.

```
/* Sample RSCS initialization PROFILE */
'CP ATTACH C08 RSCS 308'
'CP SPOOL CONSOLE START TO CONSOLES'
'START VM1WEST'
'START HPLASER'
```

The above file provides commands executed only at initialization.

External files

External files exist on non-SVM minidisks which are linked read-only. If an SVM reads parameter files from the minidisk only at startup or upon command, parameters in external files are easy to change. An authorized user can change files and signal the SVM to reACCESS the minidisk and read and process the parameter file. (The reACCESS is required for the SVM to obtain the minidisk directory as updated by the user; for files residing in the CMS Shared File System, no reACCESS is necessary.) This puts new parameters into effect with no interruption in SVM availability. If the minidisk is read-only but the SVM cannot be told to process new parameters during operation, changes will take effect only when the SVM is restarted. If continuous operation of the SVM is not critical it can be FORCEd and AUTOLOGged.

A sample RSCS parameter file follows:

```
*************************************************************
*                  RSCS LOCAL NODE-ID SPECIFICATION        *
*************************************************************
*              LOCAL       GMT
*              NODE-ID      OFFSET
*              --------    --------
      LOCAL    9370          5
*              NODE-ID NAME  = HOME
*              GMT OFFSET    = 5 (EASTERN STANDARD TIME)
*************************************************************
*                  RSCS OPERATOR FORM NAME SPECIFICATION   *
*************************************************************
*              OPERATOR
*              FORM NAME
*              --------
      OPFORM   STANDARD
*************************************************************
*                     RSCS LINK-ID SPECIFICATIONS          *
*************************************************************
*              LINE     VIRTUAL TIME TASK SPOOL KEEP
*      LINK-ID DRIVER   ADDRESS ZONE ID   CLASS SLOTS
*      ------- ------   ------- ---- ---- ----- -----
      LINK PST4381 DMTNJE 040     5    VMBT *     2
*************************************************************
*                  RSCS AUTHORIZED OPERATOR SPECIFICATIONS *
*************************************************************
*              LINK-ID    USERID    LOCATION   CP
*              --------   --------   --------   --
      AUTH     *          OPERATOR   *          CP
*************************************************************
*                     RSCS SUPERVISOR SPECIFICATIONS       *
*************************************************************
*              ---------------------------------------
      TAGS     384        NUMBER OF TAG SLOTS TO GENERATE
      DUMP     VM  DUMPS  DUMP TYPE AND USERID TO SEND IT TO
      MSGNOH              SPECIFY NO HEADER (RSCS MUST BE
*                         PRIVILEGE CLASS B TO USE THIS)
```

This file is processed at initialization to determine the number and type of communication links, users authorized to control RSCS, and other options. Lines beginning with "*" are comments.

Internal files

Internal files exist on SVM minidisks. If the parameter minidisk is accessed read-only, parameters can be handled as if they were in external files. If the SVM accesses the disk read/write, files can only be changed from the SVM (with normal operation interrupted) or from another userid with the SVM logged off, or through commands provided by the SVM.

Embedded in code

SVM options should not be specified in SVM software, whether it is an EXEC or a compiled language. Such options can only be changed by taking the SVM out of service, and such changes blur the SVM maintenance history.

Reconfiguration and Maintenance

Ideally, it should be possible to completely reconfigure or apply maintenance to an SVM without disrupting service. This is, in practice, often impossible. Some reconfiguration can be done by externally changing parameters as described earlier. Allowing an SVM to execute CP and CMS commands at the direction of authorized users provides an added degree of external control, allowing (for example) minidisks to be DETACHed, LINKed, or reACCESSed while SVM execution continues. An SVM should include a list of commands which can be executed in this manner, excluding self-destructive commands such as DEFINE STORAGE or SET MACHINE.

Users should be informed when an SVM will be out of service; applications which invoke SVM services should be disabled or issue warning messages. Users should not be left to determine from lack of response (or a hung terminal) that an SVM is unavailable. Similarly, an SVM upon which other SVMs rely should be taken out of service under controlled conditions, since client SVMs may have no means of detecting the outage or protecting their own clients. An SVM which provides critical function may be defined with duplicate software minidisks so that changes can be applied to one set and tested in another userid while the production SVM operates normally; minidisks can then be swapped with only a brief interruption in service.

Termination

SVMs should have a procedure for orderly termination of operation, closing files (SPOOL or minidisk), and logging off.   An external signal for termination should be available; it should not be necessary for an operator or system programmer to reconnect to a server to terminate it.   Typically, the normal communication technique (SPOOL file, VMCF, IUCV, secondary console) will be used; the SVM should verify that the termination request was sent by an appropriately authorized (by the SVM, not CP-privileged) user.

The command or function sent to the SVM to signal termination should *not* be named SHUTDOWN.   SHUTDOWN should be reserved for requesting CP system termination; using it in another context risks (and has caused!)   accidental shutdown of production VM systems—not a pleasant experience.   Sadly, some IBM products (e.g., DIRMAINT, RSCS) use SHUTDOWN to signal termination; installation-written SVMs should standardize on a command such as STOP, EXIT, or END.

Reliability and Restart

Disabled wait

Program checks in critical CMS modules, some CMS file system errors, paging errors, and program interrupt loops cause CMS to load a disabled wait PSW. This stops virtual machine execution and prevents any internal (for example, timer interrupts) or external (user requests, I/O interrupts, etc.) event from causing it to resume. Little can be done within a virtual machine to prevent or recover from disabled wait conditions. The RTM VM/ESA SVM, however, can be instructed to monitor critical SVMs, and, if they become DISConnected and disabled, notify the system operator or other designated user. RTM can notify another userid of such conditions via VMCF, which allows automatic recovery by FORCEing and reAUTOLOGging the disabled SVM.

When CMS is about to enter a disabled wait, it first obtains the address of a routine and gives it an opportunity to restart the virtual machine. The routine's address must be stored in field AUSERRST, which is contained in the CMS nucleus data area (NUCON). This routine should not attempt to simply re-start the SVM program, as it might not be safe to continue CMS execution at that time. The usual use of AUSERRST is to initiate a re-IPL of CMS instead of simply loading a disabled-wait PSW.

Use of CP SET CONCEAL is usually preferable to the AUSERRST method (see "CONCEAL" on page 207).

Program check

Through programming or data errors, SVM software can encounter program checks or other application ABENDs. Normal CMS processing of these conditions results in program execution ending and a read being issued to the virtual machine console. These actions are fatal to an SVM. The CMS ABNEXIT macro can establish an exit routine which receives control in the event of an application ABEND. This exit can log the problem, collect diagnostic information, take corrective action, and either restart the SVM or (in the case of unrecoverable problems) log it off. The OS STAE and SPIE macros are also available for intercepting SVM application failures, though native CMS macros such as ABNEXIT are preferred.

Disk full

An SVM which creates or maintains disk files (even if only for log, audit, or accounting data) may fail if a minidisk fills up. Minidisk occupancy must be monitored at time intervals or when transactions start or complete. If occupancy is too high (or, alternatively, if not enough space remains free) an SVM should recover space by erasing or compressing files or (as a last resort) temporarily storing files in CP SPOOL. Any of these actions should be reported to the system operator and other appropriate users. If no minidisk space can be recovered, an SVM should cease operation before a minidisk fills completely, since errors caused by writing to full minidisks can lose or corrupt data.

SVMs using the CMS Shared File System should also be sensitive to exhausting their allotment of SFS space, and should use the

QUERY LIMITS command and the DMSQLIMA and DMSQLIMD CSL calls to monitor their SFS usage.

It is important to understand the concept of **committed** vs. **uncommitted** SFS work, since uncommitted work may legitimately exceed the defined space allotment.

Missing/invalid/duplicate input

SVMs can encounter problems with internal data, such as control files, or external data, such as SPOOL files. All assumptions about data should be validated; no data should be trusted without validation. The unexpected must be anticipated and handled: required files will not always arrive, or will arrive in the wrong order, or will be duplicated. An SVM must ensure the correct origin, time/date, size, datatype, and other attributes of data files. The datatype of information provided must be verified. Within an installation, standard facilities should be used for controlling and processing SVM files, to ensure consistency and facilitate implementation of new SVMs.

CONCEAL

The SET CONCEAL ON command and CONCEAL directory option instruct CP to "protect" a virtual machine. In a protected virtual machine, terminal activity such as attention or break key interrupts will not enter CP, a disabled wait PSW results in an automatic virtual machine re-IPL, and CP attempts to continue execution if a shared memory page is altered. The reason for an automatic re-IPL is passed to the virtual machine as an IPL parameter, enabling intelligent recovery from permanent conditions. Protecting an SVM greatly increases the reliability of the service it provides.

Notification

SVMs should automatically report problems they encounter to the proper authorities, typically the system operator and one or more people responsible for SVM maintenance. If the list of userids to notify is stored in a CMS NAMES file, an SVM can use the TELL and SENDFILE commands to notify one or several users simultaneously. In many cases both commands should be used: TELL provides imme-

diate notification with a message; SENDFILE provides an electronic
note if users to be notified are not logged on when a problem occurs.
As an external file, the NAMES list can be changed without impacting
the SVM, though the SVM must reACCESS the minidisk containing
the NAMES file to ensure that the most current copy is used. Alternatively, if problem messages only appear on an SVM's console, the
system operator or other userid running PROP can be made a
secondary SVM console with SCIF. Messages can then be handled
or redirected by PROP action routines.

Debugging

Detect being (re)connected

SVMs which handle errors by dumping their virtual machines
and/or logging off or re-IPLing should detect when they are operating connected and suppress normal error handling. When operating connected, SVMs should report errors to the virtual machine
console and enter a debugging mode where virtual machine activity
is displayed on the console. SVM commands should be provided to
end debugging mode and to begin disconnected operation.

Console

An SVM's SPOOLed console file is often the most useful tool for
problem analysis. All SVMs should start console SPOOLing early in
initialization. When many SVMs are used, printed console logs
become burdensome. A simple SVM can receive and archive
SPOOLed console files so that they need not be printed but remain
available for debugging. The archiver can maintain several days or
weeks of console files, erasing files as they age or as storage disks
fill. The benefit of the archiver SVM can be increased by having all
SVMs close their consoles at least once a day, so that in case of a
system failure, console files covering many days or weeks will not be
lost.

Dumps

When all else fails, an SVM should attempt to provide as much
information about the failure as possible. This should include at

least a full-storage dump via the CP VMDUMP 0-END DSS command. An SVM can use the SET AUTODUMP ON command to request that CMS take a dump when it detects a serious error; however, the default for this dump is largely worthless. Issuing the SET AUTODUMP ON ENTIREVM command will change the AUTODUMP action to perform a full-storage dump.

Performance

SVM performance can affect overall system behavior and response to individual SVM transactions.

Measurement

The load an SVM places on the system can be observed from any VM performance monitor (RTM VM/ESA, VMPRF, etc.) or reported by the SVM itself. An SVM can use the CP QUERY TIME command periodically to determine its resource consumption; responses can be recorded with SVM activity statistics to measure the resources used by specific or average transactions. By time-stamping input and responses, an SVM can measure elapsed time for user requests. Statistics can be useful in reporting service levels to users or countering complaints about service unavailability or delays.

Tuning

SVM performance can be affected by factors external to and within the SVM. An SVM cannot deliver satisfactory service if it is denied adequate CPU, I/O, or memory resources. A critical SVM (typically, one on which interactive users depend) on a heavily loaded system must be designated for improved processing. CP commands SET SHARE, SET QUICKDSP, SET RESERVED, and LOCK can improve SVM performance but can degrade operation of other virtual machines. Critical SVM minidisks can be cached to improve I/O service.

Internal SVM operation can be changed to minimize resource demands. SVM software can be made resident (to avoid repeated fetching from minidisk) with EXECLOAD and NUCXLOAD. SVM applications can be implemented or operated with performance in mind: databases can be compressed or reorganized periodically; data files can be retained in virtual memory to avoid repeated reads, since CP paging is much more efficient than minidisk I/O.

Security

Audit trail

An SVM's SPOOLed console log can be an audit trail if the SVM uses it to log arriving transactions, actions performed, and problems encountered. It has the disadvantages of not being directly under the SVM's control, being at risk of CP SPOOL difficulties, being somewhat free-form, and occupying more space than needed. CMS files are more efficient and accessible locations for audit trails, allowing fixed-format data to be stored compactly. An audit trail is useful only if it is used; exceptions (errors, access violations or attempts, etc.) should be highlighted to allow easy manual or automatic detection.

Command authority

At least two classes of authority should be defined: general user and privileged. Only privileged users should be able to invoke functions that reconfigure an SVM or affect other users' service or data. Complex SVMs may require multiple levels of authorization, possibly under configuration control.

SVM-specific authorization should be required for privileged SVM functions, rather than granting SVM privileges based on CP command privileges (as RTM VM/ESA does). If privileges are granted to users designated in the system directory as members of an ACI group, an SVM can use DIAGNOSE X'A0' to verify group membership.

If users can request an SVM to issue CP and/or CMS commands (and this should be carefully considered and implemented, since it can compromise SVM integrity), destructive commands (LOGOFF, DEFINE STORAGE, and some SET options) must be disallowed. In addition, checks must be made for illicit execution of multiple commands in a single transaction, for example, by embedding X'15' (the line end character) in a CP command.

Accounting

SVMs should gather transaction and resource consumption information to allow charging for service. Even if SVM service will not be charged, planning for or actually gathering accounting information greatly simplifies charging later. Accounting information can also provide valuable insights into how an SVM is being used, whether charged for or not.

DIAGNOSE X'4C'

This facility places information in the CP accounting file. This integrates SVM and other accounting data in time sequence, and can simplify processing of aggregate data.

Internal

Instead of or in addition to placing SVM data in the CP accounting file, SVM data can be kept in SVM-managed storage (minidisk or SFS). This simplifies detailed analysis of an individual SVM's data but can complicate integration into system-wide reporting. In addition, SVM retention of the data requires space management and, ultimately, disposition of data to avoid space exhaustion.

SVM examples: IBM

AUTOLOG1

AUTOLOG1 is one of the very few userids known specifically to CP. When CP is initialized, AUTOLOG1 is AUTOLOGged if it is defined in the system directory. A PROFILE EXEC on AUTOLOG1's A-disk can serve as a system-wide profile, by AUTOLOGging assorted other SVMs and issuing CP commands. After the PROFILE completes, AUTOLOG1 can log off or remain available as an SVM.

A 30-second delay in the PROFILE before executing standard automatic commands provides a window in which to FORCE AUTOLOG1 and prevent the commands from being executed. This can be useful for bringing up a system for testing or benchmarking.

DIRMAINT

The VM Directory Management Program Product, more familiarly known as DIRMAINT, manages the VM system directory. It can automate directory changes, including minidisk allocation and password maintenance.

PVM

VM/Pass-Through provides terminal connectivity between VM systems or between VM and MVS or VSE systems. It allows VM terminals to log on to these remote systems.

RACF/VM

RACF enforces security access rules for LINK and LOGON commands.

RESLIM

The VM Resource Limiter (RESLIM) is an SVM-based IBM product which automates computer load management functions and detects and reports situations requiring intervention. RESLIM periodically examines system and user-specific resource consumption, and applies rules to ensure proper resource allocation.

RSCS

Remote SPOOLing Communication Subsystem (RSCS) provides file transfer services between VM systems or between VM and MVS or VSE systems.

SFS

CMS files can be stored in Shared File System (SFS) file pools, in addition to traditional personal and shared minidisks. Each file pool is owned and managed by an SVM which processes user and administrator requests.

SQL/DS

Structured Query Language/Data System (SQL/DS) is an IBM database management system implemented as an SVM. SQL/DS provides data sharing between users, multiple concurrent updates, different views of data for different users, access control, and data recovery. SQL/DS servers communicate via IUCV or APPC/VM.

VMUTIL

VMUTIL, part of IBM's CMS Utilities Feature, is a general time-of-day event processor. It is controlled by the WAKEUP module with a parameter file giving specific actions to perform.

Error recording

Hardware error information is captured by CP. Under VM/ESA 370 feature, it is written to CP-owned DASD space and can be monitored as it is collected by an SVM via the *LOGREC system service. Under VM/ESA ESA it is only available to an SVM, which must record it for later processing. This processing, similar to that of accounting data, is controlled by the CP RECORDING command.

SVM examples: Non-IBM

Accounting

Accounting data is usually collected and processed by an SVM (the alternative being manual interactive processing, an unreliable technique). While collection techniques differ between VM/SP (and HPO) and VM/ESA, the issues are the same: accounting data often represents data center revenue, and must be reliably processed. At the same time, this function contributes to overhead, and so must be done as efficiently as possible. Processing usually consists of accepting arriving data immediately, to avoid risk of loss, and batching it for later reporting.

Dump processor

While dump analysis is not yet suitable for automation, some dump-related tasks may be implemented in an SVM. The destination userid for dump files is specified in VM module DMKSYS (for VM/ESA 370) or HCPSYS (for VM/ESA ESA). If this is not an individual's userid, dump files can collect without being noticed, especially on systems which are sometimes unattended or which can take a dump without restarting. If the dump destination userid is periodically AUTOLOGged, it can detect newly arrived dump files and alert the proper staff. New dumps may be processed automatically with data extraction tools to provide basic problem determination information and load the dump onto disk before manual analysis begins.

Special SVM Examples

GCS

Group Control Subsystem (GCS) is a virtual machine operating system. It manages subsystems (SVMs) that support a Systems Network Architecture (SNA) network. SVMs in a GCS group can share common read/write virtual memory and communicate with each other. Some GCS-based SVMs are VM SNA Console Support (VSCS), which lets SNA network terminals be virtual machine consoles; and Remote Spooling Communication Subsystem (RSCS) Version 2, described above.

MVS

MVS is IBM's "other" major operating system. While sometimes used without VM, it often operates as a virtual machine under VM.

SRPI

CMS can provide a different kind of service machine: connected to a PC providing host services to it. Enhanced Connectivity Facilities (ECF) is a facility for sharing resources between personal computers (PCs) and 390 computers. The Server-Requester Programming Interface (SRPI) allows PCs to access host servers.

TSAF

The Transparent Services Access Facility (TSAF) provides access to SVM resources within a VM processor or across VM processors. The TSAF SVM handles communication between systems by letting APPC/VM (Advanced Program-to-Program Communication/VM) paths span VM systems.

AVS

The APPC/VM VTAM Services (AVS) facility allows APPC/VM programs using TSAF to communicate with programs running on other processors on an SNA network. The other processors need not be running VM. AVS functions transparently, without modifications to either program.

Future Developments

Many new interfaces for SVMs have been created in recent years. New facilities will continue to be introduced, primarily (as always) to support IBM function and products, but available as well for non-IBM innovation.

Intra-system interfaces (VMCF, IUCV, SPOOL files) are well understood and widely used. Cross-system facilities such as TSAF, however, have yet to be widely exploited. Cooperative and distributed processing are just beginning to reach production applications.

Rules and Recommendations for SVM Construction

1. Do not rely on software executing in user virtual machines for security, accounting, or data integrity.
2. Do not grant users SVM privileges based on CP command privileges; require SVM-specific authorization for privileged SVM functions.
3. Create open, robust, general SVMs that use (when possible) standard interfaces.
4. Localize and document any non-standard interfaces used.
5. Verify SVM environment attributes and any required resources during initialization.
6. Begin SPOOLing the SVM console early in initialization.

7. Consider using XA or XC mode in SVM development and maintenance to exploit current architecture and facilities.
8. Validate the identity of clients and verify any assumptions about data received in user transactions.
9. Provide complicated or critical SVMs with duplicate software minidisks to simplify applying maintenance and testing.
10. Gather statistics on SVM transaction service times for capacity and performance analysis, or for evaluating user complaints about SVM availability and performance.
11. Gather transaction and resource consumption information to allow charging for service.

Chapter

8

Server Tasking Environment/VM

By Joel A. Farrell and Stephen E. Record

Overview

The Server Tasking Environment/VM (STEVR/VM) is a CMS extension which provides a multitasking, parallel, distributed execution environment for applications and service virtual machines. It addresses some of the most critical performance and structural requirements of multi-user servers on VM. To increase throughput and decrease response time, servers must overlap operations, respond to events in a timely fashion, and, to an ever-growing degree, exploit the multiprocessor capabilities of the underlying computer complex.

These requirements are not new. Many servers on VM incorporate their own specialized tasking supervisors to address the need to overlap operations. These generally have proven to be difficult to maintain, support only assembler language, and do not provide multiprocessor execution. STEVR/VM aims to be the tasking base for all service virtual machines, meeting the needs of both existing

STEVR/VM as a runtime extension

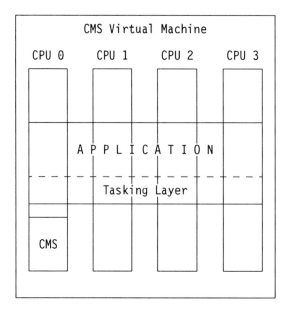

and newly written servers, and supporting both Assembler H and C/370 programming environments. It is flexible enough to be integrated into existing servers as a replacement for their tasking supervisors, and to provide powerful building blocks for creating new servers designed according to modern concurrent programming paradigms.

While the customer community has expressed the need for other types of multitasking capability for CMS, this extension addresses what appears to be the most pressing set of requirements. It implements a sufficient subset of the full CMS process model described below to meet the needs of a large class of high-performance server applications. In particular, STEVR/VM provides multiple lightweight execution threads and disciplined capabilities for exploiting parallel processing under application control. It further includes queueing interfaces for message communication within or between STEVR/VM applications, and a suite of event management services for defining, signaling, and responding to asynchronous events. Those event services are employed internally to provide facilities for system- and application-level accounting, robust error recovery, timing, and tracing.

STEVR/VM is distributed as a library of functions that are bound into the exploiting application as an extension to the language runtime environment.   It provides multitasking support for programs written in C/370 Version 2 or Assembler H. STEVR/VM functions establish and maintain a multitasking execution environment while allowing the C/370 application to use the C/370 function library and the native CMS application programming interface. Support for other languages can be supplied by users in the form of a set of programming language execution environment exits.

STEVR/VM is supported for execution on the following VM products and their corresponding releases:

- VM/SP Releases 5 and 6, with or without HPO
- VM/XA SP Release 2.1
- VM/ESA 370 and ESA features

The recommended operating environment for STEVR/VM is VM/ESA; earlier VM releases are supported to provide a smooth migration path. Multiprocessor exploitation is supported in VM/ESA in XA- and XC-mode virtual machines.   Basic multitasking is equally supported on all the supported VM releases and VM architectures.[1] Only EC-mode virtual machines are supported on VM/SP, VM/SP HPO, and VM/ESA 370 feature.

Functions provided are logically fundamental parts of the operating system, and were originally distributed in this form to address the most urgent multitasking requirements in a timely fashion and to provide a smooth transition to VM/ESA; they are integrated into CMS as of VM/ESA Release 2.0.

The remainder of this chapter offers a more complete introduction to the features and functions of STEVR/VM. To set the context, the CMS multitasking process model, of which STEVR/VM is the initial realization, is described.   Then the most important areas of the STEVR/VM application programming interface are examined, including an illustration of how servers may be constructed to take full advantage of these facilities. For further information, including an exhaustive description of the STEVR/VM application programming interface (API), consult the *Server Tasking Environment/VM Programmer's Guide and Reference, SL26-0027.*

---

[1]   C/370 Version 2 is not supported on VM/SP Release 5 with or without HPO.

Multitasking Process Model

A process model specifies the rules and relationships involved in writing multitasking applications and performing concurrent activities. It primarily defines execution units, how they interact, and how resources are managed relative to them.

The Server Tasking Environment/VM process model defines concurrent programming concepts that promote distributed and parallel computation. In particular, its structure supports Programmable Workstation (PWS) affinity and exploits the multiprocessing capability of the underlying VM system. In its fundamental concepts, the process model of STEVR/VM closely resembles that of OS/2; and, where possible, the process management interfaces presented by STEVR/VM are a superset of those of OS/2. This should tend both to facilitate porting applications between CMS and OS/2, and to promote development of cooperative applications distributed across the CMS and OS/2 environments.

This process model defines some concepts not implemented by STEVR/VM. These concepts are included to show how the implemented subset fits into the larger context. Also, some concepts from the full model are embodied in some STEVR/VM services to allow for extending the implementation.

Basic constructs

The basic dispatchable entity in the system is the **thread**. The thread represents an instance of execution of a unit of program code. Its environment is characterized by a PSW, a set of register values, and a savearea stack. At creation time, the system assigns an identifier to each thread. This identifier is unique within the process containing it and is not reused during the life of that process.

The locus of resource ownership in the system is the **process**. A process consists of a collection of threads (at least, but not necessarily more than, one) performing related work. Other resources associated with a process include but are not limited to storage subpools, queues, open files, and APPC conversations. All threads in a process have equal access to the resources associated with the process. When a process terminates, its resources are relinquished to the system or terminated, as appropriate. The system assigns an identifier to each process. This identifier is unique within the session containing it and is not reused during the life of the session.

While this model defines some relationships between multiple processes, STEVR/VM does not implement the capability for an application to create additional processes.

The collection of processes, accessible devices, and addressable storage embodied in a virtual machine is the **session**.   This is similar to a user's logon session.   Each session has a primary address space that is shared by all its processes.   The session may also have access to one or more data spaces that may be shared with other sessions occupying the same real memory.

Interactions of threads and processes

The process model defines interactions between and within processes. Although STEVR/VM allows only one user process per virtual machine, the processes in different virtual machines can communicate and synchronize. In addition, there are actually two processes in each session: the user process and a process in which some STEVR/VM functions execute. This system process is established as the initial process and is called the **root process**.   It performs session initialization and creates a number of threads dedicated to performing standard system functions or managing shared facilities (for example, the virtual machine timers). The root process subsequently creates the process that runs the user application. The user process cannot create additional processes in this implementation.

Interprocess communication in STEVR/VM is based on queues. Creating a process establishes a **primary queue** on which messages may be sent to the process. The primary queue bears the name of the process and has session-level scope by default. The primary queue may not be deleted except during process termination. The threads in a process can communicate and coordinate work using queues. Additionally, queues can be used to communicate between processes, possibly in different sessions.

Creating a process also creates an initial thread on which the specified program starts executing.   Any thread may create, suspend, resume, terminate, or alter the priority of any other thread in the same process. All threads within a process are peers: normal termination of one thread has no effect on other threads in the process. When the last thread in a process terminates, the process itself terminates.

At creation, each thread is assigned a priority relative to other threads in the same process. The priority of a thread may be altered by any thread, including itself, in the same process.

Threads may be grouped in dispatching classes to control both preemption and parallelism. A thread can be preempted only by a thread in a different class and can never be preempted by a thread in its own class. Threads in different classes may execute in parallel, but only one thread from a given class may execute at a given time. A thread may allow another thread in its class to be dispatched either by yielding control explicitly or by calling a blocking function—that is, one that includes the possibility of stopping the execution of the thread until a condition is met.

STEVR/VM provides facilities that let processes recognize and respond to the occurrence of named events either internal to the process or elsewhere in the session. STEVR/VM defines system events, such as **exception occurred, trace data became available**, and **accounting data became available**, that it signals at the appropriate times. Applications may also define their own events and may signal occurrence of any defined event. A process may establish an event handler to be "driven" (called) asynchronously when the event occurs, or may create a thread to wait explicitly for the occurrence.

Normal termination of a thread occurs implicitly when it returns control through the last savearea on its stack; other threads in the process continue unaffected. A thread may also explicitly request termination of itself alone or of the entire process containing it; either one of these methods also constitutes a normal termination. Normal termination of a process, whether by explicit request or as a result of normal termination of the last existing thread, causes process end event handlers to be driven and resources associated with the process to be released.

Abnormal termination of a thread may be requested either by the system, if a program check or other error has been detected; or by the thread itself, by explicitly signaling an error event. If the process has previously established an error event handler, it is driven with all other threads in the process suspended; the event handler may elect either to let termination continue or to recover. If the process has established multiple error event handlers, they are driven in LIFO (last in, first out) order until one has elected to recover or all have chosen to continue termination. If no applicable error event handler has been established in the process, or if all applicable error event handlers choose not to recover, abnormal termination of a thread induces abnormal termination of the entire process.

Process Management

Process management is the set of services that lets an application create, interrogate, and manipulate the threads within a process. Application threads share process resources while processor time allocated to the virtual machine in which the application is running is distributed among them.

The threads created through the process management services are termed **lightweight** because they own only their execution state, or context. This implies that threads require minimal overhead for the system to create, maintain, and delete. The lightweight thread approach to multitasking lets the programmer create threads dynamically to handle new work and use threads to wait for asynchronous conditions or events. In general, the simplest programming approach is to allow concurrency between threads to handle asynchrony while program code running under the thread proceeds in a purely synchronous fashion. Later examples return to this point.

Creating threads

A concurrent (or multitasking) application is a program with multiple threads of execution proceeding through the program's code over the life of the program. When an application is started, a process is created by the STEVR/VM services with an initial thread that begins execution at the main program entry point. This thread can then use the ThreadCreate function to create additional threads. The ThreadCreate function takes as input the address of the entry point at which the thread should begin execution, and returns a unique identifier of the thread, called the **thread ID**. All later references to the thread are made through its thread ID.

When a thread is created, it is also assigned a priority and a thread class. These determine how the thread acts relative to other threads in the process. Threads are dispatched in priority order; the highest priority runable thread is always the next to be dispatched. Priority values fall in a range of 0 through 32,767, with higher values denoting higher priority. If all threads are assigned equal priority, a round-robin dispatching effect is achieved.

Dispatching classes

In addition to assigning priority, creating a thread also assigns it to a dispatching class. A dispatching class is a set of threads with two properties:

- No thread in the class is ever given control in place of another in the same class unless the executing thread voluntarily gives up control.
- No two threads in a class are ever dispatched in parallel: that is to say, they are never in execution at the same time on different processors (CPUs). However, any thread can be preempted by or dispatched in parallel with any thread in a different class.

A parameter on the ThreadCreate call controls assignment of the new thread to a class. The new thread is assigned either to the class of the creating thread or to a new class, putting the thread in a class by itself. Other threads can join this new class through subsequent ThreadCreate calls or through the class reassignment function, ThreadSetDispatchClass.

These dispatching classes provide a means to control parallelism. For example, if the application is a server that needs to use all the power of a large multiprocessor complex, each thread could be assigned to a different class, thereby allowing each thread to be dispatched in parallel. If, however, some part of the server could not execute in multiprocessor mode, the threads that execute in that particular code could be assigned to the same class. This would let those particular server functions execute without explicit thread synchronization.

Process termination

The point at which the last thread in the application ends its execution is called **process termination**. Since STEVR/VM supports only one user process, process termination is the same as application termination. At this point, STEVR/VM cleans up storage and other resources. In addition, it signals an event, called the **process end event**, that can cause application post-processing to occur. This is similar in concept to the service call for nucleus extensions done by CMS. The event handler for this event can do any clean-up needed.

Multiprocessor Configuration Control

Many service virtual machines and some computationally intensive applications require **parallel processing** to cope with heavy processing loads. Parallel processing means the execution of more than one thread of a particular application at the same time on different real CPUs of the real processor complex. For example, a numeric application may process each column of a table in parallel, if the computations performed on the rows are independent of each other. A different type of example involves a multi-user server like a file server or a database manager. These servers may become saturated with requests. By exploiting parallelism they can potentially handle several requests at the same time. In general, the goals of parallel processing are to reduce the time a computation takes, or to increase capacity and/or improve the responsiveness of a server.

STEVR/VM provides parallel processing capabilities through use of CP's virtual multiprocessor support. CMS virtual machines running STEVR/VM-based applications can have more than one virtual CPU, each of which will execute threads. These virtual CPUs, in turn, are dispatched independently by CP. CP can have none, any one, several, or all of the CPUs for a particular virtual machine in execution at a given time.

The use of virtual CPUs is controlled by CP information and command input. The user directory entry determines how many virtual CPUs can be defined and how many are to be predefined for a particular virtual machine. If the application requires more CPUs than those automatically defined, it can use the VCPUCreate function to dynamically define additional virtual CPUs (up to the limit specified in the directory) while the application is running. As soon as the CPU is defined, STEVR/VM begins dispatching threads on it within constraints imposed by dispatching classes. Essentially, the number of CPUs that can be used is equal to the number of thread dispatch classes the application has created. If all threads are assigned to different classes, all CPUs can be exploited to the fullest.

For most parallel applications, the number of virtual CPUs should be equal to the number of real CPUs in the real processor complex. However, an application whose threads make use of synchronous CP facilities, such as DIAGNOSE instructions, can efficiently make use of more CPUs. This is because most synchronous CP operations serialize only the issuing CPU: an application may have multiple CPUs in CP-wait while other CPUs are still runnable.

Event Management

Events define or represent activities that occur during program execution that may be of interest to application programs or to STEVR/VM itself. These activities may include both hardware events, such as interrupts, and software events, such as abnormal termination. Event management enables a process to monitor these events and perform specific functions based on their occurrence. The occurrence of an event is indicated by a system call to generate a signal and is thus always associated with the process under which that system call executed. An event may be defined such that its occurrence is recognizable either only within the process in which it occurred, or throughout the session containing that process. A process may monitor both events which occur within itself and those events whose occurrence has session-wide visibility and which occur in other processes in the session.

Event management functions provide the capability to create and delete event names, to monitor the occurrence of a set of events, and to take action based on the occurrence of some or all of that set of events. STEVR/VM uses its event management services in support of process management and in implementation of other facilities which provide or demand sensitivity to asynchronous interrupts or equivalent phenomena (error handling, accounting, tracing, and timing). User applications may avail themselves of event management services to exploit these system facilities, to augment or replace the standard response to system-defined events, to simulate occurrence of system-defined events, or to define and manipulate their own events.

System events are defined by STEVR/VM either during session initialization or at first invocation of the service that employs the event, and their occurrence is signaled by STEVR/VM as appropriate. The set of system events includes:

VMACCOUNT	Production of an accounting record
VMERROR	Beginning of abnormal process termination
VMIPC	Arrival of a message on a queue
VMPROCESSEND	End-of-process clean up
VMTIMER	Expiration or cancellation of a timer
VMTRACE	Production of a trace record

Application programs may define other event names for their own use; CMS provides identical event management services for system and user events. Any program may signal any event defined to the process in which it is executing; in particular, application programs are free to signal events defined by other applications or by STEVR/VM itself. It is the responsibility of the signaling program to determine when it is appropriate to signal any particular event.

Event identification

An **event name** is a character string of arbitrary length and composition which provides the primary identification of an event. The event name is provided by the issuer of the EventCreate function which creates the event definition and is used to identify the event for signaling and monitoring purposes. The event definition may have either process or session scope; in either case, the event name must be unique among all event names known within that scope. By convention, system event names consist of upper- and lowercase alphabetic, numeric, and underscore characters; begin with the reserved prefix **VM**; and have a maximum length of 24 bytes.

A particular occurrence of an event may be further characterized by an additional character string of arbitrary length and composition called an **event key**. For example, a VMTIMER event carries a key that is the unique identifier of the particular timer that has resulted in this signal. The key is provided by the issuer of the EventSignal function and may be used by the issuer of the EventMonitorCreate function to specify which occurrences of a particular event are of interest. The key may be omitted by the issuer of EventSignal if secondary characterization is not required by an event definition or for an isolated occurrence of an event. Similarly, the issuer of EventMonitorCreate may specify a partial key, possibly including wildcard characters, or omit the key entirely to match a broader range of occurrences.

Event monitoring

The occurrence of an event or set of events may be observed by establishing an **event monitor** defining the condition to be satisfied and an action to be taken when requisite events have occurred. An event monitor is established by the EventMonitorCreate function. Asynchronous event handling may be accomplished by associating a trap routine with an event monitor through the EventTrap function, and synchronous event handling may be performed either by testing the condition of the monitor with the EventTest function or by waiting for the condition to be satisfied with the EventWait function. Deletion of an event monitor is performed by the EventMonitorDelete function and occurs automatically at termination of the process in which the event monitor was created. An event monitor which is required for a single activation only, such as for an individual timer event, may be created with an option that specifies automatic deletion when its first activation is complete.

The condition under which an event monitor may be activated is defined by one or more pairs of event names and event keys denoting events to which the monitor is sensitive, and by a count which specifies the minimum number of those events which must occur to satisfy the condition. Event names to be monitored must be specified exactly, but event keys may contain wildcard characters, be abbreviated, or be omitted entirely to broaden the range of occurrences of interest. Once the monitored condition is satisfied, the monitor is eligible to become active. If there is an outstanding EventWait or EventTrap associated with the monitor, the monitor is activated immediately, causing the waiting thread to be unblocked or the trap routine to be scheduled for execution. Otherwise, the monitor remains inactive until an EventWait, EventTest, or EventTrap is issued for it. Thus, possible activation states of a monitor are as follows:

active The monitored condition is satisfied, and an event handling program is executing, either as the result of an EventWait being completed, a trap routine being invoked, or an EventTest being conducted.

waiting The monitor is not active, the monitored condition is not satisfied, and there is an outstanding EventWait associated with the monitor.

trapping The monitor is neither active nor waiting, the monitored condition is not satisfied, and there is a trap routine associated with the monitor.

testable The monitor is not active, waiting, or trapping; the monitored condition may or may not be satisfied, but there is neither an outstanding EventWait nor a trap routine associated with the monitor.

Each event name and event key pair specified in the definition of the event monitor establishes the beginning of a list of zero or more matching signals which are **bound** to the monitor in order of delivery. At the point of activation of the monitor, the first signal on each such non-empty list is collected to form the **current signal set** of the monitor. During each activation the current signal set may be examined and manipulated by EventTest, EventRetrieve, EventDiscard, and EventMonitorReset functions. Signals which arrive while the monitor is active are not added to the current signal set and are not visible, at least until the current activation is complete; however, a signal which is delivered while the monitor is inactive, even after sufficient signals have been bound to satisfy the monitored condition, becomes part of the current signal set at activation if no equivalent signal is already bound. The number of bound signals which are retained is specified at creation of the monitor; when that limit is exceeded, the oldest bound signal of a particular type (excluding a member of the current signal set if the monitor is active at the time) is automatically removed to make room for a new arrival.

The current activation of a monitor is considered complete when a trap routine returns control or an EventWait is reissued. At inactivation, the current signal set is automatically released and any bound signals are examined to determine whether the monitored condition is again satisfied; if so, the monitor is eligible for immediate reactivation. The EventMonitorReset function may be invoked explicitly to force inactivation of an event monitor, either to allow a trap routine to be re-entered or to permit any bound signals to be interrogated by the EventTest function.

Event signaling

Event signaling provides the mechanism by which the occurrence of events is defined and communicated to processes through event monitors. All events are signaled explicitly by the EventSignal function, which specifies the event name, an optional event key, and other event-related data. The interpretation of the event-related data rests on a private protocol between the event signaler and the event handler(s) and must be established separately for each named event; event management simply provides a conduit for delivering this data. The scope of the event definition determines whether the signal is confined to the process in which it is issued or delivered throughout the session.

Each process in the range of the signal which is enabled for the event being signaled is examined for **qualifying** event monitors (i.e., those whose definition contains an event name and event key pair which match the signal). If one qualifying monitor exists, the signal is delivered to it and the event-related data is saved for ultimate presentation to an event handling routine through the EventRetrieve function. If qualifying monitors exist in multiple processes, the signal is delivered to all of them concurrently. If multiple qualifying monitors exist in a single process, the protocol by which the signal is delivered is determined by the definition of the event: it may be broadcast to all monitors in the process simultaneously, or presented to one qualifying monitor at a time in either FIFO or LIFO order of their creation. In either case, the set of qualifying monitors is established at the time the signal is received; once the delivery of a signal to a sequence of monitors has begun, no newly created monitor will be added to the sequence.

Signals which are presented sequentially are said to be **propagated** from one qualifying monitor to the next. Propagation does not occur until the signal is released from the current signal set of the first monitor, either implicitly as a result of the monitor going inactive, or explicitly through a call to the EventMonitorReset function. Each propagated signal is bound to the next qualifying event monitor and ultimately becomes part of its current signal set; when the last qualifying monitor has released the signal, it is finally discarded. Propagation of a signal along a sequence of event monitors in a process may be terminated prematurely by the use of the EventDiscard function; this allows one event handler to prevent another of lower **precedence** (i.e., farther down in the propagation order) from being notified of, and attempting to respond to, a particular occurrence of an event.

If no process in the range of the signal is enabled for the event or has created a qualifying monitor, the signal is termed **loose** (i.e., not bound to any event monitor). The number of loose signals of an event which are retained is established when the event definition is created; when that limit is exceeded, old signals are discarded as new ones occur. Whenever an event monitor is created or a disabled process containing an event monitor re-enables, any loose signals for which the monitor qualifies are delivered as though the events they represent had just occurred.

Event handling

Event management provides facilities to support both asynchronous and synchronous event handling. An asynchronous event handling program is associated with an event monitor by the EventTrap function, but its invocation occurs during subsequent program execution at a point dependent on the occurrence of one or more events rather than during the execution of a specific system call. Synchronous event handling, by contrast, is effected with the EventWait or EventTest functions, and the invocation of the event handling program is implicit on return from a satisfied EventWait or successful EventTest.

Once the event monitor is active, it makes very little difference to the event handling program whether it was invoked synchronously or asynchronously; the environment in which it executes is equivalent and the event management facilities available to it are identical in either case.[2] The event handling program can execute the EventRetrieve function to obtain the event-related data from each signal in the current signal set. If necessary, the event handler can also use the EventDiscard function to prevent some or all of the current signal set from being propagated to event monitors of lower precedence.

Only one activation of an event monitor at a time is permitted; however, multiple event monitors may be active simultaneously, and one event handling program may be interrupted for the asynchronous invocation of another so long as it is associated with a different event monitor. While an event monitor is active, signals for which it qualifies are queued to it (subject to the bound signal limits established at monitor creation) for consideration when the current activation is complete. Activation of an event monitor is associated with the thread on which the event handling program is executing. Termination of a thread automatically resets all event monitors active on that thread.

When the event handler has finished processing the current signal set, it must indicate to event management that the monitor is going

---

2   A distinction arises from the difficulty in supporting exit routines written in languages that require a runtime environment: the asynchronous event handler must issue the EventTest function to determine the contents of the current signal set.

inactive and the current signal set may be released. This may be accomplished in a variety of ways:

- An event trap routine may simply return.
- A program using EventWait may simply flow to another EventWait on the same monitor.
- Any program, in particular one using EventTest to poll for event occurrences, may issue the EventMonitorReset function explicitly.

After the current signal set is released, remaining bound signals are checked to see whether the monitored condition is again satisfied. If so, the monitor is eligible for immediate reactivation.

Interprocess Communication

STEVR/VM provides queue-based interprocess communication (IPC). Queue operations form a general mechanism for communication and coordination among processes and among threads within a single process. They are intended to aid both distributed processing and object-based programming. To describe how such programming approaches are supported by IPC, a few definitions are required.

To define a queue, its elements must be defined first. A **message** is a data element that is transferred by IPC. Each message consists of a **prefix** containing control information describing the origin and contents of the message, and the **message text**, the actual data to be conveyed, including a key describing the content or meaning of the data. A **queue** is simply a list of such messages. Each queue is identified by a name assigned to it by its creator at the time it is created.

A thread creates a queue at a certain visibility scope. The operation of placing a queue in one of these scopes is called **exporting** the queue to that scope. This placement occurs when the queue is created, and is fixed for the life of the queue. The export operation guarantees that the queue name is unique among all queue names exported to the target scope by processes sharing the target scope with the exporter.

The defined queue scopes are listed on the next page.

Level	*Definition*
Process	The queue is visible only within a specific process, and the queue name is unique only among process-level queues in that process.
Session	The queue is visible to any process executing in the same session as the exporting process, and the queue name is unique among all names exported to the session level by processes executing in the same session as the exporting process.
Network	Like a session-level queue, the network-level queue is visible to any process executing in the same session as the exporting process. The queue name is unique among all names exported to the network level by processes executing in the same session as the exporting process. The queue is visible to processes outside the owner's session, subject to capabilities of the underlying communication carrier.

Each of these export levels promotes distributed processing. In particular, network-level queues promote interprocess communication from one userid to another.

The QueueCreate function returns a numeric token, called a **queue handle**. All threads in the creating thread's process use this handle to identify the queue on all subsequent function calls. Threads in other than the creating process must open the queue with the QueueOpen function to use it, much like opening a file for I/O. The QueueOpen function returns both a queue handle and an indication of the level at which the queue to be opened was found. The QueueOpen function searches the name scopes in the order requested by the invoker. If the invoker does not request a specific order, the QueueOpen function searches the name scopes outward from the locus of the function caller; in other words, the function first searches for process queues, then session queues, and so on.

Threads may send messages to the queue, perhaps choosing to block until the message is received (the QueueSendBlock function) to perform a rendezvous, or to specify that STEVR/VM should provide reply assistance (the QueueSendReply function) for client/server interactions. With QueueSendReply, a process transmits a message and identifies the queue in which the receiver of the message is to place a reply. STEVR/VM tags the message with a token, which is passed to the receiver for use with the QueueReply function in place of a queue handle. The replying process need not have opened the reply queue; in fact, the reply queue need not even be visible to the replying process.

When a message is sent, the sender may identify a substring of the message text as a **message key** to identify the content or intent of the message. The specific use of the key is left for the sender and receiver to decide. One or more threads in the creating process issue receive calls to gather up the messages waiting in the queue (the `QueueReceiveBlock` or `QueueReceiveImmed` function). The receiver provides a **match key**, possibly containing wildcard characters, and only queues messages whose message key matches the specified match key are eligible to be received. To facilitate coupling message arrival waits with other kinds of waits, STEVR/VM optionally signals a process-level event, **VMIPC**, when a message arrives on a queue.

Messages emanating from a single thread to a single target queue are guaranteed to arrive on the target queue in the order sent. Within a single session, messages emanating from multiple threads to a single target queue are guaranteed to be placed on the queue in the overall order sent. Across sessions, no such guarantee is made.

When a sender is finished, it closes the queue (with the `QueueClose` function). Closing the queue does not disturb the queue's contents. When the receiver is finished, it closes and deletes the queue with the `QueueDelete` function. Only the process that created a queue may delete it. When a process terminates, queues created by that process are deleted and messages waiting in those queues are deleted. Threads waiting on receipt of such messages are notified that the messages were deleted. STEVR/VM queues are volatile; once a queue is destroyed, its contents cannot be recovered.

Network-level queues

Network-level queues allow IPC to occur between processes in different sessions. Such operation represents IPC at the widest possible scope, that is, from one userid to another. This facility can let multiple users run a single cooperative application based on queues. It can also be used to implement servers based on IPC.

When a network-level queue is created, it resides in the same session as the process that created it. Other processes in that session can access the queue with the same speed as they have for session-level queues residing in that session. Processes in other sessions access the queue more slowly, because STEVR/VM uses a communication carrier on their behalf to reach the remote queue. In either case, the primitives (API calls) used to reach the queue are the same as those used to reach queues of other scopes.

In general, programs using the queue API need not be sensitive to whether queues being manipulated are located at the network level. One point to keep in mind, though, is that network-level queues are one of the few constructs in STEVR/VM where *inter*process aspects of the CMS process model, that is, those process model traits relating to interaction of one user process with another, come to light. When two STEVR/VM application programs communicate with one another through network-level queues, they are exposed to timing, synchronization, and scope-of-recovery effects not seen within a single STEVR/VM application. Programmers must remember to account for such effects when writing distributed applications with STEVR/VM.

For example, consider a client/server situation where the client and server components are separate STEVR/VM applications, each residing in its own virtual machine. Each must be written to expect that the partner might not yet be started, that the partner might fail, and so on. A more subtle situation is the one in which requests from the client *cause* the server to be started; in this case, the client might see startup transients as the server springs to life. These situations come about because the client and server reside in separate processes, *not* because they reside in different virtual machines.

To facilitate selection of retry strategies, the queue API provides reason codes indicating the kind of retry an application might choose to attempt. One such reason code indicates that an operation might succeed if the application simply retries it. The "out of storage" indicator is an example of this kind of reason code. Another reason code, returned only when network-level queues are involved, indicates that the connection to the remote STEVR/VM application has been lost. In this case, the application's only recourse is to try to re-establish the connection to the remote application by reopening the remote queue. Depending on the nature of the application, this more serious retry attempt might need to be coupled with some application-dependent recovery procedure.

STEVR/VM provides code supporting network-level queue operations using the APPC/VM private resource manager facility as the carrier.[3] This allows applications to send messages to one another's queues within a VM collection (through TSAF) or across collections (through AVS). STEVR/VM also contains interfaces that allow customers to write line drivers to support queue operations over other carriers.

Service queues

In client/server relationships, it is sometimes necessary to let a server hide the identity of a service queue from its clients. For example, a server may choose to create and delete work queues dynamically, hiding the true identities of said queues. In addition, it might be desirable to let a diagnostic tool or trace facility place itself between a server and its clients so that the requests and responses might be debugged or otherwise monitored. Insulating clients from the true identity of a queue enables these kinds of functions, among others.

To facilitate this, STEVR/VM provides the notions of **service IDs** and **service queues** and integrates these concepts into the queue API. The queue API provides a function for associating a session-level queue with a service ID, and it lets clients use service IDs in place of queue handles in the `QueueSendReply` and `QueueSend` functions. With these two features, STEVR/VM provides a way for clients to send messages to a server's queue, identifying the service queue by service ID. The client need not open the service queue to send messages to it. In fact, the client need not know the name of the service queue.

Other Facilities

Synchronization

Threads within a single process share all resources owned by the process. This implies that threads must coordinate access to these resources by implementing serialization and mutual exclusion policies. The synchronization functions provided by STEVR/VM allow sets of threads to implement coordination and mutual exclusion poli-

---

3   The APPC/VM carrier runs on VM/SP Release 6, VM/SP HPO Release 6, and all releases of VM/ESA (both the 370 and ESA features).

cies. They are primitives upon which more elaborate and special purpose synchronization mechanisms can be built by programming languages and applications. These primitives are designed to be highly efficient in a parallel execution environment. They provide support for structured synchronization techniques and for basic locking.

Timer services

STEVR/VM provides a comprehensive, callable timer facility. This facility allows timers to be started, stopped, and interrogated. Threads can wait for a time interval to expire, test to see if it has expired, or be asynchronously signaled on timer expiration. Since expiration of a timer is indicated by occurrence of the **VMTIMER** event, the full power of Event Management may be used in responding to timer expiration, and timer events may be handled either alone or in combination with other events defined by STEVR/VM or an application.

Accounting services

Accounting for resource utilization is an optional facility which is enabled and controlled by the application. Interfaces are provided by which the application may specify both the frequency and the selectivity of accounting. STEVR/VM gathers the account information and presents it by signaling the **VMACCOUNT** event. The application then uses event management services to obtain the accounting data.

STEVR/VM also provides the means to associate a given thread or process with an application-defined **account ID**. Among other things, this capability lets servers charge requesters for server processing performed for the requesters. For example, the userid of a virtual machine on whose behalf a set of threads is working can be used as an account ID and assigned to each thread in the set. This account ID is part of the accounting record and so can be used to relate work done by these threads to the requester they were serving. When a thread begins work for another requester, the account ID can be reset.

ABEND services

During execution of an application, a serious error may be detected by CMS, STEVR/VM, or the application itself. An unrecoverable error in a CMS service or an unexpected program check causes an ABEND to be issued. STEVR/VM provides facilities for the application both to request its own abnormal termination and to be notified of, and to attempt to recover from, ABENDs requested by itself or CMS.

All ABEND notification and recovery facilities are provided through event signaling and monitoring. When abnormal termination is requested, STEVR/VM signals the **VMERROR** event. The application defines an error handler by creating an event monitor for the VMERROR event and associating a trap routine with that monitor. The error handler may examine the error event data and either attempt recovery, let termination continue, or signal a different error condition. If multiple monitors are defined for the VMERROR event, the error handlers associated with these monitors are driven in LIFO order. If an ABEND is not recovered by any error handler, the application process is abnormally ended.

Trace services

For good serviceability, STEVR/VM accumulates and maintains trace information to permit trace entries to be written without significantly affecting the load and timing characteristics of the system, and to be processed in real time using a broad range of criteria and without loss of data. Event management furnishes the fundamental support for tracing. Additional interfaces are provided to permit the application to regulate the generation of trace records and to generate its own trace records in a standard format. STEVR/VM emits trace data by signaling the **VMTRACE** event. Application programs may selectively collect trace data by creating event monitors sensitive to the VMTRACE event, and may process the trace information by associating event handlers with such monitors.

System exits

To provide for installation tailoring and extension of the product, STEVR/VM provides a set of exits and tailoring functions. User add-on routines can modify thread creation and deletion and other significant functions, provide support for other programming languages or language runtime environments, and provide communications carriers for remote queue operations using other connectivity mechanisms.

General Programming Interface Information

Services provided by STEVR/VM are requested by applications by means of procedure calls. STEVR/VM procedure calls each perform a single, well-defined function. This results in a large number of calls compared to what would be seen in an equivalent assembler macro API design. However, each call tends to be simple, performing one function and requiring few parameters. Functions are called by C/370 programs just as any invocation of a function that returns void. Assembler programs invoke functions using BALR 14,15 linkage.

Parameter lists

All parameters specified in the function descriptions in this chapter are required. That is, no STEVR/VM functions support optional or omitted parameters. The following conventions are used for the two supported languages:

C/370   Although C/370 header files provided by STEVR/VM specify os linkage on the #pragma linkage statement for each function, the usual C/370 call-by-value approach is maintained for the C/370 programmer. All input parameters are passed by value and for output parameters addresses of variables to receive values are passed by value. For example, the ThreadYield function takes one input parameter, the thread ID, and returns two values, the return code and the reason code. So a call to ThreadYield from C/370 would look like this:

```
Call ThreadYield(&retcode,&rsncode,tid);
```

Notice that the "address of" operator (&) is used with the two output parameters.

Assembler Calls to STEVR/VM functions from assembler use standard type-1 parameter lists. The register conventions are:

R1   Address of a list of addresses of the parameters

R15   Address of the entry point for the function

R14   Return address

STEVR/VM functions can be called by a program running in access register mode in an ESA/XC virtual machine, but all parameters must be in the primary address space. STEVR/VM does not use access registers to reference storage in a data space.

Programming language binding files

STEVR/VM provides C/370 header files and assembler macros to aid in using the Application Programming Interface (API). These files are called **programming language binding files.** They define the entry points, declare the data types of function parameters, map long function names to external symbols, and define constants for return and reason codes and other values. In the documentation of functions in this chapter, values that can be assigned to option parameters and values of return and reason codes are given by the symbolic names defined in the binding files. Each value has the same symbolic name in both the C/370 and assembler binding files. These symbolic names are part of the formal API definition and should be used by programmers in place of their corresponding numeric values.

The C/370 binding files are included in a C/370 program using the C/370 #include statement and in an assembler program by coding the macro name with no parameters.

In addition, assembler binding files include DSECTs that map the parameter list address block defined by type-1 linkage. An assembler call to the ThreadYield function would look like this:

```
USING R1,VMTHRYI_PLIST
MVC    VMTHRYI_PLIST_RC,=A(RC)    Address of return code
MVC    VMTHRYI_PLIST_RE,=A(RE)    Address of reason code
MVC    VMTHRYI_PLIST_TID,=A(TID)  Address of Thread ID
L      R15,=A(THREADYIELD)
BALR   R14,R15                    Invoke ThreadYield
```

In addition, the call can be made using the CALL macro provided by CMS. Using it, invocation of ThreadYield would be coded as:

```
L     R15,=A(THREADYIELD)
CALL  (R15),(RC,RE,TID)
```

Note that the register form of entry point address, rather than a symbol, must be specified.

The use of the API can be seen in the following example of a very simple application. In it, the main entry point of the application receives control and creates a thread to perform some processing. The C header file vmcmt.h includes the declarations that make the STEVR/VM API accessible. The function new_thread is specified as the entry point for the new thread. It is at that address that the new thread will begin execution.

```
#include "vmcmt.h"             /* lang. binding files */
#pragma linkage(applmain,OS)

int applmain (extpl,tokpl)     /* use applmain entry  */
    char * extpl;              /* extended plist      */
    char * tokpl;              /* tokenized plist     */
{
    extern int new_thread (void);   /* new thread      */

    int rc,...etc.;            /* declare variables   */

    ThreadCreate               /* create a thread     */
    (
      &rc,                     /* return code         */
      &re,                     /* reason code         */
      &thread_id,              /* returned thread id  */
      tc_flags,                /* thread create flags */
      2,                       /* flags length        */
      1,                       /* +1 priority offset  */
      (int) new_thread,        /* new entry point     */
      tc_plist,                /* plist for thread    */
      0                        /* plist length        */
    );
    ⋮
  (more processing)
    return(0);
}

    ⋮

#include <stdio.h>             /* standard I/O          */
#include "vmcmt.h"             /* language binding file*/

#pragma linkage(new_thread,OS)

int new_thread()

{
    ⋮
  (new thread processing)
    return;
}
```

The next example shows the same program in assembler.
External symbols for API entry points are defined in macro
VMASMMT, included at the end of the example.

```
APPLMAIN CSECT
         LR       R12,R15          EP address
         USING    APPLMAIN,R12
*
* Process parms in tokenized/extended plists if any
*

         :
*
* Create a thread to execute at label THREAD1
*
         L        R15,=A(THREADCREATE)
         CALL     (R15),(RC,RE,TID,FLAGARRAY,              *
                  VM_PRO_RELATIVE_PRIORITY,                *
                  THREAD1,PLIST,PLISTLEN)

         :
         LM       R14,R12,12(R13)  Restore regs
         BR       R14
         :
THREAD1  DS       0H

         :
*
*   Perform Concurrent Work
*

         :
         LM       R14,R12,12(R13)  Restore regs
         BR       R14
*
*  Data definitions
*
         VMASMMT                        Assembler binding file

         :
         END      APPLMAIN
```

Server Structure

STEVR/VM gives server writers a powerful set of tools and building
blocks for construction of high-performance servers. Server writers
must decide, based on requirements of particular servers, what
concurrent program structure to use for the application foundation.
Facilities introduced so far, together with concepts described in the
process model description, are enough to describe several structures.
   The simplest concurrent program structure is one having some
number of threads, each having a unique function to perform and
none interacting with each other until the end of the computation.

Some numeric mathematics problems and some classes of transactions may be approached in this fashion. For example, a transaction composed of updating a file, a database, and a tape log could have three threads, each assigned to one of the three output objects, and each performing its update in parallel with the others.

For many servers, a more sophisticated structure may be more appropriate. In these servers, threads can be dedicated to individual services, individual clients (users of the server), or individual managed resources. Widely differing levels of coordination and synchronization may be required depending on the choice of structure.

A basic, but widely applicable, server structure is the queue-based model. In such a server, requests arrive from the client on a queue. The queue, being owned by the process, is equally accessible to all threads in the process. Each thread processes a request based on the contents of a message received on the queue and then sends a reply back to a queue owned by the client. Each thread can handle a specific request (thus resulting in a server with one thread for each type of request supported by the server) or each thread can handle any of the possible requests.

In either case, the basic structure of a thread in this model is:

```
Do While (server running)
   QueueReceiveBlock the request

      :

      Process the request

      :

   QueueReply the result back to the client
End
```

When the thread issues the `QueueReceiveBlock` function, it is left waiting until a message arrives on the queue. When processing is complete, the thread sends a response back the to client. It then loops back to receive the next request.

The next diagram illustrates the queue-based model.

Queue-based structure

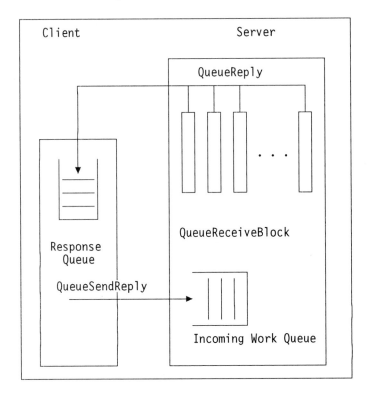

Another applicable structure for servers that use APPC/VM or IUCV to communicate with their clients is an event-based model. The approach translates interrupts to signals that can be handled using the event services. Instead of reading messages from a queue, server threads wait on an event monitor. An interrupt exit, such as one established by CMSIUCV, handles interrupts by collecting the interrupt information and signaling an event. This signal then satisfies an event wait, letting a thread process the request. The result is sent back by the thread using the appropriate communication mechanism, such as APPC/VM.

A thread in this model closely resembles its counterpart in the queue model:

```
Do While (server running)
   EventWait for the request
      :
   Process the request
      :
   APPC/VM Send the result back to the client
End
```

The next diagram illustrates the event-based model.

Event-based structure

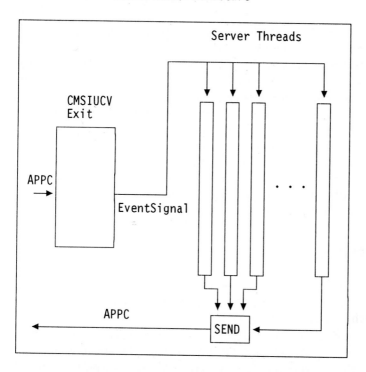

As in the queue model, the thread waits at the top of the loop for the next request. In both models, the threads process their work sequentially, with concurrency and asynchrony provided by using multiple threads.

Within either model, the server still must deal with some familiar problems. In the case of a parallel server, these problems can be compounded by multiprocessor concerns. The problems common to most servers include how to communicate with clients, how to handle interrupts, and how to interact with CMS in an efficient manner. The following suggestions are given in light of the STEVR/VM execution environment to provide help in finding the best solutions to these problems and others that might occur.

Interrupt handling

Most CMS-based servers are interrupt driven. They handle interrupts for communications, I/O, and timer handling. This is accomplished through exit routines established with the CMS HNDEXT, HNDINT, HNDIO, HNDIUCV, and CMSIUCV macros.

STEVR/VM provides mechanisms to allow threads to perform their functions in a synchronous manner, with concurrency among threads providing the asynchrony. So, to combine CMS interrupt handling with STEVR/VM multitasking, the exit routine should convert the interrupt into either a message or a signal. The exit routine, which continues to execute in the restricted environment of CMS second-level interrupt handlers, should gather data from the interrupt, build either a queue message or event data for a signal and issue the QueueSend or EventSignal function. A thread can then process the interrupt in an environment without the CMS interrupt handler restrictions. The server should spend as little time as possible in the interrupt handler exit routine.

Communication

Most service virtual machines communicate with clients by using the Virtual Machine Communication Facility (VMCF), the Inter-User Communications Vehicle (IUCV), or Advanced Program-to-Program Communication/VM (APPC/VM). The server uses each of these by means of HNDEXT or HNDIUCV exits. In other words, the server handles interrupts to receive messages and learn of completion of communication functions.

If the server needs to use one of these communication methods, the technique to apply is to turn the interrupt into a signal or a queue message, as described above. In this way, the client can continue to communicate with the server using the communication mechanisms it currently uses.

If the client is another CMS virtual machine in a VM collection or connected through an SNA network, both the client and the server can communicate with queues. This method best integrates communication into the natural concurrent programming structure of the server; however, the client must be on a VM system.

A variation of the queue approach is to use the `QueueIdentifyCarrier` function to provide the carrier with queue communication. The server can use the queue API, with the installed queue carrier sending and receiving data according to whatever communication protocol the client uses. This allows the server to exploit the concurrent programming power of queues and still allow the client to use the communication mechanisms available on its system. However, to accomplish this, server writers must provide the queue carrier, and some component on the client system must understand the line flows.

Another alternative is to use the SAA Common Programming Interface. This high-level language API for APPC communications is made up of synchronous calls. Because of its synchronous nature, it results in more serialization than is acceptable for many multi-user servers. However, it is applicable for single-user servers and multi-user servers that perform significant amounts of computation per request.

For more information, see *SAA Common Programming Interface Communications Reference.*

Data management

The main consideration when managing data in the server is how various types of file operations affect the synchrony of the virtual machine. Read and write operations on CMS minidisks are synchronous and as such do not allow for overlapping file I/O with other processing. Many other services are synchronous as well. For servers with intense file I/O requirements, asynchronous interfaces should be used.

The CMS Shared File System (SFS) provides asynchronous interfaces for file I/O. This is particularly true for VM/ESA Release 1.1 and less so for previous releases. By using the asynchronous interfaces and distributing work between several CMS work units, both overlap and parallelism can be achieved.

For more information on the CMS Shared File System, see *CMS Application Development Guide* or *CMS Shared File System Administration*, depending on the level of the VM system.

Another alternative is to use CP services directly for high speed data management. The DASD Block I/O System Service provides block-oriented I/O directly to a minidisk in an asynchronous manner. CP also provides services to map DASD volumes into VM data spaces. Data can be manipulated in the data space with a high degree of parallelism. These approaches provide the best performance but require the most work by the server writer.

For more information on the DASD Block I/O System Service and VM data spaces, see *VM System Facilities for Programming.*

Summary

The Server Tasking Environment/VM augments the suite of CMS application programming services with general and flexible tools for parallel and distributed processing. This step in the evolution of the CMS execution environment is aimed chiefly at addressing the requirements of high-performance servers and large scale applications. VM application writers are writing new sophisticated service virtual machines while at the same time moving their existing servers and other applications into an environment in which performance and capability demands are increasing dramatically. STEVR/VM provides fundamental building blocks to allow VM applications to achieve required performance levels, provide new function without building elaborate infrastructure into the application, and address the new challenges of providing services to LAN-based clients.

9

Exploiting the Shared File System

By Scott Nettleship

Most VM/ESA customers probably see the Shared File System (SFS) as something new to VM/ESA. SFS has actually been in use since 1988, when it was introduced with VM/SP Release 6. Most VM/ESA customers are seeing SFS for the first time in their installations for two reasons: VM/SP Release 6 was not a smashing marketplace success, and the SFS could not run on VM/XA SP because of missing facilities in CP. This chapter examines:

- What makes up the Shared File System
- How and why it can be used by VM/ESA users
- How the SFS is administered
- How to write and use CMS applications for data managed by SFS

Introduction

SFS has been around since 1988 with the introduction of VM/SP Release 6 (and VM/SP HPO Release 6). When the Shared File System was being developed, IBM believed that it would revolutionize the way CMS users would work with their VM systems. Since then the Berlin Wall has fallen, the Soviet Union is really no longer a union of states, and European countries are ready to form their economic alliance, but the SFS has not quite materialized as a revolution to the CMS user community. So, to determine what SFS can provide to the CMS user community, one must look at the CMS file system as most people are familiar with it.

CMS users throughout VM history have used the concept of a **minidisk,** which is a contiguous allocation of a real DASD volume, owned by a VM user. Since a minidisk can be a subset of a real volume, multiple minidisks can exist on a real volume. VM users generally have one or more minidisks on which to store their data in the form of CMS-format files. Minidisks in many ways are similar to the hard disks of today's personal computers. The restrictions on the amount of data that can be stored and the individual file size that can be accommodated depend directly on the size of a disk. Minidisks were intended by design for single-user service.

CMS minidisk files and space may be shared, but only with care. The normal situation is that each CMS user has a private minidisk that is not shared with other users. This means that each user has a reserved allocation of DASD space. Any unused minidisk space is not available to other users, even for temporary files. This leads to some amount of wasted space for the installation. Also, if a user outgrows an allocation, a system admistrator must create a new minidisk on a real volume, allocate it to that user, copy the user's files to the new minidisk, and remove the old minidisk. It is obvious that DASD space management can be time consuming.

A minidisk owner may authorize other users to read from or write to that minidisk. Typically, minidisk sharing is done in read-only mode. Large tools disks or data disks are examples of this. When a user accesses the disk (via the CMS ACCESS command), the user gets a "snap-shot" of the disk. If the disk is updated while the user has it accessed, it must be reaccessed in order to see the updated contents. When users try to share a minidisk in read/write mode, much care must be taken to protect the files on that minidisk. The danger in minidisk sharing is that the ACCESS command reads the minidisk directory into a user's storage. The directory contains the names of files, file location on the minidisk, and file attributes such as record length. Having this information in storage is extremely important in achieving desired CMS performance. CMS uses this directory to find files and free space. Therefore, if the owner creates a new file, other users must reACCESS the disk, which rereads the directory, in order to see the new file. If the owner erases a file, other users, unless they reACCESS, will think that the file still exists; if the owner then creates a new file that uses the same space as the erased file, those other users may see parts or all of the new file. If multiple users are sharing the minidisk in write mode, each user's CMS thinks it controls allocation of space based on its in-storage directory and allocation map. Clearly, because there is no point of control for data sharing, the sharing of minidisk files can be very complicated.

Another limitation of the minidisk file system deals with data integrity. CMS "commits" the minidisk—or makes all minidisk file changes permanent—when the last file that was open for write on the minidisk is closed. It does this by writing the minidisk directory and allocation information to the minidisk. If a failure occurs before this is done, the minidisk contains the data as it was after the previous commit. This has two implications. The first is that if one program, with a file open for write, calls a second program that writes data and closes its files, the data will not be committed until the first program closes its file. The second implication is that if the second program decides to close all files on that minidisk in order to ensure that its data is committed, the first program's data will also be committed. There is only one commit scope on a minidisk, and that is the entire minidisk. There is no separation between programs that call each other. Applications must be very conscious of the state of files they are using, and—in many cases—what other applications may be doing while they are running.

Many aspects that make CMS minidisks ideal for CMS users make them cumbersome in an environment for sharing data among many users. As minidisks can be equivalent to a hard disk of a personal computer user, the Shared File System can be compared to a Local Area Network (LAN) environment of CMS users. File data is managed by an SFS server machine which services requests for data from CMS client machines. This system is very different from that of traditional CMS users with their data on their own minidisks.

The SFS server owns and manages a collection of minidisks. Yes, minidisks. As mentioned earlier, minidisks are excellent when used by a single user—in this case, the SFS server. The collection of data that is owned by an SFS server is known as a **file pool**.

The file pool contains files for numerous users, who are **enrolled** in the file pool. To manage these user files, each file pool has a certain number of files and minidisks devoted to control information.

Every file pool needs a control minidisk that keeps track of all data in the file pool. Each minidisk is divided into 4096-byte (4K) sections called blocks; the control disk contains a map of all the blocks in the file pool. The map tells the file pool server machine which blocks are being used and which are not.

The last item of the control data is the Catalog Storage Group, or, as it is often called, Storage Group 1. Catalogs contain information about files and directories that exist in the file pool, who owns them, and who is authorized to read and write them.

To help protect control data integrity, as well as user data, each server maintains a **log**. Copies of the log are kept on two separate minidisks. In the logs, the server records changes to the file pool so that if the system failed in the middle of an operation, the file pool would not be corrupted. It is also needed so that applications can roll back (undo) changes. It is recommended that the log minidisks reside on separate physical volumes for both performance and integrity reasons.

The rest of the space in the file pool is for user data. To allow control over which users have files on which minidisks, the server uses a concept called storage groups. A **storage group** is a collection of minidisks within the file pool. Storage groups are identified by numbers ranging from 1 to 32767. Storage group 1 is used for catalog information; storage groups 2 through 32767 are for user data.

To access a file pool, a userid must be enrolled in it. When a userid is enrolled, it can be assigned an allocation of space in a particular storage group, and files can be created using that space. All the userid's files will reside on one or more of the minidisks assigned to the storage group. The user's allocation of space is referred to as the user's **file space**. The file spaces of many users can be assigned to a single storage group. Each user can have, at most, one file space in a given file pool.

A file space is a logical allocation. That is, no physical DASD space within the storage group is set aside for the user. The file pool server allocates physical disk space as needed until a user reaches an assigned limit of allocation (file space). A user only uses the amount of physical disk space required to hold data in existing files. The unused portion of their file space can be shared by other members of the storage group. This method of DASD management can produce a great deal of DASD savings. Since there is no static allocation of physical DASD space for each user, all space is either in use by an individual user or is available to all other users in the storage group. There have been reported savings of up to 30 percent of physical DASD space when files are kept in SFS.

Using the Shared File System

One of the most common comments about SFS is that it "looks like something one might use someday but right now there is no time to learn anything new". SFS was in many ways designed to be a logical addition to the CMS file system. Most users familiar with CMS commands such as ACCESS and FILELIST can start to use SFS right away without a significant learning effort.

Organizing file data

The minidisk file system is a "flat" file system. Files have no implicit organization on minidisks. CMS minidisk users have devised all sorts of interesting ways to organize their files. Usually these revolve around naming conventions using the filename and filetype fields. The Shared File System supports hierarchical directories. The hierarchical directory structure is similar to the MS-DOS file structure. Users enrolled in an SFS file pool are given **root** directories. The root directory name is the same as the owning userid. From there, users can create subdirectory structures below the root directory. Subdirectory names can be up to 16 characters in length, and there can be up to eight subdirectory levels below the root directory.

Using this hierarchical structure, a user can place related files together in the same subdirectory, rather than trying to enforce artificial naming conventions. This concept, while certainly not new to many users, allows them to organize data in the same manner as they would on personal computers or other operating systems.

Along with this ability to organize files into hierarchical directories, SFS also provides the ability to reference files from other subdirectories. This is done by using file **aliases**. A file alias is simply a pointer to another file. In SFS terminology, the file containing the actual data is called a **base file**. The base file can be referenced in the same ways as would be expected for a minidisk file. A file alias is a pointer to a base file. Examples show the power of using file aliases:

- Programs (EXECs, etc.) from tools disks can be migrated to SFS. Since many different tools files can reside on the same disk, a subdirectory can be created for each type of tool (XEDIT, REXX, BookMaster, and the like). This enables the tools to be organized into their logical groupings. Another function that would also be desired is the convenience of having these tools accessed at the same filemode letter in the search order as they were on a minidisk. This can be done by creating a tools subdirectory and placing a file alias in that directory for every tool to be accessed at that one filemode letter. In this way, only one copy of a file exists, but it may referenced in multiple ways.
- No matter how many tools users have, there are always other people who have something else that can help do VM work. Traditionally, this meant that users would exchange, ship, and store each others' files on minidisks. With SFS, as long as the owning users keep the tools in an SFS directory, other users can simply create aliases in their own directories to the base file. This allows users to have access to the owner's one copy of the file, and allows them to see changes if the tool is "improved". Also, an alias name that is different than the name of the base file can be chosen, which might be more meaningful to that individual user.

As these examples show, the ability to use file aliases can greatly enhance the organization of file data in SFS.

File security

With minidisks, security is at the minidisk level. A user with the password to a minidisk can link it and access all files on that minidisk (including files supposedly protected by filemode 0 naming). As with any password-based system, there is no real control of who can get the password and no real means to audit who has obtained access to the files.

The Shared File System lets users assign authorities to individual files. A user can be given authority to read or write another user's files by using the GRANT AUTHORITY command. Thus, authorities are controlled by the owner of the file and the owner can grant or revoke another user's authority to any file or group of files. The following is a list of the types of authorities for SFS files:

Read   A user with read authority on a file may only read that file.

Write   A user with write authority may read and write the file.

New Read   A user with New Read authority has read authority to future files in the directory; this, however, does not imply that the user has read authority on the directory or on any existing files in that directory.

New Write   A user with New Write authority has write authority to future files in the directory; this, however, does not imply that the user has write authority on the directory or on any existing files in that directory.

New Read and New Write give the directory owner the ability to grant authority to directories that are dynamic without individually granting authorities when new files are added.

Authority may be granted to another user, a group of users (using nicknames), or to all users that can connect to the file pool. For the last case, authority is granted to PUBLIC, thus letting all users read or write the file. Similarly, the owner of the directory can grant read or write authority to other users. Directory authorities are separate from file authorities; that is, read authority on the directory does not necessarily imply read authority on all the files in that directory. Directory level authorities are:

- Read—a user with read authority can see the list of files in that directory. It does not imply, though, that the user can read any of these files. This authority is required to use the ACCESS command to reference an SFS directory.
- Write—a user with write authority can add or delete files in that directory. Files, once created in the directory, then belong to the owner of the directory. The creator of the file is automatically given write authority to the file.

With these file and directory authorities, users can give access to a file or group of files to a single user or a group of users. The GRANT command allows the owner to give other users authority to files and directories.

The difference between granting file level authority and directory level authority depends on the scope of the data to which other users are to have access. To give another user the ability to reference a file but not the directory, only file level authority is appropriate. An example of this is granting a user read authority to execute an EXEC in a tools directory. What the other user would commonly do is create an alias into one of his or her directories to this EXEC. This avoids the need for authority on the directory to reference the file. On the other hand, to allow another user to modify the EXEC requires granting write authority on the file and at least read authority on the directory. The authority on the directory is necessary to allow the second user to use the ACCESS command to assign the directory to a filemode letter so the file can be edited.

Types of SFS directories

There are two types of SFS directories. The first is called a **FILE-CONTROL** directory. This directory type allows users to grant authorities on individual files. All SFS directories in VM/SP Release 6 are file control directories. The second type of SFS directory is known as a directory control (**DIRCONTROL**) directory. This type of directory resembles a CMS minidisk and is new with VM/ESA Release 1. There are no individual file level authorities. Read authority on a directory implies read authority on all files and all future files in that directory. Also, only one user can access a DIRCONTROL directory read/write at a time. All other users get read-only access until the user with read/write access releases the directory. A DIRCONTROL directory is in many ways similar to a CMS minidisk. When moving applications that store file data on minidisks to SFS, consider using a DIRCONTROL directory, especially for "read-mostly" data.

The following authorities have implications on both directory and files contained in that directory:

- Directory Read—a user with Directory Read authority has the same authority on the directory as if it were a CMS minidisk. This implies that the user has read authority on the directory, all existing files within the directory and all future files within the directory. This authority may only be used with Directory Control (DIRCONTROL) directories.
- Directory Write—a user with Directory Write authority has the same authority on the directory as if it were a CMS minidisk. This implies that the user has write authority on the directory, all existing files within the directory and all

future files within the directory. This authority may only be used with Directory Control (DIRCONTROL) directories.

File sharing

Now that many of the functions of the Shared File System have been described, consider how these can be used to share data among many CMS users (after all, sharing is in the name of SFS). SFS lets CMS users share files and file data without needing to know when the data was changed or having to reaccess the owner's files. Files are shared at the file level. That is, there are no conflicts when users are referencing different files. Also, many users can use the same file concurrently.

Multiple readers and one writer may access a file at the same time. When a user opens a file with the intent of reading it, that user gets a consistent view of the file, even if another user is writing data to that file. In this way, a user will not get a partially updated file. This is of particular importance for users sharing programs such as EXECs: problems will occur if such users execute a partially updated copy.

File updates will not be seen by readers of that file until the updates are complete, and the writer has committed those updates to the file system. After the file system has these updates committed, any future readers of the file will see the new version. However, if any users opened the file before the updates were committed, they will still see the previous version of the file. In order to see the new updates, they must close and then reopen the file. This differs greatly from the minidisk file system, which requires a user to reACCESS an entire minidisk to see file updates.

Once many users have authority to access SFS files, a method is needed to avoid concurrent updates to those files. In SFS, this is done by placing locks on a specified file or directory. There are two categories of locks, implicit and explicit. An implicit lock is one that SFS acquires and releases automatically. To allow greatest concurrency, SFS acquires locks only when needed and frees them as soon as possible. A lock is acquired, for example, when a file is opened. The type and duration depends on the intent of the open (read or write) and when the file is closed. This can prevent other users from attempting to update the file while it is being updated. It does not prevent other users from reading the file.

CMS provides a way to lock files and directories explicitly, to prevent simultaneous updates. When actively working with SFS files and directories, CMS automatically creates and deletes implicit locks. The CREATE LOCK command creates an explicit lock on a file, a group of files, or a directory. The type of lock and the duration are specified to CREATE LOCK. The QUERY LOCK command displays information about the locks that have been created. The DELETE LOCK command deletes explicit locks.

In CMS, XEDIT allows users to edit SFS files in the same manner as minidisk files. When several users XEDIT a file, explicit locking is necessary. This is due to the fact that XEDIT reads the file into memory, then closes it. Once the file is closed, the SFS implicit lock is released and another user can update the file. New XEDIT options (LOCK and NOLOCK) have been added to control this process. The default is LOCK. XEDIT gets an Update Session lock on the input file being edited. Another user can XEDIT the same file, but will receive a warning message saying it cannot be updated. In a sharing environment, it is best to use the NOLOCK option when it is known that the file will not be updated. This avoids preventing others from updating the file.

Interactive Use of the Shared File System

Users often ask for a "brief" education on using SFS. Most times people set aside an hour or so and then prepare themselves for a significant learning experience. While there are many commands and concepts that must be learned in order to maximize SFS exploitation, it is very quick and easy for most CMS users to absorb the basic concepts.

The place to start is to explain that instead of having minidisks, users have root directories named the same as their userid. Most people are familiar with the concept of hierarchical directories; if they are not, simply leaving them with a single, root directory is essentially the same as giving them 191 disks. In most cases, people start using SFS when they need to access data that belongs to someone else. They are less interested in moving data into SFS initially and more interested at getting at data already in SFS. Instead of explaining the concepts of accessing directories, base files, and aliases, simply tell them about the DIRLIST command. From this one command, a CMS user can effectively use SFS.

When users want to access data in someone else's directory, they can issue the command DIRLIST userid.. This allows them to see the part of the directory structure to which they have been granted authority. This also relieves them of the problem of remembering the name of the directory where the data resides. DIRLIST only shows directories to which they have authority.

```
SCOTT     DIRLIST  A0   V 319   Trunc=319 Size=16 Line=1 Col=1 Alt=0
Cmd   Fm  Directory Name
      -   SERVER8:SCOTT.
      -   SERVER8:SCOTT.GOODIES
      -   SERVER8:SCOTT.PCTOOLS
      -   SERVER8:SCOTT.PCTOOLS.BACKUP
      -   SERVER8:SCOTT.PCTOOLS.PS1
      -   SERVER8:SCOTT.PITCHES
      F   SERVER8:SCOTT.SESSIONSERVICES
      -   SERVER8:SCOTT.SESSIONSERVICES.MORETOOLS
      -   SERVER8:SCOTT.SFSTOOLS
      -   SERVER8:SCOTT.SHARE
      -   SERVER8:SCOTT.SHARE.PITCHES
      -   SERVER8:SCOTT.SHARE.TRIPREPORTS
      B   SERVER8:SCOTT.TOOLS
      -   SERVER8:SCOTT.TOOLS.EXECS
      -   SERVER8:SCOTT.VMTOOLS
      -   SERVER8:SCOTT.VMTOOLS.SFSTOOLS


1= Help      2= Refresh  3= Quit   4= Sort(fm)  5= Sort(dir)   6= Auth
7= Backward  8= Forward  9=        10=          1= Filelist   12= Cursor
```

From the DIRLIST screen, which is reminiscent of a FILELIST screen, users can put the cursor on the directory desired and press PF11 to ACCESS it. From there, they are presented with a FILELIST screen, from which they can edit, copy, and perform functions familiar in their normal environment. Using DIRLIST and FILELIST screens, users can also find out information such as file and directory authority, alias names and subdirectory structures. Usually after this point, people become interested in getting their own data organized into this structure and get in touch with the local SFS administrator to get enrolled. So the best advice when telling users about SFS is to start with the DIRLIST command and then move on.

The next concept to describe is using the ACCESS command to get at SFS data. The ACCESS command is used to read in a minidisk "directory" off a physical volume, store information regarding files in virtual storage, and place the minidisk somewhere in the CMS search order at a filemode (A–Z). Just as the design goal was to be able to use as many existing programs written for minidisks as possible for SFS data, the same concept is used with SFS directories. An SFS directory can also be accessed as a CMS filemode letter. In this way programs that use a filemode reference can use an SFS directory as well as a minidisk. All CMS commands work with accessed SFS directories. When people see that SFS has hierarchical directories, they begin to think that there may be a relationship between subdirectories in the structure. In other operating system environments, a search of a directory may also imply searching subdirectories below the original directory. This is not the case with SFS. All searching in CMS is still done through the traditional search order. The only way that an SFS directory can be a part of that search order is when it is accessed.

What this means is that the end-user typically uses the ACCESS command directly or uses the DIRLIST screen to use an SFS directory. Since many more subdirectories can exist than minidisks, the limitation of 26 filemode letters is more of a problem. The use of file aliases can help this problem, but as yet there is no way of using the CMS search order to access more than 26 SFS directories and minidisks at a time.

With the concepts of hierarchical directories, accessing SFS directories, and productivity aids such as DIRLIST and FILELIST, many CMS users should feel comfortable with using SFS in their daily work. This of course can only happen if there is an SFS file pool available to the user community. One of the most commonly asked questions at user groups is "Why would I want to worry about the administration necessary to support SFS in my shop?"

This is a difficult question, because the answer depends on the type of environment. Instead of trying to explain it, the following are two examples that illustrate how SFS can be used to solve problems.

At a large university, VM is used for functions such as office automation, administration, and teaching. Many classes need VM minidisk space for students to perform programming assignments. In the past with minidisks, each student was allotted one cylinder of space. If for some reason they needed more, it was usually up to the professor (more commonly the student assistant) to send a request to the system adminstrator to find a bigger minidisk, format it, and copy the data from the old one to the new one. This was not only time-consuming but usually had one or more distressed students waiting for space. The university VM installation switched to SFS for the following reasons.

First, the minimum allocation in SFS is one 4K block of DASD storage (this is actually zero blocks of data, since one block is required for file information). This enables university staff to give out only the amount of storage the students need. Since DASD cylinders are getting larger all the time, this allows them to better allocate their DASD resources. If students need more space, it can be given to them online by changing their file space allocations. This allows university staff to be more responsive to their users. Finally when the class is over, they can delete students from SFS. There is no worry of residual minidisks that could be used by someone later.

The second case is a large company that has many internal documents that must be viewed by and shared among many users. In the past, documents were created by a user or group of users, then stored on a minidisk. People who wanted to access the document would either give the minidisk password to people or would send the document (via SENDFILE) to those users. This was then copied onto the reviewer's minidisk, read and commented on. The comments were sent back to the document owner who then updated the original copy and would send periodic notes to say when a refreshed copy was available. The procedure would likely begin all over again. Clearly, this was wasteful in two ways: people reviewed sometimes unstable versions of the document, and multiple copies of the data were generated, either on multiple people's minidisks or in the system SPOOL space (commonly used as an extension of a user's minidisks).

Since the large company switched to SFS, documents are placed in a single SFS directory, and reviewers are given read authority to the files and the directory. Some reviewers are also given write authority if appropriate. Reviewers now either access the owner's directory to review the files, or place an alias to the files in their own directories. As a matter of fact, the files they review could be alias names instead of real filenames, which might be needed for security. There is usually only one copy of the data kept and it is not passed around the network to multiple users. Also, when the file is updated, the next time it is opened (typically using XEDIT) the changes are seen by the reviewers. In this way, reviewers know they are looking at the most current copy of the document, and need not worry that it has changed since they last accessed the minidisk.

These are two examples of what SFS can do for a VM installation. In no way is this the full extent of how it can be used. A few more examples:

- SFS removes the minidisk restriction of a minidisk being only as large as a physical volume. A file space in SFS may greatly exceed the size of a physical volume.
- The same is true of a CMS file size. An SFS file may be as large as the user's file space, which again can be greater than a physical volume.
- SFS is a resource controlled by the Transparent Services Access Facility (TSAF) in VM. This allows the resource to be transparent within a TSAF collection of up to eight VM nodes. Given that, users can access SFS directories and not know which VM node owns the data. In fact, this directory may be a resource in the network. The access of this directory may go through the Virtual Telecommunications Access Method (VTAM) to get to the data. To users, this is again transparent. This can reduce the need for worrying about shared DASD and allow users to get at data when they would previously need to log on to another VM node.

While these alone may not be compelling arguments for why SFS can be good for an installation, there are many other persuasive reasons to seriously consider using SFS as a part of VM/ESA.

SFS Use of VM Data Spaces

Installations running VM/ESA Release 1.1 on an ESA/390 platform have a virtual machine architecture called **ESA/XC** available. One of the facilities of this architecture used by SFS is **data spaces**. A data space is an area of virtual storage that can be accessed by several virtual machines. What is described here is SFS use of the data space facility and how this can be managed.

One of the most significant performance aspects of SFS, or any server-based file system, is the amount of communication resources that is used to access the data. Consequently, a tremendous amount of work is done for both the server and the user machine to reduce the number of calls to the server. Many improvements have been made to SFS in this area since its introduction, but it still is not possible to achieve performance characteristics comparable to using CMS minidisks. The primary use of data spaces for SFS is to obtain minidisk-like performance (with minidisk caching).

In order to use data spaces, files must reside in an SFS directory control (DIRCONTROL) directory. The primary reason for this is that the attributes of a DIRCONTROL directory map very well to managing data in a virtual storage environment that will be shared across virtual machines. After a DIRCONTROL directory has been created (and presumably has files in it) it can be made "data space eligible" via the SFS DATASPACE ASSIGN command. At this point, the directory and its contents can be placed in a data space.

When an SFS data-space eligible directory is ACCESSed, SFS maps the directory to a data space. The mapping causes CP to associate data space pages with the appropriate file pool minidisk blocks on disk. SFS maps the blocks for all the files within the directory and the control blocks relating to those files. When an authorized user accesses the directory in read-only mode, all access to the files in that directory are done directly to the data space. There are no communications to the SFS server machine. This provides a great performance advantage because the data is retrieved directly from shared virtual storage. When the user machine is running in XC-mode, the SFS does not use CMS virtual storage to maintain the control blocks associated with the directory. Instead, the control blocks residing in the data space are used. This can reduce the virtual storage requirements within the user machine as well as the real storage requirements of the machine in general.

The performance gain in using directories is best for XC-mode virtual machines, but 370- and XA-mode virtual user machines may also access the data in the data space. When the data space eligible directory is accessed in these modes, the data space is created as before but the control blocks are also copied into the user's virtual machine storage. Any file data access is done through a CP DIAG-NOSE by CMS when a file is referenced. While this takes longer than using the direct reference of an XC-mode virtual machine, it is still considerably faster than using the communication path to the SFS server.

Data spaces are not intended for private data or data that is commonly updated. Data spaces are a system-wide resource that should be managed as such. Data spaces work very well for SFS data that needs to be shared among more than one virtual machine and is **read-mostly**. This term means files that are updated infrequently or updated when no one is typically accessing the files (an off-shift type of update).

When a user accesses a data space eligible directory in read-only mode, it is mapped into a data space (if it has not been already) and the pointer information for data space access is passed back to the CMS user machine. The CMS file system uses this information on all file accesses in the future. When a directory is accessed in read/write mode CMS uses the normal communication path to SFS. The performance gain achieved by not communicating with the SFS server on read-only data cannot be achieved with read/write data because the server must know about files that are being updated (e.g., which another user may have locked). When the files are placed in a data space, the user sees a "snapshot" of the directory at the time it was accessed. If another user modifies the directory by either updating a file or adding or deleting a file, the next user who accesses the directory as read-only will see a new snapshot of the directory. This causes SFS to create a new data space in addition to the one that was created for the previous user. Thus data spaces can proliferate when data is being modified.

The best way to remember how data spaces are used by SFS is that every time a user accesses a data space eligible directory, a unique version of that directory and its contents are put in a data space. As long as every future access of that directory matches the version that is in the data space, that copy is used. If the contents of the directory have changed a new data space is created.

The SFS administrator can:

- Assign DIRCONTROL directories to be data space eligible
- Remove that eligibility
- Query who is accessing a data space and how many versions of that data space are currently in use

Also, the maximum number of data spaces and the maximum number of total bytes being created by data spaces can be declared in the CP directory of the SFS server machine. This helps prevent "runaway write" types of scenarios with data spaces.

Another recommendation is to have data space-eligible directories in a file pool of their own. This should be done for several reasons:

- Since the files that typically would be put in a data space are intended for multiple users, it is easier for people to remember the file pool name of these directories.

- Administration of these data spaces can be localized to one SFS server machine instead of over several server machines.
- Since the data in this file pool is by definition read-mostly, a more liberal backup plan can be used on that file pool.
- Again, since the data is read-mostly, the amount of time that the file pool is unavailable should be reduced. This is due to the fact that a read-mostly file pool has less administrative overhead.

In summary, data spaces can be used by SFS to provide the performance characteristics of minidisks with the benefits of having the data reside in the Shared File System. This is best used for read-mostly data such as tools disks and product libraries (note: the S- and Y-disks are not eligible. These disks use auxiliary directories and cannot be placed in SFS). Relative to using minidisks, the benefits include:

- For XC-mode user machines, they share the file control blocks (FSTs) in the data space instead of being copied into each user's virtual machine storage. Also, changes to files in these directories are managed by SFS where shared FSTs for minidisks must be managed manually.
- Each read-only access of the directory provides a consistent version of the directory and its contents until it is released.
- These directories can be accessed by authorized users on other VM systems. Only those users on the local system have the benefit of the data spaces, however.
- Access to the files is controlled by the GRANT/REVOKE method of authorization vs. the password protection of minidisks.

With VM/ESA Release 1.1, SFS offers the performance characteristics necessary for many types of data as well as the enhanced function needed for file sharing and data access.

Application Programming Using SFS

One of the most important benefits that SFS can provide to a VM installation is through its application interfaces. The CMS environment over the years has been regarded as one of the best interactive operating system platforms. One area in which CMS fell short was application programming interfaces, especially those to the file system. Areas needing improvement included:

- Access to CMS files from high-level languages
- Ability to control when data is actually written to files
- Ability to undo file changes
- Ability to separate work from multiple applications

In all of the above cases, application writers learned tricks to code around the shortcomings of the minidisk file system. File system access routines were coded using assembler or through the command interface (via EXECIO). The CMS Pipelines facility now helps REXX programmers achieve better productivity. Applications repetively issue the FINIS function to insure that data is actually written to disk. Once a write is completed to a minidisk file, there is usually no practical way of undoing it. For this reason, applications commonly use a temporary file to receive data, then replace the entire file at once with the temporary file. Finally, when more than one application is running in a CMS machine, applications always risk modifying data that other applications are using.

These issues are all dealt with using SFS interfaces. First, one must review basic concepts behind the SFS interfaces.

Using existing programs with SFS

One of the most important design issues with SFS was to allow most existing programs that use minidisks to use SFS, preferably with minimal changes. For example, EXECs that ACCESS a minidisk and then use CMS commands to manipulate files should work with SFS by simply replacing the minidisk LINK and ACCESS with the ACCESS of a SFS directory. Other CMS interfaces that allow access to SFS files are:

- CMS file system macros (FSOPEN, FSSTATE, etc.)
- OS and DOS macro simulation

Applications that do not share data or that use only read-only sharing should run unchanged. This is usually—but not always—the case. Probably the most irritating problem is the fact that many applications (usually EXECs) use the QUERY DISK command to find accessed modes. For minidisks, this returns information about the size of the disk and the amount of free space available. For an SFS directory, a "-" is returned in these fields. The original intent was to avoid misleading applications that the cumulative amount of space available on accessed filemodes was greater than it actually was (since multiple SFS directories may be accessed, but the file space limitation remains the same). For such cases, change to use the QUERY SEARCH command instead. In most cases existing programs will run unchanged.

CMS Work Units

When writing SFS applications, even relatively simple REXX programs, the concept of the CMS work unit should be understood. Once programmers understand work units, the amount of effort needed to code successful SFS applications is reduced.

In CMS, applications must be concerned with the integrity of data and to some extent the data of other applications. With the CMS minidisk file system, applications can interfere with the commit of each other's data. **Commit** means making the changes permanent on disk, either by adding new data or replacing old data. The reason for the interference is that CMS does not commit data until the last file opened for write is closed. If, for example, an application always keeps a trace file or log file open on the A-disk, and the application writes to the A-disk, even though the application closes its files, they are not committed because of the open log file. When the application closes its A-disk file, probably at termination, all open A-disks file are committed. If an error occurs before then, it is possible that the application's changes will be lost even though it closed its files. Applications may circumvent this by issuing FINIS * *, which ensures that its files are closed and committed, but which also closes and commits the files of other applications on the same filemode.

With the addition of the Shared File System, the concept of the CMS work unit was implemented. The work unit is the CMS unit of commit for recoverable data, which currently includes SFS, Structured Query Language (SQL), and APPC protected conversations. Minidisks behave as before. The work unit allows applications to coordinate changes which need to be made together and to separate changes which should not interfere with each other. When a file is opened, it is associated with a particular work unit, through either the specification of a work unit or the current default. The important commit rules for a work unit are:

1. All changes in a work unit are committed together or fail together. CMS guarantees that if any file in the work unit

cannot be committed because of an error condition, all changes to the other files in the work unit are thrown away (rolled back).

2. Open files do not prevent a commit. Changes to open files are committed and the file remains open. Note that this is not true for FSCLOSE, which requires that all files open for write be closed.

3. Commit of one work unit does not affect files open on other work units.

An application can separate its work into multiple work units. CMS assigns a default work unit, called work unit 1, at the beginning of the application. If the application takes no action, all changes are done on that work unit. The application can also request additional work units. If the application requests an additional work unit from CMS, and is assigned work unit 10, it can write to some SFS files on work unit 1 and to other SFS files on work unit 10. If it opens file A and file B on work unit 1 and file C on work unit 10, writes to all three files, closes file A and commits work unit 1, the changes to files A and B are made permanent. The commit does not interfere with file C in that its changes may still be committed or rolled back.

The CMS file system interfaces to SFS support work units. The FSREAD/FSWRITE interface, which includes OS simulation and EXECIO, does not allow work unit specification, but always uses the default work unit. The FSCLOSE/FINIS function includes an implied commit at the point that the last file open for write on the work unit is closed. A CMS work unit stack is provided so that programs using these interfaces can still use work units. Any time a function or command is called, the **currently active** work unit, also known as the **default** work unit, is used. If an application wants to change the default work unit—for example to call a subroutine and separate the work—it can use CMS functions to get, push, and pop the work unit off the work unit stack.

The SFS callable interface supports the specification of the work unit on all SFS functions. When opening a file, that work unit is then used for the life of the open. If a work unit is not specified, then the current default is used. With this interface, the close function does not include an implied commit. There are separate commit and rollback functions. These commit or roll back the entire work unit, including current changes to open files. In the rollback case, the files are then closed.

As shown above, the concept of work units is very powerful in CMS. Not only can these concepts be used to develop or enhance applications, but this also may prove useful in debugging applications where file updates may or may not be seen depending on how work units are being used.

SFS callable routines

As mentioned above, there are separate callable routines that are used to provide functions to SFS. All SFS routines reside in the Callable Services Library (CSL) called vmlib, shipped with VM/ESA. SFS routines are callable from supported high-level languages and can also reside in a segment or within the virtual machine of the user. Obviously if SFS will be used by more than a few users, the CSL routines should be loaded into a saved segment.

When writing applications that work with SFS files, programmers should use CSL interfaces wherever they can. These CSL interfaces provide the following advantages:

They are callable from high-level languages: Equivalent function requires an assembler-level routine or CMS command (if a command exists for that function).

CSL routines provide direct file reference: All CSL routines accept SFS directory and filenames. Using other interfaces usually requires use of accessed filemode letters. CSL may make accessing directories unnecessary in many cases.

Explicit control of work units: CSL routines allow applications to specify the work unit that the function will use. This allows for explicit controls of the committing or rolling back of changes. Both CMS command and macro interfaces will attempt to do commits at predefined times, usually at the completion of each function call.

The next two figures contain short examples of coding CSL calls in REXX and in PL/I. There are several SFS sample EXECs shipped with VM/ESA (on the MAINT 193 minidisk) that provide some administrative functions and also demonstrate how to use CSL calls in REXX.

A REXX example of using CSL calls:

```
/*   REXX program to RENAME an SFS file or directory */
say 'Enter Fileid of source file or directory:'
pull fileid
say 'Enter Fileid of target file or directory:'
pull fileid2
rc = 0; rs = 0
call CSL 'DMSGETWU rc rs workunit'        /* Use private workunit */
if rc ¬= 0 then do
   say 'Error from Get Workunitid, rc = ' rc ' rs = ' rs
   exit
end
fileidlen = length(fileid)
fileidlen2 = length(fileid2)
commit = 'COMMIT'                         /* COMMIT the RENAME */
commitlen = length(commit)
call CSL 'DMSRENAM rc rs fileid fileidlen fileid2 fileidlen2
                  commit commitlen workunit'
select
   when rc = 0 then say fileid 'successfully renamed to' fileid2
   when rs = 44000 then say 'File or Directory not found'
   otherwise
   say 'Error: rc='rc ', reason code='rs 'from RENAME function.'
end
```

A PL/I example of using CSL calls:

```
/* PL/I example of using the Exist for File function in SFS   */
DCL DMSCSL     OPTIONS(ASM INTER RETCODE) ENTRY,
    RTNCODE    FIXED BIN(31),  /* return code */
    REACODE    FIXED BIN(31);  /* reason code */
 DCL DIRNAME CHAR(153) VARYING;   /*Directory name*/
 DCL FILENAME CHAR(8);
 DCL FILETYPE CHAR(8);
 DCL LEN_OPEN FIXED BIN(31) INIT(8);
 DCL COMMIT_PARM CHAR(10);  /* Parameter to issue commit */
 DCL LEN_COMMIT FIXED BIN(31) INIT(8);
 DCL 1 FILESPEC,
       3 FNAME CHAR(9),
       3 FTYPE CHAR(9),
       3 DIRNAME CHAR(153);
FILESPEC = ' ';
FILESPEC.FNAME = FILENAME;      /* Fileid to look for */
FILESPEC.FTYPE = FILETYPE;
FILESPEC.DIRNAME = DIRNAME;
COMMIT_PARM = 'COMMIT  ';
CALL DMSCSL('DMSEXIFI',        /* Does file exist? */
            RTNCODE,
            REACODE,
            FILESPEC,
            LEN_FILESP,
            COMMIT_PARM,
            LEN_COMMIT);
PUT SKIP EDIT('Return codes from Exist:') (A);
PUT SKIP DATA(RTNCODE);
PUT SKIP DATA(REACODE);
```

Modifying existing programs using SFS

As stated earlier, many programs that use minidisk files can use SFS files with little or no changes. This is true if the SFS directory containing the files resembles a minidisk. What is meant specifically by this is:

- A file has no authorities granted to other users.
- No aliases have been created for the file.
- There are no dependencies on use of minidisk addresses.

If at least one of the first two cases is false, then the files are considered shared. When users migrate files to SFS, both of the first two cases will be false, so all files start off shared. Since one of the major functions is ability to share files between users, users will move quickly to the read/write sharing environment.

In the most common file sharing environment, the owner of a file will grant other users read authority to the file. When an application opens a file, it gets the last committed version. That is, applications see file updates only when files are opened: file images remain consistent until files are closed and reopened. It is important to note that directories containing such files need not be reaccessed in order to see the changes.

Files for this application can reside on either a minidisk or in an SFS directory. Existing applications using File System (FS) macros as well as EXECs using EXECIO can reference files in SFS directories. In this case, an application used by either the reader or writer may encounter situations that are new in this file sharing environment. Applications may have to change to account for an updated strategy for handling temporary files, for minidisk "assumptions" (now invalid), and for new CMS return codes.

In many CMS applications, it is common to use temporary files for file integrity. With CMS minidisks, when an application must replace an existing file's data, it writes the data to a temporary file, erases the old file, and renames the temporary file to the old filename. In the Shared File System, a file may have authorities and aliases associated with the file. When a file is erased, any authorities and aliases associated with that file are also deleted.

Applications have several options when handling temporary file data:

- When using the FS interface, use the FSOPEN macro with the REPLACE option (OPENTYP=REPLACE). This relieves the application from having to erase and rename the file being written.
- Use COPYFILE with the REPLACE option. This retains authorities and aliases: it simply replaces the file data.

It is important to note that writing to an SFS file is done within a CMS work unit. When FSOPEN is used with the REPLACE option, the file is erased when the first write is issued to the file. If at anytime during that processing the system fails, the work is rolled back and the file returns to its original state. Also, higher-level languages that use CMS OS simulated macros such as OPEN as well as EXECIO, will work correctly because they are translated into the correct FS macro by the file system.

The second item to look for is minidisk application "assumptions". There are some assumptions that applications may have made which may no longer be valid for SFS directories:

- Assumption: "If one file on an accessed filemode can be written to, then all files on that filemode can be written to". Not all files on a read/write filemode may be written to in SFS. An SFS directory accessed as read/write may have an alias that points to a file over which the issuer has read-only authority. In this case, an error could result from attempting to write to the file through the alias name.
- Assumption: "I can always read or write an existing file". A file may exist but be locked. Applications that check for existence of a file, then assume it can be read, may run into cases where it is locked by another user.
- Assumption: "The attributes of a file do not change". Applications that get file information using FSSTATE, then use that information later may want to consider using the FSOPEN macro. Issuing FSSTATE does not prevent other users from writing to the file. Attributes of the file (including its existence) may change from the time that the FSSTATE is issued and the next operation on that file. The FSOPEN macro prevents other users from writing to the file so that the version is consistent until the file is closed.

An application that uses files in SFS directories may encounter situations not previously possible in a non-sharing environment. Anyone who has ever coded logic in an EXEC to put out a message and exit when a non-zero return code is encountered can appreciate this. With SFS, there are new return codes that can be returned from existing commands and macros. These are all documented in the *CMS Application Development Reference.* Programmers may need to review applications to see if they should quit when these new error cases occur, or try and recover. The commit/rollback functions provide applications with the ability to handle file data in ways that were not possible before with minidisks.

The *CMS Application Development Guide, CMS Application Development Reference,* and the *CMS Migration Guide* are all excellent places to look for information regarding how to code and modify existing code for both SFS and minidisk applications.

SFS Administration

There are many items that the people who will administer SFS servers should know. These include:

- Generating and starting SFS servers
- Enrolling users
- Setting and modifying space allocations
- Allocating physical DASD
- Backup and Restore functions

Instead of discussing these items in detail in this book, it is much better to refer to the *CMS Planning and Administration Guide.* There are 17 chapters covering over 250 pages of information on SFS topics. There is no better or more complete reference to SFS administration than this manual. It cannot be stressed enough that the proper planning for SFS via this manual will be returned many times over in both performance of SFS servers and the amount of unnecessary maintenance that will be avoided.

There are a few things that have been found by people administrating SFS from practical experience. First, there can be occasions when it is necessary to bring up the SFS server without a certain storage group available. This may occur if a storage group assigned to a DASD is inoperable due to an error. While the DASD is unavailable, it is certainly necessary to make the file pool available to the remaining users. If the device is operable (can be linked) but is having errors:

- Issue the DISABLE GROUP (DETACH command to make the storage group unavailable. Once the device is available or the FILESERV RESTORE is done to a new device, the storage group can then be enabled.

If a volume becomes inoperable and cannot be linked by the server, the SFS server will not be able to start. In order to get the server running while the device is "offline" the following procedure can be used:

- Stop the server via the STOP IMMEDIATE or STOP NOBACKUP commands.
- Change the file pool ID in the DMSPARMS file so that when the server restarts, the file pool name will be hidden from the users. This will allow an administrator to make changes on the running server without other users accessing it.
- Create a new POOLDEF file by copying the existing POOLDEF file to the new file pool name:

```
COPYFILE oldfp POOLDEF A newfp POOLDEF A
```

- After affected minidisks have been found, define temporary disks that are the same size and address as the inactive minidisks. These will be used when the file pool is restarted.
- RESERVE the temp disks for the file pool server.
- Now restart the server using FILESERV START. The file pool is now available but only under the new file pool name.
- Next, disable the storage group or groups where the inactive minidisks reside. Since these are temporary disks at the moment, no user should be allowed to use these disks until the actual file pool is made available.
- Again, stop the server.
- Rename the file pool ID in the DMSPARMS file back to the correct file pool name.
- At this point, it is safest to re-IPL the server machine. Remember not to execute the PROFILE EXEC if it automatically starts the server.
- At this point the FILESERV START command can be issued to bring up the server again for the rest of the users. It always pays to issue a QUERY DISABLE GROUP command to make sure the storage group or groups used by the affected users are still disabled once the server has been restarted.

•   Once the inactive minidisks are ready to be used, the server must be brought down, the temporary disks released, server restarted, and the storage groups that were disabled enabled.

What this procedure points out is the tradeoff of performance aspects of using multiple volumes in a storage group versus reliability aspects of dedicating volumes to only one storage group. If a volume fails, the number of storage groups that reference that volume will be affected. It is still desirable to use multiple volumes for storage groups because it allows the SFS server to overlap I/O to these different volumes.

One of the most common areas of discussion concerning SFS is with server backups. As was mentioned earlier, the details of doing SFS backups are discussed in the *CMS Planning and Administration Guide*. The backup being referred to is the native SFS FILEPOOL BACKUP command. Vendor products also can backup and restore SFS data. The individual product owners should be consulted to determine which features are most suitable for a given installation. As installations plan for SFS, it is good to understand what resources will be needed for these backups. Here are some examples of SFS servers and the tapes needed for backups:

```
SERVER1 -- 13126 3380 cylinders -- 1315 users -- 38 3480 tapes
SERVER2 --  5197 3380 cylinders --  632 users -- 21 3480 tapes
SERVER3 --  2382 3380 cylinders --  457 users --  9 3480 tapes
```

Previous to VM/ESA Release 1.1 all blocks within a storage group were backed up. This included non-allocated (zero) blocks. In VM/ESA Release 1.1, these blocks are skipped. So if storage groups are not too full, backups will take less time and less tape or DASD space.

Another important thing to know about backups is that they can be inhibited by files currently open or directory control directories being accessed read/write by other users. If an automated backup procedure is used, it must handle these situations. One automated procedure could try to disable a storage group in order to perform the backup. If it fails, determine via QUERY LOCK CONFLICT which user is preventing acquiring the lock to perform the disable operation. If after 25 tries the disable cannot complete, it forces the server connection for that user and sends a note indicating what happened. If the backup runs with SET FILEWAIT ON, it will wait for the implicit lock to be released. Often this is no problem, if a file is opened for a short period of time. However, if a user has a file open

and disconnects, this can cause the backup to be suspended indefi-
nitely. Again, this is a case where installation staff must decide
what action to take. Knowing that it can happen is usually enough
so that a procedure can be defined for handling such cases. Also, if
RACF is used, the LINK NOPASS option should be considered for
backup automation.

One last area to discuss is basic problem determination techniques. Typically, from one to many users will call support
personnel saying they cannot get at their data and the server is
"down". Here are a few basic troubleshooting techniques:

- Send a QUERY LIMITS command to the server. This determines if it is up at all. If users are trying to access the
  server from another node in a TSAF collection, try the
  command from the node where the server resides. If it
  responds, that may indicate a networking problem to the
  server for users not on that node.

- Log on to the server and check for a dump. Typically the
  SFS server will be AUTOLOGged, so it may be back up again
  even if it ABENDed. Always have the server console
  SPOOLed! Consider calling the support center to check for
  problems even if the server is again operational.

- If users cannot access data but the server is up, try a
  QUERY DISABLE on the storage group and file space of the
  user. If the storage group is disabled, it may indicate a
  backup or some other automated procedure has failed.

- If for some reason the server is stopped (in CP READ), take a
  VMDUMP (using #CP VMDUMP 0-END DCSS). Any information
  that can be gathered close to the actual error will aid the
  IBM support center in problem determination.

- One last thing that can be tried is checking the minidisks in
  the storage group of the affected users. There may have
  been a DASD error. The SFS server writes messages to the
  server console, so check the SPOOLed console for messages
  having information regarding device errors.

These are basic steps to help solve some of the more common SFS
problems. The more an installation uses SFS the quicker it will be
able to isolate these types of calls to their administrators.

Summary

This chapter provided an idea of functions offered by the Shared File System. As users begin to move data onto SFS, the more they will like it, and the more they will ask from the support organization that provides it. This should be anticipated before the first file pool server is started.

This chapter covered many functions that SFS can provide, as well as benefits that SFS offers in the way of DASD savings. This chapter concentrated on the user presentation of SFS and how SFS can be used by applications.

Acknowledgments

I would like to thank the people that have given me help and advice, both directly and indirectly, in the completion of this chapter. Special thanks go to Dick Stone and Dave Crockett, who have influenced many aspects of SFS and then put them down in writing so people such as myself could learn from them later. I would also like to thank Cherie Barnes, Maria Jenny, Terri Perrone, and others for their technical and grammatical help in the final preparation of this chapter.

10

SQL/DS and VM Data Spaces Support

By Peter Kohlmann and Terrence D. Sole

Introduction to the SQL/DS Product

A **database** is any collection of data. It may be a collection of notes
in a book, a more formal filing system, a computer system file, or a
complex management system that can store and manipulate millions
of data records.

A **relational database** presents data as a logical grouping of
tables. A tabular format is often easier to visualize than a hierarchical or network database system, since most people are used to
working with tables.

The Structured Query Language/Data System (SQL/DS) product is
a Relational Database Management System (RDBMS). It is easily
installed and managed, and can be used by end-users as well as
data processing professionals. Facilities are provided for data query,
data manipulation, and reports capabilities for data integrity,
recovery, and security.

A sample SQL/DS table might be as simple as this EMPLOYEE table:

EMPNO	LASTNAME	FIRSTNAME	PROJECT
29381	Smith	Sandy	Moonglow
36457	White	Pat	Jupiter
17463	Adamski	Kim	Muskox
46284	Loden	Bryce	Jupiter

Tables

SQL/DS tables are structures made up of **columns** and **rows**. At the intersection of every column and row is a specific data item called a **value**. A **column** is a set of values of the same type. A **row** consists of a sequence of values: one for each column of the table. There is no inherent order to rows within a table.

Indexes

When the number and the size of tables in an SQL/DS database are large, it becomes necessary to have available a search strategy to find needed information. An **index** is an ordered set of pointers to rows in a database table, based on the values of data in one or more columns, but separate from the data in the table. When an index is requested, the database manager builds it and maintains it automatically.

Indexes are used to:

Improve performance: In most cases, access to the data is faster than without an index.

Ensure uniqueness: A table with a unique index cannot have rows with identical index **keys**. (A key is a column, or an ordered set of columns, on which the index is created.)

Catalog

A set of tables that contain information the RDMS needs about tables, views, and indexes is maintained. The catalog is actually a set of SQL/DS tables that contain information about all tables in the database. Information such as number of tables, number of columns in each table, index keys, data types, and users authorized to work with data are some of the information found in the catalog.

Views

Views provide alternative ways of looking at data in one or more tables.

Like tables, they have rows and columns. Views can be used like tables in SQL statements. Database administrators (DBAs) create views and authorize their use: through use of views DBAs can control what information a user sees, or control operations that can be performed. For example, a PERSONNEL table may contain names, addresses, and salaries of employees. Many departments may need the names and addresses but only Payroll needs salary information. A table view consisting of only names and addresses will satisfy most departments, while a view consisting of names, addresses, and salaries is available only to Payroll. This allows a single entry of name and address to be used by all departments, eliminating the need for each department to have its own copy of the information.

A table has a storage representation, but a view does not. When a view is created, its definition is stored in the catalog. No data is stored, and, therefore, no index can be created for a view. However, an index created for a table on which the view is based may improve the performance of operations on the view.

SQL Language

The Structured Query Language (SQL) is the language used to access data in a relational database. Unlike many other programming and data languages, SQL programmers need not code a sequence of instructions explaining **how** to get to the data: all that is needed is a single statement directed to the database manager, which then determines how to access and maintain the data.

Suppose there is an EMPLOYEE table as shown above. A plausible request is to list all employee names and employee numbers (EMPNO), with output sorted by last name. The SQL statement is:

```
SELECT LASTNAME, FIRSTNAME, EMPNO FROM EMPLOYEE ORDER BY LASTNAME
```

This statement produces the following output:

LASTNAME	FIRSTNAME	EMPNO
Adamski	Kim	17463
Loden	Bryce	46284
Smith	Sandy	29381
White	Pat	36457

Note that the column arrangement has been changed to the sequence specified by the SELECT statement, and that information not requested (PROJECT) has been omitted. The ORDER BY clause, on the SELECT statement, told the database manager to sort rows by last name. The SELECT statement clauses could also be used to limit the number of rows selected, thereby producing a subset of the data. For example, to restrict the list to just persons working on the **Jupiter** project, the statement would be:

```
SELECT PROJECT, FIRSTNAME, LASTNAME, EMPNO FROM EMPLOYEE -
    WHERE PROJECT='JUPITER'
```

Resulting output would be:

PROJECT	FIRSTNAME	LASTNAME	EMPNO
Jupiter	John	Traxler	36457
Jupiter	Bryce	Loden	46284

SQL/DS statements

SQL/DS statements can be entered interactively or embedded within application program statements. There are three major categories: **DDL**, **DML**, and **DCL**. Each is discussed below.

Data definition language (DDL)

DDL statements allow users to create and modify tables, to establish referential structures (parent-dependent relationships between tables), and to create and delete views and indexes. DDL statements are:

- CREATE TABLE
- CREATE VIEW
- CREATE INDEX
- ALTER TABLE
- DROP TABLE
- DROP VIEW
- DROP INDEX

Data manipulation language (DML)

DML statements allow users to retrieve, insert, or change data. Each time a DML statement is issued, one or more rows in a table are affected. DML statements are:

- SELECT
- INSERT
- UPDATE
- DELETE

Data control language (DCL)

DCL statements allow users to control who can see and use the information in the tables, and to control when changes take effect. DCL statements are:

- GRANT
- REVOKE
- LOCK
- COMMIT WORK

- ROLLBACK WORK
- CONNECT

Static and dynamic statements

SQL statements are either **static** or **dynamic**.

Static or embedded SQL

SQL statements can be embedded in application programs (such as C, COBOL, FORTRAN, REXX, or assembler programs). Before a program is compiled, the appropriate SQL preprocessor flags SQL statements as comments, checks their syntax, and includes the code necessary to invoke the database manager.

Dynamic or interactive SQL

Dynamic SQL statements are entered at a terminal or built by a program: they are not provided to the database manager until the program runs. Programmers can write programs that read information from terminals and then build SQL statements; in this sense, the process is similar to the SQL-handling processes used by the database manager's interactive facilities. Programmers use dynamic SQL to process SQL statements and present the results to users. Dynamic SQL allows users to create their own query programs, tailored and designed for their specific needs.

Using the Database

The SQL/DS database manager is easy to use and to administer: with relatively little effort, it can be set up so that application programmers and end-users can begin to use it almost immediately. In a development environment, it provides database capability for interactive dynamic use, supports changing requirements, and is a useful tool for modeling data designs and developing uses of data.

VM users of an SQL/DS database manager can be on the same processor as the **database machine** (a virtual machine dedicated to the RDMS to which user machines send their queries) or on a different processor (as a remote users). They can also switch from accessing one database to another within an application.

VSE users can access VM database machines as guest users. The VM SQL/DS database manager may be on the same VM system as the VSE guest, on a different VM system if the VM systems are part of the same TSAF collection (if TSAF is activated), or connected using an SNA network (if a gateway is used).

Components of the SQL/DS RDBMS

The SQL/DS RDBMS is composed of four main components:

Database: This is composed of:

- A collection of data contained in one or more storage pools. A **storage pool** is composed of one or more **database extents** (dbextents). Each dbextent is a VM minidisk.
- A directory of where data is stored in storage pools. Each database has one directory disk.
- A log of operations performed on the database. Each database has either one or two log disks.

Database Manager: The program that provides access to the data in the database. The database manager is loaded into the database virtual machine from the production disk.

Application Server: The facility that responds to requests for information from and updates to the database. It is composed of the database and the database manager.

Application Requester: The facility that transforms a request from an application into a form suitable for communication with an application server.

The diagram on the next page shows these components.

Basic Components of the SQL/DS RDBMS

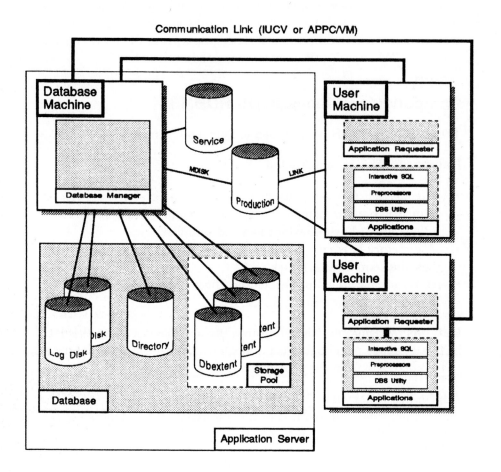

Communication Link (IUCV or APPC/VM)

Using Application Programs

Data in SQL/DS databases can be accessed by application programs. Application programs operate in virtual machines, and may be interactive (online) or noninteractive (batch). These programs are controlled by the VM Conversational Monitor System (CMS), by the Customer Information Control System/Virtual Machine (CICS/VM), or by equivalent facilities. When the VM/ESA ESA feature is used, application programs can employ 24-bit or 31-bit addressing, and can operate in virtual machines with more than 16 million bytes of memory. Programs work with SQL/DS data through SQL statements embedded in them. The detailed task of accessing SQL/DS data is done by the database manager. Therefore, programs are less affected by changes in data format. Putting data-handling operations in SQL statements embedded in programs uses the power of the SQL/DS database manager and decreases the data handling done by the programs themselves. Programs that access SQL/DS data can also access data from other sources such as CMS files, VSAM files, and CICS data.

The SQL/DS product provides preprocessing for C, COBOL, FORTRAN, PL/I, and assembler language. By using the SQL/DS **extended dynamic** statements, a programmer can write a preprocessor for any host language.

Data Independence

Having data in SQL/DS tables lets workstation users and programmers ignore details concerning physical data storage. The choice of columns in the tables is made by considering the various demands that might be made on the data. Usually, data independence is greater if each table contains only one type of data (such as inventory data or employee data). This approach decreases duplication or redundancy of data. It also makes data more flexible.

Each user or program then works with a portion or view of data in the tables. As new needs arise, new columns may have to be added to existing tables, but users and programs not concerned with the need are not affected.

Data independence means that users and programmers need not spend time changing their access methods and programs just because data elements they do not need have been modified. They can work on whatever are their current needs.

Data Integrity

When a group of related changes is made to the database, the database manager ensures that either all changes are made or none are made. An example of related changes would be financial transaction that subtracts from one account and credits to another. When related changes are made, other users and programs never see inconsistent data.

Entity integrity

Entity integrity is required for some data: it means that each value in a set must be different from the other values in that set. For example, an EMPLOYEES table can not contain duplicate employee identifiers, such as serial numbers. The database manager provides a way to specify that the values must be unique, and it ensures that duplicates do not occur.

Referential integrity

When data in one table references data in another, a third type of integrity is needed. Consider, for example, an EMPLOYEES table and a DEPARTMENT table. When new employees are added to the EMPLOYEES table, the departments to which they are assigned must exist in DEPARTMENTS. If a department is deleted from DEPARTMENTS, no employees can be associated with that department.

To ensure that references from one table to another are informed, DBAs can define rules that are automatically enforced when any data in these tables changes. These rules, called **referential constraints**, ensure **referential integrity** between the tables.

Data Administration

Data administration entails determining what data is stored in the database and controlling how it is used. There can be one administrator or many; each site decides how centralized this control should be. In addition, users can do much of their own data administration, subject to levels of security authorization granted to them. For example, depending on privileges they have, users may be able to design, create, and delete their own data.

Catalog tables contain information about data in the database and each user's authority to access parts of that data. Together, they serve as an integrated data dictionary and directory. When a user defines a database object (creates a table, for example) the catalog tables are updated automatically to reflect the current status of the database. These tables are under the control of and can be updated only by the database manager.

The database manager is normally run so that many users and programs can access the database at the same time, and so that the administrator can perform database maintenance tasks while the system is being used by other users. This state is called **multiple-user mode**. It can also run in **single-user mode** when maximum performance is required for involved, time-consuming tasks such as loading large quantities of data.

Data Security

Security features control access to data and to the database manager itself. Administrators specify what data each user can access, and the type of access (read or update) allowed.

In addition, a Security Audit Trace facility records who uses the database manager, what authorizations they have, and how they used their authorizations.

Each user is defined to the database manager by a user identification (userid), a password, and a level of authority. Users first log onto VM with a system identifier (userid) and password. The database manager then uses this information to determine proper user access. A user's level of authority determines his or her freedom in using the database manager. At a typical installation:

- All users are granted CONNECT authority to access the database manager.
- Some users are granted RESOURCE authority to enable them to acquire space for tables. (They consume some of the system's resources.)
- A few users are granted DBA (Database Administrator) authority. They can perform administration tasks, such as adding new users or assigning table space to other users.

Users can grant and revoke to others the privileges of working with data or programs that they control. For example, the creator of a table can authorize another user to work with only certain rows or columns of that table. The creator can also limit the type of work that others may do: for example, usage can be limited to query (SELECT statement) activity.

Data Recovery

The database manager helps to keep data in a consistent state, even in the face of abnormal situations (such as program ABENDs or media failures). A consistent state means that no change is left only partially completed.

For example, a change that requires updating two tables requires two SQL statements. An abnormal ending between the first and the second statement would leave the data in an inconsistent state.

To prevent (or repair) an inconsistent state situation, the database manager uses **Logical Units of Work** (LUWs). A logical unit of work is a group of change statements that must all be completed in order for a desired change to be effected.

If an LUW ends without an implicit or explicit commit instruction, the database manager undoes all changes made by that LUW.

Logging

A log is maintained of all changes completed by each LUW and of control statements that delineate the LUW. For each change, the database manager writes a log record consisting of old and new values of the updated object. The log itself can reside on a dedicated disk. This disk can also be duplexed so that if there is a media failure on one log, database operations can continue using the other.

When initializing the database manager in single-user mode, the operator also can choose whether or not to maintain a log for recovery purposes. A log is always needed for internal SQL/DS operations, even though it might not be used for recovery of user data.

Dynamic backout of a program

If a logical unit of work is not completed for some reason, it can itself issue a ROLLBACK statement. Similarly, the database manager can terminate an in-progress LUW when an authorization violation, SQL/DS quick shutdown, or deadlock occurs. In such an event, the database manager undoes all changes made by uncommitted LUWs to preserve a consistent state. Data is left as though the LUW never started. User or operator involvement is not needed.

Restart recovery

Restart recovery relies on internal log checkpoints. At the time of a checkpoint, the database status information is recorded in the log.

All changes are then forced to be written to the database. This procedure minimizes work at restart time, by eliminating the need to redo any work done before the checkpoint.

If the system fails some time after the checkpoint was taken, the database manager recovers when the system is started again. The log containing the checkpoint state is used to recover the database to a consistent state. The database manager reconstructs a consistent state by:

- Undoing updates made before the checkpoint by LUWs that were uncommitted when the system failed.
- Redoing updates made between the time of the checkpoint and the time of the failure by LUWs that were committed by the time of the failure.

Media recovery

The database manager provides a method of recovering from a system failure that caused a loss of disk-storage integrity. This method entails periodically placing a backup copy of the database or the log on a file (archiving). Archiving can be started explicitly by the SQL/DS operator, or implicitly by itself. The database manager starts archiving when it nears the log overflow point. While archiving is in progress, other work continues. Logging occurs normally, except that checkpointing is not done.

When starting the database manager after a media failure, the operator restores the database from the archive files. The manager then applies to the database changes recorded on the log after the archive file was created.

The database manager uses tape for database archive files. VM facilities can also be used to archive a database to disk.

Features of SQL/DS

Database services utility

The SQL/DS Database Services Utility (DBSU) is an SQL/DS application program that is run using an SQL/DS-supplied EXEC, or invoked from an application program or from a user EXEC. It does the following:

- Loads (INSERTs) data into SQL/DS tables from a sequential (SAM) file, allowing a user to specify periodic commit inserts to the database. Inserts are saved in the database whenever a specified number of records have been processed. This way, if an error occurs during the processing, only database changes made since the last commit point must be re-entered. If a referential structure is defined, INSERT rules (referential constraints) apply when loading data with DBSU. This means that parent (primary key) rows must be loaded before their dependent (foreign key) rows.
- Unloads all rows of a table or view into a specially formatted file or a SAM file.
- Reloads (INSERTs) rows into a table from data that was previously unloaded. The source and destination database machines need not be the same.
- Executes SQL statements against the database in interactive or batch mode.

VSE guest sharing

When VSE/AF is run as a guest operating system under VM, VSE users and programs may access either:

- An SQL/DS database in a VSE partition
- An SQL/DS database running under VM CMS

The latter technique offers several advantages, detailed on the next page.

- A single database may be shared by VM and VSE users.
- The installation, administration, and operating workload are reduced, compared to supporting separate databases for VSE/AF and VM.
- VSE users may be able to exploit SQL/DS functions that are available only with VM, such as access to remote databases.

Use of a VM database by VSE does not restrict VM users of the database in any way. When it is necessary to operate a VSE database and a VM database, DBAs may either:

- Run two VSE guest operating systems under VM. One VSE system can access a VSE database in a partition and then access a VM database.
- Run a single VSE guest system, and specify at IPL time whether VSE should use a VM database.

It is possible to share a VM database with multiple VSE guest systems. In addition, CICS users can use the CRIB transaction to specify the name of the database to be accessed. When multiple CICS partitions are used, each partition can access the same or different VM databases.

Distributed relational databases

A distributed relational database (DRDB), like a local database, also consists of a collection of tables. However, these tables are distributed across multiple computer systems which may be far apart.

Each computer system in a network has its own relational database management system to manage tables in its own environment. Additionally, each RDMS can process a request for locally stored data or data stored on another computer system. In fact, the user or the program that makes the data request need not be aware that the data is in another computer system. Essentially, the same SQL request can be issued whether the data is local or remote. The local database management system determines where the data exists and passes requests across the network to the correct computer system. The relational database management system in the remote computer system services the request and returns the information to the originating system.

An important element of this process is that integrity, recovery, and security of the data are maintained by the participating database management systems.

The Distributed Relational Database Architecture (DRDA) protocol is IBM's architecture for enabling customers to obtain and provide enterprise-wide relational data across diverse locations and operating systems. The SQL/DS DBMS running under VM/SP Release 6 or VM/ESA uses it to support requests between SQL/DS and other SAA database manager such as DATABASE 2 (DB2), Operating System/400 database managers, and Distributed Database Connection Services/2 for Operating System/2.

Improving Performance with VM/ESA 1.1

The **VM Data Spaces Support** (VMDSS) feature can dramatically improve performance of an SQL/DS application server by using the data spaces facility found in VM/ESA 1.1. Data spaces give the server access to vast amounts of fast storage, and use a high performance DASD I/O system that has many advantages over the standard SQL/DS DASD I/O system (IUCV *BLOCKIO).

The feature can also distribute data across multiple dbextents, which helps balance the load on DASD and allows the operating system to read and write data in parallel. Finally, the performance of the DASD I/O system can be monitored for individual storage pools, to control the amount of system resource they use.

Understanding VM data spaces

To understand how data spaces work and why they are an improvement over existing systems, it is important to first understand how VM uses its **paging system** to manage virtual machine storage.

Standard virtual machine storage

Each virtual machine within a VM system has its own **virtual address space** (also called a **primary address space**), which is where programs are loaded and run. Because this space is **virtual**, the operating system does not dedicate a piece of main storage (also called real storage) to each virtual machine. Thus 16MB of main storage does not need to be purchased for each 16MB virtual machine. Instead, VM only uses main storage for those parts of virtual storage required right now, or that are likely to be required in the near future.

These parts of storage are divided into 4096-byte (4K) blocks called **pages**. When a virtual machine needs a page that it has not accessed before, the operating system will retrieve it from its location on DASD, and load it into an empty page frame in main storage. (Before a virtual machine can use a page, the page must be in main storage.)

When the operating system runs out of free pages in main storage, it will move the least recently used ("oldest") page to auxiliary storage to create a free space for a new page. While the virtual machine is still active (logged on), the page will remain in either main or auxiliary storage.

VM/ESA uses two types of auxiliary storage: system paging DASD and optional expanded storage. If expanded storage is available, a page will be moved there first. If expanded storage is full, the least recently used page in expanded storage will be moved to system paging DASD by way of main storage. When a virtual machine needs a page that it has previously used, the operating system will move it back to main storage from expanded storage, or from system paging DASD, if it is not already in main storage.

This paging system accomplishes two things. First, it allows each virtual machine to use much more storage than could be accommodated in main storage alone. Second, it keeps the most recently used pages in the storage devices that are the fastest to access. (The most recently used pages are the ones most likely to be used again in the near future.) Main and expanded storage are much faster than system paging DASD, and while expanded storage can be as fast as main storage, it is effectively slower because the operating system still needs to move the page into main storage before it can use it.

Data spaces storage

In VM/ESA 1.1, a program running in a machine's primary space can dynamically create additional address spaces for data, called **data spaces**. Like a virtual machine's primary address space, a data space is a virtual space with its real pages in main storage, in expanded storage, and on DASD. However, unlike a primary space, a program cannot run in a data space. Also, in VMDSS the VM paging system manages data space pages differently than virtual machine pages. In VMDSS this means that data spaces do not use system paging DASD. (Unmapped internal dbspaces are the exception. See "Unmapped internal dbspaces:" on page 306.)

The next two diagrams illustrate SQL/DS use of virtual machine storage with and without VMDSS.

Standard Virtual Machine Storage

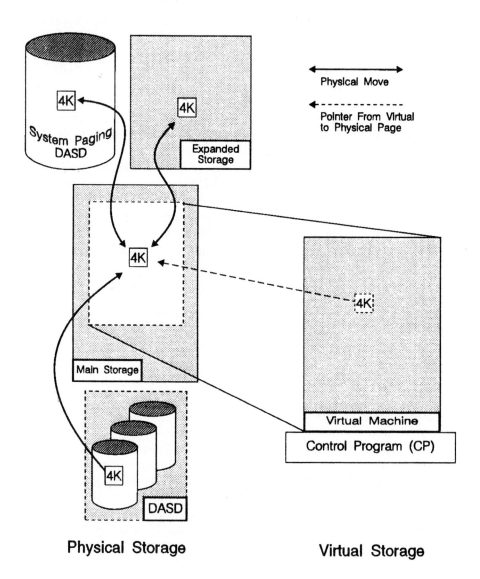

Physical Storage   Virtual Storage

Data Spaces Storage

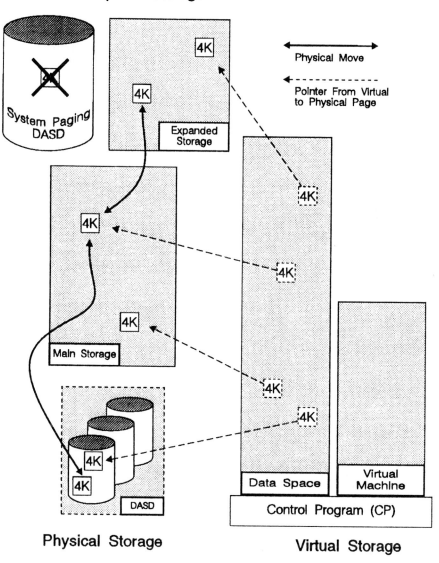

Physical Storage   **Virtual Storage**

With VMDSS, if there is no longer any free space in main or expanded storage, the operating system will simply replace an old unmodified data space page there with a new page. If the old page is needed again, it will be reread from its original DASD source. If the old page was modified while it was in main storage, the operating system ensures that the modified page is written back to its original DASD source before it is overwritten.

This expands a machine's effective storage by providing additional addresses for data, thereby making more room in the primary address space for larger programs.

How VMDSS uses data spaces

Reading pages

Before a page of data can be used by the SQL/DS database manager, it must be located in its data page **buffers**. The buffers are two areas of storage in the primary address space, and are created when the database manager is started. One area is reserved for pages from the SQL/DS directory disk, and the other for pages from SQL/DS storage pools. They are called the **directory buffer pool** and the **local buffer pool**, respectively.

With VMDSS off: When the database manager needs a page, it looks for it in the appropriate buffer pool. If it does not find it there, it uses a VM service called IUCV *BLOCKIO to read the page from DASD into a free space in the pool.

Since the buffer pools are part of a primary address space, the operating system treats them like part of the database manager code. If a buffer page is not referenced frequently, it may be moved out to expanded storage or system paging DASD by the VM paging system. (For more information, see "Asynchronous page fault processing" on page 303.)

The database manager explicitly directs the operating system to move pages to and from DASD with the IUCV *BLOCKIO facility. Once database machine pages are in main storage, they may be moved out to either expanded storage or system paging DASD by the VM paging system.

The diagram on the next page shows page movement with VMDSS off.

Page Movement in the Standard SQL/DS DASD I/O System

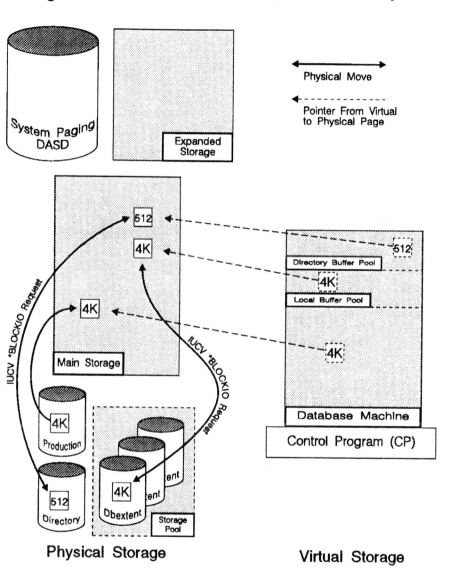

Physical Storage   Virtual Storage

With VMDSS on: If the database manager cannot find a page in its buffer pools, it "retrieves" it from a data space and stores it in a free space in its pool. When this happens, the operating system actually does most of the work. If the page is already in main storage, the database manager can move it directly to the buffer pool. If the page is in expanded storage or in DASD, the operating system moves it into main storage, and then copies it into a buffer.

In a processor that supports **Enhanced Move Page for VM**, pages are moved from expanded storage directly into a buffer.

This system has several advantages over the standard SQL/DS system, which uses the IUCV *BLOCKIO facility. In the latter, each page move must be explicitly requested by the database manager, whereas here paging is done by the VM paging system. This is faster and more efficient for several reasons, including:

- Shorter path length
- Asynchronous page fault processing
- Striping
- Blocking and prefetching
- Dynamic storage size management
- More asynchronous writes

See "Advantages of the VMDSS DASD I/O system" on page 303 for a detailed description of each advantage.

The next figure shows a page being read into main storage from DASD and then into a buffer pool. The page will be in two places in main storage until either the data space page is released or the database manager releases the buffer page (see "Releasing pages" on page 301).

Page Movement with VM Data Spaces Support

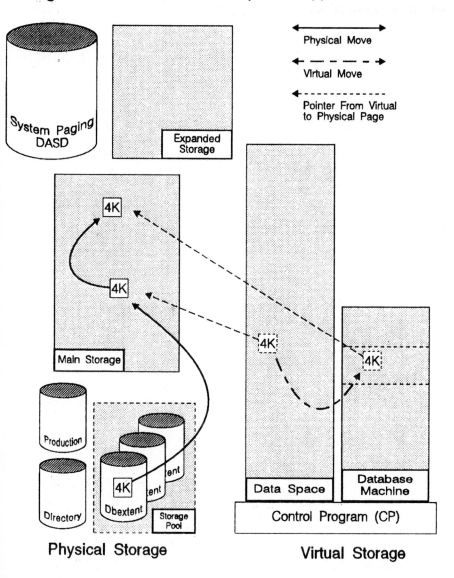

Physical Storage   **Virtual Storage**

Releasing pages

With VMDSS off: When the database manager needs a buffer
for another page, it overwrites the "oldest" unmodified page in the

pool with a new page. This is referred to as **releasing** a page or **stealing** a buffer.

With VMDSS on: When the database manager needs a buffer for another page, it does so in the same way that it would with VMDSS off.

When the operating system needs main or expanded storage for itself or for other virtual machines, it may release data space pages from main storage. Pages may also be released at the request of the database manager. There are several parameters that control when the database manager will start releasing pages and which pages it will choose (see "Dynamic working storage size management" on page 304).

Modifying pages

With VMDSS off: While a page is in the buffer pool, the database manager may modify it. To ensure data integrity, a modified page will not be released until it has been written back to DASD. If the database manager needs a buffer occupied by a modified page, it will first write the page to DASD, then load the buffer with a new page.

With VMDSS on: Instead of writing the modified page to DASD, the database manager moves it to a data space.

Once again, the operating system does most of the work. It takes the page from the database manager, moves it into main or expanded storage, and marks it as being modified.

If the operating system needs a main storage page that is occupied by a modified page, it will move the modified page to expanded storage or to DASD before it uses the main storage page. Similarly, if it needs an expanded storage page that is occupied by a modified page, it will move the modified page to DASD by way of main storage.

Checkpoints

At SQL/DS checkpoints, the database manager writes a summary status record to the SQL/DS log and makes sure that all modified data pages and status information are written to DASD. This ensures that a permanent record of the database is on DASD.

*With **VMDSS** off:*   The database manager writes all the modified pages that are still in the buffer pools to DASD. Until it is finished, it cannot serve any users.

*With **VMDSS** on:*   The database manager moves modified pages that are still in the buffer pools to data spaces. It then directs the operating system to save all modified pages that are still in data spaces (main and expanded storage) to DASD. (Modified pages will only be in main or expanded storage.   Once a page is written to DASD, it is no longer considered **modified**.)   Until the operating system is finished, the database manager is forced to wait: it cannot serve any users until the checkpoint is complete.

Advantages of the VMDSS DASD I/O system

The paging system in VMDSS can be much faster and more efficient than the standard SQL/DS DASD I/O system (IUCV *BLOCKIO).

The data spaces act as a large DASD cache, keeping the most frequently used data in the fastest storage. While this is similar to using a large pool of SQL/DS buffers or DASD caching, there are significant advantages to using VMDSS over these two methods.

Shorter path length

There is a series of internal processes between when the database manager requests a page from DASD and when the operating system transfers it to main storage. This series is shorter with Data Spaces Support than with the standard DASD I/O system.

Asynchronous page fault processing

Since the operating system treats buffers like part of the database manager code, it may page them out to CP paging DASD if it needs main storage. Whenever the database manager needs a piece of code (or a buffer) that has been moved to paging DASD, it and all its users must wait for that page to return from DASD.

With VMDSS, a smaller pool of local buffers can be used, decreasing the chance of a buffer being paged out. If a page fault occurs in a data space (the operating system cannot find the page in main or expanded storage), the database manager can proceed with other users and return to the original user when the fault has been resolved.

Striping

The VMDSS feature will attempt to evenly distribute, or **stripe**, data across all the dbextents in a storage pool.

With striping switched off: The database manager allocates pages in a storage pool in sequence, usually allocating all the pages in one dbextent before using the next.

With striping switched on: The database manager allocates 16 pages in sequence on each dbextent in the storage pool. The operating system can then read and write the pages to and from DASD in parallel. This may significantly improve DASD performance, depending on how the DASD, their controllers, and their channels, are configured. The optimal configuration would include several dbextents in the storage pool, each on a separate channel, controller, and physical storage device.

Blocking and prefetching

When VMDSS is used, the operating system tracks the way the database manager accesses pages. It records which pages are used together (in a **block**), and the order in which they are used. Then, when the database manager requests a page from a data space, if it is on DASD, CP will start retrieving (**prefetching**) other pages in the same block in the order previously followed. Since DASD I/O can proceed in parallel (due to striping), this effectively places pages in main storage before the database manager needs them.

In some cases, the database manager will pass information to the operating system about how it expects to use pages. The operating system uses this information to modify its own reference pattern and thereby further improve prefetching.

Dynamic working storage size management

The VMDSS feature provides three new parameters to manage how the database manager uses main and expanded storage. They can be specified at startup, or changed dynamically while the database manager is running.

Target Working Storage Size: This parameter controls how much main and expanded storage a database machine uses. While this target may be exceeded, the database manager will try to keep storage use at or below it if possible. (Of course, the target may never be reached if the operating system is heavily loaded.)

Working Storage Residence Priority: Each storage pool has its own working storage residence priority, which can be used to favor pages from some storage pools over others. When the database manager copies a page from a data space into its buffers, it checks the residence priority of the pool where the page is located. While the database manager keeps the buffer pool page, it either keeps or immediately releases the data space page, depending on:

*   Its priority
*   Whether the current working storage size is above or below the target
*   Whether the page is an index or a data page.

This gives the option of improving the performance of critical storage pools, even when the amount of main and expanded storage is limited.

Save Interval: To make checkpoint processing faster, this parameter can limit the number of pages modified by the database manager in main and expanded storage. At a checkpoint, the database manager makes sure that all the modified pages in main and expanded storage are written to DASD. If there are many modified pages, it can take a long time to complete the checkpoint, and until it is complete the database manager cannot serve any users.

When the number of modified pages in a data space exceeds the save interval parameter, the database manager directs the operating system to save all modified pages in that data space to DASD. Unlike the save that occurs during checkpoint, the database manager can continue to service users while this is being done.

Also, VMDSS does not just use expanded storage: unlike minidisk caching, it can use main storage as well. The operating system will use main storage whenever possible, moving the least recently used pages to expanded storage.

More asynchronous writes

With VMDSS, the database manager can write modified pages back to DASD (see "Modifying pages" on page 302) *more* asynchronously than without it.

With VMDSS off: If the database manager needs a buffer occupied by a modified page, it first writes the page to DASD, then loads the buffer with a new page.

When it does this, it puts the current user (also called an **agent**) into an I/O wait state until the write is complete. Since the database manager continues to service other agents that are not in wait states, this process is asynchronous **between agents**.

With VMDSS on: When the database manager writes a modified page to a data space, the current agent is not put into a wait state. The operating system ensures that the page is eventually written to DASD (before the next checkpoint) without stopping the current agent. This process is asynchronous **within an agent**, and is therefore more asynchronous than without VMDSS.

Turning VMDSS on and off

Individual SQL/DS storage pools and the SQL/DS directory can be used either with or without VMDSS. While internal dbspaces can be used either with or without Data Spaces Support, an additional choice is possible. Internal dbspaces may be either mapped or unmapped. (Internal dbspaces are areas of working storage dynamically created by the database manager for operations such as sorting or creating indexes.)

Mapped internal dbspaces: Since internal dbspaces are assigned to a specific storage pool, Data Spaces Support can be turned either on and off for them by turning support on and off for that pool. This type of VMDSS is similar to the support for any other storage pool. Since the system assigns, or **maps** each data space page to a physical page in an SQL/DS dbextent (contained in a storage pool), it is referred to as **mapped** support.

Unmapped internal dbspaces: The VMDSS feature also supports **unmapped** internal dbspaces. Instead of mapping pages onto SQL/DS dbextents, VM/ESA manages them as normal virtual storage paged to VM system paging DASD. The internal dbspaces are still assigned to a storage pool, but they do not use any DASD in that pool.

The basic advantage of unmapped internal dbspaces over mapped is that the database manager never writes unmapped pages to DASD. This reduces the overall DASD I/O, without affecting the integrity of the system. (A record of internal dbspaces is not required to recover a database.)

Performance counters

Several counters are available in the VMDSS feature to monitor the performance of the SQL/DS DASD I/O systems. Each storage pool has its own set of four counters. There is also a set of four counters for unmapped internal dbspaces and a set for the SQL/DS directory. These counters are different depending on whether or not a particular component is using data spaces. (Unmapped internal dbspaces always use them.)

These new counters provide insight into the effectiveness of local database buffer pools, VM data space usage for each component, as well as the load being placed on various VM subsystems as a result of the database.

VSE guest sharing

Although the VMDSS feature does not support application servers running in VSE, VSE users can access a VMDSS database in VM/ESA through guest sharing. The database manager runs in one virtual machine, while the VSE users run under a VSE guest system in another virtual machine. Since the VMDSS feature affects only the database manager, VSE guest sharing users will benefit from the same performance improvements as VM users.

Summary

The SQL/DS product is a general-purpose relational database system that can be used by laypersons and application programmers alike, on both local and distributed databases. Its table-based structure makes conceptual understanding of the data organization easy, while its simple English-like commands (for example, SELECT, UPDATE, DELETE) enable even inexperienced users to learn how to issue queries and other operations quickly and easily. Among the features provided are utilities that help to ensure minimal downtime and maximum data security and integrity.

Bibliography

1. *SQL/DS Application Programming for IBM VM Systems*, SH09-8086

2. *SQL/DS Database Administration for IBM VM Systems*, GH09-8083

3. *SQL/DS Database Services Utility for IBM VM Systems*, SH09-8088

4. *SQL/DS General Information for IBM VM Systems*, GH09-8074

5. *SQL/DS Interactive SQL Guide and Reference for IBM VM Systems*, SH09-8085

6. *SQL/DS Operation for IBM VM Systems*, SH09-8080

7. *SQL/DS SQL Reference for IBM VM Systems and VSE*, SH09-8087

8. *SQL/DS System Administration for IBM VM Systems*, GH09-8084

9. *SQL/DS VM Data Spaces Support for VM/ESA*, SH09-8107

11

Exploiting OfficeVision/VM

By Liston Tatum

Introduction

OfficeVision, IBM's Systems Application Architecture office automation package, provides three distinct services: **electronic mail**,
appointment calendar, and **electronic document** processing
functions. Less obviously, it provides a centrally administered
storage and distribution mechanism, which can be accessed from
any point within the organization. Finally, it can be used to provide
integrated, menu-driven access to these functions and other applications, in lieu of the CMS command line interface. It is often set up
to start automatically when users first log on, giving rise to the
widely held misapprehension that OfficeVision **is** VM/CMS.

   Started as a joint development effort between IBM and AMOCO,
OfficeVision was first introduced as the Professional Office System
(PROFS) PRPQ (Programing Request for Price Quotation), a class of
software product often provided with little or no support and eligible
for withdrawal at any time. As it gained market acceptance, IBM
formalized the support and development organization, designating
PROFS a Program Offering (a somewhat more formally supported

product class), and finally making it available as a Program Product in June 1982. In May 1989, PROFS was renamed OfficeVision/VM, mostly to herald IBM's intention to make it and their MVS CICS-based office system, DISOSS (now known as OfficeVision/MVS) look the same to end-users. Various features have been added over the years, and other improvements have been made, but change has been evolutionary; OfficeVision/VM is not the replacement the new name might suggest.

Electronic mail is the feature most frequently mentioned in the context of office automation. Electronic notes facilitate communication within an organization, typically reducing the time required to make routine decisions from more than a week to less than an hour. Like memoranda, electronic correspondence tends to be concise; the high-speed distribution mechanism makes it possible to hold asynchronous conversations with as many participants as appropriate. In addition, the inherent convenience encourages information exchange outside the normal reporting structure, often resulting in a certain amount of corporate culture shock when the system first enjoys widespread distribution.

OfficeVision provides a central **electronic calendar** feature which makes it possible to keep appointment schedules on the system so that they may be cross-referenced for meeting arrangements. The system can check schedules of all intended participants, as well as conference room schedules, and return a list of available time periods. The person requesting the meeting selects the best time from among the alternatives, and a note is sent automatically to the list of participants, who can add it to their calendar with a single action. No organizational directive is required to elicit cooperation; typically, users need to be invited to a meeting only once on a planned day off to see the value of keeping calendars up-to-date! Also, like electronic notes, the accessibility provided by OfficeVision facilitates meetings that otherwise might not have occurred.

The third major service provided by OfficeVision is **centralized document management**. For organizations that require it, Office-Vision will maintain a single copy of a document, serializing updates, while maintaining previous versions. Read and update access can be restricted to specific individuals, while changes and approvals are routed automatically. The document can be stored, ultimately in an unmodifiable form, so that if subsequent changes are required a copy must be made of the existing finalized version, which remains on file. Keywords can be associated with the document to facilitate subsequent retrieval, but a certain amount of discipline must be exercised because, unlike a manual filing system, it is not possible to view a list of all keywords in use.

Document processing provides access to mainframe text editors like VM's XEDIT or DisplayWrite/370, and page formatting facilities provided by markup languages such as IBM's Document Composition Facility. "Fill-in-the-blank" forms can be created to duplicate paper forms currently in use in an organization, and be associated with routing slips to automate existing approvals processing (of purchase orders, for example). Unfortunately, the amount of effort customers must invest in learning to use this aspect of the system is considerable, in contrast to electronic note and calendaring functions, and it is not unusual for installations to remove document processing from the main menu.

Architecture

OfficeVision is implemented as a collection of four service virtual machines (SVMs) which are started at system initialization and run disconnected, that is, not directly attached to a terminal. These virtual machines provide independently dispatchable address spaces, or tasks, to the VM scheduler. The first three characters of the SVM names are chosen by the site but must be consistent; following is a brief description, using **OVM** as the SVM name prefix, of the role of each of the SVMs:

OVMDBM   Is the database manager; it maintains the user attribute data set (the **UAD**), a registry of those authorized to use the office system. The active copy of this file is held in memory, and may be updated interactively without affecting the availability of the system. The database manager also maintains a collection of minidisks for document storage. It assigns a unique chronological number (a **CRON** number) to each document, distributes pointers to the active copy, and handles the retention of previous versions.

OVMCAL   Is the calendar virtual machine; it maintains the calendar database. Like the database manager, calendars are kept on a collection of minidisks owned by OVMCAL. The centralized calendar database facilitates the search for commonly available unscheduled times, as mentioned previously.

OVMMAIL Is the mail carrier; it handles transfer of electronic notes from sender virtual machines to appropriate mailbox managers, and places tickler files in recipients' virtual readers, to inform users of the existence of unopened mail.

OVMMBX Is the mailbox manager (there can be more than one of these); it keeps unopened mail, as well as the inbaskets of users who have delegated mail authority to others, on disk. When users open their mail, unopened mail (or their entire inbaskets) are fetched from disk, decompressed, and sent to their virtual machines with a memory-to-memory transfer, using VM's Inter-User Communication Vehicle (IUCV).

Executable code required by office system users is owned by a fifth virtual machine, the **system administrator** userid, who also owns minidisks used for maintenance. Over 1.5 megabytes of code is located in a shareable virtual memory area called a **Discontiguous Saved Segment** (DCSS), which appears to be part of each user's address space (virtual machine). The DCSS is not used by the SVMs.

Installation

The first installation step consists of defining the directory entries of the four SVMs and the office system administrator's virtual machine. The documentation contains suggested configurations. Also, the DCSS must be defined, although this can be done after the code is moved to disk and other configuration decisions have been made (this is discussed in more detail later). Again, there is sample code in the installation documentation. A privileged VM/ESA ESA feature user can define the DCSS dynamically using the CP DEFSEG command. For VM/ESA 370 feature, the VM system maintenance userid can add the DCSS definition using the system name table (SNT) override file and the OVERRIDE command.

Once the OfficeVision system administrator has been defined (e.g., SYSADMIN), installation consists of logging on to this userid, attaching the tape, and answering a series of configuration questions posed by the install EXEC. It may be a good idea to work through these questions in the manual in advance; there is no restart mechanism. However, the DCSS build and save operation can be performed later, and should be postponed until installation is otherwise complete and verified.

After the code has been installed, apply the current level of service; OfficeVision will not run correctly without it. The code on the product tape is not changed between releases so as to provide a common base at all customer sites. When problems are discovered, object code replacements are added to a cumulative maintenance tape, which must be incorporated into the customer's running version. This is accomplished using a library search sequence (SYSADMIN's base, delta, zap, merge, and run minidisks) which, among other things, makes it possible to remove maintenance that has proven to be defective. Use the EXEC on the service tape to move the code to disk in the same fashion as the installation. Once this code is available, the OfficeVision initialization module and the DCSS should be generated using the EPSDCSSL EXEC provided for the purpose.

A LINK statement must be added to user virtual machines' directory entries to provide access to the minidisk containing the Office-Vision user code (the installation default is SYSADMIN's 399). Place this statement in a directory profile entry along with links to other shared code, such as the CMS system residence minidisk, and include it in the user virtual machine's directory entry using an INCLUDE *profilename* statement. Using directory profiles significantly reduces overhead associated with updating the online copy of the system directory, and facilitates global changes required to make new program products available.

Finally, log the SVMs on, starting with OVMDBM, and disconnect them. Add AUTOLOG statements for the SVMs to AUTOLOG1's PROFILE EXEC, so the system will resume operation automatically whenever VM is re-IPLed. Log on to the database manager (OVMDBM), define users in the user authorization directory with the UAD INPUT command, then refresh the in-memory copy with the UADLOAD command (note that unlike UAD INPUT, UAD LIST, etc., UADLOAD is a single word).

PROFS to OfficeVision Migration

Migration to OfficeVision is straightforward; keep in mind that OfficeVision is really PROFS Version 3. The only substantive change is the way OfficeVision handles inbaskets, including addition of the mailbox manager. The documentation contains several migration scenarios, ranging from simply dropping the code on top of the existing PROFS system to creating a parallel set of virtual machines. A parallel system minimizes the time the office system must be offline for the transition, and provides the fastest backout in the unlikely event that one proves necessary. A publication that covers various approaches to reverse migration is available from an IBM representative.

Release 1.0 (or service level 100) was shipped so that all inbaskets were returned to the mailbox manager when they were closed, but the impact on performance was so great the code was changed. With release 1.1 (or service level 101) the inbasket is returned only in cases where its owner has delegated processing authority to someone else. They are, however, stored in a new format; existing inbaskets get converted when they are first opened, which imposes a significant one-time load on the system. Although from the user's perspective the system is essentially unchanged, the inbasket migration process is sufficiently I/O- and CPU-intensive that delays may occur on the first day. This may be avoided by performing a batch migration, using the PROFS INBASKET QIB command, either from an entry in the CMS system profile (SYSPROF EXEC) or equivalent. Add code to check whether the virtual machine is disconnected; if so, stack a pair of null lines to accept the default responses to questions posed by the INBASKET command, invoke the command, then log the user off:

```
/* addition to facilitate a batch OV migration */
   'TERMTYPE'
   if rc = 20 then do       /* If disconnected */
      push ''               /* Accept default responses */
      push ''
      'PROFS INBASKET QIB'  /* Causes migration */
      'CP LOGOFF'
   end
```

Fetch the user entries from the system directory, using XEDIT or the tools provided by a directory management product such as DIRMAINT or VMSECURE. Create an EXEC that AUTOLOGs small groups of OfficeVision user virtual machines, posting a VM console read between each group to allow monitoring progress and retain control of the process.

Configuration Suggestions

Installing OfficeVision usually implies extending service to a large community of individuals who are not expected to be "computer literate". Consider placing a SETUP EXEC on a minidisk created for the purpose, and add a LINK in user virtual machine directory profiles as virtual address 192. CMS will automatically access this address as a D-disk. Include the CMS minidisk accesses necessary to run OfficeVision (and others appropriate to the installation) in the SETUP EXEC, and call it from the users' PROFILE EXECs. By keeping a single copy of this code, it is possible to make changes available to the entire user community without affecting the SVMs. The system profile (SYSPROF EXEC) on the CMS system residence minidisk (virtual 190) can also be used to this end, and has the benefit of being executed by default, but also affects every userid. SVMs must be specifically exempted from executing the setup code, perhaps by running an alternate CMS, and modifications must be carried forward to new releases of VM. See Chapter 7, *Exploiting Service Machines,* on page 177 for specific svm tips.

OfficeVision can be invoked automatically by the SYSPROF or the default user PROFILE EXEC, but stack the line to invoke PROFS or OV rather than invoking it directly. This allows the calling EXEC to exit; although it is legal to call OfficeVision from an EXEC, doing so may cause conflicts with other products.

The first time users process their NAMES files, OfficeVision creates a copy of the sample OFS OFSMCNTL (from SYSADMIN's 399 minidisk); the same is true when they process their alternate nickname file (OFS2 OFSMCNTL). OfficeVision address resolution searches OFS OFSMCNTL first, then follows a chain of NEWFILE statements found at the end of each file. In order to maintain a central copy of system-wide information, add a NEWFILE statement to SYSADMIN's sample OFS2 OFSMCNTL file, and move the LOCAL and other control statements to the file, which becomes third in the sequence. This prevents OfficeVision from creating private copies of global parameters which may need to be changed.

OfficeVision displays a full-screen IBM logo with copyright information the first time it is invoked after a user logs on, requiring the user to press the ENTER key to continue. This annoyance can be suppressed by adding an EXIT statement to the beginning of EPRWDCPR EXEC, causing it to exit quietly whenever called. Copyright information remains on the main menu. Finally, the way to avoid working after hours to update any of the shared files that define the office system configuration (nickname lists, the printer definition file, etc.) is to edit the file, but rename the existing copy from the XEDIT command line with the CMS RENAME command before committing (FILEing) the changes. This preserves the existing data on disk in the location where those who have already accessed the shared minidisk expect to find it, while creating a new copy that will be available the next time the user accesses the disk. The old copy can be erased after a reasonable interval, or the next time the file needs updating.

Performance: Operating System Configuration

With the exception of certain operations, like SENDMAIL address resolution, OfficeVision/VM can deliver consistent subsecond response time to a very large number of concurrently logged-on users. Despite this fact, performance is the complaint voiced most frequently, perhaps in part due to the fact that the system's reaction to keyboard input suffers in comparison to personal computers. Be careful not to underestimate the impact of performance on customer satisfaction, and the relative importance of this issue to the organization. OfficeVision is likely to be management's primary (or only) point of contact with the online services offered by the information systems division.

As is typical for interactive applications, OfficeVision is a memory-intensive system, so provision of adequate real memory is the most important single factor affecting performance. VM/ESA 1.0 is capable of addressing memory above the 16MB line, while release 1.1 adds the ability to access VM Data Spaces, which, in combination with VM's Shared File System, can be used to create an essentially memory-resident file system for OfficeVision user code normally located on SYSADMIN's 399 disk. Note that OfficeVision does not currently support allocation of user A-disks in the CMS Shared File System.

In general, telecommunications SVMs should be given the best service, followed by multi-user data servers. The OfficeVision SVMs operate on behalf of the user community as a whole, and should be serviced accordingly; they tend to require only small amounts of processor resources between I/Os, but need to be dispatched frequently.

Experience indicates that 4MB is a good minimum virtual machine size for user virtual machines, which is significantly more than previous versions required. OfficeVision can have memory allocation problems with large amounts of unopened mail; it may be worth defining users with a large volume of correspondence at 6 MB. Note that the DCSS must not overlap the address range of the user virtual machines (the SVMs do not use it).

Performance: OfficeVision Configuration

The mailbox manager represents a departure from previous PROFS versions that kept notes in system SPOOL space. (SPOOL space is where reports are queued for printing, among other things.) This change enhanced the security and reliability of OfficeVision and the VM system itself, because SPOOL space is volatile and tended to fill with unopened mail. Notes from external systems are still kept in SPOOL (so it must be carefully backed up with the CP SPTAPE command or a third-party product), but this tends to be only a fraction of the previous volume.

On very active systems some performance improvement may be obtained through use of multiple mailbox managers. The general rule is one mailbox manager per 200 concurrently logged-on users. Clients are assigned to specific mailbox managers; if possible, those who communicate with each other often should be assigned to the same mailbox manager, to minimize the transfer of notes between them. Standard OfficeVision compresses mail before it is written to disk, but this can be stopped by changing the INBKPACK flag in the OFSNUCON macro and reassembling the nucleus, in the unlikely event that processor resources are more constrained than I/O throughput.

Document and calendar database managers keep user information on a collection of minidisks, which should be located on separate (real) drives. Schedules are written to the calendar minidisks based on a hashing algorithm which, as delivered, is keyed to the first letter of the userid and assumes an English language name distribution. Modify this to suit the installation by editing EPSSMODE ASSEMBLE (and reassemble the module), then monitor calendar disk space utilization and adjust the algorithm to balance the load. The document database manager has access control mechanisms called **document subdatabases**, which are mapped to separate minidisks.

Organizations that use the document facility must monitor space availability in the document databases, which is done from the database manager's (OVMDBM) console.

The OfficeVision main menu includes a time-of-day clock, which is updated every minute, causing roughly 60 pages to be transferred into main memory for each inactive user. If there are many concurrently logged-on users, a significant reduction in system paging load can be achieved by changing this interval in the OFSNUCON macro and reassembling the OfficeVision nucleus. Setting it to 0 (legal but undocumented) stops automatic refresh. Note that the clock is also updated whenever the main menu is redisplayed, either by returning to it from another function or by pressing the enter key.

Much of OfficeVision is written in REXX; OfficeVision 1.1 is compatible with the REXX compiler. Modest improvements in responsiveness can be obtained by compiling frequently used EXECs (e.g., OPENMAIL), although this is less effective than might be expected: the REXX interpreter is already very efficient. Either way, these EXECs can be loaded (and shared) in an installation DCSS.

Distributed Access

Either TCP/IP or VTAM (or both) can be used to provide distributed access to the system, depending on environment. IBM 3270 terminals or terminal emulators are generally required, which means the user end of TCP/IP TELNET connections must support TN3270 (as IBM's does). The OfficeVision main menu takes full advantage of 3270 data stream commands, which makes it the acid test of terminal emulation. If this causes problems that cannot be resolved, the OFFICE2 menu set (once known as PASF, the PROFS Application Support Facility) can be used, but this sacrifices the interrupt-driven mail waiting indicator.

Multi-session access is useful for those needing to work with other mainframe systems such as CICS or TSO. These sessions may be backed by memory in communications controllers, or provided by the terminal emulator software in network attached personal computers, or driven by a VTAM session manager (e.g., IBM's Netview/Access). This makes it possible to maintain a background connection to the office system so that incoming mail can be answered promptly.

Note that activity on OS/2 or Windows-based PCs may cause the terminal emulator to be paged out of memory, resulting in a sluggish start when the session is brought to the foreground. Graphic emulators in general are noticeably less responsive than their character-oriented counterparts (e.g., the PC/DOS Version of IBM's Personal Communications/3270), but do make it possible to mail business graphics.

IBM's new Microsoft Windows-based OfficeVision interface, Current, provides an alternate access mechanism. Current establishes a connection to the mainframe and transfers mail, calendars, and documents to the PC for local processing, replacing them at the end of the session. It is a High-Level Language Application Programming Interface (HLLAPI) application, so it supports token ring or Ethernet attachments, or coax with a 3270 emulation card. It is especially useful when access to the system is via modem and dial-up line. OS/2 Office was IBM's OS/2-based token ring connection, but it has been stabilized (with no new enhancements planned) in favor of alliances with Lotus Notes and cc:Mail.

Inter-system Connectivity

The usefulness of a communication system is based in part on the number of people that can be reached with it, which suggests connecting systems together. The software for doing this depends on the communications protocols supported by the various machines, and that used in existing networks. Either TCP/IP or VTAM can be used; however, in part because IBM's support for TCP/IP is relatively recent, a more complete integration of OfficeVision systems is possible in a VTAM environment. Local calendars, for example, can be cross-referenced with those on another VTAM-connected node using VM's Transparent Services Access Facility (TSAF).

The Remote SPOOLing and Communications Subsystem (RSCS) is the transport mechanism when VTAM is used to interconnect Office-Vision systems. It is also required to support OS/2 Office. With the required VTAM communications links in place, RSCS makes it possible to access IBM's IBMMAIL service, which can be used to exchange correspondence with IBM and other participating organizations (for a small fee). It will also drive network printers, including those attached to PCs (using PC/3270 for example), which allows users to print notes or documents at their workstations. RSCS is the most appropriate mechanism for connecting systems in an IBM environment.

Equally interesting for different reasons, TCP/IP's Simple Mail Transfer Protocol (SMTP) provides mail transfer between dissimilar systems. With the addition of the PROFS/Extended Mail program offering, and an Ethernet or token ring connection, OfficeVision can exchange mail with Unix, VAX VMS and other non-IBM systems. SMTP makes it possible to access the Defense Advanced Research Projects Administration (DARPA) Internet, which is widely supported by educational, research, and commercial organizations. The Internet is connected to similar networks in most other countries, and so provides world-wide connectivity. Many universities and nonprofit research institutions maintain SVMs for special interest lists; these SVMs distribute mail directed to the list to all members. This provides a diverse group of global electronic forums. Also, most private electronic mail networks, including IBM, maintain bridges to the Internet. It is becoming increasingly common for an installation to run both protocols.

Finally, IBM Business Partners (e.g., Soft-Switch) and other companies market protocol conversion software which allow Office-Vision to interconnect with most other electronic mail systems. Similarly, most competing systems offer OfficeVision bridges, including local area network-based workgroup systems such as WordPerfect Office. A recent PC Week article listed more than two dozen personal computer-based mail systems; all but two featured connections to OfficeVision. While these are primarily intended for notes, some provide document exchange using IBM's Revisable Format Text Document Content Architecture.

Co-requisite Products

In addition to the communications products mentioned previously, several OfficeVision features are implemented using other IBM program products. The least obvious of these is the Interactive System Productivity Facility (ISPF). OfficeVision's nickname and distribution list processing screens (to avoid confusion, IBM calls them panels) are handled by ISPF. Although these lists can be manipulated with VM's XEDIT, uninitiated users find the Office-Vision feature much easier to use. ISPF is also required to support DOS Office Direct Connect.

OfficeVision uses other IBM program products to provide an integrated set of office automation functions. Graphics can be included in notes and documents with the assistance of the Graphical Data

Display Manager (GDDM). Support for Advanced Function printers (AFP) also requires GDDM. The Document Composition Facility/SCRIPT is a markup language which can be used in conjunction with OfficeVision document processing to produce camera ready copy. DisplayWrite/370 (DW/370) enhances text editing facilities available for document processing. DW/370 is required if it is necessary to exchange documents with other systems using IBM's Revisable Format Text/Document Content Architecture (RFT/DCA), such as OfficeVision/MVS.

Finally, there are high-level language runtime libraries which are necessary to support certain features. OfficeVision Version 1 Release 2 provides a new inbasket processing facility called OVMAIL (see the list of new features below), which requires access to the REXX compiler's runtime library. Although the older inbasket function is still supported, OVMAIL answers numerous complaints about the way incoming mail is handled. In addition, IBM's C/370 runtime library is required to support DW/370, as well as TCP/IP; TCP/IP is required to correspond via the Internet.

Enhancements

By far the most valuable addition to a VM/CMS system running OfficeVision available from IBM is a collection of REXX EXECs written by Charles Naul. Previously available as **CUA Application Coding Techniques in VM REXX**, the product is generally known as **Terrific New Tools** (TNT), and replaces a collection called **PUPPIES**.

In February 1992, a greatly enhanced version of TNT was announced, called the **CUA 2001 Tool Kit**. This product is a joint offering by the IBM Customer Education and VM Office Technical Support groups.

CUA 2001 is intended, in part, to provide a means of rapidly implementing CUA applications on non-programmable terminals, either as prototypes of systems planned for other software platforms or as production applications in themselves. It offers tutorials on writing REXX code, and to a lesser extent, OfficeVision interfaces, including REXX code to display a selectable list of note logs, an address book/telephone directory, a centrally managed bulletin board, and examples of intelligent forms.

The CUA 2001 Tool Kit is much more extensive than the previous version, providing support for action bars, pull downs, pop-ups, contextual help, selectable fields, data entry with prompting; in short, a collection of routines that implement all the features of the SAA CUA environment, and instructions in their use.

However, while TNT was a bargain at $75; CUA 2001 is considerably more expensive, costing $3,000, or $4,500 with a one-day training class via telephone conference call.

Unfortunately, beginners may find the EXECs somewhat difficult to follow; they are functionally rich, and could be improved somewhat by a more rigorous application of structured programming techniques.

IBM's VM Office Systems group has begun marketing enhancements to OfficeVision built on the CUA 2001 "Core Services" (the tool kit is not needed). One of these enhancements, the AWAY facility, allows users to leave a message, and optionally defer to another user, in the event that they would be unable to answer their mail. Attempts to send notes to users who are AWAY display the message left by the recipient; the sender can then send the note anyway, save it, or send it to someone else. This solves the problem of a "hot" item languishing unopened in somebody's inbasket. The package, including the CUA 2001 Core Services, costs $4,000.

One very serious problem with electronic mail results from the relatively few characters used to specify an address. This makes it difficult to associate them with the people they refer to, while at the same time greatly increasing the possibility that an error will produce a valid match. The OfficeVision nickname facility mitigates this problem somewhat (as a security recommendation, do not provide a company-wide nickname file), although they too are limited to eight characters. The solution is an online mechanism to translate a person's full name, department, or other identifying information directly into an address. The TNT tool kit's address book application does this by making it possible to identify addressees from a selection list, with search capabilities. As another alternative, IBM's **Callup** (a Program Product as of March 1992) provides a similar function, with fuzzy matching capabilities, and extensive intersite synchronization facilities. Callup allows individuals to update their own directory entries, and works with Current (see new features list below). Both systems allow addresses to be copied directly into the note.

For sites requiring access to electronic mail systems based on other protocols, such as the Internet, the PROFS/Extended mail program offering is appropriate. Written in REXX, this package sends mail in a simple text format suitable for Internet SMTP transfer, or X.400. It provides code to obtain addresses from the traditional VM/CMS USERID NAMES file, which is functionally equivalent to OfficeVision nicknames, but accommodates long format addresses. It also provides a screen which makes it possible to enter the long Internet-style address directly. Sadly, the code does not integrate well with OfficeVision, which transfers control to extended mail address resolution when a note is sent to an invalid address. Provision for various addressing formats adds significant overhead to both SENDMAIL and INBASKET functions. Also, users must be shown how to use the CMS NAMES command, or XEDIT, to add Internet addresses to their *userid* NAMES files.

Finally, access through OS/2-based 3270 terminal emulation can be enhanced by IBM's CM MOUSE Support/2, which provides mouse selectable fields on the 3270 screen. Instead of using PF keys, the mouse pointer is positioned over the desired option, which is activated by the standard double click. CM MOUSE helps to integrate the 3270 screen image into the desktop as though it was an OS/2 application running locally, although with significantly different performance characteristics.

Client Support

The simplicity of the menu-driven user interface makes it possible to introduce the system into some environments by simply bringing it online. IBM's introductory manual, *Jump Start on OfficeVision*, is useful in this respect. The tutorial includes instructions on how to log on, so learning to use the system can be self directed. Depending on the level of comfort the user community feels with computers, Helpdesk support may be sufficient, or an organization may schedule small group demonstrations.

Integration of various functions available to users helps give a monolithic feel to the installation. As mentioned previously, user accounts can be set up to start OfficeVision from their PROFILES. Local applications can be included in the main menu by editing OFS $SYSPROF and adding the executable program name followed by a brief description. This integration can replace the CMS command interface for users who access a limited number of functions, and individualized versions of the main menu may be provided if appropriate (these are named OFS $PROFILE and maintained on the users' 191 minidisks).

Installations with connections to external mail systems should provide instructions on the use of the Extended Mail address resolution screen; it is not intuitive. The CMS NAMES command is also useful, particularly to those unfamiliar with XEDIT. It is a good idea to provide a printed sample showing how to fill in the various fields, because it is not obvious how they are used.

New Features of OfficeVision

The most significant usability enhancement that was introduced when PROFS was renamed OfficeVision is the user's ability to delegate authority to process mail. An obvious concession to the way executive correspondence is often handled, this also makes it easier to continue business functions in someone's absence. Mail classification was introduced with this feature, so that correspondence may be designated as addressee-only, personal, unclassified, and so on. Access can be granted to unclassified mail, for example, while withheld on correspondence marked personal or addressee-only. This facility includes the ability to answer mail on the addressee's behalf. Note that PROFS/Extended mail changes OfficeVision's default of unclassified to addressee-only; this can be prevented by adding IN-BASKET-CLASSIFICATION: as the last line of PROFS/Extended's PSPMAIL USERPROF file.

A criticism of OfficeVision has been lack of availability of text editing functions from within notes. Release 2 note processing provides access to XEDIT, so it is now possible to split a line to insert text or join two lines using the XEDIT SPLIT, JOIN, and SPLTJOIN macros. In addition, the improved inbasket processing function OVMAIL makes it possible to perform the same action (delete, for example) on a group of notes at one time. Inbaskets are refreshed when mail is received, which solves the problem of having to leave inbasket processing to gain access to new mail. Also, notes sent locally that have not been opened can be retrieved.

Surprisingly late to support the SAA Common User Access guidelines, release 2 uses PF7 and PF8 to page up and down in notes. Using earlier releases, people accustomed to SAA-compliant software sometimes mailed notes they intended to review. PF1 is now the HELP key, and PF3 is quit. Although the system, or individual users, can use an override file to preserve the old layout, this is probably not a good idea in the long run.

Perhaps the most exciting change to OfficeVision is addition of the personal computer component **Current**. After the somewhat lack-luster market acceptance of OS/2 Office, IBM developed a Microsoft Windows application which enables a high level of integration with the mainframe system. Mail and documents are moved to the PC and processed locally; as long as the mainframe connection is available, users are notified of mail arrival immediately. The Current address book function interacts with Callup to provide transparent access to the organization's directory, while the scheduling system works with the standard OfficeVision calendar. Significantly, Lotus spread sheets, WordPerfect documents, .PIF images, and various other PC-based files can be attached to notes and mailed intact through OfficeVision to other Current users.

Current uses IBM's High-Level Language Application Programming Interface (HLLAPI) to work with the mainframe, which in essence simulates a terminal operator by placing information in the appropriate locations of a virtual 3270 screen, so it can be used anywhere a 3270 session can be obtained. The graphical user interface is provided by Windows calls, which means Current runs on most existing DOS-based PCs and works well using OS/2 version 2 Windows support.

Conclusions

Despite its great value, it is unlikely that the cost of installing a mainframe and communications network can be justified simply to provide electronic mail, except in the very largest companies. More reasonably, the value of an existing network can be enhanced, or a collection of requirements may be met (as with a new installation), allowing hardware and software costs to be distributed over several functions. In cases like these, other requirements such as an MVS CICS-based financial system may argue against selecting OfficeVision/VM. However, recent improvements in packaging, such as the VM/ESA Software Delivery Option, minimize the system programmer support required. The installation of VM, in a logical partition or on a small machine, should be considered to run Office-Vision, if access can be integrated with other networking requirements. In many cases the inherent flexibility of the VM environment is worth the cost. Obviously, the greatest incremental value may be obtained where there are other reasons for running

VM, in which case various software dependencies and most system support requirements will have been satisfied already.

The OfficeVision installation process is relatively straightforward and the system performs well. It is so user-friendly that it can be introduced with only minimal assistance, although the greatest value can be realized by identifying a support group. Provisions have been made for extensive customization, and the product can be well integrated into the organization's information systems environment or even used to package existing systems into an integrated shell. Unfortunately, the benefits of office automation are intangible and somewhat difficult to quantify; however, once the system is operational, users often wonder how they got along without it.

12

MOSAIC—The VM/ESA Imaging Solution

By Dave Hemsath and Dan Hunsinger

The Problem with Paper

Borrowing from the American author, Mark Twain, "rumors of the 'paperless office' have been greatly exaggerated." Paper is the life-blood of enterprises around the world. Office automation systems have increased, rather than decreased, the amount of paper produced—and that paper has to be processed. According to *IMC Journal*:[1]

- 1.3 trillion documents are currently stored by enterprises
- 900 million additional documents are generated each day
- 2.7 billion pieces of paper are put into folders every day

The Association of Information and Image Management (AIIM) states that:

---

[1] International Information Management Congress (IMC) Journal, May–June, 1987

- 95 percent of information in the U.S. is stored on paper
- 4 percent on microfilm
- Only 1 percent stored electronically[2]

There are problems associated with this information:

- Storing it
- Retrieving it
- Routing it
- Sharing it
- And so on

What Is a Document Imaging/Management System?

Imaging system basics

Imaging is converting information on "paper" to computerized digital format using an electronic "camera."

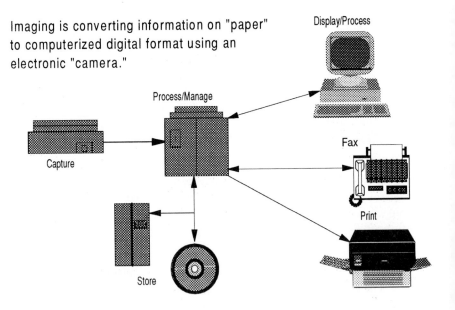

---

[2]   AIIM, 1990

Definition

A document imaging/management system can eliminate or greatly reduce these problems. The major components and operations of such a system are shown in the next diagram. Hardcopy information is captured and brought into the system as bitmaps using scanners or facsimile transmissions. Pages are organized (indexed) for subsequent search, retrieval, and routing (workflow) operations.

Benefits

Many benefits are derived from this system. File storage space is reduced or eliminated when documents are stored on DASD or optical media. Access times for information improves from days or hours to mere seconds. The same information can be shared concurrently by users of the system. Electronic security ensures sensitive information is available only to authorized personnel. The movement of the "virtual paper" from person to person can be automated and integrated with existing applications. An enterprise's procedures are often redesigned to optimize use of new capabilities in the document imaging/management system. The evolution of imaging/managment systems (henceforth called **image**) benefits an enterprise as shown below.

Benefits of Image

Task Savings on labor, space, equipment, supplies for paper handling, overnight express charges, micrographics

Process Improved productivity, processing, work quality, documentation, and control; elimination of callbacks; cost reduction in the office and warehouse for new equipment; asset protection through protection against liability claims and catastrophic losses

Strategic Improved customer service and field agent support; improved ability to promote new products/services and organizational changes; better competitive edge

Performance challenges

Image creates a much heavier demand on system capacity. Digital images are non-coded data. They require much more storage than their coded data equivalent. For example, a standard typewritten page might have 2,000 characters on it. A black and white or **bitonal** scan at 200 scan points per inch in horizontal and vertical directions produces 3,740,000 bits of information. (Bitonal images are the only kind discussed in this chapter; an excellent source of information about other kinds of images and image processing in general is *Practical Digital Image Processing*, by Rhys Lewis, ISBN 0-13-683525-2.) Each bit represents a dark or light spot at the sampling point (at 200 scan points per inch there are 40,000 samples per square inch). Images are usually compressed before storage and then decompressed after retrieval and before viewing, editing, etc. Compression results in about an order of magnitude reduction in storage required to hold the image.

Even though images are much larger than traditional coded data objects, users of image systems still expect performance roughly equivalent to what they experience with other computer applications. This represents a large demand on all aspects of the system: CPU cycles, central storage, secondary storage, networks, and so on. These demands on the system necessitate a system design that distributes functions to system components best suited for each task.

Building on the basics

More functions can be added for additional productivity gains. Some sample functions are:

- Bar code and checkbox recognition for automated indexing of documents or routing of facsimiles.
- OCR to create coded text from scanned images. The output from the OCR operation may be integrated with a text search/retrieval system such as IBM's STAIRS/CMS product.
- Computer Output Micrographics (COM) replacement.

MOSAIC Document Imaging/Management

Science Applications International Corporation (SAIC) developed a document imaging/management solution for VM and VM guest customers. SAIC is an IBM business partner in the United States for this solution, which is named **MOSAIC**. MOSAIC was announced by SAIC in April 1991 and became generally available later that year.

MOSAIC development history

Virtually all document imaging/management systems use a combination of workstations and "hosts" (servers). Workstations provide image capture, processing, display, output, and the like; this is best accomplished by powerful processors and specialized hardware. Hosts act as centralized repositories for electronic documents.

In 1989 and early 1990 SAIC worked in cooperation with IBM Data Systems Division (DSD) to port an existing PC-DOS LAN document imaging solution to a VM server environment.

The effort began with a VM/SP (Virtual Machine/System Product) Release 6 host and SAIC's PC-DOS plus Windows 2 image workstations. SAIC believed that VM was a good target for the existing server. VM's rich development environment, its high SAA content, and ability to work cooperatively with workstations were all pluses.

The major impediment to SAIC's first porting effort was the memory-constrained environment of the image workstation. PC-DOS only provided 640KB of memory. This proved insufficient to accommodate the operating system, network drivers, Windows 2, APPC/PC and the image workstation applications. The PC-DOS LAN system used NetBIOS for communications between the image workstations and the server. NetBIOS was unavailable for the workstation-VM environment. SAIC evaluated using a 3270 (SNA LU Type 2) base for workstation-host communications, but performance was inadequate. APPC (SNA LU Type 6.2) communication provided requisite performance, but imposed too high a DOS memory requirement.

In March 1990, SAIC was briefed on the VM PWSCF Programming RPQ under development at the IBM Endicott VM Development Lab. VM PWSCF provided the SAA CPI for Communications (an evolution of APPC) and fit within the image workstation's available memory. SAIC became a Field Test site for VM PWSCF and its follow-on program product, VM PWSCS.

The relationship between the MOSAIC development team and the VM PWSCx[3] developers has been mutually beneficial. Use of VM PWSCx enabled SAIC to proceed with porting. The Endicott developers got good feedback from "real world" use of their product.

With the memory/communications problem solved, SAIC proceeded with porting the image system's server from PC-DOS to VM. A working prototype was complete three months later in June 1990. The next year was spent restructuring the VM image server to work efficiently in the VM environment. During this year, about two months were spent moving the MOSAIC workstation code to the Windows 3 environment, including testing new VM PWSCS Windows 3 support functions.

MOSAIC functional overview

MOSAIC is a complete document imaging/management solution for VM and VM guest customers. Hardcopy (paper, micrographics, etc.) information is captured electronically and this electronic version of the information is subsequently used in lieu of hardcopy.

MOSAIC provides the standard suite of functions, i.e., capture, storage, retrieval, viewing, printing, and so on.

MOSAIC meets or exceeds the expected average performance for image systems, that is, five seconds or less to retrieve the first image from host DASD (ten seconds or less for a mounted optical platter) to an image workstation, and one second or less to display the next sequential page in a multiple-page document (read-ahead caching at the workstation is under the user's control).

MOSAIC provides an excellent file-folder indexing system. Image objects and associated information can be indexed into container objects such as documents, folders, filing cabinets, etc. by simply clicking on an object's icon and dragging it into another object. More powerful indexing and search capability is available by using MOSAIC's keyword application, which enables multiple keyword fields and data to be associated with image objects. The MOSAIC administrator can dynamically create and/or modify these image

---

[3]   PWSCx is used to represent both VM PWSCS 1.1 on the workstations and VM PWSCF 1.2 on the VM/ESA (Virtual Machine/Enterprise Systems Architecture) Release 1.0 370 feature host. The host functions of VM PWSCF are replaced by ISFC on VM/ESA Release 1.1.

databases without requiring a SYSGEN. Also, for the "power user", all facilities of SQL/DS are available for keyword searches.

MOSAIC currently provides workflow functions as a simple customization of the base electronic mail capabilities. More sophisticated workflow can be implemented by custom code using MOSAIC APIs to access MOSAIC queues.

MOSAIC provides integrated inbound and outbound facsimile. No paper need be handled by a MOSAIC user.

MOSAIC can recognize bar codes and checkboxes on captured hardcopy. This facilitates automating some data entry activities from forms. For example, a large pharmaceutical company uses MOSAIC with bar coded new drug clinical trial reports to automatically provide most of the indexing information, such as drug number.

MOSAIC provides a common set of APIs for both workstation and host CMS environments, making it straightforward to integrate MOSAIC with existing or new custom applications.

Systems application architecture conformance

MOSAIC is an SAA-conforming client/server solution. Specifically, MOSAIC implements the following SAA elements:

- Cooperative structure
- CUA (Common User Access) 1989 Workplace
- VM environment
- CPI-Communications
- CPI-Database (with SQL/DS Version 3)
- CPI-C
- CCS-IOCA[4]

Exploitation of VM/ESA data spaces

MOSAIC uses SQL/DS Version 3 to store global indices and knowledge about objects, users, security, etc. It uses the VM Shared File System (SFS) to keep page objects on host DASD. A very exciting result of this is that MOSAIC implicitly exploits VM Data Spaces on ES/9000 systems with availability of VM/ESA Release 1.1 and

---

[4] Function Set (FS) 10—CCITT G4 compressed bitonal images.

SQL/DS Version 3.3, since these releases of SFS and SQL/DS exploit VM Data Spaces. Preliminary performance measurements indicate that SQL/DS Version 3.3 with VM Data Spaces Support feature makes elapsed times up to 3.3 times faster than without it for complex queries, and up to 39 times faster for database scans.

The MOSAIC desktop

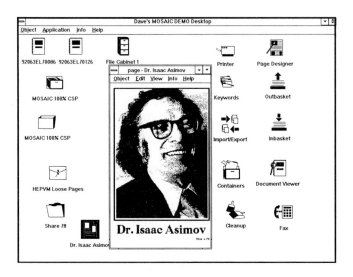

MOSAIC users access the system via the MOSAIC Desktop. This SAA CUA-conforming GUI provides a simple "point and click" interface to all of MOSAIC's facilities. All benefits of a GUI on a powerful PWS are realized. Users unfamiliar with GUIs (or even computers!) can rapidly learn to use MOSAIC because of its desktop application. MOSAIC end-users are unaware of the work the VM host server performs on their behalf in an invisible manner: they are not even logged onto VM. And because MOSAIC is a Windows application, all other facilities available to Windows users are also available concurrently, for example, 3270 "termulator," spreadsheet, and DTP.

The sample desktop in the preceding figure shows image and container objects, as well as most applications. Most users would not have all the applications, but only those they are authorized to use. Icons for the electronic mail system (Inbasket and Outbasket) denote applications that are used to mail individual pages up through entire filing cabinets to other MOSAIC users. The Cleanup application only removes image and container objects from the desktop, not the system. The Container and Keywords applications were previously mentioned in discussing MOSAIC's excellent file-folder capabilities. Containers can be created dynamically to organize information the way end-users, workgroups, or entire enterprises do their work. There is complete flexibility in types of containers that can be defined, and in inter-object relationships. The Page Designer application uses the Windows clipboard to cut and paste new page images from existing pages, Windows applications, etc. Original captured pages are never altered. The Document Viewer application is a convenient way to examine a multiple-page document. The user simply clicks on a document icon and drags it onto the Document Viewer application icon. The Import/Export application supports exporting MOSAIC images to IOCA, TIFF or PSEG3820 formats. IOCA and TIFF files can be imported into MOSAIC at the workstation.

MOSAIC administration

The MOSAIC administrator's role is to support the MOSAIC end-users. Thanks to MOSAIC's power and flexibility, most administration tasks can be done with little or no impact on the MOSAIC users. At the most, users may have to log off and re-log on to MOSAIC for changes to take effect; for example, when a new image database has been defined and must be accessed. This is analogous to a CMS user having to reaccess a minidisk or SFS directory; it is certainly an improvement over older computer applications requiring a complete system regeneration.

The administrator works primarily from a set of ISPF dialogs in a CMS session as shown in the next figure.

MOSAIC provides a CUA-conforming front end to a series of complex SQL commands that the administrator never sees. MOSAIC maintains global awareness of all users, resources, attributes, workstations, etc. through a series of SQL tables on the VM host.

```
            MOSAIC System Administration Menu

            Version 2.0
            Copyright (c) SAIC 1990, 1991
            Science Applications International Corporation
            All Rights Reserved

   Select option:

        1. User maintenance
        2. Group maintenance
        3. Mail distribution
        4. Printers
        5. Fax directories
        6. Keyword categories
        7. Optical volumes
        8. Optical pools
        9. Configuration
       10. Backup/Restore
        X. Exit MOSAIC

   Command ===> _____
    F1=Help  F2=Split  F3=Exit  F4=Return  F12=Cancel
```

Some of the MOSAIC administrator's tasks are discussed in more detail below:

User maintenance: MOSAIC users are defined to the system with all their attributes, for example, password, group affiliation(s), application suite, security, and other authorizations.

MOSAIC maintains security levels at the page object level and up. For example, two users with different authorization clearances might have the same folder open on their desktops and might not have the same contents displayed if one user is not authorized for some of the documents. No indication of the existence of a restricted object is given.

Another example shows the power of global awareness provided by the VM host: if two users have the same object (such as a folder) open on their respective desktops and one user adds to or deletes from the folder, the other user sees changes immediately. MOSAIC keeps only one permanent instance of any object within itself. The same physical object can "reside" in multiple container objects and when information about the object or its contents change, knowledge of the change is instantaneously available throughout the system.

Group maintenance: One or more workgroups can be defined with the MOSAIC system, permitting partitioning/organizing of users, resources, and the like. For example, Personnel and Accounting departments would probably be in separate groups.

Mail distribution: One use of this function is to set up "mail room" userids that can be used as designated recipients/routers of inbound facsimiles that do not have standard destination information. Distribution lists can also be defined.

Printers: Background printer resources on the LAN can be set up and made available to all or selected users of the system.

Fax directories: Predefined sets of facsimile numbers are, as always, available to whatever subsets of the whole user community are defined to aid the outbound facsimile application.

Keyword categories: This is one of the more often performed tasks. Here, all various keyword fields, their attributes, enumerated lists, etc. are created and maintained.

Optical volumes, optical pools and backup/restore: The DFSMS/VM product suite is currently in its infancy. Therefore, MOSAIC provides SMS-like functions in the area of storage management sufficient for its own needs.

Distribution of processing

The basic philosophy of MOSAIC design is the same as most client/server solutions: "*all* resources are used for tasks for which they are best suited."

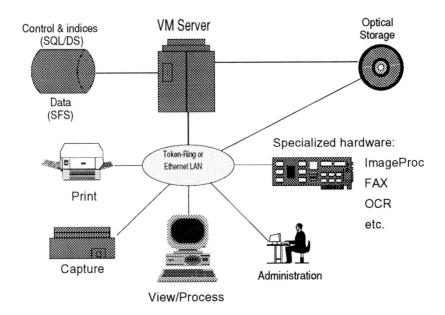

Thus, as shown above, the VM host acts as the central control and coordination point, providing security, network management, storage management, and backup capabilities. The VM host serves as the solution database engine and image repository for images on DASD (using VM's SFS) or the optional OSS. With its world-class SQL/DS DBMS and standard server architecture, the VM host provides a transparent, scaleable server with good price/performance.

The workstations control the end-user interface and perform all the "bit-twiddling" image functions with hardware assists for performance.

Connectivity

MOSAIC can exploit VM PWSCx in various ways:

LAN: Token Ring and/or Ethernet, IEEE 802.x and/or IPX
WAN: SNA, TCP/IP
LAN-host server connnection: Channel/ESCON, SNA, DEA, integrated Token Ring

MOSAIC coexists with other LAN "citizens".

It is appropriate now to take a closer look at the method used to connect MOSAIC client workstations with VM host servers. Because performance is a critical success factor in imaging solutions, the method used for PWS-host communication is a very important factor in the overall solution design. Also important is adherence to standards.

As shown above, the use of VM PWSCx by MOSAIC satisfies both these requirements. VM PWSCx provides high performance, low system overhead, and reduced complexity for client/server applications. VM PWSCx applications are written using the SAA CPI for Communications (CPI-C). Use of CPI-C helps ensure long-term viability of MOSAIC. A private protocol, optimized for this environment, achieves the requisite price/performance parameters. VM PWSCx provides growth through multiple domain support and access to WANs. In addition, VM PWSCx, in conjunction with other products (e.g., OS/2, Network Services/2, ACF VTAM, VM/ESA, TCP/IP), can provide SAA CPI-C connectivity to resources within a wide area network (WAN).

A variety of LAN-host connection methods are available. Choosing connection method(s) for MOSAIC is based on mutiple parameters, including price/performance, installed infrastructure, strategic LAN directions for the enterprise, etc. Not all VM PWSCx connectivity services (and hence the many possible MOSAIC configurations) are discussed here. For more information on all the connectivity options provided by VM PWSCx (e.g., NetWare IPX, TCP/IP, AIX, X.25, Ethernet, etc.) refer to *VM Programmable Workstation Communication Services: Managing VM PWSCS*, SC24-5585.

In the example, MOSAIC workstations communicate with an OS/2 EE 1.3 **domain controller** using the IEEE 802.2 protocol over a Token Ring LAN. The domain controller provides a gateway to the VM/ESA host's ISFC component to complete peer-to-peer connection between MOSAIC workstations and MOSAIC server virtual machines. The domain controller uses the S/370 Channel Emulator Adapter/A in the PS/2 to communicate via an MCCU.

The domain controller is used for five purposes:

1. Improve network performance
2. Provide Ethernet connectivity
3. Support attachment to the host via an MCCU
4. Support attachment to the host via a WAN
5. Provide access to resources throughout a WAN

When using VM PWSCx, the best data transfer rates and bandwidth are available using an MCCU (channel-to-channel) connection.

As VM PWSCx evolves, providing additional functions for peer-to-peer communications, MOSAIC will be able to exploit these enhancements without requiring any code changes. This is the advantage of using SAA CPI-C.

An example of the power and flexibility of VM PWSCx is shown below.

Real-world example of VM PWSCx-enabled connectivity

SAIC Corporate MOSAIC Network

SAIC CHQ, Campus Point

MOSAIC Development
Sorrento Valley

4381-R13 CPU
VM/ESA 1.0 370 Feature
VM PWSCF 1.2
SQL/DS 3.2
C/370 2.1.0 RTL
ISPF/DM 3.2
MOSAIC/VM 2.x

9377-90

CTC

Local/Remote
MOSAIC PWSs

Domain Controller 1
OS/2 EE 1.30.2
PWSCS 1.1
TCP/IP 1.2

16 Mb/s   Br   T1   Br

16 Mb/s
Token-Ring
LAN

Ethernet (802.3)

SAIC, McLean, VA

Local MOSAIC Workstations

T1
TCP/IP
Backbone   DC2

Remote MOSAIC Workstations

SAIC's corporate headquarters will use MOSAIC for daily operations, including handling of Material Safety Data Sheets (MSDS). There are three sets of users for this system: the headquarters staff, using Ethernet-connected workstations; the MOSAIC development group, using Token Ring-attached workstations connected to the central VM PWSCS domain controller via a high-speed remote LAN bridge; and users at a subsidiary location in the Washington, D.C., area, also using Ethernet and connected back to San Diego over a transcontinental TCP/IP link. The MOSAIC workstations and VM/ESA server do not require any changes; VM PWSCx provides the SAA CPI-C interface and hides underlying connection/network details. This includes the ability to coexist with and support heterogeneous media and protocols.

MOSAIC VM server architecture

MOSAIC's server architecture

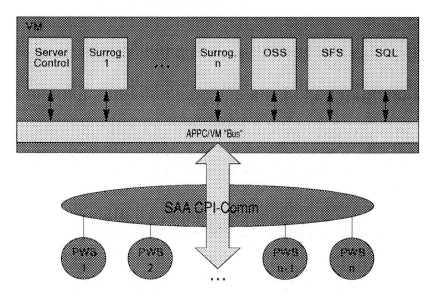

As shown above, MOSAIC is optimized for the VM environment in two important respects.

First, a surrogate virtual machine is allocated for each logged-on MOSAIC user to provide host resources transparently to the user. This enables VM's efficient scheduler/dispatcher to manage the host resources for each MOSAIC user. The multitasking SQL and SFS servers can service surrogate machines in an effective manner.

Second, VM PWSCx software provides a high-speed, low-overhead connection optimized for the VM-workstation environment.

The MOSAIC host services also provide policy/logon management so that the number of the concurrent MOSAIC users cannot exceed the license count.

Customization and integration

MOSAIC's scripting facility

The scripting facility consists of a script editor, used to create scripts, and a script interpreter that executes the scripts. A script is a 4GL-like language (akin to a hybrid between C and REXX) and is executed at the workstation. Full programmability is provided. The editor has powerful pre-fill functions to create scripts rapidly. The interpreter accesses 3270 sessions via MS-Windows Dynamic Data Exchange (DDE). It can get and put 3270 status information and data; 3270 fields and data can be declared as triggers that cause the interpreter to execute specified routines. Thus, for example, a student-number field in a CICS/VSE application might get filled in and automatically trigger the interpreter to initiate a series of actions resulting in the student's folder being brought up and opened on the Desktop, all without requiring any new or overt action by the CICS application user. The interpreter can create/interact with custom Windows dialogs, and has access to the MOSAIC APIs. This ability to add document imaging and object management functions to existing 3270-based host applications, without requiring either modifications to the existing applications or changes to users' interactions with their systems, is a powerful step towards realizing the promise of operational image technology.

Integrating existing applications with MOSAIC

As previously discussed, MOSAIC's baseline system provides a complete turnkey solution for standard document operations, for example, electronic filing cabinet archives. This provides good value, but operates essentially stand-alone. A much greater benefit can be realized when document imaging and object management services are integrated with core line-of-business operations: for example, insurance claims processing, loan applications, university admissions/student records, Material Safety Data Sheets (MSDSs), purchase orders, invoices, etc. The key is that today, people process these mountains of non-coded information, often with the assistance of computerized systems. So it is essential to integrate electronic imaging and object management functions with these processes/applications, often reengineering the processes/applications to intelligently use the new capabilities.

There are three levels of integration possible for applications using the existing MOSAIC solution. In order of increasing coding effort and payback, these are:

1. Run the MOSAIC Desktop in a window and the application in another window side-by-side on the same MOSAIC workstation. Information may be transferred between applications using the Windows Clipboard. For example, an OfficeVision/VM note in a PC/3270 2.0 window can be copied (as a bitmap) into MOSAIC's Page Designer application via the clipboard and then saved in MOSAIC. This level of integration requires no additional programming. It is applicable to workstation and (3270-based) host applications.

2. Still workstation-based, but using the scripting facility, custom applications can be rapidly prototyped/implemented. Scripts can use Windows DDE to exchange information with one or more 3270-based host applications. Scripts also have access to MOSAIC's functions/APIs and other resources. For example, a 3270 window may be running a CICS/VSE application that brings up an insurance policy number and associated information. A custom script could bring up the electronic folder associated with the policy number automatically by using triggers. This has several advantages to an enterprise:
   - Benefits (productivity, cost savings, et al.) of image
   - No user retraining required, existing 3270 application interface still used
   - No modifications to 3270 applications required

   More than 80 percent of most enterprise integration requirements can be met using scripts.

3. Using the Windows and CMS environments API libraries, custom applications, either new or as additions to existing ones, can be written. API functions include:
   - Put and get IOCA images
   - Put, get and change index information
   - Invoke workstation printer servers
   - Invoke workstation fax servers
   - Invoke E-mail system
   - Share data with VM applications
   - Communicate with custom VM applications
   - Invoke custom workstation applications

Customizing and enhancing MOSAIC

Myriad possibilities exist for customizing MOSAIC using the API libraries at the workstation and host levels. Because virtually all resources are available within the VM/CMS environment it is very easy to perform value-added customization of MOSAIC and/or integrate MOSAIC's functions into existing applications. Customization examples include support for viewing MOSAIC images on Graphical Data Display Manager (GDDM)-supported displays, support of host all-points addressable (APA) printers, and remote print/fax request from a 3270 CMS session. Another example is Computer Output Micrographics (COM) replacement, either by intercepting/indexing/storing coded data from a line-printer, 3800-1, or AFPDS data stream for subsequent search/retrieval operations, or converting an AFPDS output file into IOCA page images and storing them in MOSAIC rather than printing them.

The scripting facility provides the capability of quickly creating libraries of reusable custom applications/applets. Custom dialogs are a snap, so additional features to the base system are produced quickly and at low cost.

Recent Enhancements

MOSAIC continues to evolve in function and architecture. The following MOSAIC enhancements have recently become available as part of MOSAIC Version 2.1A:

- Support for the LAN-attached models of the IBM 3995 optical storage subsystem (OSS), a.k.a. "jukebox." This provides support for 20, 94, or 188GB of write-once read-many (WORM) storage with one OSS (multiple OSSs can also be supported).
- Support for the Lexmark 4019 and 4029 Laserprinters.
- Support for the IBM 2456 scanner.
- Software decompression option for view-only workstations
- Proportional scaling.
- Enhanced object reordering (editing a container object's order/content).

The Brave New World

Document imaging/management systems form an exciting new technology that is starting to move into mainstream use by enterprises. The impact of imaging is often compared to that of timesharing and online transaction processing systems in the 1970s. Imaging creates new demands and roles for an enterprise's computing resources — including a requirement for distributed/cooperative processing. VM/ESA, with its high SAA content, data spaces, synergy with programmable workstations, and friendly application environment is well-suited to the role of image database and repository.

Glossary

DDE: Dynamic Data Exchange.

DEA: A Data Exchange Adapter is a high-speed connection between the S/370 and PS/2 planars of an ES/9371 MicroChannel 370 system. VM PWSCx can use the DEA for LAN-host communications.

IOCA: Image Object Content Architecture.

ISFC: Inter-System Facility for Communications is a function of the VM/ESA Release 1.1 control program (CP) that supports high-performance communication between programs running in a VM/ESA Release 1.1 system and programs running in channel-attached local area network (LAN)-based workstations. Workstation applications written to the Common Programming Interface (CPI) Communications program interface provided by VM PWSCS may communicate with VM/ESA Release 1.1 applications written to the Advanced Program-to-Program Communications/VM (APPC/VM) assembler language or CPI Communications programming interfaces to take advantage of this high-performance connection between VM PWSCS and ISFC. VM PWSCS and ISFC enhance the VM/ESA host/workstation synergy and fulfills the VM/ESA statement of direction announced September 5, 1990.

MCCU: A Multisystem Channel Communications Unit) provides a channel-to-channel (CTC) connection between two or more (depending on the model) "host" systems. Some processors, such as the ES/4381 and ES/9221 have integrated CTC capability as a feature.   The 3088 is an external MCCU.   In pre-ESCON days, MCCUs provided the highest-speed interprocessor communication link.

13

VM Communications

By Stuart McRae

Overview

VM/ESA has one of the richest communications products portfolios among today's operating system platforms. It has not always marketed these capabilities, but it should be remembered that when the 9370 was launched, the Endicott laboratories responsible for designing the hardware and the VM system which ran on it saw one of its roles as replacing the Series/1 as IBM's all-purpose communications processor. Although the 9370 has not really lived up to that role, one of the benefits of the intent has been the very rich set of communications capabilities developed for VM to support distributed systems of all kinds.

In addition to this, the Endicott Programming Lab has for some time focused on development of VM as a host platform for cooperative processing, the interface between intelligent workstations and mainframe based applications. As **client/server computing** has become one of the hot topics of the computing industry, it is no accident that the Endicott Programming Lab has taken on a worldwide mission within IBM in this area.

Communications of every kind

It has been said that VM was the first local area network, but implemented entirely in software. The virtual machine model of computing, where each user appears to have a personal stand-alone computer system, led very early on to realization that effectively utilizing the system required a mechanism for communication between separate virtual machines. This models very well the subsequent discovery, in the Personal Computer Age, that once everyone has a real machine, the next problem encountered is allowing those real machines to communicate with each other.

To provide these facilities in VM, the ability to use the SPOOLing system to pass files between virtual machines was developed. It was soon realized that virtual machines on different VM systems needed to communicate in the same way, and the sequence of products which became VNET (on IBM's internal systems) and RSCS (the **Remote SPOOLing Communications Subsystem** to the outside world) was developed. As well as providing a way for users to transmit files to each other, this provided a mechanism whereby the Remote Job Entry stations (used to feed the batch-oriented computer systems of those days with cards, and to output results) could connect to VM.

Soon the ability to exchange files between virtual machines was extended to message passing via VMCF and then IUCV, but initially this remained a capability only within one VM system. What did develop was the idea of allowing users connected to one system to log on to another, remote VM system. This was provided first by the VM/Pass-Through product, universally known as PVM, and subsequently by allowing VTAM to run in a guest and then natively on VM. Now a user connected to any VM, MVS, or VSE system via VTAM can log on to that VM system remotely and use its services.

Over time, the total domination of SNA over the networking world has waned, and VM has responded by offering both strong TCP/IP support, and also (though VTAM) increasing levels of OSI support. These protocols are now widely supported from the lowest levels (Ethernet and HDLC) up to the application layer (SMTP and X.400 mail, FTP, NFS and FTAM file transfer, and Telnet terminal emulation). Even network management is increasingly integrating SNMP (from the TCP/IP world) and CMIS/CMIP (from OSI) within the SNA NetView umbrella.

The restriction on allowing inter-virtual machine communications only within one VM system was finally relaxed by adopting the SNA

LU 6.2 protocol, **Advanced Program-to-Program Communi-cations** (APPC) and implementing it in VM (as APPC/VM). At first this could only be used within one system or across systems by clus-tering up to eight local 9370s on a LAN using TSAF (the **Trans-parent Services Access Facility**, a VM component), but subsequently a gateway was also offered to allow an APPC/VM session to be established via VTAM with any remote SNA applica-tion using the APPC protocol (not just on VM, but on any platform, including CICS, AS/400, OS/2 EE, PC-DOS, or AIX as well as other vendors' products).

VM Programmable Workstation Communication Services (VM PWSCS) product extends this APPC/VM support to offer a very high speed (non-VTAM) communications link between a VM host and personal computers on a local area network. This was the first of a series of products which allow VM to act as a server for a LAN community of PC workstations (an area pioneered by VM/PC Bond and its successor the **Enhanced Connectivity Facilities**, ECF). This family now includes products like LANRES/VM, for Novell NetWare connectivity, and WDSF/VM, for host backup and archiving of workstation files.

Many of these more advanced products can be used to build upon VM's role as the original "software LAN". In the past, giving users virtual machines was cheaper than giving them real ones. The revo-lution in PC technology is beginning to change these dynamics. It is a natural consequence of the VM architecture and the extension of inter-virtual machine communications outside the host VM system using industry standard protocols, that a service virtual machine, which provides a service for other virtual machines, can also provide a similar service for other real machines, namely intelligent work-stations distributed locally and around the world.

It is therefore practical today both to consider distributing proc-essing performed in user virtual machines out to user real machines, while still offering the same centralized services, and also to use VM as a platform for delivering services which existing workstation users need in a controlled, reliable, and integrated way. Indeed, to borrow a marketing phrase from Sun, increasingly "the Network is the Computer" and the concept of using only a single real machine to offer services to a user is as dead as batch processing (which, however, is itself enjoying a strong afterlife!). What the user should see is a single integrated service, even though it is actually imple-mented on an integrated, heterogeneous network of real and virtual machines.

VM/ESA Connectivity Options

Terminal support

Originally, all VM terminals were ASCII asynchronous terminals (Teletypes or TTYs) connected in linemode. Subsequently the norm became 3270-type devices, locally attached via a 3274 control unit, or remotely connected using binary synchronous (bisynchronous) protocols (now obsolete).

Although linemode TTY support was originally dropped from VM/XA SP (except for VTAM devices), it was added back and is thus available in VM/ESA. However, linemode use of VM is no longer a widely used option, and many modern applications have limited support for linemode users. Most terminals today are either 3270 devices, workstations (e.g., PCs) emulating 3270 devices, or ASCII Teletypes emulating 3270 devices.

3270 terminals

Today, when a real 3270 terminal (or a PC emulator containing a coax card) is used, the connection is normally to a 3174 or 3274 controller. This controller may be either channel attached to the host directly, or remotely connected via an SNA SDLC communications line, or over a token ring LAN, to a 3745 or equivalent front-end processor (which may itself be remotely connected to the host in the same ways). SNA also now allows these protocols to be carried to a remote site over X.25.

As an alternative, when an intelligent workstation is used (normally a PC), it is possible to use a token ring connection to talk to a 3174 connected to the LAN, or to another PC which acts as a gateway between the LAN and a 9221 or a front-end processor.

Two final options available for workstation users are a version of the TCP/IP **TELNET** terminal protocol implemented in an alternative Telnet client application called **TN3270** (available on a wide variety of platforms including PCs and Unix systems), and an X Windows-based terminal emulator called **x3270** which emulates a 3270 within a window under X.

In the future, it seems likely that IBM will also support 3270 emulators connected to hosts over APPC sessions.

ASCII asynchronous communications

When an ASCII asynchronous teletype terminal is used today, it is likely to be using 3270 emulation so that it looks like a 3270 screen to the VM application. Sometimes the protocol converter supports a variety of different "glass teletypes" capable of performing such emulation (such as the VT100 and IBM's 3101), sometimes it is designed to be used with a specially written PC application, and sometimes it supports both mechanisms.

One option is a hardware protocol converter, such as an IBM 3708, the ES/9000 workstation subsystem on 9221 models, the **ASCII Emulation Adapter** on a 3174, or a third party emulator such as Hydra or solutions marketed by Adacom, Rhumba, Attachmate, and others. In addition to supporting dumb teletypes, the two IBM solutions support a specially written PC application called FTTERM (although they cannot be used with IBM's Personal Communications/3270 package). The Rhumba solution is designed for use with Rhumba's Windows 3-based terminal emulator and application front-end tool.

An alternative is to provide 3270 emulation via a protocol converter package running on VM, such as SIM3278, RELAY, or Packet/3270. This sort of product may run either in VM or as a VTAM application. In addition to supporting dumb teletypes, these packages normally include intelligent PC front ends, and perhaps a Macintosh front end as well. A variety of transports such as TCP/IP may be supported as well as asynchronous dial-up. They often also offer sophisticated techniques for improving performance, such as data stream optimization and SIMWARE's ability to maintain a local cache of screen images on the workstation.

In addition to using these packages on a directly dialed telephone line, they may be used over the public X.25 packet switched networks to provide lower cost access from remote locations or traveling laptop computers. Indeed, Packet/3270 was specifically written for this environment, although some of the other packages now work equally well in this environment.

An alternative approach for remote access is to provide a VTAM link from the target VM system to IBM's Information Network (IIN), which then provides access points around the world into which the remote or laptop user can dial using FTTERM or a dumb teletype emulation package. In some countries, IBM offers special ASCII asynchronous dial-in ports to IIN which support ASCII asynchronous capabilities of its high-end Personal Communications/3270 terminal emulator.

In addition to terminal emulation, PC packages normally offer a file transfer capability to upload/download files, and the **High-Level Language Application Program Interface** (HLLAPI, pronounced "Hullappi") which allows applications to control the host session to automate routine tasks or implement application front ends. They may even offer an APPC option.

File transfer

The most common networking mechanism used with VM is RSCS, which allows file transfer to other VM systems, to MVS and VSE systems, and to AS/400s (using IBM's Network Job Entry, NJE, protocols), as well as to any other system supporting the *de facto* remote job entry protocol 2780 and its SNA successor 3780. Links may be SNA based, may use a Channel-to-Channel Adapter for direct connections between CPUs, or may use the old bisynchronous protocol. Additionally, RSCS drives 3270 printers and suitably connected ASCII printers and plotters.

For MVS systems, RSCS communicates with NJE to allow files to be exchanged with the JES SPOOL. Files from MVS application may be routed to printers on VM or to virtual card readers of specific virtual machines (via the ROUTE JCL card). TSO also supports the NETDATA file format used by VM's SENDFILE and NOTE commands. In addition to file transfer, messages may be sent cross-system (and on VM, are delivered as CP messages).

On VSE systems, RSCS communicates with POWER. Although traditionally VSE systems running under VM have passed files to VM and its devices via the virtual punch of the VSE system, use of a POWER-to-RSCS link provides more flexibility and better routing capabilities.

RSCS runs under the control of the Group Control System (GCS) component of VM/ESA. When used in conjunction with an SNA link, RSCS runs in the same group as VTAM and uses its services. When used only with non-SNA links, RSCS still runs under GCS but does not require VTAM to be installed.

RSCS provides a logical extension of the VM SPOOL to allow files placed in the SPOOL to be moved to either the SPOOL area of a remote (VM or non-VM) system, or to be transmitted to a device not directly connected to the VM system.

An alternative, increasingly important networking product for VM is TCP/IP. The File Transfer Protocol (FTP) of TCP/IP allows files to be exchanged between systems supporting the protocol. Unlike the RSCS (SPOOLing system based) approach, FTP uses explicit GET and PUT commands to allow a user to move a file from one location on one system to another location on another system. TCP/IP is widely used in the Unix world, and is becoming a popular way to link workstations to servers in client/server systems.

The third inter-system file transfer mechanism supported by VM is the OSI FTAM standard, as implemented in IBM's **OSI/File Services** (OSI/FS) product. However, this protocol is not widely deployed.

Remote file access

Another mechanism for distributing files, closely related to file transfer, is remote file access. VM supports two protocols of this type. The VM Shared File System (SFS) communicates with remote VM systems to allow users on one system to remotely access files in an SFS on the remote system. This support uses APPC/VM to communicate between the two systems, and so a remote APPC communications path is needed between the VM systems (i.e., either via VTAM and an SNA network, or locally in a TSAF cluster).

The second remote file access mechanism supported is Sun's Networked File System (NFS), the *de facto* standard for remote file access over TCP/IP. TCP/IP for VM offers NFS **server** support, allowing remote workstations to access files on the VM system and create files on VM. Note that client support is not currently offered, so CMS users cannot access files stored on remote systems.

As yet, VM/ESA does not support the Systems Application Architecture (SAA) remote file access protocol, **Distributed Data Access** (DDA).

3270 file transfer

Another file transfer mechanism to/from VM is the IND$FILE command. This allows workstations to transfer files to and from VM over 3270 terminal sessions, and is used by many workstation terminal emulators from IBM and third parties on PC-DOS, OS/2 EE, and AIX (or indeed other Unix systems).

Note that the "$" in "IND$FILE" is, in fact, the currency symbol, and hence varies according to character set used. In the USA, this is the dollar sign; in the UK, it is the pound sign, although the utility is still often referred to as "IND-dollar-FILE". In other countries, various other graphics are associated with this character.

Care must therefore be taken when using a terminal emulator supporting IND$FILE to configure the file transfer command to be used according to the code page in use on both the workstation and the host (or rather the 3174 control unit, or the hardware/software providing the equivalent function). Although this is comparatively straightforward when the workstation and controller are in the same country and configured the same way, when connecting remotely to systems in other countries (e.g., via ASCII asynchronous terminal emulation) experimentation is normally required to make this function work. A frequent solution to this problem is to create an INDFILE EXEC which calls IND$FILE, and configure the terminal emulator to use that command for file transfer instead.

The user interface to IND$FILE normally takes the form of SEND and RECEIVE commands on the workstation which allow a file to be stored on VM, or downloaded from VM to the workstation.

The **Enhanced Connectivity Facilities** also provide a mechanism to transfer files between a workstation and VM by allowing the host file system to appear as an additional drive on the PC.

Electronic mail protocols

In addition to these file transfer mechanisms, a number of special purpose electronic mail protocols are supported by VM.

SNA Distribution Services (SNADS) is a mail file transfer protocol widely used in MVS (by DISOSS) and other systems (e.g., the AS/400). This protocol is not directly supported by VM or OfficeVision/VM, but instead the OfficeVision/VM DISOSS bridge will send mail via RSCS to an MVS application which will give the mail to DISOSS (which can turn it into SNADS traffic for, say, an AS/400). Similar *ad hoc* solutions are available for direct links to the AS/400 (again using an RSCS link) and OfficeVision/2 (using RSCS and a service virtual machine which communicates with the OfficeVision/2 server over a 3270 session). Alternatively, IBM offers Soft-Switch Central if native SNADS support is required on VM.

Simple Mail Transfer Protocol (SMTP) is the TCP/IP electronic mail protocol, is supported by TCP/IP for VM, and also offers a replacement for the CMS NOTE command which is able to format mail for delivery to SMTP destinations.

X.400 is the OSI standard for electronic mail interconnect, and is supported both by a set of products running with IBM's OSI product, OSI/CS, and also by Soft-Switch Central.

Application program support

The primary mechanism for inter-application communications on distributed VM systems is APPC/VM. This implements the APPC verb set to allow a CMS application to communicate with:

- Another CMS application on the same system
- A CMS application on a different VM system
- An APPC application connected anywhere in the SNA network running on any platform

Indeed, a virtual machine can even have an APPC/VM conversation with itself, but this is not likely to be useful unless it is running a multitasking supervisor (e.g., **CMS Pipelines** or the **Server Tasking Environment/VM**).

CMS offers an assembler level interface to APPC/VM. This is implemented via a small number of new APPC/VM-specific macros, plus some extensions to the existing IUCV interface (note that APPC does not define a platform-independent application programming interface, rather it defines the functions which must be implemented).

The **Common Programming Interface Communications** (CPI-C, now called CPI-CI in SAA) is the Systems Application Architecture (SAA)-defined application programming interface (API) to APPC. This is implemented via CMS Callable Services Library (CSL) calls to provide an interface to APPC/VM from REXX or other high-level languages.

APPC provides a mechanism for establishing **sessions** between applications, passing data, and terminating the session.   Each session is half duplex (i.e., transmission is permitted in only one direction at a time), but applications normally establish two sessions to allow full duplex, bidirectional **conversations**. An application may normally define any number of parallel sessions, up to a defined limit.   APPC also defines security mechanisms to allow authorization of conversations. In SNA terms, each APPC/VM application is a **Logical Unit** (LU) of type 6.2.

One of the additional (optional) facilities of LU 6.2 which is offered by VM/ESA is the **sync point** architecture, which provides application coordination, resynchronization, and logging to assist in implementing **two-phase commit** protocols. It is implemented in CMS as **Coordinated Resource Recovery** (CRR). This allows multiple applications to perform updates to external objects in a coordinated fashion, with all updates being either **committed** or **rolled back,** and is implemented over APPC/VM in a similar way to CPI-C.

The ability to establish APPC/VM conversations within one VM system may be convenient, but the mechanism really blossoms by allowing communication between applications on different VM systems or between a CMS application and an application running on a different host system.

The TSAF service virtual machine provides a mechanism for linking up to eight VM systems into a **TSAF collection**, which allows applications running on any of the systems to communicate with each other via APPC/VM.

In a TSAF collection, the different TSAF service virtual machines can be linked via:

- A Channel-to-Channel Adapter (or a 3088 link)
- A bisynchronous communications line
- An Ethernet or Token Ring connection using the appropriate adapter on a rack-mounted ES/9000

Within a TSAF collection, protocols used are designed to be highly reliable, supporting multiple routes between nodes and full, automatic recovery on link failure (providing an alternative path exists), without the application being involved. Collections may also be dynamically partitioned and then reunited when links fail and are reconnected.

The TSAF collection is designed to work as a local cluster of machines, and one or more of the TSAF machines in these collections may be linked over an SNA wide area network via **APPC/VM VTAM Support** (AVS) to another TSAF system in a different collection. AVS is a VTAM application which runs under GCS in the same group as VTAM on the VM system, and implements a **gateway** to the whole TSAF collection for the rest of the SNA network. This allows multiple collections, each between one and eight systems, to be inter-linked over a wide area via the SNA backbone network. Note that every VM system in the TSAF collection need not run AVS (or indeed VTAM): only one gateway somewhere in the collection is needed.

APPC/VM documentation and implementation assume that there are fundamentally two types of APPC application, **resource managers** (**servers** in normal terminology), and **user programs** (or **clients**). APPC provides a general mechanism which can be used just as easily to provide communications between two servers, or even two users, as it can to provide what has recently become a traditional client/server model. In practice, of course, given the single-tasking nature of CMS, it is unlikely that APPC-style communications will occur between users (as both users must run their respective applications for communication to occur). This is why the service virtual machine model was created in VM, and this is why the APPC/VM client/server model works well in that environment. Similarly, many server-to-server applications use a master/slave protocol, and hence the client/server model can still be applied.

APPC/VM defines three resource types. **Local** resources are unique to the local VM system, but not to other systems in the TSAF collection or through the AVS gateway. **Global** resources are known throughout the TSAF collection and may be accessed via the AVS gateway.

There is one significant distinction between access to global resources within the collection and access to the same resources via the AVS gateway. When an application identifies itself as a local or global resource, CP records its name dynamically so that access can then be granted to any requesting APPC/VM application on the same system. In addition, for global resources, TSAF is informed when the resource identifies itself, and so makes that resource name available throughout the TSAF collection. However, this sort of automatic registration does not occur for the AVS gateway. If a global resource is to be accessed by remote applications via AVS, it must be statically defined in the appropriate AVS configuration table. Indeed, AVS will map global resource names to an external LU 6.2 name (an LU name plus a transaction program name), thus removing the need to have the resource name be unique throughout the SNA network.

On the other hand, the third resource type—**private**—does not identify itself dynamically in this way. Rather it is defined in the local system directory as a virtual machine, with the userid being the same as the target LU name for the resource. When a user connects to this APPC/VM resource, from inside or outside of the TSAF collection, the virtual machine will be logged on via AUTOLOG, ready to process the request. When the virtual machine becomes idle (i.e., has no IUCV or APPC connections and has been inactive for 30 minutes), it will be forced off. A single virtual machine may be defined to provide multiple private resources, but the requests will be handled sequentially, not in parallel.

Configuration and use of APPC/VM, TSAF, and AVS is described in detail in the *Connectivity Planning, Administration and Operation* manual for VM/ESA. The assembler level interface to APPC/VM and the CPI-C and CRR interfaces are described in the VM/ESA *CMS Application Development Guide for Assembler* and *CMS Application Development Guide*, respectively.

Other application interfaces

In addition to SNA-oriented APPC support, VM offers support for the **sockets** interface (on top of which many TCP/IP applications are built) through its TCP/IP product.

Alternatively, in the OSI world, **OSI/Communication Services** (OSI/CS) offers an OSI protocol stack on VM/ESA allowing applications to communicate over X.25 and LAN networks with other applications supporting the OSI protocols. The **VTAM OSI Remote Programming Interface** feature allows applications using the same application program interface to be run on a system not connected to the OSI world and to communicate across an APPC session to an OSI/CS system. This provides a gateway to an OSI network, thus allowing such applications to be distributed in an SNA network without requiring wholesale deployment of OSI protocols in parallel to SNA protocols.

The VTAM Product Family

A full overview of the SNA capabilities offered by VTAM, or even the full set of VTAM and related products available, is beyond the scope of this chapter. However, a few specifics are worth mentioning.

When ACF/VTAM Version 3 Release 3 is used with the VM/ESA ESA Feature, it is able to exploit the 31-bit addressing capabilities of GCS, thus providing storage constraint relief for large VM systems. In addition to core VTAM services being 31-bit exploitative, **VM SNA Console Services** (VSCS), the VTAM component which interfaces to VM/ESA **Console Communication Services**

(CCS) to allow remote terminals to log on to VM or dial to VM applications, can also utilize memory above the 16MB line.

This release of ACF/VTAM also supports ESCON channels on VM/ESA and the VTAM **First Failure Data Capture** (FFDC) capabilities for non-disruptive generation of dumps for certain error conditions. VTAM Version 3 Release 4 for VM/ESA provides many additional VTAM capabilities including Token Ring, IEEE 802.3 (Ethernet), and FDDI connections via the 3172 Interconnect controller, and the OSI Remote Programming Interface (described elsewhere).

The NetView family of products, which provides network management for host-based SNA networks, is also supported on VM. Broadly, their function is the same on VM as on MVS (although sometimes the products lag a release or so behind). There is therefore little VM specific functionality (indeed, NetView on MVS is the major user of REXX on that platform, allowing it to maximize compatibility between the two systems).

A specific example is **NetView Distribution Manager** (NetView DM) which uses **SNA/File Services** (SNAFS), a derivative of SNADS, to distribute service to remote systems, and microcode to 3174 controllers (SNAFS, together with SNA/Management Services and SNADS, provide the architectural basis for the NetView products). This is provided to allow centralized system management of distributed systems, and can be used (on VM or MVS) together with the **Distributed Systems Node Executive** (VM/DSNX) running on VM at the remote site to distribute new versions of VM components, applications, data, or other objects. NetView DM can then invoke procedures to update the remote systems to use these new objects—DSNX effectively acts as a "catcher" for service distributed by NetView DM.

Another NetView product, the **NetView File Transfer Program**, offers high volume, store-and-forward data transfer via APPC between VM, MVS, VSE, and AS/400 systems over APPC links in an SNA network (with optional file compression). This includes transmission of VSAM files.

NetView Access Services is a VTAM-based multisession terminal monitor. It also offers security features (allowing RACF, or an equivalent, to define which user can access which VTAM applications) and a shadow capability (allowing a helpdesk operative, for example, to look at a user's session). Similar multisession products have been available on VM for some time (for example, TUBES), and the latest version of VM/Pass-Through (PVM) has similar capabilities.

Remote SPOOLing Communications Subsystem

RSCS is the prime file transfer and printer SPOOLing mechanism for VM. Originally included as part of VM/370, RSCS was split out as a separate program product, **RSCS Networking**, when VM/SP was announced. Version 2 of that product offered SNA support for the first time by running under GCS, alongside VTAM, and allowing the use of SNA transports to communicate with remote systems.

RSCS Version 3 represents a major enhancement to the product, not so much because of any major new features, but because it provides numerous incremental improvements to help implement robust, powerful, and easy-to-administer networks. Key new features in version 3 are:

- Significant performance improvements over Version 2
- A **Generalized Programming Interface** to allow customers and vendors to write new line drivers
- Enhanced command responses, and a new **Command Response Interface** to deliver the results of a command in a parsable form to a user application
- Return of undeliverable SPOOL files to sending users
- An **Event Scheduling Manager** to perform certain functions automatically at specific times
- A line driver included for the AS/400 (previously requiring a PRPQ)
- The inclusion of sample security exits (e.g., to intercept files with specific names)
- A procedure to automatically exploit RSCS **List Services**, allowing files sent to remote locations to be sent once and "fanned out" only when necessary

VM/Pass-Through Facility

The **VM/Pass-Through Facility** (PVM) connects multiple VM systems together, and then lets users on terminals connected on any one of them to log on to any of them. It utilizes the **Logical Device Support Facility** (LDSF) in CP to create a logical 3270 session. CP then gives PVM the 3270 data stream which it would normally send to the terminal, and PVM transmits it to the remote user's terminal instead.

When users connect to the Pass-Through Virtual Machine (PVM, from which the product gets its common name) they are presented with a menu of remote systems to which they may connect. Users can connect to PVM via CP DIAL from a 3270 terminal, or via a command from CMS. In the latter case, the ability to temporarily disconnect from the remote session and return to the local CMS session is provided, as well as a screen capture capability which writes the remote screen image to a CMS file.

PVM acquired bisynchronous (3270) terminal and printer support when VM/XA SP was announced without this function, and PVM also provides this support for VM/ESA.

PVM must be implemented on each VM system to which the user is to be provided access. The links between these systems may be CTCA (including a 3088 and ESCON with Version 2), bisynchronous telecommunications line, or APPC/VM session (which may be implemented via VTAM over an SNA network, or locally within a TSAF cluster).

Version 2 of PVM adds multiple session support and the ability to program in REXX macros to automate session establishment and other activities on the remote session. It also provides a VTAM gateway to allow 3270 sessions with VTAM to be established without the need to create a local CP 3270 session and then dial that to VTAM.

TCP/IP for VM

TCP/IP Version 2 for VM (often called "FAL" from its product number, 5735-FAL) is the implementation of the Transmission Control Protocol/Internet Protocol suite on VM.

TCP/IP products are also available from IBM for PC-DOS and OS/2; there is TCP/IP support in AIX/ESA and AIX for the RS/6000; and there are host products for MVS and the AS/400, showing IBM's commitment to providing TCP/IP across its whole product range.

TCP/IP for VM supports the major applications in the protocol suite:

TELNET: Remote terminal logon both inbound to VM and outbound from VM terminals. Both line mode support and 3270 data streams are supported. The 3270 support both allows a convenient method for a user on one VM system using TCP/IP to log on to a remote VM system in full-screen mode (in much the same way as using PVM from a CMS session), and also allows a suitable workstation implementation (such as **TN3270**, provided with many workstation TCP/IPs, or the **x3270** application for X Windows on Unix systems) to access the VM system in full-screen mode.

FTP: The File Transfer Protocol, as either a client (originator) or server (target) of a transfer request. Specific support is provided to preserve fixed record format file structure in transfer between VM systems, as well as supporting traditional, stream-oriented file transfer. ASCII, binary, and EBCDIC file transfers are supported. RACF support allows CMS file access to occur without logging on to the target system.

SMTP: The Simple Mail Transfer Protocol allows the exchange of electronic mail with other TCP/IP systems (or non-TCP/IP systems via appropriate gateways). Alternative versions of the CMS NOTE and SENDFILE commands are provided to allow notes and files to be sent via SMTP mail. Received notes are sent to the user's reader. Access to the SMTP gateway may optionally be restricted to a list of registered users, with mail to/from other users being rejected.

REXEC: The Remote Execution Protocol client allows CMS users to execute commands on remote systems providing REXEC servers, and receive back the results.

LPR/LPD: Support for TCP/IP "line printing" applications allow remote applications to print files on local VM printers and RSCS printers, and also allows VM users to print on remote systems supporting LPR/LPD.

X Windows: Support for X Windows clients allows applications running on VM to drive an X server (i.e., terminal) on a remote system. This allows a user on an X terminal, a PC with X Windows support, an RS/6000, or any other workstation running X to access VM-based X applications. A VM terminal cannot access remote X applications, however.

MOTIF: A provision of the Open Software Foundation's MOTIF toolkit allows applications written to this interface to be implemented on VM and be used by remote X users, giving them the typical MOTIF "look and feel".

GDDM: Graphics support allows users on remote X Windows terminals to access GDDM applications on VM within an X Window. This allows all of the GDDM applications to be used (such as ICU for charting) as well as supporting user written applications which use the GDDM libraries to drive the screen.

SNMP: Support for the both the Simple Network Management Protocol agent and monitor protocols is offered. SNMP monitor support allows TCP/IP for VM to act as a NetView focal point to allow TCP/IP based networks utilizing SNMP to be managed from NetView. For example, asynchronous events (SNMP TRAPS) can be forwarded to NetView, and sample NetView CLISTs written in REXX are provided to demonstrate the use of NetView to manage an SNMP system. The agent support allows TCP/IP for VM to be managed by other SNMP management products.

Sockets: The Berkeley socket library is the *de facto* standard application programming interface to TCP/IP, and may be used by user applications. IUCV communicates between the socket library running under CMS and TCP/IP service virtual machines.

RPC: Sun's Remote Procedure Call library is provided for application use, using the External Data Representation (XDR) protocol to allow data exchange between applications with different hardware architectures.

NCS: Apollo's Network Computing System libraries serve as an alternative remote procedure call protocol (using the OSI ASN.1 data encoding standard for transmission).

Domain Name Server: This allows VM to hold domain data for name resolution. SQL/DS is a prerequisite for full use of the Domain Name Server. An SMSG interface is offered for management of the server.

Kerberos: Support for the Kerberos authentication service is provided to perform validation of communication requests for access control to servers. Specifically, the Kerberos server is provided, together with administration and database management applications. In addition, the Kerberos library is provided for applications that need to authenticate conversations. Kerberos is actually provided as two non-chargeable features, one for use in the U.S. and

Canada (with DES encryption) and one for use outside (without DES).

Additional features offered with TCP/IP for VM include:

NFS (chargeable feature): Offering server support for Sun's Network File System, this is the *de facto* standard for remote file access over TCP/IP. This allow NFS clients to access the CMS file system from remote workstations (although client support, which would provide access to files stored remotely from CMS, is **not** offered). A RACF interface and user exits are also offered for access control.

Softcopy Documentation: This is a free feature, that offers online publications in BookManager READ format.

Various application programming interfaces are provided for C. In addition, both C and Pascal interfaces to the TCP and UDP protocol boundaries are offered. Authorized CMS userids may also access the IP layer directly.

TCP/IP for VM supports a rich set of connectivity options:

3172: The 3172 Interconnect Controller (model 1) channel attaches to the VM host and may be configured for Ethernet or Token Ring attachment. The 3172 is a MicroChannel-based control unit for high performance connectivity to LANs. The model 3 extends this support to offload processing from VM to the 3172.

8232: The predecessor to the 3172, the 8232 LAN Channel Station installed in an Industrial PC gives Token Ring, Ethernet, or PC Network support.

9221: The following integrated controllers are supported on rack-mounted ES/9000 (9221) systems:

*   Ethernet adapter (not supported for NFS)
*   Token Ring adapter (4 or 16 Mbits/second)
*   X.25 Communications Subsystem

37xx: A 3745 or 3720 front-end processor (or equivalent), together with VTAM, NCP, and NPSI.

HYPERchannel: The NSC HYPERchannel with an IBM channel adapter.

One particularly interesting application of TCP/IP for VM is to allow access to an SNA backbone network to carry TCP/IP traffic between locations. The SNALINK component communicates over the backbone via an LU 6.2 session (although it does not use APPC/VM, instead implementing its own APPC support to VTAM).

As an alternative to SNALINK, multiple TCP/IP for VM systems can be linked via PVM sessions between hosts. This allows connection across any PVM-to-PVM link, including a CTCA or TSAF cluster without VTAM, as well as over an APPC/VM link via VTAM.

OSI Products

As user demand for open systems has increased, IBM has implemented more and more **Open Systems Interconnect** (OSI) products, and incorporated an increasing amount of OSI into Systems Application Architecture. In the future, therefore, the ability to use OSI standards for interconnecting between enterprises and between systems within enterprises will become increasingly important, even for an SNA-oriented installation.

The following is a brief summary of the OSI products available for use in the VM/ESA environment.

X.25 support

X.25 support for VM is provided through the **X.25 Network Control Program Packet Switching Interface** (**NPSI**) which runs in a 3745 or 3720 front-end processor, and offers an interface for X.25 devices to connect to host applications. In addition it provides a mechanism for attaching remote front-end processors (running NPSI) or 3174 control units (including systems emulating such control units, for example RS/6000 AIX systems) over an X.25 network via QLLC (**Qualified Logical Link Control** Protocol, a packaging of SNA protocols with X.25 protocols). On rack-mounted ES/9000 systems, this support can also be offered via the integral X.25 controller and VM/VTAM.

Originally this support was exploited by a pair of products, OTSS and OSNS, which implemented the full OSI protocol stack to provide the platform upon which IBM's OSI applications were implemented. These products have now been superseded by **OSI/Communication Services** (OSI/CS), which provides the platform for IBM's current range of OSI applications.

For users wishing to implement OSI applications, IBM originally offered the **General Teleprocessing Monitor for Open Systems Interconnect** (GTMOSI, sometimes pronounced "Je t'aime OSI"). This application also offered terminal emulation for "glass teletype" terminals connected over the X.25 network. GTMOSI has been replaced by the **Communications Subsystem for Interconnection** (CSFI), which also includes an interface to OSI/CS and NetView (and is upwardly compatible with GTMOSI).

It should be noted that IBM increasingly offers PS/2-based alternatives for facilities such as X.25 support on the host where a full front-end processor implementation is not justified. For example, **Programmable Network Access** (PNA) on OS/2 offers 3270 emulation for X.25 connected terminals, while connected to the host over an SDLC link. Users with a large X.25 network can also use IBM's PS/2-based **X25Net** family of products to run a parallel X.25 network, which can be interconnected with VM via NPSI or PNA as required.

Alternatively, if the requirement is merely to carry X.25 protocols over the SNA backbone to allow them to connect to another X.25 device, this function is provided via the **X.25 SNA Interconnect (XI)** product, which is managed by the **Network Supervisory Function** running on VM.

OSI applications

OSI/CS is IBM's platform for the provision of OSI application on VM/ESA. This includes both products and customer-written OSI applications (in C and COBOL). Support is provided for both X.25 connections via NPSI (over leased lines, switched lines, or ISDN) and 802.3 (the IEEE standard for Ethernet) LAN connections via a 3172 controller. Token Ring and FDDI interfaces are expected.

A subset of the CCITT X.500 Directory Service is provided (providing only support for a local directory, not remote directory access). In addition, OSI/CS offers a NetView interface for operator commands and alert processing, as well as support for the OSI CMIS/CMIP Network Management protocols for event reporting and logging. Over time, IBM will provide more comprehensive OSI Network Management (CMIS/CMIP) support in NetView.

The VTAM OSI Remote Programming Interface feature allows an application running on one system and using the OSI/CS programming interface to utilize an OSI/CS system running on a remote

system.   This applications uses an APPC communications session
with the OSI/CS system to allow multiple applications to be spread
over a set of VM, MVS and VSE systems and all access a common
(set of) OSI/CS gateways.   No OSI/CS support need be installed on
the non-gateway systems.

An application which uses OSI/CS is **OSI/File Services** (OSI/FS),
which implements the OSI **File Transfer, Access, and Management (FTAM)** standard.   This provides remote file creation,
transfer, and deletion across an OSI network, in synchronous and
asynchronous modes of operation.   Both an interactive command
level interface and a C or COBOL programming interface are
provided.

The other major OSI application offered on OSI/CS is X.400 electronic mail.   The **Open Network Distribution Services X.400
Feature** offers X.400 Message Transfer Agent functionality on
VM/ESA.   Together with the **X.400 PROFS Connection** it can offer
electronic mail interchange between PROFS and OfficeVision/VM
and other X.400 applications.

As an alternative solution for X.400 applications, IBM also cooperatively markets the Soft-Switch Central X.400 gateway, which
provides similar functionality but distributes the X.400 implementation and the OSI protocol stack onto a separate gateway processor
instead of running it on VM with NPSI.   This gateway uses an
APPC communications path to communicate with Soft-Switch
Central on the host, and supports X.400 over both X.25 and
Ethernet transports.

PC Connectivity Products

Terminal emulation programs

IBM offers three major terminal emulation programs for 3270 access
to hosts.   All provide basic 3270 capabilities, IND$FILE file transfer
capabilities, and the HLLAPI programming interface.

PC/3270 Emulation Program, Entry Level (3270EE) supports
a single CUT (Control Unit Terminal) mode host connection over a
coax link to the host (IBM's 3270 connection for MCA system or PC
3278/79 emulation adapters for ISA systems).   This is basically a
single session connection to the host, although the control unit may
provide multisession support.   3270EE supports EEHLLAPI, a

common subset of HLLAPI available on all of the emulators. If file transfer or application access to the connection is to be used, and a 3174 control unit is being used, correct configuration is essential (specifically the "File Transfer Aid" bit in the 3174 configuration).

Personal Communications/3270 is a high end package, offering Distributed Function Terminal (DFT) support (which moves much of the intelligence from the control unit into the terminal, and provides multiple sessions) over coax, as well as comprehensive connectivity options via Token Ring, SDLC, and Ethernet. It also offers **3174 Peer Communication** (commonly known as "LAN over coax") with Configuration Support C of the 3174.

When used with Token Ring, the LAN may be connected either directly to the control unit, or alternatively, to a gateway PC running Personal Communications/3270 which is then connected onto the host.

Personal Communications/3270 offers Windows support as well as a DOS interface. It also provides mouse support (sensitive to screen content).   It supports EHLLAPI (a version of HLLAPI also supported by Communications Manager), together with a DDE interface to allow access to the API under Windows.

Personal Communications/3270 offers limited ASCII asynchronous support, but only for dial-up to special protocol converters provided for IIN access in the U.S.. For all other asynchronous 3270 access, IBM offers **PC/Host File Transfer and Terminal Emulator Program** (FTTERM).   This allows connection to a 3174 with the ASCII Emulation Adapter feature, or a 3708 protocol converter. It offers FTHLLAPI, a subset of HLLAPI compatible with those offered by the other emulators (with minor restrictions imposed by the unusual method of communication).   Its key feature is support for IND$FILE file transfer to and from the host system, over a dial-up ASCII asynchronous link.

FTTERM uses a superset of IBM's 3101 "glass teletype" control codes for its 3270 emulation.   FTTERM can also be used to access other hosts via *de facto* industry standard terminal emulations (e.g., VT100) and file transfer protocols (XMODEM and YMODEM).

Assorted other 3270 emulators are available from other vendors, both Windows-based and non-Windows-based, CUT- and DFT-based, supporting an array of different transports for host connection (often including support for the IBM connectivity options, as well as proprietary ones and even mechanisms such as TCP/IP).

IBM's emulators do not offer the ability to emulate graphics terminals (for use with GDDM applications). If this is required, IBM offers a GDDM-PCLK (GDDM PC Link) product, which operates over any HLLAPI session and, together with a host component (an feature of GDDM), provides similar function in a far less usable way (an equivalent product for OS/2 Communications Manager works with OS/2 Image Support to provide a much more effective implementation of this function). Many third-party emulators either have graphics mode built in, or offer it as an add-on component.

Enhanced Connectivity Facility

The **Enhanced Connectivity Facilities** (ECF) is a cooperative processing application which comes in two parts: one runs on CMS and one runs on the workstation (DOS or OS/2 EE). These applications communicate over a 3270 session (supporting HLLAPI), and offer access to host services from the workstation. The interface used between the host and workstation components is called the **Server Requester Programming Interface** (SRPI).

Services offered include:

1. Host files may appear to reside on an additional drive on the workstation. In this case an accessed CMS minidisk is mapped on to a workstation drive, and individual CMS files may be accessed from either system (EBCDIC to ASCII translation will be performed if required).
2. A workstation disk drive may physically reside on the host. In this case the workstation volume appears to be a single file on CMS, and the individual files cannot be accessed from the host (although the whole volume may be backed up as a single file).
3. SRPI can issue a host command from the command line of the workstation (or from a .BAT file) and have the results displayed on the PC console.
4. SRPI has the ability to queue PC files to be printed on host printers.
5. Host database access (for SQL/DS) is included.

VM PWSCS

VM Programmable Workstation Communication Services (PWSCS) provides an implementation of the **Common Communications Protocol for Communications** (CPI-C), the SAA defined programming interface to APPC, for workstations or servers running PC-DOS, Windows, OS/2, or AIX (on the PS/2 or the RISC System/6000). This allows customer- or vendor-written applications on the workstation or server to communicate with VM applications using APPC/VM, or via VTAM on VM to any APPC application.

The PWSCS gateway (termed the domain controller) runs on a PS/2 under OS/2 Extended Edition. Each gateway may connect to two different LANs. PWSCS then offers channel attachment to VM via either an integrated channel or a 3088 Multisystem Channel Communication Unit (using the Channel Adapter/A), or attachment via the Data Exchange Adapter on the 9371 Model 14 or 114, or via the integrated Token Ring adapter on the ES/9000. In addition, by installing **SAA Network Services/2** on the PWSCS server, PWSCS can act as a gateway between the CPI-C applications and any APPC application directly accessible to the OS/2 server, without requiring the VM channel connection.

Connection between the CPI-C application on the workstation and the PWSCS server may be provided:

- For PC-DOS and Windows clients via the IBM LAN Support Program
- For OS/2 clients via Communications Manager
- For AIX and OS/2 clients over TCP/IP
- For PC-DOS, Windows, or OS/2 clients via Novell NetWare (using its TCP/IP support).

For example, an application can issue CPI-C calls that are carried over TCP/IP to the PWSCS server, and hence over an SNA LU 6.2 session to communicate with an SNA-based application anywhere in the network.

VM PWSCS is able to generate NetView alerts for network management.

LANRES/VM

LAN Resource Extension and Services/VM (LANRES/VM) is an interface between Novell NetWare 386 and a VM host. It is implemented as a NetWare Loadable Module (NLM) on NetWare file servers. This communicates with the VM host component directly via a channel card, or indirectly via a PWSCS/VM gateway.

Specifically, LANRES/VM allows:

A NetWare disk image to reside on the VM host: The volume is stored as a single CMS file (and hence the individual files in the disk image cannot be accessed from the host). For example, this allows such volumes to be backed up to host tapes.

Data transfer from the Host to the NetWare file store: Files may be moved between the NetWare file store and the VM filing system via host commands (commands to get and put files). This can be used to make a file available to PC users (but does not allow transparent PC access to host files in the way that ECF does).

Administration from the host: NetWare administrator commands can be issued from the host (from any authorized, connected terminal or from an EXEC). This allows REXX procedures to be written to perform NetWare administration. In addition, LAN directory can be built from host data.

Printer server on VM: This allows PC users to print on host printers (system or RSCS printers) transparently. ASCII data and AFP (Advanced Function Printing) or PostScript data streams may be supported.

WDSF/VM

The **Workstation Data Save Facility/VM** (WDSF/VM) is a backup/restore and archive/retrieval system for workstations. Full and incremental backup of data is offered to host DASD, as well as on-demand archiving. On VM, data may be staged through multiple storage areas on disk and then on tape (or cartridge). Multiple versions of files may be retained.

On multitasking workstations, backup can occur automatically at set times of the day. Data may be compressed before it is transmitted to the host. Individual files or entire directories or subdirectories may subsequently be restored.

Workstation client support is currently offered for PC-DOS (over a 3270 session), OS/2 Extended Edition (over a 3270 session or a TCP/IP connection), AIX for the RISC System/6000, SunOS for Sun workstations (over a TCP/IP connection), and Apple Macintosh (over TCP/IP).

The product can be used for auxiliary purposes other than straightforward backup, such as archiving data to the host so that it may be retrieved by other users. Automatic migration to tape allows long retention periods to be specified, and the creation of multiple tape copies allows for offsite archiving.

In addition, the workstation-to-host communication protocol is documented so that vendors and users may implement WDSF/VM clients.

Other OS/2 products for VM

Communications Manager in OS/2 Extended Edition (OS/2 EE) offers both 3270 terminal emulation and APPC (LU 6.2) support which can be used to communicate with VM (as discussed above).

Two additional products should be mentioned. CM Mouse Support/2 is an add-on to the Communications Manager that allows the mouse to be used intelligently on host 3270 sessions. A Mouse click can have a script associated with it which is not only sensitive to the data underneath the mouse pointer at the time, but also to other data on the screen (for example the PROFS screen number, which tells it which menu is currently displayed). The product comes with a set of scripts to make the mouse useful for OfficeVision/VM and PROFS users. **SAA Application Connection Services** (AConnS) is an extension to the OS/2 Extended Edition desktop manager to allow VM applications to be invoked via icons placed on the desktop. This includes automatic host logon, and the initiation of the desired application within a 3270 window. Applications may reside on multiple, different hosts.

In addition, workstation access to host Advanced Function Printers is provided via a separate product, **SAA PrintManager**. AConnS is a prerequisite for other SAA applications for host/workstation integration, such as the **SAA Delivery Manager** and the **SAA Asset Manager**.

Summary

VM has the richest set of communication offerings among IBM host systems. It is often the developing and proving ground for products subsequently provided for MVS as well (e.g., TCP/IP, LANRES).

It has good SNA connectivity, good TCP/IP connectivity, and a growing level of OSI connectivity. These are the three cornerstones of IBM's future SAA communications strategy.

Not only does VM provide facilities in all three areas, it also allows an unparalleled ability to mix-and-match the environments: for example, carrying TCP/IP over an SNA backbone, SNA over X.25 communications, OSI over SNA, RSCS and PVM over APPC, and client/server communications over 3270 protocols, TCP/IP, and APPC.

The choices can be bewildering. However, only by being aware of the breadth of possibilities is it possible to build a communications infrastructure which is responsive to individual business needs.

14

VM/ESA–Workstation Synergy

By Chip Coy

Introduction

This chapter discusses many of the ways to connect and use DOS and OS/2 workstations with VM/ESA systems. It has two main goals:

1. To show how workstation programs can communicate with VM/ESA host programs.
2. To provide a glimpse of the coming world of cooperative applications.

This chapter does not discuss all the cooperative applications available for DOS and OS/2; such a listing would be immediately out of date. Intead, supplement it by reading current periodicals or by contacting vendors—IBM and others—to discuss specific needs and find the appropriate products.

This chapter does not discuss every possible communications mechanism. Rather, it focuses on two program-to-program mechanisms, one of which is likely to be at the center of most enterprise networking strategies: **SNA LU 6.2** and **TCP/IP**.

These topics, and the example programs that go with them, provide insight into how DOS and OS/2 workstations can be used in a cooperative fashion with VM/ESA.

Connectivity

There are two main connectivity topics to describe: the type of physical connection used and the connectivity software employed.

Physical connectivity

There are three general types of physical connections:

Coaxial cable: or **coax** is probably the most common connectivity for workstations connected to VM. The connection typically consists of a small piece of bare copper wire on the end of a black cable sticking out of the wall of an office. The bare copper wire is inserted into a **3270 adapter** card. Data rates for coax reach the 2 megabit range.

A possibility for providing more than 3270 emulation with a coax connection, for workstations connected to an IBM 3174 control unit, is the **Peer Communication feature**, which allows workstations to communicate as if in a local area network (LAN) with other workstations. The other workstations may be coax-attached to the same 3174 control unit; or when the 3174 is attached to an IBM Token Ring Network (TRN), they may be attached directly to the Token Ring, coax-attached to another 3174 within the TRN, or attached to other IBM TRN systems.

Token ring: or **T/R** is an up-and-coming connectivity technology for workstations connected to VM. The connection is a short cable with a workstation connection on one end (similar in appearance to a serial connector, but with fewer holes) and a three tier connector on the other end (meant to fit into an IBM Cabling System wall plate). The two ends are quite different in appearance and difficult to confuse. Maximum data rates are either 4 or 16 megabits/second, depending on the type of workstation adapter used.

Ethernet: Ethernet is another popular workstation connectivity technology. Ethernet physical connections come in a wide variety, from coaxial cable to thick orange cables. The maximum theoretical data rate is typically 10 megabits/second.

Connectivity software

Connectivity software also comes in a wide variety. Some connectivity software is tied to a particular physical connectivity, but this is becoming less so over time.

OS/2 Communications Manager

OS/2 Communications Manager provides both 3270 and non-3270 terminal emulation, as well as access to SNA Advanced Program-to-Program Communications facilities.

SAA Networking Services/2

Networking Services/2 Version 1.0 enhances the OS/2 Advanced Program-to-Program Communications (APPC) Application Programming Interface (API) by providing significant performance improvements and substantial reduction in network definition effort. It also supports the SAA Common Programming Interface for Communications, (CPI-C) enabling greater portability of applications across different environments.

Networking Services/2 also provides Advanced Peer-to-Peer Networking (APPN) capability. Networking Services/2 provides both end node (EN) and network node (NN) support, allowing workstations to participate in a peer network with other small, midrange, and large systems. This support enables greater flexibility in network design.

The OS/2 sample program shown in "OS/2–VM Sample Application" on page 382 is easily changed to work with Networking Services/2 by changing the line:

```
address PWSCS
```

to:

```
address CPICOMM
```

TCP/IP

IBM TCP/IP products are available for VM/ESA (product number 5735-FAL), OS/2 (product number 02G6-968), and DOS (product number 02G7-087).

These TCP/IP products, or separately priced features of these products, provide the following functions:

- Network File System (NFS) support
  - DOS and OS/2 can act as NFS requesters
  - OS/2 and VM can act as NFS servers
- Terminal emulation to other systems via the TELNET command
- Program-to-program communications via TCP and UDP sockets
- Remote procedure call programming interface
- File transfer
- Remote command execution
- Remote line printing
- Send and receive mail facility

The VM and OS/2 products provide these additional facilities:

- Server for remote line printing
- Simple Network Management Protocol support (SNMP)
- Kerberos services for development of secure client/server applications

The OS/2 product provides these additional facilities:

- Presentation Manager 3270 emulator (PMANT)
- X Window System server

The VM product provides these additional facilities:

- Domain Name Server
- X Window System support
  - Application development toolkit
  - GDDM applications support to X Window System servers
- Access to SQL/DS data
- Connections to other VM or MVS TCP/IP systems via SNA LU0

Examples

Presented here are simple examples of a TCP/IP server application
on VM and a TCP/IP client application on OS/2. These examples,
while not extensively tested, show how C programs can communicate using TCP/IP sockets.

The OS/2 client shown here is invoked via:

```
timeclnt hostname hostport
```

where hostname is the name of the VM system running the server
portion, and hostport is the port number specified to the server
portion.

```
/* Include files */
#include <manifest.h>
#include <bsdtypes.h>
#include <in.h>
#include <socket.h>
#include <netdb.h>
#include <stdio.h>

/* This is an OS/2 C user program that gets the */
/* current date and time from a server running on VM */
void main(int argc, char **argv)
{
    unsigned short port;       /* port client will connect to */
    char buf-20=;              /* data buffer for receiving */
    char datestr-9=;           /* date from the host */
    char timestr-9=;           /* time from the host */
    char datecmd-16=;          /* date command */
    char timecmd-16=;          /* time command */
    struct hostent *hostnm;    /* server host name information */
    struct sockaddr_in server; /* Server address */
    int s;                     /* client socket */

    /* Check arguments passed: should be hostname and port */
    if (argc != 3)
    {
        fprintf(stderr, "Usage: %s hostname port\n", argv-0=);
        exit(1);
    }

    /* The host name is the first argument: get server address */
    hostnm = gethostbyname(argv-1=);
    if (hostnm == (struct hostent *) 0)
    {
        fprintf(stderr, "Gethostbyname failed\n");
        exit(2);
    }

    /* The port is the second argument */
    port = (unsigned short) atoi(argv-2=);

    /* Put the server information into the server structure */
    /* The port must be put into network byte order */
    server.sin_family      = AF_INET;
    server.sin_port        = htons(port);
    server.sin_addr.s_addr = *((unsigned long *)hostnm->h_addr);

    /* Get a stream socket */
    if ((s = socket(AF_INET, SOCK_STREAM, 0)) < 0)
    {
        perror("Socket()");
        exit(3);
    }

    /* Connect to the server */
    if (connect(s, &server, sizeof(server)) < 0)
    {
```

```
        perror("Connect()");
        exit(4);
    }

    /* Get the time from the server */
    if (recv(s, buf, sizeof(buf), 0) < 0)
    {
        perror("Recv()");
        exit(6);
    }

    /* Close the socket */
    close(s);

    /* Build and execute the DATE/TIME commands */
    sscanf(buf, "%s %s", datestr, timestr);
    sprintf(datecmd, "DATE %s", datestr);
    sprintf(timecmd, "TIME %s", timestr);
    system(datecmd);
    system(timecmd);

    /* Done! */
    exit(0);

}
```

The VM server shown here is invoked via:

```
timesrv port
```

where *port* is the number of any unused TCP/IP port (the NETSTAT command shows which ports are in use).

```
#include <manifest.h>
#include <bsdtypes.h>
#include <socket.h>
#include <in.h>
#include <netdb.h>
#include <stdio.h>
#include <time.h>

/* This is a VM TCP/IP server that answers any incoming connect */
/* with the current date and time in the form yy/mm/dd hh:mm:ss */

/* The server takes one argument: a TCP/IP port number (e.g., 9998) */

int main(int argc, char **argv)
    {
    unsigned short port;      /* port server binds to */
    struct sockaddr_in client; /* Client address information */
    struct sockaddr_in server; /* Server address information */
    int s;                    /* socket for accepting connections */
    int ns;                   /* socket connected to client */
    int namelen;              /* length of client name */
    char timemsg-18=;         /* buffer for sending the time */
    int  timelen;             /* length of buffer */
    time_t now;               /* current time */
    struct tm *now_tm;        /* current time (broken down) */
    int  i;                   /* index for EBCDIC->ASCII translate */

    /* Check arguments: should be only one (port number to bind to) */

    if (argc != 2)
    {
        fprintf(stderr, "Usage: %s port\n", argv-0=);
        exit(1);
    }

    /* First argument should be the port */
    port = (unsigned short) atoi(argv-1=);

    /* Get a socket for accepting connections */
    if ((s = socket(AF_INET, SOCK_STREAM, 0)) < 0)
    {
        tcperror("Socket()");
        exit(2);
```

```
      }

      /* Bind the socket to the server address */
      server.sin_family = AF_INET;
      server.sin_port   = htons(port);
      server.sin_addr.s_addr = INADDR_ANY;

      if (bind(s, &server, sizeof(server)) < 0) {
          tcperror("Bind()");
          exit(3);
          }

      /* Listen for connections, specify the backlog as 1 */
      if (listen(s, 1) != 0) {
          tcperror("Listen()");
          exit(4);
          }

      /* Handle each incoming connection */

      for (;;) {

          /* Accept a connection */
          namelen = sizeof(client);
          if ((ns = accept(s, &client, &namelen)) == -1) {
              tcperror("Accept()");
              continue;
              }

          /* Get the current time */

          now = time(NULL);
          now_tm = localtime(&now);

          timelen = sprintf(timemsg, "%d/%d/%d %d:%d:%d",
                  now_tm->tm_mon+1, now_tm->tm_mday, now_tm->tm_year,
                  now_tm->tm_hour, now_tm->tm_min, now_tm->tm_sec);

          /* by subtraction) */
          for (i = 0; i < timelen; i++)
              if (timemsg-i= == ' ')
                  timemsg-i= = 0x20;
              else
                  if (timemsg-i= == ':')
                      timemsg-i= = 0x3A;
                  else
                      if (timemsg-i= == '/')
                          timemsg-i= = 0x2F;
                      else timemsg-i= -= 0xC0;

          /* Send the message back to the client */
          if (send(ns, timemsg, timelen, 0) < 0)
              tcperror("Send()");

          close(ns);
          }
  }
```

VM Programmable Workstation Connectivity Services

VM PWSCS is connectivity software optimized for high-speed communications between a System/370 or System/390 running VM/SP Release 6, VM/ESA Release 1.0 370 feature, or VM/ESA Release 1.1 and workstations attached to local area networks. These workstations may run IBM OS/2, IBM DOS, Microsoft Windows Version 3.0, IBM AIX PS/2, AIX Version 3 for RISC System/6000, or Novell NetWare.

VM PWSCS provides the SAA Common Programming Interface for Communications.

In addition to connecting directly to a VM system, VM PWSCS workstation applications may access SNA LU 6.2 network resources via an OS/2 Communications Manager gateway, Networking Services/2 gateway, or a VM host VM/VTAM gateway.

OS/2–VM Sample Application

Presented here is a simple example of a VM LU 6.2 server application accessible from workstations via either SNA LU 6.2 (using SAA Networking Services/2 for example) or VM PWSCS and a trivial example of a VM PWSCS client application. These examples, while not extensively tested, show how SAA Procedures Language programs can communicate using the SAA CPI for Communications.

The OS/2 client shown here is invoked via `timeclnt` *host name*, where *host name* is the name assigned on the workstation via the VM PWSCS "View Configure" utility that identifies the target host.

```
/* This is an OS/2 REXX user program that gets the */
/* current date and time from a server running on VM */

   pwscs_directory='C:\PWSCS'        /* Set PWSCS installation directory */
   arg destname .

   if destname='' then
      do
         say 'You must enter the symbolic destination name.'
         signal QUIT
      end

   address PWSCS                      /* Direct commands to PWSCS */

/* Read program constants from the file ACPHREXX.CPY */

   copyfile=pwscs_directory||'\ACPHREXX.CPY'  /* Set REXX def'n file */

   call stream copyfile,'C','Open Read'  /* Open the definitions file */

   do while stream(copyfile,'S')=='READY' & lines(copyfile)
      interpret linein(copyfile)        /* Interpret each definition */
   end

   call stream copyfile,'C','Close'    /* Close the definitions file */

/*-----------------------------------------------------------------
   Before we can communicate to the resource, we must initialize a
   conversation path.  To do this we call the CMINIT
   (Initialize_Conversation) routine.  The parameters are:
   - An output conversation id, which we must remember to
     specify on other calls to communication routines for this
     conversation.
   - The name of the destination which we are attempting to use.
   - A return code variable.
   ----------------------------------------------------------------*/

   'CMINIT conv_id destname conv_rc'
   if conv_rc <> CM_OK then
      do
         say 'Unable to initialize conversation to destination' destname
         signal QUIT                    /* Quit now */
      end

/*-----------------------------------------------------------------
   Get the partner LU name using the CMEPLN routine
   (Extract_Partner_LU_Name).
   ----------------------------------------------------------------*/
```

```
       'CMEPLN conv_id plu plu_length conv_rc'
       say 'Partner LU = "'plu'"'

/*------------------------------------------------------------------
    Now we are ready to actually allocate the conversation to the
    resource we wish to use.  We use the CMALLC (Allocate) routine
    for this.  The parameters are:
      - the conversation ID of the initialized and tailored conversation
      - a return code variable
    ------------------------------------------------------------*/

       'CMALLC conv_id conv_rc'

       if conv_rc <> CM_OK then
         do
           say 'Unable to allocate conversation to destination',
              destname', rc =' conv_rc
           signal QUIT                     /* Quit now */
         end

/* Get the date and time from the server */

     status_flag = CM_NO_STATUS_RECEIVED

     do while status_flag <> CM_SEND_RECEIVED
       'CMRCV conv_id buffer 256 data_flag received_length status_flag',
            'rts_flag conv_rc'
       if conv_rc <> CM_OK then
         do
           say 'Unable to receive data from destination - rc =' conv_rc
           call CLEANUP conv_rc            /* Clean up the conversation */
           signal QUIT                     /* Quit now */
         end
       else
         if data_flag <> CM_NO_DATA_RECEIVED then
           do   /* Set the date and time */
             parse var buffer sdate stime
             address '' 'DATE' sdate
             address '' 'TIME' stime
           end
     end

/*------------------------------------------------------------------
    At this point, we have displayed the entire contents of the file.
    For simplicity, this program is designed to request a single file
    and then sever the path.  Our last Receive should have indicated
    that the resource switched us back to Send state
    (status = CM_SEND_RECEIVED).

    Now we are ready to deallocate the conversation.
    ------------------------------------------------------------*/

       'CMDEAL conv_id conv_rc'
       if conv_rc <> CM_OK then
         say 'Unable to deallocate the conversation - rc =' conv_rc

/*------------------------------------------------------------------
         All done
    ------------------------------------------------------------*/

QUIT:
   exit 0

/*------------------------------------------------------------------
    Clean up the conversation following abnormal termination.
    ------------------------------------------------------------*/

CLEANUP:
   arg conv_rc .

   if conv_rc = CM_PARAMETER_ERROR |,
      conv_rc = CM_PRODUCT_SPECIFIC_ERROR |,
      conv_rc = CM_PROGRAM_ERROR_NO_TRUNC |,
      conv_rc = CM_PROGRAM_ERROR_PURGING |,
      conv_rc = CM_PROGRAM_ERROR_TRUNC |,
      conv_rc = CM_PROGRAM_PARAMETER_CHECK |,
      conv_rc = CM_PROGRAM_STATE_CHECK then
      do
        say 'Abnormally terminating conversation' conv_id'.'
        'CMSDT conv_id CM_DEALLOCATE_ABEND cleanup_rc'
        'CMDEAL conv_id cleanup_rc'
      end

   return
```

The VM server shown here is not invoked directly; rather, a small bit of setup work (as described in the example) is performed to allow the incoming request to automatically invoke the EXEC.

```
/* This is a VM CPI-C server that answers any incoming allocate with */
/* the current date and time in the form: yy/mm/dd hh:mm:ss */
/*
    Create a $SERVER$ NAMES file containing one line:

    and place two commands in the PROFILE EXEC of the server:

        'SET AUTOREAD OFF'
        'SET SERVER ON'

    the TIMESRV EXEC will be executed each time a client connects.

*/

/* Get constants */
    'EXECIO * DISKR CMREXX COPY * (FINIS STEM JUNK.'
    do i = 1 to junk.0; interpret junk.i; end
    drop junk.

/* Direct commands to CPI-C */
    address CPICOMM

/* Accept a connection (using CMACCP) */

    'CMACCP conv_id conv_rc'

    if conv_rc <> CM_OK then do
        say 'Unable to accept conversation, rc =' conv_rc
        exit                                /* skip this one */
        end

/* Now wait for the requester to give us SEND state */

    do while status_flag <> CM_SEND_RECEIVED
        'CMRCV conv_id dummy 80 data_flag',
                'received_length status_flag rts_flag conv_rc'

      if conv_rc = CM_DEALLOCATED_NORMAL then
          do
            say 'Conversation' convid 'disappeared.'
            exit                            /* Wait for next req */
          end

      if conv_rc <> CM_OK then
          do
            say 'Unable to receive data on conversation' conv_id', ',
                'rc =' conv_rc
            call CLEANUP conv_rc            /* Clean up the conversation */
            exit                            /* Wait for next req */
          end
    end

/* If the conversation went away, just wait for the next one */
    if conv_rc <> CM_OK then exit

/* We are in SEND state, so send date and time (translate to ASCII) */

    buffer= translate(date('U') time(),,
        '2030313233343536373839 3A2F'x, ' 0123456789:/')
    bufferl = length(buffer)
    'CMSEND conv_id buffer bufferl rts_flag conv_rc'    /* Date/time */
    if conv_rc <> CM_OK then
        do
            say 'Unable to send date/time, rc =' conv_rc
            call CLEANUP conv_rc            /* Clean up the conversation */
            exit                            /* wait for the next one */
        end

/*  Wait for requester to deallocate the conversation */

    do while conv_rc = CM_OK
        'CMRCV conv_id buffer 80 data_flag received_length status_flag',
            'rts_flag conv_rc'
    end
```

```
/* Done! */

  exit

/*  Clean up the conversation following abnormal termination */

CLEANUP:
  arg conv_rc .

  if conv_rc = CM_PARAMETER_ERROR |,
     conv_rc = CM_PRODUCT_SPECIFIC_ERROR |,
     conv_rc = CM_PROGRAM_ERROR_NO_TRUNC |,
     conv_rc = CM_PROGRAM_ERROR_PURGING |,
     conv_rc = CM_PROGRAM_ERROR_TRUNC |,
     conv_rc = CM_PROGRAM_PARAMETER_CHECK |,
     conv_rc = CM_PROGRAM_STATE_CHECK then do
     say 'Abnormally terminating conversation' conv_id'.'
     'CMSDT conv_id CM_DEALLOCATE_ABEND cleanup_rc'
     'CMDEAL conv_id cleanup_rc'
     end

  return
```

Applications and Application Enablers

IBM Workstation DataSave Facility/VM

IBM Workstation Data Save Facility/Virtual Machine (WDSF/VM) provides key services for backing up, archiving, and restoring disk or diskette data files by allowing a VM system to act as a server for workstations. It moves responsibilities of backup/archive media management to VM while providing client applications for PC/DOS, OS/2 EE, AIX Version 3 for RISC System/6000, SunOS, and MacOS. WDSF/VM communicates from the workstation to the host using either a 3270 connection (with either Personal Communications/3270 on DOS or OS/2 EE Communication Manager) or a TCP/IP connection.

IBM Executive Decisions/VM

IBM Executive Decisions/VM addresses executive and staff needs to access, analyze, and communicate critical business information. IBM Executive Decisions/VM is a versatile executive support system that helps improve executive and staff productivity. It provides a simple, consistent, icon-oriented user interface based on OS/2 EE to access specialized functions and office tools such as mail, calendar, address book, and telephone as well as external news services. IBM Executive Decisions/VM is an integrated IBM System/370 and Personal System/2 (PS/2) application.

AD/Cycle

AD/Cycle is IBM's solution for SAA Application Development. Many AD/Cycle components span the boundary between the workstation and the VM host.

OfficeVision/VM

The DOS Direct Connect and OS/2 Office features are other examples of traditional VM applications that now span the boundary between the host and the workstation. These OfficeVision features provide workstation based access to OfficeVision/VM functions.

IBM SAA Distributed Database Connection Services/2

IBM SAA Distributed Database Connection Services/2 (DDCS/2) provides read/write access to host databases for OS/2 Extended Services database client and client/server workstations. DDCS/2 implements the SAA Distributed Relational Database Architecture (DRDA) to supported host database systems. Supported host database systems include SQL/DS, DB2, and OS/400. In addition to supporting single-user access from an OS/2 workstation with IBM Extended Services, this product also supports multi-user access to a host database from LAN-attached DOS, DOS Windows, or OS/2 workstations through a DDCS/2 server in conjunction with IBM Extended Services with Database Server for OS/2.

DDCS/2 uses APPC or APPN to connect to the host system.

IBM SAA Application Connection Services

IBM SAA Application Connection Services (AConnS) extends the OS/2 EE environment into the mainframe world. It simplifies the use and administration of application programs. Application invocation (including automatic host logon) is made consistent for *all* applications (local, host, and cooperative) in the enterprise information system. Host AFP printers can appear logically connected to the workstation. AConnS is prerequisite for IBM cooperative applications such as SAA Delivery Manager.

IBM SAA Delivery Manager

IBM SAA Delivery Manager provides the customer with a flexible means of customizing, controlling, and delivering programs and files from the MVS or VM host processors to IBM OS/2 programmable workstations. IBM SAA Delivery Manager may be used to manage customer programs and data, IBM licensed programs and other vendor's programs, information, and files. Using IBM SAA Delivery Manager, end-users may select packages to be delivered, installed, and/or updated on their workstations, or the host administrator can initiate the delivery, installation, and/or updating to end-user's workstations. IBM SAA Delivery Manager is a cooperative application that uses IBM SAA Application Connection Services with part of the application in the host and part in the workstation.

IBM SAA PrintManager

IBM SAA PrintManager provides common access to printing, including Advanced Function Printing (AFP) across VM and MVS. Through the use of the PrintManager Interface and the application programming interface (API), customers can employ a common set of print options from within an application program. Print files can then be sent to the system SPOOL in a simplified, consistent manner.

Besides providing a general solution to these difficult print problems for VM and MVS, SAA PrintManager accepts print jobs for OS/2 applications via the IBM SAA Application Connection Services/VM or MVS.

Summary

This chapter covered many topics of connecting and using DOS and OS/2 workstations with VM/ESA systems. Hopefully these topics, and the example programs that accompany them, have provided a view of how DOS and OS/2 workstations can be used in a cooperative fashion with a VM/ESA system.

This is a rapidly evolving interface area; IBM and myriad other vendors are continually introducing new products and facilities to couple workstations to VM/ESA.

15

Apple Macintosh Synergy with VM/ESA

By Pat Ryall

This chapter discusses how the Apple Macintosh personal computer "plugs and plays" in an IBM VM/ESA mainframe world. It begins by reviewing key features of the Macintosh that are exploited when the Macintosh user connects to IBM systems, whether a 9371 or an ES/9000. It then details how and where these features are used. The emphasis is on connectivity options including 3270, database access, and personal productivity such as mail.

The main topics discussed are:

- An overview of the Macintosh and its features
- Communication in an IBM world, with terminal emulation and file transfer, including connectivity options and challenges
- 3270 connectivity choices, players, options, gateways, and APIs
- APPC (Apple had the first IBM-approved non-IBM LU 6.2 implementation) and recent APPN announcements

- Database including generic and specific access plus external calls from Macintosh applications including HyperCard, host- and server-based databases
- Personal productivity including mail, word processors, file transfer, and file filters/translators
- Implications of the Apple/IBM alliance agreement

Products and services mentioned are for illustrative purposes and are neither an inclusive list nor recommendations of particular manufacturers or vendors. Rather, references illustrate the type of capabilities available to the Macintosh-to-VM/ESA mainframe user. Although the purpose of this chapter is to discuss Macintosh-to-VM/ESA connectivity, most references apply equally to IBM's other mainframe operating systems as well.

Even though Apple Macintosh computers are traditionally viewed as desktop computers, they connect extremely well to IBM main-frames running all the main IBM operating systems including VM/ESA. For example, Apple's SNA*ps family, described below, delivers a comprehensive, integrated set of protocols and services for Macintosh users to communicate in IBM's Systems Network Architecture (SNA) environment. Apple's Data Access Language (DAL) interface to host databases, also described below, permits database users to incorporate Macintosh front ends in their client/server database solutions while giving Macintosh users transparent access to thousands of SQL applications.

How did this ease of connecting come about? It has been a result of conscious decisions by Apple and third-party vendors such as Avatar and DCA (DCA and Avatar have now merged) to provide the infrastructure, tools, and applications required.

The Macintosh User Interface

Macintosh system software differentiates Macintosh computers from all other personal computers. It provides the consistent, common sense way of working with the computer—with commands in plain English and a graphics-based user interface that offers straightfor-ward access to the computer's resources. Because Macintosh system software is an integral part of Apple's system architecture, Apple has always provided Macintosh users with the four important advantages listed on the next page.

- Superior personal computing power and ease of use
- Consistent, intuitive applications that work together
- Built-in networking and multi-vendor connectivity
- Growth without disruption, which protects the user's investment

Superior personal computing power and ease of use

The Macintosh user interface provides a consistent and familiar computer environment in which people can perform their many tasks. The Macintosh user interface—the result of years of research into the interaction of people and computers—was designed to make all levels of computer users—from novices to experts—more productive and effective. The Macintosh user interface is graphics-based; that is, control of computer functions is accomplished by pointing to and selecting graphic representations of real-world images, called **icons**, displayed on the computer screen. This interface intentionally provides a natural and intuitive computing environment; so natural that users become unaware of the tool being used, and can concentrate on the task at hand. This characteristic of the Macintosh user interface is often referred to as **transparency**. Because this interface is integrated into the Macintosh system, rather than added on separately, all software written for Macintosh operates similarly, maximizing the user's ability to accomplish diverse tasks.

The direct results of these Macintosh attributes have been confirmed by several independent studies: users can exploit powerful new technology faster and with less disruption than can users of other systems. These studies revealed that both MIS managers and computer users are more satisfied with Macintosh overall; that Macintosh has lower training costs per user; and that users give Macintosh higher ratings in key performance categories.

Consistent, intuitive applications that work together

These elements created a foundation for applications that all work in the same way, sharing graphics and other information through the simple metaphor of cutting and pasting. Although the Macintosh system has continually evolved since 1984 to bring more power and functionality to the user, the basic design principles of the Macintosh are unchanged. Ten principles that have guided the development of the Macintosh desktop interface are summarized below (see *Human Interface Guidelines: The Apple Desktop Interface*, Reading, MA, Addison-Wesley, 1987.)

1. Metaphors from the real world: Use concrete metaphors and make them plain, so that users have a set of expectations to apply to computer environments. Wherever appropriate, use audio and visual effects that support the metaphor.

2. Direct manipulation: Users want to feel that they are in charge of the computer's activities.

3. See-and-point (instead of remember-and-type): Users select actions from alternatives presented on the screen. The general form of the user action is noun-then-verb. Users rely on recognition, not recall; they should not have to remember anything the computer already knows. Most programmers have no trouble working with a command-line interface that requires memorization and Boolean logic. The average user is not a programmer.

4. Consistency: Effective applications are both consistent within themselves and consistent with one another.

5. WYSIWYG (What You See Is What You Get): There should be no secrets from the user, no abstract commands that only promise future results. There should be no significant difference between what the user sees on the screen and what eventually gets printed.

6. User control: The user, not the computer, initiates and controls all actions.

7. Feedback and dialog: Keep the user informed. Provide immediate feedback. User activities should be simple at any moment, though they may be complex taken together.

8. Forgiveness: Users make mistakes; forgive them. The user's actions are generally reversible—let the user know about any that are not.

9. Perceived stability: Users feel comfortable in a computer environment that remains understandable and familiar rather than changing randomly.

10. Aesthetic integrity: Visually confusing or unattractive displays detract from the effectiveness of human computer interactions. Different things should look different on the screen. Users should be able to control the superficial appearance of their computer work places to display their own style and individuality. Messes are acceptable only if the user makes them, applications are not allowed this freedom.

The power of the Macintosh computer lies in the thousands of applications and peripherals available. Many applications such as Aldus PageMaker, Microsoft Excel, and 4th Dimension from ACIUS, have broken new ground in the industry, while maintaining Macintosh ease of use and consistency. Peripherals such as large capacity disk drives, laser and color printers, CD-ROMs, optical scanners for text and graphics, and an array of communications devices have multiplied the original power of the Macintosh many times over. Because of ongoing efforts with its third-party developers, and interface tools built into the Macintosh computer, products from Apple have a significantly larger base of consistent, graphics-based programs than the rest of the PC industry.

The Macintosh computer's success can be directly traced to the fundamental vision of the engineers who designed it: build a computer that will be accessible, engaging, and exciting to use, while insulating users from the technical complexities traditionally associated with computing. To accomplish this, they added two key elements to the hardware and operating system:

1. An environment based on the desktop metaphor that uses real-world graphic images and a see-and-point user interface
2. A toolbox of common routines upon which all applications can draw

Built-in networking and multi-vendor connectivity

The Macintosh personal computer family has a robust ability to communicate with other computer systems and environments. Every Macintosh system has hardware and software networking capabilities that are integral to the architecture. The networking capability provides an AppleTalk protocol stack with built-in LocalTalk, EtherTalk for Ethernet, and TokenTalk for Token Ring. This includes session-based protocols such as the Apple Data Stream Protocol (ADSP) and Apple Filing Protocol (AFP) for file sharing.

Apple's goal is to enhance users' environments and extend their reach by integrating intuitive communication capabilities into the Macintosh and accessing remote information and services in a way familiar to them. Apple recognizes the multi-vendor needs of its users and is committed to providing Macintosh integration into other computing environments that represent the majority of the market requirements. These environments already include: IBM's large and small systems, Digital Equipment Corporation's VAX, Open System Interconnection (OSI), and Transmission Control Protocol/Internet Protocol (TCP/IP). Because the Macintosh was designed for networking from the start, it's easy for Macintosh users to set up a local area network to share files and printers, and to connect to other computing environments, such as DEC, IBM, OSI, and TCP/IP.

The **Macintosh Communications Toolbox (CTB)** is an integral part of the system software that provides Macintosh applications with standard access to communications services, including data connection, terminal emulation, and file transfer protocols. It is Apple's strategic communications development platform to support multi-vendor connectivity. The Communications Toolbox consists of four key managers: Connection, Terminal, File Transfer, and Communications Resource managers. These managers are designed to work in concert with communications tools created by Apple and third-party developers to provide applications with standard communications functions. Apple provides TTY, VT102, VT320 terminals; text and XMODEM file transfer; and Serial, AppleTalk ADSP, and LAT (DEC's Local Area Transport) connection tools.

The CTB allows developers to easily create protocol-independent applications and eliminates the need for driver remapping, providing applications with access to all registered communications devices. It features an open, modular and extensible architecture, while its communications tools provide consistent, intuitive network configuration user interfaces.

Growth without disruption, protecting user investment

Because the Macintosh architecture was designed to grow, all Macintosh owners—even buyers of the original Macintosh computer—have a clear growth path to system software version 7.0 (System 7), available since 1991, version 7.1 in 1992, and beyond. System 7 brings greater power and ease of use to Macintosh users:

- Built-in features such as the Finder for powerful multi-tasking, with background file sharing, copying, and printing, and fast file finding. Because the system automatically installs them, users can quickly add items such as fonts and desk accessories simply by dragging them into the System Folder.
- See a font or hear a sound simply by double-clicking its icon in the System Folder.
- Use built-in HELP called **Balloon Help**.
- Have file sharing without a dedicated server.
- TrueType outline fonts for great-looking documents on the screen and the printed page.
- Sound input can add voice comments to voice-capable applications through the familiar Macintosh user interface.
- In most cases use virtual memory with 32-bit addressing.
- Aliases allow users to store an application or document in more than one place without duplication. Users access hard disks or frequently used network services (e.g., a server) by simply double-clicking an alias from any Macintosh computer on the same network or remotely from a modem-equipped Macintosh.
- WorldScript provides built in support for virtually every written language including non-Roman languages. Apple can quickly localize the Macintosh computer for nearly simultaneous delivery of computer products throughout most parts of the world.
- The QuickTime system-software extension manages sound, video and animation. It includes large screen size for video playback; support for full-screen, full-motion digital video cards; fully integrated support for the Kodak Photo CD; 1-bit fast dithering for playback on monochrome screens; generic media handlers that let developers create new movie-track types; and closed captioning.

System 7 provides new features that software developers are building into their applications including InterApplication Communication and AppleEvents with "Publish" and "Subscribe" to create live links between applications for automatic document updating. The Data Access Manager provides built-in access to remote databases and can extract data from remote mainframes. All System 7 features are fully integrated, using the familiar Macintosh interface, providing users with even more power. For example, users can combine "Publish" and "Subscribe" with built-in networking to update documents automatically across a network.

Growth is without disruption and protects users' investments since System 7 works with all Macintosh computers that have 2 megabytes of RAM and a hard disk. Thousands of applications continue to work together with powerful new capabilities for Macintosh applications in business, education, science, and entertainment.

Communicating in an IBM VM World

The main ways a Macintosh connects to a VM host, typically for terminal emulation, are via serial (asynchronous and synchronous) connections, 3270 coax, and, perhaps most common today, LAN-based connections. The Macintosh supports many terminal emulation programs from both Apple and third-party vendors. Terminal emulators support asynchronous (TTY), 3270, and TCP/IP access to VM across various media. 3270 supports both Control Unit Terminal (CUT) and Distributed Function Terminal (DFT) emulation of IBM 3270 Information Display Systems. Emulators are differentiated by how they provide the connection to VM: their features, how well they exploit the Macintosh desktop (such as background operation under the Finder and the Macintosh user interface), and the number of sessions supported. Terminal emulator applications also usually provide an application programming interface or API. APIs allow other applications and utilities to exploit the terminal emulator functionality programmatically. This is the building block on which front-end tools rely (i.e., they treat the 3270 as a buffer to transport data and screens to an application on the Macintosh).

It is very important that terminal emulators exploit the Macintosh capabilities. Just meeting the definition of a terminal emulator is not enough. In the Macintosh world, an emulator must make it easy to change font size and colors independent of the VM host. The emulator window should be able to move about just as any other Macintosh window does. Having copy-and-paste is a basic requirement. Tear-off palette windows for PF keys and frequent commands are very handy features. Printing should just print the current screen. Keyboard remapping should be as simple as dragging keys around on a graphic display of the keyboard in use.

For example, Apple's MacTerminal (for asynchronous connections) can save terminal sessions to disk automatically. Apple's SNA*ps

3270 emulator lets users resize windows by using a dialog box after a menu selection, or by simply dragging the grow box (in the lower right hand corner) smaller or larger. Avatar's MacMainFrame provides icons on the window border to simplify changing fonts, remapping the keyboard, changing the operator information area (OIA), and others.

Serial access

Asynchronous serial connections use a software product such as the above-mentioned MacTerminal, which uses the Communications Toolbox. It provides standard serial (TTY) access to VM and other hosts. MacTerminal also supports DEC VT100 access to IBM systems so that 3278 emulation (typically 24 line) is also possible through a protocol converter at the host such as Simware or hardware such as a 3172.

Apple's **MacX25** links Macintosh computers to packet-switched data networks (PSDNs) supporting CCITT (International Telegraph & Telephone Consultative Committee) recommendation X.25. The MacX25 Server allows Macintoshes to be set up as single-entry points to the PSDN. Server-based access makes it easy to add users and reduces costs by maximizing use of expensive resources such as leased lines. Access to host computers and end-user services on the PSDN is distributed from the server to Macintosh computers over the AppleTalk network. **MacPAD** software, included with MacX25, works with the server software and provides packet assembler/disassembler (PAD) connectivity to the PSDN (X.3, X.28, X.29). MacPAD is implemented as a Communications Toolbox connection tool and allows terminal applications using the toolbox to connect to host systems on the PSDN. The MacX25 Programming Library works in conjunction with the MacX25 server to provide X.25 access by applications.

An easy-to-use address book with a standard Macintosh user interface allows users to select available services by name without learning PAD commands. A graphics-based administrator application facilitates software installation and administration of user access. User passwords prevent unauthorized users from accessing the server. It does not require a dedicated server and can run with other applications. It operates as a DTE or a DCE with a maximum of 64 virtual circuits. A single link is supported for each Apple Serial NB (NuBus) card but multiple cards can be used for each

Macintosh. It operates at up to 19.2 KBPS with a V.24/V.28 connection and up to 64 KBPS with a V.35 connection. Multiple servers are allowed for each AppleTalk network.

3270 connectivity

The 3270 world is a bit more complicated than the asynchronous world since there are more options available. The Macintosh computer can have either a serial SDLC card, a 3270 coax card, or a LAN card (Ethernet or Token Ring), or perhaps use the built-in LocalTalk connection to access VM hosts. There are also variations based on whether or not AppleTalk distributes 3270 sessions to other users on the LAN via a gateway. But to users of terminal emulators and APIs, there are few differences in how they are used; only in how they connect. 3270 emulators support most models of the 327x, 317x, 3180, and 319x in both Control Unit Terminal (CUT) and Distributed Function Terminal (DFT) modes, including Multi-Function Terminals (MFT). They also support base and extended attributes, have extended color support, and include Operator Information Area (OIA) status line symbols.

What distinguishes the different 3270 terminal emulators are their exploitation of Macintosh features, their naturalness as Macintosh applications, their extensions to the standard 3270 features, and the power and ease of use of their APIs. An example of an extension is type-ahead, which 3270 hardware does not support. A feature that is mandatory is support for basic Macintosh features such as cut, copy, and paste. An emulator should offer complete 3270 emulation, exploit Macintosh power, and feel natural to experienced Macintosh users. Apple's SNA*ps products are a good example of emulator/Macintosh synergy.

Apple's **SNA*ps** (Systems Network Architecture protocols and services) family delivers a comprehensive, integrated set of protocols and services for Macintosh to communicate in SNA environments over a wide range of media. (SNA*ps replaces Apple's MacDFT and MacAPPC products.) The family gives Macintosh users flexible and transparent access to data, applications, and services on IBM host systems. SNA*ps offers concurrent support for terminal emulation and peer-to-peer communication (APPC) in an SNA environment and provides high performance and flexible access to SNA networks from a single Macintosh or an AppleTalk network. The SNA*ps

Gateway, described below, also incorporates the first level of support for IBM's Advanced Peer-to-Peer Networking (APPN) protocols.

Balloon HELP Example

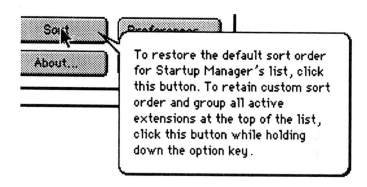

Avatar's **MacMainFrame** product fully supports System 7 including virtual memory, "Publish" and "Subscribe", AppleEvents, TrueType, and 32-bit addressing.   MacMainFrame has System 7 HELP Balloons for all basic features, such as MacMainFrame menus and dialog boxes, and also includes specific HELP Balloons for status and error conditions that can occur during MacMainFrame connectivity operations.   For example, some balloons interpret the 3270 status line symbols, add additional information about host errors, and suggest when to contact the system administrator.

MacMainFrame support of System 7's "Publish" and "Subscribe" allows users to take information from a MacMainFrame 3270 window and "Publish".   For example, a MacMainFrame user can access a mainframe financial application, select/highlight an area of data, and "Publish" it to an edition file.   When a Microsoft Excel spreadsheet document subscribes to that edition file, the host data will then be incorporated into the Excel document for further use. This type of usage shows the ease of transparent connectivity between the Macintosh and IBM mainframe environments. Because of products like MacMainFrame, Macintosh users can easily access mission-critical data that is usually kept on the corporate mainframe and transparently use it within Macintosh applications.

Both Avatar (MacMainFrame graphics) and DCA (MacIRMA PCLK graphics and MacIRMA GraphStation) emulate IBM's 3179G and 3192G color graphics terminals in both workstation and gateway configurations. They let Macintosh computer users access IBM mainframe computer graphics applications. They use the DFT All Points Addressable (APA) graphics method in addition to implementing host graphics manipulation with CUT, such as PC Link (PCLK) or Program Symbols. They allow host Graphics Data Format (GDF) and PC Interchange Format (PIF) files to be accessed, manipulated, transferred, and converted to Macintosh formats, including EPS, PICT, MacDraw, and MacPaint files. Users can also export these graphics to various output devices connected to their Macintoshes.

3270 workstation

The terms "stand-alone workstation" and "client of a gateway" are used to describe connection types. If a user has a direct connection to an IBM controller via SDLC or coax card, the user is usually described as a 3270 workstation. Even a LAN-based Token Ring user can be defined as a downstream PU and hence be thought of being directly connected to a host. The advantage of this approach is that the user has a direct connection or simple connection through the LAN to the host, with reduced LAN traffic. The downside is that each user's workstation must be defined to VTAM at the VM host and that resources such as DFT sessions may not be shared easily by other users on the LAN.

SNA*ps 3270 gives a Macintosh computer stand-alone access to VM hosts. SNA*ps 3270 includes CUT and DFT capabilities for direct coaxial SNA connections. It supports all IBM screen display formats and attributes, uses the IBM standard protocol for file transfers, and integrates mainframe data into Macintosh applications using standard Macintosh copy-and-paste techniques. SNA*ps 3287 enables LaserWriters to emulate IBM's 3287 printers for printing host application documents.

As another example, DCAs MacIRMA WorkStation software with the MacIRMA coax card also supports light pen applications plus enhanced support for file transfer, including MacBinary and cross-platform file translation.

3270 gateways

With gateways, a shared Macintosh (or a PC in the case of the DCA IRMALAN product) serves as an SNA gateway emulating a 317*x* cluster controller. The gateway can also be a dedicated controller, such as the Netway 1000 from Tri-Data (now part of Avatar), that supports both AppleTalk and SNA protocols (i.e., a remote 3174). 3270 sessions can be distributed across the LAN or internetwork via AppleTalk, which includes LocalTalk, EtherTalk, and TokenTalk. SDLC and coax cards typically support a maximum of five DFT sessions. With Token Ring gateways, up to 64 concurrent users and 128 host sessions can be supported. To the host, these nodes appear as remote 3270 controllers.

The advantage of a gateway is that sessions can be shared; many more sessions can be supported, at higher speed; and configuration is easier than with individual workstations. The disadvantages can be more LAN traffic as users converse with the gateway and then the gateway converses with the host over the same Token Ring. With a gateway there is an additional step needed by users to specify location of the gateway on the network.

The **SNA*ps Gateway** is a complete implementation of IBM LU 2, LU 6.2, and NT 2.1. Users can configure it as an AppleTalk network gateway to enable any Macintosh to communicate with IBM systems running the VM, MVS, OS/400, and OS/2 operating systems. The SNA*ps Gateway supports multiple interface cards and adjustable performance parameters, and combines 3270 terminal emulation with APPC. It provides access to existing 3270 terminal-based applications and a Macintosh interface to host applications, databases, and OfficeVision services. Implemented on an intelligent NuBus card, it offers parallel sessions and independent LU support. This design gives users multiple gateways in a single machine and frees the main Macintosh processor to run applications without affecting the Macintosh's performance. The design frees the main Macintosh processor to run other LAN applications that provide file, mail, and database services. It is easily upgraded to support new features without hardware changes. The SNA*ps Gateway supports 8, 32, and 64 sessions. The gateway software supports the Apple Token Ring NuBus cards for Token Ring networks, the Apple Serial NB Card for SNA/SDLC connections, and the Apple Coax/Twinax Card for cluster controller/DFT connectivity.

File transfer

The ability to transfer files is an important part of Macintosh-to-VM mainframe connectivity. Most file transfer mechanisms are compatible with IBM's **IND$FILE** (3270-PC file transfer program for VM, program number 5664-281). Some also support their own protocols (e.g., Avatar's CMSHFT and DCA). While many options are available, the main consideration is the ability to transfer Macintosh files in either document, binary or text format quickly and accurately. 3270 emulator vendors supply options to interactively transfer files in standard Macintosh format including in the background or programmatically though the APIs (or XCMDs/XFCNs from Hyper-Card, etc.). In addition, MacMainFrame offers extensive security features for user and data protection. Various online HELP screens are available at any time.

3270 APIs

The 3270 Application Programming Interface (API) is a key part of 3270 terminal emulators, allowing programmatic access to emulator capabilities. Most 3270 emulators provide an API. The APIs may be a subset of IBM's High Level Language API (HLLAPI) or Extended HLLAPI (EHLLAPI) or may be vendor-unique. They allow program access to the presentation space (see also "Front-Ending" on page 414, especially MitemView) and to file transfer capabilities. Vendors provide additional services such as 3287 print support with their APIs. Other applications, including Apple's DAL, can use the 3270 presentation space as data transport via the API. APIs are also building blocks for other Macintosh-based external functions (sometimes just called externals) such as HyperCard XCMDs, ACIUS' 4th Dimension externals (4DEX), C code, etc. Externals for different products may differ due to the calling sequences, but are conceptually the same.

Third-party developers can build on the flexibility provided by APIs. For example, the SNA*ps 3270 Developers Kit enables third-parties to build LU 2 applications, including alternative 3270 terminal emulators, graphical front ends to 3270-based applications, and host interface development tools. Users and developers can generate "programmed operator"-style applications to simulate routine operator functions, such as log on procedures and file transfer, as well as complicated data transfer operations to move data from a host database to a Macintosh spreadsheet. Avatar supplies with its API an IBM3270 XFCN and IBMXFER XCMD that give the HyperCard developer the ability to create HyperTalk scripts that perform all functions of the IBM terminal and the ability to transfer files to and from a VM host.

Avatar's MacMainFrame also supports the SNA*ps 3270 Developers Kit. If developers or organizations write a front-end application based on the SNA*ps Developers Kit, MacMainFrame hardware can be used. Because the MacMainFrame application software supports the SNA*ps API, Macintosh users running MacMainFrame application software will be able to access the host via the SNA*ps hardware product. Organizations may choose this scenario because of the richness of the MacMainFrame application user interface or for APA graphics support. Current MacMainFrame-based front-end applications have been developed with products including Apple's DAL, Mitem's MitemView, and Connectivite's **Both** development tools.

TCP/IP

Since the Macintosh system supports a TCP/IP protocol stack with Apple's MacTCP driver, both Telnet TN3270-style access and FTP (File Transfer Protocol) are also supported over Ethernet and Token Ring. In addition, other TCP/IP protocols, including file access, are supported from Macintosh to VM hosts with IBM's 5798-FAL support. The focus is the same: the Macintosh gives access over the LAN to a gateway that supports multiple 3270 DFT sessions. Any user with client software can access the gateway and get terminal emulator support and file transfer.

For example, **TCP/CONNECT** from InterCon Systems provides IBM 3270 emulation for the Macintosh emulating 327x models using the TN3270 protocol over TCP/IP networks. TCP/CONNECT features multiple sessions, multiple hosts, and full support of extended keyboards with function keys and editing key clusters. The program contains implementations of both FTP server and FTP client. This means users can initiate file transfers either remotely from another machine or locally from the Macintosh computer. The TCP/CONNECT FTP server runs in the background on the Macintosh computer. It allows another machine to transfer text and binary files to and from a Macintosh computer, with optional automatic translation into and out of the MacBinary format. Users can also optionally set up lists of user names and passwords to limit this capability to authorized users. The TCP/CONNECT FTP Client allows users to initiate file transfers from a Macintosh computer using the standard Macintosh user interface.

Another example is Advanced SoftwareConcepts' **asc3270**, which is a communication toolbox tool for 3270 terminal emulation using the standard access interfaces of the CTB.

File translators

The ability to translate files from one vendor's file format to another's, or from EBCDIC to ASCII, is also important. Some Macintosh applications such as MacWrite or Microsoft Word provide ways to save files directly in different formats. This eases file transfer from a Macintosh to another PC running DOS or to a mainframe. One example is being able to convert a MacWrite file to DCA-RFT format for later use by DisplayWrite and PROFS. MacWrite uses Apple's XTND technology, described below, and can save files in this format directly. The Apple File Exchange application can also assist in converting file formats and transferring files from DOS-based media.

Apple's **XTND** architecture and the Easy Open system extension allows Macintosh applications to read and write files in a potentially unlimited number of file formats. XTND is important because the process of importing and exporting foreign file formats is seamlessly integrated into the Macintosh "Open" and "Save As" operations, minimizing extra steps required to read and write such files. Users can customize their machines by installing only required translators. Applications can share translators.

XTND-capable applications are linked with a library of "glue" routines that load dynamically. XTND lists an open-ended set of file translators to select for the file format for reading or writing through an XTND search path in a modified Macintosh standard file dialog box, loads the appropriate translator, and then allows the application to communicate directly with the translator. A standard text document model specifies the grammar and objects of text documents (e.g., headers and the order of objects and their dependent relationships), as well as an API for reading and writing such documents. This API is used to communicate between the application and the translator. Each translator file contains resources for reading and writing one or more file formats.

In the standard Open Dialog box, XTND places a pop-up menu below the file list.

When the default option ("All available") is in effect, all available files that can be opened are displayed in the file list. If the user chooses one of the pop-up menu selections, only files that match that file specification are displayed. For a "Save As", the pop-up menu is similarly located.

After identifying the file and file format, the user clicks the "Open" (or "Save") button to initiate the operation. The appropriate XTND translator will import (or export) the file.

MacLinkPlus/Translators from DataViz is an extensive library of more than 250 file translators for converting Macintosh files or documents from one application format into another. These include translators for spreadsheets, word-processing documents (MacWrite, Wordstar, Microsoft Word, etc.), database files (e.g., Dbase) and graphics [Macintosh PICT, AutoCAD (DXF), PC Paintbrush, etc.]. Translators preserve file formatting attributes, such as tabs, margins, underlines, bold, and the like. They can translate files to or from the Macintosh SuperDrive floppy, 5.25-inch DOS drives, or file servers. The supplied DOS Mounter software makes DOS disks visible on the Macintosh desktop and from within Macintosh applications.

3270 as transport

Besides using the 3270 as a presentation space—something users can see and read—it can also be thought of as a buffer that can be used to transport data between a Macintosh and a mainframe. File transfer programs, described above, use the presentation space to move character and binary data between hosts and Macintosh computers. Using the 3270 presentation space as transport is a bit anachronistic since it was never designed for that purpose. DFT structured fields (type D0 is used for IND$FILE) are better since they avoid presentation space control characters and have better transfer rates. APPC is even better since it avoids the presentation space. The key point is that the tradeoff is one of performance versus complexity (most applications support a 3278 but only a few might exploit APPC). Also, in many ways, thinking of the 3270 as a data transport service means it can be exploited for various uses including database as described below (see "Database World" on page 407).

Advanced Program-to-Program Communication (APPC)

Macintosh APPC software is one of a family of connectivity products supported by SNA*ps Gateway that let the Macintosh function in mainstream SNA environments. The SNA*ps APPC Developers Kit offers tools for creating LU 6.2 applications, including communication with IBM's OfficeVision, host-resident databases, and emerging distributed applications through the familiar Macintosh user interface. SNA*ps APPC provides a complete implementation of SNA Logical Unit 6.2 and makes it possible to develop applications that provide access to other Macintosh and non-Macintosh environments using LU 6.2 services. It also allows development of applications that tightly integrate Macintosh personal computers with established environments that support LU 6.2. Interface files for the LU 6.2 device drivers are available for the Apple MPW 68000 assembler, MPW C, and MPW Pascal languages, among others.

XCOM 6.2, from Spectrum Concepts, is a facility for transferring data (including reports, jobs, and files) between Macintosh computers and IBM mainframes, Token Ring LANs, LAN gateways, and others. It provides a consistent user interface regardless of the computer on which it is installed. XCOM 6.2 permits high-speed peer-to-peer transfers to be initiated at either end, unattended, with error checking and automatic error recovery. It supports dial-up or dedicated lines, CPU channels, coax, and Token Ring LAN. XCOM 6.2 is fully PU 2.1 compatible.

Advanced Peer-to-Peer Networking (APPN)

APPN is IBM's extension to SNA networks that provides the means for mainframe, departmental, and workstation systems to communicate as peers through standardized connectivity and directory services. Currently, Macintoshes can communicate over the IBM SNA network as peers, but the network lacks the directory and routing services needed for transparent communications. In 1991, Apple announced support for IBM's new SNA extensions that will further extend the Macintosh computer's capability to easily communicate with IBM and other computers.

Apple plans to support APPN in two phases: first, the LAN support included in the current SNA*ps Gateway release; second, full APPN end-node support in a future SNA*ps Gateway release. SNA*ps's support of APPN enables a new generation of Macintosh applications that provide truly transparent access to IBM host data and services and integration of AppleTalk, Apple's network protocols, into enterprise-wide SNA networks. As more APPN products are delivered by IBM, Apple will continue to evolve its SNA products. As part of this effort, Apple will migrate its SNA APIs to conform to IBM's Common Programming Interface for Communications (CPI-C).

Apple's APPN support will allow Macintoshes to be automatically integrated into the IBM environment as part of Apple's commitment to serve its users' needs through support for *de facto* as well as industry standards. APPN will play a major role in meeting the growing needs of users who use various manufacturers' computers and need access to IBM SNA networks. APPN support on the Macintosh will also allow effective integration of AppleTalk into wide-area SNA networks. This enables any Macintosh computer on an AppleTalk network to have full access to any resource in the SNA network. It also allows the SNA network to be used as a backbone, transparently connecting remote AppleTalk networks into a single network.

Database World

The Macintosh supports a wide variety of database facilities. These include generic access to remote databases from standard queries such as Apple's Data Access Language and SequeLink from TechGnosis, access to remote databases from Macintosh-based databases such as 4th Dimension, HyperCard, and others, and also Macintosh versions of databases such as Oracle, which can connect to remote Oracle databases. This support includes both client code and servers. For example, Oracle running as a server on a Macintosh can communicate with a remote Oracle database. As described above, these tools often use the 3270 presentation space to log on and transfer the SQL requests to a VM system and return the answer to the Macintosh client.

The Macintosh has always been the platform for unique and innovative applications—and this extends to the database world. Products like 4th Dimension from ACIUS, Omnis 5 from Blyth, Foxbase+/Mac from Microsoft and Helix from Helix Technologies provide Macintosh users with state-of-the-art data management and application-development capability. In addition, all major cross-platform, corporate-database, and application-tool vendors have also endorsed the Macintosh and delivered both client and server products, including Oracle for Macintosh. Apple intends to continue providing all elements needed to make the Macintosh a complete database client platform for stand-alone and client/server database applications.

Apple's **Data Access Language** (DAL), formerly CL/1, is Apple's client/server protocol for *ad hoc* remote data access. DAL client software and the Data Access Manager (DAL was a separate component before System 7) mean that Macintosh developers can write their applications once and use the same applications to access data transparently in local or remote locations. With this infrastructure in place, Apple is working closely with third-party vendors to provide its users and developers with the database tools needed to implement mission-critical applications.

DAL supports a generic ANSI Structured Query Language (SQL) to access to various relational databases and flat files supporting more than 40 host systems (e.g., SQL/DS for VM). The beauty of DAL is that all DAL-supported remote databases are accessed transparently via the same SQL; there are common error messages; and DAL simulates features missing from specific implementations, such as multiple cursors. DAL requires adapter (server) code to run on the host system.

DAL is optimized for decision-support applications with uniform access to data, regardless of different brands of databases, host platforms, operating systems, database management systems, or network connection. DAL gives Macintosh application developers the flexibility of using an open, standard, host database access language (API). It enables plug-and-play connectivity for accessing data from different data sources between desktop applications and organizational host data. Host databases can be relational, hierarchical, or flat-file in nature. DAL insulates the desktop application from these details and differences, allowing it to concentrate instead on providing better interaction between "personal" processing on the desktop and organizational computing on the host system. DAL provides communications as part of its runtime environment through network adapters (communication drivers) which relieve the programmer from the burden of communications programming. Developers focus on integrating corporate data into their applications, rather than low-level networking and programming tasks.

Using DAL, the desktop application describes a host data access request in a uniform, high-level way. The DAL server for the host system then carries out the request and returns the results to the desktop application. DAL provides automatic data translation when transferring data between client and host systems. The language supports a set of standard data types which represent all host data manipulated by DAL programs. Data from a host data source is automatically mapped into these standard data type when data is accessed. DAL sources include local Macintosh databases, remote Macintosh database servers, and Apple and third-party remote host database servers, such as DEC VAX/VMS and IBM mainframes. DEC VAX/VMS includes Rdb, Informix, Ingres, Oracle, and Sybase; DEC also provides DAL as a part of its PathWORKS product. IBM sources include SQL/DS for VM/CMS and DB2 and Teradata DBC/1012 for MVS/TSO and MVS/VTAM.

The **Data Access Language Server for VM/CMS** provides uniform support for DAL-compatible applications, regardless of the type of personal computer used (it could even be a Windows-based or MS-DOS PC). It works with existing SQL/DS databases, operating under the standard security and integrity of VM and SQL/DS. Asynchronous operation allows the user to continue other work while the DAL Server performs a command.

The architecture of the data access manager is tailored for future extensibility. The Macintosh Data Access Manager provides two levels of interface for applications:

- A high-level interface is a standard way for desktop applications, such as a graphical charting package, to access data. With the Macintosh File menu "Open Query" command, a user can choose a query like "Monthly Sales" to launch a request for data. This request returns the sales information for the month into an application, for example a charting package. The Data Access Manager's query builder makes it easier for in-house developers to create data-access pathways to different data sources. Thus, it delivers the flexibility to use such queries to create custom reports and presentations.
- A low-level interface is intended for in-house or custom developers who use tools like HyperCard and 4th Dimension to build highly customized data-access interfaces. This low-level interface permits developers of data-intensive commercial applications, like statistical packages, to build sophisticated query interfaces for their desktop applications.

DAL is intended for Macintosh applications that need *ad hoc* access to data from multiple data sources, not performance-oriented applications like transaction-processing systems. Such applications, especially in a single database-vendor environment, may be better served by the many solutions available from third-party Macintosh database and tool vendors like Informix, Ingres, Oracle, Sybase, and others.

In addition to the VM Server, the DAL Server for MVS/VTAM provides DAL access to IBM DB2 and Teradata DBC/1012 databases on MVS hosts without the need for a MVS/TSO logon. This includes concurrent access to multiple subsystems and databases from within one desktop application, 3270 data-stream and APPC support, and SNA (i.e., through SNA*ps) or non-SNA connections.

As a member of the SQL access group, Apple will support the SQL access standard the group ultimately establishes. Apple is also working with software and hardware vendors to extend DAL client and server support to other industry platforms.

For example, in 1992 Apple and Microsoft endorsed the combination of DAL and Microsoft's **Open Database Connectivity** (ODBC) specification as a complete cross-platform solution for decision support applications requiring *ad hoc* access to host data residing on a broad range of servers and databases. This means that through a combination of ODBC and DAL technologies customers with both Windows and Macintosh systems will be able to have consistent data access for applications on both platforms, using one API, one SQL language, and one client. This in turn will make it easier to develop and deploy client/server databases across multi-platform environments. Apple plans to extend the Data Access Manager to include the ODBC functions and to build, distribute, and support a Macintosh ODBC/DAL client that translates ODBC calls and information into DAL functions and requests to enable ODBC applications access to DAL servers. Apple will develop and Microsoft will distribute and support an ODBC/DAL client for the Windows operating system.

Along with Apple, Computer Associates (CA) will distribute and support Apple's DAL Servers for VM/CMS, MVS/TSO, and MVS/VTAM, accessing DB2, SQL/DS and Teradata databases. CA will also develop DAL servers for data in CA-IDMS, CA-Datacom, and CA-DB databases. It will also port the DAL server for the CA databases to IBM's DOS/VSE operating system. Pacer Software will support the DAL Server Unix platforms for TCP/IP and asynchronous connections for Ingres, Oracle, Informix, and Sybase databases. Novell will support the DAL Server for Tandem and NetWare. Tandem is currently shipping the DAL Server for Tandem. Data General also plans DAL Server support. Blyth has DAL Toolkits for

MS-DOS and plans kits for Windows, OS/2, and Unix. Lotus 1-2-3 for Macintosh was announced with DAL support.

Like DAL, **SequeLink**, from TechGnosis, allows cooperative processing between Macintosh and VAX computers and IBM AS/400 hosts. Users write Macintosh front ends to transparently access a relational database residing on a VAX/VMS or the AS/400. The SequeLink API for Macintosh programs closely mirrors SQL-based relational databases and includes a rich programming environment. It is suited for both decision-support applications and online transaction-processing applications using Oracle, Ingres, Rdb and Sybase databases. SequeLink supports the native SQL used by the remote database system. Hence, unlike DAL, there is no need to rewrite complex and lengthy SQL statements developed for host application. Direct access to host SQL databases from HyperCard or 4th Dimension is possible with the supplied with XCMD and 4DEX packages. Multiple opened cursors allow complex operations and many SQL operations are available on the Macintosh including multi-row fetch, transaction commit, rollback, security control, and others. Network access is completely hidden and automatic with support for Apple-Talk or DECnet plus APPC for the AS/400.

DataPrism, from Brio Technology, and **ClearAccess**, from Fairfield Software, are examples of Macintosh database query tools that enable Macintosh users to copy data from remote databases into spreadsheets, word processors, and charting programs without programming. Analysts can use a visual data model or just point and click on the data items they want to create SQL-type queries to (most) relational databases without relying on database experts. They can deliver a single, consistent interface to all client/server computing since they can access mainframe databases and provide local processing for quick analysis. They can use System 7 "Publish" and "Subscribe" to reflect the new data instantly with spreadsheets, word processors, or charting tools. Complete turnkey client/server applications can be created, without requiring developers to master the complexities of SQL, networks, or data server operating systems. Both can use DAL (plus other networking services such as Oracle) to provide remote database access.

DataPrism supports the entire analytic process, from raw data to meaningful results through a full-featured user interface, interactive reporting, built-in charting, and complete export capabilities. Clear-Access queries can be recorded as scripts while they are being executed, then saved anywhere on the network and run by other users from their own workstations. Query results can be automatically moved into any other application for further analysis and manipulation, even providing upload capability. DataPrism can be integrated with Macintosh applications, such as Microsoft Excel spreadsheets, HyperCard, and 4th Dimension.

For a specific vendor example, **Oracle for Macintosh** from Oracle provides access to a relational database on the Macintosh and remote systems using the SQL language from within Hyper-Card, Oracle Card, and C environments to more than 100 Oracle-supported platforms including VM. Oracle transforms HyperCard into a full-function SQL database. It allows developers to create sophisticated and diverse Macintosh applications that access Oracle, DB2, SQL/DS, or VAX/RMS data. With **Hyper*SQL**, HyperCard developers can make simple queries, such as extraction of local data, or construct complex multi-table joins and updates that involve several tables on different computers. The Query Tool allows users to build queries graphically and then output results to favorite Macintosh applications.

Oracle card for Macintosh is a portable, end-user database query and application development tool combining the power of Oracle's RDBMS with the point-and-click ease of HyperCard. Programmers and non-programmers can build front-end applications for Oracle client/multi-server systems through an easy-to-use, point-and-click interface without programming. Users can create and manage local and remote database tables with the Table Builder. Users can query the database and build simple on-screen and text reports graphically with the Query Builder. Oracle Talk enables developers to build more sophisticated applications. Oracle card users can integrate images and graphics into their applications. Oracle Card can be used against a local database, or, using SQL*Net network interfacing software, transparently access Oracle databases on any Oracle-supported computer platform.

The **Pro*C** precompiler permits Oracle users to create custom applications to access a database by including SQL commands within C programs. Oracle includes networking software and drivers to permit applications built with SQL commands to share data with other existing systems on a network. For advanced usage Oracle works with Apple's Macintosh Programmers Workshop (MPW).

Oracle's Data Server enables users to base applications on Oracle (including local Macintosh) and move databases from one platform to another without modification as demands change, and then export them to other Oracle-supported environments. **SQL*Star** open system architecture and **SQL*Net** networking software make Macintosh applications front ends to all networked data. SQL*Net automatically establishes the communication channel between the application front end and database back end. It supports asynchronous, DECnet, TCP/IP, 3270, and APPC protocols. SQL*Star ties all Oracle, plus DB2 and SQL/DS distributed databases, together into a single, logical database, even if they are located on multiple, dissimilar computers. The data server protects data from unauthorized access and system failure. **SQL*Connect** allows Oracle databases to access other databases such as DB2, SQL/DS, and RMS on a VAX. **Oracle Server for Macintosh** is an open database server for Macintosh workgroups that provides Macintosh networks with high-performance multi-user database capabilities. Users can develop and implement production database applications in Macintosh environments. Because Oracle Server for Macintosh is fully integrated with the Macintosh operating environment, database administration and installation are simple and straightforward.

In 1991, Information Builders (IBI) and Apple announced a strategic relationship in which IBI's **Enterprise Data Access/SQL (EDA/SQL)** client/server software products will provide Macintosh computers access to non-relational data from a broad array of databases. IBI will develop System 7 Data Access Manager support for its EDA/SQL client. This product will enable Macintosh users to transparently access enterprise data residing in 45 different databases and file structures on 35 hardware platforms including IMS, VSAM, and other legacy databases. EDA/SQL also enables a single request to join relational and non-relational data.

EDA/SQL for Macintosh will enable Macintosh products to participate in IBM's Information Warehouse framework of database management systems, interfaces, tools, and facilities that provide access to multi-vendor systems and enterprise-wide data.

EDA/SQL provides an ANSI SQL API for the Macintosh computer. The EDA/SQL HyperCard Extender allows HyperCard developers to easily integrate EDA/SQL with their applications through a set of XCMDs. Other EDA/SQL Extender Products provide direct interfaces from popular tools, such as Lotus 1-2-3 and SmallTalk. EDA/SQL servers for MVS, VM, and VMS were available in 1991 with servers for other hosts to follow.

Front-Ending

Front-ending is a technique whereby screens (usually 3270) from host-based applications are captured by a Macintosh and reformatted to exploit the look and feel of the Macintosh. There are several advantages to this technique. No changes to host applications are required. The amount of development effort required to program the Macintosh front end can be reduced significantly. The users benefit from a new interface for improved productivity and consistency with all the other Macintosh applications.

Several tools are available to front-end applications. They usually consist of a driver to talk to the presentation space (i.e., the 3270 data streams), an API, filters and pattern matchers, and an interface builder. Drivers are supplied by 3270 card or gateway manufacturers. Access to the presentation space is through the API via calls from C or Pascal, HyperCard or 4th Dimension externals, or proprietary front-end building tools. These tools consist of filter or pattern matchers which allow developers to quickly and reliably recognize specific host screens and the data contained on them. These filters can be changed easily to reflect the inevitable yet often subtle changes to host screens. The filter then passes control to code that builds the user interface, be it HyperCard in the case of MitemView or a high-level interface builder with little or no formal coding required, such as Connectivite's Both.

The direct use of an API from a programming language, Hyper-Card, or specialized tool is usually a tradeoff between speed of development, knowledge of the Macintosh and details of its toolbox, and overall functionality required—that is, how well the tool lets front-end application developers do what is required. There are always tradeoffs. Sometimes the resultant front-end application is unacceptably slow. The tool may limit access to the Macintosh toolbox unacceptably. The Macintosh front end, though visually more attractive and many times easier to use, cannot make up for limitations in original design and functionality of host applications. These can stem from the design of many host applications, which are hierarchical (where users traverse a series of menus, e.g., ISPF) and deterministic, such that what the user can do next may be very limited. Macintosh applications are event-driven, where the user decides what to do next, and almost never deterministic, as the full power of the Macintosh is available most times. The only time to stop or warn a Macintosh user is when danger looms (e.g., a file may be erased unexpectedly).

Front-ending should be thought of as an interim step on the path to true client/server applications, where the VM host becomes a server to the Macintosh.

MitemView, from Mitem Corp., is a developer's toolkit for creation of "Point-and-Click" graphical user interfaces (GUIs) to mainframe applications without host system modification. It is a stand-alone operating environment that can be used with non-sequential, non-deterministic scripting languages of HyperCard, SuperCard, or others to produce cooperative front ends or distributed function applications using the Macintosh. From a user's standpoint, MitemView combines the comfort of a Macintosh-style interface with the expertise and efficiency of a power user. To the mainframe, MitemView looks like a terminal and does not affect performance, security, or host code.

The MitemView environment provides a separate pattern-recognition capability that dramatically simplifies the process of developing applications. MitemView applications can communicate with IBM, DEC, Tandem, and asynchronously connected host systems. Multiple sessions on each type of system via various protocols are supported. MitemView operates in conjunction with the scripting languages of HyperCard or SuperCard and can exploit a wide range of existing HyperCard stacks and third-party external commands and functions to extend local functionality. MitemView-enabled stacks can operate as modules in larger, integrated systems, providing access to existing terminal-based applications, as well as transaction-based applications (SQL, AppleLink, etc.).

Another example is **Both** (formerly Masquerade 3270), from Connectivite Corp. It is a non-intrusive, rapid front-end development environment. It links a Macintosh workstation to a 3270-based mainframe and allows a host application to be redesigned without modifications to look, feel, and behave as a standard Macintosh application. All IBM 3270 fields and functions are supported. It can add new functionality to a host application; share processing workload with the host, customize the flow of information and/or navigation paths in host applications, and integrate a Macintosh graphical user interface into any mainframe application. Features include: ease-of-use; full programmability, including arithmetic, logic functions, sort routines, built-in business graphics, and the like; support for all workstations and gateway hardware, including Apple, DCA, Avatar and Tri-Data; full Window management; minimized development time; and point and click development to create the desired user applications and can create complex applications with no programming expertise required.

Another approach to front-ending is with a tool called **MacWorkStation** (MWS), acquired from Apple by United Data Corp. MacWorkStation helps exploit the ready pool of host-based programming talent in many organizations. It provides access to Macintosh desktop services (e.g., Windows, pull-down menus, dialog boxes, graphics, file system, and print facilities) via simple command strings from the host without requiring knowledge of the details of Macintosh programming. Host programmers replace the traditional 3270-based and TTY user interface with Apple Terminal Service (ATS) commands to build a traditional Macintosh application. MWS allows host programmers to extend applications on the Macintosh by writing MacWorkStation externals in C or Pascal. MacWorkStation uses a client/server model similar to the X Window System, with the Macintosh computer as the server. The key differences from X are in its access to the full Macintosh desktop, ability to extend the application on the Macintosh with externals, and simple yet powerful ATS commands. Sometimes even limitations of the hierarchical nature of typical host applications can be eliminated, because the main programming is done at the host.

MWS includes protocols which are messages sent to or received from a host; directors which form a high-level toolbox including alerts and dialogs; exec modules which are Macintosh code resources that eliminate redundant host-based activities, improve performance or add new functionality; the Communications Connection Language (CCL), a scripting language for accessing remote locations; and communications modules which are Macintosh code segments that allow Macintoshes to work with different communications protocols (3270, TTY, AppleTalk ADSP, and TCP/IP). The **MWS Dialog Builder** is an interface builder that allows developers to quickly build MWS dialog resources. The **MWS Event Handler** enables MWS messages (events) to be handled locally on Macintoshes without going back to the host, and allows prototyping of user interfaces without host or local coding.

Mail and Personal Productivity

Many Macintosh users live almost completely within the LAN environment, accessing VM and other hosts only occasionally. Many standard tools and applications for which one would have used a VM system are available directly in a Macintosh LAN environment. This environment includes thousands of applications including word processors, spread sheets, drawing packages, application builders, mail, and scheduling tools. This is a significant change from the early use of VM hosts, which provided the central and perhaps the only source of applications and of course data. In many cases today VM hosts are used only for printing, mail servers (e.g., PROFS), and data access. Users access these services directly via terminal emulation (e.g., to get to PROFS) and file transfer utilities (e.g., IND$FILE). They may also use a front end such as MacProff (described below) to provide a Macintosh look to the more traditional PROFS 3270 access.

More and more LAN-based services are used to:

- Access VM host mail services through mail gateways such as Soft-Switch's SNADS Gateway (described below)
- Enable LAN-connected LaserWriters to emulate 3287 print data streams
- Get access to databases through tools such as DAL, ClearAccess, or vendor-supplied tools (e.g., Oracle) as described above

In summary, people use VM hosts as repositories from which to get and store the data they need to do their jobs.

For example, both **Microsoft Mail** from Microsoft, and **QuickMail** from CE Software, are sophisticated, fully integrated electronic mail systems that allow users on any number of local or remote AppleTalk networks to communicate with each other by sending memos, files, telephone messages, and graphics. They provide personalization, customizable address books, prioritizing, return receipts, password and security features, and so on.

MacProff, from Mariette Systems International, is a HyperCard-based front-end application for IBM's PROFS, OfficeVision, and PASF electronic mail systems. MacProff is designed to make the process of interacting with the IBM mail system more pleasant by providing Macintosh features such as cut-and-paste, pull-down menus, and point-and-click buttons. It includes more than 100 predefined cards that match the most commonly used electronic mail screens. MacProff does not impact the PROFS, OfficeVision or PASF system because all MacProff work takes place on the Macintosh, not the mainframe. It includes a set of tools that make it simple to change the look and feel of the interface to the main-frame-based system. Features include the ability to:

- Send multiple page notes
- Allow full-screen Macintosh note editing
- Provide a "Hot Calendar" by allowing users to click on a date to view the daily schedule
- Support schedule and calendar functions with point-and-click
- Send multiple-page Macintosh text as PROFS notes
- Use the Macintosh to store nicknames, userids and distribution list names
- Save and search notes in local HyperCard stacks display multiple-page notes in scrolling list; delete multiple
- Notes in a batch
- Print notes directly on a Macintosh printer.

Products from **Soft-Switch** can transparently interconnect multi-vendor electronic mail networks and provide tools to manage these networks and even mail-enabled applications to exploit them. Users see the network as if everyone uses the same system; messages, editable documents, and binary files can be freely changed. With Soft-Switch's **SNADS Gateway/MS Mail**, Microsoft Mail users can exchange mail as final-form messages (i.e., ASCII messages are converted into FFT-DCA), modifiable documents (e.g., RFT-DCA), and binary files (for example, spreadsheets) with users of other systems that are connected to a Soft-Switch Enterprise Mail Network or DISOSS. With the gateway, Microsoft Mail users exchange mail with SNADS users as if they were Microsoft Mail users in other areas. The gateway performs bidirectional mapping between the Microsoft Mail user name format and SNADS user name format. By connecting an SNADS Gateway/MS Mail to a Soft-Switch SNADS Gateway/MVS or Gateway/VM over LU 6.2 Sessions, Microsoft Mail users can access any services (e.g., library services, translation services, distributed print services, or directory services) available on the Soft-Switch Enterprise Mail Network.

Though not related to VM/ESA directly, many vendors, including Apple, support X.400 Mail and TCP/IP Simple Mail Transfer Protocol (SMTP) gateways. Through such gateways, mail can pass transparently between the Macintosh and VM. For example, Retix's **RetixMail for Macintosh**, allows Macintosh users to send and receive messages and data files with other users on PCs, minicomputer, and mainframe systems and other Macintosh computers with

X.400 protocols. (X.400 is the OSI global messaging standard adopted by many organizations, including the U.S. government.) Users of RetixMail share a common Retix OpenServer 400, an X.400 message server that operates on an IBM PC-compatible microcomputer. A large number (30 to 150 users per LAN) of PCs and Macintosh computers may be served by one OpenServer 400.

Collaborative computing

Apple's strategy is to bring collaborative computing to all Macintosh personal computer users through planned enhancements to System 7. The **Apple Open Collaboration Environment (AOCE)** architecture will further user interaction and collaboration through personal computers. Traditionally, electronic collaboration has been restricted to electronic mail. AOCE products will include a consistent, intuitive, and integrated facility for directory look-up, security, and transport, and it will provide common collaborative functions such as addressing and mailing letters and documents from any application as well as the Macintosh desktop. Macintosh users will be able to interact with others anywhere, anytime, and regardless of their locations—home, office, classroom, or on the move. Key characteristics are:

- A full suite of tools and programmatic interfaces for messaging, directory, privacy, security, public-key based digital signatures, and electronic mail, which extend and complement the InterApplication Communication (IAC) capability of System 7
- An open-system architecture providing the ability to integrate existing and emerging alternative message transports, directory services, electronic mail, and emerging industry standards like X.400
- Interfaces that include support for the vendor-independent messaging (VIM) interface specification (see below), for mail and messaging services, which will enhance portability of mail-enabled applications across different computer platforms

These features will provide system software services aimed at overcoming barriers to collaboration such as physical separation, non-simultaneous availability, lack of trust, and data incompatibility.

Vendor-Independent Messaging

In 1992, Apple Computer, Borland International, Lotus Development Corporation, and Novell signed a memorandum of understanding to jointly develop and support the **Vendor-Independent Messaging (VIM)** interface specification. The companies have formed a steering group and will serve as the trustees of the VIM interface specification. The specification provides a non-proprietary, industry standard programming interface to help software developers and corporate developers write messaging- and mail-enabled applications. The specification was first provided, royalty-free, to interested parties in 1992. The specification alleviates the confusion created by disparate programming interfaces on multiple computer platforms and messaging systems. Support of VIM in AOCE products demonstrates Apple's commitment to promoting multi-platform development. Lotus' earlier OMI proposal served as a catalyst for the formation of the joint effort. Apple, Borland, Lotus, IBM, and Novell will support VIM in future versions of their products.

Implications of the Apple/IBM Agreement

In 1991, Apple and IBM announced a series of comprehensive agreements. These agreements, in which Motorola plays a key technology role, cover a range of hardware and software initiatives and follow the terms of the companies' letter of intent announced in June 1991. The announcements complement an existing array of products that help support interoperability between Apple desktop computers and IBM networks. Some functions these products address include workstation-to-mainframe hardware and software, local and wide area connectivity, application-to-application communication, and more specialized functions such as workstation data backup and archiving. For users, the benefits of the alliance begins with Macintosh computers communicating even more readily in large-system networks. These agreements then will extend the benefits of IBM RISC and Macintosh technologies across a broader range of open-systems platforms. In the longer term, two software joint ventures formed by Apple and IBM will create new capabilities, make computers easier to use, and make computer programming simpler and much faster. For the industry, these initiatives will make open systems even more powerful and easier to use.

The alliance consists of five distinct technology initiatives. Three expand the companies' current technologies; two focus on the creation of new foundation technologies.

Expansion to current technologies

- Through new development and technology and software licensing, Apple and IBM, for both planned and existing products, will allow users to integrate their Macintosh computers more effectively with IBM mainframe, midrange, and departmental networks. Macintosh computers acting as clients to IBM servers will be able to access a more comprehensive set of services on IBM-based networks. Such services for local and wide area networks include file and printer sharing, database access, terminal services, client/server applications, and network management. The agreement will also enhance IBM's role as a total systems provider for users who require multi-vendor networking, where equipment from many different manufacturers must work together flexibly and seamlessly.
- Apple, IBM, and Motorola will create a new family of powerful Reduced Instruction Set Computing (RISC) microprocessors optimized for personal computers and entry-level workstations. Derived from IBM's single-chip implementation of its POWER RISC architecture, the new PowerPC chips, to be used in some future Macintosh and IBM products, are expected to be available in two to three years.
- Apple and IBM announced PowerOpen, a new open-systems environment. PowerOpen is derived from the Open Systems Foundation kernel, AIX (IBM's version of Unix), the Macintosh interface, and the POWER architecture. The environment enables a system to run both Macintosh and AIX applications on RISC-based hardware from both companies. Examples of PowerOpen systems will include future RISC System/6000s and RISC-based Macintosh systems. This easy-to-use, standards-based environment is expected to be available in two to three years. IBM will continue to enhance its RISC System/6000 independently. Apple will also continue to enhance its A/UX Unix product.

New foundation technologies

- Kalieda is a new independent company formed by Apple and IBM to create and license multimedia technologies for a wide range of companies and industries. Products resulting from the joint venture will be available in the mid-1990s.
- Apple and IBM formed an independent joint venture called Taligent, to develop a next-generation operating environment based entirely on object-oriented technology, expected to be available in the mid-1990s. The joint venture will license the technology widely, and both parent companies will use it in future products. Apple will integrate aspects of this technology into Macintosh and IBM will integrate aspects of technology into OS/2 and AIX.

The networking announcement highlights five areas:

1. AppleTalk Services for OS/2 will allow Macintosh, OS/2, and DOS-based personal computers to share files, query corporate databases, and access a broad range of communications services through a common OS/2 server. The IBM 6611 Network Processor, announced in January 1992, supports routing of AppleTalk, TCP/IP, DECnet, and NetBIOS network protocols; IPX and XNS networks; and SNA data link switching.
2. As part of the effort to ensure interoperability between its current and future environments, Apple licensed and incorporated IBM's Token Ring technology for use in its Token Ring 4/16 NB Card product announced in 1991.
3. Macintoshes will be able to participate more fully in SNA. A key development will provide Macintosh users with full access to APPN directory and routing services [see the APPN discussion in "Advanced Peer-to-Peer Networking (APPN)" on page 406].
4. Network management integration will enable users to manage networks with Macintosh personal computers with IBM's LAN Network Manager or centrally through IBM's NetView network management product. This will promote more cost-effective and efficient management of networks consisting of Apple and IBM products.
5. Macintosh personal computers and IBM's AS/400 systems will communicate more effectively for improved access to

AS/400 data and applications. Enhancements for the Macintosh will include terminal services as well as more advanced client/server functions of the AS/400. Apple implemented its DAL server for the AS/400 in 1992.

Summary

As discussed, any service, tool, or application must fit naturally into the Macintosh environment to be successful. Complexities of the command-line interface native to the VM world are not acceptable for the Macintosh. The applications that are most widely accepted are those that fit into Macintosh naturally and extend the VM experience naturally.

For 3270 emulators, this can be in the way they allow users to tailor font point size, perhaps just by changing the window dimensions or allowing color to be remapped transparently on the Macintosh. In the case of 3287 print support, it means allowing users to simulate 3287 printers on the Macintosh directly using Apple Laser-Writers or without printing, browsing files and only printing when required. Macintosh support for all popular LAN topologies both as stand-alone 3270 workstations and as clients to a gateway adds to Macintosh value. File transfer works in a very natural Macintosh fashion. Vendors support fast file transfers using 3270 structured fields and APPC. Using the 3270s to transport data between VM and a Macintosh computer is a valuable for a large number of applications.

File translation utilities such as those provided by DataViz help move files easily from the IBM EBCDIC world to the Macintosh ASCII world and the Macintosh applications that reside there.

Databases are the entry into the client/server future. Tools such as Apple's Data Access Language and others from vendors such as Oracle allow Macintosh users to transparently access VM databases and files. DAL provides flexibility to access databases from different vendors and hosts with no Macintosh changes except for different connection methods. These tools use existing 3270, serial, and TCP/IP connections as transport. They are also beginning to support APPC for transport as well.

Front-ending tools allow Macintosh developers to add new faces and in some cases new capabilities to existing, hard-to-change and learn VM applications. For example, MacProff has Macintosh-compliant access to VM PROFS and OfficeVision. With LAN-based mail servers connected to gateways such as from Soft-Switch, Macintosh users can access VM-based and X.400-based mail transparently without the need to log on directly or even use a front end. Front-end applications can be written with third-party tools such as MitemView which uses the 3270 API provided by most 3270 vendors. In some cases, they even support each other's APIs, for example, Avatar's MacMainFrame support for Apple's SNA*ps API. Fourth generation tools such as HyperCard and 4th Dimension offer users the ability to build significant, new applications besides front-ending 3270s. Apple's plans for an Open Collaboration Environment continue its strategy to add base facilities, in this case access to mail primitives, to the Macintosh operating systems. Apple recognizes the multi-vendor needs of its users and is committed to providing Macintosh integration into other computing environments

In the near term, the IBM/Apple alliance provides for improved connectivity between the Macintosh and VM hosts. Support for APPN is planned. In the longer term, new strategic platforms, such as PowerOpen, based on the Open Systems Foundation kernel, IBM's AIX, Apple's A/UX, and Macintosh adapters, increase VM and Macintosh synergy.

A key attribute is that when the Macintosh connects to the VM mainframe world, it does not compromise the features that make the Macintosh valuable. New applications will look and feel natural and will support Macintosh system software and hardware features.

16

Overview of VM/ESA Printing/Publishing

By P.C. McGrew and W.D. McDaniel

Publishing is, by nature, a resource-intensive task, regardless of whether final output is directed to a printer or a terminal for soft-copy delivery. VM/ESA supports several programs and products that work in concert with IBM's System Application Architecture (SAA) and Information Interchange Architecture (IIA) to help design strategies for information dissemination that best use available resources.

Publications listed at the end of this chapter provide more infor-mation about IBM publishing, printing, and information delivery strategies, program products from IBM and other vendors, and general management information that may be useful when consid-ering changes to information dissemination strategies.

This chapter examines using the VM/ESA environment to exploit offerings from IBM and other vendors to optimize publishing activ-ities. This environment is so powerful that many companies find it both possible and desirable to use VM-based publishing, even if they primarily use CICS, MVS, or VSE.

Printing versus Viewing

This chapter generally uses the phrase **information dissemination** rather than **printing** or **publishing**. This deliberate choice emphasizes the fact that information is developed and distributed for varied reasons.

For most information developed within a corporate enterprise, the default is to get it onto paper and circulate it. This is an expensive default reaction. Those who look carefully at information dissemination within and outside the corporate enterprise generally find it helpful to review information flow in terms of:

- Where information should be created
- What should be made available online
- What should be printed
- Where information should be maintained

As stated above, many enterprises find answers in VM publishing solutions because of their diverse offerings, ease of use, and speed of implementation. For a complete information dissemination environment, consider both print and view components, and review what types of information should be handled by each. New offerings described below show how easy it is to integrate and expand with VM/ESA-based solutions.

Positioning for VM printing

VM-based printing can be as simple as sending line data to an impact printer, or as complex as building a fully functional Print Services Facility (PSF) Version 2.0 environment supporting multiple vendors' Intelligent Printer Data Stream (IPDS) printers. There may also be a requirement to support multiple printer data streams. A very complex print environment might include printers that use one or more of the following printer command sets:

Carriage Control: found on impact printers and other types of line printers. These printers may be attached to VM hosts or PCs.

AFP: Advanced Function Printing developed by IBM and supported by a variety of printer vendors. AFP output can be routed to 3800 Model 3 Printers and those that emulate that environment without the use of PSF, although this limits the flexibility and functionality of print output. A fully functional AFP environment includes Print Services Facility (PSF), which provides support for all IPDS functions on IPDS printers.

Metacode: developed by Xerox for their high speed printers. This print environment is easily supported from VM, requiring no additional print drivers, such as PSF in the AFP environment.

Hewlett-Packard (HP) PCL: generally supported by word processing and other PC programs.

PostScript: developed by Adobe to support all-points-addressable printing in the PC environment. There are variations and levels of PostScript, which means that PostScript generated by any given program may require special header files or special environmental setup programs to print on some PostScript printers.

It can also include implementing environments that emulate the Advanced Function Print Data Stream (AFPDS) normally sent to PSF using cards and boards on the printer available from various vendors. A VM-based printing environment can also serve as a print server and print manager for other operating systems, and as such provide support for HP and PostScript output to PC-based printers.

Another key element to understanding print requirements is recognizing that host printing may involve more than just multiple data streams or command sets; there may also be the problem of multiple resolutions. Printers place toner on paper in small units called **dots**, **pels**, or **spots**. A dot is generally the smallest addressable print object on a page. IBM host-based printers place toner on the page at 240 pels or dots per inch in each direction. The next generation prints at 480 dots per inch (dpi) in each direction. By contrast, Xerox printers and most PC-attached printers are usually 300 or 600 dpi printers. This is important because resolution differences between various print environments is the primary hurdle in creating sharable printer objects, such as fonts, graphics, overlays, and job descriptors. This issue is addressed in detail in *In-House Publishing in a Mainframe Environment* by McGrew and McDaniel (McGraw-Hill, 1991).

To understand more about the AFP environment, the role of PSF, and the connectivity options for other print data streams, refer to the list of publications at the end of this chapter.

To begin to understand where VM printing fits within an enterprise, determine where and how printing currently occurs. This may be performed internally or by a consultant in printing and publishing in corporate environments. It will allow an analysis of what implementing a VM-based print environment can accomplish.

The flexibility of the VM environment, the vast array of publishing tools and products, and ease-of-use of the VM environment make it possible to build and maintain a highly sophisticated print environment that grows as the technology surrounding printing changes. "Getting to Print in VM/ESA" on page 435 provides more information on establishing the environment for productive information dissemination via print.

Positioning for VM viewing

The other half of the VM publishing story is positioning not to print, but to view. IBM calls it a **softcopy delivery strategy**. Other vendors call it **online viewing**, and some even refer to it simply as **hypertext**. Regardless of what it is called, the net result is viewing text and graphic information on terminals.

VM-based viewing can involve an environment as simple as the ability to call up a file formatted for terminal display, or as complex as development of a display environment that contains structures to permit information within any file to be found using structured search techniques. It may even include mapping to related information in other text files and application programs.

From the point of view of positioning, the more sophisticated the online view environment, the more time must be spent on its design and implementation. However, a well-designed and integrated viewing system can start small, grow, and still provide great savings. By providing instant access to correct information about any topic related to a worker's environment, online access to information can dramatically increase productivity. Everyone with access to a terminal can reach to the most up-to-date information, although that flexibility can be restricted as needed. Not only is the cost of creating, purchasing, and distributing thousands of sheets of paper almost eliminated, but security surrounding those documents can be enhanced.

The question of updating documents held by users is also eliminated. It becomes unnecessary to create, print, and distribute revisions, Technical News Letters (TNLs), or entire documents whenever text changes. By maintaining text in an online environment, changes can be entered, reviewed, approved, and made available in a fraction of the time required for the paper equivalent. This quicker access to current information can eliminate countless problems, not to mention saving time and money. However, the requirement to notify users of changes to files must not be ignored.

Both positioning for online information delivery and implementing an online viewing strategy are generally quite easy in a VM environment. They can include the simple addition of online help for commonly used utilities, implementation of online books from vendors, and the development of online books from in-house documents.

The next figure shows a panel used by the authors to execute the Document Composition Facility (or BookMaster) in a VM environment on an ES/9000. The same panel exists on a 9375 and GTI PubStation running VM/ESA. Note the window built around the DCF Release field and the box opened to provide information about valid values. This method provides information about the program without the requirement to print an internal user's guide.

Most online display environments use the full terminal screen. In the example shown, screen real estate is handled so that the HELP information and the application are available at the same time. See *Online Text Management: Hypertext and Other Techniques* (McGraw-Hill, 1989) for more information on setting up VM-based screen environments for online viewing.

VM-based viewing can go beyond simple HELP information by providing programs which provide access to files composed for line devices or application data designed for line devices. This is similar to results of accessing most online databases or information retrieval services.

The most sophisticated online environments are those that were pioneered on workstations, but have been implemented in VM for the past several years. These include some method of access to a text library, and the additional ability to directly find pieces of text directly related to the current inquiry or to browse through a variety of files on a learning expedition. "Getting to View in VM/ESA" on page 441 provides more information on positioning an enterprise for viewing in VM.

```
    DCFPANEL            GenText, inc. DCF EXEC


 Use this screen to execute DCF.


 Input File:   Name: FIPROP2   Type: SCRIPT    Mode: *


 Output File:  Name: FIPROP    Type: LIST3820  Mode: BG


 Script Options ( Profile: DSMPROF4  Dev: 3820A    Bind: 1I 1I     DCF Rel 4.0


 Lib: DSMGML4   Page:            Fpasses: 2   Message: ID       Copies : 1


 Quiet(Y/N): QU  Continue (Y/N): CO  Index:(Y/N)    Sysvar: X NO D YES


 +---------------------------------------------------------+
 |                 INPUT FILE NAME                         |
 | This is the name of the DCF file to be processed.       |
 | It must be supplied; there is no default.               |
 +---------------------------------------------------------+


 PSF  Options List: OPTION(DUPLEXP  OPTIONS) ME NO



 F1=Help F2=Exit Help F3=Exit F11=Help Index F12=Cancel
```

Information Development

As a publishing environment, VM provides access to a wide variety of information development tools. Some are markup-based composition languages, some are markup-based forms-design languages, and others are word processors. All VM publishing products offer access to a wide variety of print devices, and with a little creativity online text can be created using any of them.

Document Composition Facility

IBM's **Document Composition Facility (DCF)** is the extension to **SCRIPT**, the original control-word-based text composition language offered by IBM. SCRIPT uses control words to invoke formatting routines. With development of DCF, a generalized markup language was added to permit intent-based markup.

In a VM environment, invoking DCF is generally a simple matter of executing the SCRIPT command while pointing at the appropriate document. While not a "What You See Is What You Get" text processor, most users find that with practice a final document can be produced with as few as two tries.

As of this writing the current DCF release is 4.0. Enhancements in this release include:

- Exploitation of virtual storage above 16MB line
- Support for file sizes greater than 65,535 records
- Renaming disk-resident modules, discontiguous saved segment, and the bootstrap module at installation
- AFPDS, PostScript, IPDS, and various line printer outputs
- Use of the PRINT option on the SCRIPT command to send AFP files directly to SPOOL, saving process time and DASD
- Shading
- Definition and use of separation masters
- Merging variable data using the .VT control word and a post-processor
- Definition of custom generalized markup tags
- Online HELP for SCRIPT commands and error messages
- Direct inclusion of overlay objects
- Inclusion of IOCA objects using Segment Include control word

While BookMaster has been identified by IBM as the strategic mainframe publishing product, DCF provides a significant amount of flexibility, the ability to define custom applications, and distinctly reduced resource consumption when compared to BookMaster. DCF is generally updated more quickly to exploit new printers and new features of AFP and IPDS.

BookMaster

What began as an IBM internal tool for developing product and service manuals is now sold as **BookMaster**. It is an extensive library of generalized markup tags (a **tagset**) designed to provide high-quality intent-based markup for creating a variety of technical documents, including user manuals, training documents, parts catalogs, maintenance applications procedures, and program logic documents.

BookMaster also includes internal macro code to link headings, figures, and targets of those references when used in a BookManager viewing environment. Additional tags allow document creators to add links between pieces of information within a book or defined library.

BookMaster Release 4, current as of this writing, supports functions needed in a BookManager environment (BookManager is IBM's softcopy delivery environment). It does not support all control words or DCF features, such as Overlay Include, text merging, or the Copy Group control word to invoke alternate AFP copy groups from within documents.

If the requirement is to be fully compatible with IBM publishing and exploit the IBM softcopy delivery initiative, consider BookMaster; remember, however, to calculate program overhead when beginning document development or transforming documents to be BookMaster-compatible.

Overlay Generation Language

The Overlay Generation Language (OGL) is IBM's forms design product used to create AFP Overlays in a host environment. It consists of a handful of commands that allow the forms creator to place text, lines, boxes, and graphics on a page to create either a freestanding document or an overlay onto which variable data can be merged. The new release of OGL/370 can draw lines along defined paths, and circles as well as straight lines.

In a VM environment, output of the program invoked with the OVERLAY EXEC is a set of object files which should be placed in an overlay library for most efficient use. These Overlay objects are specifically designed for AFP environments and are not natively supported for online applications or printing outside of the AFP environment.

Waterloo SCRIPT

This product, marketed by WATCOM and developed by the University of Waterloo, has the same roots as IBM's Document Composition Facility, as its name implies. Just as DCF includes diverse features to support IBM strategic printing directions, Waterloo

SCRIPT finds wide acceptance among publishers who require a low-cost product that permits host-based document markup and composition output to host-attached printers. In the case of Waterloo SCRIPT, those printers include AFP, Xerox, PostScript, HP, and typesetters.

It is a rich markup-based language with extensive symbol manipulation features that make development of text-based applications quite easy. Waterloo SCRIPT includes a variety of tagsets for special purposes, such as agreements, letters, technical documents, scientific documents, and academic documents. It also includes a set of tags similar to the DCF Starter Set.

CompuSet 6.0

This host-based document markup environment readopted the name by which it entered the marketplace. It spent several years as the **Xerox Integrated Composition System (XICS)**, but has been spun off as a Xerox Technology Venture company under the management of Document Sciences Corporation (DSC) as CompuSet 6.0. The new version supports a wide variety of output devices, including PostScript printers.

Host Forms Description Language

The Host Forms Description Language (HFDL) is the Xerox offering for development of overlays (called **forms** in the Xerox environment). Like OGL, it has a small set of commands that are used to place text, lines, boxes, and graphics on a page to create either a freestanding document or an overlay onto which variable data can be merged.

In the Xerox environment the forms generally reside on the printer and not on the host. Just as OGL was designed to support only the AFP environment, HFDL is specific to the Xerox environment.

Word processors

In addition to the text markup languages that depend on use of XEDIT or some other text editor to create source code, VM environments support several word processors. Word processors differ from text composition languages in that they do not support the addition of author-intent markup to the document. Word processors simply provide a means for formatting a document using font calls and positioning information. They usually support output to HP and Post-Script printers, and also support interchange formats such as Revisable Format Text (RFT) and Fixed Format Text (FFT).

Some word processors available for VM, like EdWord from Trax Softworks and WordPerfect 370 from WordPerfect Corporation, support a variety of line print environments. At this writing only WordPerfect 370 supports AFP and PostScript. IBM's DisplayWrite/370 supports RFT/FFT output, but not AFP or Post-Script. None of these products supports online viewing, either directly or indirectly.

IBM's original VM Office Automation product, PROFs, and its follow-on, OfficeVision/VM, support IBM word processors and Word-Perfect 370, but neither VM office environment supports the type of industrial-strength publishing normally associated with text mark-up-based products like DCF and BookMaster, or a softcopy delivery environment like BookManager.

Graphics Development

Graphics development on the host is generally painful. Most users find that they can better support their print and view graphics requirements by integrating a PC-based product. The number of PC products on the market that support development of graphics to be used in VM-based publishing is almost limitless. Many that are marketed by IBM Business Partners provide intuitive user interfaces and sophisticated features, and some are provided free with a new mouse or PC.

Almost any of them can create acceptable graphic files and most can create PostScript files, but none can create IBM Page Segments, IOCA (Image Object Content Architecture) raster objects that can be scaled by the new generation of IBM AFP printers, or Xerox IMG (raster) graphic files directly. These types of printers require investigation of or writing a transform program to create the correct file format from the PC format.

Graphic conversions

In a VM environment, PostScript output can be routed to AFP printers using services of the IBM product called the PostScript-to-AFP Interpreter. It can transform text-only, graphics-only, or compound documents into AFP. Since it is a VM application, PostScript files from PCs must be moved to the VM environment using a file tranfer protocol.

ProcessMaster, an IBM Publishing product, can also be used through its **Convert Graphics/Image Files** facility to convert chart data files (ADMCDATA) created with IBM's Graphical Data Display Manager (GDDM) to Graphic Data Files (ADMGDF). These can then be converted to PSEG files also using GDDM. Graphical Data Display Manager is a set of host-based graphic support utilities and routines. It also provides a conversion path from ADMIMG image files to PSEG3820 files.

This environment requires up-to-date versions of related IBM software; for example, GDDM must have the 2.3 Small Programming Enhancement (SPE) installed to be able to create the IO image objects (IOCA) and to get Graphics Object Content Architecture (GOCA) support for GDDM-created vector graphics objects.

Generally, conversions like these on the host are resource-intensive. Unless the publishing environment executes on a dedicated VM system, it may be wise to investigate PC-based transforms and upload results for use in printing.

Also consider offerings from vendors other than IBM. Corel handles several transforms in **Corel DRAW!** product, as does **HiJaack** from Inset Systems. GenText, Inc., sells **Bit2Bit**, a graphics transform product that "fills the gaps" by providing conversions from most popular PC formats to most popular host formats. It runs under VM/SP Release 5 and later, on PCs running PC-DOS/MS-DOS and Windows, and under MVS and Unix.

Getting to Print in VM/ESA

To exploit the full power of publishing in a VM environment, and especially printing managed from a VM environment, the best approach is to implement a print server architecture incorporating a wide variety of features. There is no single-vendor answer to these requirements as of this writing, but as demonstrated in later sections, most components exist in the market and can be assembled with help of a skilled consultant. The feature list for a comprehensive print environment under VM/ESA includes:

Simple interface: A simple human interface at the user's personal terminal, regardless of whether it is a PC attached to the host or a 3270-architecture terminal, and regardless of the type of system the user normally uses: TSO under MVS, VM, or even the operator's console. This interface should allow print jobs to be specified and defined by users or by background environmental definitions and activation or cataloging of these same jobs. The ideal interface should provide facilities for users to retrieve document and printer resource code to personal accounts for updating and recompiling.

Rather than having to know what is necessary to print a document, users should specify either where to print it or the type of printer it is to print on. The ideal interface takes over from there to determine required protocol conversions, accumulate resources, transform them as necessary, then manage final print queues.

Users should not have to know or care what jobs or documents consist of, or what processing is required to construct them; concern should be on where documents should print: local printer (associated with the user in a table), fastest printer, shortest queue printer, overnight printer, or some outside resource.

Security for resources: There should be an administrative function to define and control the printing environment. Most environments require security locks to prohibit unauthorized persons from using resources and printers not allowed by corporate policy.

Distributed processing: It is rare to see a requirements list from large enterprise publishers that does not include local and remote distributed processing. VM provides an excellent vehicle to support IBM's Print Services Facility (PSF) for IPDS printers, execute transforms, and communicate with other environments and other machine classes.

VM hosts are easily networked to other IBM and non-IBM computers. Links are necessary to transfer print, printer resources, and commands, and to merge data from disparate environments.

Data collection and merging: Most enterprises need to accept data from anywhere in the internal network, or from customers, and to merge that data onto print resources stored in the enterprise. These resources must be available for creation and use anywhere in the network.

Planning a robust print server architecture allows building an environment that permits data to be merged to be transferred to the print server machine using standard IBM or other vendor transfer products. In this scenario, data must contain merge instructions. In some cases, data is simple print line data plus job-level information defining particular print resources needed and merging to be performed.

Consistent "look and feel": Less for Common User Access compliance than attention to the desire (and sometimes the requirement) enterprise publishers have to comply with using identical fonts and other printer objects, regardless of what the actual print device is. Positioning for consistency requires attention to font selection for corporate documents, attention to graphics creation platforms and graphics printing requirements in documents to be printed on multiple types of printers, and development of resources to ensure that adjustments are made in print jobs to start print at the same place on the page regardless of the actual device.

This attention to consistency provides two benefits:

1. Users deal with a single, consistent interface for all printing needs regardless of type and style.
2. Common printer resources ensure ability to produce consistent look and feel in documents and customer materials.

Support for diverse Page Description Languages: Positioning for a versatile print environment should include the ability to support several Page Description Languages (PDLs) including AFPDS/IPDS, PostScript, and Computer Output Microfiche (COM) environments. Transforms to and from word processing languages should be carefully considered to enable a complete **print anything anywhere** strategy.

Repository for static print objects: There should be a central repository for such static objects as fonts, overlays/forms, pagedefs, formdefs, other types of printer information files, and graphics objects (page segments, IOCA or GOCA objects, or encapsulated PostScript files). In addition, source code for these objects must also be available within the enterprise.

A central repository provides a library of form definitions, overlays/forms, style files, templates, and clip art for use in varied printing environments. Centralized storage of these objects also makes it possible to determine early if a resource is undefined or missing, thus avoiding extra processing cycles in error.

Composed or compiled objects should be available for use in simple printing or complex data merging/mass mailing uses. Interfaces must be designed and provided for defining large merging print jobs using these objects.

Modular design for growth: Printing and publishing requirements change as new technologies move into the market. The VM environment is often the first host environment to implement new technology, so positioning for growth is essential. The overall print environment should allow introducing and supporting printers and transforms as needed. A robust base set should support AFP and PostScript devices and varied form and font objects.

Under the assumption that IBM IPDS/AFP printers will always be supportable by PSF, that leaves the requirement to support for other types of printers required. Other printers may require different drivers or interfaces, so the most versatile print environment will accommodate inclusion and activation of these using a device-driver approach.

Transforms and protocol converters may be added or withdrawn in the same manner. Providing access to new transforms and defining their attributes and interfaces should be all that is required to integrate a new transform or protocol converter.

Support for different resource object types: Graphic and image objects from diverse environments should be supported in a manner that does not require the user to be knowledgeable about the form of the graphics. Routines should be incorporated into the environment to automatically convert graphic files in ADMGDF format to page segments when a particular page segment is requested by an incoming print stream and it is not found in that format.

Image formats must also be handled transparently. If images are stored as a Tagged Image File Format (TIFF) class B (black and white) file (most common output from scanners), but requested for printing on a PostScript device, the transform should be available to create the Encapsulated PostScript file without users being aware of the need to do so.

Support for compound and complex documents: The environment should allow simple designation of print tasks, batch submission of standard print jobs, and support for compound and complex documents. Compound documents consisting of text, image, and graphics should be produced on demand with one-step efficiency for the user. Complex printing requirements should be satisfied by providing user access to the library of resources and by providing an ability to define complex print requirements in a cataloged print job.

This discussion assumes that the requirement is printing in an IBM AFP environment. If the requirement is printing on a non-AFP device, such as a Xerox metacode printer, most of the environment remains as described above, but programs that must be put in place include transforms into Xerox fonts and Xerox .IMG (image) files. Xerox resource objects (print description files, job descriptors, fonts, and graphics) generally exist on the physical printers. The means that the mechanisms to manage the resources are somewhat different than when all resources can reside in the host environment.

Print Services Facility

Print Services Facility for VM is IBM's printer driver that converts device-independent Advanced Function Printer Data Stream (AFPDS) files to device-dependent Intelligent Printer Data Stream (IPDS) files. This is a large job, considering the number of printers involved.

Release 2 of PSF/VM added support for:

- 4028 coax-attachable 300 dot IPDS printer.
- 3900 high-speed, fanfold, 2400 dot IPDS printer.
- 3835 MICR post-processing interface.
- 3828 MICR printer.
- Advanced Function Image and Graphics (AFIG) on 3825 and 3835 printers. This environment supports printer-based decompression of image objects to speed print time on image-intensive print jobs.

In addition to new printer support, IBM enhanced the data stream to use a common SPOOL File Conversion Machine (SFCM) to ensure cross-system consistency.

As with any complex print environment product, installation and implementation can be time consuming and frustrating if quality advanced planning is not done. Advanced planning should include a careful review of print requirements, existing methodologies, and requirements defined by users. Print windows, composition windows, turnaround requirements from start to completion of a print job, and similar issues should be considered during planning. Then, with the help of a qualified internal or external consultant, plans can be laid for the development of a print environment that can grow with user requirements.

VM to PostScript overview

In a VM publishing environment, PostScript as well as AFP output may be desirable. DCF and BookMaster can generate PostScript natively.

PostScript generated by DCF (or BookMaster) is not simple Post-Script with all text and data in ASCII. Text to be printed is in EBCDIC and all fonts are remapped to EBCDIC codepages specified during composition. IBM took this approach to insure that characters available to users of System/370 and System/390 systems would be available to PostScript generators. However, this means that PostScript files generated by VM/ESA systems may not function properly with other PostScript files from other sources. To transfer DCF-generated PostScript files to a PC or PS/2 for printing requires transferring them as binary files: do not allow any EBCDIC to ASCII translation.

Once transferred to a DOS or OS/2 system, DCF-generated Post-Script can be transferred to parallel or serial PostScript printers. However, intermixing DCF-generated PostScript with PostScript generated by a DOS or OS/2 application such as Windows causes unpredictable results. This is due to PostScript code generated by DCF encoding PostScript fonts into an EBCDIC codepage. If this is mixed with pure ASCII PostScript code which does not reset these codepoints, the result is likely to be unrecognizable.

PostScript generated by CompuSet 6.0, on the other hand, can be routed to most PostScript printers without any difficulty since CompuSet was designed to support ASCII printers.

Getting to View in VM/ESA

BookManager

IBM's strategic offering for softcopy delivery is BookManager. Initially offered in VM only, it now has READ (view) and BUILD (compose) components available for most SAA platforms. READ is the component that permits a user to view a document and use links within the document to navigate it in a nonlinear manner. BUILD, designed to work with BookMaster, also supports Starter Set GML and the CALS SGML tagsets. It is used to compose the document, which has been marked up to support the location of linked objects by the READ program.

BookManager is a large program that invokes BookMaster to build a data file, and then postprocesses the file to identify sources and targets for hypertext links, TOC entries, index entries, and cross reference items. It performs sophisticated processing that can be CPU intensive, even in the best VM/ESA environment.

Under VM/ESA, BookManager provides full-screen document viewing on 3270 terminals with color mapping to emulate font changes. Text searches are allowed both within documents and across document boundaries within a BookManager Bookshelf. Annotations are stored in the BookManager file.

Text searches can be precise or "fuzzy", taking into account synonyms and related concepts. These features, while quite sophisticated, impact BookManager's performance and are best used only when needed. As of this writing, building a book is quite time consuming and does not benefit from availability of VM/ESA's extended memory above 16MB. This is due to extensive lexical scanning and indexing necessary to provide the fuzzy search capability. Searches against such indexed books are also very resource-intensive and do not benefit from greater storage availability.

BookManager offers support for viewing graphics from GDDM sources. These include GDF and ADMIMAGE files.

Another offering for viewing in VM: ViewGlas

ViewGlas from GenText, Inc., is a hypertext-based online viewing system for IBM mainframe environments. Using **ViewGlas**, IBM DCF Starter Set, custom DCF applications, Waterloo SCRIPT, and other markup languages can be made available as online hyperdocuments accessible through a hypertext interface.

Hypertext systems provide a mechanism for reading related documents in a natural topic-oriented manner. **Documents** can be traditional manuals, or nothing more than chunks of information linked together as in a catalog or information textbase. The **ViewGlas** hypertext paradigm provides automated and user-encoded links connecting one information node to another. **ViewGlas** also offers hypertext creation tools and environments.

The **ViewGlas** system contains **ViewGlas Author**, **ViewGlas Browser**, and **ViewGlas Consulting**.

ViewGlas Author

ViewGlas Author provides authors with tools to create original **ViewGlas** hyperdocuments and to convert existing DCF documents into hyperdocuments. It includes the custom GML tagset and pre-processors necessary to generate **ViewGlas** hyperdocuments from IBM DCF source code. A basic hypertext document can be created with no changes to original source files.

ViewGlas Browser allows viewing text, performing searches, creating annotations, placing bookmarks, and following links to other text, graphic displays, or user-written programs. **ViewGlas Browser** is the delivery system for hyperdocuments created with **ViewGlas Author**.

Any string may be sought. Fuzziness allows:

- Treating multiple blanks between words as a single blank
- Performing case-insensitive searches
- Matching strings spanning up to five lines of a window

The next occurrence of strings, all occurrences in the current document, or all occurrences in the current HyperLibrary can be sought. Annotations and bookmarks can also be searched.

Searches in ViewGlas benefit from availability of ESA storage as does the entire product. Larger HyperLibraries, with more Hyper-Documents, may be viewed at much deeper levels as the amount of virtual storage grows. In addition, availability of ESA storage speeds document writing and viewing considerably. Searches, in particular, benefit greatly when very large documents (1000–2000 pages) must be rapidly searched.

Any number of annotations may be made to any number of lines; a single text line may have any number of annotations attached to it. These can be stored as private to the annotator or as public comments on works. Annotations linked to target nodes will remain in revised versions.

Bookmarks can also be attached—as many as desired—to as many lines as desired. These also travel with document revisions if they are attached to surviving target nodes.

The ability to search for annotations or bookmarks which match a string pattern allows a high degree of group authoring and revision processing within a ViewGlas environment.

ViewGlas supports all IBM 3270-type terminals to their fullest capabilities. From the oldest 3277 to the latest PS/2 Intelligent Workstation, **ViewGlas** provides as much flexibility and capability for the user as is possible with the terminal at hand. Any document can be viewed on any terminal, without maintaining more than one copy of the document. Nor is **ViewGlas** limited in connectivity. Regardless of how 3270 terminal sessions are connected to the mainframe—locally, remotely, or via LAN—all **ViewGlas** users have full access to hyperdocuments.

In addition, ViewGlas offers more than just full-screen viewing. Documents may be viewed using the ViewGlas windowing system which allows for varied window sizes, styles, and placements to help organize text information being presented.

ViewGlas supports both vector graphics (with IBM GDDM) and bit-mapped images (IBM page segments), for all graphics terminals.

Online applications

Applications of online document viewing are many and varied. These include:

- Online access to manuals and documentation allows end-users, technical support, and helpdesk personnel rapid, efficient online access to manuals, documentation, procedures, protocols, standards, updates, and changes. This is ideal for customer support functions.
- Intelligent online HELP facilities provide an online HELP environment which allows easily modifiable text, multiple users of the same documentation, HELP facilities tailored to specific groups, and multiple levels of help sophistication

from detailed background information to brief syntax examples.

- Shared authoring environment supplies a design or development team with common access to current levels of documentation while allowing for individual annotation and modification. All authors and reviewers can read and annotate simultaneously. No hardcopies need be printed and distributed.

Benefits of such systems include:

Reduced printing and distribution costs: Documents are no longer printed, stored prior to distribution, distributed, and stored upon receipt.

Reduced warehousing costs: Documents are no longer kept in inventory, and costs associated with destroying obsolete documents are avoided.

Reduced lead times: The time required to make new information available to employees and clients is reduced to only the time it takes to key and recompose a document, eliminating time required for printing and distribution.

Protection from incorrect or out-of-date information: Only current information is available to employees and customers because information is updated and made available in an *ad hoc* mode with little lead time required.

Reduced problem research time: Search facilities of ViewGlas- or BookManager-type products allow rapid access to specific information needed, without thumbing through pages, referring to indexes, and manually following cross-references.

Enhanced document review environment: All authors can read and annotate simultaneously. All authors have online access to the most current revision, so there is no need to print and redistribute copies after changes are made.

Enhanced customer support: By using online document viewing, organizations benefit by solving the business problem of providing up-to-date information to people who need it quickly and in an easily and effectively used form.

VM/ESA and Small 370 Server-Based Publishing

Although not available in a preconfigured form, VM/ESA provides the basis for a comprehensive and powerful publishing environment that supports creation, composition, revision, online distribution, and printing capabilities. Using any of the small 370 systems, such as the 9371, GenText PubStation (see below), or even 9375 and 9221, anyone can construct such an environment from existing software available from IBM and other vendors. With the addition of a simple graphical interface consisting of two parts:

- Client interface
- Server interface

it can be constructed to ensure that it can communicate with other VM systems and non-VM systems. Add programming to provide bridges and interfaces to all the components listed, and the system is complete.

To be comprehensive, it must connect to other systems via such protocols as:

- An MVS interface driven by MVS Job Control Language
- Multi-protocol network support including
  - FTP (File Transfer Program)
  - TCP/IP (Transmission Control Program/Internet Protocol)
  - SNA LU 6.2 (System Network Architecture)
  - RJE 3780, 3777 (Remote Job Entry)
  - IBM Token Ring
  - Ethernet

It must also provide:

- Open architecture to incorporate new protocols
- Transparent conversion into AFPDS of a variety of print data streams:
  - PostScript
  - HP PCL
  - Flat ASCII (carriage control and line feed at the end of each line)
  - Smart ASCII (limited document formatting, using control characters)

Graphics and image must be handled through transparent conversion of varied image and graphic data streams such as:

- CCITT 3 and 4 (FAX standards)
- TIFF Class B
- IOCA
- GOCA
- GDDM

into AFP-compatible forms. Raster image formats should always be transformed into raster forms. Vectorization is not really worth the effort or resources because it will be less important as printers emerge which can handle both vector and compressed image formats.

Dynamic merging of application-generated data into final documents should be supported two ways:

- AFPDS-driven merging of text, graphics, and image
- Control file-driven merging of text, graphics, and image

Any image or print format supported by the transforms listed above should be eligible for merging into the AFP output data streams.

A print queue manager function is needed to receive incoming data streams, coordinate transform and merging activities, and schedule output printer production. The queue manager can be implemented as a "black box" multitasking system which spawns necessary tasks within a host processor to perform conversions and merging.

VM/ESA, treated as a software LAN which can have multiple servers started and waiting for work, can provide an effective and elegant solution to these requirements. A collection of virtual machines, controlled by the print queue manager described above, can play "pitch and catch" with incoming print streams to be routed, converted, merged, and transformed into final AFPDS. The final AFP print output can then be directed to a common print queue managed by an operator using the graphical interface mentioned above.

A Page Description Language (PDL) Interpreter is needed to transform print and graphic data streams into AFPDS. This component can be managed and driven by the queue manager's scheduling subsystem. The final AFPDS data stream can be returned to the queue manager, which will schedule it for output, then use IBM's

Print Services Facility (PSF) to send it to the selected printer. PSF operates in this overall system as a final device driver rather than a true print queue manager. The management functions are provided by the queue manager.

A resource manager is needed to construct the AFP resources necessary to support AFP printers. Objects to be managed include:

*   Pagedefs
*   Formdefs
*   Page Segments
*   Overlays
*   Fonts

Tools to produce pagedefs, formdefs, and overlays are required. Since the system being described uses PSF to drive AFP printers, the rest of the AFP software suite must be available as well. The system should, however, offer interfaces to some of these products to make them more usable. These primarily consist of front ends to IBM's AFP resource construction tools. Font creation will not be supported, although font modification via IBM's Font Library Service Facility (FLSF) will be available.

Tracking of changes to these resources should be part of the resource manager as should coordination of resources downloaded to those printers and print servers which need them.

AFP printers are attachable via IBM 370 Channel, COAX, or serial connections. Channel speeds vary from 3 to 4.5 megabytes per second.

Since PSF is the device driver for the AFP printers, device level support of the IOCA and GOCA formats is supported automatically. In addition, this architecture will grow as IBM expands its capabilities, and the server system described here takes advantage of enhancements as they become available.

The Operator Interface should be graphical in nature, conforming to CUA standards. The operator will have a variety of functions available:

*   Print starting, stopping, and restarting.
*   Page range selection.
*   Print job rerouting.
*   Multi-copy print.
*   Print job cancellation or suspension during print conversion sub-tasks or after jobs have been submitted to a printer.

- Print job and queue status displayable with a variety of information fields available to aid operators in managing the printing environment controlled by the server. The overall operator interface will be structured as an "Object-Action" interface.
- Print job prioritization, including prioritization of print conversion tasks. The operator will be made aware of all the conversion tasks to perform and will be able to raise and lower priority of remaining subtasks as well as overall priority of entire print jobs.

The system will provide data recovery and automatic or manual backup of queues and resources. The system will return to a stable state after power or software failure. The system will contain an option for specifying automatic and continuous backup of queued print and resources.

Security and administration facilities will be provided to allow operators or administrators to control and configure the following options:

- Adding and deleting users
- Defining read, write, and access capabilities by user, to include control of access to individual devices and the system as a whole
- Specifying print job class
- Defining operator capabilities and operator view of print queues and resources
- Defining system administrators and capabilities

Billing statistics will be accumulated and available for use in billing systems as flat files. These will include data such as:

- Job identifier
- Job origin
- Userid
- Pages printed
- Lines printed
- Data records in job
- Destination device
- Conversions performed

Platforms for publishing

The publishing system described above will function adequately on older System/370 systems, but will benefit greatly from the extended capabilities System/390 as driven by VM/ESA. Consequently, such a system is best implemented on a System/390 platform.

The 9371 is not a 390 platform and does not have sufficient processing power for the print manager described. The 9371 does provide a networked server capability which can be driven from the primary system, but probably needs a higher power driver to manage and control the queues and the transforms.

A GenText PubStation, a System/370 processor implemented on a single chip coupled with both VM/ESA and OS/2 publishing software, runs the VM/ESA 370 feature in a PS/2. This platform generally runs about four times faster than a 9371, and is more than powerful enough for the system described above. This system, networked to a larger corporate host, can provide an excellent platform for implementing AFP printing and publishing management in a distributed manner. Even in a local environment, such a system can provide an offloading of processing from the main host to a cost-effective dedicated processing environment.

PubStations are available in several configurations to meet particular needs. They can be attached to each other using OS/2 LAN Manager and can be attached to larger VM/ESA systems using Transparent File Access, a facility that allows local VM/ESA users to access the host VM/ESA minidisks as if they were their own.

This scalable VM/ESA power, from 9371s to PubStations to ES/9000s, makes VM/ESA an excellent platform for implementing publishing solutions. As needs grow and complexity increases, users can transport out of one platform into another with a minimum of conversion effort. The same cannot be said for moving through the ranks of other operating systems such as MVS.

VM/ESA offers substantial improvements in printing functionality as supporting products such as PSF and DCF begin to exploit the ESA architecture. Extending these products with management systems produces an umbrella printing solution which operates under VM/ESA to exploit those new features to their fullest.

Read More About It

Embarking on any new publication plan, especially with all of the offerings available, is best done after a healthy dose of information. The following list includes only some of the many publications available to help:

AFP Publications Listing

Advanced Function Printing (AFP)	
Publication Title	*Number*
A Guide to IBM's AFP	S544-3095
AFP: Data Stream Reference	S544-3202
AFP: Host Font Data Stream Reference	S544-3289
AFP: Printer Information	G544-3290
AFP: Printer Summary	G544-3135
AFP: Software General Information	G544-3415
Intelligent Printer Data Stream Reference	S544-3417
Page Printer Migration: General Information	S544-3227
Page Printer Migration: Programming Guide	S544-3228
PSF/VM Programming Guide	S544-3466
Remote PrintManager Version 3.0: User's Guide	S544-3293
Remote PrintManager: User's Guide	S544-3439
Why Enterprise Printing?	G544-3642

IBM Page Printers	
Publication Title	*Number*
ABOUT TYPE: IBM's Guide for Type Users	S544-3122
ABOUT TYPE: IBM's Guide for Using VM Print Management Facility with Type	G544-3517
ABOUT TYPE: IBM's Technical Reference for 240-Pel Digitized Type	S544-3516
ABOUT TYPE: IBM's Typographic Primer for Digitized Type Program Products	G544-3183
Supplement to ABOUT TYPE: IBM's Typographic Primer for Digitized Type Program Products	G544-3186

Xerox Corporation publications listing

Xerox	
Publication Title	*Number*
Font Data Base Management Utility Reference	892176-11
HFDL User Guide (VM)	896017
PDL / DJDE Reference	720P90050
Xerox 4045 User Guide	6000P87278
Xerox 4090 Operators Guide	720P90170

General publications listing

General	
Publication Title	**Publisher**
In-house Publishing in a Mainframe Environment P. C. McGrew and W. D. McDaniel	McGraw-Hill, 2nd ed., 1991
Online Text Management: HyperText and Other Techniques P. C. McGrew and W. D. McDaniel	McGraw-Hill, 1989
The State of the Electronic Printing Market	A. D. Parker and Associates
Proceedings (3 times yearly)	GUIDE, Inc.
Proceedings (2 times yearly)	SHARE, Inc.
Proceedings (one time yearly)	XPLOR, Inc.

VM/ESA Application Development

This section describes the environment in which VM/ESA applications execute, conversion of applications from earlier VM versions to exploit VM/ESA, application tuning, SAA compliance, and application debugging.

17

Native Application Development and Execution

By Chip Coy and Eleanor Coy

Introduction

This chapter provides an overview of programming languages and interfaces available in VM/ESA for developing CMS applications. Application development for other platforms is not covered in any great detail. Some programming experience is assumed.

Why is CMS a good application development platform?

In many ways the success of CMS as an application development platform for System/390 comes from the twin advantages of an easy-to-use file system and reasonable—if at times undocumented—programming interfaces to system function when compared with other System/390 application development environments such as TSO under MVS or ICCF under DOS/VSE.

The CMS file system, both minidisks and the VM Shared File System, allows programmers to create files without pre-allocating each individual file, as MVS and DOS/VSE require.

The CMS Application Programming Interface provides straightforward interfaces to most system functions, and reasonable interfaces to all system functions.

Programming Languages

Programming language choices for CMS applications can be influenced by many factors. Languages may be dictated by the environment: for example, Ada for Department of Defense applications. The choice of a language may be strongly influenced by knowledge of that language and previous programming experience. The ultimate decision is influenced by languages available on both the development and target VM systems.

A partial list of IBM programming languages available for VM/ESA includes:

- VS COBOL II
- PL/I
- VS Pascal
- VS FORTRAN (Includes parallel processing and S/390 Vector Facility support)
- AD/Cycle C/370 (full ANSI C implementation)
- Ada
- Assembler (F, H, L)
- REXX
- APL2
- RPG
- Cross System Product (CSP)
- The LE/370 family of languages and libraries

A partial list of common vendor languages available for VM/ESA includes:

- C (WATCOM C, SAS/C, SAS/C++)
- SAS
- RAMIS
- ADABAS (runs on GCS)
- NOMAD

Most applications are written either in assembler or REXX, with REXX the language of choice. C is new to VM but growing in popularity. Many programmers know C, and good programming toolkits, like the new IBM LE/370 Runtime library, are now available for CMS. Most "old timer" VM system programmers and developers write application code almost exclusively in REXX, with some assembler used for high-performance functions or to provide facilities not available in native REXX. They write in other languages only if working on an existing application not written in REXX, or when writing for an operating system where REXX is not supported. Because REXX is so easy to use and debug, and is so well integrated into CMS, it makes little sense to use anything else. The deciding difference between, say, COBOL and REXX, is that COBOL is extremely self-contained: the division between what belongs to and what is external to COBOL (data, other programs, system commands) is very clear. Anything that is "not COBOL" must be very carefully and verbosely defined before it can be used. The verbosity and precision required to do this in COBOL (and PL/I and FORTRAN, to a lesser extent) is troublesome. In REXX, required setup is greatly reduced.

Like APL and BASIC, REXX is an interpreted language. An interpreted language processor translates each line of source code into object code, then executes the results all in one step. Compiled languages separate the translation and execute steps. Compiled language source is completely translated into object code in one step (the compilation or assembly). The execution step is usually separate and independent of the translation. Interpreted language programs tend to be much easier to debug than compiled language programs, because it is always evident what line of code failed. Most interpreted languages also have a facility that allows immediate examination of contents of variables at the point of failure (or at any time during program execution). Before REXX compilers were available, compiled languages had an execution speed advantage. With availability of REXX compilers, this advantage is greatly reduced. COBOL is still the premier business application language at many established data centers, while FORTRAN is still extensively used for numerically intensive and scientific applications.

APL, REXX, and, to a lesser extent, BASIC are excellent prototyping languages because of their easy setup. APL, though daunting because of its quirkiness, is a very terse and powerful general-purpose language. It is also the champion vector and matrix manipulator. Prototyping the major logic paths of a complicated application saves a tremendous amount of work later in development. It is much easier to detect unexpected side effects and identify sections not thoroughly thought through when there is a working model to analyze.

Environment

VM provides several CMS machine environments: 370 mode, XA mode, ESA mode, and XC mode. CMS, used for more than 20 years, contains a lot of history.

370 mode simulates an old hardware architecture and is provided for existing applications' hardware-specific dependencies. 370 mode supports 24-bit addressing (maximum 16 megabytes of virtual storage) and XA/ESA/XC modes support 31-bit addressing (maximum 2 gigabytes virtual storage).

XA mode and ESA mode are functionally identical on ESA-capable hardware, although selecting ESA mode is disallowed on non-ESA-capable hardware. Thus ESA mode implies availability of ESA features, although XA mode does not imply their unavailability. The only difference is in the output of CP QUERY SET and INDICATE USER, which show XA or ESA.

There is good compatibility between ESA and XC modes, although XC mode also provides VM data space support. There are significant differences between 370 and ESA/XC modes, sufficient to require significant effort to migrate applications between them.

Unless there is a very specific need, new applications should not be developed for 370-mode execution. The choice between ESA and XC mode should be determined by where applications will execute. XC mode is only available on VM/ESA Release 1.1 or later and is only useful if VM is running on ESA-capable hardware.

Programming Interfaces

VM/ESA has two official classes of programming interfaces: **preferred** and **compatibility**. There is a third class that is rarely discussed in official IBM documentation: "other" interfaces.

Preferred

Preferred interfaces provide the highest level of function in all machine environments (370, XA, or XC). The newest additions to VM, they were introduced to support hardware architecture changes.

Compatibility

Compatibility interfaces support historical interfaces in CMS. Most compatibility interfaces became compatibility interfaces either because they could not be extended to the new XA/ESA architecture or could not fully support new CMS function. OS simulation and CMS DOS also fall into the category of compatibility interfaces, but in this case, the compatibility is with MVS and VSE. CMSDOS is woefully outdated and used exclusively for access to VSE/VSAM. Some attempt has been made to keep OS simulation current with MVS. It is used extensively by applications shared between VM and MVS.

Other

The other interfaces in the VM/ESA system are either undocumented or not intended as part of the general programming interfaces (GPI). They came into use because early releases of VM lacked many necessary application programming interfaces. Application programmers exploited undocumented interfaces to address system control blocks or invoke system routines directly. Older VM establishments are rife with applications that use CMS internals, which have have changed significantly with the introduction of function like the Shared File System and 31-bit addressing support, often breaking these applications. CMS is rectifying this problem by providing documented user exits in some frequently invoked system modules, providing "preferred" programming interfaces to system function via the Callable Services Library (CSL), and allowing some CMS source code to remain available. However, continued use of undocumented internal interfaces in applications is dangerous. CMS internals will continue to change as CMS continues to evolve. If use of other interfaces is unavoidable, it should be extensively documented. Every attempt should be made to replace undocumented interfaces with documented, supported interfaces as new releases of VM/ESA introduce them. Also, submit requirements via a major user group (for example, SHARE or GUIDE) or IBM representative (as a PASR—Product and Support Requirement) for improvements to the VM/ESA product, describing additions needed to the VM/ESA general programming interface. The VM/ESA organization in Endicott, NY is seriously interested in practical experiences with shortcomings of VM/ESA programming interfaces. There is no guarantee that all interface problems will be fixed immediately, but all PASRs receive a response from a knowledgeable person.

Program Characteristics

Program structure

To facilitate discussion, CMS application programs are divided into four basic categories: **interactive** or **single-user** programs, **client** programs, **server** programs, and **batch** programs. Each category has distinguishing characteristics.

Interactive

Interactive or single-user applications run in a user's virtual machine and perform tasks solely for that user. This category probably varies the most in terms of program complexity—from simple applications cobbled together in a few minutes and intended for a single user, to very complicated routines that just happen to run self-contained in a single CMS machine. An example of the latter type is IBM's DCF (familiarly known as SCRIPT), a text processing product. Many PC applications are examples of complex single-user programs. REXX is the language used under CMS for quick simple tools, basically because REXX does not require the elaborate setup/teardown of compiled languages. REXX also allows in-line use of CMS and CP commands.

Client

Client applications share most characteristics of interactive applications except for isolation. Client applications run in a user's virtual machine, and offer some form of terminal interface. The distinguishing difference is that client applications are not self-contained:

they depend on interaction with a server to finish processing. In many cases, clients and servers are considered a single program structure and discussed as such (the term "client/server" is common in development discussions). However, there are many client applications that are separate from their servers, so they can be considered a separate category. IBM's QMF (Query Management Facility) is an example of such a separation of client from server. Actually, QMF communicates with different servers, depending on the operating system under which it executes. On VM, QMF uses SQL/DS; on MVS, it uses DB2.

Server

Server applications, generally characterized by simultaneous use by multiple individuals, are almost always request-driven. Servers often control access to protected and/or shared resources, such as databases, and may require authorization to use. Servers run in their own virtual machines, usually disconnected (without an attached console and normally not monitored by a human operator). Applications that request services from a server are called clients (see above). Servers may or may not reside on the same system as their clients.

In general, interactive or single-user applications are easiest to design and write. The client/server structure is both more complex and almost always slower in execution. The need to adhere to a communication protocol when building either a client or a server adds significantly to program complexity. Protocols define a standard structure which must be followed step-by-step without deviation. The need for a communication path between client and server also adds significantly to program overhead. The major reason for choosing a client/server structure is to protect a shared resource or to provide a privileged function to users who normally would not be authorized. SQL/DS is an example of a server that provides data sharing with protection. Users can share SQL data, but must be authorized for data access first. DIRMAINT is a server which provides a privileged function. Through DIRMAINT, CMS users can manipulate their entries in the VM system directory, a function they are normally restricted from performing directly. DIRMAINT provides verification and control, thus making such updates safe for end-user use.

Batch

Batch applications are often regarded as inappropriate for execution under CMS. They are usually characterized by absence of a user interface and relatively long run times. Batch programs are either I/O-intensive and perform repetitive processing on enormous amounts of data, or perform complex, CPU-intensive calculations. However, batch programs can be and often are run under CMS with success.

Instead of using CMS, batch applications can be run under VM's Group Control System (GCS). Execution under GCS provides many useful facilities, but is not well documented.

Batch programs are also often developed and tested under CMS using either CMS DOS or OS simulation interfaces, then moved to VSE or MVS for execution.

Program-to-Program Communications

When programs run together in a single virtual machine, inter-program communication is simple, since programs can pass data via a number of mechanisms. Under CMS, the most common data sharing methods are data files, the CMS program stack, and GLOBALV variables. Less common, but worth mentioning, are control blocks and data buffers in memory. CMS data files generally reside on disk (DASD), although tape is also used. Methods for reading and writing files also depend on programming language. The Callable Services Library (CSL) provides file system interfaces for use by most major high-level languages (HLL) and the assembler.

Writing files to disk to pass data between applications is a slow way to move information. It makes sense only when applications are at constant risk of failure. The batch term for this type of data recording is **checkpointing**. OfficeVision/VM is infamous for littering users' primary disk space with notes to itself on where it left some function when it exited. OfficeVision uses this information to reconfigure itself when it is next invoked so users start where they left off. CMS provides a native facility called GLOBALV (for global variables) to do this type of level setting. GLOBALV is generally used to save user tailorable application defaults.

Control blocks and data buffers in memory are similar constructs. They are both areas of memory, separate from applications, that are located via pointers containing their memory addresses. The major difference between the two is volatility. At best, buffers exist only for the duration of application execution. They are usually associated with files resident on disk or tape. Control blocks tend to persist and are usually used to pass information that controls application execution. Control blocks and data buffers are most frequently used by assembler programs, less often in HLL applications. High-level languages have language constructs which perform tasks similar to data buffers and control blocks, but creation and management of such entities is usually masked from programmers and not under application control.

The CMS stack

The CMS stack is a data buffer (or queue) that CMS maintains and manages for application use. Many CMS commands have a STACK parameter and can receive input from the stack and, optionally, place output into the stack. The CMS stack can be segmented or partitioned into smaller buffers. This ability is particularly useful for nested applications. Stack segmentation allows multiple programs use the stack without interfering with one another. In some cases, the stack is the only way a program can communicate with VM commands. It is also a convenient way to transmit small amounts of data between programs written in different programming languages without needing data conversion. Until recently, the CMS stack could only be manipulated from assembler or REXX programs. One of the nicer CSL facilities is a set of callable services that allow HLL access to CMS stack functions.

Client/server communication

Client/server applications move program-to-program communications outside a single virtual machine. Client/server communications are conducted via communications protocols. These are special interfaces that establish, maintain, and terminate communication paths between applications. These paths are also called **conversations**. The main VM protocols are **APPC**, **CPI-C**, and **IUCV**.

APPC and CPI-C allow program communication across systems and networks. On VM, this is accomplished through APPC/VTAM Support (AVS). AVS is the bridge to VTAM and the SNA network. APPC is an assembler language-level interface and CPI-C is the high-level language interface of APPC. Both APPC and CPI-C can be used to communicate to non-VM (heterogeneous) systems as long as applications use the correct protocol. IUCV is an older communications protocol that is also still extensively used because it remains the fastest communications path. IUCV, an assembler-level interface, is limited to a single VM system. Some old CMS applications also use VMCF. VMCF is an early precursor to IUCV. It offers no real advantage to new applications and is mentioned here solely for completeness.

Two other communications mechanisms are used enough use to deserve mention. One is sending files between virtual machines through the VM SPOOL. This is the slowest and most primitive way of moving data between virtual machines, but is also the simplest. SPOOL files can be sent to CMS users on the same system, on remote VM systems, and to other operating systems.

Data spaces is another VM facility that can facilitate communication between server and client. Introduced in VM/ESA 1.1, it exploits new ESA hardware facilities. A data space is a separately addressable memory area usable by either a single virtual machine or shared among several virtual machines. New registers, called **access registers**, establish data space addressability. Data spaces can be used to exchange large amounts of data at memory speed. Data spaces can contain up to 2 gigabytes; each processor can manage up to 1024 data spaces. Communication is limited to a single VM system.

The type of communication path chosen depends on many factors—how well a server must perform, whether it must communicate outside the VM system on which it resides, what language the application is written in. Communicating via VM SPOOL files is not a good choice for a high-performance server, but is perfectly acceptable for an application whose results are not needed quickly. An example of this type of application is a batch server that queues CPU-intensive calculations and runs them when the machine is lightly loaded.

Many familiar CMS applications are a combination of interactive and server. They provide interactive "front ends" for CMS users to converse with and server "back ends" for access to protected or shared resources. OfficeVision/VM is an excellent example of this type of application structure. OfficeVision/VM has both interactive tools to maintain individual notelogs (which are resident in the user's virtual machine) and calendar or document database server machines, which contain information that is protected against unauthorized access, but can be shared with other OfficeVision/VM users.

End-User Interaction

Types of user interfaces

CMS applications may have a command-level interface only or a more elaborate, menu-driven interface. CMS commands are good examples of command-level interface applications. Many IBM program products such as ISPF and Query Management Facility (QMF) have panel-driven interfaces; so do some built-in CMS commands such as FILELIST, SENDFILE, and NAMES. The choice of user interface generally depends on the amount of dialog the program needs to conduct with its users. Most CMS commands perform narrow, well-defined tasks. They usually require little or no input; what input they accept is well-defined. Only the HELP facility, which contains a lot of information, is a panel. A command-level interface operates in linemode. It is contained in a single line on the terminal screen. Under CMS, menu-driven interfaces control the entire terminal screen, unlike some PC window interfaces which allow the screen to be divided into multiple active windows. Menu-driven interfaces usually exploit advances in terminal technology and use features like color, highlighting, protected fields, and the like. Almost all new professional applications are menu (panel)-driven. This reflects both industry fashion and advances in hardware technology (the most important being the mouse). Three of the most commonly used panel managers available on CMS are ISPF, GDDM, and CMS Session Services (also known as **Fullscreen CMS** or **CMS Windows**). ISPF and GDDM are separate program products, while CMS Session Services is an integral part of CMS.

An advantage the virtual machine concept provides to the CMS application user is isolation from interference by other users and applications. CMS is a single-user system, very similar to a PC. This isolation gives application programmers and application users extensive leeway in custom tailoring applications to individual needs and tastes. This tailoring is normally done through use of user profiles and the GLOBALV command. Typically, users tailor their screens—selecting colors, setting PF keys—creating a comfortable screen layout. They can also establish and save other default settings. What can be defaulted is literally limited only by imagination and program design.

Program Development

Program coding under CMS is generally done using either the XEDIT editor (also known as the System Product Editor) or the ISPF editor, PDF. Some users also use their favorite PC editors, then upload program source files to VM.

XEDIT creates files with characteristics appropriate to the programming language being used, if the special reserved filetypes are used when naming files.

Some special filetypes recognized by various language processors are:

Language	Filetype
assembler	ASSEMBLE or ASM
FORTRAN	FORTRAN
PL/I	PLI or PLIOPT
PASCAL	PASCAL
COBOL	COBOL
C	C
REXX	EXEC
RPG	RPG

This chapter does not describe XEDIT use; that is done more than adequately in IBM documentation such as the *VM/ESA XEDIT User's Guide.* Chapter 4, *Exploiting XEDIT,* on page 107 discusses some advanced XEDIT techniques. XEDIT provides a powerful update facility to aid in program maintenance that is worth discussing since it is not a "normal" editor function.

Update facility

The CMS update facility offers several advantages over maintaining programs as single source files:

- Ability to selectively apply and remove changes
- Ability to view a module up to a particular change level
- Ability to easily obtain list of changes to a module

This brief overview of CMS update does not provide a complete source control system, but rather shares a possible use of CMS update to assist in providing effective source code change control.

The CMS update facility offers a number of different ways to maintain a program; this section only covers the method that allows multiple updates.

One file, called a **control file**, lists filetypes of lists of module updates, called **auxiliary control files**, or **AUX** files. An example control file is shown below. The first record, TEXT MACS, is required. The second record indicates that for each program, a file with file-type AUXR1, which will list filenames of updates, may exist:

```
TEXT MACS
TEXT AUXR1
```

To create the first update to a program, create a file with the same filename as the source program and filetype AUXR1. Place a line in the file to indicate the filetype of the update file. The sample AUXR1 file below shows a single update with filetype FIX1:

```
FIX2 - skip program name
```

To create an update, issue the XEDIT command with the CTL option as shown below. This example shows creating an update to a program called SHOWPARM using control and AUX files created above:

```
xedit showparm c (ctl cdev
```

To create subsequent updates, just add new lines to the *top* of the AUX file and issue the XEDIT command again.

To view the program including changes only up to a specific update, use XEDIT with the UNTIL option. For example, to see the program with just the FIX1 update but no later updates, issue:

```
xedit showparm c (ctl cdef until fix1
```

There is a significant chance that changing a file when XEDITing with the UNTIL option will cause other, "later" updates to fail. It is best to use the UNTIL option only to view intermediate updates, and if changes are required, add another update.

To apply all updates, issue the CMS UPDATE command with the CTL option as shown below. This produces a file with the same file-type but with a filename with a "$" prefix. Typically, this output file is compiled or printed and then erased.

```
UPDATE SHOWPARM C * CDEV CNTL * (CTL SEQ8
```

Programming Tools

The following programming tools are various aids for building applications.

LE/370 (Language Environment/370)

High-level languages have been available under CMS since VM's early days, but originally CMS was intended for application development targeted at MVS or VSE. The idea of CMS as a production environment in its own right has come slowly to IBM. This is changing with recent introduction of LE/370 and CSL (Callable Services Library). LE/370, an IBM program product, provides a common runtime subroutine library for many high-level IBM languages. C, PL/I, COBOL, and FORTRAN are supported. Compilers have had subroutine libraries for a long time. Major advantages to LE/370 are:

1. It is a runtime library
2. It is common across 370/390 operating system platforms
3. It is common across supported languages

The advantage of a runtime library is that programs using library routines need not be recompiled if a routine is updated. Library subroutines are loaded at execution time (or **runtime**, hence the name) rather than at compile time. Commonality across operating system platforms aids code portability. CMS is still used for application development for both VSE and MVS due to its excellent interactive interface and XEDIT editor. For cross-system applications, this commonality is a big plus. Commonality across supported languages means the call structure and the subroutine name remain essentially the same whether using COBOL or FORTRAN or C. This is a boon when dealing with multiple languages.

LE/370 provides services for initializing and terminating programs, allocating storage, handling conditions and messages, manipulating date and time, common math routines, interlanguage communication, and interfaces to operating system functions. A caveat: LE/370 documentation has its own vocabulary. What CMS calls a "stack", it calls a "heap"; what CMS calls a "return code", it calls a "function code"; and so on.

The next example shows a sample LE/370 call from a C program.

```
/* Call LE/370 from C */
#include <leawi.h>
int main(void)
{
CEESERV(&parm1,&parm2,&parm3,...,&fc);
}
```

Callable Services Library (CSL)

While LE/370 is just being accepted as an application development tool, CSL (Callable Services Library) has been available under CMS since VM/SP Release 6 and is available on all releases of VM/ESA as an integral part of CMS. CSL is also a runtime library. It provides two major services to the application developer. The first is a high-level language call interface to VM system services. The second is a set of tools for user extensions to CSL. The Callable Services Library is meant to be extended. While it provides extensive services, more are always needed. Facilities are provided that easily create new CSL routines and CSL libraries. CSL provides automatic parameter list checking (datatype, length, number of parameters) and program linkage for CSL subroutines; the programmer need only supply the logic. The one restriction is that CSL subroutines must be written in 370 assembler language.

CSL routines are callable from COBOL, PL/I, REXX, FORTRAN, Pascal, 370 assembler, and C. The CSL library shipped with CMS is called VMLIB. It includes routines to:

- Use CMS Shared File System (SFS) facilities
- Use VM data spaces from CMS applications
- Perform error checking and debugging
- Use CPI-C (the SAA Common Programming Interface for Communications)
- Use Coordinated Resource Recovery (CRR)
- Manage workunits
- Obtain or modify selected CMS system information

Typical CSL use from a PL/I program:

```
PLISAMP: PROCEDURE OPTIONS(MAIN);
/* Sample PL/I program. Uses CSL to call a REXX EXEC (named   */
/* REXXSAMP in this program) which executes a VM command, also */
/* passed from this PL/I program. The REXX EXEC returns the    */
/* command response in the variable "RETURN_AREA"; it is then  */
/* edited and displayed on the terminal.                       */
/* Declare for call to REXX EXEC */
DECLARE DMSCSL    ENTRY EXTERNAL OPTIONS(ASSEMBLER INTER);
DECLARE LENGTH    BUILTIN;
```

```
DECLARE SUBSTR    BUILTIN;
/* DMSCCE is the REXX/CSL interface. The number, type, and       */
/* position of the arguments needed by a CSL subroutine are      */
/* defined in the template distributed with the CSL system       */
/* library.                                                      */
DECLARE DMSCCE CHARACTER(8) INITIAL('DMSCCE');
/* Parameter list to be passed                                   */
DECLARE EXEC_NAME CHARACTER(8) INITIAL('REXXSAMP');
DECLARE ARGUMENT   CHARACTER(60) INITIAL ('IDENTIFY(STACK)');
DECLARE RETURN_CODE    FIXED BINARY(31) INITIAL (-1);
DECLARE NUMBER_ARGS    FIXED BINARY(31) INITIAL(1);
DECLARE ARG_LENGTH     FIXED BINARY(31);
DECLARE RETURN_AREA_LENGTH     FIXED BINARY(31);
DECLARE RETURN_AREA   CHARACTER(200);
/* Initialize Length variables                                   */
ARG_LENGTH = LENGTH(ARGUMENT);
RETURN_AREA_LENGTH = LENGTH(RETURN_AREA);
/* Call REXX EXEC REXXSAMP and execute CMS IDENTIFY command. */
CALL DMSCSL (DMSCCE, RETURN_CODE, EXEC_NAME, NUMBER_ARGS,
     ARGUMENT, ARG_LENGTH, RETURN_AREA, RETURN_AREA_LENGTH);
/* Extract USERID from information returned. */
/* Display "HELLO FROM userid" on terminal screen. */
PUT LIST ('HELLO FROM',SUBSTR(RETURN_AREA,1,8));
END PLISAMP;
```

Typical REXX program called from PL/I:

```
/* Execute CMS command, pass back argument to HLL program */
arg command
command
parse pull answer .
return answer
exit
```

CMS Pipelines

CMS Pipelines is a powerful and elegant enough application development tool to be worth mentioning, even though the only language it formally supports is REXX. CMS Pipelines provides an extensive library of built-in functions along with the means to add functions easily if the system library is found lacking. CMS Pipelines was introduced into the VM product in VM/ESA Release 1.1, and is available on prior VM releases with IBM product number 5785-RAC. The pipelines concept is that of data flowing in and out of a discrete series of (relatively) simple operations, much like water flows through pipes. It is a concept familiar in the Unix world to which traditional CMS programmers must adjust. Instead of doing everything to the data in one monolithic routine, Pipes chips away at data in a series of small steps. It make take a little more up front thinking to decompose an application, but Pipes applications are much easier to debug or modify, and often run much faster than more "traditional" routines. *The REXX Handbook* (McGraw-Hill, 1992, ISBN 0-07-023682-8, available as IBM publication SB20-0020), contains a chapter about CMS Pipelines written by the author of CMS Pipelines, John Hartmann, that is very useful for getting the flavor of real-world programming with CMS Pipelines.

CMS Multitasking

CMS Multitasking, integrated into VM/ESA 2.0, is the successor to the Server Tasking Environment/VM (STEVR/VM) PRPQ. Both STEVR/VM and CMS Multitasking provide high-level language APIs to CMS multitasking services. These services allow programmers to create multiple threads of execution, serialize resources between multiple threads, and communicate between threads both within a single virtual machine and between virtual machines. CMS Multitasking also provides exploitation for multiple virtual processors.

Compilation and Assembly

Unlike interpreted languages, compiled languages separate translation and execution steps. For the sake of brevity, assemblers and compilers are listed together under the single term "compiler", since they behave similarly enough to be discussed together. Compilers translate program source code to object code. While doing the translation, compilers check for syntax errors. Syntax errors are incorrect use of the compiler language. These are different from logic errors, which are errors in program design. Syntax errors can range from misspelling command names and variable names, to neglecting to define variables, to using conflicting options when specifying variable characteristics, to forgetting necessary punctuation, to starting a program field in the wrong column. Assemblers are fussiest about correct syntax. Compilers usually generate three outputs: a TEXT file, a LISTING file, and terminal messages. Compiler options are available to suppress generation of one or more of these outputs. The TEXT file contains translated source code, which is not yet executable: one more step is necessary, the **linkedit**. If syntax errors are severe enough, many compilers will not generate a TEXT file. The LISTING file lists errors detected in the source code, and any messages or warnings from the compiler. It may or may not also contain the source code. Some compilers also generate messages on the terminal screen.

If a program contains references to MACRO or COPY files, those files must be available during compilation. MACRO and COPY files reside in macro libraries (filetype MACLIB). The CMS command that makes the contents of a library available is GLOBAL followed, in this case, by the MACLIB parameter and the names of needed libraries. CMS supplies the following system macro libraries for assembler language programs:

HCPGPI   General purpose interfaces to CP function.

DMSGPI   General purpose interfaces to CMS function.

OSMACRO   Simulated MVS macros. Programs using these interfaces will execute correctly on both CMS and MVS.

OSMACRO1 Non-simulated MVS macros used to support MVS program development under CMS. Programs using these interfaces will not execute correctly under CMS.

OSVSAM   MVS/VSAM macros supported under CMS. Contains a subset of MVS/VSAM function.

CMS also includes DMSOM, HCPPSI, IXXOM, and OSPSI macro libraries for its own maintenance. Most compilers also include their own libraries.

Compiler invocation

Various commands invoke compilers and assemblers:

Language	Invocation Command
PL/I	PLIOPT
FORTRAN	FORTVS2
COBOL	COBOL2
assembler	ASSEMBLE (Assembler F)
assembler	HASM (Assembler H)
assembler	HLASM (High-Level Assembler)
REXX	REXXC
C	CC
ADA	ADA
PASCAL	VSPASCAL

This is not a complete list of commands which invoke available compilers and assemblers. Older compilers have used COBOL, FORTRAN, FORTVS, and PLI. These may still be available on some VM systems. Not all systems have all compilers or assemblers.

The following example shows compilation of the very simple PL/I
program whose source was listed earlier.

```
list plisamp *
PLISAMP  PLIOPT    A1
Ready;
pliopt plisamp
5668-910 IBM OS PL/I OPTIMIZING COMPILER V2.R3.M0     21 AUG 92  16:38:22
NO MESSAGES OF SEVERITY W AND ABOVE PRODUCED FOR THIS COMPILATION
MESSAGES SUPPRESSED BY THE FLAG OPTION:  1 I.
COMPILE TIME     0.00 MINS          SPILL FILE:      0 RECORDS, SIZE  4051
END OF COMPILATION OF PLISAMP
Ready;
list plisamp *
PLISAMP  PLIOPT    A1
PLISAMP  LISTING   A1
PLISAMP  TEXT      A1
Ready;
```

AMODE and RMODE

Two options that should always be specified, if appropriate, are
AMODE 31 and RMODE ANY. These options can be specified at program
load or module generation time as options on the CMS LOAD and
GENMOD commands.

The AMODE (addressing mode) program attribute defines the
address length programs can handle. AMODE has three possible
values: 24, 31, or ANY. AMODE 24 specifies that the program entry
point receives control from the system in 24-bit addressing mode.
Or, less technically, the program can only handle 24-bit addresses.
AMODE 31 indicates that the program entry point receives control in
31-bit addressing mode unless the program is running in a 370-
mode virtual machine. Since 31-bit addressing is not supported in a
370-mode virtual machine, the program will receive control in 24-bit
addressing mode. AMODE ANY specifies that the program entry point
can handle either 24-bit or 31-bit addresses, and receives control in
the addressing mode of its caller.

The precise technical definition implies that every entry point in a
program can have a different AMODE. This is true, and there are
examples of this unpleasant practice. In general, the AMODE designation applies to an entire program and is consistent across all
program entry points.

The RMODE (residency mode) program attribute defines where
programs can reside in storage. RMODE has two possible values: 24
or ANY. RMODE 24 indicates that a program contains only 24-bit
addresses and must execute below the 16MB line in virtual storage.
RMODE ANY specifies that a program can run in any virtual storage
location, either above or below the 16MB line.

At first glance, it seems that AMODE ANY RMODE ANY would be the optimal combination of options. Alas, that combination has unexpected side effects that make it invalid under certain circumstances. Use AMODE ANY RMODE ANY with caution. *MVS Extended Architecture System Programming Library 31-bit Addressing* is a booklet of approximately 100 pages that explains in detail all combinations of AMODE and RMODE and what to look out for. There is also a short but good section on AMODE and RMODE in the descriptions of the CMS LOAD and GENMOD commands in *Virtual Machine/Enterprise System Architecture CMS Command Reference*.

High-level languages (anything but assembler) do not have difficulty with AMODE 31 RMODE ANY as long as the compiler supports the options. Most older applications will continue to operate in 370 mode, and many in XA, ESA, and XC modes; however, some will require minor or, in some cases, major updates.

At worst, older applications compiled before the AMODE and RMODE options were available must be recompiled and relinked. Assembler language programs require more work. Reference has been made earlier to various virtual machine modes which CMS supports: 370, XA, ESA, and XC. 370 mode supports 24-bit addressing only. XA, ESA, and XC modes support 31-bit addressing. Assembler programs coded when 370 was the only virtual machine mode tend to use high-order register bytes for flag bits since they were not used to form storage addresses. This is disastrous in ESA/XA/XC machine modes, where all register bytes are used for addresses. The result is that 370 assembler programs often require significant work to run in AMODE 31.

Linkediting: building executable files

Once a program has been successfully compiled (all flagged errors corrected), it is ready to be **linkedited**. Linkedit is an old batch programming term used to describe resolving external program references. An external reference is a reference to a routine or program that exists separately and independently from the program being linkedited. The CMS command that performs this step is LOAD. The CMS loader performs a number of functions. It loads programs into memory and relocates internal addresses. It resolves external references. It provides a memory map of the program called a LOAD MAP (discussed later), which is an extremely useful debugging tool. For complex applications consisting of multiple programs which must be loaded into memory together, CMS provides the INCLUDE command.   INCLUDE is supplemental to and must always be used in conjunction with LOAD.

As for the compile step, libraries needed by the LOAD command must be specified prior to program loading. The command to do this is still GLOBAL but it takes two new parameters: TXTLIB and/or CSLLIB, depending on what types of libraries are called.   The example below shows loading the PL/I sample program. The first LOAD command is done without any libraries available and generates errors. The errors, all unresolved external references, are resolved by making the PL/I system text libraries and and the VM system CSL library available to the loader via the GLOBAL command.

```
load plisamp
DMSLIO201W The following names are undefined:
 IBMBPIRA IBMBPIRB IBMBPIRC IBMBCEDB IBMBOCLA IBMBSIOA
 IBMBSLOA IBMLLIST
Ready(00004);
global csllib vmlib
Ready;
global txtlib plilib pliibm
Ready;
load plisamp
Ready;
```

The next example shows a portion of the LOAD MAP produced by the LOAD in the previous example.

```
Control card - ENTRY PLISTART
PLISTART SD 00010000          RMODE ANY AMODE ANY
PLISAMP1 SD 00010080          RMODE ANY AMODE ANY
PLISAMP2 SD 00010220          RMODE ANY AMODE ANY
DMSIBM      00010000
PLICALLA    00010004
PLICALLB    00010008
PLIMAIN  SD 00010300          RMODE ANY AMODE ANY
PLISAMP     00010088
SYSPINT  SD 00010308          RMODE ANY AMODE ANY
 ⋮
```

The most common and frustrating error in linkediting is unresolved external references. It is not always obvious what libraries are needed. Notice that the PL/I library names all start with the characters PLI. This is relatively standard for compiler libraries. VM system libraries always reside on the S-disk. A search must be made for library names by filetype (MACLIB,   TXTLIB,   CSLLIB, LOADLIB). Compiler libraries reside on the Y-disk by IBM convention, but some installations move them to conserve disk space or limit access to a compiler. Compiler libraries have some identifying three- or four-character prefix. PL/I is PLI; FORTRAN is VSF2; COBOL is VSC2. Information on various compiler libraries is documented in IBM language publications, but they are not always within easy reach.

Where the loader places a program in memory is governed by a number of considerations: virtual machine mode, virtual machine size, the SET LOADAREA command, any RMODE settings in effect, and whether the ORIGIN option was specified on the LOAD command. 370 mode precludes loading above the 16MB line no matter what the other options specify. SET LOADAREA does not normally need to be modified. For the curious, its effects are well-documented in the *CMS Command Reference*. SET LOADAREA is useful only for applications that must run in all three virtual machine modes. The ORIGIN option on the LOAD command forces the loader to start loading programs at the address specified with ORIGIN.

In an XA/ESA/XC-mode virtual machine, if RMODE is not specified on the LOAD command, the RMODE defaults to the most restrictive RMODE encountered during the load. In other words, program source may have been compiled with the RMODE ANY option, but if any external reference is RMODE 24, the whole load defaults to RMODE 24. If RMODE ANY is specified on the LOAD command, CMS loads the program in the largest area of contiguous free storage available above the 16MB line. If RMODE 24 is specified or encountered during the load, CMS loads the program in the largest free storage area below the 16MB line. Once the program is successfully loaded, the next command is START.

Testing and Debugging

Up until this point, all the steps beyond writing the program source pertained to compiled languages and assemblers only. Interpreted languages do not require separate compile and linkedit steps in order to execute, but all programs, no matter what the language, need to be tested and debugged. Interpreters will now balk at both syntax and logic errors indiscriminately, while compiled language programs have had their syntax errors corrected at compile time. Despite this, interpreted language programs are still usually quicker to debug. The line that failed is always evident and so, usually, is the reason for failure. Interpreted languages do not have to be recompiled or relinkedited after changes are made to the program source code. REXX also has an extensive and powerful trace facility built into the language.

Although REXX is particularly easy to troubleshoot, when testing HLL applications it is usually pretty obvious why a program ABENDs and where ABENDs occur. It may take a while to figure out what causes a problem, but tracing through the operating system is normally not a necessary step towards problem resolution. Placing statements in a failing program to display variable contents immediately before executing a failing line of code is usually sufficient. Once it is clear which variable or variables are incorrect, it becomes an exercise in determining whether a program is being passed bad data or is incorrectly processing something earlier on. A useful VM tool helps with problem determination: the console SPOOL. VM records almost everything that displays on a terminal screen in the console SPOOL, if spooling has been turned on. This is ideal for testing applications, since a record can be kept of every test and any system or application messages generated. The console SPOOL, created as a print file, can also be routed to a virtual reader and read onto disk if a hardcopy is not wanted. The console SPOOL only captures output generated when VM is in control of the terminal screen. Full-screen applications take control of the terminal screen from VM; their output is not captured in the console SPOOL.

Every now and then, either something goes wrong that requires digging into system code, or an application being tested and debugged is written in assembler. Assembler allows programmers to get into trouble that HLLs are designed to prevent. VM provides several tools for debugging system and assembler problems. According to a brief and unscientific survey, the most useful commands are TRACE, DISPLAY, and STORE. TRACE is a powerful command that captures information about instruction execution, register alteration, storage alteration, and I/O activity within a virtual machine. DISPLAY shows contents of storage, registers, and control areas (virtual, real, or guest). STORE alters the contents of storage, registers, and various virtual machine control areas. None of these commands are useful without knowledge of assembler. The next example shows a short trace of I/O instructions.

```
spool console start
Ready;
load plisamp
Ready;
trace i/o
Ready;
```

```
  :
B
  -> 00E1B5E6  SSCH  B233B5FC      00001B1C      CC 0     SCH 000E    DEV 0009
               CPA 00001AC0    PARM 00000000     KEY 0  FPI C0  LPM FF
start
B
*** 00E1AE28    I/O DEV 0009 -> 00E0DDB0        SCH 000E    PARM 00000000
B
  -> 00E0DE86  TSCH  B235D090 >> 000013F8      CC 0     SCH 000E    DEV 0009
               CCWA 00001AD0    DEV STS 0C  SCH STS 00   CNT 00FA
               KEY 0    FPI C0   CC 0    CTLS 4007
B
DMSLIO740I Execution begins...
  -> 00E1B5E6  SSCH  B233B5FC      00001B1C      CC 0     SCH 000E    DEV 0009
               CPA 00001AC0    PARM 00000000     KEY 0  FPI C0  LPM FF
  .
  .
  .
TRACE END
Trace ended
begin
Ready;
spool console stop
Ready;
```

While troubleshooting a program, typing in commands to recompile, relinkedit, reload, and restart a program after making changes can become tedious. It is very easy to write a short procedure in REXX to handle everything. The following is a very simple example of such a procedure:

```
/* Simple REXX program for compiling and executing PL/I program */
/* First step: Compile program */
   address command
   'PLIOPT PLISAMP'
   if rc <> 0 then do                      /* Check return code */
      say 'Compile failed with return code' rc
      'XEDIT PLISAMP LISTING'
      exit
   end
/* Second step: linkedit program */
'GLOBAL CSLLIB VMLIB'
'GLOBAL TXTLIB PLILIB PLIIBM'
'LOAD PLISAMP'
   if rc > 4 then do /* Check rc; 4 is warning and can be ignored. */
      say 'Load failed with return code' rc
      'XEDIT LOAD MAP'
      exit
   end
/* Third step: Run program */
   'START'
   exit
```

As written, the sample EXEC includes the name of the program to be compiled, the compiler call, and libraries needed. With a bit more effort, the EXEC could be generalized to accept a program name or names as input, select the compiler based on the program filetype, and select libraries based on the compiler. The amount of time taken to write the sample EXEC shown was limited by typing speed—little design was required, since it mainly consists of the commands normally typed manually. The sample EXEC is executed by typing its filename and pressing ENTER—which is much easier than entering all the commands individually.

Putting a program into production

The following are several ways to place VM applications into production.

Disk-resident MODULEs

The easiest method is to create a disk-resident MODULE file. The command used to create CMS MODULEs is GENMOD. GENMOD options that should always be specified are AMODE 31, RMODE ANY, and RLDSAVE. Reasons for using AMODE and RMODE were discussed earlier in this chapter in the section on compiling programs. GENMOD used with the RLDSAVE option creates a relocatable MODULE, which CMS does not load at a specific storage address. Instead, CMS finds the best place to load it, starting from the top of storage (highest available address in the CMS virtual machine) and working down. This goes a long way towards eliminating the problem of two programs needing the same storage addresses. Before CMS supported relocatable MODULEs, such conflicts were common and catastrophic. GENMOD defaults to creating non-relocatable MODULEs for compatibility with older CMS releases. A current topic of debate is whether to change the default on GENMOD to RLDSAVE. An example of using LOAD and GENMOD:

```
global csllib vmlib
Ready;
global txtlib plilib pliibm
Ready;
load plisamp
Ready;
genmod plisamp
Ready;
list plisamp *
PLISAMP   PLIOPT    A1
PLISAMP   LISTING   A1
PLISAMP   TEXT      A1
PLISAMP   MODULE    A1
Ready;
```

The GENMOD command is always used in conjunction with LOAD and (optionally) INCLUDE commands. Once a MODULE is created, it can be executed by typing its filename and pressing ENTER. In many cases, application modules are prefixed with front-end EXECs. These are stubs, usually written in REXX, that set up proper execution environments for MODULEs, making available any data files needed; setting up the virtual printer, reader, or punch if necessary; ensuring adequate storage or disk space is available; and so on. Usually, creating a MODULE or MODULEs and a front-end EXEC is sufficient to place single-user applications into production.

Nucleus extensions

For high-performance applications, two more steps can be taken. First, make the disk-resident module a **nucleus extension**. Nucleus extensions provide a method for loading programs into storage for later execution. Their advantage is that later invocations do not require CMS to read the program from disk. This option is most beneficial for programs called frequently during a single CMS session. The benefits of a nucleus extension accrue each time the application is called. Nucleus extensions remain in memory until either they are explicitly deleted or CMS storage is cleared.

A note about nucleus extensions and changing programs: if changes are made to a program that has been loaded as a nucleus extension, be sure to explicitly delete the nucleus extension before starting to test, since nucleus extensions are invoked before nearly anything else. Much time and frustration has been spent wondering why a program change failed to fix a problem, due to failure to purge the nucleus extension—resulting in execution of a nucleus extension containing the old code.

Nucleus extensions, with proper options on the NUCXLOAD command, can be called at the end of each command (the ENDCMD option), during ABEND processing, or when a NUCXDROP command is issued (the SERVICE option), or as a CMS Immediate command (the IMMCMD option).

Programming considerations for nucleus extensions are covered in *CMS Application Development Guide for Assembler*.

Segments

The major drawback to nucleus extensions is that they load into user storage. If an application is large and/or is used simultaneously by several CMS users, demands for extra virtual storage can place a significant extra load on real system resources, especially the paging subsystem. This type of an application should be placed into a **saved segment**. Saved segments, also known as **DCSSs** or (incorrectly) as **discontiguous shared segments**, do not load in user storage. The storage they occupy is attached to user machines as an extension while the segment is being used, and a single copy of the pages can be shared among many virtual machines. Segments provide both a significant performance boost to applications and significant savings in real system resources. Offering two such important benefits, most commercial VM applications use segments.

A relatively new facility in CMS called **logical segments** is highly recommended for the flexibility it adds. Code to be placed in a DCSS must be reentrant, since shared saved segments cannot alter their storage. Whenever possible, generate segments above the 16MB line. Doing so of course requires that code residing in the segment support 31-bit addressing.

More information on segments is available in the *VM/ESA CMS Application Development Guide* and *VM/ESA CP Planning and Administration*.

Conclusion

This chapter provided a brief overview of procedures and techniques for developing applications under CMS for CMS. Most topics introduced in this chapter are covered in more detail elsewhere in this book. For further reading, a good place to start is the *VM/ESA CMS Application Development Guide*.

18

Converting Applications to VM/ESA

By Charles T. Boeheim and Steven L. Jones

Introduction

Conversion is the process of transferring a set of applications to a new system environment. Historically, relatively little application-level conversion has been required to move from one level of VM to another. However, VM/ESA includes the major restructuring of CMS that was introduced by CMS Release 5.5 in VM/XA SP because of the significant architectural differences between the 370 and XA instruction sets.

Applications that have already been converted to VM/XA SP have already had much of the necessary work done for conversion to VM/ESA. Applications that have been converted to VM/SP Release 6 have already encountered the restructuring of CMS for the new architecture, but not the new architecture itself, which may require more conversion effort. Applications still running under VM/SP or VM/SP HPO Release 5 or earlier may involve substantial conversion effort due to major changes in machine architecture, CMS structure, and CP interfaces.

For this discussion, the VM/ESA 370 feature is similar to VM/SP Release 6. This version of VM/ESA includes all of the CMS changes of CMS 6, but no XA or ESA architecture changes.

Applications already running under VM/ESA Release 1.0 ESA feature should require little or no conversion. Such applications should still be examined, however, to see if they might benefit from exploitation of new facilities.

Objectives

It can be difficult to delimit the conversion task. Conversion can be taken to mean only investing the bare minimum of work to keep an application running, or it can mean performing substantial work to use newer and more functional interfaces. For instance, some installations may find it sufficient to execute all applications in 370-mode virtual machines, for which conversion is fairly minimal. Other installations may need to convert all or most applications to XA- or XC-architecture virtual machines to exploit larger address spaces, VM Data Spaces, or SFS performance enhancements.

This chapter primarily describes conversion to XC-architecture virtual machines, with at least toleration of the XA instruction set. For many applications it will be unnecessary to convert further to 31-bit addressing: XA toleration enables exploitation of the XC architecture for such items as saved segment management.

The March Towards Preferred Interfaces

The most charitable statement that can be said about CMS programming interfaces is that they have never been formally defined. For assembler programmers, the programming interface was a set of assembler macros and a collection of control block descriptions. The macros often had little consistency among them, and the descriptions of control blocks found in the CMS macro libraries were considered fair game by most programmers.

For REXX programmers, the programming interface was mostly the same commands that were meant to be used interactively, with the same syntax and output meant for human interpretation. For good measure there were a few commands such as EXECIO that looked like CMS commands but were only useful when called from

within an EXEC. There were even a few confused functions such as
NUCEXT that would provide simple return codes to an EXEC, but also
provide information in registers for assembler programmers.

When CMS 5.5 was written to exploit the XA architecture, much
of this started to change. Old macro interfaces often did not support
the 31-bit addresses that were needed, so a new set of macros called
the Preferred Interface Group was introduced. These macros were
generally more consistent than the old set, were more flexible in
accepting different argument types, and provided in-line, list, and
execute forms.

At the same time, macros that had been in CMSLIB MACLIB and
DMSSP MACLIB were reorganized into DMSGPI MACLIB and DMSOM
MACLIB. DMSGPI contains those that can be relied on as general
programming interfaces, and DMSOM contains those that are considered internal and which may change from release to release. Of
course, just knowing that the macros and control blocks used in an
existing program are out of bounds does not help the conversion
effort if there are no other ways to accomplish a programming task.
The good news is that the macros are still available in DMSOM since
IBM did not remove them entirely; access them by changing the
GLOBAL MACLIB list to include DMSGPI and DMSOM. If the program
still assembles, it will likely continue to run without change (at least
for control block reasons). However, if the program uses macros in
DMSOM, think about finding different ways to accomplish the same
task, since these may change in future releases of VM.

Should programs that use macros in the Compatibility Group be
converted to use new macros in the Preferred Interface Group? Not
necessarily! The older macros will continue to work in 370-mode
virtual machines, and in most cases will work in XA- or XC-mode
virtual machines in programs running below the 16MB line. Only if
the programs must be loaded above 16MB do macro calls need to be
changed to the Preferred Interface Group.

The antidote to the use of the CMS command language as a
programming interface is the Callable Services Library (CSL), introduced in VM/SP Release 6. The CSL provides a program-call interface for requesting system services, and for querying and setting
many environmental settings. Appropriate CSL calls can be used to
insulate a program from future changes in command syntax or
responses.

Do EXECs that use CMS commands and their responses need
conversion? More often than one might like, they do. Between
VM/SP and VM/XA, responses to many CP commands changed, and

VM/ESA in general uses the same responses as VM/XA. Many CP message numbers have changed, device addresses have grown from three to four digits, and there are often more lines of responses from commands. When changing an EXEC because of command syntax or response changes, consider looking for a CSL routine that performs the same function. The CSL routine will be more robust in future releases of VM. If it turns out that there is no CSL routine to do what the program needs, let IBM know through marketing representatives or user groups; the CSL is expanding and growing, and IBM solicits input on functions needed.

In practice, EXECs that deal with disks or SPOOLed devices are the most likely to need work. EXECs that trap and parse command output may need attention, although this is somewhat less likely. EXECs that are more purely computational or command procedures are the least likely to require any conversion.

Learn about the new preferred interfaces right at the start. When a program needs changes to keep it running in VM/ESA, that is the time to convert to the new interfaces. However, there is probably little need to change existing programs that continue to run.

Storage Management

One of the most basic areas of CMS changes is in storage management. The changes are so basic that they affect the operations of both user programs and CMS itself. These changes were first introduced in CMS 5.5, and are found in CMS 6 and all later CMS versions. Applications already converted to run under CMS 5.5, CMS 6, or CMS 7 should need little or no additional change under CMS 8.

Prior to CMS 5.5 there was not a lot of emphasis on the management aspect of storage management. Native CMS storage, requested by the DMSFREE assembler macro, was simply the storage beyond the end of the current program until it ran into something else. OS storage, requested by the GETMAIN assembler macro or by most high-level languages, was simply the storage from the highest available storage address down until it ran into something else. The management of this storage was only to detect when these two areas ran into each other.

Now CMS storage is organized into many **subpools**. There are subpools for general user program storage and for OS simulation storage, but there are many new subpools as well, for program loading, XEDIT, CMS internal use, and many other purposes. Each subpool has a name, such as USER, NUCLEUS, DMSOS000, and so on. The subpool name can be used to collect together storage allocations, give them common attributes, and to perform some manipulations of the entire collection.

Storage is now allocated to individual subpools in units of one page, starting from high addresses and working down. Storage from various subpools is intermingled according to the order in which it was allocated, rather than the previous two large amorphous heaps. While this arrangement provides much greater flexibility and control over a program's storage usage, there are still a few opportunities for programs to break when encountering the new architecture.

One breakage opportunity comes from intermingling storage from different subpools. Programs have occasionally had long-standing bugs that caused them to use storage that they did not allocate, perhaps by using more elements of an array than were declared. In the past, there may have been a high probability that no other program was using the physically adjacent blocks of storage into which this program was writing. Now there may be a much greater chance that an ill-behaved program will "step on" storage being used by another program. The new storage management structure can make this sort of long-hidden bug painfully visible.

Another frequent problem in storage management is fragmentation. Fragmentation is not a new problem, but the changes in storage management can cause programs that did not previously encounter fragmentation to begin to have problems. For instance, if a program uses OS GETMAIN storage, but calls a subroutine or service that uses CMS DMSFREE storage, those two types of storage are now intermingled rather than coming from separate areas. This can cause certain patterns of storage acquisition to break up available storage into small, unusable pieces, and cause the program to either need a larger virtual storage size, or even to always run out of storage no matter how much it is given.

Another, harder-to-solve storage problem is the storage eater. This is a program that gradually uses up all available storage until it fails with an out-of-storage condition. Typically, storage eaters are disconnected service virtual machines that run for many hours or days without re-initialization. Often, they must be watched with one of the new tools that are discussed at the end of this section, to determine why storage is not being reclaimed properly.

The persistence of various sorts of storage allocations has also changed. Previously (CMS 5 and earlier), storage obtained with OS GETMAIN would persist until the next return to the CMS command prompt, CMS storage with TYPE=USER would persist until an ABEND occurred, and TYPE=NUCLEUS storage would persist forever. Now there is some degree of control that can be exercised over the persistence of storage, but there have also been changes to the defaults.

OS GETMAIN storage is by default connected to the program that allocated it, and is released as soon as that program returns to its caller. Technically, the storage is associated with the SVC 202/204 that invoked the program, and the return that unstacks the SVC also releases the storage. This means that GETMAIN storage will not persist as long as it previously did, and this can cause problems if the program expects otherwise. A new command, SET STORECLR ENDCMD/ENDSVC controls whether this default clean up at end of SVC is performed, or whether it should be deferred until the return to the CMS command prompt.

CMS storage is by default in a globally known subpool named USER, and this storage is only cleaned up during ABEND processing. A subpool named NUCLEUS contains the former TYPE=NUCLEUS storage, and is never explicitly cleaned up. A program that wishes more control over the time of clean up can define a new named subpool, and can choose to have it cleaned up at end of SVC or to have it never explicitly cleaned up.

Programs that obtain storage for interrupt handlers, or programs that are nucleus extensions or that may be re-entered during their lifetime must be particularly careful about choosing storage that has an appropriate persistence. Storage that does not persist long enough will cause strange addressing exceptions, possibly long after the event that released the storage. Storage that persists too long will cause the fragmentation or memory eaters mentioned above.

Each storage problem seems to be unique in its cause and manifestation, and the only thing they seem to have in common is the painstaking research needed to find the cause. This research is fortunately eased by several new tools introduced in VM/ESA to diagnose storage management problems. The SUBPMAP command reports how many pages of storage are allocated to each subpool. Issue this command as a program runs to watch changes in allocations in subpools. The STORMAP command gives a much more detailed mapping of individual storage allocations. Direct output from this command to a disk file to detect patterns of allocations

over time. However, very detailed analysis of the output will probably be required to make effective use of this tool.

The third tool, STDEBUG, is the most powerful of the three, but also
the one that takes the most skill and persistence to use. This
command traces operations that obtain and release storage, sending
output to the virtual console, a virtual punch, or a virtual printer.
The trace can be restricted by type of request, address range of the
requester, subpool name, or several other criteria. Nonetheless, the
volume of output from this command can be truly daunting. One of
the most frequent tasks when debugging a storage allocation
problem is searching through this output for obtains not paired with
releases, or patterns of obtains that create fragmentation. The
XEDIT ALL subcommand can display subsets of this trace, and the
SORT subcommand can organize the trace in various ways: chronolog-
ically, by caller address, or by storage address.

The CMS Pipelines facility can also process, reduce, aggregate,
and report on this data.

Program Loading and Management

Just as storage is now managed, so are loaded programs. CMS
acquires the storage that a program will occupy before loading it,
and will refuse to load it if it cannot acquire the space. While this
sounds like (and is) a proper way to do it, difficulties can arise in
older programs that were either sloppy or clever.

The first part of the process that this affects is LOAD/INCLUDE
handling. A LOAD command implicitly deletes all previously loaded
programs from memory. Programs that run afoul of this are usually
either trying to generate complex modules and should be using
INCLUDE instead of LOAD, or are trying to do dynamic linking, and
should be using the LOAD macro instead. The PRES option of LOAD
may be used to request that other programs not be deleted; however,
this request is ignored if the program overlaps another, so this
option cannot be used to create overlay structures.

It may also occur that some portion of storage needed to load the
program is in use by some other object that cannot be moved. The
confusing part of this is that the address specified in the message
specifies the start of the area into which the program attempted to
load, not the address of the storage in use. This can make it difficult to guess what prevented the load from completing.

Another difference is that the start of the user area can float between X'10000' and X'20000'. The new SET LOADAREA command specifies whether programs are always to load at X'20000' as they did in past CMS releases, or whether they are to use the lowest possible address. The default for 370-architecture virtual machines is to load at X'20000', while the default for XA and XC virtual machines is for the load point to float. This can affect a few programs that are sensitive to their execution addresses.

Similar rules govern the loading of modules, with the additional complication that there are two kinds of modules: **relocatable** and **non-relocatable**. Non-relocatable modules load at the address at which they were generated, and by default delete other inactive non-relocatable programs from storage. They cannot create program overlays any longer, since overlapping programs are deleted when a new program is loaded, even if the PRES option of LOADMOD is used.

Relocatable modules load at the highest address appropriate for their Residency Mode (RMODE). This again can cause problems for programs that have expectations about where in storage they load, though programs designed to be relocatable should have few such expectations. Opportunities are created for storage fragmentation if a program allocates storage that outlasts the program lifetime. For instance, if a relocatable program accesses a disk, the disk directory could very easily be left in an awkward location in storage, causing fragmentation.

The largest opportunity for problems in program management is with programs that cooperate with each other, or that have expectations of how long they remain in storage after returning control to their caller. The new rules for program lifetime are complex, and merit careful study if the programs are complex. They are in the *CMS Application Development Guide*.

Program Linkage

There are two major kinds of program linkage to consider: **supervisor assisted** and **direct branch**. Supervisor assisted linkage is the mechanism used by CMS to locate, load, and transfer control to CMS modules. Direct branch linkage is used to transfer control within a program, or between already loaded and established programs.

Supervisor assisted linkage was performed with SVC 202 in older CMS versions. SVC 202 is still supported by CMS, but has a number of restrictions on its use. SVC 202 cannot be used by programs that reside above the 16MB line, and there are restrictions on its use between programs in different addressing modes. The replacement for SVC 202 is SVC 204, which is normally coded by use of the CMSCALL macro. SVC 204 can be used in any addressing mode, and handle linkage between programs of unlike residency or addressing modes.

SVC 204 has been available since CMS 5.5, and APAR VM34760 is available to implement limited use of it in CMS 5. However, programs that may run in older releases of CMS, including CMS 5 without the compatibility APAR, may have to contain dual-path code to conditionally use SVC 204 only on newer CMS releases.

Formerly, programs received information in the high order byte of register 1 about how they were called. For compatibility, that information is still presented there for AMODE 24 programs. However, AMODE 31 programs must find that information in the USERSAVE DSECT pointed to by register 13 instead, since all bits of register 1 are required for the parameter list address. A program that will only run on releases of CMS from 5.5 onward could simply check USERSAVE for this flag, since it is always presented there. A program that must execute under previous releases of CMS must know to retrieve the flag from register 1 instead.

Is there a need to convert existing programs to use SVC 204? Probably not, if the program need not run above the 16MB line. SVC 202 will continue to function, and CMS will handle most necessary translations transparently to the program. However, for new work, CMSCALL is easier to code, more flexible, and ensures that the program is ready to exploit new system services.

Direct branch linkage was traditionally a BALR instruction to transfer control and a return address to a called routine. However, this cannot accommodate routines that are in different AMODEs, so CMS provides a new macro, AMODESW, to assist in writing architecture-independent program calls. AMODESW can call a routine that may be in a different AMODE, switching AMODE in the process and preserving the calling AMODE to be restored upon return. For instance, to load a routine dynamically from a TXTLIB and transfer control to it, use the following code:

```
LOAD    EP=MYPROG        Load routine
LR      R15,R0           Get entry point
AMODESW CALL             Call MYPROG in correct AMODE.
```

The LOAD macro loads MYPROG into storage, and returns its entry point in R0, with the high order bit indicating the addressing mode. The AMODESW CALL macro invocation saves the current program's return address and AMODE in R14, switches AMODE to match MYPROG, and transfers control. Presumably, MYPROG will use the AMODESW RETURN instruction to switch back to the AMODE of its caller.

The CMS loader can fill in V-type address constants (VCONs) with the correct addressing mode bit. In CMS 5.5 through CMS 7, the loader sets the addressing mode bit for VCONs that refer to SD-type entries, that is, the symbols that appear on CSECT statements. In CMS 7, APAR VM46641 introduced a new option for the LOAD command to control the setting of this bit: the HOBSETSD option continues the existing behavior and is the default; the HOBSET option sets the AMODE bit for both CSECT and ENTRY symbols; and the NOHOBSET option does not set the AMODE bits. In CMS 8, the default changes from HOBSETSD to NOHOBSET to be compatible with behavior of the MVS linkage editor.

OS Simulation

With CMS 5.5, OS simulation was upgraded to MVS SP 2.2.0 level for those parts of OS simulation that CMS supports. This allows use of MVS macros that support 31-bit addressing for programs that run above the 16MB line. There are a few changes to note during the conversion task.

The broadest change is to storage management, as described earlier in this chapter. MVS GETMAIN requests are mapped directly to CMSSTOR OBTAIN requests and to the CMS subpool structure. A nice benefit is that CMS now supports the subpool parameter of the GETMAIN and FREEMAIN macros, as well as FREEPOOL and related macros. CMS subpools are created for each MVS subpool, with names in the form of DMSOSnnn, where nnn is the MVS subpool number.

Also alluded to earlier is the change in persistence of GETMAIN storage to more closely match that in MVS. All GETMAIN storage allocated by a program is released when the program returns to its caller, rather than the previous behavior of releasing GETMAIN storage only on return to the CMS command level. Previously, many programs attempted to control this clean up with the STRINIT macro, which released all existing GETMAIN storage at all levels.

The new default behavior cleans up storage more often, and the STRINIT macro has become a null operation.

For instance, if program A calls program B, and B does not explicitly release storage that it allocates, the new behavior will now automatically release the storage. Previously, program A may have contained a STRINIT call to release that storage so that A could regain its use. However, if another program C calls a program D, and D returns information to C in some allocated storage, the new behavior will release that storage before it can be returned to C. Programs like C and D may use the SET STORECLR ENDCMD command to request the previous behavior. This command will cause storage to be retained until the return to CMS command level, and STRINIT to regain its previous function. However, unless this program runs in an isolated environment where it can be certain that STORECLR will be set properly, consider reworking the programs to use native CMS services to obtain storage with the needed persistence.

A problem in converting programs that use MVS data management services to use 31-bit addressing is that these I/O services use 24-bit addressing only. DCBs must be allocated below the 16MB line, as must any I/O buffers that they refer to, and any exit routines. Further, the OPEN, GET, PUT, READ, WRITE, and CLOSE macros must also be expanded only below the 16MB line, since they operate in AMODE 24. The best approach is to create a library of routines that perform these data management functions, and assemble them with AMODE 24. Then use the LOAD macro to load them dynamically during execution. LOAD will automatically load them below the 16MB line, since they are marked AMODE 24. Then AMODESW CALL can transfer control to them in AMODE 24, regardless of whether the program has loaded above or below the 16MB line, and whether it is in AMODE 24 or AMODE 31.

High-Level Language Considerations

Conversion is generally much easier for programs written in high-level languages such as FORTRAN, PL/I, COBOL, or C. Compilers generate code that is already AMODE 31, and their runtime libraries handle differences in system services. Many programs are ready to run above the 16MB line as soon as enough storage is defined for them to do so.

One of the first tasks may be getting programs to load above the 16MB line. In general, the best way to do this is to make modules relocatable, so that CMS automatically loads them in the highest area that can accommodate them.   However, some languages are known to generate so many internal symbols that the relocation directory cannot be saved, or takes up too much disk space to be practical. VS FORTRAN with the TEST option is particularly noted for this behavior. Options for such programs include always doing a LOAD/START sequence rather than generating a module, or creating a non-relocatable version of the module. A non-relocatable module will require either two versions for use above and below the 16MB line, or a restriction on its use only to virtual machines at least as large as the one that generated the module.

Other difficulties may arise from libraries of subroutines that may have been obtained from other vendors or developed locally. If some of these libraries contain AMODE 24 subroutines, use of these subroutines can restrict the program to execution below the 16MB line. The load map now contains the AMODE of each subroutine included within the module, as well as the name of the library that supplied that routine. Inspect the load map to find which routines restrict the module, and either update them to AMODE 31 or replace them. If necessary, use dynamic loading to load them below the 16MB line during execution, though an assembler subroutine will be needed to do so.

Some of the worst difficulties may come if some subroutines contain architecture-dependent instructions, for example, for I/O libraries.   These may restrict the program to 370-architecture virtual machines until these routines are replaced or reengineered.

The good news is that CSL routines are available now that perform many tasks that were previously accomplished by library routines written in assembler.   That library can potentially be replaced with CSL calls to system services. Become familiar with the services available in the CSL that are documented in the *CMS Application Development Reference* before working with libraries that provide system services, and be ready to replace routines with CSL calls rather than converting them.

Segments

Planning saved segments

The basic problem faced when converting from a System/370 environment to an ESA/390 environment is congestion below the 16MB line. If this were a perfect world, conversion would be a simple matter of moving all segment-based applications to saved segments defined above the 16MB line, as XA-mode virtual machines now have up to 2GB of address space. However, the world is not perfect and many segment-based applications must still reside below the 16MB line. The most frequent reason for this restriction is that at least one application in the application set being used cannot tolerate the ESA architecture. This means that the application set must be executed in a 370-mode virtual machine and therefore all addressability above the 16MB line is unavailable.

Know which products run in which mode. If a product is 370 mode only, it can only be used in a 370-mode virtual machine. All other products that are used with this product must be defined below the 16MB line, even if they can execute above the 16MB line, because of the 370-mode dependency of one of them.

If a product can tolerate an XA-mode virtual machine, it may then reside below the 16MB line as in 370 mode; however, it may now invoke programs above the 16MB line. Therefore, in this environment all products capable of execution above the 16MB line may be placed there, even if one product in the mixture must reside below the 16MB line.

Programs defined in a segment above the 16MB line may invoke programs above or below the 16MB line; however, they cannot execute in a 370-mode machine.

For several reasons (discussed later), there is simply less room for saved segments below the 16MB line for a virtual machine on VM/ESA than there is for a similar virtual machine on VM/SP. This is also true to a much smaller extent for conversion from VM/XA to VM/ESA.

Architecture differences

System/370 segments were 64KB (16 pages) in size. In contrast, ESA/390 segments are 1MB (256 pages) in size. This difference means that there are only 16 segments below the 16MB line under

VM/ESA ESA feature, whereas there are 256 segments below the 16MB line under VM/SP or the VM/ESA 370 feature. The obvious conclusion is that conversion of the VM/SP segment layout to the ESA feature is more than just replicating the existing structure.

Learn about CP segment packing before starting to convert the existing segment structure. This support allows multiple **members** in one VM/ESA 1MB segment **space**. The basic 1MB segment architecture remains unchanged; however, CP segment packing allows the segment manipulation programming interfaces (DIAGNOSE X'64', SEGMENT LOAD, etc.) to reference members within the 1MB structure as separate entities that can be as small as one 4K page in size.

While planning this segment packing, determine which saved segments are used together and whether there are any that are **not** used together. Segments that are used together should be packed together. Segments that are not used together should be placed in different spaces that load at the same address, as they will not be required at the same time.

Segment members may belong to spaces with different global sizes. Two segment spaces that are different sizes can have the same member in both of them to take advantage of segment overlay support.

CMS nucleus size

The CMS nucleus continues to grow with each release of CMS. In addition, for the ESA feature the CMS named saved system is defined in megabyte increments rather than 64K increments. CMS under VM/XA required two full megabytes for the named saved system. These were the two megabytes (X'E' and X'F') immediately below the 16MB line. In VM/ESA Release 1, CMS 7 still occupies these two segments; however, the nucleus has grown sufficiently large within this space that the storage required for saving the shared S-stat and Y-stat has become a concern. There may be severe degradation in overall system performance by not having both shared S- and Y-stats.

Part of this problem was alleviated in CMS 7 via APAR VM49762, which made more space available; however, installations having large shared Y-stats must consider this as a potential inhibitor. One solution is to skip conversion to CMS 7 altogether and go directly to VM/ESA Release 1.1 and CMS 8.

CMS 8 solves this problem by utilizing a third 1MB segment for the CMS nucleus. This third segment is placed above the 16MB line and is used in 370 virtual machines as well as XA-mode and XC-mode virtual machines. This segment contains read-only data such as messages. By moving this data from the two segments below the line to the new segment above the line, sufficient space is made available for the shared S-stat and Y-stat in their traditional location, between the end of the executable portion of CMS and the end of the second segment which is normally the 16MB line.

The segment below the CMS nucleus

The X'D' segment needs special consideration when defining saved segments. The portion of the CMS nucleus below the 16MB line normally occupies from X'E00000' to X'FFFFFF', which consists of the 15th and 16th megabyte. If the virtual machine (VMSIZE) size is greater than 14MB (X'E00000') there will be free storage used by CMS in the high end of the 14th megabyte which is the X'D' segment.

For example, in a 16MB machine free storage starts at the top end of the 14th megabyte; thus, at IPL, CMS gets free storage here because storage management allocates free storage from the top down. This effectively renders the X'D' segment useless for saved segments except for virtual machines less than 14MB in size. In virtual machines less than 14MB in size, the X'D' segment cannot be free storage and is therefore available for segment loading.

Even if CMS usage extended down only a few pages into the X'D' segment and the target saved segment to be loaded had not defined these pages in the original DEFSEG, a DIAGNOSE X'64' LOADSEG would affect the whole megabyte including the CMS control blocks in the high end of the segment and CMS would fail. The SEGMENT LOAD command or macro would fail because SEGMENT processing makes sure the whole megabyte is unallocated prior to the SEGMENT LOAD. There is no way to reserve the 14th megabyte early enough because DMSINS calls CMS modules at IPL for initialization long before any PROFILE is executed, and many of these modules are AMODE 24, meaning they obtain storage at the highest possible address below 16MB.

This problem also exists when the VMSIZE is greater than 16MB because the AMODE 24 modules cannot get their free storage above 16MB. Again, storage comes from the highest address below 16MB, which will be the 14th megabyte because the CMS nucleus is in the 15th and 16th megabytes.

The only time the 14th megabyte can be used to load a saved segment is when VMSIZE is less than 13MB (X'D00000'), because then all free storage is below the target DCSS. The trick is in saving the segment, because to do so VMSIZE must be greater than the segment space.

There are two ways to save the segment:

- The portion of the 14th megabyte to be saved is below the area used by CMS and does not collide with it. This can be done because page ranges can be specified on the DEFSEG and the rest of the megabyte is not saved (the CMS used storage). When the whole megabyte is loaded by the SEGMENT LOAD, VMSIZE **must** be less than 13MB, so the SEGMENT command does not attempt to obtain the storage, which would fail.

- If the objects that are being loaded into the 14th megabyte collide with the CMS control blocks in the high end, it is necessary to generate a CMS NSS that is low—say, at the 8MB line—and IPL it in a 16MB machine. Then CMS will have the 15th and 16th megabytes for its control blocks and the 14th megabyte should be free. Again, after it has been saved it should be loaded only in a virtual machine of less than 13 megabytes, so segment processing will not attempt to acquire storage allocated at IPL.

CMS storage requirements

CMS on VM/ESA requires more virtual storage than VM/SP 5. A user who might have been able to function in a 4MB virtual machine on VM/SP 5 may require a larger virtual machine on VM/ESA even though the same application set is being executed. The difference in virtual storage requirements is far less for a conversion from VM/XA or VM/SP 6.

Additional storage required will be taken from what might have been previously reserved as segment space, leaving less room for saved segments.

Conversion hints

Converting DMKSNT

When converting from VM/SP (including HPO) it is necessary to convert DMKSNT segment definitions to equivalent CP DEFSEG commands. This conversion should be one of the first steps done to indicate how well the previously defined 64K segments group into the 1MB segment structure. It allows comparing apples to apples instead of apples to oranges. Once DMKSNT conversion has been accomplished, related applications should be combined into packed segments by manipulating DEFSEGs for those applications. The process of converting DMKSNT definitions to DEFSEG commands is documented in the *VM/ESA Conversion Notebook*

When converting to the 370 feature of VM/ESA the process is much simpler. The 370 feature no longer uses DMKSNT files; however, they may be used if desired. The 370 feature is shipped with an SNT OVERRIDE file which replaces DMKSNT. The SNT OVERRIDE file is used as input to the OVERRIDE command to dynamically change saved segment definitions. The process is documented in the *VM/ESA Release 1 CP Planning and Administration for 370*.

The MIGROVRD EXEC is supplied with the 370 feature of VM/ESA to perform the one-time conversion of an existing DMKSNT to an OVERRIDE source file.

Segment maintenance

Consider writing an EXEC to define, install, and save segment members that will belong to segment spaces with different global sizes. They should be defined in the smallest space first. The EXEC will automate the process and remove the human error frequently introduced into the process of segment maintenance because of the complexity involved. The EXEC can be executed whenever changes are made to any saved segments within the system, and ensure the all the required steps are taken and done in the correct order.

Some product installation procedures rely on attaching "empty" pages via DIAGNOSE X'64'. This allows small service machines to get addressability to page ranges that require initialization. In other words, a "dummy" segment is loaded outside the virtual machine to gain addressability to the page range where the final segment will be built and saved. This assures that no overlay condition will exist during installation since all work is performed outside of the virtual machine.

VM/ESA uses **skeleton** and **active** segment definitions for dynamic segment management. They ensure that only active segments are attachable, rather than copies in the process of being defined, or "old" copies.

Installation procedures relying on "empty" page attachment require additional steps:

- SAVESEGs issued after DEFSEGs to create "empty" segment
- DEFSEGSs issued again to meet VM/ESA "skeleton" requirement

Control Blocks and Internals

There are internal changes and restructuring with every new release of VM. However, internal changes introduced in CMS 5.5 and CMS 6 were perhaps the most dramatic ever. Some applications depending on CMS internals have been extremely difficult to move from VM/SP 5 to a new CMS. Changes to CMS control blocks and internals are too numerous to mention. Below are a few examples, followed by general guidelines on how to approach the task of converting applications that depend on internals.

Storage management

CMS storage management was completely rewritten in CMS 5.5, and the NUCON following fields were removed:

- MAINLIST
- MAINSTRT
- FREELIST
- FREENUM
- MAINHIGH
- FREELOWE
- FREELOWR
- FREEUPPR
- FRERESPG

These fields' labels were removed, and the fields are now reserved, with values of 0. Applications that reference these fields and are reassembled with the new version of NUCON will produce assembly errors, as these fields will be undefined. Programs allowed to execute from previous releases will fetch a 0 value from these areas in NUCON and process it accordingly. For example, an application subtracting MAINHIGH from FREELOWE to determine the size of the largest contiguous block of free storage will compute a value of 0.

Some of these fields have no equivalents in CMS 7 and an altivernate method must be found to perform the same operation as had been done previously. In the example above of subtracting MAINHIGH from FREELOWE, there is an internal entry point in CMS Storage Management (DMSFRUMX) that will accomplish the same result.

Other changes in Storage Management included replacing the DMSFRT control block pointed to by ADMSFRT in NUCON to a new control block structure. The same location in NUCON was relabeled as NUCFRWRK and now points to the DMSFRWRK control block. The NUCXFRES field in NUCON is now ignored by CMS and no longer needs to be updated with the amount of Nucleus Key Storage being obtained by the application. Entry point DMSFRES was made a NOP and the services provided by it are no longer available. Restructuring of Storage Management internals has obsoleted the AREA=LOW and AREA=HIGH parameters on the DMSFREE macro, because free storage is no longer grouped into low and high USER or NUCLEUS key storage. These parameters are ignored. Finally, the internal FREE and FRET entry points were removed.

Program management

The size of the CMS Loader Table entry has increased, and programs examining the loader tables must take this into consideration. This also can be a problem when a module is created on CMS 7 with a map appended, and is executed on CMS 5; however, APAR VM40766 gives CMS 5 "knowledge" of the new loader table entry size.

The module header record was greatly restructured due to the new information required to be saved such as relocation, AMODE, RMODE, architecture requirements, and the like. Existing fields in the module header record are compatible with previous releases of CMS and the changes are primarily the addition of new fields. For the first time, the module header record has a mapping macro, MODHDCB, contained in DMSOM MACLIB. It is not supported as a programming interface; however, it illustrates the format of the module header for debugging or general education.

Another factor to consider is the location where OS loaded (loaded via the MVS LOAD macro) programs are resolved. The location is resolved as a fixed value beyond the current position of the location counter, not the actual location to which it points. The current increment (subject to change) is X'50000' bytes beyond the location counter value. This algorithm is intended to leave space for INCLUDEd programs at the point of the location counter while placing OS loaded programs above this area.

Device support

DEVTAB entries have been enlarged, so programs scanning DEVTAB must take the new entry size into consideration. Also, when a Shared File System directory is accessed as a minidisk, the corresponding DEVTAB entry has a virtual device address of 0, which can be misinterpreted as meaning there is no entry.

CMS console support has been restructured, and CCWs in OPSECT are no longer used, so programs that modify them may no longer get the same results.

File system

The AFT was extensively restructured in CMS 6. Programs using the AFT must be examined for possible incompatibilities.

Fields in the ADT pertinent to minidisks are not always reliable for a Shared File System Directory. An example of such an unreliable field is ADTLEFT, the number of remaining free blocks on the minidisk.

A significant amount of the file system was rewritten in PL/AS for CMS Release 6, causing source code to become unavailable. This impacts the ability to carry local enhancements forward.

Updating an FST in storage to alter file attributes, commonly performed on minidisk FSTs, will not achieve the same results for Shared File System FSTs. Essentially, Shared File System FSTs are *copies* in storage of the real FSTs kept by the server. Updates to the storage copy are not reflected to the server original.

Many file system internal interfaces are AMODE 24. Applications converted to AMODE 31 that call these internal interfaces must switch to 24-bit addressing before calling them. The module prologues contain the only documentation as to which internal interfaces are 24-bit and which are 31-bit.

XEDIT

XEDIT places zFONC above the 16MB line if storage is available. Applications executing in 24-bit addressing mode that manipulate XEDIT control blocks will fail in such an environment and must be changed.

Conversion tips

The first step that should be considered is reassembly using the new macro libraries. This will find references to fields that no longer exist. If it is known which internal interfaces and control blocks a program is using, manual inspection comparing their usage to their new format should be done to determine if that usage is still appropriate. When applications fail that successfully executed on previous releases of CMS, the possibility of CP or architecture dependencies must first be eliminated. When that has been eliminated, begin to look for an internal dependency that may have been overlooked.

Finally, attempt to remove as many internal dependencies as possible. Many dependencies on CMS internals can be removed because the CMS restructure removed the limiting factors that necessitated the use of internals. Some internal entry points (scan and stack) have been externalized and CMS macro interfaces have been provided.

The Extract/Replace Callable Service is a possible alternative to direct manipulation of CMS control blocks; however, the number of control blocks (or fields in particular control blocks) is limited; this may not help every such need.

The next section describes in more detail some interfaces that may remove dependencies on the use of CMS internals.

Interfaces and Commands

Overview

There have been significant enhancements with respect to application programming support. Unfortunately, there are also significant incompatibilities.

Examples on the positive side are facilities like enhanced interrupt support (HNDEXT, HNDIO, CONSOLE, etc.) that provide more complex interrupt handling and eliminate much need to perform stealing of PSWs and other architecture-dependent operations. The differences between 370- and XA-based I/O interrupt reporting can be masked through use of these interfaces. Segment management interfaces allow loading saved segments inside virtual machines. VM/ESA enhanced OS/MVS storage management interfaces provide a wealth of function not available with the DMSFREE/DMSFRET interfaces. VM/ESA has the CMS Shared File System with programming interfaces to exploit it. There are also interfaces in VM/ESA 1.1 to exploit VM Data Spaces.

The price of this is a set of programming interfaces that generally are not backward compatible, meaning if exploited, applications are prohibited from execution on previous releases of VM. This problem is aggravated by the fact there are so many levels of VM currently in production environments and fully supported. If an application elects to exploit new CMS storage management function, it will not execute on a VM/SP 5-based CMS unless the new function is dual-pathed or inhibited in that environment. Coding efforts to support all releases of VM currently in use can be cost-prohibitive, and often force the choice of the lowest common denominator, such as the Compatibility Group described later in this section.

Other changes that impact applications (though many have been fixed via APARs) are more internally oriented items such as loader table restructure, module format changes, command option default changes effecting module execution, changes in storage management internal algorithms impacting application storage usage, and many, many others. Most of these can be overcome in the process of application conversion; however, often there is not sufficient documentation warning of these pitfalls and they are encountered by trial and error. For VM/XA, a document was published titled *VM/XA SP Bimodal CMS Application Programming Considerations* that provides a description of many of these types of conversion problems.

There is no VM/ESA equivalent of this document; however, though the VM/XA version is outdated, it still provides much useful conversion information.

Two IBM publications, the *CMS Application Development Guide* and, more importantly, the *CMS Application Development Guide for Assembler*, document a significant amount of the work required to convert existing interfaces to execute in VM/ESA and exploit the new function available. Read these books prior to beginning the actual conversion, as they provide many examples of interface usage that are lacking in the *Application Development Reference*.

Interface structure

VM/ESA has the same interface structure that was introduced in CMS 5.5. This structure consists of:

- The CMS Preferred Interface Group
- The CMS Compatibility Group
- OS/MVS DOS/VSE group
- Other interfaces that are internal to CMS and not supported

Some interfaces that existed prior to CMS 5.5 were altered to provide 31-bit support and placed in the Preferred Interface Group. Other previously existing interfaces were left unchanged. These interfaces make up the Compatibility Group and usually have an equivalent interface in the Preferred Interface Group which was introduced in CMS 5.5.

Most previously existing interfaces have remained upward-compatible from release to release, meaning they will provide function equivalent to their earlier versions; however, they will not exploit any new function. For example, the DMSFREE macro (with a few exceptions) on VM/ESA is functionally equivalent to the DMSFREE macro on VM/SP 5. It will continue to work unchanged.

The *VM/ESA Conversion Notebook* is a valuable source in identifying the changes made to interfaces, messages, return codes, commands, etc. Compatibility tables list conversion requirements for each component of the system.

Use of these compatibility interfaces minimizes the work required to convert applications to VM/ESA; however, it also limits the ability to exploit new facilities such as 31-bit addressing and storage above the 16MB line. It is generally necessary to convert interfaces in the

Compatibility Group to the equivalent in the Preferred Interface Group to exploit new architecture or CMS function.

The Preferred Interface Group also contains is a library of callable service (CSL) routines. A significant portion of these routines are related to Shared File System exploitation. Existing interfaces such as FSREAD, FSWRITE, FSOPEN, etc. work with the Shared File System, but generally do not provide more function than is provided for minidisks. For complete exploitation of the Shared File System it is necessary to convert to CSL routines. It may be necessary to make some changes to existing file system calls if they are to be used with files in the SFS because status such as exceeding threshold limits can be reported, which will involve return codes the application might not expect.

The OS/MVS DOS/VSE group simulates a subset of the MVS and VSE operating systems. Though by no means complete, there was a significant upgrade of OS-simulated macros from the VM/SP 5 level, including 31-bit and XA support, as well as additional operands not previously supported. Significant changes to DOS/VSE support allow VSAM interfaces to be invoked in an XA-mode virtual machine under VM/XA, and in VM/ESA 1.1 to allow them to be invoked above the 16MB line.

The largest conversion effort will be to convert use of internal interfaces that have been changed.

Commands

Session Services commands were changed except for QUERY and SET. Three new commands, PSCREEN, VSCREEN, and WINDOW replace VM/SP 5 Session Services commands. The SET OLDCMDS migration enhancement of VM/SP 6 and VM/XA has been disabled under VM/ESA. A CONV2WD command converts EXECs containing Session Services two-word commands to the new windowing commands.

Other command related changes may require attention. Some are changes in error message suppression, case sensitivity, option parsing, return codes, etc. This does not imply that all changes are negative. Some provide useful function lacking in previous releases of CMS; however, the changes may affect existing applications.

Architecture-related

Another major area is conversion of architecture-sensitive usage to interfaces designed to provide architecture independence. For example, use of the Set System Mask (SSM) instruction should be converted to the ENABLE macro to execute in XA-mode virtual machines. It may be necessary to convert usage of DIAGNOSE codes such as X'58', X'14', X'18', and X'20' because of differences between the VM/SP 370 implementation and the VM/ESA ESA feature which is based on VM/XA. Often changes are not required; however, there are differences that in some cases will change application behavior.

Interrupts, I/O, and Other Architecture Changes

Familiarity with XA architecture is essential for conversion of 370-based applications that use architecturally sensitive instructions or storage locations. Interrupt processing, I/O, and PSW manipulation all depend on the virtual machine architecture being used.

Interrupt handling

The basic difference between SVC, program, and external interrupt handling in 370 mode and XA mode is the location of interrupt information. When executing with a BC-mode PSW, applications commonly examine the interrupt code portion of the SVC old, program old, or external old PSW to determine what event occurred. An XA-mode PSW does not have an interrupt code field. Instead, interrupt information is placed in fixed locations in page zero. Each type of interrupt (external, program, and SVC) has its own reserved location for interrupt information. Applications that reference the old PSWs must be converted to use these architecturally defined fields in an XA-mode virtual machine.

Another possibility to consider is use of CMS programming interfaces rather than direct low memory/PSW referencing. For example, external interrupt handling has been improved in CMS and many reasons for direct PSW manipulation have been removed. There may now be multiple external interrupt handlers, defining separate handlers for each unique code to be intercepted.. There may also be a default handler to take care of external interrupts that do not have a specific handler. There is also a mechanism to post an ECB

associated with an external interrupt which will satisfy a WAITECB
condition.

I/O handling

I/O is handled very differently in XA architecture. Applications
providing their own SIO/TIO support must be dual-pathed with the
XA equivalent SSCH/TSCH instructions. In addition to conversion of
operation codes for I/O, differences in I/O interrupt handling and
status reporting must be accommodated. For example, I/O in the
XA architecture does not use the CSW field in page zero to report
channel status. I/O status is reported through control blocks
pointed to by I/O instructions themselves. Also consider using
format-1 (XA) CCWs rather than format-0 while converting I/O
routines. The XA architecture supports both formats; however, it
may be useful to convert the CCWs at the same time, to move more
quickly to 31-bit exploitation.

If programs use the CMS HNDINT macro to handle I/O interrupts,
examine the new HNDIO macro. It provides more function and helps
minimize the difference between 370 and XA modes. By using CMS
macros to handle I/O interrupts, it is possible to handle interrupts in
either 370 or XA mode without distinguishing between them.

Applications performing I/O with DIAGNOSE X'18' or X'20' must
also be converted for the XA architecture, as these DIAGNOSE
codes are 370 mode only. The replacement diagnose codes are
DIAGNOSE X'A4' (for DIAGNOSE X'18') and DIAGNOSE X'A8' (for
X'20'). Note that DIAGNOSE X'A4' and DIAGNOSE X'A8' are not
provided by the 370 feature of VM/ESA.

Applications using CMS macro interfaces to perform I/O will
require minimal conversion. Generally, only reassembly will be
required.

Instruction set differences

When converting applications, also consider:

- Some 370 instructions do not exist in XA
- Some XA instructions do not exist in 370
- Some instructions exist in both 370 and XA, but behave
  differently in the two environments.

When a 370-mode-only instruction is executed in XA mode or an XA-mode-only instruction is executed in 370 mode, an operation exception results, the cause of which is relatively easy to determine.

Instructions that execute in both modes but execute differently can have more subtle results. Usually, differences are caused by instructions being sensitive to the current addressing mode. For example, the BAL and BALR instructions place link information into the high order byte of the first operand register in 24-bit addressing mode (which is the only addressing mode available for a 370-mode virtual machine); however, in 31-bit addressing mode, the full 31 bits of the first operand are used as the resultant address and no linkage information is present. The only way to obtain the equivalent linkage information is with the IPM (Insert Program Mask) instruction.

This topic is discussed in detail in *VM/ESA Application Development Guide for Assembler* and *ESA/370 Principles of Operation*.

A common instruction that requires conversion in order to allow XA-mode execution is SSM (Set System Mask). SSM is generally used to enable and disable for various maskable interrupt conditions. SSM is an XA-mode instruction; however, the common mask of X'FF' is not valid in an XA-mode virtual machine and results in a program check. The easiest conversion of SSMs is to replace them with the ENABLE macro which is documented in the *VM/ESA Application Development Reference for Assembler*.

4-digit device addresses

VM/ESA supports 4-digit device addresses (as did VM/XA). Consequently, many CMS commands support and return 4-digit device addresses as part of their processing. An application must be aware of this and make programming adjustments as part of the conversion process. Generally, problem areas are column-dependent parsing where parsing is based upon 3-digit device addresses, or fields in control blocks that are coded to accommodate 3-digit device addresses only.

Some CMS commands that report or use 4-digit device addresses are:

- ACCESS
- CMSBATCH
- FILEDEF

- FORMAT
- LANGMERG
- QUERY DISK
- QUERY SEARCH
- RELEASE
- TAPE
- VMFPLC2

Note that to help with this situation, CMS commands such as QUERY DISK suppress the left-most digit if it is 0. For example, QUERY DISK reports 191 instead of 0191.

Also, all CP commands and DIAGNOSE codes that use device addresses report and use 4 digits: they do not suppress the left most digit if it is 0. For example, the CP QUERY command will always report back 000E for a printer at X'E' rather than 00E as it would on VM/SP.

Conclusion

Approached methodically, this conversion should prove worth the effort for the wealth of new features to be found in CMS 8. For installations already on VM/XA, the conversion should be straight-forward. For installations converting from VM/SP or VM/HPO, the ground has been well covered by others, and substantial help should be available from vendors, other installations, and user groups.

The main points to check during a conversion (some may not be relevant, depending on previous system level) are:

- Contact vendors to obtain the most current level of all software. Ensure that all versions are supported on VM/ESA.
- Check locally written EXECs for dependencies on command response formats.
- Check locally written programs for control block and architecture dependencies.
- Decide on the target environment for programs: 370, XA, ESA, or XC mode. Catalog programs as 370-only, XA-tolerant, or XA-exploitative.
- Plan the new saved segment layout.
- Test programs in their expected running environments.
- Develop fallback plans in case the unexpected happens after conversion.

Chapter

19

Interlude: Exploiting VM Data Spaces

By Romney White

VM Data Spaces Support (hereinafter **VMDSS**) is a new feature introduced in VM/ESA 1.1. It provides a way for virtual machines with DAT (Dynamic Address Translation) off (i.e., CMS) to use data spaces in new and interesting ways. The way I used VMDSS in one application is described below.

Application Overview

XAMON, the **VM/ESA and VM/XA Real-Time Monitor**, is a CMS-based real-time monitor data analysis program that I develop and support. As the next diagram shows, a user virtual machine (XAMON User) formulates a request to extract performance data and sends it to a server (XAMSERVE). The server processes the user's request, constructs a response to it, and sends it back to the user. The user machine manipulates the performance data it receives to produce visual output (Performance Displays and Graphics). The communication between the user and the server is performed using IUCV or APPC.

XAMON Structure

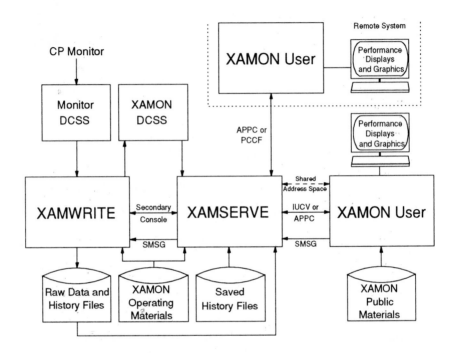

Using VM Data Spaces Support

When I considered how to use VM Data Spaces Support with this architecture, I concluded that it might be possible to improve the performance of XAMON's inter-machine communication. However, it was not clear what the benefits of using VMDSS would be, since some other form of inter-machine communication would still be required. Consequently, it became clear that I would have to perform some experiments in order to evaluate the alternatives. In the process, by using VMDSS, I would come to understand it more thoroughly.

Experiments

I designed a series of experiments to test the performance of three separate forms of communication. The existing IUCV protocol was measured to provide a starting point for evaluating other tests. The basic architecture of the environment is shown below.

IUCV Test Environment

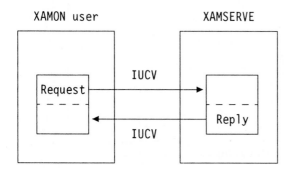

VMDSS was measured using the user's primary address space to pass the request and response back and forth. The structure of this environment is shown below.

Primary Space Sharing Test Environment

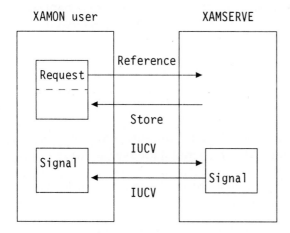

VMDSS was measured using a shared data space to hold the request and response. The structure of this environment is shown below.

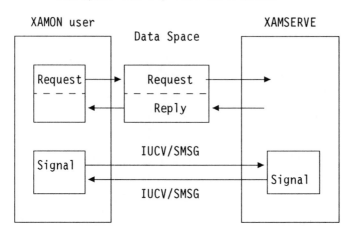

Data Space Sharing Test Environment

Initially, the following test scenarios were planned:

IUCV in 370 mode: Measure IUCV communication between two 370-mode virtual machines to establish a baseline.

IUCV in XC mode: Measure IUCV communication between two XC-mode virtual machines to determine the incremental cost of XC-mode use.

Primary space sharing with IUCV: Measure data transfer via the user's primary address space using IUCV to signal data availability.

Data space sharing with IUCV: Measure data transfer via a shared data space using IUCV to signal data availability.

Based on the results of these tests, I designed three more test scenarios:

Data space sharing with SMSG: Measure data transfer via a shared data space using SMSG to signal data availability.

Data space sharing with IUCV Quiesce/Resume: Measure data transfer via a shared data space using IUCV Quiesce/Resume as a semaphore to signal data availability.

Primary space sharing with IUCV Quiesce/Resume: Measure data transfer via the requester's primary address space using IUCV Quiesce/Resume as a semaphore to signal data availability.

Test Characteristics

I obtained the test measurements by issuing two QUERY TIME commands, one before the test started and one after it ended. This allowed me to calculate the elapsed time, virtual CPU time, and total CPU time consumption.

The system I used to collect the measurements was a 64MB ES/9000 Model 130 running VM/ESA Release 1.1. During the measurement period there was no other appreciable activity on the system. In particular, there was no paging activity.

Test Methodology

I wrote test programs to perform the activities to be measured. Only essential operations were carried out by the programs so that measurements would focus on performance of communication functions.

Each program on the requester side was invoked 1,000 times to obscure the overhead of establishing the communications environment. A REXX program was used to drive the tests to avoid delays. The inter-machine communication path and any shared data space constructs were maintained from one iteration to the next, again to ensure that the data transfer function cost dominated the results.

The programs in the server ran continuously. The requester programs were executed in the CMS transient area to avoid the overhead of loading them repeatedly.

Results

The measurement results are shown in tabular and graphical form on the next page.

Sharing the primary address space and using IUCV Quiesce/Resume to signal data availability offers the best performance. It consumes 50 percent less processor time than IUCV to perform the same function. Sharing a separate data space is almost as efficient and offers the ability to protect the primary space from inadvertent alteration by the server.

Experiment Results Table

Communications Method	Elapsed Time	Client Virtual	Client Total	Server Virtual	Server Total	Overall Total
370-mode IUCV	14	2.37	4.68	1.62	8.16	12.84
XC-mode IUCV	15	2.51	4.81	1.64	8.20	13.01
Primary (IUCV)	17	2.94	8.28	2.31	7.59	15.87
VMDSS (IUCV)	19	3.11	8.43	2.10	7.58	16.01
VMDSS (SMSG)	18	2.93	8.17	2.26	7.52	15.69
VMDSS (Q-R)	8	2.73	4.17	1.39	2.80	6.97
Primary (Q-R)	8	2.14	3.58	1.41	2.86	6.44

Graphical experiment results

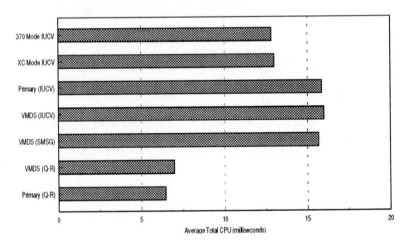

In the preceding figures, the following abbreviations are used:

Abbreviation	Meaning
Primary	Primary Address Space shared
VMDSS	VM Data Space shared
Q-R	IUCV Quiesce/Resume protocol employed

Conclusions

VM Data Spaces Support can be used to provide a superior alternative to IUCV. Communication between the user and the server is still required in order to disclose the data space identifier and to signal data availability. This notification is automatic when IUCV is used, by virtue of the communications protocol architecture.

Unfortunately, there is no such facility with VMDSS. Finding an efficient inter-machine signalling mechanism is essential to making data space use feasible for this application.

While the requirement for User Directory authorization in order to give another user permission to access a data space is valuable in some circumstances, it limits the usefulness of VMDSS in others. This same authorization is required to permit the primary space to be shared. A more flexible authorization scheme would avoid the need to make wholesale directory changes when address space sharing is used widely.

When a virtual machine's primary address space is shared, it is restricted in certain ways. In particular, it cannot use most functions of DIAGNOSE X'64', saved segment manipulation. This restriction limits the flexibility of CMS while the primary address space is shared and makes VMDSS less useful than it would be otherwise.

Despite its limitations, VM Data Spaces Support has interesting potential for expanding the function and performance of VM/ESA. Were the restrictions removed, VMDSS could be exploited much more.

20

The IBM OEM Personal/370 Adapter/A

By Chuck Berghorn and John A. Hupcey

Introduction

PS/2 systems are today as powerful as the original mainframes that VM and CMS supported, but users wishing to run System/370 applications on them have a difficult choice: either pay to port the applications to the personal computer world (and maintain two versions of the programs) or stay with a mainframe and forego advantages of the personal computer.

The **IBM OEM Personal/370 Adapter/A** (P/370) resolves that dilemma! A single card that plugs into a MicroChannel PS/2, it exploits IBM's VM/ESA (370 feature) mainframe operating system. Along with VM come the great 370 applications: programs like Book-Master, GDDM, CADAM, CICS, etc. The P/370 brings mainframe applications to the desktop.

The P/370 works with OS/2 Version 2.0, which supports OS/2, DOS, and Windows applications. With a P/370 installed in a PS/2, that capability expands to include VM and VSE applications. The

P/370 makes the PS/2 a System/370 workstation that runs main-frame programs and applications.

The P/370 lets customers and application developers "right size" applications without changing computer architectures. It propagates existing mainframe applications into smaller environments without modification. This offers both customer and developer advantages:

- Less work and less time invovled in conversions
- Only one version of software to maintain
- Growth path to larger platforms
- Less retraining for application users
- No data conversion (ASCII vs. EBCDIC, IBM vs. IEEE floating point)

The P/370 can reduce communications costs, improve response time, reduce maintenance, and provide backup/recovery systems. It can support portable sales demonstration systems, training and education, application and system development, and other features.

Although most users currently see the P/370 as a way to migrate existing applications to smaller, distributed environments, its poten-tial as a base for new applications is substantial. By writing new programs for the P/370 environment, problems of mainframe compatibility and upgrading to larger hardware are solved. With introduction of the P/370, System/370 processors come in every size: from small, portable, single-user systems to large, water-cooled, thousand-user mainframes. Customers buying P/370 applications will always be able to upgrade to larger IBM hardware that runs the application.

Uses for small System/370 processors are numerous. This chapter introduces details of this product and how it works.

History

VM and CMS were originally designed as interactive operating systems with individual users in mind. That concept, which fits perfectly with the idea of a personal computer, has intrigued people for many years. The first "personal computer-based" VM system was the IBM XT/370. It was a great idea, but was seriously hampered by the power of PCs available at the time, the high cost of memory, etc.

The IBM AT/370 was next. It was a little faster and had more memory, but suffered from the same performance problems. These systems had another disadvantage: they ran a special, single-user version of VM called **VM/PC**. While this seemed like a good idea at the time, many applications were moving toward multiple virtual machine implementations, which VM/PC did not support.

Next came the IBM 7437 VM/SP Technical Workstation. This was a MicroChannel-based System/370 workstation. It supported the full System/370 architecture, so it could run multiple virtual machines and the standard VM/SP operating system. However, its technology did not allow it to be built on a single card, so it was housed in a separate box attached to the PS/2 by a cable and an interface card.

These systems were on the right track, but were ahead of their time. Technology did not allow a single-card System/370 processor until today.

Hardware

The Personal/370 adapter card executes all System/370 instructions, including features such as VMA (VM microcode assists) and square root. The P/370 works in conjunction with OS/2 to provide I/O for the System/370 operating system. Several special-purpose OS/2 device drivers perform System/370 channel functions to emulate System/370 devices on PS/2 hardware, and to provide processor control functions.

Although the P/370 is small—a single card measuring only 3.5 by 11.5 inches—it is complex. The main card components are:

- System/370 processor module, a horizontally microcoded VLSI CMOS module with about 110K gates and 391 pins
- 16 megabytes of System/370 main storage with Error Checking and Correction (ECC)
- Control Store for P/370 microcode
- System/370 Key Array
- Indy Bus Master modules for MicroChannel protocol
- Bootstrap PROMS for adapter initialization

Communication between the P/370 and the PS/2

The P/370 works with PS/2 programs to provide a full System/370 environment. P/370 hardware and microcode communicate with the

PS/2 by interrupts, I/O ports, and memory windows. Two types of memory windows are used: a **control window** and **data windows**.

Data windows can be moved by the PS/2 over any part of the 16MB of 370 memory. The channel uses these windows to fetch Channel Command Words (CCWs) and transfer data between PS/2 I/O devices and System/370 memory. The control window allows the PS/2 to access the storage protection key array, the microcode control store, and a special area called the **Communications Buffer** or **COMBUF**. The COMBUF is where the P/370 microcode and PS/2 program communicate about I/O operations, external interruptions, and manual operations such as Start, Stop, Address Compare, etc.

When the P/370 executes an I/O instruction, it puts the device address, Operation Code (opcode), and Channel Address Word (CAW) into a fixed COMBUF location and interrupts the PS/2. PS/2 programs examine the COMBUF data, fill another area with "initial status", and execute CCWs associated with the request. Once initial status is returned, the 370 executes new instructions, while simultaneously the channel executes the CCWs. When the channel finishes, it fills another COMBUF area and interrupts the 370. At this point, the 370 either accepts or rejects the interrupt depending on channel masks. If the interrupt is rejected, the channel stacks the interrupt until channel masks change.

The PS/2 and P/370 thus work closely together. From the P/370 viewpoint, the PS/2 serves as both channel and service processor. From the PS/2 point of view, the P/370 is just an intelligent adapter card that requires periodic OS/2 service.

Channel and I/O Software

The Personal/370 channel is implemented as an OS/2 application. It works in parallel with the P/370 adapter card, executing channel programs to transfer data between P/370 memory and PS/2 I/O devices. Since PS/2 devices differ from the System/370 I/O architecture, device emulation programs called **device managers** map System/370 device types to corresponding PS/2 devices.

By implementing the channel as an OS/2 application, OS/2 device drivers and I/O software can emulate System/370 devices. This simplifies effort when implementing new device managers. Often new PS/2 I/O devices can be supported with no changes to emulation software. It also makes it easier for P/370 users, since "System/370

DASD devices" appear to OS/2 as ordinary PS/2 files that can be located on any PS/2 device (fixed disk, diskette, network file server, optical disk, etc.) and can be moved, copied, and backed up with ordinary OS/2 commands.

Device managers are written as separate OS/2 processes. They can execute independently of one another, and OS/2 protection mechanisms limit interference between them. This is especially important when developing and testing new managers.

Emulators exist for the following device types:

```
System/370 Device               PS/2 Device
------------------------        ------------------------
3370 DASD                       -> PS/2 files
3270 Terminal                   -> OS/2 Communications manager
3215 Terminal                   -> OS/2 Presentation Manager
3420 Tape drives                -> Diskettes
3480 Tape drives                -> Tape drive
Communications Controller       -> PS/2 Communication ports
Printer                         -> PS/2 Printer
3088 Multisystem Unit           -> Token Ring Local Area Network (LAN)
```

In addition to emulating System/370 I/O, the P/370 can drive real System/370 devices such as tape drives, printers, and other control units using the **IBM System/370 Channel Emulator/A** card which connects the MicroChannel to the System/370 OEMI channel.

The P/370 can also drive IBM High Function Graphic Devices (HFGD) such as IBM 5085 or IBM 6095 Graphics Processors for application such as CADAM. Additional PS/2 adapter cards are required to attach HFGD displays.

Networking

While Personal/370 systems can operate as stand-alone systems (with no connections to the outside world), exciting possibilities exist when they cooperate. A group of P/370s can be connected over a Token Ring Local Area Network (LAN). Device emulation programs make the LAN appear as a 3088 Multisystem Unit to the P/370. VM services such as RSCS and the Shared File System can thus be distributed between P/370 workstations in the same manner as between ES/9000 mainframes. With this support, P/370 users use commands such as SENDFILE, NOTE, and TELL to communicate with other P/370 users on a LAN—the same commands that communicate between mainframe users.

In addition, P/370 users can share files by placing them on NetWare+ or OS/2 file servers. These networking capabilities allow

P/370 users to collaborate on projects while each has a dedicated computer. Networking also creates an easy horizontal growth path. As new users join a department, instead of seeing performance gradually degrade until the mainframe is upgraded, users receive dedicated P/370 processors, and performance remains constant.

The Processor Console and Manual Operations

The *System/370 Principles of Operation* defines several control operations for processors, which monitor or debug System/370 programs and operating systems. They are not intended for end-users, but rather for system programmers. They were originally provided by lights and dials on the console. Starting with the System/370 Model 158, these hardware switches, knobs, and lights were replaced by a CRT that physically resembled an IBM 3277 Display Station.

As systems have become larger and more complex, consoles have been used less for debugging and more for processor control and system monitoring.

The P/370 processor console is provided by an OS/2 Presentation Manager application. When the P/370 is running normally, the processor console application need not be started. The application user has no need for the processor console. With that in mind, the console application is designed specifically for system programmers.

Console application features include:

- Flat menu hierarchy—just two levels
- Multiple memory windows
- Real and virtual memory windows
- Automatic memory display in hexadecimal and EBCDIC
- Memory alteration in hexadecimal or EBCDIC
- Memory search capability
- Double click on addresses to position memory display.
- Automatic decoding of VM CP trace table
- I/O tracing level control
- I/O device debugging
- Fake device interruptions and status
- Standard facilities such as Reset, Address Compare, and Instruction Step
- Online HELP, including System/370 Reference Card

These features make it easier for system programmers to debug operating system problems. They can also be used by application programmers to debug difficult problems that do not succumb to standard virtual machine debuggers.

Configuration

The P/370 must know how to map 370 device addresses to PS/2 resources. The 370 Configuration application, an interactive OS/2 program, performs this mapping.

The System Devices menu below summarizes current device allocations. The configuration program reads an ASCII version of DMKRIO ASSEMBLE (the VM real I/O device configuration) to guide a user during configuration. On the left, the Type column shows the device type that DMKRIO expects for that address. The MGR column shows the device manager assigned to handle that address.

```
+================================================================+
|Type Addr Label Atype Size  Mgr Filename/Parameters  Disk:>E<   |
+----------------------------------------------------------------|
|    >    >     >    >       >   >                                |
|3215 009                    8   System Operator                 |
|3215 00A                    8                                    |
|1403 00E                    3   C:\VMPRT.LST                     |
|2703 024                    B   COM1:1200,N,7,2,O                |
|3370 100 MNT191 PERM   8M   1   D:\VMSP\MAINT.191                |
|3370 101 SPOOL  TEMP  10M   1   D:\VMSP\SPOOL.101                |
|3278 200        DSPY        2   Local VM 1                       |
|3278 201        DSPY        2   Local VM 2                       |
|3370 300 SYSRES PERM   2M   1   D:\VMSP\SYSRES.300               |
|3088 440                    A   PKVMWFBH.NET                     |
|3088 450                    4   AWSHOST1                         |
|3420 580                    6   A:\TAPE.580                      |
+----------------------------------------------------------------+
MGR Codes: 1=AWS3880 2=AWS3274 3=AWS2821 4=AWSTFA  5=AWSPCSRV 6=AWSTAPE
7=AWS5080  8=AWS3215 9=LAN3274 A=AWS3088 B=AWS2703
+----------------------------------------------------------------+
| F1 Help Alt-F1 Function Key Definitions ESC/F10 Main Menu      |
+----------------------------------------------------------------+
```

Manager names reflect device types they are intended to support. A user can override these suggestions and assign any device manager to an address, but this will probably result in an error when VM tries to communicate with the device using CCWs that the manager does not understand.

To allocate new devices, a user types characteristics on the top line where the ">" symbols are. For example, to add a new DASD volume, a user enters volume label, CP allocation type, disk size, and the PS/2 drive, path, and filename where it will be located. The configuration program creates the PS/2 file and automatically performs CP Format/Allocate processing.

For other device managers, a user enters device-specific parameters. For example, for terminal sessions, text can be entered which will be displayed as the OS/2 window title for the session, or for a 2703, PS/2 serial communications port parameters. Each device manager interprets the Parameters field differently. HELP is available by positioning the cursor under the manager name and pressing the F1 key.

Unlike mainframe DASD allocation, P/370 guidelines suggest that minidisks be placed on separate device addresses. That means each minidisk occupies its own PS/2 file, which simplifies backup and restore, as well as reallocating PS/2 disk space. While it is possible to allocate several minidisks on a single PS/2 volume and use a product such as DIRMAINT to maintain the disks, it is generally simpler to use the P/370 Configuration program.

The P/370 Configuration program also has menus to maintain the VM user directory. The directory is stored as a PS/2 ASCII text file, imported to VM by the system operator's PROFILE EXEC, and applied to the system. This helps non-system programmers manage their workstations: they can add userids, minidisks, etc., without knowing VM user directory specifics.

Host Connectivity and Transparent File Access

The **Transparent File Access** (TFA) feature allows P/370 users to access data on VM mainframes over a 3270 connection. When a CMS user initiates TFA, three new commands are available: HLINK, HQUERY, and HDETACH.

These commands correspond to CP commands LINK, QUERY, and DETACH, but are implemented as CMS nucleus extensions, and manipulate disks located on the VM mainframe (the "host" system). TFA users must log on to the host from 3270 sessions and start CMSSERV. After that, the HLINK command can be issued, which allows the disk to be accessed. For example:

```
HLINK MAINT 19E 29E RR
ACCESS 29E Z
```

Now the local CMS user can access all programs and data on the host 19E disk (probably the Y-disk) as the workstation Z-disk. Using the COPYFILE command, files can be downloaded from the host Y-disk to the local A-disk. Alternatively, programs on the host disk can be invoked: they will by dynamically downloaded into P/370 memory for execution and then discarded. TFA is truly transparent to the CMS application.[1]

Requests are intercepted at the disk block I/O level and sent to the host for execution. Reading and writing host files is supported, so upload and download can be done with COPYFILE. Two differences exist between host disks and local disks:

1. Access time is slower
2. CP commands do not recognize the virtual address associated with the host disk (hence the HQUERY and HDETACH commands)

TFA avoids security problems sometimes associated with workstation access to host data, because all requests are made through the logged-on host user. Any data the user can access from the host userid can be accessed from the workstation. Access restrictions (read, write, multi-write passwords, RACF protection, etc.) are enforced by the same host mechanisms.

TFA does not require host operating system modifications or support from an I/S organization. It uses the **Server Requester Protocol Interface** (SRPI) supported by VM and the OS/2 Communications Manager. The host side of the interface consists of the standard CMSSERV program and two unique P/370 files, a SRPI profile and a module, which can easily be uploaded to the host by an end-user.

Import/Export

Because OS/2 and CMS store files in different formats, utility programs are required to move data from one operating system to the other. One way to do this is with standard OS/2 communications manager upload/download programs such as IND$FILE, but between the OS/2 session and a local P/370 CMS session. In this case, upload/download activity is initiated from OS/2.

An alternative is to use the PCOPY command provided with the P/370. PCOPY is a CMS command that imports or exports files betwen CMS on the P/370 and OS/2. PCOPY, modeled after the CMS COPYFILE command, provides standard CMS options such as LRECL, RECFM, and TRUNC, as well as "PS/2" options such as BINARY, ASCII,

---

1 OS-formatted disks are not supported.

NOEOF (no end-of-file character), etc.   Unlike IND$FILE programs, PCOPY does not require a 3270 session, so it can be issued from disconnected service machines. This PCOPY command copies the user directory from OS/2 to CMS, for use as described above:

```
pcopy c:\p370\user.dir user direct a (recfm f lrecl 80 replace
```

PCOPY and IND$FILE give programmers flexibility to move data between CMS and OS/2 and to build the best interfaces for end-user applications.

Conclusion

Priced very reasonably—less than the cost of the PS/2 it enhances—the Personal/370 introduces a new era for the VM operating system and System/370 applications. Previously, the drive for VM applications was to support larger systems with more users. This new hardware balances that trend. Hardware is now available that, in a sense, returns VM to its roots in small systems or even single-user environments. With this product, developers can concentrate on applications, and worry less about supporting different platforms, architectures, operating systems, etc.   Many of these considerations arose because hardware was not scalable.   That problem is solved with this product. Applications which run on VM can be used in a portable, stand-alone environment, in a small departmental complex, or on a large data center mainframe. The Personal/370 returns the choice of where to run applications back to where it belongs—the user.

P/370 platforms and application-specific solutions are offered by vendors such as GenText, Inc., in Dallas, TX and Interprocess Systems, Inc., in Atlanta, GA.

For more information on the Personal/370, contact the authors or IBM's OEM Business Unit at (800) IBMS-OEM.

21

CMS Application Performance

By William J. Bitner

VM is an ideal platform for understanding application performance. One can consider virtual machine processor, storage, and I/O requirements to be like those of a real machine. There are often tradeoffs among the three. These resources, though virtual, should not be taken for granted. The goal of performance management is to keep a balance between the three areas. Like a stereo system, the quality of sound produced is only as good as the weakest component.

Processor resources are consumed by execution of virtual instructions. In VM/ESA, this occurs while the virtual machine is running under SIE (Start Interpretive Execution), also called emulation mode. SIE is both a (privileged) machine instruction used by CP to begin virtual machine execution and an environment in which a virtual machine executes under hardware control. A key difference between real and virtual machines is the scope of system services available. The system services for a virtual machine include CP commands, various DIAGNOSE functions, IUCV, VMCF,

APPC/VM, and block I/O. All of these require processing by CP outside the virtual machine.

I/O resource requirements can involve various virtual devices. Virtual I/O can be performed to unit record devices (punch, reader, printer), console, tape, channel-to-channel adapter, or minidisk. Virtual minidisk I/O can use CMS-formatted minidisks or application-specific formats. CMS applications have a choice between the traditional minidisk-based file system and the newer Shared File System (SFS). Except for special cases, virtual I/O operations require processing by CP. On a real machine, cache devices may be exploited for better I/O performance. **Minidisk cache**, a feature provided by CP, can provide improved minidisk I/O performance by using expanded (real) storage.

On the real machine, there is a limited amount of storage available. A virtual machine in VM/ESA has a primary address space of up to 2047 megabytes in size, which is managed by CMS storage management. In addition, VM Data Spaces, discontigous saved segments, and dedicated expanded storage may be available to the virtual machine. For virtual machines, exploitation of VM Data Spaces makes storage virtually unlimited (at least by today's standards). However, remember that the virtual storage must reside in real storage when referenced by the virtual machine.

CPU

Processor resources are usually the best understood of the three resources. **Pathlength** is the term that is often associated with processor requirements, and refers to the number of machine instructions executed. However, simulation and CP processor time must be considered to view the complete picture. Processor or CPU requirements of an application are affected by the following:

- Program management
- Choice of algorithm
- System services
- Interfaces

Program management includes modularity and program packaging. An application may involve several thousand lines of code, so breaking it down into a series of modules and subroutines can make design, testing, and maintenance easier. When determining structure, consider performance. The **mainline**—routines used in the most frequent cases—should be grouped together. This minimizes overhead associated with calling other modules or routines.

For example, a subroutine to find a free virtual address may typically be used at the same time as a subroutine to find a free filemode. Making the two subroutines a single routine and placing them in the same module keeps linkage overhead low. Another case deals with error handling routines. Checking for error conditions in the mainline code and only branching if error processing is required makes the application more efficient.

The choice of programming language is an important performance factor. Consider the language to be a tool and know the tool's strengths and weaknesses. The most efficient programs are often written in assembler, but high-level languages may be required for productivity or maintainability goals. Using a combination can meet all goals; for example, key performance-sensitive areas can be written in assembler. For high-level languages, spend time learning available compiler optimization options. Most languages have a chapter or section in their manuals on performance.

Choosing an appropriate algorithm can make the greatest impact on performance. Tradeoffs are often made between ease of implementation and performance. It is important to know the requirements of the application. For example, implementing a heap sort instead of a simple insertion sort for a list of records that never numbers more than 20 is not worthwhile. Searching is another key area in which algorithms play a major role. Again, knowing the environment can help determine whether sequential, indexed, or hashing search methods are more appropriate.

Use and abuse of system services can lead to performance problems. System services include the following:

- CMS services and commands
- CP services and commands
- Simulation of privileged instructions by CP

Some instructions are more expensive than others, such as those that require simulation by CP. These look like single instructions, but become hundreds with CP simulation. CP commands and system services cause breaks from SIE and should be minimized. CMS commands and services may not require CP processing, but can still be expensive in CPU resources. Get the most from these services when they are used. For example, to acquire information on several CMS minidisks it is more efficient to issue a single

QUERY DISK command instead of individual QUERY DISK commands for each minidisk.

Interfaces

Interfaces between components can be important to performance. If an interface is costly, it should be crossed as few times as possible. Getting in your car and traveling to the grocery store requires time and fuel. Therefore, it is more efficient to make a list of items you need and take it with you than to drive home after getting each item to check for the next item on the list. Some program management concepts discussed earlier can be used to minimize interface crossings.

Various options exist for CMS linkages, with different performance characteristics. SVC linkage is more expensive than BALR linkage, but may be required for non-performance reasons. The Callable Services Library, or CSL, provides many functions for programs in high-level languages and assembler. The flexibility of the CSL functions costs a little extra in resources for linkage. However, there is a "fastpath" CSL linkage available to assembler language applications. Setting up for the fastpath requires extra processing for the initial call, but thereafter linkage costs approach those of the BALR type. Choosing the right linkage involves making tradeoffs.

Giving CMS additional information can decrease costs associated with interfaces. An example is appropriate use of the ADDRESS instruction in REXX programs. This minimizes the work CMS must do to resolve whether a call is a CMS command, a CP command, or another EXEC.

Macros and compile time functions can improve performance by moving overhead from execution time to assemble or compile time. Examples of this are checking for appropriate parameters or calculating an index.

I/O

Some approaches which minimize I/O requirements involve tradeoffs with other resources. Program management topics mentioned earlier are also related to I/O. The fewer modules that need to be referenced or loaded for mainline processing, the fewer I/Os processed.   Data management methods of caching, buffering, and blocking can lead to efficiencies.

Caching involves keeping data where it can be accessed more efficiently. Picture yourself in the kitchen, adding spices to a new dish. After each pinch of a spice, you could return the spice jar to the cupboard, or you could cache the key spices by leaving the jars on the counter. The same can be done with your computer data. Instead of repeatedly reading data from disk, a portion of storage can be assigned to cache the data. A minimal amount of storage for cache can greatly improve performance. However, adding more and more storage for the cache quickly hits a point of diminishing returns.

Buffering data can compensate for differences in speed of data movement and time of need for data. Going back to the kitchen, the analogy can be made to baking a cake. Various ingredients such as eggs and milk will be needed at different times, but making one trip to the refrigerator and buffering them on the counter can save time. Likewise, reading multiple records into a buffer can save I/O compared to a doing I/O for each record. Buffering on output is useful when working with slow devices or where parallelism can be used.   Buffering differs from caching, in that the data passes through the storage area and does not remain to be reused.

Blocking is a third approach to improving I/O efficiency, and involves processing multiple items together. The number of items in a group is known as the **blocking factor**. The kitchen analogy is the size of the measuring cup used to move 3 cups of flour. Using three 1-cup scoops is more efficient than twelve 1/4-cup scoops. Blocking data at 4096 bytes is often more efficient than at 512 bytes. However, large blocking factors are inefficient when dealing with small random records, and may waste storage.

The VM/ESA minidisk cache feature greatly improves virtual I/O performance. This feature provides a global cache for minidisks in the system with control of cache handled by CP. MDC supports only 4096-byte formatted minidisks and certain types of I/O.

Applications that use file I/O have a choice in VM/ESA of the traditional minidisk and the Shared File System (SFS) for files. The Enhanced Disk Format (EDF) is the formal name for the CMS minidisk file system. Both file systems have their strengths. The choice to use one or the other may depend on non-performance issues, which are discussed elsewhere in this book.   There are several methods to improve performance with these file systems.

A factor in file performance is the number of files currently accessed. This part of I/O or data management affects CPU and storage. The number of files in the search order can be reduced by appropriately grouping files on minidisks, and therefore minimizing the total number of minidisks that must be accessed. By accessing a minidisk as a read-only extension, the files can be further reduced by giving a fileid mask on the ACCESS command. For example, ACCESS 291 B/A BIT* * accesses only filenames starting BIT.

A minidisk file directory can be shared by all users when the SAVEFD facility is used to create a discontigous saved segment (DCSS). This is particularly useful for read-only minidisks that contain many files and are accessed by a large number of users.

SFS offers different approaches to minimize required resources to deal with files. As with minidisks, the number of files in an accessed SFS directory affects performance. Use of aliases can reduce the number of accessed files. A separate directory can be created tp contain aliases of a subset of required files from a different directory. Accessing this directory of aliases minimizes the number of files accessed. The hierarchical SFS directory structure can also create smaller, more meaningful directories to use instead of accessing a single large directory with many unused files.

The cost of accessing an SFS directory can be avoided altogether by using the direct access capabilities provided in the Callable Services Library. Direct access allows functions to be performed on a file without the directory being accessed. Storage resources are saved by not accessing a directory, but there is additional CPU cost for each direct access file function. Therefore, a tradeoff must be made. In general, unless an application is very storage constrained, it is better to use the direct access only when a few file functions will be performed.

VM/ESA 1.1 provides VM Data Spaces, which can be exploited by SFS DIRCONTROL directories. SFS data kept in the VM Data Spaces can provide significant performance benefits. Most end-user-to-SFS server communication can be avoided, thus eliminating CPU overhead. In addition, sharing one copy of data among all users decreases system storage requirements.

Application I/O is usually synchronous, but sometimes asynchronous I/O is more appropriate. For server applications where synchronous functions serialize many users, an asynchronous method like Block I/O could be used. Block I/O functions exist for increased synergy with minidisk cache. When an I/O can be satisfied from minidisk cache, it completes very quickly and makes asynchronous processing unnecessary. A Block I/O option exists to allow the function call to complete synchronously when the data is in minidisk cache. Another Block I/O option can force minidisk cache to be bypassed. This bypass option is useful when the cache would otherwise be flooded with data that would never be referenced again.

Storage

The goals of storage management are to minimize pages referenced by the application. As described earlier, storage is often traded for savings in CPU or I/O. Storage management functions are examples of system services which involve significant processing. For performance-sensitive areas, an application-specific storage management routine can improve efficiency. Initial storage can be acquired via the CMS Storage Manager, and then managed by the internal routines. A stack implementation can be very efficient as opposed to the standard dynamic storage manager calls.

The principles discussed in program management apply to storage management. The distribution of fields within control blocks is as important as the placement of routines within modules. Clustering frequently referenced data can minimize storage references and requirements. The CMS storage management SUBPOOL concept can further separate control blocks to reduce page references.

Storage fragmentation can be a problem. This applies not only to fragmentation by unallocated data, but also by unreferenced allocated data. When allocating storage, allocate long term storage before short term areas. Likewise, allocate large amounts of storage before smaller sizes.

Control block attributes

Understanding key attributes of a data structure or control block during design prevents performance-related problems. Combining some of the following attributes can provide valuable information:

- Size
- Number
- Content
- Use
- Obtain

- Release

Size attribute: Both the size of a control block and whether it is a fixed size is important. When a control block is just over or under 4096 bytes in size, it is worth the effort to make it an even 4096 bytes. This allows it to fit evenly in a page so that any or all fields in the control block can be used while only referencing a single page. Likewise, the size may be modified so that an even number of the control blocks fits in a page. Ordering fields is very important for control blocks or structures that are several pages in size. The size can be changed to match other control blocks. Having a common size allows storage to be used for multiple purposes and could be used in conjunction with a specialized storage manager. For example, if control blocks A and B are the same size, a storage manager could be created to process storage requests for either control block in the same manner. If the control block is very small and static, efficiencies may be gained by preallocating it, giving the ultimate control in placement. (Of course, the program must handle the problem of exhausting the supply of preallocated control blocks, perhaps by allocating more dynamically.)

Number attribute: The number of the required control blocks is another attribute. This might be a range or a relative number, such as one per disk. Using the size and number attributes gives the total storage requirement, which shows how many pages are required for the control blocks.

Content attribute: This attribute describes the contents of the fields and specifies whether these fields are read-only or read/write. Highly referenced fields should be grouped together. Infreqently referenced fields may be placed in separate control blocks. Reordering fields for reuse may provide efficiencies such as clearing several fields at once or using a subset of a control block as a parameter list or other control block.

Use attribute: How a control block is used, that is, the way the control block is referenced and from which modules, is important. Control blocks that are frequently referenced should be grouped with other frequently referenced control blocks. Avoid frequent sequential searches of linked lists that contain many control blocks.

Obtain attribute: Control blocks can be obtained dynamically, at thresholds, or preallocated. *Where* the storage is obtained from can be as important as *when* it is obtained.   When storage is requested from the CMS Storage Manager, a page reference is usually made to set up internal information. This happens regardless of whether the requested storage is ever used.   The CMS Storage Manager can manage user-defined subpools to group related control blocks.   Explore alternatives—such as creating a pool of control blocks or using a stack—for frequently obtained control blocks.

Release attribute: This attribute is similar to the Obtain attribute. *When* and *how* control blocks are released is important. The creation of a user-defined CMS storage subpool can lead to efficiencies in releasing of storage. Multiple CMSSTOR RELEASE calls can be replaced by a SUBPOOL call that releases all storage associated with the subpool. When releasing a partial page of storage, the page is referenced when internal control blocks are manipulated. Instead of releasing frequently used control blocks, reuse them.

VM Data Spaces

VM Data Spaces, added in VM/ESA 1.1, provide alternatives for storage management. VM Data Spaces dramatically increase virtual machine addressability, thus allowing an application to keep more information in storage and minimizing I/O to read data. However, remember that virtual does not mean free. CP requires real storage to hold the virtual storage and I/O is required for management of VM Data Spaces. However, virtual I/O is replaced by more efficient CP page I/O. Another strength of VM Data Spaces is the ability to share them between virtual machines.   Sharing decreases system-wide storage demands, and in some cases may replace more expensive data transfer methods such as APPC/VM or IUCV.

Performance Improvement Process

When performance is considered during application design and implementation, the application should perform well.   When performance falls short of expectations, it is necessary to determine the distribution of overhead. The majority of overhead can usually be found in a small portion of the application, known as **hot paths** in the mainline code. A guideline is that 80 percent of the overhead can be attributed to 20 percent of the code. Improving the hot paths leads to significant improvements at low cost.

VM/ESA provides several vehicles to understand application performance. Performance information of applications running from the command line is found in the long version of the CMS ready message, which is invoked by the SET RDYMSG LMSG command. This provides the virtual and total CPU used.

The CP INDICATE USER command can also be used to measure the application performance by providing a snapshot of current resources consumed by the virtual machine. By issuing a command several times and noting the differences between results, resources consumed between invocations can be determined. Including the command at strategic points in the application allows one to determine where the processing occurs.

Applications can also be **instrumented** by collecting data internally. CP DIAG X'0C' collects virtual and total CPU consumption. This approach can be implemented with a macro, but does have the weakness of requiring modifications to the application.

It is also possible to gather detailed information without modifying an application. CMS Storage Management utilities such as STDEBUG show how applications use storage management functions. In addition, the CP TRACE command can gather very detailed information. When using either of these methods, it is important to be consistent in measurement comparing different application implementations. Ensure consistency with the number of filemodes in search order, number of files, virtual storage size, and previous commands. It is sometimes worthwhile to re-IPL CMS before each measure. However, be careful of first-time processing overhead in both CMS and applications.

The CP TRACE command can provide a great deal of information, which can be minimized with its RANGE option. The following EXEC, which uses CMS Pipelines, can make the data more manageable. See Chapter 3, *Exploiting CMS,* on page 87 for more information on CMS Pipelines.

```
/* Summarize trace data */
   'PIPE < TRACE OUTPUT B |',
     'SPEC 5-12 10 15-20 35 |',
     'SORT COUNT |',
     'XLATE 20-27 0-9 a-j |',
     'SORT 20-27   |',
     'XLATE 20-27 a-j 0-9 |',
     ' > TRACE SUMMARY B'
```

Running this results in output similar to the figure below. The first column shows the number of times the instruction was executed. The second column shows the virtual address of the instruction. The final column shows the instruction mnemonic.

```
        1            000100E4                    LTR
        1            000100E6                    BNZ
        1            000100EA                    ST
        1            000100EE                    L
       30            000100F2                    L
       30            000100F6                    STCK
       30            000100FA                    LM
       30            000100FE                    L
     1500            00010102                    STM
     1500            00010106                    L
     1500            0001010A                    AR
     1500            0001010C                    BCT
       30            00010110                    LA
       30            00010114                    LA
       30            00010118                    DIAG
       30            0001011C                    BCT
        1            00010120                    L
        1            00010124                    L
        1            00010128                    LA
        1            0001012C                    B
```

The output above suggests a set of nested loops. The outer loop extends from addresses 100F2 to 1011C and the inner loop from addresses 10102 to 1010C. Improvements, such as pushing work outside of the loop, might be made in these areas. Matching addresses to an application program listing can show program execution at the virtual instruction level. Since the module was loaded at 10000, the addresses in the listing below must be adjusted to match the above data.

```
LOC       Source Statement
----      -----------------------------------------------------------
00EE            L       R6,NUMLOOPS    Get number of loops for BCT
00F2      MAINLOOP DS   0H
00F2            L       R1,REFSTART    Get address of reference area
00F6            STCK    TODSTART       Get current TOD
00FA            LM      R2,R3,TODSTART Load for storing into pages
00FE            L       R5,NUMPAGES
0102      PAGELOOP DS   0H
0102            STM     R2,R3,0(R1)    Store into page
0106            L       R4,F4096       Bump R4 to next page
010A            AR      R1,R4          Bump to next page
010C            BCT     R5,PAGELOOP    Loop for NUMPAGES
          * Issue SLEEP Command for required amount of time
0110            LA      R10,CMDSLEEP   Point to command for DIAG 8
0114            LA      R11,LCMDSLEP   Pick up command length
0118            DIAG    R10,R11,X'0008' Issue the SLEEP command
011C            BCT     R6,MAINLOOP    Loop for NUMLOOPS
0120      PREEXIT  DS   0H
0120            L       R4,SIZDWRDS    Get number of dwords used
0124            L       R3,REFSTART    Get address to release
```

There are several statements that can be moved in this code. The most significant is the L R4,F4096 at offset 0106. Moving this one instruction to before MAINLOOP reduces the pathlength of this code segment by almost 25 percent!

Summary

Programmers who write well-performing CMS applications share the following characteristics:

Know the tools used: Programmers' chief tools are the languages in which they code. Knowing performance strengths and weaknesses is important.

Code with mainline path in mind: Using the 80-20 rule, 80 percent of the overhead is attributed to just 20 percent of the code. Concentrating on key mainline functions, programmers can produce efficient applications and optimize use of their time.

Design for performance: Designing for performance creates fast applications; coding for performance only makes fast (or slow) applications faster.

Remember details: Efficient use of buffers and information previously obtained can minimize code that reinvents the wheel.

Understand the law of diminishing returns: There is a point after which additional improvements will not noticeably improve performance.

Make the proper tradeoffs: If an application uses a great deal of CPU, do not implement an improvement to save storage if the change would require additional CPU.

Following these guidelines leads to efficient CMS applications. Every language and environment has unique tools and facilities for measuring and improving performance. Learn and exploit them, along with the fundamental language or environment syntax.

Chapter

22

Application Development
for Guest Systems

By Jim Hughes

Why Do Guest System Development in CMS?

The Conversational Monitor System, CMS, is an operating system
that runs in a virtual machine and provides a wonderful interactive
environment. Besides native VM/ESA functions such as communicating with other CMS users, CMS also allows users to write, test,
and debug application programs to run under CMS or MVS, and to
share data between CMS and MVS systems.

The CMS component of VM/ESA is bimodal. This means it operates in System/370-mode using 24-bit addressing, or in
System/390-mode using either 24-bit or 31-bit addressing. This
bimodal flexibility gives complete freedom to develop and test
programs both for System/370 guests such as DOS/VSE and for
System/390 guests such as MVS/ESA.

Powerful interactive debugging tools allow monitoring virtual
machine events. VM/ESA allows tracing most events, including

instruction execution, storage alteration, register alteration, and I/O activity.

Goals of Using CMS for Development

The goal of guest system development under CMS is to produce applications faster and with minimal latent software failures affectionately called **bugs**. Another benefit of using CMS for development is improved software integrity, by using the VM update philosophy of update files applied to an unchanging base source file.

All programs require maintenence during their lifetimes. CMS allows program maintenance history to be easily traced to the source code statement level. This is valuable when regression testing requires reviewing previous software versions to determine when and how a problem was introduced.

VM/ESA program maintenance is usually performed using a function conceptually similiar to the MVS IEBUPDTE program, a utility which uses an input file to update a source program. This input file consists of lines to be added, deleted, and/or replaced. IEBUPDTE uses only one input file to create a new source program or update an existing one, while the CMS UPDATE command only updates existing programs, but can use many input files to do so. VM/ESA programmers can also use the standard system editor, XEDIT, to create update input files during a normal editing session.

The power of multiple update input files is easily demonstrated. XEDIT and UPDATE use a two-level control file to control the order in which update files are created and applied. Control files have filetype CNTRL. For example, VMESA CNTRL might look like this:

```
TEXT MACS OSMACRO OSMACRO1
* Use UPDTBUG for emergency fix filetypes
FIX BUG
* AUXREL3 contains the base updates for release 3
REL3 AUXREL3
```

This simple CNTRL file indicates that an **auxiliary control** or **AUX** file called AUXREL3 should be used (if it exists) to apply updates to base program source. This AUX file would list filetypes of any update files to be applied as the first token on lines, followed optionally by other tokens describing update purposes and/or information to be used by other maintenance tools.

To edit program BILLIO using VMESA CNTRL as the control file, the command would be:

```
XEDIT BILLIO ASSEMBLE (CTL VMESA
```

XEDIT reads the source program and then applies the updates, starting at the bottom of the control file. The first update applied is the one listed on the *last* line of BILLIO AUXREL3, if that file exists. If it does not exist, no error is generated. This allows specifying multiple AUX files in a control file, many of which only exist for specific modules or under specialized conditions.

The next update applied is BILLIO UPDTBUG, if it exists. This is an example of an update implied directly by the control file; such updates are used less frequently than updates listed in AUX files, because a single AUX file can imply a set of updates, rather than listing them individually in the control file. For example, VMESA CNTRL might also list AUXREL1 and AUXREL2 auxiliary control files, if updates from those releases have not been merged into the base; the programmer examining recent changes to the program will be less interested in those updates, and will not even wish to see them listed.

Once updates have been applied, the user edits the changed file; subsequent changes, when saved, are recorded in file BILLIO UPDTBUG. This file will contain update control records indicating source records to be added, deleted, and replaced.

This very powerful XEDIT feature makes it simple to create discrete, removable program updates. It also provides some automatic problem avoidance: since XEDIT maintains the line sequence numbers, and does not reuse them when a line is merely changed, if more than one person changes the same line in a program, an error will be raised at update time when the conflicting updates attempt to alter the same line. This is a vast improvement over simply changing the base source program, which requires saving entire previous versions to allow regression testing, and also allows lost updates if two programmers change the same source without consulting each other.

CMS also supplies a procedure to apply updates and assemble source programs, called VMFHASM. VMFHASM executes the UPDATE command to apply updates and create a temporary file before invoking the assembler. The output of the assembler is an object file, commonly called a **text deck**. The assemble procedure renames the text deck from BILLIO TEXT to another filetype, depending on the control file format and options used; for example, if the UPDTBUG file were found, the file would be called BILLIO TXTFIX. The text deck created by VMFHASM also contains a record of the macro libraries used and the updates applied as a means of determining the updates applied to create a particular object file.

The final step of the update philosophy is linking the new text deck. CMS includes a procedure called VMFLKED which uses MVS-style linkage editor commands and the control file to determine the text deck(s) to use when creating the load module. The records in the text deck that originated from the control file are included in the linkage editor map, leaving yet another track of program currency.

For a description of control files, see "Updating your source program" in the CMS Application Development Guide, SC24-5450.

Brief Overview of MVS (OS) Simulation

Introduction

CMS simulates the functions of many MVS macros, SVCs, and services to provide the capability of running and developing MVS programs in a CMS virtual machine. MVS simulation is not complete, but it is robust enough to cover writing and supporting applications such as the MVS H Assembler. Since CMS does not provide multitasking support, the resultant function of MVS simulated multitasking support works differently in CMS. For instance, the MVS ATTACH macro does not support all parameters even though no assembly errors are generated. The ATTACH service in CMS will not return control to the next sequential instruction until the ATTACHed program completes.

MVS simulation support includes three areas of concern to software developers. Items such as real storage management, I/O support, and program management are very important to developers of systems which run in both CMS and MVS. Maintenance time and effort are reduced when a single program operates in both systems, since it is much more costly to maintain two programs when one will do the job.

Real storage management

Real storage management is of interest mainly to assembler programmers, since high-level language programmers are not exposed to this aspect of MVS simulation. IBM COBOL and

FORTRAN compilers used in VM/ESA are MVS versions with front-end programs to allow invocation under CMS, so they use MVS simulation routines to provide real storage management.

I/O support

I/O support is important to all program developers. Without input and output, a program cannot do much! MVS simulation supports three types of data organization: **sequential**, **partitioned**, and **direct**. **Sequential** files are arranged in physical rather than logical sequence: record 1 is read, then record 2, and so forth. **Partitioned** files are independent groups of sequentially organized records called **members**. Members have simple names stored in a directory that is part of the dataset, and this member name is used to reference a group of records without requiring that the entire dataset be read. **Direct** files require the dataset to exist on disk; records may be accessed in any order by specifying addresses by which the records are stored and retrieved directly.

Program management simulation

Program management deals with bringing programs into real storage, transferring control to them for execution, and deleting them when they have served their purpose. MVS simulation supports the MVS/XA linkage editor at DFP level 2.3.0 and provides AMODE and RMODE support. CMS treats RMODE and AMODE attributes in the same manner as MVS/XA, and MVS services run in the same addressing modes in a CMS virtual machine as they would in an MVS partition.

CMS supports 31-bit addressing for the LOAD, LINK, ATTACH, XCTL, and DELETE macros. After completion of a LOAD function, bit 0 of register 0 indicates the LOADed program's addressing mode. A program which receives control as a result of a LINK, ATTACH, or XCTL macro has bit 0 of register 14 set to the addressing mode of the program which issued the program management macro.

MVS and CMS terminology

CMS uses many MVS terms. The following is a summary of MVS terminology and its CMS equivalent.

Catalogued procedure: CMS **EXECs** (procedures) can execute command sequences similiar to catalogued procedures and provide conditional execution based on return codes from previous steps.

Dataset: Datasets are called **files** in CMS.   CMS simulates certain MVS dataset organizations and can read real MVS sequential or partitioned datasets; CMS cannot write to real MVS datasets without modifications.   CMS reads and writes VSAM datasets.

Data definition (DD) card: The FILEDEF command performs the functions of the DD statement to specify device types and output file dispositions.

Dataset control block (DSCB):   Information about CMS disk files is contained in **file status table** entries (FSTs).

EXEC card: CMS program execution requires specifying only the name of the program for native commands, EXECs, or a linkedited program (filetype MODULE); to execute an object file that has not been linkedited (a text deck), the LOAD and START commands are used.

Job control language (JCL):   CMS and user-written *commands* (often REXX programs) perform the functions of JCL.

Job step: Invocation of a CMS command or EXEC is the equivalent of an MVS job step.

Linkediting: The CMS LKED command creates LOADLIB libraries from CMS TEXT files and MVS object modules.   The CMS LOAD command loads TEXT files into virtual storage and resolves external references.   The GENMOD command creates MODULE files which can be loaded or executed.

Load module: Load modules are members of CMS LOADLIB libraries.   LOADLIB members are loaded, relocated, and executed by the OSRUN command, and LOADLIB members are loaded and relocated by the NUCXLOAD command.   LOADLIB members can also be accessed by the LINK, LOAD, ATTACH, and XCTL macros.

Object module: Language compiler output is placed in CMS files with a filetype of TEXT.

MVS: In CMS, the term **MVS** refers both to the OS and MVS operating systems.

STEPCAT, JOBCAT: VSAM catalogs can be assigned for jobs or job steps in CMS by using special DDNAMEs IJSYSCT and IJSYSUC when identifying catalogs.

Partitioned dataset (PDS): CMS simulates PDSs in LOADLIBs and MACLIBs.

STEPLIB, JOBLIB: The GLOBAL command establishes the libraries to be used (macro libraries, or MACLIBs; text libraries, or TXTLIBs; and program libraries, or LOADLIBs). Job libraries may be controlled indirectly by accessing and releasing CMS minidisks or SFS directories containing files and programs needed.

Task: A CMS **SVC** or program level of execution is essentially an MVS task, albeit single-threaded, since CMS does no native multi-tasking.

Utility program: Functions similiar to those performed by the MVS utility programs are provided by CMS commands such as TAPE, COPYFILE, UPDATE, and DDR.

Volume table of contents (VTOC): The list of files on a CMS minidisk or in a CMS Shared File System directory can be displayed using LISTFILE or FILELIST commands.

High-Level Language Support

VM/ESA supports two COBOL compilers: OS/VS COBOL and VS COBOL II.

OS/VS COBOL products can be ordered as:

    Compiler and Subroutine Library (5740-CB1)
    Subroutine Library (5740-LM1)

VS COBOL II products can be ordered as:

    Compiler and Library (5688-023)
    Compiler, Library, and Debugger (5688-958)
    Library (5688-022)

OS PL/I Version 2 products can be ordered as:

    Compiler, Library, and PLITEST (5668-909)

Compiler and Library (5668-910)
Library (5668-911)

VS Pascal products can be ordered as:

Compiler and Runtime Library (5668-767)
Runtime Library (5668-717)

VS Fortran products can be ordered as:

Compile and Library (5688-087)
Library (5668-805)
Compiler, Library, and Interactive Debugger (5668-806)

C/370 products can be ordered as:

Compiler (5688-040)
Library (5688-039)

These compilers support calls to routines in a **Callable Services Library** or **CSL**. One such CSL library, called VMLIB, is supplied with VM/ESA. Calls to CSL routines are not resolved until program execution; this allows changing CSL routines without having to relinkedit the routine to the application program, recompile the program, or modify any program source statements.

Callable Services Libraries are described in detail in the *VM/ESA CMS Application Development Reference* manual, and the *VM/ESA CMS Application Development Guide*.

Two other IBM compilers supported by VM/ESA, Ada, and APL2, do not support CSL calls.

Ada products can be ordered as:

Compiler (5709-025)
Runtime Library (5709-027)

The APL2 licensed program can be ordered as program number 5668-899.

Connectivity

Application programs often must communicate with other programs
to acccess a resource not present or not available in the local virtual
machine.   VM/ESA supports **Advanced Program-to-Program
Communication/VM (APPC/VM)**, which provides native inter-program communication.   VM/ESA provides two programming interfaces to APPC/VM. Systems Application Architecture (SAA) defines
an interface called the **Common Programming Interface for
Communications** (**CPI-C**), which is intended for programs written
in REXX or other high-level languages; there is also a low-level
APPC/VM interface intended for programs written in assembler.
The CPI-C interface uses this low-level interface internally.

MVS has an APPC/VM counterpart called APPC/MVS, which can
communicate with APPC/VM programs. Programs written using the
CPI-C interface can be easily ported to other IBM SAA environments.

APPC/VM lets programs in a VM/ESA environment communiciate
with APPC programs located in:

- The same VM/ESA system
- A different VM/ESA system
- A VM/ESA system in a different TSAF collection that has
  AVS and VTAM running
- A VM/ESA system in an SNA network that has AVS and
  VTAM running
- A non-VM/ESA system in an SNA network that supports the
  APPC protocol
- A non-IBM system in an SNA network that supports the
  APPC protocol
- A workstation in an SNA network that supports the APPC
  protocol

MVS MACLIBs in CMS

Several macro libraries are provided as part of MVS simulation
support. The macros in these libraries provide functions as follows:

OSMACRO   macros for programs using 370-mode MVS interfaces.

MVSXA   macros for programs using XA-mode MVS interfaces.

OSMACRO1 versions of MVS macros not simulated and are provided only for assembly on CMS.

OSVSAM the subset of supported OS/VSAM macros.

Making macro libraries available to the assembler is discussed in "GLOBAL MACLIB" on page 555

MVS (OS) Simulation and Storage Management

This section explains what occurs when a program requests storage from CMS using MVS simulation; it is not a control block-level description of how CMS performs storage management for MVS simulation.

CMS translates GETMAIN and FREEMAIN requests into appropriate CMS storage requests. This means that CMS supports only one storage management system, which is based on the CMSSTOR and SUBPOOL macros.

Since CMS storage management was significantly restructured in CMS Release 5.5, programs written for prior CMS versions that use NUCON pointers for GETMAIN storage must be changed.

CMS 5.6 and above return GETMAIN free storage in a different manner than in CMS Release 5. If a program depends on other programs that are invoked by SVC 202 or SVC 204 (CMSCALL) to obtain and return GETMAIN free storage, it may require use of the SET STORECLR command. See "SET STORECLR" on page 551 for details on this command.

CMS has always allowed specification of subpools on calls to GETMAIN and FREEMAIN. In CMS Release 5, subpool calls were not simulated; in later releases, specifying the SP parameter on GETMAIN and FREEMAIN calls results in an internal call to the CMS SUBPOOL macro.

CMS supports almost all GETMAIN and FREEMAIN options, including the list options (LC, LU, and L), subpools (SP), and location control options (RC, RU, VRC, and VRU) which cause CMS MVS simulation to use the LOC= parameter on CMSSTOR to obtain and release storage above or below the 16MB line. The only unsupported operand is the RELATED keyword, which is accepted but ignored.

CMS simulation of MVS subpools is identical to subpool support in MVS/XA, with one exception: only subpools 0 through 127 are valid in CMS. Specifying any other subpool causes an ABEND.

One of the biggest recent changes to CMS MVS simulation is in the way CMS manages MVS GETMAIN storage. In VM/SP Release 5, CMS cleaned up or released GETMAIN storage at end-of-command, which in CMS is when the ready message Ready; is displayed. This method was inconsistent with MVS and made GETMAIN storage management more difficult.

In VM/ESA, the default case is that CMS releases GETMAIN storage at termination of each SVC 202 or SVC 204 (CMSCALL) level. This method is consistent with MVS and provides a programming environment where clearly defined boundaries exist between programs at different SVC levels.

The most significant impact is felt with the ATTACH macro. Even though CMS does not support multitasking, the ATTACH macro does in fact transfer control to another program. This is a clearly defined boundary and thus is at a different SVC level, so any GETMAIN storage is released when the attached program terminates. Previous releases of CMS did not work this way: the GETMAIN storage was not released until the ready message was displayed.

SET STORECLR

Problems presented by this change were recognized, so IBM developed the SET STORECLR command to allow controlling when GETMAIN storage is freed.

SET STORECLR has two options, ENDCMD and ENDSVC.

ENDCMD enables use of previously developed programs on VM/ESA without modification; however, such programs should be converted whenever possible to support running with STORECLR ENDSVC to behave in an MVS-compatible manner.

VM/SP Release 5 and earlier releases behave as if STORECLR ENDCMD existed and were in effect; later CMS releases all default to STORECLR ENDSVC.

The FILEDEF Command

The CMS FILEDEF command provides the equivalent of an MVS DD statement, with some necessary differences.

Consider an MVS DD statement to create a dataset name of HANDBOOK for a disk-resident file, which is to be retained after the job step completes. The file's data control block (DCB) attributes are:

- Record format is fixed block standard.
- Records are 80 bytes long.
- Blocks contain 800 bytes or 10 records.

An assembler program would code a DCB macro:

```
THEDATA DCB DDNAME=MYFILE,MACRF=(PM),RECFM=FBS,
            LRECL=80,BLKSIZE=800,DSORG=PS
  Corresponding JCL is:
//MYFILE DD DSN=HANDBOOK,UNIT=DISK,DISP=(NEW,KEEP),
//           DCB=(RECFM=FBS,LRECL=80,BLKSIZE=800)
```

The equivalent CMS FILEDEF statement with a CMS fileid of HAND BOOK A1 would look like this:

```
FILEDEF MYFILE DISK HAND BOOK A1 (RECFM FBS LRECL 80 BLKSIZE 800
```

This creates a file with filename HAND and filetype BOOK on the A-disk.

A complete description of the FILEDEF command is found in the *VM/ESA CMS Command Reference.*

Accessing MVS Data from VM

It is often useful to test programs with input from a remote guest operating system. CMS can read data from existing OS volumes, but (without local enhancements or vendor products) cannot create or write to MVS-formatted volumes.

CMS programs using MVS simulation can read MVS datasets by specifying the dataset name and volume on the FILEDEF statement.

For example, using the same parameters as the previous example, but using an MVS dataset name with multiple qualifiers:

```
THEDATA DCB DDNAME=MYFILE,MACRF=(PM),RECFM=FBS,
            LRECL=80,BLKSIZE=800,DSORG=PS

//MYFILE DD DSN=VM.ESA.HAND.BOOK,UNIT=DISK,DISP=(NEW,KEEP),
//           DCB=(RECFM=FBS,LRECL=80,BLKSIZE=800)
```

Assuming that an MVS volume is linked to the virtual machine and accessed as an R-disk, the equivalent CMS FILEDEF statement would look like this:

```
FILEDEF MYFILE R1 DSN VM.BOOK (RECFM FBS LRECL 80 BLKSIZE 800
```

If the DSN parameter is specified as a question mark ("?"), CMS prompts for the dataset name. This is necessary when the name is longer than eight characters.

For example:

```
FILEDEF MYFILE R1 DSN ? (RECFM FBS LRECL 80 BLKSIZE 800
DMSFLD220R Enter dataset name:
vm.esa.hand.book
```

CMS also includes a command called LISTDS to review the contents of MVS-formatted disk volumes.

The format of the LISTDS command is

```
LISTDS diskmode (options
```

where:

    diskmode is the mode at which the MVS volume is accessed.

    options   are display options such as EXTENT, FREE, etc. If no options are specified, all datasets on the volume are listed.

BDAM restrictions

The four methods of accessing BDAM records are:

1. Relative Block (RRR)
2. Relative Track (TTR)
3. Relative track and key (TTK)
4. Relative Address (HHR) (MBBCCHHR)

CMS restrictions on these access methods are:

- Only the three-letter BDAM identifiers listed above can be used to refer to records, since CMS simulation of BDAM files uses a three-byte identifier.
- CMS BDAM files are always created with 255 records on the first logical track and 256 records on all other logical tracks, regardless of the blocksize. If BDAM methods 2, 3, or 4 are used with RECFM U or V, a program must either write 255 records on the first track and 256 records on every other track, or must not update the track indicator until a NO SPACE FOUND message is returned on a write. For method

3 (WRITE ADD), this message occurs when no more dummy records can be found on a write request; for methods 2 and 4, this does not occur and the track indicator is updated only when the record indicator reaches 256 and overflows into the track indicator.

- Variable-length BDAM files (in PL/I they are regional 3 files) must be created entirely under CMS. In addition, the exact number of records to be written must be specified with the XTENT option of the FILEDEF command. When reading variable-length BDAM files, the XTENT and KEYLEN information specified for the file must duplicate information specified when the file was created. CMS does not support WRITE ADD of variable-length BDAM files; that is, a program cannot add additional records to the end of an already existing variable-length BDAM file.

- Two files of the same filetype, both using keys, cannot be open at the same time. This is because the CMS BDAM support maintains the keys for such files in a temporary file called $KEYSAVE *filetype*. Thus, if a program that is updating keys does not close the file it is updating for some reason, such as a system failure or another IPL operation, the update may be completed by rerunning the program.

- Variable-length BDAM files must be created under CMS in their entirety, with the XTENT option of the FILEDEF command specifying the exact number of records to be written. When reading variable BDAM files, the XTENT and key length information specified must duplicate what was specified at file creation time. CMS does not support adding variable-length records to BDAM files.

- Once a file is created using keys, additions to the file must not be made without using keys and specifying the original length. There is limited support from the CMS file system for BDAM-created files (sparse files). Sparse files can be manipulated with CMS commands, but are not recognized as such by most CMS commands: the number of records in the FST is treated as a valid record number.

- The number of records in the dataset extent must be specified using the FILEDEF command. The default is 50 records.

- The minimum logical record length for a CMS BDAM file with keys is 8 bytes.

Assembling Programs in CMS Using MVS MACLIBs

Assembling MVS programs under CMS in VM/ESA requires the H assembler, which supports options not available using the XF assembler. The MVS/XA macro library (MVSXA) also contains macros which require assembler H.

GLOBAL MACLIB

MVS macro libraries are made available to the assembler by the CMS GLOBAL MACLIB command, which defines macro libraries the assembler uses to resolve macro invocations.

For example, to assemble a program named HANDBOOK with macro libraries OSMACRO and OSMACRO1, use:

```
GLOBAL MACLIB OSMACRO OSMACRO1
HASM HANDBOOK
```

The assembler produces an object deck with filetype TEXT. This is important because the LKED command requires object files to have filetype TEXT.

Using the LKED Command

MVS programs executed in CMS should be from a CMS load library, or LOADLIB. LOADLIBs are created and maintained by the LKED command. The CMS LOADLIB command is a utility program that copies members from one LOADLIB to another, compresses LOADLIBs, and lists member names in LOADLIBs.

The LKED command uses the MVS/XA linkage editor for the actual link of the TEXT file to the LOADLIB as an executable module.

In the earlier example, a program named HANDBOOK was assembled, producing an object file called HANDBOOK TEXT. The following command linkedits this program and creates load library HANDBOOK:

```
LKED HANDBOOK
```

This uses the MVS/XA linkage editor to linkedit the text file and create an executable module. The LKED command uses FILEDEF commands to determine alternate means of input. A FILEDEF must be issued before the LKED command to define a unique ddname for files to be included as secondary linkage editor input.

Default FILEDEF commands issued by the LKED command for the DD names presented to the linkage editor are:

```
FILEDEF SYSLIN    DISK fname TEXT * (RECFM F BLOCK 80 NOCHANGE
FILEDEF SYSLMOD   DISK fname LOADLIB A1 (RECFM U BLOCK 260 NOCHANGE
FILEDEF SYSUT1    DISK fname SYSUT1 *
FILEDEF SYSPRINT  DISK fname LKEDIT A1
```

Consider an example of linkediting a program with input from various places: some from a text library (TXTLIB) and some from one or more TEXT files. The new program module is named NICEBOOK, and it is to be linkedited into a LOADLIB named ESABOOK. The contents of the primary input file, INPUT TEXT, are (starting in column 2):

```
INCLUDE TXTLIB1(CHAPTER1,CHAPTER2)
INCLUDE TXTFILE
NAME NICEBOOK(R)
```

The CMS commands to perform this are:

```
FILEDEF TXTLIB1 DISK CHAPTER TXTLIB B1
FILEDEF TXTFILE DISK INDEX TEXT A1
LKED INPUT (LIBE ESABOOK
```

The CMS LKED command also supports the automatic call function of the MVS linkage editor.

FILEDEFs may be issued prior to issuing the LKED command to override defaults.

For example, activating an automatic call search to a LOADLIB called CHAPTER would use the following command:

```
FILEDEF SYSLIB DISK CHAPTER LOADLIB A
```

The LIBRARY linkage editor statement (in INPUT TEXT) could be used to add additional libraries to the automatic call. The LIBRARY statement must include the DDNAME from its related FILEDEF as well as the member names to be searched. The CONCAT option of the FILEDEF command is not valid for LKED input datasets.

An example of using LIBRARY statements entered into the SYSLIN file to expand the automatic call search (starting in column 2):

```
LIBRARY CHAPTERS(SECTION1,SECTION2,SECTION3)
LIBRARY KEYWORDS(MVS,CMS,INDEX)
NAME BOOKPART(R)
```

Commands issued to execute the linkage editor and define the automatic call libraries are:

```
FILEDEF CHAPTERS DISK BOOKPART LOADLIB A
FILEDEF KEYWORDS DISK WORDLIST LOADLIB A
LKED INPUT (LIBE ESABOOK
```

A linkage input file can be used to create multiple load modules when the entire LOADLIB is linkedited. The MODULE option of the LKED command controls which load modules are relinked.

For example, if program CONTENTS is reassembled and only those load modules which have CONTENTS defined as input are to be relink-edited, the following command would be used:

```
LKED INPUT (LIBE ESABOOK MODULE CONTENTS
```

To summarize, the MVS/XA linkage editor can control the maintenance of CMS LOADLIBs in the same manner as the MVS/XA linkage editor in MVS. Linkage editor input control statements can be moved back to MVS at a later date along with the TEXT files to create executable modules in real MVS load libraries for execution in MVS.

Executing Programs in the CMS Environment

The OSRUN command executes programs from CMS and MVS load libraries. For the LINK, LOAD, ATTACH, and XCTL macros, the libraries specified in the LOADLIB global list are searched. The PARM option of the OSRUN command passes OS-style parameters to the program. If the parameter contains special characters, the parameter must be enclosed in quotes; double quotes are used to indicate the presence of quotes in the parameter quotes.

Programs executed by the OSRUN command must reside in one of the libraries specified in the GLOBAL LOADLIB command. For example, if the library name is BOOK LOADLIB A and the program name is TESTPROG, the sequence of commands is:

```
GLOBAL LOADLIB BOOK
OSRUN TESTPROG
```

CMS can load and execute programs from MVS load libraries on MVS-formatted volumes, if the libraries are defined with the FILEDEF command. Assuming an MVS volume accessed at mode M

and an MVS load library named VMESA.LOADLIB, the FILEDEF
command would define the library as OSRUN LOADLIB M with a
DDNAME of $SYSLIB and a DSN of VMESA.LOADLIB:

```
FILEDEF $SYSLIB DISK OSRUN LOADLIB M DSN VMESA LOADLIB
        (DSORG PO RECFM U BLOCK nnnnn
GLOBAL LOADLIB OSRUN
OSRUN MYPROG PARM='THIS DATA''s ALL MINE.'
```

EXECs written using the original CMS EXEC language cannot
pass parameters to programs invoked via OSRUN; only EXEC 2 and
REXX procedures may do so.

The CMS NUCXLOAD command can also load a program from a load
library and prepare it for execution. Rather than invoking it
directly, NUCXLOAD loads a program as a CMS nucleus extension.
This means the program is loaded into virtual storage and stays
resident there, and may be invoked as a CMS command.

For example, given a CMS load library called VMESA LOADLIB A
containing a program called TESTPROG, the following commands
would load and execute the program:

```
FILEDEF MYLIB DISK VMESA LOADLIB A
GLOBAL   LOADLIB VMESA
NUCXLOAD TESTIT TESTPROG MYLIB
TESTIT
```

This loads TESTPROG from VMESA LOADLIB as a nucleus extension
named TESTIT. TESTIT can then be executed as a command from
the CMS command line or as a command from a REXX or EXEC 2
procedure.

Debugging the Program

Nucleus extensions are useful for debugging, because they allow
programs to be loaded into storage without actually running them.
Programs can then be located and examined in storage, and tracing
commands can be issued, before execution begins; this is not possible
using OSRUN.

The NUCXMAP command finds a NUCXLOADed program in storage and
displays the program name, load address, entry address, program
length, and options issued on the NUCXLOAD command. This information is very useful when setting traps with the CP TRACE command.

A common technique used to trace instruction paths through a
program involves the use of assembler NOP (no operation)

instructions: null branch instructions that do not branch. The CP TRACE command can be used to look for NOP instructions during execution, and to stop execution and/or display a message when one is located.

All NOP instructions need not be identical, however: operands may be specified, and CP TRACE traps set to find specific examples. It is possible to have over a million unique NOP instructions in a single program—certainly enough for most applications! For example:

```
NOP   X'000'(0)     yields   4700 0000
NOP   X'234'(1)     yields   4700 1234
NOP   X'345'(1,2)   yields   4701 2345
```

Consider a test program with NOP instructions at various locations. Each NOP can be visualized using the CP TRACE command. Assume the program is NUCXLOADed at address X'50000' and is X'12000' bytes long. The CP TRACE command to display all simple NOP instructions within the bounds of the program is:

```
CP TRACE Instruction DATA 4700 Range 50000.12000 RUN
         CMD Display G10 T51000.20
```

This TRACE command displays the location of each NOP instruction executed, does not stop at the NOP instruction, displays the contents of general purpose register 10, and displays 32 bytes of storage starting at X'51000'.

The CP TRACE command is extremely powerful and can reduce debugging time dramatically.

Summary

MVS simulation, in conjunction with native CMS facilities, provides a powerful yet easy-to-use program development environment. Developers can use native CMS commands to create, maintain, assemble, and test programs without ever having to leave the CMS environment.

The productivity of CMS program development makes it the environment of choice for many developers of non-CMS programs.

23

Systems Application Architecture in VM/ESA

By Chip Coy, Susan Cirulli, and Dean C. DiTomasso

Introduction to SAA

Systems Application Architecture, typically abbreviated **SAA,** is IBM's structure to provide cross-system consistency between major hardware and software platforms for application programmers and application users. The SAA definition contains hardware and software platforms, a common programming interface, a common user interface, common communications support, and a set of composite applications. The SAA definition is controlled and supported by an IBM management process.

The SAA definition—or, more accurately, the systems and products that implement the SAA definition—allow applications to be moved among systems, to span systems, and to provide applications with an end-user interface that has a style in common with other applications implemented using SAA standards. Beyond the application, use of SAA facilities also allows portability of programmers and end-users. Programmers find the SAA programming interface on each of the SAA environments, and end-users find applications with a familiar end-user interface.

Hardware platforms

Hardware platforms for SAA are System/390, Personal System/2, and Application System/400. The SAA operating systems are MVS/ESA (with one or more of MVS/APPC, TSO, IMS/DC, and CICS/ESA providing the SAA environment), VM/ESA (with CMS providing the SAA environment), OS/2 Extended Edition, and OS/400.

Common programming interface

The SAA Common Programming Interface (CPI) comes in two parts: **languages** and **services**. The CPI languages are programming languages needed by application programmers and users. The CPI services are the callable services needed by application programs written in CPI languages.

Languages

CPI languages are a bit different than the SAA operating systems; the languages are specifications that do not specify a particular IBM product (the SAA operating systems are directly specified in the SAA publications). For current information on exactly which IBM product provides the implementation of a CPI language refer to *SAA CPI Summary*. Detailed information on products implementing particular CPIs is available from an IBM representative, by obtaining a copy of the ENVR3820 PACKAGE by A. J. Cubbon (CUBBON at ATLVM1) from the MKTTOOLS IBM conference disk. The current set of CPI languages and their implementing products are summarized on the next page.

Information Warehouse Framework—VM/ESA

CPI	Product	Support
C	C/370 V2 SAA AD/Cycle C/370	Full Full
COBOL	VS COBOL II 1.3.2 SAA AD/Cycle COBOL/370	Full level 2 Full level 2
FORTRAN	VS FORTRAN V2R5	Full
PL/I	OS PL/I V2R3	Full
RPG	RPG/370	Full
Procedures Language	VM/ESA (REXX)	Full level 1+ Partial level 2
Application Generator	CSP/AD, AE V3R3	Full + AD

Services

Services in the SAA CPI are much like the languages—they make up a set of specifications that do not specify a particular IBM product. Refer to the SAA CPI Summary for specifics of the current services set and which IBM products implement the specification. Current services are:

Database: Interface to databases through Structured Query Language (SQL).

Query: Access to relational data and control over data appearance in formatted reports.

Communications: Interface for program-to-program communication based on IBM's SNA logical unit type 6.2 (LU6.2). Facilities include starting and ending conversations, sending and receiving data, and synchronization primitives.

Repository: Access to organized, shared, integrated information supporting business and data processing activities.

Print manager: Interface to Advanced Function Printing, including option specification and validation and submission of either program buffers or external files for printing.

Resource recovery: Interface to two-phase commit processing.

Language environment: A common set of interfaces needed by SAA Languages (currently required by AD/Cycle C/370 and AD/Cycle COBOL/370).

CPI Services Summary—VM/ESA

CPI	Product	Support
Database	SQL/DS V3R2 SQL/DS V3R3	Partial level 2 (3.2) Full level 2 (3.3)
Query	QMF V2R4	Full
Communications	VM/ESA CMS	Full
Repository	(none)	(none)
Print manager	SAA PrintManager	Full
Resource recovery	VM/ESA CRR	Full
Language environment	AD/Cycle LE/370	Full

Common communications support

The SAA Common Communications Support (CCS) provides protocols needed to allow SAA systems to communicate with one another.

These protocols include everything from the base-level line protocols (SNA and OSI) thru higher level protocols, such as APPC, network management, and object content architectures.

The current set of protocols and the names of the implementing IBM products can be found in the *SAA CCS Summary*.

Common user access

SAA Common User Access (CUA) defines rules for the dialog between humans and computers in three different areas:

Physical consistency: The actual hardware used for human/computer interaction. This covers areas such as keyboard layout (to ensure that the ESC key is in the place the user expects it to be) and the use of the mouse.

Syntactical consistency: The sequence of elements on the display and the order of keystrokes to request actions—for example, putting the title in the same place on an application screen and always using double-click on the mouse to open an item.

Semantic consistency: Having the elements of CUA have the same meaning everywhere (having QUIT and CANCEL clearly differentiated and always performing the same action no matter which system or application is involved).

CUA is important for all applications to reduce the personal frustration that results when going between applications and having syntax and semantics shift, or when moving from one system to another and losing one's way on the keyboard itself!

Composite Applications on VM

Generally, applications are thought of as individual programs or groups of programs that form a single entity. However, as problems that applications are attempting to solve become larger and more complex, there comes a point where the problem itself is too large to be solved by a single application or organization. **Composite applications** is the name given to an open architecture where components (or applications) define the framework for integrating independently developed programs. This integration is illustrated by incremental improvements in functional fit, interoperability, and consistency of behavior by participating applications.

Composite applications have several key attributes that set them apart from other applications:

- They recognize that the problem to be solved is too large and complex for it to be handled within a single application.
- They define and manage incremental steps in the improvement of how a set of independent applications work together.
- They allow replacement of applications (components) that make up the composite. This may be advantageous because an alternative application may be better suited for solving the problem at hand than the current one in the composite.
- They provide a design that allows for adding new applications to the existing composite.

Composite applications under the SAA umbrella include AD/Cycle, Information Warehouse, and SystemView. In addition, there are several industry-specific and cross-industry application areas which could qualify as composite applications in the future. OfficeVision, Computer Integrated Manufacturing (CIM), and Insurance are candidate frameworks. The following sections discuss how AD/Cycle and Information Warehouse are exploited on the VM/ESA platform.

AD/Cycle

Introduced in 1989, AD/Cycle is IBM's solution for SAA application development. It is designed to help application developers improve their productivity, quality, and management of the development cycle. The application development life cycle consists of a series of distinct but related tasks. AD/Cycle is the framework that supports the life cycle and integrates application development tools.

AD/Cycle is made up of two major components: tools and a platform. The AD/Cycle tools support application development activities that make up the development life cycle:

- Requirements gathering
- Analysis and design
- Development
- Build and test
- Maintenance

Some tools extend across all phases of the life cycle while others support a particular phase. For example, project management and documentation tools apply to all phases of the life cycle, while enterprise modeling tools, generators, test tools, etc. are used in particular phases of the life cycle.

Enterprise modeling tools are used to define the data and processes that are used in the enterprise or corporation. Relationships between the data, processes, and organizational elements are also defined through enterprise modeling. Then, data produced by the enterprise model can be used by analysis and design tools to produce data flows and/or create the application design.

Generators and knowledge-based tools are designed to increase the productivity of application developers. A combination of generators and knowledge-based tools is most effective for increasing productivity.

Common Programming Interface (CPI) languages (described earlier in this chapter) are considered part of AD/Cycle, since they are used to develop the applications themselves. These languages are enhanced periodically in an effort to increase programmer productivity and to conform to newer ANSI or other standards. The CPI language enhancements also include the integration of various language-sensitive editors, pre-processors, compilers, and other support functions. Integration of function facilitates code integration from generators and knowledge-based tools.

AD/Cycle provides a comprehensive verification environment with test, maintenance, and redevelopment tools. These tools are used in verification of new applications and maintenance of existing ones. These tools include such functions as test data creation, management, and analysis.

The Application Development Platform is the term given to the base on which application development tools are built and used. The Application Development Platform includes the user interface, workstation services, AD information model, tool services, and repository services. The repository manager is a place for storing common definitions that can be accessed by the various tools. (For further information about AD/Cycle concepts, refer to *AD/Cycle Concepts*, publication number GC26-4531.)

VM supports a rich set of AD/Cycle tools, while participating in the AD/Cycle environment. It should be understood that the AD/Cycle environment is evolving; the entire set of tools need not be selected to take advantage of the AD/Cycle structure and improve programmer productivity. Only those tools which best complement the current development environment need be used. The development environment may evolve over time, becoming more CASE-like, simply by adding more of the pieces.

The workstation, because of its graphical and windowing capabilities, is the sensible place to front-end development tools, such as design and analysis aids, etc. VM can be used to manage resources shared among developers, such as common code or data definitions, printers, and other devices.

The following tables list the AD/Cycle tools which run under VM today, and the phase(s) with which they are associated.

Cross-life cycle tools

Product Name	Description
Application Development Project Support (ADPS)	Management of development projects
BookMaster, BookManager	Documentation
Software Common Services Library (SCLM, part of ISPF/PDF)	Build and manage libraries of common code

Maintenance tools

Product Name	Description
COBOL Structuring Facility (CSF)	Tool for restructuring COBOL code
Software Analysis Test Tool	see next table
Workstation Analysis Test Tool	see next table

Development, build/test tools

Product Name	Description
COBOL, FORTRAN, C, PL/I, RPG	SAA high-level languages
REXX (part of VM/ESA)	General-purpose programming language for editing macros and writing procedures and programs
Interactive System Productivity Facility (ISPF)	Dialog and panel development
CoOperative Development Environment (CODE)	Integrated edit, compile, and debug environment across languages
Language Environment/370 (LE/370)	Integrated cross-language execution environment, also provides additional callable services
Cross System Product (CSP)	Application generator
The Integrated Reasoning Shell (TIRS)	For development of knowledge-based applications

The following section discusses some of the workstation products that can be used to develop VM applications. These products are oriented toward the earlier phases of the life cycle: requirement gathering, analysis, and design. Further information about these and other AD/Cycle tools can be obtained from **AD/Cycle ... A Guide for Evaluating Tool Integration**, publication number G580-0024. The vendors listed are all members of the new International Alliance for the AD/Cycle framework.

AD/Cycle Tools—Workstation

Company	Product
BACHMAN	A series of tools for enterprise modeling, analysis, design, and development
Digitalk	Smalltalk/V for creating advanced graphical user interfaces
Easel	Workbench for developing CUA-compliant interfaces for existing applications
IBM	Workstation Platform/2 (WSP/2), a set of common services for integrating AD/Cycle tools BookMaster, BookManager for documentation SAA languages: COBOL, FORTRAN, C, PL/I, RPG CSP for development, build/test Software Analysis Test Tool (SATT) for software structure analysis Workstation Interactive Test Tool (WITT) for building test scripts TIRS for development of knowledge-based systems
INTERSOLV	PVCS Series, Excelerator for analysis and design
KnowledgeWare	Application Development Workbench, a series of tools for planning, analysis, and design
Micro Focus	COBOL compiler and workbench

VM will continue to evolve with SAA and the industry. VM is focused on continuing to improve its application development environment by supporting the needs of the marketplace today and into the future. With the growth of intelligent workstations, VM will work to extend its capabilities for cooperative processing. VM is a natural fit for this kind of structure because of the model of "virtual machine" it offers.

Since application development tools can be viewed as applications themselves, the customer can take advantage of those services and products VM will offer in this area. VM will work with the workstation to improve the overall capabilities of the development workbench.

Information Warehouse

The Information Warehouse (IW) framework was announced by IBM in September 1991. Information Warehouse is a composite application that defines a set of database management systems, interfaces, tools, and facilities that manage and deliver reliable, timely, accurate, and understandable business information for decision making.

The Information Warehouse framework consists of products that allow access to data wherever it is located in the enterprise. It is designed to provide access to data on heterogeneous systems—IBM systems and systems from other vendors.

The Information Warehouse framework is composed of three major parts:

1. The **Enterprise Data** element is the heart of the warehouse. It consists of the data in the enterprise and full-functioned database management systems that provide data integrity, security, recovery, reliability, availability, and performance. It includes both operational and informational data. It is built on the base provided by the SAA relational database managers. It includes both IBM and non-IBM files and databases throughout the enterprise.

2. The **Data Delivery** element is the vehicle that automates data access. This is accomplished by placing it where it can be accessed by programs and end-users. Distributed database capability is a key part of the Data Delivery element.

3. **Decision Support** applications enable knowledge workers to transform data into information. This is achieved by formulating a request for selection of data, manipulating the retrieved data, and analyzing and presenting the transformed data in various information formats and graphical charts.

IBM recognizes that customers face challenges in accessing and using data across the enterprise. The Information Warehouse framework addresses those challenges. It can be implemented with a set of products from both IBM and vendors. IBM will market business partner software products that address the data environment described by the Information Warehouse framework.

Information Warehouse includes access to distributed relational data from databases supporting Distributed Relational Database Architecture (DRDA). It also includes access to heterogeneous relational and non-relational data.

The Information Warehouse framework extends the power of informational applications and Decision Support Systems by helping to remove inhibitors that prevent the availability of pertinent data to authorized knowledge workers.

VM/ESA provides support for products that cover all three major parts of the Information Warehouse framework. The next table lists IBM products supported by VM/ESA.

IBM Information Warehouse products

Element	Category	Product
Enterprise Data Element	Relational Database Management System (RDBMS)	Structured Query Language/Data System (SQL/DS) Version 3
Data Delivery Element	Extractor	Data Extract Version 2
Decision Support Services / Informational Applications	Executive support Broad Range Natural Language Spreadsheet Management Office Management	Executive Decisions/VM Application System (AS) SAA Language/Access Lotus 1-2-3/M (tm) OfficeVision/VM Series

An example of VM/ESA participation in IW is its support of SQL/DS (Structured Query Language/Data System), a relational database management system (RDBMS) which provides the foundation for storage and management of data in the Information Warehouse framework. VM/ESA also supports the Query Management Facility (QMF) which enables access to relational data across DB2 and SQL/DS databases. The Remote-Unit-Of-Work (RUOW) distributed database query functions, defined by DRDA, allow users to access data remotely from DB2 databases in the MVS environment and SQL/DS databases in the VM environment.

VM/ESA will continue to enhance its support of the Information Warehouse framework by broadening its support for additional products that implement parts of the framework.

SAA management process

To maintain consistency in SAA, IBM established a management team to keep order and encourage progress in the SAA arena. The management team includes the SAA Executive, Earl Wheeler, who created SAA and has managed it since the first SAA announcement in March 1987. In addition, for each SAA interface, there is an SAA Interface Owner with responsibilities for:

- Definition, maintenance, and publication of the SAA interface specification (typically published as a book in the SAA library)
- Use of a change management process to ensure release-to-release compatibility in all SAA environments
- Specification and assignment of levels to authorized versions of the specification
- Definition of a compliance tool or process to be used by each implementing IBM product when certifying the product for compliance with the SAA interface specification

SAA Directions

IBM will continue to invest in the SAA vision. The SAA infrastructure of CUA, CPI, and CCS architectures will be extended. Client/Server computing environments will remain a key thrust in the evolution of SAA. IBM plans to continue incorporating advanced technology into SAA architectures and the products that enable them.

IBM will continue to build on the SAA base with integrated frameworks and composite applications. IBM business partners and other leading software vendors intend to participate in extending and enhancing the SAA base. The common base provided by SAA architectures and industry standards is an important part of the foundation for composite applications. The SAA direction is designed to move toward increased openness and interoperability with AIX and non-IBM systems. SAA architectures and systems form a key part of the foundation for IBM's support of the open enterprise.

The SAA direction will continue to emphasize support for industry standards. A key area of SAA activity is occurring with the Open Systems Foundation Distributed Computing Environment (OSF/DCE). IBM has stated that it intends to support elements of OSF/DCE on SAA platforms.

VM plans to continue to be a full SAA system into the future. VM will continue to make investments in SAA interfaces in support of business solutions on the VM/ESA system. VM/ESA has a strong focus on the open enterprise distributed environment. VM will evolve with SAA as it extends and enhances its support of the open enterprise.

References

1. *System Application Architecture Overview*, 12/90, GC26-4341.
2. *SAA ... A Guide for Evaluating Applications*, 12/91, G320-9803.
3. *Information Warehouse Framework*, Announcement Letter, 9/11/91, Number 291-471.

24

CMS Application Diagnosis

By David Kreuter

The art of problem diagnosis, or debugging, is a skill unto itself. VM/ESA provides—by design and implementation—many powerful debugging tools for the CMS user. By combining techniques in debugging with knowledge of specific tools, most CMS problems are solvable.

This chapter describes diagnosis of problems in CMS virtual machines. Problem areas discussed focus on application programs that rely on CMS system functions, such as program and storage management.

The context of applications for diagnosis includes compiled object code, calling user or system commands and routines, and exploitation of CMS programming facilities.

CMS debugging tools fall into two general contextual categories: **historical** and **real-time**.

Historical Debugging

Historical debugging is accomplished by producing a snapshot of the CMS virtual machine environment—a.k.a. a **dump** file—at the instant of problem occurrence, processing the dump file into a CMS file, and then using a software package designed to assist in dump analysis.

Several commercial dump analyzer products are on the VM software market. The product used in this chapter is IBM's **Dump Viewing Facility**, a component of VM/ESA.

Dump analysis in CMS is an under-utilized method of problem determination and resolution. Understanding the context of the CMS virtual machine provides a variety of useful techniques to assist the dump debugger.

Part of the reason this method has not been popular is certainly attributable to CMS's traditional set of excellent commands, and the power of CP class G commands. Certain situations, such as quickly running through chains of control block pointers, lend themselves naturally to the historical approach.

The goal of historical debugging is for the practitioner to bring a knowledge of the surrounding environment (CMS) into a picture of the virtual machine when an abnormality occurred. The tool set enables the practitioner to piece together the state of the machine and lead logically to the failure cause.

Real-Time Debugging

Real-time debugging is a method whereby the practitioner starts from an observance of normal state, and proceeds to run the program in conjunction with debugging tools until the problem deviation point is reached. A slight variant on this is for the practitioner to wait until the problem occurs, and then issue online commands.

CMS by nature and implementation is an ideal real-time debugging environment. CMS depends on CP to provide a complete view of virtualized architecture. One function that CP provides to a virtual machine is console function commands.

Console function commands available to CP class G users provide the capability of architecture-level debugging. Over the evolution of CP and CMS, the class G tool set has improved tremendously. VM/ESA class G commands invaluable for debugging include TRACE, DISPLAY, STORE, and BEGIN.

The virtual machine model, which means that any facility described in the hardware *Principles of Operation* manual is available to a virtual machine, is also a natural debugging environment. Virtual device participation (console, printer, etc.) allows real-time input and output as well as an accurate record through collected SPOOLed console logs of what occurred during an online debug session.

The CP TRACE command permits tracing at the architectural level. Trace functions include instruction execution tracing, register alteration, storage alteration, interrupts, and I/O events. When performing instruction tracing, a successful trace event is raised after completion of the instruction.

CMS uses the SVC instruction for supervisor services, and the DIAGNOSE instruction for hypervisor (CP) services. When a DIAGNOSE instruction has been traced, CP has completed performing the service for the virtual machine. The DIAGNOSE instruction is one virtual machine instruction, but requires many CP instructions.

This differs from an SVC instruction trace, which occurs after the SVC instruction has completed (interrupt PSW swapping has been performed) but before the CMS supervisor service has executed.

An extensive range of control options includes the ability to trace select interrupts, instructions issued in an address range, instructions by operation code or mnemonic, and bit settings in registers or storage. It can also stop or run the virtual machine.

The DISPLAY command lets the issuer display at the console storage contents, register contents, program status words (current, and by specifying interrupt class, old and new PSW values), and storage keys. Storage contents may be translated to EBCDIC (including lowercase), or disassembled to display mnemonics. Particular ranges of addresses and specific registers are also available for issuer control.

The STORE instruction alters specific contents of registers, storage, and PSWs. When altering any aspect of the virtual machine, the debugger should be aware that any change may risk program or data integrity. Virtual machine alteration is a powerful part of online debugging, but should always be executed judiciously.

The BEGIN command resumes execution at the current address in the PSW, or at the address specified as an operand. The BEGIN command is used to step through a trace session.

A common approach to debugging involves the TRACE PROG, STORE, and BEGIN commands. When a program check is trapped by TRACE PROG, it is often useful to modify the virtual machine with STORE commands, and then issue a BEGIN pointing back to the failing instruction to see if it works.

When using the BEGIN command in this fashion after a program check, the program will run in PSW key 0. This is because the program new PSW that was instated by the program check contains PSW key 0. Inadvertant execution in key 0 may be harmful to the virtual machine. PSW key 0 programs may destroy the CMS file system and other critical pointers and data areas.

In this case, it is better to to use a STORE PSW command to alter the instruction address and reinstate the user PSW key (X'E').

These architecture-level debugging commands offer an exceptionally strong approach to understanding the behavior and characteristics of virtual machine code. By coupling techniques with these tools with knowledge of the attributes of CMS, many CMS problems are solvable through online debugging.

A recommended approach to solving problems in CMS applications is to perform an instruction trace on two specific mnemonics, DIAG and SVC. These two instructions allow applications to access services from CP (DIAGNOSE instruction) and the CMS supervisor (SVC).

The hypervisor function desired from CP is indicated in the function code specified on the DIAG instruction. Primary SVCs that CMS applications use are X'CA' (202) and X'CC' (204). When these SVCs are issued, general purpose register 1 points to the parameter list. The first 8 bytes of the parameter list represent the command the application is issuing.

In addition to CP console function commands, VM/ESA has several robust new commands that deal with storage management issues: STDEBUG, SUBPMAP, and STORMAP. Existing facilities from prior releases are incorporated into the VM/ESA fold.

Many standard CMS commands and macros have uses in debugging particular CMS errors. Experienced CMS problem solvers frequently find standard errors, such as disk search order problems. It is interesting how the LISTFILE command may be the only tool required to solve a fair number of CMS problems, no matter the intricacy of the problem or skill level of the debugger.

Perhaps the most exciting real-time debugging approach is coupling CMS commands with architectural interfaces (such as interrupt capabilities) and CP console function commands for virtual machine debug and control.

CMS Structure Relevant to Problem Solving

CMS as a virtual operating system is characterized as:

Single-tasking: There is no intrinsic concept in CMS of task suspension or resumption under control of a dispatcher. Work is not ordered by importance or deadline characteristics by a set of scheduler algorithms. Rather, CMS provides a program manager that permits calling and returning from nested programs. The program manager percolates back to the next level of program routine.

A task is completed when the program manager surrenders control to a host environment such as an executing REXX program, or—when there is no other work to process—the Ready; message appears.

CMS multitasking—available as a PRPQ for VM/ESA Releases 1.0 and 1.1 and integrated into VM/ESA Release 2.0—is an important facility, especially for service machine products; see Chapter 8, *Server Tasking Environment/VM,* on page 217. This chapter deals exclusively with the current standard single-tasking CMS environment.

Command-driven: Upon completion of a task, CMS checks for another task ready to start by sequentially examining commands residing in:

1. **Program stack**—A logical stack in storage where a program may place a command to be executed

2. **Terminal input buffer**—A lookahead command buffer where data following the terminal linend character (usually the # character) is placed

If both are empty, CMS waits for a console I/O interrupt (a command typed at the terminal).

Real storage: CMS always presents a real address to its virtual processor. Architecturally, this means that CMS uses a program status word with the dynamic address translation bit off. The VM community has traditionally referred to this mode of operation as a **System/360-style** virtual machine.

For example, if a CMS routine wants to run at location X'15000', the machine expects X'15000' to be present as an absolute address. The fact that in reality it might be present in real (Control Program)

storage at, say, location X'1D05000', or in the paging system on expanded storage or DASD, is irrelevant to CMS. It remains a Control Program (CP) and architectural responsibility to manage virtual addressing schemes and formats.

This no-DAT architecture continues even in the CMS data space world of VM/ESA 1.1 with the **ESA/XC (ESA Extended Config-uration)** virtual machine mode, which allows CMS users to exploit data spaces without concern for manipulating the DAT bit. The DAT bit is required architecturally to use data spaces.

CMS publications and documentation consistently refer to virtual storage. CMS knows of no such thing as virtual storage: all storage is real to CMS.

Single-user: The CMS operating system is run and controlled by one user, the virtual console operator.

Program Management Concepts

Supervisor call instructions (SVCs)

CMS provides program management through a supervisor call mech-anism. This mechanism is provided by the architecture through the SVC instruction, operation code X'0A', which generates an **SVC interrupt**. The SVC interrupt cannot be masked in the program status word, and is a problem state instruction.

When an SVC interrupt is presented, a PSW swap occurs, with the PSW at storage location X'60' becoming the current PSW. The address portion of a new PSW for any interrupt class is referred to as the **First Level Interrupt Handler (FLIH)**. The CMS FLIH for SVCs is routine DMSITS.

CMS is sensitive to three categories of SVC interrupts:

1. Program management codes
2. Simulated DOS and OS codes
3. User-defined codes

The codes and basic functions are:

X'CA' (202)   Call a CMS routine using a parameter list addressed by general purpose register 1. This parameter list must reside below the 16MB line.

X'CC' (204)   Call a CMS routine using a parameter list addressed by general purpose register 1. This parameter list may reside above or below the 16MB line.

X'C9' (201)   Return control.

X'CB' (203)   Call an internal function.

The call routine codes play a significant role in debugging CMS applications. These codes are entered from a program calling a routine, or from the terminal command manager, which converts it to proper parameter list format.

Call SVCs

For call SVC codes (202 and 204), DMSITS performs processing known as the **CMS command search order**. When the routine or command name is found, the search stops and the routine or command is given control. The DMSITS command search order is:

1. Search for name as SUBCOM function
2. Search for name as NUCLEUS extension
3. Search for named routine loaded in transient area
4. Search CMS nucleus for specified name
5. Search currently assigned filemode letters for routine name with filetype MODULE
6. Perform these routine name conversions:
    a. Search translation tables; if found, perform search in steps 2–5 again
    b. Search synonym tables; if found, perform search in steps 2–5 again

The above searches are subject to variations, which depend on the value of the flag submitted with the calling SVC. When the calling code is X'CA' (202), the flag bits are inserted into bits 0–7 of general purpose register 1. When the calling code is X'CC' (204), the flag bits are inserted into storage, in a predefined savearea location that is available for interrogation by DMSITS and the called routine.

SVC control blocks

There are significant clues placed in CMS control blocks. Control block NUCON maps CMS's page 0. This control block includes hardware fixed storage locations, and key software information describing the state of CMS in the machine.

At SVC interrupt occurrence, the address of the instruction following the SVC instruction is stored in location X'20'. The instruction length code and interrupt code are stored at locations that depend on the particular architecture in use in the virtual machine.

DMSITS saves information concerning this SVC in a control block called SVCSECT. SVCSECT, a static control block, is addressed by NUCON entry ASVCSECT. There may be multiple SVC calls nested, so there will also be a series of dynamic SVC system save ares. These dynamic saveareas are mapped by the SVCSAVE control block.

The static SVCSECT is filled in by DMSITS to contain information including a pointer to the current allocated SVCSAVE savearea and the number of nested SVCs. In the case of applications that create unique SVC handlers with the HNDSVC macro, SVCSECT contains pointers to a list of the user-handled SVC interrupt codes, and the address of the user handlers. The fields are known as JFIRST and JLAST. The current SVCSAVE block is also addressed by NUCON field CURRSAVE.

Dynamic SVCSAVE saveareas contain the address of the SVC instruction issuance, name of the CALLEE (routine desired), the caller's general purpose registers, and pointers to other system and user saveareas. One quirk of CMS is its lack of the trace table found in most other operating systems. Instead, for SVC system saveareas at least, the designers inserted two check word fields. Each system SVC savearea contains eyecatchers ABCD and EFGH, which are used to validate the savearea on return from calling user programs. The ABCD eyecatcher is followed by the address of the next system savearea, previous system savearea, and the address of the user savearea, making it easy to locate these useful fields in a dump or storage display.

By following the chain of system saveareas, a debugger can accurately determine the flow of CMS commands. The following scenario exemplifies this technique.

SVC savearea chaining example

In the example, three programs are involved: FIRSTCAL, which invokes: SCNDCALL, which invokes: CALLTWO, which enters a CP READ state.

At the CP READ state (which to CMS is virtual processor stop state), expected saveareas are:

- SVCSECT pointing to CALLTWO (callee) with SCNDCALL as caller
- Current dynamic system savearea pointing to CALLTWO (callee) with SCNDCALL as caller
- Previous dynamic system savearea point to SCNDCALL (callee) with FIRSTCAL as caller
- Previous dynamic system savearea points to (FIRSTCAL) as callee

Each savearea has a related user savearea.

All three example programs contain their names in storage as eyecatchers. In the following console log, the CP class G DISPLAY command was used to display the contents of storage.

Location X'674' in NUCON points to the static SVC workarea (SVCSECT):

```
D 674
R00000674 00001000                              F6
```

Examine the SVCSECT. Offset X'14' points to the current savearea, offset X'1C' contains the nested SVC depth, and offset X'30' is the callee name (routine being called).

```
Location X'1000' is an SVCSECT, filled out for every SVC:

D T1000.120
R00001000 00000000 0000000C 00000000 00000000 F6 *................*
R00001010 00000000 000022C8 000022C8 00000003    *........H...H....*
R00001020 00000000 00000000 00000000 00000000    *................*
R00001030 C3C1D3D3 E3E6D640 001E8FE8 80E0F9E6    *CALLTWO ...Y..9W*
R00001040 000022C8 00E0F4B0 00E104B0 00E114E0    *...H..4.........*
R00001050 00000000 E3E6D640 C3C1D3D3 00E0FE18    *....TWOCALL....*
R00001060 00001000 40E0F4BC 00000010 90E0F9F4    *.....4.......94*
R00001070 00000000 00000000 00800E08 00E1D8F0    *.............Q0*
R00001080 C3C1D3D3 E3E6D640 000000CA 50000000    *CALLTWO....&...*
R00001090 001E8FD8 001E8FD8 00000E08 001E8FE8    *...Q...Q.......Y*
R000010A0 001E8FE8 80E0F9E6 000021B0 00E0F4B0    *...Y..9W......4.*
R000010B0 00E104B0 00E114E0 00000000 E2C3D5C4    *............SCND*
R000010C0 C3C1D3D3 00E0FE18 001E8FB8 00008650    *CALL.........f&*
R000010D0 00E102C2 0000A000 00000000 00000000    *...B............*
R000010E0 00000000 00000000 00000000 00000000    *................*
R000010F0 00000000 00000000 C1C2C3C4 00000000    *........ABCD....*
R00001100 00000000 000085E8 000052F8 0000E000    *......eY...8....*
R00001110 00000000 00000000 00000000 00000000    *................*
```

This shows that CALLTWO is the currently called program; several other fields in the SVCSECT are also useful:

22C8	Current SVCSAVE savearea
22D0	Callee name
22D8	SVC old PSW
22E8-2324	Caller's registers
2348	ABCD eyecatcher
2350	Previous SVCSAVE savearea

```
D T22C8.A0

R000022C0 00000000 00000000 00900E08 001E8FD6 F6  *..............O*
R000022D0 C3C1D3D3 E3E6D640 FFE000CC 501E8FD8      *CALLTWO ....&..Q*
R000022E0 001E8FD8 001E8FD8 00000E08 001E8FE8      *...Q...Q.......Y*
R000022F0 001E8FE8 80E0F9E6 000021B0 00E0F4B0      *...Y..9W......4.*
R00002300 00E104B0 00E114E0 00000000 E2C3D5C4      *............SCND*
R00002310 C3C1D3D3 00E0FE18 001E8FB8 00008650      *CALL.........f&*
R00002320 00E102C2 001E8FB8 00000000 00000000      *...B............*
R00002330 00000000 00000000 00000000 00000000      *................*
R00002340 00000000 00000000 C1C2C3C4 00000000      *........ABCD....*
R00002350 000021B0 000086B8 00000000 00000400      *......f.........*
R00002360 00000000 00000000 00000000 00000000      *................*
```

Examine the callee's address, as pointed to by R12 in the callee's saved registers (at location X'2318'):

```
D T1E8FB8.30
R001E8FB0 C5D9E840 E3C9D4C5 18CF900F D00047F0 E6  *ERY TIME.......O*
R001E8FC0 C012E2C3 D5C4C3C1 D3D34120 C0301BFF      *..SCNDCALL......*
```

Now look at the previous SVCSAVE savearea, at X'21B0':

21B4	Address of SVC issuer
21B8	Callee name (routine being invoked)
21D0-21FC	Caller's registers
2230	Eyecatcher

```
D T21B0.A0
R000021B0 00900E08 001E801E E2C3D5C4 C3C1D3D3 F6  *........SCNDCALL*
R000021C0 FFE000CC 501E8020 001E8020 001E8020      *....&...........*
R000021D0 00000E08 001E8030 001E8030 80E0F9E6      *..............9W*
R000021E0 00002098 00E0F4B0 00E104B0 00E114E0      *...q..4.........*
R000021F0 00000000 C6C9D9E2 E3C3C1D3 00E0FE18      *....FIRSTCAL....*
R00002200 001E8000 000085E8 00E102C2 001E8000      *......Ey...B....*
R00002210 00000000 00000000 00000000 00000000      *................*
R00002220 to 00002230 suppressed line(s) same as above ....
R00002230 C1C2C3C4 000022C8 00002098 00008650      *ABCD...H...q..f&*
R00002240 00000004 00000000 00000000 00000000      *................*
```

Again, examine the callee's address, as pointed to by R12 in the callee's registers (at location X'2200'):

```
D T1E8000.40
R001E8000 18CF900F D00047F0 C012C6C9 D9E2E3C3 E6 *.......0..FIRSTC*
R001E8010 C1D34120 C0301BFF 181256F0 C0400ACC    *AL.........0...*
R001E8020 980FD000 0AC90001 00000000 00000000    *q....I..........*
R001E8030 E2C3D5C4 C3C1D3D3 FFFFFFFF FFFFFFFF    *SCNDCALL........*
```

The user savearea pointer is at offset X'8C' in SAVESAVE (location X'223C'); this contains X'8650'. Display that savearea:

```
D T8650.60
R00008650 00000E08 001E8030 001E8030 80E0F9E6 E6 *..............9W*
R00008660 000021B0 00E0F4B0 00E104B0 00E114E0    *......4.........*
R00008670 00000000 E2C3D5C4 C3C1D3D3 00E0FE18    *....SCNDCALL....*
R00008680 001E8FB8 00008650 00E102C2 001E8FB8    *......f&...B....*
R00008690 00000000 00000000 00000000 00000000    *................*
R000086A0 to 000086AF suppressed line(s) same as above ....
```

R12 in that savearea is at X'8680'; examine the address that points to:

```
D T1E8FB8.50

R001E8FB0 C5D9E840 E3C9D4C5 18CF900F D00047F0 E6 *ERY TIME.......0*
R001E8FC0 C012E2C3 D5C4C3C1 D3D34120 C0301BFF    *..SCNDCALL......*
R001E8FD0 181256F0 C0400ACC 980FD000 0AC90001    *...0. ..q....I..*
R001E8FE0 00000000 00000000 C3C1D3D3 E3E6D640    *........CALLTWO *
R001E8FF0 FFFFFFFF FFFFFFFF 0000A000 00000000    *................*
R001E9000 00000000 C6C9D9E2 E3C3C1D3 001E8000 E6 *....FIRSTCAL....*
```

Now repeat the process one more time for the lowest-level SVCSAVE savearea, at location X'2098' (as pointed to by offset X'88' in the SVCSAVE savearea just examined). Useful offsets:

20A8	SVC old PSW
20A0	routine being called
20B0-20EC	caller's registers
2118	ABCD eyecatcher
211C	Next SVCSAVE area

```
D T2098.A0
R00002090 00000000 00000000 00900E08 00E1D4A6 F6 *..............Mw*
R000020A0 C6C9D9E2 E3C3C1D3 000000CC 50E1D4A8    *FIRSTCAL....&.My*
R000020B0 00E1D4A8 00E1D4A8 00000E08 00000848    *..My..My........*
R000020C0 00000000 001FF000 00000848 00000003    *......0.........*
R000020D0 00000848 000084C8 00001E08 001EF000    *......dH......0.*
R000020E0 00008000 000018F8 00E1CEB0 00000000    *.......8.......°*
R000020F0 90E1D2DE 0B00B000 00000000 00000000    *..K.............*
R00002100 00000000 00000000 00000000 00000000    *................*
R00002110 00000000 00000000 C1C2C3C4 000021B0    *........ABCD....*
R00002120 00000000 000085E8 000052F8 0000E000    *......eY...8....*
```

The fact that the previous SVCSAVE savearea pointer is 0 shows that this is, indeed, the lowest-level SVCSAVE.

Other useful areas in NUCON

Other NUCON pointers describe loaded programs:

LASTCMND (X'2A0') Last command issued from the CMS or XEDIT command line. It is useful in conjunction with SVC system and user saveareas to determine program flow; contains EXEC when an EXEC is invoked. This field does not necessarily contain the currently executing command: it contains the last command received *from the terminal*.

PREVCMND (X'2A8') Next-to-last command issued from the CMS or XEDIT command line. Contains EXEC when an EXEC is invoked.

LASTLMOD (X'2B0') Name of last MODULE loaded into storage by LOADMOD.

LASTTMOD (X'2C8') Name of last MODULE loaded into the transient area by LOADMOD.

NUCXCBLK (X'E3C') Pointer to start of nucleus extensions present in storage.

CMNDLIST (X'848') Tokenized parameter list: 8-byte, uppercase tokens—command, operand, options, and CMS command fence (X'FFFFFFFFFFFFFFFF').

CMDLINE   (X'740') Command as entered from the terminal.

CURRSAVE (X'528') Pointer to current SVCSAVE dynamic savearea.

Examples of using NUCON command fields

This example runs a small REXX program called TRYEXEC, which simply types a line including the invoking userid and then issues a CMS QUERY DISK A command:

```
type tryexec exec

/* */
say 'Hi' userid()
'QUERY DISK A'

Ready; T=0.01/0.03 14:44:56
tryexec
Hi KREUTER
LABEL  VDEV M  STAT  CYL TYPE BLKSIZE  FILES  BLKS USED-(%) BLKS LEFT BLK TOTAL
-      DIR  A  R/W    -   -   4096      35      -            -         -
Ready; T=0.01/0.03 14:45:02
```

After executing the REXX program, some NUCON fields contain potentially useful information;

```
2A0  LASTCMND
740  CMNDLINE
848  CMNDLIST

#CP D T2A0
R000002A0 C5E7C5C3 40404040 E3E8D7C5 40404040 F6 *EXEC      TYPE
*

#CP D T740
R00000740 A399A8F2 81F04040 40404040 40404040 F6 *tryexec           *

#CP D T840.30
R00000840 C5E7C5C3 40404040 D8E4C5D9 E8404040 F6 *EXEC      QUERY  *
R00000850 C4C9E2D2 40404040 C1404040 40404040    *DISK      A      *
R00000860 FFFFFFFF FFFFFFFF FFFFFFFF FFFFFFFF    *...............*
```

The LASTCMND field shows that the last command was EXEC; CMNDLINE contains the command typed at the terminal; and CMNDLIST contains the last command executed in that EXEC. Two fields in NUCON, LASTEXEC and PREVEXEC, do not contain meaningful information when REXX or EXEC 2 programs are executed: the fields are only filled in when programs written using the original CMS EXEC language are executed.

Next the QUERY command is removed from TRYEXEC, and the test is repeated:

```
type tryexec exec

/* */
say 'Hi' userid()
/* */

Ready; T=0.01/0.03 14:47:10
tryexec
Hi KREUTER
Ready; T=0.01/0.02 14:47:13

#CP D T2A0
R000002A0 C5E7C5C3 40404040 E3E8D7C5 40404040 F6 *EXEC      TYPE   *

#CP D T740
R00000740 A399A8F2 81F04040 40404040 40404040 F6 *tryexec           *

#CP D T840.20
R00000840 C5E7C5C3 40404040 E3D9E8F2 C1F04040 F6 *EXEC      TRYEXEC*
R00000850 FFFFFFFF FFFFFFFF C5E7C5C3 40404040    *........EXEC   *
```

The results are the same, except that since no other CMS commands were executed by TRYEXEC, the CMNDLIST field contains TRYEXEC followed by the CMS command fence.

If the called command is a MODULE, the results are similar. The next example runs TRY MODULE, which calls ABC MODULE:

```
2A0    LASTCMND
2C0    LASTTMOD
740    CMNDLINE
848    CMNDLIST


try
Ready; T=0.01/0.03 14:48:00

#CP D T2A0
R000002A0 E3D9E840 40404040 C5E7C5C3 40404040 F6 *TRY       EXEC      *

#CP D T2C0
R000002C0 C1C2C340 40404040 E3E8D7C5 40404040    *ABC       TYPE      *

#CP D T740
R00000740 A399A840 40404040 40404040 40404040 F6 *try                 *

#CP D T840
R00000840 C5E7C5C3 40404040 E3D9E840 40404040 F6 *EXEC      TRY       *
```

Since TRY is not an EXEC, it appears in LASTCMND; since ABC is loaded after TRY, it appears in LASTLMOD.

CMS Processing of Program Interrupts

When CMS is notified by the architecture (CP, really) of a program interrupt, program check routine DMSITP, is invoked. DMSITP places the program old PSW and contents of general purpose registers at ABEND into two control blocks, PGMSECT and ABWSECT. When an application ABENDs on a program check, DMSITP displays a message at the virtual machine console. Do not rely on the information returned from a CP DISPLAY G command at this point: these registers have been used by ABEND processors. The relevant register contents are available in PGMSECT and ABWSECT areas.

Once again, NUCON points to blocks involved in debugging:

APGMSECT (location X'654') Points to PGMSECT.

AABWSECT (location X'C98') Points to the ABEND work section (ABWSECT). The ABEND work section is useful during all CMS ABENDs. The CMS ABEND handler fills in this block during its processing. In most cases, ABWSECT contains the meaningful registers at the instant of problem occurrence.

Since a program check is presented by the architecture, it is also important to examine low memory hardware information. This information in NUCON is the instruction length code, interrupt code, and program old PSW.

This example shows where the low core information for a program interrupt resides:

```
370 BC-mode machine (PSW bit 12 is 0):
PGMOPSW (Program old PSW):   X'28'  8-byte field.
Program interrupt code:      PGMOPSW bits 16-31
Instruction length code:     PGMOPSW bits 32-33

370 EC-mode, 370/XA-mode, and 370/ESA-mode machines:
PGMOPSW (Program old PSW):   X'28'  8-byte field.
Program interrupt code:      X'8E'  2-byte field.
Instruction length code:     X'8C'  Bits 13-14 meaningful.
```

The bits of the ILC represent in halfwords the length to be decremented from the address portion of PGMOPSW:

```
ILC bits    Halfwords
00          Not applicable
01          One halfword
10          Two halfwords
11          Three halfwords
```

Since CMS virtual machines may be of different architectures, debuggers must be aware of the current architecture. The CP QUERY SET command returns the current machine mode.

The following scenario shows the same program check (a protection exception) from PROGIT MODULE in different architectures. In this example, the DISPLAY command reveals register and storage contents.

```
progit
DMSITP141T Protection exception occurred at 02000E in routine PROGIT
CMS

* The registers AFTER the message are not related to the problem!
#CP D G
GPR  0 =  00000000  00008094  C3D6D5F1  00001368
GPR  4 =  00000000  00000000  00000028  00000000
GPR  8 =  0000026C  00003E40  00000028  000045E8
GPR 12 =  00E1A918  00006884  40E0E782  00E1A918
```

```
* The ABWSECT contains the registers at time of ABEND:
#CP D c98
R00000C98 00006838                              F6
```

```
* 6838 is the ABWSECT; the registers are at the beginning
* (note that since DISPLAY with translation always starts at a
* quadword boundary, the registers start 8 bytes into the display):
#CP D t6838.120
R00006830 00E57D94 00000000 00000E08 0B000848 F6 *.V'm............*
R00006840 00000848 80E0F9E6 00002098 00E0F4B0    *......9W...q..4.*
R00006850 00E104B0 00E114E0 00000000 00001000    *................*
R00006860 C9E34040 00E0FE18 00020000 000085E8    *IT  .........eY*
R00006870 00E102C2 00020000 FFE000C4 A002000E    *...B.......D....*
R00006880 90F0430C 50F052E4 8702FF5C 85C20000    *.0..&0.Ug..*eB..*
R00006890 00000006 007200E6 BEA80570 00006688    *.......W.y.....h*
R000068A0 027200E6 BEAA0570 00006684 0AE20000    *...W.......d.S..*
R000068B0 20A00800 00000000 00000740 001EF000    *...........0....*
R000068C0 00008058 00F03DC0 00F04DC0 44C4D4E2    *.....0...0(..DMS*
R000068D0 C9E3D7F1 F4F1E340 D79996A3 8583A389    *ITP141T Protecti*
R000068E0 96954085 A7838597 A3899695 40968383    *on exception occ*
R000068F0 A4999985 844081A3 40F0F2F0 F0F0C540    *urred at 02000E *
R00006900 89954099 96A4A389 958540D7 D9D6C7C9    *in routine PROGI*
R00006910 E3404040 40404040 40404040 40404040    *T              *
R00006920 40404040 40404040 40404040 00000000    *            ....*
```

Display the program old PSW:

```
#CP D PSW PROG
PRG 0004  28 OLD FFE00004 A002000E   68  NEW 00000000 00E6B6B8
```

Display APGMSECT from NUCON:

```
#CP D 654
R00000654 00006628                              F6
```

Important PGMSECT values:

7C	registers at time of ABEND
58	PGMOPSW
60	ILC and interrupt code

```
#CP D T6628.120
R00006620 00F06278 00000000 00000000 00000000 F6 *.0..............*
R00006630 00000000 00000000 C5D7C9C5 00000000    *........EPIE....*
R00006640 00000E08 0B000848 00000848 80E0F9E6    *..............9W*
R00006650 00002098 00E0F4B0 00E104B0 00E114E0    *...q..4.........*
R00006660 00000000 00001000 C9E34040 00E0FE18    *.........IT ....*
R00006670 00020000 000085E8 00E102C2 00020000    *......eY...B....*
R00006680 FFE00004 A002000E 00040004 00000000    *................*
R00006690 00000000 00000000 00000000 00000000    *................*
R000066A0 00000000 00000E08 0B000848 00000848    *................*
R000066B0 80E0F9E6 00002098 00E0F4B0 00E104B0    *..9W...q..4.....*
R000066C0 00E114E0 00000000 00001000 C9E34040    *...........IT  *
R000066D0 00E0FE18 00020000 000085E8 00E102C2    *..........eY...B*
R000066E0 00020000 00000000 00000000 00000000    *................*
```

```
R000066F0 00000000 00000000 00000000 00000000   *................*
R00006700 to 0000674F suppressed line(s) same as above ....
```

The ILC is stored at different locations, depending on the hardware architecture being emulated. In a 370-mode virtual machine:

```
progit
DMSITP141T Protection exception occurred at 02000E in routine PROGIT
CMS

#CP Q set
:
MACHINE 370, SVC76 CP, NOPDATA OFF, IOASSIST OFF
CCWTRAN ON
```

The DISPLAY PSW PROG instruction shows the old and new program PSWs, and the interrupt code. Note PSW bit 12 is 0, indicating BC-mode:

```
#CP D PSW PROG
PRG 0004  28 OLD FFE00004 A002000E   68  NEW 00000000 00E6B6B8
```

The failing instruction:

```
#CP D i2000a
R0002000A ST    50C90000                              E6
```

This is an approach in an ESA-mode machine:

```
progit
DMSITP141T Protection exception occurred at 0002000E in routine PROGIT
CMS

#CP Q set
:
MACHINE ESA, SVC76 CP, NOPDATA OFF, IOASSIST OFF
CCWTRAN ON
```

Examine the program old PSW. PSW bit 12 is 1, so the virtual machine must be in ESA or XA mode:

```
#CP d 28.8
R00000028 03EC2000 0002000E                        F6

#CP D PSW PROG

PRG 0004  28 OLD 03EC2000 0002000E   68  NEW 00080000 80E6B6B8
```

Location X'8C' contains the instruction length and program interrupt; Bits 13–14 at X'8C' are 10 meaning an ILC of two halfwords.

The X'0004' at location X'8E' indicates the program interrupt code: a protection exception (program interrupt 4):

```
#CP D 8c
R0000008C 00040004                                    F6
```

Structure of CMS Storage Management

CMS provides storage management services for its routines and user programs. CMS manages storage in **subpools**. A subpool is a unique name associated with a grouping of storage. All of CMS storage is assigned to a subpool. Subpools are mapped by the SUBBK control block.

CMS tracks the use of all 4096-byte storage pages by an indexable series of STOBKs (storage origin blocks). The collection of STOBKs is referred to as the **Page Allocation Table**, or **PAT**.

SUBBKs and STOBKs reside in the FRWRK block, which is the master storage management control block. The STDEBUG, STORMAP, and SUBPMAP CMS commands provide powerful windows into the current status of FRWRK.

> STDEBUG   Provides dynamic displays of storage obtains and releases
>
> STORMAP   Reports on use of storage (STOBK) of particular storage ranges
>
> SUBPMAP   Reports existence and details of subpools

The most exciting new facility in VM/ESA debugging is the EXTSET option available on STORMAP and SUBPMAP. This option permits a virtual machine to go from a virtual stopped state (CP READ) to CMS, report some information, and return to the CP READ. This has never existed in VM.

Once again, it is architecture—defined by the hardware, provided by CP—that facilitates this scenario. When an external interrupt is fielded, a PSW swap occurs. A virtual external interrupt with a specific code is generated by issuing the CP class G EXTERNAL command.

When STORMAP or SUBPMAP are issued with the EXTSET option, the CMS FLIH for external interrupts returns control to STORMAP or SUBPMAP. The routine can then perform its work, and display results at the console.

By combining these CMS commands with CP class G tracing facilities (TRACE, DISPLAY, and STORE) insightful debugging of storage problems is possible.

The following example shows use of commands to debug a CMS problem. The STORIT MODULE exemplifies a standard CMS application approach:

- Runs as a MODULE in the user area (location X'20000') on first invocation.
- Obtains user free storage in which to house itself in for subsequent calls.
- Copies itself to the acquired storage using move character long (MVCL); this is referred to as **self-relocating** code.
- Declares itself as a nucleus extension at the obtained storage address.
- Calls itself to run as a nucleus extension.
- Subsequent calls run from the nucleus extension: the MODULE version will never be used again unless explicitly LOADMODEd.

STORIT MODULE runs successfully only on first invocation (when loaded as a MODULE, and on the first self-invocation as a nucleus extension). When subsequently invoked as a nucleus extension, an operation exception program check results.

The annotated console log extract shows the use of the storage management debug commands.

```
* Self load, NUCEXT, runs once...
storit
This routine is running from: 001E5000
Ready; T=0.01/0.02 15:08:31
```

The NUCXMAP command tells us where STORIT is located at:

```
nucxmap storit
Name       Entry     Userword Origin   Bytes    Amode (Attributes)
STORIT     001E5000  00000000 001E5000 0000001D   24
Ready; T=0.01/0.02 15:08:34
```

When invoked as a nucleus extension, an operation exception occurs:

```
storit
DMSITP141T Operation exception occurred at 1E5002 in routine STORIT
CMS

* After an IPL CMS....
storit
This routine is running from: 001E5000
```

```
Ready; T=0.01/0.02 15:18:14
nucxmap storit
Name      Entry    Userword Origin  Bytes   Amode (Attributes)
STORIT    001E5000 00000000 001E5000 000000E8   24
Ready; T=0.01/0.02 15:18:20
```

The address shown does does not look like a likely address for
USER storage. CMS reserves subpools starting with DMS for internal
routines:

```
stormap 1e5000.e8
                              Storage Map
                              ------- ---

Address Range: 001E5000 - 001E50E7

Subpool   Start     End      Bytes    Pages  Key  Attributes
DMSUSRM   001E5000  001E5EAF 00000EB0     p   E0   ALLOC    GLOBAL
Ready; T=0.02/0.06 15:18:32

nucxmap storit
Name      Entry    Userword Origin  Bytes   Amode (Attributes)
STORIT    001E5000 00000000 001E5000 000000E8   24
Ready; T=0.01/0.01 15:20:14

* The Class G CP DISPLAY command has a disassembler:

* There are no valid instructions present!
#CP D I1E5000.E8
R001E5000 ***** 0000       ***** 0000       ***** 0000
  E4
R001E5006 to 001E50E4 suppressed line(s) same as above ....
R001E50E4 ***** 0000       ***** 0000       ***** 0000
```

After another IPL CMS, notice the different address used by
STORIT:

```
nucxmap storit
Name      Entry    Userword Origin  Bytes   Amode (Attributes)
STORIT    001E8000 00000000 001E8000 000000E8   24
Ready; T=0.01/0.01 15:29:30
```

STORMAP still does not think of it as USER storage:

```
stormap 1e8000.e8
                              Storage Map
                              ------- ---

Address Range: 001E8000 - 001E80E7

Subpool   Start     End      Bytes    Pages  Key  Attributes
          001E8000  001E8FFF 00001000     1   --   UNALLOC
Ready; T=0.01/0.04 15:29:38

* Cannot even drop it properly:
nucxdrop storit
DMSFRR161E Invalid free storage release call from 0000E278,
```

```
           error code 6
DMSNXD617E Error code 6 from CMSSTOR RELEASE while unloading
           STORIT module
Ready(00003); T=0.01/0.01 15:29:52
```

After another IPL CMS, observe the results after loading the
module version and dynamically tracing storage acquisition from
within the program's range.

```
loadmod storit
Ready; T=0.01/0.01 15:53:14
progmap
Name       Entry       Origin      Bytes       Attributes
STORIT     00020000    00020000    00000208    Amode 24   Non-reloc
Ready; T=0.01/0.01 15:53:17
modmap storit
STORIT     00020000
SYSREF     00000600
NUCON      00000000
Ready; T=0.01/0.03 15:53:28
```

Request dynamic displays of storage obtains and releases called
within the address range of STORIT MODULE.

```
stdebug( from 20000.1000 ob rel cons stop msg cons
Ready; T=0.01/0.02 15:53:53
storit
*                                      Bytes    Address   Subpool
Call Adress
 15:54:03  * MSG FROM KREUTER : OBTAINED 000000E8 007DB000 UsEr
 0002003A
B
This routine is running from: 007DB000
Ready; T=0.01/0.03 15:54:17
```

Notice that it matches the origin and byte size of the nucleus
extension:

```
nucxmap storit
Name       Entry     Userword Origin    Bytes    Amode (Attributes)
STORIT     007DB000  00000000 007DB000  000000E8   24
Ready; T=0.01/0.01 15:55:22
```

It is no longer the subpool we worked with:

```
stormap 7db000.e8
                              Storage Map
                              ------- ---


Address Range: 007DB000 - 007DB0E7

Subpool    Start      End        Bytes     Pages   Key Attributes
DMSUSRM    007DB000   007DBEAF   00000EB0   p      E0   ALLOC    GLOBAL
Ready; T=0.01/0.04 15:55:36
```

This extract highlights the STORMAP command with the EXTSET operand used in conjunction with the CP EXTERNAL command. The STORIT MODULE is traced using the CP class G trace command, with instructions executed in the storage addresses of STORIT being the targets.

This approach will instruct CMS to pass external interrupt code 1 to STORMAP and show how storage is used in conjunction with tracing instructions from MODULE invocation.

The STORMAP command will be sensitive to external interrupt code 1:

```
stormap ( all extset 1
Ready; T=0.01/0.03 15:58:31
loadmod storit
Ready; T=0.01/0.02 15:58:46
```

PROGMAP command shows the location and length of TEXT or MODULE currently loaded:

```
progmap
Name        Entry       Origin      Bytes        Attributes
STORIT      00020000    00020000    00000208     Amode 24   Non-reloc
Ready; T=0.01/0.01 15:58:51
```

The TRACE instruction will stop after every instruction between X'20000'–X'20020' is executed:

```
#CP TR I R 20000.208
start
DMSLIO740I Execution begins...
 -> 00020000  LR    18CF         CC 0
B
    00020002  LA    4120001D  = 0000001D   CC 0
B
    00020006  NOPR  0700         CC 0
B
    00020008  LA    41F0C010  = 00020010   CC 0
B
    0002000C  B     47F0C030 -> 00020030   CC 0
B
 -> 00020030  LR    1802         CC 0
B
    00020032  LR    181F         CC 0
B
    00020034  SR    1BFF         CC 0
B
    00020036  ICM   BFF4C200     00020200   CC 1
B
```

When SVC 204 is issued, GPR1 points to the tokenized plist:

```
    0002003A  SVC   0ACC      -> 00E0F4B6   CC 0
```

Display the registers and then the contents of the location addressed by general purpose register 1:

```
D G
GPR  0 =  0000001D  00020010  0000001D  000085E8
GPR  4 =  000001F4  001E5000  40E46F76  00000850
GPR  8 =  00E46B50  00E44930  E3404040  00E46B50
GPR 12 =  00020000  000085E8  00E102C2  00C00000
```

The contents of register 1 point to DMSFROSV, the manager for free storage obtains:

```
D T20010.40
R00020010 C4D4E2C6 D9D6E2E5 E4A2C599 40404040 E6 *DMSFROSVUsEr       *
R00020020 00000000 00000000 00000000 80080000    *................*
R00020030 1802181F 1BFFBFF4 C2000ACC 12FF4770    *........4B.......*
R00020040 C0A61830 89300003 18931821 18824140    *.w..i....1...b. *
B
    0002003C  LTR    12FF          CC 0
B
    0002003C  LTR    12FF          CC 0
D G0.2
GPR  0 =  0000001D  007DE000
* 7DE000 IS STORAGE LOCATION
```

This is the CP Class G EXTERNAL command. The operand 1 will generate external interrupt 1. Notice the storage at 7DE000 is from subpool UsEr:

```
D P

* Notice that the PSW is enabled for External interrupts (bit 7 is 1):
PSW = FFE40080 4002003E

EXTERNAL 1
:
NUCLEUS    007DB990  007DB9EF  00000060   p  F0  UNALLOC
NUCLEUS    007DB9F0  007DBFFF  00000610   p  F0  ALLOC   GLOBAL SYSTEM
           007DC000  007DCFFF  00001000   1  --  UNALLOC
NUCLEUS    007DD000  007DDFFF  00001000   1  F0  ALLOC   GLOBAL SYSTEM
UsEr       007DE000  007DE0E7  000000E8   p  E0  ALLOC          PRIVATE
UsEr       007DE0E8  007DEFFF  00000F18   p  E0  UNALLOC
DMSCRREB   007DF000  007DF11F  00000120   p  E0  ALLOC   GLOBAL SYSTEM
DMSCRREB   007DF120  007DFFFF  00000EE0   p  E0  UNALLOC
DMSBLOKN   007E0000  007E0FFF  00001000   1  F0  ALLOC   GLOBAL SYSTEM
DMSSTORG   007E1000  007E166F  00000670   p  F0  ALLOC   GLOBAL SYSTEM
DMSSTORG   007E1670  007E1FDF  00000970   p  F0  UNALLOC
ht
DMSINTSP   007F7000  007FEFFF  00008000   8  F0  ALLOC   GLOBAL SYSTEM
    0002003E  BNZ   4770C0A6   000200A6   CC 0
B
    00020042  LR    1830          CC 0
B
    00020044  SLL   89300003   00000003   CC 0
B
    00020048  LR    1893          CC 0
B
```

```
      0002004A  LR    1821          CC 0
B
      0002004C  LR    1882          CC 0
B
      0002004E  LA    4140C110  =  00020110   CC 0
B
      00020052  LA    415000E1  =  000000E1   CC 0
B
```

The MVCL relocates the code to the obtained storage:

```
      00020056  MVCL  0E24          CC 2
```

The disassembler will show that there are instructions around:

```
D I7DE000.100
R007DE000 LR    18CF        ST    50ED0000    LA    41200023    E6
R007DE00A NOPR  0700        LA    41F0C014    B     47F0C034
 :
R007DE034 LR    1802        LR    181F        SR    1BFF
R007DE03A ICM   BFF4C0F1    SVC   0ACC        LR    1860
R007DE042 LR    1871        MVC   D2217001C0BE LA   41800023
R007DE04E STC   42807000    NOPR  0700        LA    4110C05C
R007DE058 B     47F0C076    ***** C4D4        ***** E2D4
 :
```

The SVC is issued to create a nucleus extension with the name
STORIT:

```
      00020096  SVC   0ACC      -> 00E0F4B6   CC 0
D G1
GPR  1 =  00020060
D T20060.40
R00020060 D5E4C3C5 E7E34040 E2E3D6D9 C9E34040 E6 *NUCEXT  STORIT  *
R00020070 00E00000 007DE000 00000000 007DE000    *.....'........'..*
R00020080 000000E8 50810014 5081001C 50910020    *...Y&a..&a..&j..*
R00020090 1BFF56F0 C1F80ACC 4110C100 1BFF56F0    *...0A8....A....0*
B
      00020098  LA    4110C100  =  00020100   CC 0
D GF
GPR 15 =  00000000
B
      0002009C  SR    1BFF          CC 0
B
      0002009E  O     56F0C1FC      000201FC   CC 1
B
```

This is where the routine calls itself, the STORIT nucleus extension
will be run. The running from message is displayed:

```
      000200A2  SVC   0ACC      -> 00E0F4B6   CC 0
D G1
GPR  1 =  00020100
D T20100.10
R00020100 E2E3D6D9 C9E34040 FFFFFFFF FFFFFFFF E6 *STORIT  ........*
```

Here is the message:

```
This routine is running from: 001E5000
     000200A4   BR     07FE      -> 00E102C2     CC 1
B
```

After the command completes, there is no subpool known as UsEr.
There are no instructions in the storage location. The storage is no
longer valid.

```
nucxmap storit
Name      Entry    Userword Origin    Bytes    Amode (Attributes)
STORIT    001E5000 00000000 001E5000 000000E8    24
Ready; T=0.01/0.01 16:06:10

#CP D I1E5000.10
R001E5000 ***** 0000         ***** 0000         ***** 0000
 E4
R001E5006 to 001E500C suppressed line(s) same as above ....
R001E500C ***** 0000         ***** 0000         ***** 0000

subpmap UsEr
                              Subpool Map
                              ------- ---

Subpool  Key  Anchor      Full      Part  Attributes
Ready(00010); T=0.01/0.03 16:07:06

subpmap USER
                              Subpool Map
                              ------- ---

Subpool  Key  Anchor      Full      Part  Attributes
USER     E0   007FFC2C       0         1  GLOBAL
Ready; T=0.01/0.03 16:07:13
```

Subpool names are case-sensitive. CMS was asked to name a
subpool UsEr. The subpool USER is a special subpool formed by CMS
during initialization, and available to user programs.

The default subpool attribute is **private**. All storage associated
with private subpools is deleted at the termination of the SVC that
invoked the routine.

This means that subpool UsEr was deleted at the end of the
MODULE invocation of STORIT. CMS then reused the storage,
although the nucleus extension STORIT was supposed to run from
that address.

Note that subpool names may contain mixed case (i.e., UsEr is a
different subpool than USER) and embedded blanks.

When changed to obtain storage from subpool USER, STORIT works
correctly, shown in this extract:

```
* Working version....changed CMSSTOR OBTAIN UsEr to OBTAIN USER:

storit
This routine is running from: 007E4ED8
Ready; T=0.01/0.02 16:09:42

nucxmap storit
Name     Entry     Userword Origin   Bytes    Amode (Attributes)
STORIT   007E4ED8  00000000 007E4ED8 000000E8   24
Ready; T=0.01/0.01 16:09:50
```

The storage now contains valid instructions:

```
#CP D I7E4ED8
R007E4ED8 LR     18CF
 E6
stormap 7e4ed8.e8

                              Storage Map
                              ------- ---


Address Range: 007E4ED8 - 007E4FBF

Subpool   Start      End      Bytes    Pages  Key  Attributes
USER      007E4ED8  007E4FFF 00000128    p    E0   ALLOC    GLOBAL
Ready; T=0.01/0.04 16:10:23

storit
This routine is running from: 007E4ED8
Ready; T=0.01/0.02 16:10:44

nucxdrop storit
Ready; T=0.01/0.01 16:10:46
```

Automatic Dump Creation in VM/ESA

CMS automatically dumps virtual machine contents under certain ABEND conditions. Automatic dumping is controlled by the CMS SET AUTODUMP command. The resulting dump file may then be processed from SPOOL by the DUMPLOAD command.

AUTODUMP consists of different settings, which indicate the type of ABENDs to dump on:

CMS   Dumps are produced upon program checks in nucleus code, nonrecoverable file system or storage management errors, and ABENDs resulting in disabled wait state PSWs.

ALL   Includes all conditions for the CMS setting, all program checks, and dumps induced by CMS ABEND or DMSABN macros in application code.

OFF   Disables automatic dump creation.

AUTODUMP also has a default setting for the amount and location of storage to be dumped. The defaults are:

- DMSNUC area (approximately the first 10 pages)
- Loader tables
- Page Allocation Table
- Selected pages of the master storage management workarea

When debugging application programs, this is inadequate, as the contents of pages that contain the user program are not dumped. To produce a dump with all pages, specify the ENTIREVM operand. ENTIREVM must follow an operand of ALL or CMS.

The following example uses the BADCODE program to illustrate different dump production settings.

```
* The default setting:
q autodump
AUTODUMP = CMS
Ready; T=0.01/0.01 14:09:31

* This program will cause an operation exception program check:
type badcode assemble

BADCODE CSECT
  LR 12,15
  DC X'00'
  END BADCODE

Ready; T=0.01/0.04 14:09:39

load badcode
Ready; T=0.01/0.02 14:09:44
```

Since BADCODE will run as a user program, no automatic dump will be produced with AUTODUMP CMS:

```
start
DMSLIO740I Execution begins...
DMSITP141T Operation exception occurred at 020004 in routine USERPGM
CMS
```

Change setting to dump on all ABENDs:

```
set autodump all
Ready; T=0.01/0.04 14:10:13
load badcode
Ready; T=0.01/0.02 14:10:17
start
DMSLIO740I Execution begins...
DMSITP141T Operation exception occurred at 020004 in routine USERPGM
DMSABE2047I Dump started; please wait
```

```
DMSABE1297I Dump has been taken
CMS
```

The resulting dump SPOOL file contains just 19 records. The file will not contain any of the pages occupied by user code.

```
q r all cl v
ORIGINID FILE CLASS RECORDS  CPY HOLD DATE  TIME       NAME     TYPE     DIST
KREUTER  0001 V DMP 00000019 001 NONE 12/03 14:10:19 VMDUMP   CMS      KREUTER
Ready;  T=0.01/0.06 14:10:26
```

Tell CMS that BADCODE is a system routine in a nucleus extension:

```
nucxload badcode ( system
Ready; T=0.01/0.01 14:11:39
q autodump
AUTODUMP = CMS
Ready; T=0.01/0.01 14:11:42
nucxmap badcode
Name      Entry    Userword Origin   Bytes   Amode (Attributes)
BADCODE   001F1D68 00000000 001F1D68 00000008  24   SYSTEM
Ready; T=0.01/0.01 14:11:57
```

Invoke it as a nucleus extension, notice the dump is produced. BADCODE is a system routine.

```
badcode
DMSITP143T Operation exception occurred at 1F1D6C in system routine
          BADCODE; re-IPL CMS
DMSABE2047I Dump started; please wait
DMSABE1297I Dump has been taken
DMSDIE3550I All APPC/VM and IUCV paths have been severed.
DMSWSP314W Automatic re-IPL by CP due to disabled wait;
          PSW 00020000 00E6BDAE
```

When run as a user nucleus extension, no dump is produced with AUTODUMP CMS:

```
q autodump
AUTODUMP = CMS
Ready; T=0.01/0.01 14:12:30
nucxload badcode
Ready; T=0.01/0.02 14:12:36
nucxmap badcode
Name      Entry    Userword Origin   Bytes   Amode (Attributes)
BADCODE   001E1000 00000000 001E1000 00000008  24
Ready; T=0.01/0.01 14:12:40
badcode
DMSITP141T Operation exception occurred at 1E1004 in routine BADCODE
CMS
```

Whatever the ABEND, AUTODUMP OFF prohibits dumps from being taken:

```
set autodump off
Ready; T=0.01/0.01 14:14:08
nucxload badcode( system
Ready; T=0.01/0.02 14:14:14
badcode
DMSITP143T Operation exception occurred at 1F1D6C in system routine
           BADCODE; re-IPL CMS
DMSDIE3550I All APPC/VM and IUCV paths have been severed.
HCPGIR450W CP entered; disabled wait PSW 00020000 00E6BDAE
```

The ENTIREVM operand produces dumps with all storage pages included:

```
q autodump
AUTODUMP = ALL ENTIREVM
Ready; T=0.01/0.01 14:34:56
badcode
DMSITP141T Operation exception occurred at 020004 in routine BADCODE
DMSABE2047I Dump started; please wait
DMSABE1297I Dump has been taken
CMS
```

The dump is 928 pages now. This includes the virtual machine storage and any attached segments.

```
q r all cl v
ORIGINID FILE CLASS RECORDS  CPY HOLD DATE  TIME       NAME      TYPE
KREUTER  0005 V DMP 00000928 001 NONE 12/03 14:35:01 VMDUMP    CMS
Ready; T=0.02/0.75 14:35:48
```

Comparison of Real-Time and Historical Debugging

This section compares two debugging approaches. The PROGEXMP program's goal is to write at the console its name and entry address, then invoke another routine, which displays its name and entry address.

PROGEXMP only displays one message, then ABENDs on a program check failure (an operation exception). An operation exception indicates that the address portion of the PSW contained an operation code that does not exist.

The online debugging approach uses CMS commands in conjunction with the CP class G architecture commands (TRACE, DISPLAY, and STORE). The historical approach uses the DVF DUMPSCAN command to analyze a dump after PROGEXMP fails. This is set up with the SET AUTODUMP ALL ENTIREVM command. In this example, a MODULE named PROGEXMP is created; when invoked, it ABENDs with a program check.

```
load progexmp
Ready;  T=0.01/0.02 13:20:23
genmod
Ready;  T=0.01/0.01 13:20:26
progexmp
This routine is running from: 00020000 PROGEXMP
DMSITP141T Operation exception occurred at 020186 in routine PROGEXMP
CMS
b
Ready;  T=0.02/0.04 13:20:33
```

In real-time debugging, the virtual machine can be stopped on a program check interrupt. The TRACE PROG command will place the virtual machine into CP READ on a program check:

```
#CP TR PROG
progexmp
This routine is running from: 00020000 PROGEXMP
 -> 00020184  ????  0002
```

The *** indicates that an interrupt is processed. X'20184' is the address of the program check, PROG 1 is the interrupt code, and X'E6B6B8' points to the first operation code of the program first level interrupt handler.

```
*** 00020184    PROG    0001 -> 00E6B6B8        OPERATION
```

The D G command shows the registers at the instant of the ABEND:

```
D G
GPR  0 =   00000038   000200D8   00000033   80E0F9E6
GPR  4 =   00002098   00E0F4B0   00000038   001E8FC8
GPR  8 =   00000032   D7D9D6C7   C5E7D4D7   00E0FE18
GPR 12 =   00020000   001E8000   0002010A   00020184
```

The D PSW PROG displays the old and new program check PSWs:

```
D PSW PROG
PRG 0001  28 OLD FFE00001 60020186   68  NEW 00000000 00E6B6B8
```

The following D I... instruction attempts to disassemble the instruction at X'20184', but there are no valid operation codes present:

```
D I20184.10
R00020184 ***** 0002        ***** 0198        ***** 0002  E6
R0002018A ***** 0318        ***** 0000        ***** 0000
R00020190 ***** 0000        ***** A000
```

X'2A0' in NUCON contains the last MODULE loaded into storage:

```
D T2A0.8
R000002A0 D7D9D6C7 C5E7D4D7 C2404040 40404040 F6 *PROGEXMPB            *
```

An online trace will be conducted. First, the MODULE is explicitly loaded without running it via the LOADMOD command.

Second, PROGMAP displays the address of the LOADMODed version of PROGEXMP.

```
loadmod progexmp
Ready; T=0.02/0.15 13:26:05

progmap
Name       Entry       Origin      Bytes       Attributes
PROGEXMP   00020000    00020000    00000328    Amode 24   Non-reloc
Ready; T=0.01/0.01 13:26:09
```

The TRACE will be of instructions in the range of PROGEXMP, X'20000' for 328 (hexadecimal) bytes:

```
#CP TR I R 20000.208
start
DMSLIO740I Execution begins...
 -> 00020000  STM   90ECD00C >> 000085F4   CC 0
```

The TRACE RUN option continues the trace without placing the virtual machine into CP READ. If there are not thousands of instruction before the program check, this is an effective way of seeing when a situation deviates from normal state.

```
TR RUN
B
      00020004  LR    18CF          CC 0
      00020006  NOPR  0700          CC 0
      00020008  LA    41F0C010  =  00020010   CC 0
      0002000C  B     47F0C030  -> 00020030   CC 0
 ->   00020030  LR    181F          CC 0
      00020032  L     5800C020     00020020   CC 0
      00020036  SR    1BFF          CC 0
      00020038  ICM   BFF4C194     00020194   CC 2
      0002003C  SVC   0ACC      -> 00E0F4B6   CC 0
 ->   000200C2  STCM  BE7F100B  >> 000200B3   CC 2
      000200C6  SR    1BFF          CC 0
      000200C8  O     56F0C190     00020190   CC 1
      000200CC  SVC   0ACC      -> 00E0F4B6   CC 0
* The message gets written, the failure occurred after this
This routine is running from: 00020000 PROGEXMP
      000200CE  NOPR  0700          CC 1
      000200D0  LA    41F0C0D8  =  000200D8   CC 1
      000200D4  B     47F0C0F8  -> 000200F8   CC 1
 ->   000200F8  LR    1806          CC 1
      000200FA  LR    181F          CC 1
      000200FC  SR    1BFF          CC 0
```

```
      000200FE  ICM    BFF4C194       00020194    CC 2
      00020102  SVC    0ACC      -> 00E0F4B6      CC 0
      00020104  LA     41F0C184   = 00020184      CC 2
      00020108  BASR   0DEF      -> 00020184      CC 2
  ->  00020184  ????   0002
  *** 00020184     PROG    0001 -> 00E6B6B8          OPERATION
  DMSITP141T Operation exception occurred at 020186 in routine USERPGM
  CMS
```

Based on the just completed trace, the last two instructions were a
LA (load address) and a BASR (branch and save register). Next, a
TRACE of instructions in an address range just prior to the program
check is initiated.

```
#CP TR i r 20100.40
loadmod progexmp
Ready; T=0.02/0.17 13:27:41
start
DMSLIO740I Execution begins...
This routine is running from: 00020000 PROGEXMP
 -> 00020102  SVC    0ACC      -> 00E0F4B6      CC 0
B
    00020104  LA     41F0C184   = 00020184      CC 2
```

The CP D I command disassembles the instruction at X'20108'. It
is a BASR. This BASR will branch to the address in register 15
(X'20184'). Register 15 was just loaded with that address.

```
D I20108
R00020108 BASR  0DEF
```

X'20184' contains an address, but does not contain instructions.

```
D T20184
R00020180 D7000000 00020198 00020318 00000000 E6 *P......q........*
```

X'20198', which has the contents of X'20184', *does* contain valid
instructions.

```
D I20198.10
R00020198 STM   90ECD00C    LR   18CF    NOPR  0700         E6
R000201A0 LA    41F0C010    B    47F0C030
D GF
GPR 15 =  00020184
```

The contents of GPR15 look suspect. What if GPR15 was modified
to contain X'20198'? The CP STORE command accomplishes this goal.

```
STORE GF 00020198
Store complete.
```

A reasonable idea is to always DISPLAY fields that were modified by the STORE instruction.

```
D GF
GPR 15 =   00020198
```

At this point, the LA instruction at X'20104' is suspected as being the failing agent.

```
B
     00020108  BASR  0DEF      -> 00020198     CC 2
B
This routine is running from: 00020198 PROGNXT1
     0002010A  LR    182D         CC 2
TR END
Trace ended
B
Ready; T=0.01/0.11 13:29:23
```

The preceding TRACE and DISPLAY showed that if GPR15 contained X'20198' prior to the BASR at X'20108', the program would have completed normally.

This example shows PROGEXMP being loaded into storage. Then, the failing instruction is changed to the correct instruction in storage.

Note the convenience of the disassembler operand (I). The modified program starts, and indeed completes successfully.

```
loadmod progexmp
Ready; T=0.02/0.05 11:04:40
progmap
Name        Entry      Origin      Bytes       Attributes
PROGEXMP    00020000   00020000    00000328    Amode 24   Non-reloc
Ready; T=0.01/0.01 11:04:42

#CP D I20104
R00020104 LA    41F0C184                                          E6

#CP STORE 20104 58F0C184
Store complete.

#CP D T20104
R00020100 C1940ACC 58F0C184 0DEF182D 58DD0004 E6 *Am...0Ad........*

#CP D I20104
R00020104 L     58F0C184                                          E6
start
DMSLIO740I Execution begins...
This routine is running from: 00020000 PROGEXMP
This routine is running from: 00020198 PROGNXT1
Ready; T=0.01/0.02 11:05:19
```

Now, the same problem will be solved using DUMPSCAN. Ensure all of virtual machine storage is dumped:

```
set autodump all entirevm
Ready; T=0.01/0.01 13:49:55
```

Generate the dump:

```
progexmp
This routine is running from: 00020000 PROGEXMP
DMSITP141T Operation exception occurred at 020186 in routine
PROGEXMP
DMSABE2047I Dump started; please wait
DMSABE1297I Dump has been taken
CMS

q r all cl v
ORIGINID FILE CLASS RECORDS  CPY HOLD DATE  TIME       NAME      TYPE
KREUTER  0006 V DMP 00000019 001 USER 12/03 14:36:16 VMDUMP     CMS
KREUTER  0005 V DMP 00000928 001 NONE 12/03 14:35:01 VMDUMP     CMS
KREUTER  0008 V DMP 00000020 001 NONE 12/04 11:13:50 VMDUMP     CMS
KREUTER  0009 V DMP 00000931 001 NONE 12/04 13:50:05 VMDUMP     CMS
Ready; T=0.02/0.80 13:50:59
ord r 9
0000001 FILE  ORDERED
Ready; T=0.01/0.01 13:51:03
dumpload noprint
HCPREDS8150I PROCESSING VM/ESA DUMP PRB00001
HCPEDS8168I VIRTUAL MACHINE DUMP, FORMAT=CMS, DUMPID=
HCPEDS8156A DO YOU WANT TO PROCESS THIS DUMP? (YES/NO)
yes
Ready; T=0.57/1.65 13:53:05
```

Now DUMPSCAN is invoked to analyze the dump.

The REGS subcommand returns old and new PSW values. Remember that the register contents are usually invalid.

```
    VM/ESA 1 - Dumpscan    PRB00000 DUMP A1    Type=VM Format=CMS

REGS

CPU ADDRESS - 0000                          PREFIX REGISTER - 00000000

GENERAL REGS  0 - 15
        00000000 000069BC 0000001B 00006838  90F0417C 00000000 00000044 000018F8
        000000C1 001EF000 00F05522 00F03DC0  00F04DC0 00006884 60F0563E 00000000
CONTROL REGS  0 - 15
        010000E2 00000000 FFFFFFFF 00000000  00000000 00000000 00000000 00000000
        00000000 00000000 00000000 00000000  00000000 00000000 C2000000 00000200
FLOATING POINT REGS  0 - 6
        00000000 00000000 00000000 00000000  00000000 00000000 00000000 00000000


TOD CLOCK         A4E4D3CB 7B48EE01          CSW 00008D10 0C000000

CLOCK COMPARATOR  00000000 00000000          CAW 00008D00

CPU TIMER         FFFFE6FB C1CD4900          PSW 00000000 80F05646

INTERVAL TIMER    00000000


EXT OLD FF040080 80E997D2  INT CODE 0080        EXT NEW 00000000 00E51288

SVC OLD FFE000CC 60020104  INT CODE 00CC ILC 0002  SVC NEW 00040000 00E0F4B6

PGM OLD FFE00001 60020186  INT CODE 0001 ILC 0002  PGM NEW 00000000 00E6B6B8

MCH OLD 00000000 00000000                       MCH NEW 00000000 00E6AFE0

I/O OLD FE040009 80E1AA50                        I/O NEW 00000000 00E0EEA8

* * * End of File * * *
```

The program old PSW minus the instruction length code: 20186 − 2 = 20184. X'20184' contains the failing instruction. The X'00' at X'20184' is the failing instruction. The fullword at X'20184' looks like it contains an address.

```
    ----> d t20184.10
    DISPLAY 20184      10
      00020180  D7000000  00020198  00020318  00000000 E6 *P......q........*
      00020190  0000A000  60000000  90ECD00C  18CF0700    *....-...........*
    ====>
```

The CMSPOINT subcommand works when dump format is CMS, and returns critical pointers from NUCON that are useful in debugging.

The SVCSECT, CURRSAVE, and PGMSECT fields are useful in program
check analysis. For program checks, CMSPOINT displays the general
purpose registers at the moment of the program check interrupt,
which CMS saves in PGMSECT.

```
    ----> cmspoint


    VM/ESA 1 - Dumpscan    PRB00000 DUMP A1      Type=VM Format=CMS
LASTCMND= PROGEXMP
PREVCMND= Q
LASTEXEC=
PREVEXEC=
CURRSAVE= 00002098
PGMSECT = 00006628
IOSECT  = 00001368
EXTSECT = 00003D20
ADTSECT = 001F5C88
DEVTAB  = 00003E40
DIOSECT = 00004728
SVCSECT = 00001000
TAXEADDR= 00000000
ALDRTBLS= 00014000
PGMOPSW = FFE00001 60020186
PSAVE R0-R3   = 00000038 000200D8 00000033 80E0F9E6
PSAVE R4-R7   = 00002098 00E0F4B0 00000038 001E8FC8
PSAVE R8-R11  = 00000032 D7D9D6C7 C5E7D4D7 00E0FE18
PSAVE R12-R15 = 00020000 001E8000 0002010A 00020184
* * * End of File * * *
```

The BLOCK subcommand is very handy. It formats an address
range with fields from a control block.

With CMS dumps, however, the DUMPSCAN version of control blocks
must be manually created (CP control blocks are provided with
DVF). Also, BLOCK has no way of knowing if the address passed is
actually that control block: it is up to the issuer to know what
control block is at the address.

BLOCK SVCSECT 1000 displays formatted fields:

* SVC depth (number of SVC levels active) is 1
* Current SVC savearea is at X'2098'

```
VM/ESA 1 - Dumpscan   PRB00000 DUMP A1    Type=VM Format=CMS


                 BLOCK  'SVCSECT '  AT LOCATION  1000


ADDR/OFF  NAME          CONTENTS            DESCRIPTION
00001000  SVCSECT       0000000000000000
00001000  USVCTBL       00000000            A 'HANDLE' FOR THE FOLLOWING

                                            ...
00001000  JNUMB         00000000            NO. OF DBL WORDS IN SVC
                                            NUMBER TABLE
00001004  JFIRST        00000000            ADDRESS OF FIRST ITEM (IF
                                            ANY) IN TABLE
00001008  SVCJFLEN      0000000C            (FOR BXLE)
0000100C  JLAST         00000000            ADDRESS OF LAST ITEM IN TABLE
00001010  SFLAG         04                  FLAG BYTE
00001011  *             00                  UNUSED
00001012  SVCAB         0000                SVC ABEND CODE IF ANY
00001014  CURRALOC      00002098            CURRENT ALLOCATED SAVEAREA
00001018  LASTALOC      00002098            LAST ALLOCATED SAVEAREA
0000101C  DEPTH         00000001            NESTED SVC DEPTH
00001020  ADMSOVS       00000000            ADDRESS OF DMSOVS
00001024  OVBPF         0000                'BEFORE PRINT' FLAGS
00001026  OVBTF         0000                'BEFORE TYPE' FLAGS
====>
```

The field following check word ABCD points to a savearea at X'21B0'.

```
        VM/ESA 1 - Dumpscan    PRB00000 DUMP A1     Type=VM Format=CMS
        DISPLAY 2098
        00002090  00000000   00000000   0090FFFA   00E1D4A6 F6   *..............Mw*
        000020A0  D7D9D6C7   C5E7D4D7   000000CC   50E1D4A8      *PROGEXMP....&.My*
        000020B0  00E1D4A8   00E1D4A8   00000E08   00000848      *..My..My........*
        000020C0  00000000   001FF000   00000848   00000000      *.......0.........*
        000020D0  00000848   000084C8   00001E08   001EF000      *.......dH......0.*
        000020E0  00008000   000018F8   00E1CEB0   00000000      *........8........*
        000020F0  B0E1D2DE   0B00B000   00000000   00000000      *..K..............*
        00002100  00000000   00000000   00000000   00000000      *.................*
        00002110  00000000   00000000   C1C2C3C4   000021B0      *........ABCD....*
        00002120  00000000   000085E8   000052F8   0000E000      *......eY...8....*
        00002130  00000000   00000000   00000000   00000000      *.................*
        00002140  00000000   C5C6C7C8   00000000   90000000      *....EFGH........*
```

The display continues with these important fields:

- The CALLEE field at X'21B8' shows that DMSFRRSV was the callee.
- The CALLER field at X'21B4' shows that address X'20102' contained the SVC instruction.

```
        VM/ESA 1 - Dumpscan    PRB00000 DUMP A1     Type=VM Format=CMS
        DISPLAY 21B0
        000021B0  000022C8   00020102   C4D4E2C6   D9D9E2E5 F6   *...H....DMSFRRSV*
        000021C0  FFE000CC   60000000   00020104   00020104      *....-..........*
        000021D0  00000038   000200D8   00000033   80E0F9E6      *.......Q......9W*
        000021E0  00002098   00E0F4B0   00000038   001E8FC8      *...q..4........H*
        000021F0  00000032   D7D9D6C7   C5E7D4D7   00E0FE18      *....PROGEXMP....*
        00002200  00020000   001E8000   00E102C2   00000000      *...........B....*
        00002210  00000000   00000000   00000000   00000000      *.................*
        00002220  00000000   00000000   00000000   00000000      *.................*
        00002230  C1C2C3C4   00000000   00002098   00008650      *ABCD.......q..f&*
        00002240  00000004   00000000   00000000   00000000      *.................*
        00002250  00000000   00000000   00000000   C5C6C7C8      *...........EFGH*
```

The SVCSECT also contains information concerning the last module loaded into storage:

- Offset X'334' into SVCSECT at X'1000' contains the program entry point
- X'20000' was the entry point

```
   ----> d 1334.10
 DISPLAY 1334      10
   00001330  00000000  00020000  00000000  40000000  F6  *...............*
   00001340  00000000  00002098  80000000  00000038      *.......q........*
```

Now, it has been established that:

- X'6628' is the PGMSECT
- X'7C' into PGMSECT contains the registers at ABEND time
- X'6628' + X'7C' is X'66A4'
- X'66D4' contains X'0002000' which is the value in register 12 at the program check
- X'66DC' contains X'2010A' which is the value in register 14 at the program check
- X'66E0' contains X'00020184' in register 15—the address of the failing instruction

```
 ====>
    VM/ESA 1 - Dumpscan    PRB00000 DUMP A1    Type=VM Format=CMS
 DISPLAY 6628
    000066A0  00000000  00000038  000200D8  00000033 F6  *...........Q....*
    000066B0  80E0F9E6  00002098  00E0F4B0  00000038     *..9W...q..4.....*
    000066C0  001E8FC8  00000032  D7D9D6C7  C5E7D4D7     *...H....PROGEXMP*
    000066D0  00E0FE18  00020000  001E8000  0002010A     *................*
    000066E0  00020184  00000000  00000000  00000000     *...d............*
    000066F0  00000000  00000000  00000000  00000000     *................*
    00006700  00000000  00000000  00000000  00000000     *................*
    00006710  00000000  00000000  00000000  00000000     *................*
    00006720  00000000  00000000  00000000  00000000     *................*
    00006730  00000000  00000000  00000000  00000000     *................*
    00006740  00000000  00000000  00000000  00000000     *................*
    00006750  00000000  00000000  00000000  00000000     *................*
    00006760  00000000  00000000  00000000  00000000     *................*
 ====>
```

At this point, there was a processed SVC at X'20102'. At the program check time, register 15 contained X'20184', which was the failing instruction.

The display of the storage around that area is now useful:

- X'20102' contains X'0ACC' (SVC 204, which was processed)
- X'20104' contains X'41F0C184', which is a LA instruction; it will load into register 15 the address formed by adding the contents of register 12 to X'184'
- Register 12 contains X'20000' plus X'184' = X'20184'
- X'20108' contains X'0DEF' which is a BASR
- X'20184' contains X'20198'
- X'20198' contains a valid instruction

The BASR instruction at X'20108' will save the address of the next instruction into register 14 (X'2018A') and branch to the address in register 15 (X'20184'). This is the reason for the program check, as the instruction should have been a load instruction to place the contents of X'20184' into register 15.

There is no disassembler provided by DUMPSCAN: operation codes must be manually decoded.

```
VM/ESA 1 - Dumpscan   PRB00000 DUMP A1    Type=VM Format=CMS
DISPLAY 20102
   00020100  C1940ACC  41F0C184  0DEF182D  58DD0004 E6   *Am...0Ad........*
   00020110  41F0C118  47F0C138  C4D4E2C6  D9D9E2E5       *.0A..0A.DMSFRRSV*
   00020120  40404040  40404040  00000060  00000000       *         ..-....*
   00020130  00000002  08020000  181F5800  C1281BFF       *............A...*
   00020140  BFF4C194  0ACC98EC  D00C1FFF  07FE4040       *.4Am..q.......  *
   00020150  E38889A2  409996A4  A3899585  4089A240       *This routine is *
   00020160  99A49595  89958740  86999694  7A4050F1       *running from: &1*
   00020170  40404040  40404040  40D7D9D6  C7C5E7D4       *         PROGEXM*
   00020180  D7000000  00020198  00020318  00000000       *P......q........*
   00020190  0000A000  60000000  90ECD00C  18CF0700       *....-...........*
   000201A0  41F0C010  47F0C030  C4D4E2C6  D9D6E2E5       *.0...0..DMSFROSV*
   000201B0  E4E2C5D9  40404040  00000060  00000000       *USER     ...-....*
====>
```

The same program check has been solved by using two different approaches, real-time versus historical. Real-time debugging suits many situations well, especially with the combining of CMS and CP commands.

By understanding fundamental concepts of CMS program management and concentrating attention on a handful of control blocks, determining program flow is a straightforward debugging process. The most important control block, and one certainly full of pointers in any CMS problem situation, is NUCON.

Since standard for CMS virtual machines only have CP class G privileges, the TRACE, DISPLAY, and STORE commands are available to all users for debugging. As a single-tasking environment, tracing SVC instructions in application code simply and powerfully illustrates which supervisor services an application requires and uses.

For each program call SVC, the SVC manager obtains a dynamic SVC system savearea. Even without a formal trace table, chaining through these saveareas establishes application-to-supervisor flow. A practice accepted in the CMS development community is to bypass the SVC processor by fetching pointers to control blocks and routines directly from NUCON. In the past, this practice has eliminated CP overhead incurred when simulating virtual machine SVC instructions.

In VM/ESA, CMS SVCs are emulated by the interpretive execution architecture, eliminating CP SVC simulation overhead.

Therefore, in order to provide meaningful data in storage, it is recommended that application code use standard SVC linkages. Determining application and supervisor flow without the SVC system saveareas is extremely difficult when branch linkage is used.

A small yet informative online approach to application debugging and behavior studies is to issue this command prior to invoking applications:

```
#CP TRACE SVC CA-CC CMD DISPLAY T0.40;BASE1
```

When the virtual machine enters CP READ, and the interrupt code is X'CA' or X'CC', general purpose register 1 addresses the parameter list. The ;BASE1 operand uses the contents of register 1 as a starting point to display; in this way the command requested is always shown.

The introduction of the storage management debug commands STDEBUG, STORMAP, and SUBPMAP is a huge addition to the debugging arsenal. These commands provide strong diagnostics for storage management problems. Storage management problems have been difficult to debug, as the problem may arise long after the aberrant program has exited and a Ready; prompt has been displayed. There had not been any high-level facilities until VM/ESA for storage management debugging. The CMS macro interface for debugging storage problems available in CMS 5 (DMSFRES) was cumbersome to invoke and not terribly informative.

With the CMS real-time debug lexicon of program management commands (PROGMAP, NUCXMAP), CP class G commands, and the storage management commands, CMS provides a comprehensive set of online debugging facilities.

Historical debugging with DUMPSCAN is a reasonable approach to solving problems, yet is not quite as attractive as real-time debugging. Some situations, such as full-screen applications, still require dump analysis. CP console function commands interfere with the data streams used in full-screen writes, so it is necessary to produce and process dumps in these situations, and then analyze them with DUMPSCAN or a similar product.

The DUMPSCAN full-screen with its strong XEDIT connection is a comfortable debugging environment. One of DUMPSCAN's major strengths is automatic recording of subcommands and resulting displays when the issuer SAVEs or FILEs to end the session. This file, which receives the same filename as the dump, with filetype DUMPVIEW, is restored when the dump is subsequently viewed with DUMPSCAN.

DVF's BLOCK subcommand, which "templates" control blocks online, is a helpful aid. However, DVF does not include a file of CMS control blocks (a file of most CP control blocks are provided), and the CMS DVF blocks must thus be manually created by the user.

The supplied BLOCKDEF EXEC supposedly allows creating the CMS DVF blocks, with input of the CMS macro libraries. However, it is necessary to edit the raw CMS control blocks extensively before BLOCKDEF will produce a correct set of CMS DVF blocks.

Despite the obstacles in procedurally establishing a reasonable DVF environment for CMS dumps, dump analysis is worthwhile and effective. By understanding control blocks and key anchor pointers, it is straightforward to solve problems with DUMPSCAN.

DUMPSCAN also provides a macro interface, enabling creation of REXX routines for CMS debugging.   DUMPSCAN provides subcommands for transferring data from the DVF session to the interpreter environment.

Diagnostic capabilities intrinsic to CMS virtual machines complement CMS interactive strengths tremendously. Many facilities are also expandable through macros and advanced combinations of CP and CMS commands.

The CMS operating system has traditionally been a powerful interactive end-user mainframe environment. The facilities have matured over release levels of VM, and continue to improve with the VM evolution.

With a choice of real-time or historical debugging available, the CMS programmer has a vast array of techniques and tools to employ in problem solving.

VM/ESA Resources

This section describes VM/ESA information sources and tools, including other publications, classroom and self-guided training, and softcopy publications.

25

Initial Training and Continuing Education

By David J. Chase

Understanding the way an operating system works in a variety of situations is vital to system programmers, system administrators, applications programmers, and end-users. As systems become more complex, it is clear that education must never stop, but must continue while an individual is associated with a particular system. Many people think only about traditional classroom training when education is being considered, but this is not the only way knowledge can be obtained. Education is available from numerous sources for all the different types of people who use a VM/ESA system.

Other chapters in this book describe in detail features and functions of VM/ESA systems. This chapter adds a description of where education is available in different forms, and suggests how different people with varied backgrounds can learn what they want and need to know about VM/ESA.

Types of Education

Three main types of educational possibilities are available. Documentation in the form of manuals and online HELP usually comes with a product, but other sources of information such as books and magazine articles can be obtained separately. Formal training can come from a traditional classroom either away from the work location or nearby, or from self-studies which students practice at home or in the office. VM user groups exist around the country and the world, offering students the chance to receive information from others with the same or a similar jobs.

Documentation

Documentation in the form of material to be read from the printed page or the terminal screen is available from different sources and in different forms.

Manuals

Education consists of much more than simply the traditional classroom training that many people think of first. Often the earliest educational experience is opening a product manual and reading about how to install or initialize a program. Manuals are often scorned as a source of education by people who want a more structured introduction to a product. They contain tremendous amounts of information, but they are usually arranged for reference, not for teaching. Luckily, this is not the case for VM/ESA, which has an extensive library, including many manuals specifically designed to educate users with varying needs.

End-users, who may have never used a VM system before, will find primers designed especially for them, including exercises which they can practice at their terminals. System programmers and administrators have available several manuals designed to give them introductory information for the product as well as special manuals for experienced users who only need to know what has changed since the last release. Applications programmers can use developer's guides in addition to system programming manuals to learn how best to exploit the features of VM/ESA.

HELP files

Another type of documentation often neglected is online HELP files. HELP information is duplicated in printed manuals, but often those manuals are not available to everyone who might need them. Online HELP files are as close as the terminal and are very useful when a certain command or procedure is not working as expected. Hierarchical arrangement of information in HELP files is very useful to both experienced and new users. Experienced users may simply enter the command for which HELP is required as a parameter to the HELP command; new users, or users who do not know the exact name of the command, simply enter HELP to view a task-oriented set of menus. These menus guide users through the HELP files until the desired information is found.

Magazines and books

Other sources of information are magazine articles and books such as this. *Enterprise Systems Journal* is a magazine which specializes in IBM and compatible large systems hardware and software. Subscriptions are free for qualified IS professionals in the United States, Canada, and Mexico. Send inquiries to:

Enterprise Systems Journal
10935 Estate Lane, Suite 375
Dallas, TX 75238
(214) 343-3717

Formal education

Two main kinds of formal educational training are available: in-classroom, with one or more instructors; and at the student's desk, in self-study form.

Classroom training

Often in the world of data processing the word "education" evokes an image of students going away to a classroom to listen to an instructor. This is a very popular and very common way to get education, because it offers the opportunity to ask the instructor specific questions and to interact with other students. Many education vendors offer a wide array of courses on every subject area in VM and many of these courses have lab exercises where students practice what they have just learned on a live system. Large education vendors have education centers around the country, and even around the world, where courses are offered on a regular schedule.

It is increasingly common for employers to want employees to remain at (or near) home instead of travelling to class. In response to this need, education vendors offer classes at customer locations if facilities are available, or nearby in places like hotel conference rooms. Some vendors always do business this way; for others it is an increasingly popular option. The price for offerings like this may vary from the same offering at the vendor's education center and may require a minimum number of students.

This factor comes into play a great deal when deciding how system programmers versus administrators receive education. Often a staff of administrators needs education for a new product; in this case, it might save a company a lot of travel expense money to have a vendor teach the class nearby. On the other hand, only the largest of companies have a staff of system programmers large enough to justify the cost of a local class. In this case it may be more cost effective to send students away to class.

Self-study

Self-study, an option for VM education for many years, has advantages and disadvantages. For the budget-minded the main advantage to is money saved by not paying for travel and hotel expenses. Also, self-study can be used by everyone who needs training in that subject area for a single purchase or lease price.

For students, the main advantage is the ability to study at one's own pace, and to review topics as often as necessary. For students who do not like to travel, and for companies which cannot afford to have employees away from work, self-study offers a way of providing formal education that otherwise would only be available in a classroom.

The disadvantage for some students is loss of the opportunity to ask questions; in a classroom, students can ask for points to be clarified.

Another possible disadvantage is that self-study courses rarely have real lab exercises, though they do sometimes have simulations. Simulations often provide a chance to execute certain commands or perform certain functions with realistic output appearing on the screen, but only the most sophisticated are complex enough to allow the freedom to experiment that could be had in lab exercises on a live system. This is not to say that it is impossible to provide exercises which students can execute on the system at work. As more education vendors become aware of the demand for this type of education, it will certainly become more common.

VM user groups

User groups in many cities are a very good source of education, especially for VM topics. Three large national IBM user groups hold periodic meetings where diverse VM topics are presented by users and IBM.

Since VM/ESA is the latest version of VM, many presentations are geared towards migration from older versions to VM/ESA and exploitation of new functions. Software vendors also make presentations about products which run under VM/ESA.

National IBM user groups gather together thousands of users for presentations and demonstrations in all areas. These sessions are not only product-related: all three groups also provide presentations on professional development which allow attendees to become better at the job, not just more technically knowledgeable.

SHARE

SHARE, Inc., is a non-profit, international organization, formed to: "Improve the effectiveness of members' information systems by promoting mutual support and influencing IBM's products and services."

Major meetings are held in winter and summer each year, last one week, and include over 1250 sessions. Smaller interim meetings are held in the spring and the fall. For more information, call (312) 644-6610.

GUIDE

GUIDE International Corporation is a not-for-profit association of about 2500 member companies who use medium-to-large scale IBM computers to "Improve the effectiveness of information systems for members."

Three meetings are held in the spring, summer, and fall each year, last one week, and include over 1200 sessions. For more information, call (312) 644-6610.

COMMON

COMMON is an international professional organization of more than 4400 members from 45 countries, representing the IBM midrange user community.

Two meetings are held in the spring and fall each year, last one week each, and include over 900 sessions. For more information, call (312) 644-6610.

International user groups

Internation user groups include G.U.I.D.E, SHARE Europe, Japan GUIDE/SHARE, and Australasian SHARE/GUIDE. Contact SHARE or GUIDE at the numbers listed above for information on how to contact these groups.

Local user groups

Some cities and towns have VM user groups; some have general IBM user groups which sometimes have VM-related presentations. The best way to find out about these is to "ask around" since there is not a formal registry of such organizations. Often an IBM Systems Engineer or Marketing Representative will know about local groups, or will be able to find out how to contact one.

Local user groups have varied meeting schedules: some meet quarterly, many monthly, some more frequently. Often one day in length, meetings consist of presentations by members about various tools and procedures which they have found to be of great benefit, and by software vendors explaining their products. Many times presentations will be accompanied by live demonstrations of products or procedures.

The following table lists local user groups as of this writing.

Group Name	Contact Name	Telephone
Albany, NY Users Group	Dan Heinz	(518) 473-7890
Austin VM Brown Bag Day	Tom Sarff	(512) 338-7541
British Columbia VM Users Group	Debbie Bugg	(604) 660-1618
Canada VM Users Group	Robert Botham	(416) 675-3111 x4252
Chicago Area VM Enthusiasts (CAVMEN)	Mark Suchecki	(708) 518-0058
Los Angeles VM Users Group (LAVMUG)	Rod Hroblak	(818) 841-9470 x397
Metropolitan VM Users Association (MVMUA)	Jeff Savit	(212) 807-2084
Midwest Regional VM Users Group (MVMRUG)	Doug Sinnott	(419) 537-4957
VM Enthusiasts of Michigan	Jim Bur	(313) 525-5401
Minnesota VM Users Group	Gary Garrison	(612) 333-3660
New England Users of VM (NEUVM)	Luke Marvin	(617) 461-3830

Group Name	Contact Name	Telephone
PROFS – OfficeVision/VM Users Group of Washington, DC (PUGWASH)	Julie Cochran	(202) 786-2688
San Francisco Bay Area Users (BayBunch)	VM Assist	(415) 362-3310 x727
Seattle Area VM Users Group	Hal Antonson	(206) 936-6426
Tri-County VM Users Group	Jerry Garren	(805) 967-5511 x2046
Washington, DC VM Users Group (HillGang)	Donna Walker	(703) 354-7040

Suggested Curriculum Paths

End-users

The term **end-user** describes a person who uses the system but is not responsible for maintaining it or creating application programs which run on it. Sometimes sophisticated end-users not only use the system to do their job, but also create short programs which make various tasks easier for everyone. More commonly, end-users do not have any programming skills: they simply use applications written by others.

End-users usually feel more comfortable with the system if they feel they understand a little about how it works; to that end, there is a manual designed especially for them. The *VM/ESA CMS Primer* introduces topics like the CMS file system, the editor, how to send notes to other users, and the like. It is written to lead students through terminal exercises so they can experiment and teach themselves.

Also for end-users are two more manuals: the *VM/ESA CMS User's Guide* and the *VM/ESA XEDIT User's Guide*. These books introduce their respective subjects and suggest exercises students can perform.

Many education vendors have courses for people learning VM/ESA basics—some classroom courses, some self-studies. Often the titles of these courses have words like "Concepts", "Features", "Facilities", or "Fundamentals". They tend to be short, one or two days in length, and often precede another course during the same week which covers CMS and/or REXX.

These courses are designed for end-users to get practical experience at the same time they learn basic VM structure. Often this is enough for them to feel comfortable with VM. Even if they do not understand everything in the system, they know enough about it to ask the right question when something does not function as expected. If they want to know more about things like REXX or XEDIT, it may be appropriate for them to attend a course targeted at application programmers.

Application programmers

Application Programmers create programs used by others or themselves. These programs may be created in compiled languages (for example, C or COBOL), but often REXX is the easiest tool for the job.

The *VM/ESA Procedures Language VM/REXX User's Guide* is a good place to start learning REXX fundamentals. The wonderful thing about an interpreted language like REXX is that it is so easy to experiment with it. The *User's Guide* can be used to get started by coding examples to see how the interpreter works. Gradually students can start looking inside other programs on the system to pick up techniques of REXX coding to use in their own programs.

Another topic of great interest to the application programmer is the VM system editor, XEDIT. XEDIT is a very powerful editor because of the capability for users to write command macros in REXX.

Many applications are written based on XEDIT and REXX; for this reason many education vendors have courses covering one or both of these subjects. These courses almost always have laboratory exercises to reinforce knowledge gained during the lectures. There are also self-study education packages offered by different vendors, some with built-in self-correcting lab simulations.

New system programmers

System programmers are responsible for installing and/or maintaining VM/ESA systems, often including other program products besides VM/ESA itself. Since VM/ESA and products which run in conjunction with it all use CMS facilities to install and do maintenance, a system programmer must have some understanding of basics along with REXX and XEDIT, in addition to knowledge of the components of VM/ESA.

So, beyond CMS, REXX, and XEDIT mentioned before, the new systems programmer must learn what makes up a VM/ESA system. The first manuals to read through are *VM/ESA General Information* and *VM/ESA Introduction* in order to find out, for instance, what the components are, what machine types are supported, what devices are supported, etc. More than half of the VM/ESA manual library is made up of publications for the VM/ESA system programmer—far too many to list here. Any system programmer should become familiar with these manuals so that they can easily be used as references while learning about the system.

Many companies will invest some of their education budget to send a new system programmer to class. All education vendors with full curricula offer basic and advanced courses for system programmers. The courses most appropriate for new system programmers often have titles with "Installation" or "Implementation" in them. Care must be taken to select courses at the appropriate skill level for the student, since it is possible that courses with similar titles may target students with different backgrounds. More advanced courses, covering topics such as system tuning and debugging, are available from a variety of vendors; these can be taken later.

Major IBM user groups have special session offerings for people new to VM; these are often aimed at the system programmer, since companies typically send system programmers rather than end-users to such meetings. Topics from REXX and XEDIT to introductions to VM/ESA components and common program products are discussed at most meetings. Local VM user groups usually look for suggestions of topics for presentations and are eager to be of service to members, both new and old. Very often all it takes is a call to a local user group officer with a request for a presentation on a topic such as *Servicing a VM system* to get someone with that knowledge to explain it at a local meeting.

System programmers new to VM

For experienced system programmers new to VM, the choice of education is quite similar to that for new system programmers. The difference is that basic concepts of systems operation need not be learned, so reading manuals generally suffices for the first stage of learning.

Depending on the level of experience of the system programmer, it may be possible to go directly to a course covering installation of the system without formally learning the fundamental education necessary for someone completely new to VM. Often all that is needed is exposure to the system and installation techniques for the student to be able to pick up enough to learn the rest "on the job".

There is sometimes a temptation to assume that all operating systems are similar enough that basic education is not necessary, but VM is very different from other operating systems. It is generally not advisable for a student not yet familiar with VM to start with a sophisticated topic like performance or debugging since without the proper background, many techniques or recommendations are meaningless.

Again, user groups offer much useful information in the form of presentations as well as the chance for the student to speak with other system programmers and get advice and hints. Contacts made at local user group meetings can be invaluable in emergency situations when there is a need to borrow something or get quick advice.

VM system programmers new to VM/ESA

For system programmers already familiar with VM, but who need to learn about VM/ESA, there are a number of information sources. The *VM/ESA Using Release n Enhancements* manual summarizes what is new in each new VM/ESA release. "Conversion Notebook" manuals are provided with each VM/ESA release and are very important references for planning conversion from VM/SP (with or without HPO) or a migration from VM/XA to VM/ESA. Differences between the VM/SP family of operating systems and VM/ESA should not be underestimated, and neither should the need for education about them.

Several education vendors offer courses on conversion and/or migration to VM/ESA, some with machine exercises and some without, depending on course depth. Typically, these courses are shorter than the general installation courses because it is assumed that the student already knows VM basics.

Experienced VM system programmers often look forward to user group meetings held shortly after General Availability of a VM release because of the "User Experiences" presentations usually scheduled. During these, customers who have installed the new release describe new functions used and share hints or describe pitfalls to avoid during the installation or conversion.

All system programmers

System programmers, no matter how skilled, can benefit from information published in IBM manuals outside the regular VM/ESA library. Books commonly known as "Red Books", because of the color of their covers, come from the International Technical Support Center (ITSC) in Poughkeepsie, NY. "Orange Books" come from the Washington Systems Center (WSC) in Gaithersburg, MD. Topics covered are usually about a specific subject such as installation experiences or new device support and exploitation. Because they are not part of the regular library, people do not always hear about them, but an IBM representative should be aware of any new ones published.

Education Vendors

The following are two alphabetical lists of some vendors of VM education. The first contains the three largest vendors. These offer full curricula including classroom and self-study education. The second contains the names of vendors offering specific courses: some on products they produce, some in particular areas of VM.

Some types of courses are performance (tuning), diagnostics (debugging), planning, migration, conversion, logic (structure and flow), maintenance, fundamentals, CMS, REXX, and XEDIT, to name just a few. As time goes on, some courses are dropped and others added, so specific titles and durations are not listed here since most vendors have catalogs describing their courses. Many offer courses at their own centers, customer sites, or other specified locations.

Full VM curricula:

Amdahl Corporation	(800) 233-9521
Hitachi Data Systems	(800) 543-2979
IBM Corporation	(800) IBM-TEACh

Other VM education:

American Data Group	(404) 921-1123
Benchmark Technical Services	(203) 346-4661
Goal Systems International	(614) 888-1775
Mike Teitelbaum and Associates	(212) 799-2200
Science Research Associates	(SRA) (800) SRA-1277
VM Assist	(415) 362-3310

Summary

A wide selection of educational choices are available for VM, from manuals which accompany the system, to user groups and seminars, to classroom and self-study courses. Users from the newest secretary to the most experienced system programmer can gain from one or more of the alternatives. User groups and education vendors can provide the information needed—and are just a telephone call away.

26

Information at Your Fingertips

By Pamela Christina

Introduction

This chapter describes the forms of VM/ESA information which are available online: the VM/ESA HELP facility and **online books** (soft-copy publications). Online books are manuals that can be stored and read on host systems or workstations.

Online information provides convenient access to product documentation whether users are logged on to a host system or using a workstation, virtually eliminating the need to keep paper copies of documentation at each work location. Individual users of online books also find that information retrieval of reference material is enhanced by online search capability. Distinct advantages to an enterprise include centralized control over user information, ability to share selected pieces of information, and the option to modify and reproduce documentation, as needed.

The VM/ESA HELP facility provides handy reference information about command formats, usage information, and message descriptions for the many VM/ESA components. The HELP facility is an integral part of VM/ESA and is included on the product tape. One copy of the hardcopy (paper) library is shipped with the VM/ESA product order.

VM/ESA online books are an optional feature. VM/ESA online books are created from the SCRIPT source files used to make unlicensed printed manuals. Books are read online using the IBM SAA BookManager Release 2 family of products (READ/VM, READ/MVS, READ/DOS, or READ/2). In November 1991, IBM announced a strategy for online books for licensed programs that run in IBM SAA environments, reinforcing a commitment to move towards integrated product information. The storage media, software, and the terms and conditions associated with online books are dynamic. While information contained herein is current at the time of printing, the most up-to-date information can be obtained from IBM.

Trends for minimizing the amount of information needed to use IBM products, providing more information online, and delivering less information on paper are contributing to an information evolution. This chapter provides a snapshot of online information options in the timeframe of VM/ESA Releases 1.0 and 1.1.

Features of the VM/ESA HELP Facility

The HELP facility provided with VM/ESA contains command formats and descriptions; experienced VM users have long found it to be a convenient online reference. Frequent users of HELP take advantage of fast-paths to look up command information:

```
HELP command-name
  or
HELP component command-name
```

and skip the intermediate menus to display the HELP file for a command. However, HELP is useful to both the novice and the experienced VM user. Task menus guide users to the appropriate command. People using only the fast-path and who have not seen a recent HELP menu may be pleasantly surprised at the myriad options offered by the VM/ESA HELP facility. The next diagram shows an example of a VM/ESA HELP screen.

```
        HELP TASKS        Task Help Information        line  1 of  25
        (c) Copyright IBM Corporation 1990, 1991
        Move the cursor to the task that you want, then press the ENTER key
        or the PF1 key.


        TASKS        - Help if you don't know VM/ESA commands.
                       Good choice for beginners
        MENUS        - List the HELP component MENUs
        HELP         - Explain some ways for using HELP
        COMMANDS     - List VM/ESA commands that you can use
        CMS          - Show only CMS commands
        CP           - Show only CP commands
        OPTIONS      - Show options for the QUERY and SET
                       commands of both CMS and CP
        SUBCMDS      - List VM/ESA subcommands that you can
                       use, such as XEDIT
        STATEMTS     - Show statements for REXX, EXEC 2, and EXEC
        ROUTINES     - Show callable routines
        MACROS       - Show Assembler Language Macros for
                       CMS, APPC/VM, and IUCV
        MESSAGES     - Explain how to get help for messages
        OTHER        - Show commands for other products,
         PRODUCTS      such as RSCS and SQL/DS
        LIBRARY      - Describe the VM/ESA Library
```

Efficient use of the VM/ESA HELP facility

The VM/ESA HELP facility uses the power of XEDIT to display HELP information in display mode. (HELP viewed on linemode terminals displays one line at a time.) Individual users of HELP can specify the level of detail they prefer. Three levels of HELP are provided for most commands:

Brief   Displays command description and format
Detail   Shows entire HELP file
Related   Suggests commands that are similar

HELP command options allow users to select the level of detail or specific sections to be shown, saving display time and avoiding paging through the file. Parts of the HELP file that can be requested include the description, format, parameters, options, notes, and error messages. People who know what they need may find this helpful. Of course, while any part of a HELP file is displayed, pressing the PF1 (ALL) key shows the entire file. Favorite HELP settings can be preserved permanently by specifying them on the DEFAULTS command.

In addition to providing information about basic CMS and CP commands and REXX statements, the VM/ESA HELP facility includes reference information such as assembler language macros for APPC/VM, CMS, and IUCV, as well as routines for VM Data Space Support, SFS file and directory management, SAA CPI Communications (CPI-C), and CPI Resource Recovery (CRR). Note that the VM/ESA hardcopy and softcopy libraries do not provide documentation about the EXEC statements and the EXEC 2 control statements. This information is provided only in the VM/ESA HELP facility.

Information about the VM/ESA library, including form numbers and ordering tips, can be obtained from HELP LIBRARY. This information was added at customer request.

Tailoring HELP for an enterprise

The HELP facility allows tailoring for enterprise needs. New HELP files can be created for internally developed commands and their associated error messages. Menus can be tailored to include new commands and other local procedures, thus making it transparent to end-users whether commands are site-tailored or part of VM/ESA.

HELP files for commands are separate files which are derived from the source used in printed and online books. Instead of starting from scratch, new HELP files can be created by renaming an existing file and making the appropriate changes. There are a few guidelines for naming conventions, text tagging to allow specific sections to be displayed, and hints for revising the menus. Detailed instructions for creating new HELP files that resemble the format of the VM/ESA HELP are described in the *IBM VM/ESA CMS User's Guide*.

Features of Online Books for VM/ESA

Online books place documentation at users' fingertips for use on host systems or at a workstation. Displayable versions of VM/ESA online books are delivered on magnetic tape, tape cartridge, or CD-ROM, making the VM/ESA library portable.

Online books delivered on CD-ROM are ideal for use at a single workstation or one connected to a LAN where the books can be shared. Users of mainframe-interactive terminals are not left out for lack of workstations, because online books can be read on graphics terminals (GDDM is required for viewing embedded graphics). The attraction of online books is the potential to reduce physical space requirements for using and storing product documentation, while providing everyone with a current, consistent level of information.

The remainder of this chapter identifies items to consider when providing online books throughout an enterprise—the options available, benefits from the various delivery media, and software and hardware considerations.

Examining options for reading VM/ESA books online

Enterprise practices for ordering, using, storing, and maintaining product documentation should be examined to determine the ideal softcopy solution. Consider the central library and any libraries stored at personal workareas, remembering that maintaining (ordering and updating) hardcopy libraries and the physical storage requirements (space and shelves) can be significant factors in a softcopy decision.

Implementing a softcopy solution for an enterprise depends on the following:

- How book files will be loaded into the system
- Who will read online books (users, support personnel)
- Whether books will be read from mainframe terminals or workstations
- Whether there will be a need for printing entire books
- Whether books will be customized

This section discusses the options available. Greater detail is found in BookManager manuals and in *Using VM/ESA Online Documentation*.

The choice of delivery medium—tape, cartridge, or CD-ROM—depends on the equipment available and user needs. Tape or cartridge are often thought of as the only options for efficiently loading book files onto a host, and CD-ROM is often only considered for workstation use. However, a November 1991 announcement alters these perceptions. IBM S/370 and S/390 Optical Media Attach/2 allows mainframe users to load data (e.g., online books) from CD-ROMs. This program emulates a channel-attached tape drive and moves CD-ROM files from a PS/2 over a host system I/O channel. Regardless of the media chosen, online book files stored on a host can be distributed for use on workstations.

Information needs can vary within an enterprise; therefore more than one softcopy solution may be necessary. The support staff has a critical need for all product documentation regardless of system availability. Workstation access to all product documentation can be ideal for support staff personnel responsible for maintaining system availability. However, many end-users need only a subset of product documentation. Host-based access to online books may be sufficient for their needs.

Equipment provided to the user community may be as diverse as their information needs. Users can be provided with access to online books on the host, a workstation connected to a LAN, or a stand-alone workstation with or without CD-ROM reader. An enterprise maintains a degree of control over which publications are provided online and who will be given access to them when information is disseminated from a host system.

The discussion has thus far focused on displayable book files. When are source files for online books needed? Using softcopy source files is preferable when there is a need to customize and rebuild online books or when a hardcopy printout of a book is desired. BookManager READ allows printing sections of displayable online books. However, when there is a need to print an entire manual, the softcopy source files are required. Source files for VM/ESA Releases 1.0 and 1.1 are shipped on magnetic tape or cartridge, not on compact disk. Using IBM BookMaster, VM/ESA softcopy source files can be formatted and printed. The next table specifies the types of online book files needed and products required to accomplish the following tasks on a workstation or VM/ESA system:

- Reading at workstation
- Reading on VM/ESA

- Tailoring and rebuilding softcopy on VM/ESA
- Printing topics from VM/ESA
- Printing a book on APA (all points addressable) printer (a printer which can print any image, rather than just predefined fonts)

Within many enterprises, it is not possible to replace every user terminal with a PS/2 and a CD-ROM reader solely for reading online books. Though perhaps it would be nice, suitable alternatives exist for users of workstations and mainframe-interactive terminals. Continual improvements are being made in delivery of online books, so with that in mind, the table provides a checklist for understanding the scope of what is needed, rather than serving as the definitive source. (Consult an IBM representative for particulars.)

Product requirements using VM/ESA online books

Softcopy Type or Product Name	Version	Read on PWS	Read on VM	Tailor and Build Soft-copy	Print Topics on VM	Tailor and Print Hard-copy
VM/ESA displayable BOOK files	1.1.0 or later	Yes	Yes		Yes	
VM/ESA soft-copy source files	1.1.0 or later			Yes		Yes
Book-Manager READ/VM	1.2.0 or later		Yes		Yes	
SAA Book-Manager READ/2 or READ/DOS	1.2.0 or later	Yes				

Softcopy Type or Product Name	Version	Read on PWS	Read on VM	Tailor and Build Soft-copy	Print Topics on VM	Tailor and Print Hard-copy
Book-Manager BUILD/VM	1.2.0 or later			Yes		
Publishing Systems BookMaster	1.3.0 or later			Yes	Yes	Yes
Document Composition Facility (DCF)	1.4.0 or later			Yes	Yes	Yes
Graphical Data Display Manager (GDDM)	2.2.0 or later		Yes	Yes	Yes	
Compiler for REXX/370	1.1.0 or later		Yes		Yes	
C/370 library	1.2.0 or later		Yes	Yes	Yes	

As IBM fully implements its online book strategy, online books delivered on CD-ROM will be packaged with a BookManager read facility for OS/2 and DOS. The read facility can be used to read only those books (or specified IBM books). This virtually eliminates the requirement of BookManager READ product for use on OS/2 or DOS when the sole intention is to read only IBM online books.

Reading and sharing online books on VM

Disseminating information on VM via online books is a natural extension of providing HELP and other online tools to convey information. From a user perspective, reading books online is convenient and maintains the familiar look of books (e.g., table of contents, index, etc.). With online books, a library is only a few keystrokes away. When VM/ESA online books are installed in a public library, a user can type one command, BOOKMGR, to begin using BookManager. A menu is presented listing the books available. By moving the cursor next to the selected book and pressing the ENTER key (or typing OPEN), the book is opened to a table of contents. The table of contents can be paged up or down to locate a familiar topic.

Those preferring to search using an index can select the Index from the Table of Contents list and look for the keyword. Moving the cursor to the keyword and pressing the ENTER key results in the passage being displayed. This is called a **hypertext link**. Hypertext links between books are provided within the VM/ESA release 1.1 softcopy library for the books that are registered in a BookManager public library. When a reference is made to a specific VM/ESA online book, moving the cursor to the title in the phrase and pressing the ENTER key will place the user at the title page for the referenced book. Using the search tools provided with BookManager READ, users can go to a specific section or set up a search for given topics. Search functions are easy to use and are in the form of pull-down windows. Flexibility is built into the search functions that accommodate searching a given set of books or doing "fuzzy" searches (phrases that closely match what was entered). As in hardcopy books, bookmarks can be inserted to mark a spot or several spots. The user can return to a marked passage the next time the book is opened.

From an enterprise perspective, disseminating information in the form of online books on VM makes library management more like managing software. The level of information seen by users is more easily controlled. Books that an enterprise would like to make available for general viewing can be kept in the public library. Books to which installations prefer to limit access can be stored on a separate minidisk with access controlled by IBM Resource Access Control Facility (RACF).

On VM, users share a single copy of the online books, but they may personalize the books with marginal notes. Notes are stored on users' A-disks. This capability is ideal for enterprises that create their own internal documentation, develop product information, or have proprietary information that requires controlled access. During a document review, for example, personalized notes can be distributed for others to read.

Reading and sharing online books on a workstation

There are many options for reading online books on a workstation.

- Reading on workstations
- Reading on workstations with CD-ROM readers
- Reading on workstations connected to LANs

With IBM SAA BookManager READ/2 and BookManager READ/DOS, users can read and use online books on workstations. These workstation products can be included on the BookManager READ/VM product tape and can be later downloaded for use on the workstation using the instructions provided in *IBM BookManager READ/VM Installation and Customization*. As IBM fully implements its online book strategy, IBM books delivered on CD-ROM will be packaged with a BookManager READ facility for OS/2 and DOS. This facility will be used to read only the IBM books shipped in a given CD-ROM collection. The BookManager READ product continues to be needed to read books on a host system, older online books, and non-IBM books. So, until the built-in read facility is implemented, each workstation used for reading online books continues to need a license for a BookManager READ product.

Displayable books files are needed in order to read online books on a workstation. Files can be downloaded from the host or uploaded from a CD-ROM reader and copied to diskette or stored on the hard disk. Files being moved between host and workstations should be moved in binary form (i.e., without converting EBCDIC to ASCII). Displayable book files built on VM/ESA can also be read on any BookManager READ platform, including a workstation.

The reading capability is virtually the same as that provided with the host version of BookManager READ, but is enhanced by operating systems features such as the windowing, icons, and use of a mouse, instead of the keyboard. With BookManager READ/2, a window is opened for each open book. The size of the windows can be changed (minimized or maximized) and resembles having several open books on the desk top. Hypertext links within text are more apparent on the workstation READ products than on VM. Another difference is that sections of marked text can be printed while using BookManager READ/2, and graphics can be printed, although separately from the text—contrasting with BookManager READ/VM, which can print with graphics included.

A CD-ROM reader is not required for each workstation to be used for reading online books. When only one CD-ROM is available for a small group of people, a LAN library approach can maximize online book availability by providing a central, shared library. Using a workstation connected to a LAN which has a library, users can read any book in that library. It is transparent to users whether a book is on a LAN or on their workstations. Each workstation with a requirement to read online books from the LAN will need a licensed copy of BookManager READ installed on it. Or, with OS/2 LAN server, several BookManager READ programs may be shared among a larger group, with concurrent use limited to the number of programs purchased.

Tailoring VM/ESA online books

Just as products are tailored at installation time, certain documentation can be tailored to match and make it more useful to the readers. Online books are easily updated and can ensure current, consistent information is disseminated throughout an organization. Possibilities include tailoring the enterprise operation's "Run" book, or simply updating a primer by replacing the variables with pertinent user information. Information that is updated frequently and is seemingly out of date before it can be printed lends itself to softcopy format on a host system.

Within an enterprise, BookManager BUILD can create internal online books. For example, university catalogs, as well as company product documentation, policies, and procedures, or internal specifications, are ideal candidates for online books.

Tailored hardcopy documentation is obtained by updating the VM/ESA source files (marked up with BookMaster tags), reformatting them, and printing the output on an APA printer. To create tailored online book files, source files are updated, and new online book files are built using the IBM BookManager BUILD/VM program. IBM restrictions for updates are that notices, especially safety notices, may not be removed. In general, BookManager BUILD will create online books from files marked up with:

- IBM Generalized Markup Language (GML) Starter Set
- IBM Publishing Systems BookMaster
- CALS SGML, the Standard Generalized Markup Language for the Computer-aided Acquisition and Logistics Support initiative of the U.S. Department of Defense.

Displayable online books are individual book files, one per book, with filetype BOOK (or file extension BOO on DOS and OS/2). Displayable files contain text and graphics. Books containing graphics may be larger, as picture content affects book size. Files containing graphics are delivered with source files. Graphics and pictures in VM/ESA documents were created with IBM Publishing Systems DrawMaster.

Collecting online books for VM-related products

Online books are provided for many IBM products. IBM reinforced a commitment to BookManager in a November 1991 announcement that IBM will ship BookManager-viewable books for IBM products that run on SAA platforms (VM/ESA, MVS/ESA, OS/400, and OS/2).

To demonstrate the extent of the collection of online books, The next table shows VM/ESA-related products that have announced that some or all of their documentation is available in BookManager form. Products not listed may, indeed, provide online books (but did not make this printing). It is best to consult an IBM representative or verify in an announcement letter the books which are in softcopy and those that are not. Until such time that an all-inclusive list of online books becomes available, an IBM representative can obtain information on which products have announced their intention to make online books available by requesting SOFTCOPY LIST from PSTOOLS on BLDVM1 and provide customers with the appropriate portion of the list.

VM and related products with softcopy information

Shortened Product Name	Version	Product Number	Announcement
ACF/NCP	6.1.0	5688-231	291-506
ACF/SSP V3R7 (VM)	3.7.0	5664-289	291-507
ACF/VTAM V3.4	3.4.0	5684-095	290-556
AD/Cycle C/370	1.1.0	5688-216	291-481
AD/Cycle COBOL/370	1.1.0	5688-197	291-480
AD/Cycle CoOp Development Environment/370	1.1.0	5688-194	291-477
AD/Cycle LE/370	1.1.0	5688-198	291-479
Ada Runtime Library/370	1.2.0	5706-295	291-424
Ada/370 R1	1.1.0	5706-292	290-746
Ada/370 R2	1.2.0	5706-292	291-424
Application Connection Services/VM	1.1.2	5684-099	291-296
Attachable Media Manager/VM	1.2.0	5684-140	291-230
BookManager BUILD	1.2.0	5684-026	290-377
BookManager READ	1.2.0	5684-062	290-377
BookManager READ/DOS	1.2.0	5601-453	290-375

Shortened Product Name	Version	Product Number	Announcement
BookManager READ/MVS	1.2.0	5695-046	291-103
BookManager READ/2	1.2.0	5601-454	290-376
BookManager READ/2	1.2.1	5601-454	290-754
BookMaster	1.4.0	5688-015	290-378
CALLUP (PRPQ)		5799-CZE	
CALS Application Feature, ProcessMaster	1.3.0	5664-387	289-566
SAA Delivery Manager/VM	1.2.0	5684-098	291-645
Document Composition Facility (DCF)	1.4.0	5748-XX9	
DFSMS/VM	2.1.0	5706-116	291-541
ES/9000 Models 490,570,610			191-160
ES/9000 Model 860			191-159
ES/9000 Models 340,500,580,620,720			190-125
ES/9000 Models 520,640,660,740			191-159
ES/9000 Models 820,900			191-159
ES/9000 Models 120,130,150,170			190-131

Shortened Product Name	Version	Product Number	Announcement
Expert System Consultation Environment/VM	1.3.0	5664-392	289-700
Expert System Environment/VM	1.3.0	5664-391	289-700
ISPF V3R2 for VM	3.2.0	5684-043	290-320
ISPF/PDF V3R2 for VM	3.2.0	5684-123	291-129
MUMPS/VM	3.2.0	5706-218	291-262
NetView Graphical Monitor Facility-VM/ESA	2.1.0, 2.2.0	5756-051	290-570
NetView (VM/ESA)	2.2.0	5756-051	291-514
Network Routing Facility	1.7.0	5668-963	291-510
Network Terminal Option	1.8.0	5735-XX7	291-508
S/370 and S/390 Optical Media Attach/2		5621-264	291-647
OSI Manufacturing Messaging Services VM	1.1.0	5684-107	290-626
OSL R1 MVS, VM, and AIX/370	1.1.0	5688-137	
OSL R2 MVS, VM, and AIX/370	1.2.0	5688-137	290-700
SAA PrintManager	1.1.0	5688-179	291-299

Shortened Product Name	Version	Product Number	Announcement
Process Master Text Tagger Feature VM		5664-387	289-565
Publishing Systems BrowseMaster	1.2.0	5688-224	291-248
Compiler for REXX/370	1.1.0	5695-013	291-320
Library for REXX/370	1.1.0	5695-014	291-320
IBM SAA RPG/370	1.1.0	5688-127	291-062
Screen Definition Facility II (VM)	1.3.0	5664-307	291-490
SGML Translator, DCF Edition	1.2.0	5684-025	289-567
SystemView Host Management Facility/VM	1.1.0	5684-157	291-535
TCP/IP V2 VM	2.2.0	5735-FAL	290-308
TPNS	3.2.0	5688-121	291-082
VM PWSCS	1.1.0	5684-138	291-587
VM/ESA	1.1.0, 1.1.1, 1.2.0, 1.2.1	5684-112	290-499, 291-541, 292-318, 293-271
VM/Pass-Through	2.1.0	5684-100	291-111
VM/RSCS V3	3.1.0	5684-096	290-500
WDSF/VM	1.1.0	5684-122	291-522

Summary

This chapter touched upon some considerations for providing VM/ESA information online. When planning incorporation of online information within an enterprise, it is wise to evaluate the way information is used to determine aspects which may be improved by disseminating information online. The media and tools associated with online information continue to change as new and exciting technology is developed.

27

VM/ESA References

By Pamela Christina

A wealth of product information is available from IBM and other sources. The trick is finding out where to look for the information desired. This chapter describes, for both novice and experienced users, a variety of information sources and publications pertaining to VM/ESA and VM-related products, and highlights sources for some selected topics. An alphabetical listing provides an extensive list of references.

Locating and Obtaining IBM Publications

In general, most IBM product manuals contain a listing of manuals which comprise the product library. Products with extensive libraries often provide separate library-description manuals. This section provides tips on:

- Identifying product library contents
- Locating the correct level of information
- Determining methods for ordering publications

Locating product information

Typically, most product documentation provides some reference to related documentation and may be found by looking in the table of contents or the index for **Bibliography** or **Related Information**. VM/ESA manuals each list related publications in addition to the separate manual, *VM/ESA: Library Guide and Master Index*. The *Library Guide* describes each VM/ESA manual and contains a master index, a combination of all VM/ESA book indexes, helping to locate specific items across the library. When using online books (softcopy publications), locating information is facilitated by online search functions in BookManager READ.

Other handy sources for locating VM product information are the VM HELP Facility and the *VM/ESA Library Roadmap*. Information about the VM/ESA library, including form numbers and ordering tips, can be obtained from HELP LIBRARY. The *VM/ESA Library Roadmap*, introduced for VM/ESA Release 1.1, contains a subset of the *Library Guide* that lists the following information:

- New functions and descriptions, along with pointers to their documentation
- Information which has been relocated within the VM/ESA library, with former and new locations identified
- Contents of the library (titles and form numbers)

VM veterans able to cite the book and page number of specific information often find themselves disoriented when that information moves elsewhere in subsequent library releases. While it may seem that writers move information to intentionally confuse readers, reorganizations occur primarily in response to numerous customer comments. The *Library Guide* maps reorganizations and contents of each book in the library.

How VM publication numbers are selected

Many readers wonder how VM publication numbers are determined. Within IBM, an organization that produces product information is allocated a set of publication numbers. The person in Endicott Information Development (publications), referred to as the "Controlling Party", keeps a log of publication numbers for VM and VM-related products in a large, blue notebook. There is a lot of history in that old notebook.

When a new publication number is needed, the planner or writer selects the next entry in the notebook. When numbers were obtained for VM/ESA Release 1.0, the *VM/ESA CMS Command Reference* was assigned the next entry:

```
_C24-5461
```

Information about the publication assigned to that number is written in the notebook along with its use key. Use keys are:

G   is for general (like a general information manual).
S   is the use key for books that are for sale.
L   is for licensed information and has a separate set of numbers.

The *VM/ESA CMS Command Reference* use key is S, making the complete publication form number **SC24-5461**. The controlling party and planners then provide information about these publication numbers to distribution centers via an online database.

The **suffix number** for a first edition is implied to be **-00** and is not usually shown. Subsequent releases of IBM manuals add a suffix number to the form number. Thus the number for the VM/ESA Release 1.1 *VM/ESA CMS Command Reference* includes the suffix -01: SC24-5461-**01**. While this may seem trivial, it is important to installations which support multiple levels of VM systems and require information for particular product levels.

Obtaining publications to match a system

The publication ordering system was not initially designed to accommodate suffix numbers. Specifying the eight-character form number (without the suffix) orders the latest issue of a publication. Someone wanting the latest edition of the *VM/ESA CMS Command Reference* specifies its form number, SC24-5461, which provides the most current level. However, someone needing an earlier version, for example the VM/ESA Release 1.0 edition, was required to order by its **pseudo number**. Pseudo numbers are assigned to specific publications for a given release. Pseudo numbers for prior release manuals are listed in the ever-helpful *VM/ESA Library Guide and Master Index*. The pseudo number for the CMS manual cited earlier is ST00-4690. In 1992, the publications ordering system was updated to accommodate suffix numbers and continues to support pseudo numbers.

Storage considerations

Packaging of hardcopy VM documentation has been a frequent discussion topic for customers and IBM. Some prefer loose-leaf, others want perfect binding (in which the book spine glued). Some like spiral binding for particular books, but prefer to store other manuals in binders. The conclusion is that no single method will please everyone; so, for VM/ESA, it was appropriate to offer options in storage. Nearly every book in the VM/ESA library is perfect-bound to allow storage on a shelf without requiring a binder. Not everyone agrees on the ideal binder size or the books which should be stored together, so various binder sizes are offered for VM/ESA, along with the option of sticky labels for "roll-your-own" binder inserts for grouping of manuals in binders to people's own choosing. Information about binder capacities and page counts for VM/ESA manuals is located in the *VM/ESA Library Guide and Master Index*.

Is shelf storage space for manuals a problem? Online books (soft-copy publications) are a space-saving, convenient option. Online books, available as an optional VM/ESA feature, can be read online (at the host or on a workstation) with the IBM SAA BookManager Family of products. See the general information manual for the appropriate platforms for details about using BookManager Read:

* IBM *SAA BookManager READ/2 General Information* for use on OS/2
* IBM *BookManager READ/VM and BUILD/VM General Information* for reading on VM/ESA
* IBM *BookManager READ/DOS General Information* for reading on DOS
* IBM *BookManager READ/MVS General Information* reading on MVS/ESA

For more information about online books, see Chapter 26, *Information at Your Fingertips,* on page 635.

Options for ordering publications

Hardcopy and optional softcopy (machine-readable) information can be ordered with the product (and afterwards) by IBM representatives. An IBMLink application feature for ordering information, **Publication Order Entry** (PUBORDER), enables online ordering of product information. IBMLink is available to customers at discretion of their IBM Branch Office. PUBORDER is the tool used within IBM for ordering publications. PUBORDER features include:

* Ability to search and order in the same session
* Can enter orders for both billable and non-billable items
* Online confirmation of order acceptance
* Order status query and review of past orders
* Same-day cancellation capability

Many sites have SLSSs (System Library Subscription Services), which were arranged through IBM representatives. IBM publication *Organizing and Maintaining a System Library* helps organize libraries and set up and maintain library subscriptions. An SLSS is a customized service for subscribing to IBM publications from initial shipment to updates. Subscriptions are arranged by interest profiles or specific order numbers. Prices of IBM publications can be found in the *IBM Marketing Publications KWIC Index*. IBMLink users may also review their SLSS profiles by an IBMLink feature.

When ordering a set of information, such as an entire VM/ESA library, a bill-of-forms number may be used instead of specifying an individual form number for each item in the set. Some bill-of-forms for VM/ESA are listed in the next table.

VM Release	Order no.	Description
VM/ESA 1.1	SBOF-3280	Unlicensed publications
VM/ESA 1.1	LBOF-3281	Publications for system diagnosis
VM/ESA 1.1	LBOF-3282	Licensed publications
VM/ESA 1.0	SBOF-3268	Unlicensed publications (ESA feature)

Journals and Publications

Formal product documentation, like a car owner's manual, describes product and general usage information. However, information from other sources and user experiences can be valuable. This section notes a handful of places to read about VM/ESA. To subscribe to periodicals or newsletters, contact the publisher of the publication.

Beyond Computing: This is a bimonthly IBM periodical which contains general news items about industry and technical articles about software and hardware, replacing *IBM Update.*
IBM Directions: This magazine was published by IBM to describe business issues with applications of interest to executives. The final issue was Spring 1992 and a new periodical is forthcoming.
IBM Systems Journal: This periodical is published quarterly. A notable issue is Volume 30, no. 1 (1991), which was devoted to VM/ESA (order no. G321-0102).
Profit: This magazine is a bimonthly periodical published by IBM for the small business person and entrepreneur.
Red Books: IBM Washington Systems Center publishes **Red Books** to describe various user experiences. Topics include VM/ESA performance reports, Pipelines user experience, and an SFS primer. The *Red Books* complement IBM's formal product documentation.
VM Software Newsletter: This newsletter is published quarterly by IBM. It contains information of interest to VM software vendors.

Following are a few documents that may be helpful. An IBM representative can obtain them from a marketing disk called MKTTOOLS. The word in uppercase and enclosed in parentheses following the document title is the document filename on MKTTOOLS.

VM/ESA 1.1 Performance Information (VM11PERF): This provides information on performance of VM/ESA 1.1 running various workloads on IBM 9021, 9121, 9221, and 3090 processors. The report is 340 pages long and can be be ordered via publication number GG66-3236.

VM LP Migration Matrix (VMLPMIGR): This document, also called *WHAT is SUPPORTED WHERE*, is a table of IBM VM Software products that identifies which levels of VM support which software product.

VM/ESA Guests (VMGUESTS): This table lists current releases of VM and supported guests. Guests covered are VM, AIX, MUMPS/VM, MUSIC/SP, MVS, TPF, and VSE.

VM/ESA Processors (VMCPU): This document lists current IBM processors supported in current VM environments. The matrix addresses VM Operating Systems running first level.

IBM Products Implementing IBM SAA Elements (ENVR3820 or ENVRBOOK): This package lists the IBM and Cooperative Software products that implement the IBM SAA elements in the four SAA environments.

IBM Customer-Sponsored Exchange of Information

User groups, VMSHARE electronic conferencing, and the VM Workshop are activities initiated by IBM customers for the purposes of exchanging information.

IBM user groups

Wouldn't it be nice to hear real-life experiences before starting a task? IBM user groups create an environment where an exchange of user experiences takes place, along with an opportunity to hear technical presentations and pick up some practical tips. Formal IBM user groups exist worldwide and meet for up to a week several times a year. A primary activity is to formalize requirements to be submitted to IBM. User group members meet with other IBM customers who are using similar products, learn about new products from IBM developers, and discuss and submit formal requirements to IBM. Proceedings are published and distributed to member organizations. These proceedings can include published papers, if available, and often reprints of presentation view foils. For example, the SHARE User Group Proceedings contain:

*   Volume 1, which is hardcopy and includes formal papers.
*   Volume 2, which is microfiche and contains copies of the overhead transparencies (view foils).

User groups exist around the world; a partial listing appears on the next page.

- COMMON
- GUIDE (USA)
- GUIDE Latin America
- G.U.I.D.E.
- SHARE (USA)
- SHARE Europe
- Australasian SHARE/GUIDE (Australia and Asia)
- Japan GUIDE/SHARE

See "VM user groups" on page 625 and "International user groups" on page 626 for information on how to contact these groups.

On a smaller scale, regional VM user groups offer an alternative to the commitment of formal IBM user groups. Regional groups usually meet for one day and provide three to four speakers.

User groups in general can provide technical vitality and networking opportunity for those with similar product interests.

Regional user groups are listed in "Local user groups" on page 626.

VM Workshop

What is the VM Workshop? The VM Workshop is a summer meeting of VM enthusiasts sponsored by a different university each year. A unique handout from this meeting is the workshop tape containing helpful tools and programs contributed by other VM system programmers. Harry Williams (Marist College) described the workshop in a VMSHARE append:

> The VM Workshop is an all-volunteer, self-supporting organization. It provides a forum for individuals and organizations with an interest in VM to exchange information and experiences. Attendees are urged to participate by making a presentation. Normally, parallel sessions are held throughout the day so meetings are kept relatively small, encouraging interaction among the speaker and the audience. Participants from sites which run VM (including profit-oriented and nonprofit organizations with business, research, education, and service objectives), as well as participation from vendors who provide VM utilities and applications are welcome. The first VM Workshops were held in the 1970s, and the Workshop became an annual meeting in 1981. Wichita State hosted the conference from 1981–1983, Kansas State in 1984–85, University of Kentucky in 1986, Brigham Young in 1987, Michigan State in 1988, Kansas State

in 1989, Indiana University in 1990, University of Kentucky in 1991, University of Arkansas in 1992, and Michigan State in 1993.

The University of Notre Dame hosts the 1994 workshop; contact Harry Williams at (914) 575-3252.

VMSHARE electronic conference

Many discussions which begin at user group meetings, continue online on the VMSHARE electronic conferencing facility. VMSHARE is a database of VM information which is open to SHARE VM Group members, members of the other IBM international user groups, and IBM. Some participants live by the motto "VMSHARE once a day!"

VMSHARE participants query others for tips, offer their expertise to others, and provide news at it happens. Often, the person who does the asking learns a valuable piece of information that may save time or effort. Many IBMers participate on VMSHARE by asking "What if" type of questions to test the waters. An even greater number of IBMers take advantage of the read-access available within IBM to learn more about what customers have to say.

Documentation for VM/ESA and Related Products

This section lists a few sources for a variety of VM topics. Sources listed in this section are included with form numbers in the alphabetical bibliography at the end of this chapter.

VM/ESA library and ordering information

* IBM *VM/ESA Library Guide and Master Index*
* IBM *VM/ESA Library Roadmap*
* IBM *VM/ESA Using Online Documentation*
* HELP LIBRARY on a VM/ESA system

Where to learn about new features and functions

For most product libraries, one or more pieces of information exists to describe what is new in a given release (general information manuals, release guides, features summaries, etc.).   Some IBM references for VM/ESA are listed on the next page.

- *VM/ESA: Conversion Notebook* assists with the conversion or migration from earlier versions of VM.
- *VM/ESA: Features Summary* is a licensed publication that describes how the CP functions work.
- *VM/ESA: General Information* provides general information about VM/ESA to assist in determining how it meets needs.
- *VM/ESA: Solutions* describes various VM/ESA solutions offered by VM-related products.
- *VM/ESA: Using Release 1.1 Enhancements* describes the new features and functions for the release.

Exploiting VM capability

STEVR/VM: Server Tasking Environment/VM (RPQ P81089) provides servers and applications with a service layer that extends CMS to provide a multitasking and multiprocessor environment.

- IBM *Server Tasking Environment/VM Programming RPQ P81089 Programmer's Guide and Reference*

Papers presented at user groups include:

- *Introduction to the Server Tasking Environment/VM* (author Joel Farrell)
- *Getting Started With the Server Tasking Environment/VM* (authors Joel Farrell and Christine T. Casey)

CMS Pipelines: CMS Pipelines is a tool for passing data through a series of programs. IBM Reference material for VM/ESA 1.1 CMS Pipelines includes:

- *VM/ESA CMS Pipelines Reference*
- *VM/ESA CMS Pipelines Users Guide*
- *VM/ESA CMS Pipelines Reference Card*

Presentations given at SHARE and other user groups include:

- *CMS Pipelines* (author Jim Elliott)
- *Plunging Into Pipes* (author Melinda Varian)
- *Plunging On—Apprentice Plumbing* (author Melinda Varian)

Other IBM sources include:

* *CMS Pipelines Tutorial*
* *VM CMS Pipelines User's Guide for PRPQ P81059* which contains a tutorial and reference information for the program offering 5785-RAC

SFS (CMS Shared File System): The Shared File System is an extension to the CMS file system that coexists with the minidisk file system.   IBM Product information and user group presentations include:

* IBM *CMS Shared File System Primer*, from IBM Technical Support Center
* IBM *VM/ESA CMS Administration Reference* which contains the command information for SFS administration and operation and SFS File Pool Server Machine administration
* IBM *VM/ESA CMS Planning and Administration Guide* which describes how to manage the Shared File System
* *Shared File System Overview and Administration* (author Scott Nettleship)
* *The Shared File System as a Development Librarian* (author Michael J. Donovan)
* *SFS Performance Management* (author Bill Bitner)

LEXX: Live Parsing Editor, more commonly known as LEXX, provides an alternative editor for use on VM.   It is available with the CMS Pipelines PRPQ P81059.   (Note that CMS Pipelines without LEXX is integrated into VM/ESA 1.1.1).

* IBM *Live Parsing Editor User's Guide*
* IBM *Live Parsing Editor Reference*

3270 Entry Assist: 3270 Entry Assist, available on most IBM 3270 control units, provides extended 3270 terminal features such as word tabs and word deleted.   It is documented in:

IBM *3270 Information Display System: Entry Assist User's Guide* (GA23-0119)

Sources of performance information

IBM generally publishes a performance report for new releases of VM. User groups provide exchange a wealth of information on the topic of performance and capacity planning. The Computer Measurement Group, Inc., is an annual, international conference for management of performance information and evaluation. Some areas have a local chapter.

Bulletins and Books:

* IBM *VM/ESA Release 1.0 Performance Report*
* IBM *VM/ESA Release 1.1 Performance Report*
* *VM and CMS: Performance and Fine Tuning* (author Jeffrey Savit)

Papers and Presentations about VM Tuning:

* *3990-3 Extended Function Use in VM* (author Craig A. Welch)
* *Care and Feeding of Monitor APPLDATA* (author William J. Bitner)
* *Interpreting VM/XA Monitor Data* (author W. Romney White)
* *Intro to VM Performance and Tuning* (author W. Romney White)
* *Intro to VM/XA and VM/ESA Performance Management* (author William J. Bitner)
* *Performance Information Guide* composed by the SHARE committees for VM Performance and Capacity planning (published by SHARE, Inc.)
* *Using VM Data Spaces Effectively* (author W. Romney White)
* *VM DASD Performance Update* (author Paulus Usong)
* *VM Data Spaces and ESA/XC Facilities* (authors J.M. Gdaniec and J.P. Hennessy)
* *VM/ESA Monitor Enhancements: Interpreting the Data* (author W. Romney White)
* *VM/ESA 1.0 Performance* (author William J. Bitner)
* *VM/ESA 1.1 Performance Update* (author William J. Bitner)
* *VM/XA Paging* (author W. Romney White)
* *VM/XA System Product Workload Characterization* (authors Barton Robinson and W. Romney White).
* *VMPRF Enhancements for VM/ESA* (author Joefon Jann)

Realtime Monitor VM/ESA (RTM VM/ESA): IBM *Realtime Monitor VM/ESA Program Description/Operations Manual* SH26-7000-04 for RTM VM/ESA Release 5.

VM Performance Planning Facility (VMPPF):

- IBM *VMPPF Primer*
- IBM *VMPPF Guide and Reference*
- IBM *VMPPF Usage and Experience Guide*
- IBM *Capacity Planning and Performance Management Methodology*

VM Performance Analysis Facility (VMPAF):

- IBM *VMPAF General Information*
- IBM *VMPAF User's Guide and Reference* (also provided on the product tape in LIST1402 and LIST38PP formats)

VM Performance Reporting Facility (VMPRF):

- *VM Performance Reporting Facility User's Guide*

Communication product information

RSCS:

- IBM *Introducing VM RSCS Networking Version 3*
- IBM *RSCS Exit Customization*
- IBM *RSCS General Information*
- IBM *RSCS Operation and Use*
- IBM *RSCS Planning and Installation*

VM/Pass-Through Facility (PVM): VM/Pass-Through Facility provides multi-session support across system nodes.

- IBM *VM/Pass-Through Facility Administration and Operation*
- IBM *VM/Pass-Through Facility Programmer's Reference*
- IBM *VM/Pass-Through Facility User's Guide*

Client/server product information

Workstation Data Save Facility/VM (WDSF/VM):   The WDSF family of products allows VM to act as a server to backup and archive that easily forgotten workstation data.

* IBM *WDSF/VM: Version 1 for DOS and OS/2 Clients: Implementation Experiences*
* IBM *WDSF/VM Administrator's Guide and Reference*
* IBM *WDSF/VM AIX User's Guide and Reference*
* IBM *WDSF/VM Apple Macintosh User's Guide and Reference*
* IBM *WDSF/VM DOS User's Guide and Reference*
* IBM *WDSF/VM General Information*
* IBM *WDSF/VM OS/2 User's Guide and Reference*
* IBM *WDSF/VM Programmer's Reference*
* IBM *WDSF/VM RISC System/6000 Client User's Guide*
* IBM *WDSF/VM Sun User's Guide and Reference*

LAN Resource Extension and Service/VM   (LANRES/VM):   LANRES/VM establishes a VM server environment to allow NetWare clients to access mainframe resources easily.   With LANRES/VM, NetWare local area networks may be channel-attached to System/390 or System/370 systems providing high-speed, transparent access to the varied disk and printer resources supported by VM.

* IBM *LANRES/VM Administration*
* IBM *LANRES/VM General Information*
* IBM *LANRES/VM Planning and Installation*

VM Image Solution: MOSAIC is a document imaging and management solution for VM and VM guests that was developed by SAIC (Science Application International Corporation).

* SAIC *MOSAIC Administration Guide VM Server Version 2.0*
* SAIC *MOSAIC Application Programming Interface (API) Reference—Workstation 2.0*
* SAIC *MOSAIC Installation Guide VM Server Version 2.0*
* SAIC *MOSAIC Messages and Codes Version 2.0*
* SAIC *MOSAIC Press Kit*
* SAIC *MOSAIC Quick Guide Version 2.0*
* SAIC *MOSAIC User Guide Version 2.0*
* SAIC *MOSAIC Workstation Installation Guide Version 2.0*

VM Personal Workstation Communication Services (PWSCS): VM PWSCS is a high-speed communications programming interface between workstations and VM systems.

- IBM *VM PWSCS: Host Guide and Reference*
- IBM *VM PWSCS: Installation Checklist*
- IBM *VM PWSCS: Managing VM PWSCS*
- IBM *VM PWSCS: Programming for VM*

System management product information

DIRMAINT: IBM VM/Directory Maintenance library may be obtained with a bill-of-forms number, SBOF-0483. Manuals of interest include:

- IBM *VM/Directory Maintenance: General Information*
- IBM *VM/Directory Maintenance: Operation and Use*

CMS Utilities Feature: The CMS Utilities Feature provides for VM/ESA many of the utilities which were popular in VM/IPF.

- IBM *VM/ESA CMS Utilities Feature*

Attachable Media Manager/VM: AMMR/VM controls access to tape drives and other attachable devices.

- IBM *AMMR/VM Command Language Reference*
- IBM *AMMR/VM Installation and Operations*

Database and database management information

SQL/DS (Structured Query Language/Data System):

- IBM *SQL/DS Application Programming for IBM VM Systems*
- IBM *SQL/DS Database Administration for IBM VM Systems*
- IBM *SQL/DS Database Services Utility for IBM VM Systems*
- IBM *SQL/DS General Information for IBM VM Systems*
- IBM *SQL/DS Interactive SQL Guide and Reference for IBM VM Systems*
- IBM *SQL/DS Operation for IBM VM Systems*
- IBM *SQL/DS SQL Reference for IBM VM Systems and VSE*
- IBM *SQL DS System Administration for IBM VM Systems*
- IBM *SQL/DS VM Data Spaces Support for VM/ESA*.

Programming language support information

REXX Information: Following is a sampling of the VM/REXX publications.   There have been numerous papers presented and books published on the topic.

*   IBM *VM/ESA: Procedures Language VM/REXX Primer*
*   IBM *VM/ESA: Procedures Language VM/REXX Reference*
*   IBM *VM/ESA: Procedures Language VM/REXX Reference Summary*
*   IBM *VM/ESA: Procedures Language VM/REXX Users Guide*
*   *The REXX Handbook* (authors Gabriel Goldberg and Philip H. Smith III), collected works from various REXX experts

EXEC 2:

*   IBM *VM/SP EXEC 2 Reference*
*   Note that the VM/ESA hardcopy and online books do not provide documentation about the EXEC statements and the EXEC 2 control statements. This information is provided only in the VM/ESA HELP Facility.

Miscellaneous

MUMPS/VM: MUMPS/VM is a programming language which runs as a guest on VM/ESA and looks like native MUMPS to the users. The product library may be ordered using the bill-of-forms, SBOF-3279.

*   IBM *MUMPS/VM Reference*
*   IBM *MUMPS/VM User's Guide*
*   IBM *MUMPS/VM Utilities Programmers Guide*

OfficeVision/VM: IBM *OfficeVision/VM Release 2 Functional Guide* provides detailed information about OfficeVision/VM Release 2 (cross-system calendar support and more).

Alphabetical Bibliography

- Adair, R.J., R.U. Bayles, L.W. Comeau, and R.J. Creasy. *A Virtual Machine System for the 360/40.* IBM Cambridge Scientific Center Report 320-2007, Cambridge, MA., May 1966.

- Amdahl, G. M. *The structure of System/360, Part III—Processing unit design considerations.* IBM Systems Journal, Volume 3, no. 2, 1964.

- *The Association of Information and Image Management (AIIM)*, 1990.

- Attanasio, C. R. *Virtual Control Storage—Security Measures in VM/370.* IBM Systems Journal, Volume 18, no. 1, 1979.

- Bergsten, James R. *Problem Diagnosis in VM.* VM Applications Handbook, McGraw-Hill, 1989.

- Bitner, William J. *Care and Feeding of Monitor APPLDATA.* Paper presented at SHARE 78 session O761, Anaheim, March 1992.

- Bitner, William J. *Intro to VM/XA and VM/ESA Performance Management.* Paper presented at SHARE 77 session O574, Chicago, August 1991.

- Bitner, William J. *SFS Performance Management.* Paper presented at SHARE 78 session O760, Anaheim, March 1992.

- Bitner, William J. *VM/ESA 1.0 Performance.* Paper presented at SHARE 76 session O766, San Francisco, February 1991.

- Bitner, William J. *VM/ESA 1.1 Performance Update.* Paper presented at SHARE 78 session O762, Anaheim, March 1992.

- Blaauw, G. A., and Brooks, F. P., Jr. *The structure of System/360, Part I—Outline of the logical structure.* IBM Systems Journal, Volume 3, no. 2, 1964.

- Case, R. P., and A. Padegs. *Architecture of the IBM System/370.* Communications of the ACM, Volume 21, no. 1, January 1978.

- Doherty, Walter J., and Arvind Thadhani. *The Economic Value of Rapid Response Time.* IBM form number, GE20-0752, 1979.

- Donovan, Michael J. *The Shared File System as a Development Librarian.* Paper presented at SHARE 76 session O710, San Francisco, February 1991.

- Elliott, J. L. *CMS Pipelines.* Paper presented at SHARE 78 session O705, Anaheim, March 1992.

- Farrell, Joel A. *Introduction to the Server Tasking Environment/VM.* Paper presented at SHARE 77 session O715, Chicago, August 1991.

- Farrell, Joel A, and Christine T. Casey. *Getting Started With the Server Tasking Environment/VM.* Paper presented at SHARE 77 session O716, Chicago, August 1991.

- Fischofer, William T. *CP Support for Hidden Servers.* Presented at SHARE session O615, July 1985.

- Fuller, Lloyd E. *NOMAD and Data spaces.* Presented at SHARE 78m, Anaheim, March 1992

- Gdaniec, J. M., and J.P. Hennessy. *VM Data Spaces and ESA/XC Facilities.* IBM Systems Journal, Volume 30, no. 1, 1991.

- Goldberg, Gabriel. *Automatic Operator and Modified CMSBATCH.* Paper presented at SHARE session B623, March 1982.

- Goldberg, Gabriel. *Automating Software Operation and Data Collection Under VM.* Paper presented at SHARE session O557, August 1987.

- Goldberg, Gabriel. *COUNTER—A Data Collector.* Paper presented at the annual meeting of the VM Workshop, Wichita, June 1983.

- Goldberg, Gabriel. *Service Virtual Machines.* VM Applications Handbook, McGraw-Hill, 1989.

- Goldberg, Gabriel, and Philip H. Smith III. *The REXX Handbook.* McGraw-Hill, 1992, ISBN 0-07-023682-8.

- *International Information Management Congress (IMC) Journal*, May-June 1987.

- IBM. *Application Development/Cycle Concepts.* IBM manual, order no. GC26-4531.

- IBM. *Application Development/Cycle ... Guide for Evaluating Tool Integration.* IBM manual, order no. G580-0024.

- IBM. *Attachable Media Manager/VM Command Language Reference.* IBM manual, order no. SC24-5576.

- IBM. *Attachable Media Manager/VM Installation and Operations.* IBM manual, order no. SC24-5575.

- IBM. *Automated Console Operation for VM/XA.* IBM manual, order no. GG24-3269.

- IBM. *BookManager READ/DOS General Information.* IBM manual, order no. GB35-0816.

- IBM. *BookManager READ/MVS General Information.* IBM manual, order no. GC38-2032.

- IBM. *BookManager READ/VM and BUILD/VM General Information.* IBM manual, order no. GC23-0447.

- IBM. *Capacity Planning and Performance Management Methodology.* IBM manual, order no. GG22-9288.

- IBM. *Care and Handling of the IBM Magnetic Tape Cartridge.* IBM manual, order no. GA32-0047.

- IBM. *CMS Pipelines Tutorial.* IBM manual, order no. GG66-3158.

- IBM. *CMS Shared File System Primer.* IBM manual, order no. GG24-3709.

- IBM. *CP67/CMS User's Guide.* IBM manual, order no. GH20-0859.

- IBM. *Device Support Facilities User's Guide and Reference.* IBM manual, order no. GC35-0033.

- IBM. *Enterprise Systems Architecture/370: Principles of Operation.* IBM manual, order no. SA22-7200.

- IBM. *Enterprise Systems Architecture/390: Principles of Operation.* IBM manual, order no. SA22-7201.

- IBM. *Enterprise Systems Architecture/XA: Principles of Operation.* IBM manual, order no. SC24-5594.

- IBM. *Environmental Report Editing and Printing Program (EREP) User's Guide and Reference.* IBM manual, order no. GC28-1378.

- IBM. *Introducing VM RSCS Networking Version 3.* IBM manual, order no. GX24-5265.

- IBM. *An Introduction to Advanced Program-to-Program Communication.* IBM manual, order no. GG24-1584.

- IBM. *LAN Resource Extension and Service/VM General Information.* IBM manual, order no. GC24-5618.

- IBM. *LAN Resource Extension and Service/VM Administration.* IBM manual, order no. SC24-5620.

- IBM. *LAN Resource Extension and Service/VM Planning and Installation.* IBM manual, order no. SC24-5619.

- IBM. *Live Parsing Editor Reference.* IBM manual, order no. SL26-0029.

- IBM. *Live Parsing Editor User's Guide.* IBM manual, order no. SL26-0028.

- IBM. *Maintaining IBM Storage Subsystem Media.* IBM manual, order no. GC26-4495.

- IBM. *Managing VM/SP HPO Real Storage Constraint Below the 16 Megabyte Line.* IBM manual, order no. GG66-0261.

- IBM. *Marketing Publications KWIC Index.* IBM manual, order no. G320-1621.

- IBM. *MUMPS/VM Reference.* IBM manual, order no. SB35-0503.

- IBM. *MUMPS/VM User's Guide.* IBM manual, order no. SB35-0502.

- IBM. *MUMPS/VM Utilities Programmers Guide.* IBM manual, order no. SB35-0504.

- IBM. *MVS/Extended Architecture System Programming Library: 31-Bit Addressing.* IBM manual, order no. GC28-1158

- IBM. *Network Implementation Guide Version 3 Release 4 for MVS/ESA, VM/SP, and VM/ESA.* IBM manual, order no. SC31-6434.

- IBM. *OfficeVision/VM Release 2 Functional Guide.* IBM manual, order no. GG22-9498.

- IBM. *Organizing and Maintaining a System Library.* IBM manual, order no. GE20-0731.

- IBM. *Performance Management in a Virtual Machine Environment using the Virtual Machine Performance Planning Facility.* IBM manual, order no. GG66-3143.

- IBM. *Program Directory for Use with Virtual Machine/Enterprise Systems Architecture System Delivery Offering (VM/ESA SDO).* IBM reference material.

- IBM. *Program-to-Program Communications in Systems Application Architecture (SAA) Environments* IBM manual, order no. GG24-3482.

- IBM. *Realtime Monitor VM/ESA Program Description/Operations.* IBM manual, order no. SH26-7000.

- IBM. *Remote Operation of VM/ESA and MVS/ESA Guests using Target System Control Facility.* IBM manual, order no. GG24-3679.

- IBM. *S/370 and S/390 Optical Media Attach/2 Installation and Users Guide.* IBM manual, order no. SC53-1200.

- IBM. *S/370 and S/390 Optical Media Attach/2 Technical Reference.* IBM manual, order no. SV53-1201.

- IBM. *SAA AD/Cycle Language Environment/370 Programming Guide.* IBM manual, order no. SC26-4818.

- IBM. *SAA BookManager READ/2 General Information.* IBM manual, order no. GB35-0800.

- IBM. *SAA CCS Summary.* IBM manual, order no. GC31-6810.

- IBM. *SAA Common Programming Interface: Summary.* IBM manual, order no. GC26-4675.

- IBM. *SAA ... Guide for Evaluating Applications.* IBM manual, order no. G320-9803.

- IBM. *Server Tasking Environment/VM Programming RPQ P81089 Programmer's Guide and Reference.* IBM manual, order no. SL26-0027.

- IBM. *SoftwareXcel CustomPac/VM IBM announcement letter.* 392-048.

- IBM. *SoftwareXcel SystemPac/VM VM/ESA 1.1.1 Installation Guide.* IBM reference material.

- IBM. *SQL/Data System Application Programming for IBM VM Systems.* IBM manual, order no. SH09-8086.

- IBM. *SQL/Data System Administration for IBM VM Systems.* IBM manual, order no. GH09-8084.

- IBM. *SQL/Data System Database Administration for IBM VM Systems.* IBM manual, order no. GH09-8083.

- IBM. *SQL / Data System Database Services Utility for IBM VM Systems*. IBM manual, order no. SH09-8088.

- IBM. *SQL / Data System General Information for IBM VM Systems*. IBM manual, order no. GH09-8074.

- IBM. *SQL / Data System Interactive SQL Guide and Reference for IBM VM Systems*. IBM manual, order no. SH09-8085.

- IBM. *SQL / Data System Operation for IBM VM Systems*. IBM manual, order no. SH09-8080.

- IBM. *SQL / Data System SQL Reference for IBM VM Systems and VSE*. IBM manual, order no. SH09-8087.

- IBM. *SQL / Data System VM Data Spaces Support for VM / ESA*. IBM manual, order no. SH09-8107.

- IBM. *Systems Application Architecture Overview*. IBM manual, order no. GC26-4341.

- IBM. *Systems Application Architecture: SystemView Concepts*. IBM manual, order no. SC23-0578.

- IBM. *IBM System / 360 and System / 370 I / O Interface Channel to Control Unit Original Equipment Manufacturers' Information*. IBM manual, order no. GA22-6974.

- IBM. *System / 370 and System / 390 Optical Media Attach / 2*. IBM reference material, order no. G325-5026.

- IBM. *System / 370: Principles of Operation*. IBM manual, order no. GA22-7000.

- IBM. *System / 370, 30xx, 4300, and 9370 Processors Bibliography*. IBM manual, order no. GC20-0370.

- IBM. *Systems Journal*. Volume 30, no. 1 (1991), order no. G321-0102.

- IBM. *Transaction Programmer's Reference for LU Type 6.2*. IBM manual, order no. GC30-3084.

- IBM. *Virtual Machine Performance Planning Facility Guide and Reference.* IBM manual, order no. SH24-5230.

- IBM. *Virtual Machine Performance Planning Facility Primer.* IBM manual, order no. SH24-5198.

- IBM. *Virtual Machine Remote Spooling Communications Subsystem Networking Diagnosis Reference Version 3, Release 1.* IBM manual, order no. LY24-5248.

- IBM. *Virtual Machine Remote Spooling Communications Subsystem Networking Exit Customization Guide.* IBM manual, order no. SH24-5222.

- IBM. *Virtual Machine Remote Spooling Communications Subsystem Networking General Information.* IBM manual, order no. GH24-5221.

- IBM. *Virtual Machine Remote Spooling Communications Subsystem Networking Operation and Use.* IBM manual, order no. SH24-5220.

- IBM. *Virtual Machine Remote Spooling Communications Subsystem Networking Planning and Installation.* IBM manual, order no. SH24-5219.

- IBM. *Virtual Machine/Extended Architecture: Bimodal CMS Application Programming Considerations.* IBM reference material, order no. GG24-3278.

- IBM. *Virtual Machine/Enterprise Systems Architecture: CMS Administration Reference.* IBM manual, order no. SC24-5446.

- IBM. *Virtual Machine/Enterprise Systems Architecture: CMS Application Development Guide.* IBM manual, order no. SC24-5450.

- IBM. *Virtual Machine/Enterprise Systems Architecture: CMS Application Development Guide for Assembler.* IBM manual, order no. SC24-5452.

- IBM. *Virtual Machine/Enterprise Systems Architecture: CMS Application Development Reference.* IBM manual, order no. SC24-5451.

- IBM. *Virtual Machine/Enterprise Systems Architecture: CMS Application Development Reference for Assembler.* IBM manual, order no. SC24-5453.

- IBM. *Virtual Machine/Enterprise Systems Architecture: CMS Application Migration Guide.* IBM manual, order no. SC24-5454.

- IBM. *Virtual Machine/Enterprise Systems Architecture: CMS Application Multitasking.* IBM manual, order no. SC24-5652.

- IBM. *Virtual Machine/Enterprise Systems Architecture: CMS Command Reference.* IBM manual, order no. SC24-5461.

- IBM. *Virtual Machine/Enterprise Systems Architecture: CMS Command Reference Summary.* IBM reference material, order no. SX24-5249.

- IBM. *Virtual Machine/Enterprise Systems Architecture: CMS Data Areas and Control Blocks.* IBM manual, order no. LY24-5245.

- IBM. *Virtual Machine/Enterprise Systems Architecture: CMS Diagnosis Reference.* IBM manual, order no. LY24-5244.

- IBM. *Virtual Machine/Enterprise Systems Architecture: CMS Pipelines Reference (Available with APAR VM47212).* IBM manual, order no. SC24-5592.

- IBM. *Virtual Machine/Enterprise Systems Architecture: CMS Pipelines Reference Summary.* IBM reference material, order no. SX24-5270.

- IBM. *Virtual Machine/Enterprise Systems Architecture: CMS Pipelines User's Guide (Available with APAR VM47212).* IBM manual, order no. SC24-5609.

- IBM. *Virtual Machine/Enterprise Systems Architecture: CMS Planning and Administration Guide.* IBM manual, order no. SC24-5445.

- IBM. *Virtual Machine/Enterprise Systems Architecture: CMS Primer.* IBM manual, order no. SC24-5458.

- IBM. *Virtual Machine/Enterprise Systems Architecture: CMS Primer Summary of Commands.* IBM reference material, order no. SX24-5247.

- IBM. *Virtual Machine/Enterprise Systems Architecture: CMS User's Guide.* IBM manual, order no. SC24-5460.

- IBM. *Virtual Machine/Enterprise Systems Architecture: CMS Utilities Feature.* IBM manual, order no. SC24-5535.

- IBM. *Virtual Machine/Enterprise Systems Architecture: Common Programming Interface Communications User's Guide.* IBM manual, order no. SC24-5595.

- IBM. *Virtual Machine/Enterprise Systems Architecture: Connectivity Planning, Administration, and Operation.* IBM manual, order no. SC24-5448.

- IBM. *Virtual Machine/Enterprise Systems Architecture: Conversion Notebook.* IBM manual, order no. SC24-5525.

- IBM. *Virtual Machine/Enterprise Systems Architecture: CP Command and Utility Reference.* IBM manual, order no. SC24-5519.

- IBM. *Virtual Machine/Enterprise Systems Architecture: CP Command and Utility Reference Summary.* IBM reference material, order no. SX24-5271.

- IBM. *Virtual Machine/Enterprise Systems Architecture: CP Data Areas and Control Blocks.* IBM manual, order no. LY24-5253.

- IBM. *Virtual Machine/Enterprise Systems Architecture: CP Diagnosis Reference.* IBM manual, order no. LY24-5251.

- IBM. *Virtual Machine/Enterprise Systems Architecture: CP Diagnosis Reference Summary.* IBM reference material, order no. LX24-5260.

- IBM. *Virtual Machine/Enterprise Systems Architecture: CP Planning and Administration.* IBM manual, order no. SC24-5521.

- IBM. *Virtual Machine/Enterprise Systems Architecture: CP Planning and Administration for 370.* IBM manual, order no. SC24-5430.

- IBM. *Virtual Machine/Enterprise Systems Architecture: CP Programming Services.* IBM manual, order no. SC24-5520.

- IBM. *Virtual Machine/Enterprise Systems Architecture: CP Programming Services for 370.* IBM manual, order no. SC24-5435.

- IBM. *Virtual Machine/Enterprise Systems Architecture: Customization Guide.* IBM manual, order no. SC24-5562.

- IBM. *Virtual Machine/Enterprise Systems Architecture: DFSMS/VM Diagnosis Guide.* IBM manual, order no. LY27-9589.

- IBM. *Virtual Machine/Enterprise Systems Architecture: DFSMS/VM Installation and Customization.* IBM manual, order no. SC26-4704.

- IBM. *Virtual Machine/Enterprise Systems Architecture: DFSMS/VM Messages and Codes.* IBM manual, order no. SC26-4707.

- IBM. *Virtual Machine/Enterprise Systems Architecture: DFSMS/VM Overview.* IBM manual, order no. GC26-4703.

- IBM. *Virtual Machine/Enterprise Systems Architecture: DFSMS/VM User's Guide.* IBM manual, order no. SC26-4705.

- IBM. *Virtual Machine/Enterprise Systems Architecture: Diagnosis Guide.* IBM manual, order no. LY24-5250.

- IBM. *Virtual Machine/Enterprise Systems Architecture: Dump Viewing Facility Operation Guide and Reference.* IBM manual, order no. SC24-5530.

- IBM. *Virtual Machine/Enterprise Systems Architecture: Enterprise Systems Architecture/Extended Configuration Principles of Operation.* IBM manual, order no. SC24-5594.

- IBM. *Virtual Machine/Enterprise Systems Architecture: Features Summary.* IBM manual, order no. LY24-5252.

- IBM. *Virtual Machine/Enterprise Systems Architecture: General Information.* IBM manual, order no. GC24-5550.

- IBM. *Virtual Machine/Enterprise Systems Architecture: Group Control System Reference.* IBM manual, order no. SC24-5531.

- IBM. *Virtual Machine/Enterprise Systems Architecture: Installation Guide.* IBM manual, order no. SC24-5526.

- IBM. *Virtual Machine/Enterprise Systems Architecture: Introduction.* IBM manual, order no. GC24-5441.

- IBM. *Virtual Machine/Enterprise Systems Architecture: Library Guide and Master Index.* IBM manual, order no. GC24-5518.

- IBM. *Virtual Machine/Enterprise Systems Architecture: Library Roadmap.* IBM reference material, order no. GX24-5276.

- IBM. *Virtual Machine/Enterprise Systems Architecture: Licensed Program Specifications.* IBM manual, order no. GC24-5439.

- IBM. *Virtual Machine/Enterprise Systems Architecture: Procedures Language VM/REXX Primer.* IBM manual, order no. SC24-5598.

- IBM. *Virtual Machine/Enterprise Systems Architecture: Procedures Language VM/REXX Reference.* IBM manual, order no. SC24-5466.

- IBM. *Virtual Machine/Enterprise Systems Architecture: Procedures Language VM/REXX Reference Summary.* IBM reference material, order no. SX24-5251.

- IBM. *Virtual Machine/Enterprise Systems Architecture: Procedures Language VM/REXX Users Guide.* IBM manual, order no. SC24-5465.

- IBM. *Virtual Machine/Enterprise Systems Architecture: Programmer's Guide to the Server-Requester Programming Interface for VM.* IBM manual, order no. SC24-5455.

- IBM. *Virtual Machine/Enterprise Systems Architecture: Quick Reference.* IBM reference material, order no. SX24-5259.

- IBM. *Virtual Machine/Enterprise Systems Architecture: Release 1.0 Performance Report.* IBM manual, order no. ZZ05-0469.

- IBM. *Virtual Machine/Enterprise Systems Architecture: Release 1.1 Performance Report.* IBM manual, order no. GG66-3236.

- IBM. *Virtual Machine/Enterprise Systems Architecture: REXX/EXEC Migration Tool for VM/ESA.* IBM manual, order no. GC24-5607.

- IBM. *Virtual Machine/Enterprise Systems Architecture: Running Guest Operating Systems.* IBM manual, order no. SC24-5522.

- IBM. *Virtual Machine/Enterprise Systems Architecture: SAA Common Programming Interface Communications Reference.* IBM manual, order no. SC26-4399.

- IBM. *Virtual Machine/Enterprise Systems Architecture: SAA Common Programming Interface Resource Recovery Reference.* IBM manual, order no. SC31-6821.

- IBM. *Virtual Machine/Enterprise Systems Architecture: Service Guide.* IBM manual, order no. SC24-5527.

- IBM. *Virtual Machine/Enterprise Systems Architecture: Software Vendor Product Directory.* IBM manual, order no. GC24-5461.

- IBM. *Virtual Machine/Enterprise Systems Architecture: System Messages and Codes.* IBM manual, order no. SC24-5529.

- IBM. *Virtual Machine/Enterprise Systems Architecture: System Operation.* IBM manual, order no. SC24-5528.

- IBM. *Virtual Machine/Enterprise Systems Architecture: Using Online Documentation.* IBM manual, order no. GC24-5583.

- IBM. *Virtual Machine/Enterprise Systems Architecture: Using Release 1.1 Enhancements.* IBM manual, order no. SC24-5596.

- IBM. *Virtual Machine/Enterprise Systems Architecture: Virtual Machine Operation.* IBM manual, order no. SC24-5523.

- IBM. *Virtual Machine/Enterprise Systems Architecture: VM/ESA Solutions.* IBM reference material, order no. GBOF-1439.

- IBM. *Virtual Machine/Enterprise Systems Architecture: VMSES/E Introduction and Reference.* IBM manual, order no. SC24-5444.

- IBM. *Virtual Machine/Enterprise Systems Architecture: XEDIT Command and Macro Reference.* IBM manual, order no. SC24-5464.

- IBM. *Virtual Machine/Enterprise Systems Architecture: XEDIT Command Reference Summary.* IBM reference material, order no. SX24-5250.

- IBM. *Virtual Machine/Enterprise Systems Architecture: XEDIT User's Guide.* IBM manual, order no. SC24-5463.

- IBM. *Virtual Machine/System Product EXEC 2 Reference.* IBM manual, order no. SC24-5219.

- IBM. *Virtual Machine/System Product High Performance Option: CP for System Programming.* Release 5 (SC19-6224-7), IBM reference material, order no. ST00-2743.

- IBM. *VM Batch Facility General Information.* IBM manual, order no. SC24-5572.

- IBM. *VM Batch Facility Installation, Customization, and Administration.* IBM manual, order no. SC24-5573.

- IBM. *VM Batch Facility User's Guide.* IBM manual, order no. SC24-5574.

- IBM. *VM CMS Pipelines User's Guide for PRPQ P81059.* IBM manual, order no. SL26-0018

- IBM. *VM Performance Analysis Facility General Information.* IBM manual, order no. GC23-0566.

- IBM. *VM Performance Analysis Facility User's Guide and Reference.* IBM manual, order no. SC23-0564.

- IBM. *VM Performance Reporting Facility User's Guide.* IBM manual, order no. SC23-0460.

- IBM. *VM Personal Workstation Communication Facility General Information.* IBM manual, order no. GL26-0022.

- IBM. *VM Personal Workstation Communication Services: Host Guide and Reference.* IBM manual, order no. SC24-5593.

- IBM. *VM Personal Workstation Communication Services: Installation Checklist.* IBM manual, order no. SX24-5268.

- IBM. *VM Personal Workstation Communication Services: Managing VM PWSCS.* IBM manual, order no. SC24-5585.

- IBM. *VM Personal Workstation Communication Services: Programming for VM.* IBM manual, order no. SC24-5586.

- IBM. *VM Real Time Monitor (SMART) Program Description and Operations.* IBM manual, order no. SH20-2337.

- IBM. *VM/Directory Maintenance: General Information.* IBM manual, order no. GC20-1836

- IBM. *VM/Directory Maintenance: Operation and Use.* IBM manual, order no. SC23-0437

- IBM. *VM/Integrated System: General Information.* IBM manual, order no. GH24-5119.

- IBM. *VM/Integrated System: Installing Your System.* IBM manual, order no. SC24-5341.

- IBM. *VM/Integrated System: Planning for Your System.* IBM manual, order no. GH24-5337.

- IBM. *VM/Pass-Through Facility Administration and Operation.* IBM manual, order no. SC25-5557.

- IBM. *VM/Pass-Through Facility Programmer's Reference.* IBM manual, order no. SC25-5556.

- IBM. *VM/Pass-Through Facility User's Guide.* IBM manual, order no. SC25-5555.

- IBM. VM/System Product *System IPO/Extended General Information.* IBM manual, order no. GC20-1890.

- IBM. VM/System Product *System IPO/Extended Planning Guide.* IBM manual, order no. GC20-1874.

- IBM. *VM/XA Storage Planning.* IBM manual, order no. GG66-3141.

- IBM. *VMPPF Usage and Experience Guide.* IBM manual, order no. GG24-3542.

- IBM. *VSE/ESA Master Index.* IBM manual, order no. SC33-6520.

- IBM. *Workstation Data Save Facility/VM Administrator's Guide and Reference.* IBM manual, order no. SH24-5234.

- IBM. *Workstation Data Save Facility/VM AIX User's Guide and Reference.* IBM manual, order no. SH24-5238.

- IBM. *Workstation Data Save Facility/VM Apple Macintosh User's Guide and Reference.* IBM manual, order no. SH24-5243.

- IBM. *Workstation Data Save Facility/VM DOS User's Guide and Reference.* IBM manual, order no. SH24-5236.

- IBM. *Workstation Data Save Facility/VM General Information.* IBM manual, order no. GH24-5232.

- IBM. *Workstation Data Save Facility/VM OS/2 User's Guide and Reference.* IBM manual, order no. SH24-5237.

- IBM. *Workstation Data Save Facility/VM Programmer's Reference.* IBM manual, order no. SH24-5239.

- IBM. *Workstation Data Save Facility/VM RISC System/6000 Client User's Guide.* IBM manual, order no. SH24-5240.

- IBM. *Workstation Data Save Facility/VM Sun User's Guide and Reference.* IBM manual, order no. SH24-5242.

- IBM. *Workstation Data Save Facility/VM: Version 1 for DOS and OS/2 Clients: Implementation Experiences.* IBM manual, order no. GG24-3694.

- Jann, Joefon. *VMPRF Enhancements for VM/ESA.* Paper presented at SHARE 78 session O767, Anaheim, March 1992.

- Lewis, Rhys. *Practical Digital Image Processing.* Ellis Horwood, (ISBN 0-13-683525-2), 1990.

- Marcoux, Anne-Marie. *VMSHARE: How it works, What comes out.* Paper presented at SHARE 77 session O551, Chicago, August 1991.

- McClain, Gary, ed. *VM Applications Handbook.* McGraw-Hill, ISBN 0-07-044948-1, 1989.

- McMaster, James. *How to Do a CP Enhancement.* Proceedings of SHARE 74, Volume 1, Anaheim, CA, March 1990.

- Mosteller, William S. *Systems Programmer's Problem Solver.* QED Information Sciences, 1989 (ISBN 0-89435-271-7).

- Nettleship, T. Scott. *Shared File System Overview and Administration.* Paper presented at SHARE 76 sessions O555 and O556, San Francisco, February 1991.

- Nettleship, T. Scott. *VM/ESA Shared File System.* IBM Systems Journal, Volume 30, no. 1, 1991.

- Nolan, John. *Use of the Programmable Operator Interface (PROP) as an Operator Interface.* Paper presented at SHARE session B867, August 1984.

- Plambeck, K. E. *Concepts of Enterprise Systems Architecture/370.* IBM Systems Journal, Volume 28, no. 1, 1989.

- Polya, George. *How to Solve It.* Princeton University Press, 1973.

- Relay Technology, Inc. (formerly VM Systems Group, Inc.) *KPROBE Reference Guide.* Vienna, VA, 1993

- Robinson, Barton. *Performance Facilities Usable in the VM/ESA World.* Paper presented at SHARE 77, Chicago, August 1991.

- Robinson, Barton, and W. Romney White. *VM/XA System Product Workload Characterization.* Proceedings of Computer Measurement Group, 1990.

- Roegner, Michael. *VM: May I Be of Service.* Paper presented at SHARE session O611, Anaheim, March 1987.

- Savit, Jeffrey. *VM and CMS: Performance and Fine Tuning.* McGraw-Hill, ISBN 0-07-054972-9, 1991.

- Science Applications International Corporation. *MOSAIC Administration Guide VM Server Version 2.0.*

- Science Applications International Corporation. *MOSAIC Application Programming Interface (API) Reference— Workstation 2.0.*

- Science Applications International Corporation. *MOSAIC Installation Guide VM Server Version 2.0.*

- Science Applications International Corporation. *MOSAIC Messages and Codes Version 2.0.*

- Science Applications International Corporation. *MOSAIC Press Kit.*

- Science Applications International Corporation. *MOSAIC Quick Guide Version 2.0.*

- Science Applications International Corporation. *MOSAIC User Guide Version 2.0.*

- Science Applications International Corporation. *MOSAIC Workstation Installation Guide Version 2.0.*

- Tyler, Linda, and John Dooman. *Can SQL/DS Run (Well) on VM?* Paper presented at SHARE session O672, New York, August 1988.

- Usong, Paulus. *VM DASD Performance Update.* Paper presented at SHARE 78 session O764, Anaheim, March 1992.

- Varian, Melinda. *Plunging Into Pipes.* Proceedings of SHARE 76, Volume 1, San Francisco, February 1991.

- Varian, Melinda. *Plunging On—Apprentice Plumbing.* Paper presented at SHARE 78, Anaheim, March 1992.

- Varian, Melinda. *VM and the VM Community: Past, Present, and Future.* Proceedings of SHARE 73, Volume 1, Orlando, FL, August 1989.

- VM Systems Group, Inc. *KPROBE User's Guide.* Vienna, VA, 1993.

- Wagner, Michael. *Using the Programmable Operator in Service Virtual Machines.* Paper presented at SHARE session O558, August 1986.

- Welch, Craig A. *3990-3 Extended Function Use in VM.* Paper presented at SHARE 78 session O768, Anaheim, March 1992.

- White, W. Romney. *Interpreting VM/XA Monitor Data.* Paper presented at SHARE Europe Annual meeting, Vienna, 1989.

- White, W. Romney. *Intro to VM Performance and Tuning.* Paper presented at SHARE Europe Annual meeting, Berlin, 1990.

- White, W. Romney. *Using VM Data Spaces Effectively.* Paper presented at SHARE Europe Spring meeting, Cannes, 1992.

- White, W. Romney. *VM/ESA Monitor Enhancements: Interpreting the Data.* Paper presented at SHARE Europe Spring meeting, Lausanne, 1991.

- White, W. Romney. *VM/XA Paging.* Paper presented at SHARE Europe Spring meeting, Paris, 1990.

- Wilson, T.D., and T.E. Potok. *VM Service Machine Performance.* Paper presented at SHARE session O601, San Francisco, March 1987.

Biographies

Chuck Berghorn

("The IBM OEM Personal/370 Adapter/A")
 Chuck Berghorn is a senior programmer on the Personal/370 project and team leader for the I/O subsystem. He worked on the IBM 7437 and A74, earlier versions of small System/370 systems. He was also team leader for the LANRES/VM PRPQ, and is an author of the IBM Graphics Attachment Program for the 3277GA and for the 5080. Chuck is the original author of the CMS WAKEUP utility and the Panel/2 Lineart Facility. He graduated with a B.S.E.E from Purdue University in 1973, and joined IBM in 1974.
 Chuck Berghorn, IBM Corporation, B/94/MS-P215, Building 915, P.O. Box 950, Poughkeepsie, NY 12602, (914) 433-3004.

Bill Bitner

("CMS Application Performance")
 Bill Bitner is a Staff Programmer in the Performance Evaluation department of the IBM Endicott, NY Programming Laboratory (EPL). Bill is currently EPL representative to the VM Performance and Capacity Planning project of the SHARE user group. He joined IBM in 1985 after receiving a B.S. in Computer Science from the University of Pittsburgh at Johnstown. Bill has worked on performance in various VM areas. In 1990, he received an Outstanding Technical Achievement Award for contributions to VM performance.

He loves his job and the various nicknames picked up during his VM
career: Wild Bill, Bitman, Rapmaster Bill, Bit, Uncle Rapmaster,
and Doctor of Bitology.

William J. Bitner, IBM Corporation, 1701 North Street, Endicott,
NY 13760, (607) 752-6022.

Charles T. Boeheim

("Converting Applications to VM/ESA")

Chuck Boeheim manages the Server Computing Group (encompassing VM and Unix systems) at the Stanford Linear Accelerator
Center (SLAC) in Menlo Park, CA. He has been involved with many
release-to-release conversions, having worked with VM since VM/370
Release 3.

Since receiving his B.A. from Cornell University in 1978 in
Computer Science and Cognitive Psychology he has worked in
University VM computer centers, first at Cornell University and
later at Stanford University. In that time he has worked in user
services, database support, and VM system programming. He was
responsible for porting SPIRES, the Stanford database system, from
Wylbur to VM, and for converting the SLAC VM system from
VM/SP to VM/XA.

In 1988, Chuck joined the CMS Project of SHARE, becoming
Requirements Coordinator later that year and Project Manager in
1990. In 1991 he because Deputy Manager of the VM Group. He
vigorously promotes dialogues between customers and IBM, which
have resulted in release of such internal IBM products as CMS Pipelines and LEXX. He has presented several talks at SHARE, such as
Low Overhead File Sharing in VM, *Exploiting VM/XA*, and *Pipelines Programming Paradigms: Prefab Plumbing*.

SLAC is among the top research institutes in high energy physics
in the world. SLAC operates a two-mile long electron-positron accelerator on the Stanford campus in the foothills near the San Francisco Bay. Since 1981, VM has been the primary operating system
at SLAC, providing numerically intensive computing, document
preparation, and mail services to the Stanford high energy physics
community. SLAC is entirely funded by the U.S. Department of
Energy, and is operated by Stanford University.

Charles T. Boeheim, Stanford Linear Accelerator Center, P.O. Box
4349, MS 97, Stanford, CA 94309, (415) 926-4640.

Mark Cathcart

("Wide-Open VM")

Mark is a "certified" IT Specialist(!) in the Enterprise Systems Business Unit for IBM UK. He joined IBM in 1987 and accepted his current position in 1993, where he is the Senior Professional responsible for Client/Server and Open Systems. Previously, Mark was senior professional in VM/VSE Product Management and Technical Support. He is a "Poacher turned Game-keeper" after spending 13 years as an IBM customer, more recently as assistant Manager of Technical Services, responsible for VM systems at a bank in New York.

In January 1993, he was invited to Endicott, New York to help IBM's new Client/Server Computing unit (C/SC) plan for the future. He has been and is involved in a number of customer and IBM development projects and likes to play "devil's advocate" at IBM with his unique insider's perspective.

Mark Cathcart, IBM United Kingdom Ltd., Enterprise Systems AL6, Basingstoke, Hampshire, UK RG21 1EJ.

David J. Chase

("Initial Training and Continuing Education")

David Chase is an education instructor and developer with the IBM Corporation in New York City. He most recently wrote the IBM course for the new VMSES/E installation and service tool for VM/ESA.

During nine years with IBM he has worked as a developer of VM/SP HPO and VM/XA SF and as an instructor and course developer for courses on installation and maintenance topics for VM/SP and HPO, VM/XA SF, VM/XA SP, and VM/ESA.

David has represented IBM VM Education numerous times at SHARE, and has given varied technical presentations there and at local VM user groups around the country.

David Chase, IBM Corporation, 65 East 55th Street, New York, NY 10022, (212) 230-5116.

Pamela Christina

("VM/ESA References" and "Information at Your Fingertips")

Pamela Christina is a Staff Programmer with the IBM Endicott Programming Lab (EPL). She holds a B.A. in Mathematics from State University of New York at Cortland College. Pam spent a decade in VM Information Development (fondly known as PUBS) which included an enjoyable three years as publications representative to the SHARE VM New Users Project. She recently joined the EPL Customer Support group that concentrates on VM critical situations and customer satisfaction issues.

Pamela Christina, IBM Corporation, EPL Customer Support, Department G13/Building 17, P.O Box 8010, Endicott, NY 13760, (607) 752-6125.

Susan Cirulli

("Systems Application Architecture in VM/ESA")

Susan, who has an M.S. in Applied Statistics from George Washington University, joined IBM in 1983 after working several years as an applications programmer on both IBM and non-IBM systems. Susan spent her first few years with IBM performing competitive evaluations and analysis. She then joined Marketing, working with customers to convert applications to IBM platforms. In 1988 she began working more closely on VM and application development strategy, and was the VM focal point for SAA Planning for several years. Susan is now in the Endicott Programming Laboratory Strategy and Plan Management department, where she works on market research and opportunity definitions.

Susan Cirulli, Staff Planner, IBM Enterprise Systems Line of Business, Endicott Programming Laboratory, Endicott, NY 13760.

Chip Coy

("Systems Application Architecture in VM/ESA", "Native Application Development and Execution", and "VM/ESA–Workstation Synergy")

Chip joined IBM in 1983 as a VM programmer in the Thomas J. Watson Research Center in Yorktown Heights, NY. In 1987 he moved to Endicott, NY, where his work in VM planning led to the position of focal point for VM/SAA System Planning. In 1990 Chip moved to a technical position in the Enterprise Systems Client

Server Products area, concentrating on platforms and products to enable System/390 operating systems and programmable workstations to work together to meet business needs. Chip is technical lead for the Data Facility Distributed Storage Manager (DFDSM) server on VM and MVS.

Chip Coy, Advisory Programmer, IBM Enterprise Systems, Endicott Programming Laboratory, Endicott, NY 13760, (607) 752-6392.

Eleanor Coy

("Native Application Development and Execution")

Eleanor joined IBM in 1984 as a VM programmer at East Fishkill. In 1987 she moved to Endicott as VM planning liason with VM office and printer products. In 1991, Eleanor moved to VM product planning and system design working on CMS and GCS.

Eleanor Coy, Staff Programmer, IBM Enterprise Systems, Endicott Programming Laboratory, Endicott, NY 13760, (607) 752-2583.

Dean C. DiTomasso

("Systems Application Architecture in VM/ESA")

In 1980, Dean joined IBM in Kingston, NY, with a Bachelors degree in Computer Science from the State University of New York at Potsdam. While in Kingston, he held several positions in the Data Systems Division Assurance organization. In 1987, Dean relocated to IBM in Endicott, NY, his current location. In Endicott, Dean has held Planning and Project Office positions in the 4381 Product Engineering Customer Satisfaction Center, the 9370 Packaged Solutions organization, and the Endicott Programming Laboratory. Dean's present position is in the Endicott Programming Laboratory Solutions Planning organization as laboratory focal point for VM/ESA SAA System Strategy and Planning.

Dean DiTomasso, Advisory Planner, IBM Enterprise Systems Line of Business, Endicott Programming Laboratory, Endicott, NY 13760.

Joel A. Farrell

("Server Tasking Environment/VM")

Joel Farrell is an Advisory Programmer at the IBM Endicott Programming Laboratory in Endicott, NY. He joined IBM in Endicott in 1981 in VM Development where he has worked on areas such as I/O, XA-mode execution, saved segment management, and program management. Most recently he led the effort to develop the Server Tasking Environment/VM product.

Joel received his B.S. in Computer Science from Kansas State University in 1980 and his M.S. degree in 1985 from Syracuse University, also in Computer Science. He is an IBM representative to SHARE and a member of the Association for Computing Machinery.

Joel A. Farrell, IBM Data Systems Division, P.O. Box 6, Endicott NY 13760, (607) 752-1852.

Gabriel Goldberg

("Exploiting Service Machines"; co-editor of this book)

Gabriel Goldberg is president of Computers and Publishing, Inc., and active as a consultant and writer, emphasizing IBM and VM computing. He worked for VM Systems Group, Inc. (now Relay Technology, Inc.) for six years, most recently as vice president of technology, responsible at various times for product planning, evolution, and development, along with documentation and customer support. Relay develops and markets data center and end-user software. He wrote and edited *V/Update*, the technical newsletter received every two months by more than 20,000 VM system programmers and users around the world.

Before joining VMSG, he was a senior staff member at The MITRE Corporation, where his involvement with VM began in 1972 by coordinating conversion from MVT to Release 1 of VM/370; he has been a VM enthusiast ever since. Since MITRE was among the first VM sites, many software tools developed by Gabe were widely used, aiding other installations when IBM's support of VM was very weak. Prior to MITRE, he worked in IBM's OS System Design Department in Poughkeepsie, New York. Gabe has consulted for clients such as The World Bank, The University of California, and the Association for Computing Machinery. He obtained a B.S. in Mathematics from The Polytechnic Institute of Brooklyn.

Gabe, active in many national and local IBM user groups, was a founding member and elected director of MVMUA (Metropolitan New York VM Users Association, the oldest and largest local VM user group), is a member of the Hillgang (Washington, DC, area VM user group) steering committee, and has held several management jobs in SHARE (a major national IBM user group), most recently serving as CMS project manager. He has given hundreds of presentations to these and other groups, and contributes frequently to trade publications.

Gabe co-edited *The REXX Handbook* (McGraw-Hill, 1992, ISBN 0-07-023682-8), *The VM/ESA Systems Handbook* (McGraw-Hill, 1993, ISBN 0-07-023686-0), *The VM/ESA Users and Applications Handbook* (McGraw-Hill, 1993, ISBN 0-07-023703-4), all with Philip H. Smith III, and *The AS/400 Communications and Connectivity Handbook* (McGraw-Hill, 1993, ISBN 0-07-023692-5), with John Foley.

Gabriel Goldberg, Computers and Publishing, Inc., P.O. Box 3882, McLean, VA 22103, (703) 506-1125 x237, (703) 506-0936 (FAX).

Dave Hemsath

("MOSAIC—The VM/ESA Imaging Solution")

Dave Hemsath is a Senior Programmer at the IBM VM Development Laboratory in Endicott, NY. He is technical leader of the team working with SAIC's MOSAIC development group.

He has held varied technical and management positions at Endicott and IBM headquarters in Westchester County, New York. His interests include client/server systems, computer graphics, and multimedia.

Dave joined IBM in July 1979 after receiving a B.S. in Computer Engineering from the University of Nebraska at Lincoln.

Dave Hemsath, IBM Corporation, P.O. Box 6, Endicott, NY 13760, (607) 752-2870.

Jim Hughes

("Application Development for Guest Systems")

Jim Hughes is a Software Developer with Systems and Communication Sciences in New Ipswich, NH. While working for a large database company he was responsible for design and implementation of a source code library system. The library system ran in CMS and supported a VM version of the software, OS/MVS version of the software, and DOS/VSE version of the software.

Jim has been in the software business since 1969. During his career, he has developed commercial applications, teleprocessing monitors and database systems; managed a timesharing company;

and was cofounder of a computer-based commodity trading system. He graduated from Florida Institute of Technology with a B.S. in Computer Science.

In 1988, Jim became Vice President of the New England Users of VM, NEUVM. He is currently NEUVM President.

He has written articles for *VM update* published by Xephon.

Jim Hughes, 5 Almas Street, Windham, NH 03087, (508) 486-5965.

Dan Hunsinger

("MOSAIC—The VM/ESA Imaging Solution")

Dan Hunsinger is Chief Architect and Manager of the MOSAIC development team in San Diego, CA. Dan's first assignment was working on the PC-DOS LAN predecessor to MOSAIC.

SAIC is a world-wide, diversified, high-technology research, engineering, and systems integration company with over 12,000 employees. MOSAIC is SAIC's commercial operational image offering, based on its experience in developing custom image solutions for several years.

Dan worked for other companies on imaging and micrographics projects before joining SAIC in June 1988. He received a B.S. in Computer Science from Iowa State University in 1984.

Dan Hunsinger, SAIC Commercial Systems, 10770 Wateridge Circle, San Diego, CA 92121, (619) 552-5224.

John A. Hupcey

("The IBM OEM Personal/370 Adapter/A")

John A. Hupcey received his B.S.E.E. degree in 1974 and his M.E.E. in 1975, both from Cornell University. Before joining IBM he worked on the design of digital long distance switching systems. He joined IBM in 1978 at the Thomas J. Watson Research Center to work on high-speed System/370 processor design. In the IBM Poughkeepsie Laboratory, he has worked on the Processor Controller for the IBM 3090, the IBM 7437 Technical Workstation, LANRES/VM, and the the Personal/370 workstation. In his spare time he likes to do VM system programming.

John A. Hupcey, IBM Corporation, B94/MS-P215, Building 915, P.O. Box 950, Poughkeepsie, NY 12602, (914) 433-3106.

Steven L. Jones

("Converting Applications to VM/ESA")

Steve Jones is a Senior Programmer in IBM's Rochester, MN programming laboratory, working in AS/400 SLIC Supervisor Development. Steve joined IBM in Kingston, NY, in VM/XA CP Component Test. As a member of the CMS Release 5.5 Development Team, he wrote much of the CMS Release 5.5 Storage Manager. He was also responsible for the original CMS support for VM/XA Segment Packing, and wrote the STORMAP, SUBPMAP, and STDEBUG CMS commands. He continued involvement with CMS after development of CMS 5.5 and became a regular SHARE attendee as an IBM Representative to the CMS Project. He moved from Kingston to Endicott as part of the VM consolidation. In Endicott, he worked as a CMS System Designer, and was owner of the CMS Design APAR process, with responsibility for providing technical direction to CMS development. He was also involved with evaluating customer requirements for CMS and finding delivery mechanisms.

Steve recently transferred from Endicott to Rochester, MN, to work on AS/400 product development. He has a B.A. in Computer Science from the University of Minnesota.

Steven L. Jones, IBM Corporation, Department 4A5/Building 030-2, 3605 Highway 52 North, Rochester, MN, 55901-7829, (507) 253-1425.

Peter Kohlmann

("SQL/DS and VM Data Spaces Support")

Peter Kohlmann is an Information Developer at the IBM Canada Laboratory in Toronto. As a member of the SQL/DS development team, he worked on documentation for the VM Data Spaces Support (VMDSS) Feature, and has spent the last year writing *The SQL/DS Performance Tuning Handbook*. He has a B.S. in Electrical Engineering from Queen's University in Kingston, Ontario.

Peter Kohlmann, IBM Canada Ltd., 3G/946/1150, 1150 Eglinton Avenue, Toronto, Ontario Canada M3C 1H7, (416) 448-3827.

David Kreuter

("CMS Application Diagnosis")

David Kreuter has 10 years experience with the VM operating system. Mr. Kreuter is founder and president of VM RESOURCES LTD., a company specializing in comprehensive VM consulting services.

Mr. Kreuter is an internationally respected technical consultant in the VM community. He has taught and developed courses for vendor and customer organizations throughout the U.S. and Canada, and is a frequent speaker at VM user groups.

VM RESOURCES LTD. provides technical consulting in system and application tuning and measurement, system programming, and program development for leading VM clients throughout North America.

Prior to forming VM RESOURCES LTD. three years ago, Mr. Kreuter held a variety of progressive professional positions with IBM Canada and the DMR Group.

David Kreuter, VM Resources Ltd., 60 Cantertrot Court, Thornhill, Ontario, Canada L4J 7X7, (416) 660-3639.

Tom Kumpf

("VM/ESA Fundamentals, Features, and Components")

Tom Kumpf is Product Development Manager for Relay Technology, Inc. (formerly VM Systems Group, Inc.), in Vienna, VA. He has 24 years of experience in IBM computing, 17 of which are with VM. Tom wrote VMSG products V/SEG and V/SPOOL.

Prior to joining VMSG in 1986, he was a system programmer for Boeing Computer Services, specializing in CP internals. He spends his free time with his wife Sue, daughters Alicia and Lindsay, their yellow Labrador Maggie, and Albert, their parrot.

Tom Kumpf, Relay Technology, Inc., 1604 Spring Hill Road, Vienna, VA 22182, (703) 506-0500.

W. D. McDaniel

("Overview of VM/ESA Printing/Publishing")

W. D. McDaniel, Chief Research Officer for GenText, Inc., describes himself as a VM bigot. In addition to co-owning GenText, and co-writing books and articles for the trade press with P. C.

McGrew, McDaniel functions as chief designer for all GenText products and projects.

McDaniel has a varied background in computers. From 1975 through 1982 he was employed by NCH Corporation, a Texas-based chemical manufacturer. While there he dealt with all aspects of data processing, including operations, production control, system programming, and applications, including an assignment as operations manager for the NCH U.K. office in Birmingham, England.

In 1982 he moved on to become manager of product development, and later director of research and design, for a software company specializing in providing laser printing and demand publishing products to the insurance industry.

He is involved in the SHARE Document Composition and Electronic Publishing Project as a speaker. He is also co-author of *In-House Publishing in a Mainframe Environment* (1987, 1990) and *On-line Text Management: HyperText and Other Techniques* (January 1989), both published by McGraw-Hill. McGrew and McDaniel also co-write articles for the trade press.

GenText was founded in 1989 by P. C. McGrew and W. D. McDaniel. The GenText product line and services emphasize a company philosophy that any corporate document should be viewable and printable anywhere in the enterprise, regardless of how it was created.

GenText is an IBM Business Partner and an IBM Application Specialist for Electronic Publishing in corporate environments. GenText, a member of SHARE and XPLOR, is a VM-based organization, doing code development in REXX and C.

GenText's strategy is to provide:

- Innovative solutions for enabling enterprise-wide print and view strategies
- Tactical custom solution development for integrating incompatible print and view products
- Consulting in long term print and view strategies.
- Custom application development for all aspects of electronic publishing.

W.D. McDaniel, GenText, Inc., 9400 N. Central Expressway, Suite 1640 LAB 147, Dallas, TX 75231-5045, (214) 691-0300.

P. C. McGrew

("Overview of VM/ESA Printing/Publishing")

P. C. (Pat) McGrew is President and CEO of GenText, Inc., a company based in Dallas, Texas, specializing in corporate publishing solutions, usually VM-based. With her partner, W.D. McDaniel, she has positioned GenText as a provider of corporate publishing environment studies, software enablers to permit execution of the GenText philosophy that *any* document, regardless of where it was created, should be printable or viewable anywhere in the enterprise, and IBM mainframe hypertext applications for delivering online documentation and softcopy.

Prior to forming GenText with McDaniel in September 1989, McGrew worked for software developers and manufacturers as Documentation Specialist, Documentation Manager, and Product Advisor. She has also worked in the printing industry as a type-setter, publication manager, and publication designer. Her expertise in both traditional and electronic printing and publishing, a variety of composition languages and products, and corporate publishing concepts and requirements form part of the foundation for the GenText product line.

McGrew is involved in both the SHARE Document Composition and Electronic Publishing Project of the Integrated Technologies Group and Technical Communication Project of the Management Group as a speaker, planner, and Project Officer. She is a nationally recognized consultant in both development of host-based text applications and in development of text management strategies, and is certified by XPLOR International as an Electronic Document Printer and Publisher (EDPP).

She co-wrote with McDaniel *In-House Publishing in a Mainframe Environment* (1987, 1990) and *On-line Text Management: HyperText and Other Techniques* (January 1989), both published by McGraw-Hill. McGrew and McDaniel also co-write articles for the trade press.

P.C. McGrew, GenText, Inc., 9400 N. Central Expressway, Suite 1640 LAB 147, Dallas, TX 75231-5045, (214) 691-0300.

Stuart McRae

("VM Communications")

Stuart McRae has a degree in Computing Science from Imperial College in London. He subsequently became a system programmer in the Computing Department at Imperial, working on VM/370 Release 2 and beyond. He is a past chairman of the SHARE Europe (SEAS) VM Regional Committee for UK and Ireland, and is currently on the Executive Board and Treasurer of SHARE Europe. Over the past 18 years he not only has worked with all major VM releases, but also has wide experience outside the VM world (including MVS and Unix).

Stuart McRae is currently European product manager for Soft-Switch, a vendor of mail system interconnectivity and gateway products for VM and MVS. He has been directly involved in development, design, architecture, and management of products for VM since 1983.

Stuart McRae, Imperium, Imperial Way, Worton Grange, Reading, Berks, England RG2 0TD, 011 44 734 757100.

Scott Nettleship

("Exploiting the Shared File System")

Scott Nettleship is an IBM Staff Programmer in CMS file system development in Endicott, NY. He has been part of the VM Development team since 1983. Scott has a B.S. in Computer Science from Rutgers University and a M.S. in Computer Science from State University of New York (SUNY) at Binghamton. Scott wrote a recent article on the CMS Shared File System in the *IBM Systems Journal* (Vol. 30, No. 1, 1991) and is IBM representative to the CMS File System Committee at SHARE.

Scott Nettleship, IBM Corporation, P.O. Box 6, Endicott, NY 13760, (607) 752-6208.

Ray Parker

("VM/ESA Fundamentals, Features, and Components")

Ray Parker is a product developer at Relay Technology, Inc., responsible for development and support of KPROBE, a VM system and dump analysis utility. Before joining Relay Technology, he was a Senior System Specialist for Software AG of North America, working on development and support of products running on VM/CMS, VM/GCS, VSE/SP, and MVS/XA. He began as a system programmer in 1979; with a mixture of employee and consulting experience, he has worked in several installations covering diverse industries as well as hardware and software platforms. His involvement with VM began with VM/SP Release 1, when he became an immediate VM enthusiast.

Ray has had long involvement with HillGang (the Washington, DC, area VM user group), been a steering committee member since 1988, and given occasional presentations. He has been a regular VM Workshop participant for the last six years, and reviewed *The REXX Handbook* manuscript.

Ray Parker, Relay Technology, Inc., 1604 Spring Hill Road, Vienna, VA 22182, (703) 506-0500.

Ross A. Patterson

("Exploiting CMS" and "Exploiting Service Machines")

Ross Patterson has been involved with VM as a system programmer and software developer since 1982, and has been employed as a VM Systems Architect by Sterling Software (formerly Systems Center, Inc.) since October 1989. At Sterling, he has worked on maintenance, enhancement, and design of several systems-management products, including VMBACKUP, NoteKeeper, VMSPOOL and VMARCHIVE.

Before joining Systems Center, Ross was employed by Rutgers University, where he managed VM and MVS research computing systems, and by the New Jersey Educational Computer Network, where he was responsible for maintenance and enhancement of the instructional and research computing environment.

Ross has been active in the IBM mainframe user community for a number of years, and has served as an elected member of the Board of Director of MVMUA, the oldest regional VM user group; a member of the HillGang (Washington DC VM user group) Steering Committee; and held Deputy Project Manager and Project Manager positions in several SHARE Projects.

Ross Patterson, Sterling Software, Inc., 1800 Alexander Bell Drive, Reston, VA 22091, (703) 264-8385.

Stephen E. Record

("Server Tasking Environment/VM")

Steve Record is an Advisory Programmer in the Department of Computer Sciences at IBM's Thomas J. Watson Research Center in Hawthorne, NY. He joined IBM in 1984 to participate in a research project exploring addition of multitasking capabilities to CMS, which produced the RxCMS prototype, and has since been involved in various other areas of operating systems research centered on VM. He spent 1988 and 1989 on a temporary assignment in the CMS design organization of the Endicott Programming Laboratory working on architecture and design of a new multitasking CMS, from which the Server Tasking Environment/VM product is derived.

Steve graduated from Yale in 1969 with a B.A. in History of Art, started graduate school in Forestry at the University of Montana in 1971, and eventually reemerged in 1976 from Yale with an M.A. in Statistics. Before joining IBM he held several jobs at the Yale Computer Center, finishing as a VM system programmer from 1980 to 1984. At SHARE, he has been an irregular attendee and occasional speaker since 1982, but is more recently better known as Mary Sue's husband.

Stephen E. Record, IBM T.J. Watson Research Center, P.O. Box 704, Yorktown Heights, NY 10598, (914) 784-7702.

Pat Ryall

("Apple Macintosh Synergy with VM/ESA")

Pat Ryall is Director of Technical Support at The SoftAd Group, a Marin County, CA., systems integration company specializing in sales and marketing automation solutions. He has over 20 years experience with IBM mainframes in operating systems, file systems, and networking, and over eight years of management experience.

From 1988 to 1993 Pat was a project manager at Apple's Technical Services Group (TSG) (formerly Apple Integrated Systems), managing business-critical projects with Apple's large enterprise customers. There he had the opportunity to apply mainframe knowledge and experience while learning the Macintosh in customer-related projects.

From 1983 through 1988 he was both a member and a manager of a group at IBM Research in Yorktown, NY, experimenting with VM CP structure and CMS user externals. His responsibilities included proposing and prototyping changes to operating system structure and studying the impact on the CMS user interface. His specific interests were in file systems and file servers.

Prior to working for IBM, he worked for Amdahl in Sunnyvale, CA, where he was responsible for liaison between software development and the field for Amdahl program products. His duties also included resolving high-severity software and performance problems and describing Amdahl products and services to the field and customers. During this period, he developed and taught the Amdahl CMS Internals class; jointly developed the CMS/XL program product; developed and taught a capacity planning course; and worked on Amdahl's VM curriculum. He was also an active member of user group organizations.

In the past he was an active member of the SHARE user group and held several posts within the VM Project, including CMS Project Manager.

Pat lives in San Jose CA, with his wife and the 1.5 children still at home, and, most recently two stray cats. When not busy at work, he works on projects about the house and likes to travel.

Pat Ryall, 1124 Amur Creek Court, San Jose, CA 95120, (408) 927-9626.

Philip H. Smith III

("Exploiting XEDIT"; "Exploiting REXX"; co-editor of this book)

Philip H. Smith III is manager of product development at Relay Technology, Inc. (formerly VM Systems Group, Inc.), in Vienna, VA. He has developed and enhanced successful CP and CMS products, and is now responsible for managing RTI's systems software products.

He has worked with VM since 1979, starting at Bell-Northern Research in Ottawa as a student, and continuing at the University of Waterloo in Ontario, Canada, long the home of extensive VM knowledge and enhancements. While at the University, he participated in support and enhancement of their heavily modified VM, running VM/CMS Unlimited's Single-System Image product to link two IBM 4381s and two IBM 4341s. An XEDIT expert, he has also written and distributed several extensive and popular XEDIT modifications.

He recently co-edited *The REXX Handbook* with Gabriel Goldberg, published by McGraw-Hill, ISBN 0-07-023682-8. This volume, with chapters by three dozen authors, many within IBM, provides the most definitive reference available for the SAA Procedures Language (REXX). Phil also wrote two chapters.

Phil is a member of the Washington, DC, area VM user group (Hillgang) steering committee and contributes regularly to various trade journals. He is a frequent speaker at SHARE (a major national IBM user group) and local user groups, and an avid participant on VMSHARE, the world-wide VM electronic conference, where he signs himself and is known as "...phsiii".

Philip H. Smith III, Relay Technology, Inc., 1604 Spring Hill Road, Vienna, VA 22182, (703) 506-0500, (703) 506-0510 (FAX).

Terrence D. Sole

("SQL/DS and VM Data Spaces Support")

Terrence D. Sole, Dip.Ed., B.Sc., M.Sc., born in Vancouver, British Columbia, Canada, received his education in Montreal. During postgraduate training in Parasitology and Epidemiology he conducted field research throughout the Canadian Arctic, the middle East, and India while developing an interest in using databases as a research tool. Upon graduation, Terry combined interest in database and education becoming involved in Customer Education. He is now a Staff Information Developer at the IBM Laboratory in Toronto.

Terrence D. Sole, IBM Canada Ltd., 1150 Eglinton Avenue East, Station G6, Department 946, North York, Ontario, Canada M3C 1W3, (416) 448-4343.

Liston Tatum

("Exploiting OfficeVision/VM")

Liston Tatum is a database administrator for the University of Virginia Health Sciences Center, responsible for administering an IBM MVS-based DB2 relational database. His eclectic background in operating and telecommunications systems has contributed to his concentration on intersystem interoperability; he is currently working to provide transparent, centralized access to various sources of information within the hospital from OS/2-based workstations.

Liston Tatum, University of Virginia Hospital, Medical Center Box 512, Charlottesville, VA 22908-9005, (804) 924-8289.

Romney White

("Exploiting CMS Session Services" and "Exploiting VM Data Spaces")

In August 1988, Romney White co-founded Velocity Software. There, he designs, develops, and supports performance-related products for the VM environment. In addition, as vice president and member of the board, he participates in corporate long-range planning, marketing, and sales support activities.

Prior to establishing Velocity Software, Romney was president and chief executive officer of VM/CMS Unlimited. Under his direction for three years, VM/CMS Unlimited was dedicated to solving a broad cross section of problems in the VM arena.

Before founding VM/CMS Unlimited, Romney was a principal, founder, and member of the board of The Adesse Corporation. There he played a key role in long-range planning, in addition to carrying out daily responsibilities to design, implement, and support a wide range of VM-related software products.

Prior to entrepreneurial endeavors, Romney was associate director of systems at the University of Waterloo's Department of Computing Services. In 11 years with the University, he held various positions in software engineering, many of which involved the VM operating environment. During this tenure, through his and others' efforts, the University became world-renowned as a source of VM experience and expertise.

Romney's extensive knowledge in the VM field has made his name synonymous with VM. He is frequently invited to speak at the GUIDE, SHARE, and SHARE Europe user groups, as well as at local and regional VM groups throughout the world. He has been awarded Master and Bachelor degrees in Mathematics by the University of Waterloo.

Velocity Software, Inc., is an industry leader in the area of VM performance products and services. The only company focused exclusively on VM performance, Velocity provides a comprehensive, in-depth perspective and a wealth of expertise that is unrivaled.

Romney White, Velocity Software, Inc., 60 Alban Street, Boston, MA 02124-3709, (617) 825-3599.

Index

D

E

M

O

X

ABOUT THE EDITORS

PHILIP H. SMITH III is Manager of Product Development at Relay Technology, Inc. (formerly VM Systems Group, Inc.) in Vienna, Virginia. He is a frequent speaker at SHARE (a major national IBM user group) and local user groups, and is an avid and well-known participant in the VM community. He coedited and wrote chapters for *The REXX Handbook*, and coedited *The VM/ESA Systems Handbook*.

GABRIEL GOLDBERG is a consultant, writer, and editor, specializing in IBM and VM computing. He has worked with IBM mainframe computers for nearly 25 years, most recently as vice president of technology at VM Systems Group. Coeditor of *The REXX Handbook* and *The VM/ESA Systems Handbook*, he has written dozens of trade press articles and given hundreds of presentations to groups around the world.

ABOUT THE SERIES

The J. Ranade IBM and DEC Series, with more than 90 published titles, are McGraw-Hill's primary vehicles for providing mini- and mainframe computing professionals with practical and timely concepts, solutions, and applications. Jay Ranade is also Editor in Chief of the J. Ranade Workstation Series and Series Advisor to the McGraw-Hill Series on Computer Communications. Jay Ranade, Series Editor in Chief and best-selling computer author, is a Senior Systems Architect and Assistant V.P. at Merrill Lynch.